The Flow

A Hedonist's Guide To Buddhism, Meditation & Travels in Thailand

A Travelogue Memoir

Laurence Davidson
Flip Flops Off Press

© 2025 Laurence Davidson. All rights reserved.

No part of this book may be reproduced, distributed, transmitted, or stored in any form or by any means - electronic, mechanical, photocopying, recording, scanning, or otherwise - without prior written consent of the author, except as permitted by United States copyright law for purposes such as criticism, comment, news reporting, teaching, scholarship, or research (a.k.a. "fair use").

Any unauthorized use, reproduction, or distribution constitutes copyright infringement and will result in civil and criminal penalties under the Copyright Act of 1976 (17 U.S.C. §§ 101 et seq.). The author reserves the right to seek all remedies available by law, including injunctive relief, damages, and attorney's fees.

Violators will also be subjected to my patented "snark retaliation protocol," which may include - but is not limited to - (a) sternly worded cease-and-desist letters, (b) relentless passive-aggressive social media takedowns, and (c) a letter from my lawyer written in an intimidating font.

No generative artificial intelligence (AI) was used in the writing of The Flow. AI was used to create line drawings that are included at the beginning of each chapter. The author expressly prohibits any entity from using this publication to train AI technologies to generate text, including, without limitation, technologies capable of generating works in the same style or genre as this publication. The author reserves all rights to license all uses of this work for generative AI training and development of machine learning language models.

All quotes and excerpts in this book are used for educational, commentary, informational, and illustrative purposes. Every effort has been made to identify and credit sources accurately. No infringement of copyright is intended.

This book is a nonfiction travelogue memoir. All names, characters, places, and incidents are either true and used with permission, omitted or changed by request. Any resemblance to actual persons, living or dead, is my choice and entirely intentional - unless you're all bent out of shape about it. In that case, the resemblance is purely coincidental.

Published by Laurence Davidson & Flip Flops Off Press
First Edition, August 2025
Updated, October 2025
ISBN: 979-8-9995953-0-0
Library of Congress Control Number: 2025916487

Dedicated to Tammy Louise Nelson

Greetings adventurous reader,

You are about to embark on a journey, but you won't be alone.

This is my personal story.

May my adventures resonate, educate, amuse and entice you to follow suit. If so? If you decide to pack a small bag and head out your door? May your journey be fulfilling in ways you never dreamed possible.

Love and merits to you all and thank you for allowing me to be a part of your lives, if only for a while.

Sādhu

Laurence Davidson

Table of Contents

INTRODUCTION. BABY STEPS AND FEELING STICKY 1
CHAPTER 1. OF MONKS AND MEETINGS 9
CHAPTER 2. LEAVE THE MONKEY, TAKE THE CANOLLI 23
CHAPTER 3. TAKE A WALK ON THE THAI SIDE 35
CHAPTER 4. CHIANG MAI. MUCH ADO ABOUT SOMETHING 49
CHAPTER 5. WHEN I GET OFFA THIS MOUNTAIN, I KNOW WHERE I WANNA GO 79
CHAPTER 6. ARE YOU HAPPY TO SEE ME? AN ELEPHANT IN THE ROOM 87
CHAPTER 7. WELCOME TO THE JUNGLE: NOTES FROM A FOREST MONASTERY 99
CHAPTER 8. HEADS SHAVED AND ORDINATION. A RADICAL SHIFT 131
CHAPTER 9. ALMS ROUNDS - A BEGGAR IN THE WILDERNESS 144
CHAPTER 10. CHIANG RAI AND THE GOLDEN TRIANGLE 154
CHAPTER 11. PAD THAI AND OTHER GATEWAY DRUGS 172
CHAPTER 12. DÉJÀ CHIANG 189
CHAPTER 13. WATS UP DOC? 207
CHAPTER 14. BANGKOK'S SIREN SONG 232
CHAPTER 15. KOH CHANG: FLIP THE NEW YEAR SURFING THE ISLAND VIBE 368
CHAPTER 16. SILENCE. THE LOUDEST SCREAM 395
CHAPTER 17. IT'S A BANGKOK BOOMERANG 397
CHAPTER 18. AYUTTHAYA. LESSONS FROM A COSMOPOLITAN KINGDOM 438
CHAPTER 19. AND IN THE END 448
ADDENDUM 1. PACK THESE AND PRAY: YOUR TECHS ROAD TO RUIN 453
ADDENDUM 2. LAURENCE RECOMMENDS: MY TOP 10 LIST 454
ADDENDUM 3. ASPARAGUS, FONTINA AND PROSCIUTTO 456
ADDENDUM 4. A BRIEF INTERLUDE. LAUNDRY ON THE ROAD 457

INTRODUCTION. BABY STEPS AND FEELING STICKY

I'm not lost; but I am simply and conveniently between purposes.

And so it began. October 25th, 2024. Saying goodbye at the curb for departures at Seattle's SeaTac International Airport left me hollowed out as I walked through the airport doors without looking back - partly to avoid melodrama, mostly to avoid bursting into tears in front of the TSA agents, towards an adventure that was, at that point, bittersweet.

I wasn't on a yatra binge chasing enlightenment or trying to ask the "right" questions. I just had a vague sense that answers I needed might involve monks and mountains, noodles and curries, and the kind of uncomfortable self-discovery that makes you want to fake a phone call and leave the room. I needed distance. Silence. Beauty. Something in me had gone quiet; a hum I used to hear, forgotten over time, like a song that stops playing and you don't notice until the room feels wrong. Thailand wasn't the goal so much as the direction my compass pointed to when the noise got too loud. Not to escape exactly, but to remember what it felt like to move through the world with curiosity. And maybe, if I got lucky, with a little grace. What I didn't expect was how fully my journey would nudge me out of my apathetic self through joy, stillness, love, grief and camaraderie. I wanted to feel *me* again. Or at least find out what was left when the scaffolding of my former life finally collapsed.

Thailand is a land of 65 million people where Buddhism isn't just a philosophy but the cultural heartbeat of 93.5% of the population. As I boarded that first flight, these were simply abstract statistics.

Walla Walla, Washington to Seattle to San Francisco to Hong Kong. And last, Bangkok. Thirty-five plus hours of travel tests one's soul. That kind of long travel in economy will try and eliminate it entirely. From southeastern Washington State to Bangkok is a brutal slog, even when traveling light. Planes, trains and automobiles carried me across the globe and left me even more hollowed out than when my soon-to-be-ex and I parted at the departures curb.

By the time I got to my boutique hotel in the middle of that sweltering morning I was completely wiped out physically and emotionally. My travel clothes were layered for long flights and the stale, chilly, recirculated air of airports and planes. It was late October. I had left the Pacific Northwest behind. A region in terminal velocity free-fall towards winter temperatures - into my first experience of SE Asian continental heat and humidity. It felt like an inescapable sauna. Those clothes, thick and suffocating were never meant for the subtropics.

As I stepped out of Suvanabhumi International Airport on the outskirts of Bangkok into the dripping mid-morning Thailand climate, I seriously considered burning my travel togs in a curbside sacrificial pyre no matter the consequences. I didn't, but it wasn't for lack of motivation.

And then it got worse.

The hour-long taxi ride through convoluted spaghetti-woven Bangkok highways and surface roads slipped by my exhausted, indifferent eyes. Before leaving the US, I had emailed the hotel explaining my mid-morning ETA, requesting an early check-in. When I arrived, the staff was just beginning the turn-around and the previous occupants of my room hadn't checked out yet. I was too early for my room by hours, and no early check-in was available. I sighed, swapped Birkenstock's and socks for flip-flops, left my small roll-on and daypack with the front desk to find the hotel bar.

It was outside. Of course it was. I nursed an ice-cold beer (OK, three) while waiting semi-patiently for my room - and more importantly, the shower. Concluding a fourth beer was definitely a bad idea, I strolled the block to take in the local surroundings and get my bearings. I was smack dab in the middle of Bangkok. I didn't know a soul, how to get around or where to grab a bite to eat.

Bangkok. A sprawling city of over 11 million people, spreading across nearly 607 square miles, is massive. And it is busy! Sitting at sea level, the elevation averaging just under 5 feet above, with the Gulf of Thailand abutting the southernmost district of the Bangkok Metro area, Bang Khun Thian, it radiates a brutal sub-tropical heat and humidity. That hit especially hard for a Pacific Northwest guy used to aridity and *"normal"* temperatures.

Bangkok is divided into fifty Districts. Thirty-five are to the east of Chao Phraya River, known as Krung Thep, while the other fifteen occupy the western Thonburi side. These are broken down into 224 neighborhoods. When someone tells you they "did" Bangkok, you know that they, like me, barely scratched the surface no matter how long they stayed or how widely they explored. Saying I was overwhelmed could be the understatement of the year.

I had two nights in Bangkok before heading north to Chiang Mai, another city I knew almost nothing about. What I had gleaned from research and way too many hours watching vapid Top 10 "what YOU should do because I did them" videos couldn't tell me much more beyond surface gloss.

Fun fact: Bangkok holds the record for the longest official city name in the world. Thai children learn it as a song in school and it's heartwarmingly adorable to see a local light up when they get ready to sing it. Their eyes smile first, followed by a broad, prideful grin. It's beautifully sincere. Here we go:

Krung Thep Mahanakhon Amon Rattanakosin Mahinthara Ayuthaya Mahadilok Phop Noppharat Ratchathani Burirom Udomratchaniwet Mahasathan Amon Piman Awatan Sathit Sakkathattiya Witsanukam Prasit.

... and *breathe*!

Just out the gate of my hotel, uneven underfoot, not exactly sidewalk nor street, simply a faded broken paint stripe battling for relevance and survival, to show you where, if you dare, walk. Types and shapes of vehicles, many unfamiliar to me except from pictures, whizzed by on the "wrong" side of the road from what I'm accustomed to. That alone proved to be challenging considering my state of mind and dishevelment. Pedestrian right-of-way simply does not exist in Thailand. Yeah - OK, it does, legally, but tell that to the millions of scooters, tuk tuks, cars, carts, buses, trucks and every other form of transportation plying those roadway waters.

By the time I got back to the poolside bar, my 501's and heavy long-sleeve hoodie I had worn for an eternity clung to me like clammy neoprene and smelled just as bad. I was a walking PSA for heatstroke.

Wilson, the kind, generous and perceptive concierge at the hotel, La Petit Salil Thonglor 1 in the Sukhumvit neighborhood, greeted me with impeccable English. "Mr. Davidson, what brings you to Bangkok?"

"Actually, Bangkok is only my first quick stop for a couple of nights. I'm traveling as much of Thailand as I can squeeze in over 3 months," I replied.

"Where are you going next?" Wilson's questions were direct and curious.

"To Chiang Mai for a few nights to dump the jetlag, then up to the mountains for a month to ordain as a monk."

Wilson said nothing. Just smiled, his eyes locking onto mine.

Feeling the weight of his silence, I dragged the conversation forward. "I'm going to iMonastery for the month of November. After that, I'm traveling north to south to explore Thailand. It's my first time here."

Wilson politely asked for my phone. I was curious about his request but had heard that Thais loved to connect so I handed it over. He tapped in his personal cell number into my contacts for me.

"Anytime you need advice or help - day or night - call or text me," Wilson exclaimed.

That single, quietly beautiful act of kindness and generosity told me everything about the heart of the Thai people.

Traveling to the eccentric, massive Asian canvas was my target. It was a part of the globe I'd never explored before and that needed to change. Planning undertaken through duress and depression was a daunting and lonely task. I chose the ancient, semi-mythical, exotically romantic and sensuously erotic Thailand for many reasons.

My first focus was a Theravāda Buddhist monastery that welcomes westerners to experience monastic life as a fully ordained monk. Why? I'll get to that later. Nestled high up in the mountain jungles along the Luang River, about 60k across mountainous terrain from the small city of Pai in the province of Chiang Mai, I would relinquish time and mind to Buddha in northwestern Thailand. I'd ordain as a monk in the Dhammakaya order, live a clean, insightful life, learn more about the Dhamma, strengthen my meditation practice, and hopefully become a better man along the journey.

My previous life, once full of love and laughter, now in ragged tatters like a shredded pirate flag long forsaken by her crew had come to a horrendous crash-and-burn end. I needed change and to heal myself before I could ask forgiveness from anyone.

After a monastic detox, the plan was to spend my remaining months exploring Thailand. From the northern town of Chiang Saen, where Thailand, Laos and Myanmar meet along the mighty Mekong River in the zone notoriously known as the Golden Triangle (famous for opium production, money laundering, smuggling and most recently cybercrime). Then I'd meander south to Koh Chang, a lush National Park Island in the Gulf of Thailand which is almost within swimming distance of Cambodia. This seemed like a damned fine idea. My plan also included avoidance - steering clear of the heavily infested hot spots (Phuket and Pattaya) where 90% of Thailand tourists congregate. That wasn't a mistake, it was intentional, and it carried hard-honed prejudice. I didn't need drunken hoards in rayon elephant pants with buckets of booze turning my adventure into a farcical comedy of fear and loathing.

I wanted discovery, immersion. I wanted to learn about that mysterious place historically known as Siam. To live the life of an adventurous vagabond to see how and where Thailand would blow my mind and wend its way into my heart. If things went well, seen through the lens of a surreal Cassatt landscape and impressionist illusion, this would be my first, but not last, journey to Asia.

As my plans fell into place a wise and infuriatingly insightful friend asked if I was running away or towards something. I tried with bravado to answer honestly. I blurted out, though with little conviction, "towards," but I was lying. That wasn't even half true. Painful personal life issues aside, shaking the dust off from my overly familiar town where family and friends love me, to fly someplace different in every way? I would be alone for my birthday, except for hanging out with monks chanting ancient passages in Pali. That did not have me anticipating a raucous birthday party. Then missing the warm familial traditions of winter holidays? It was a complex, anxiety-inducing chunk of work. But it was also exciting. And despite leaving hearth and home I wouldn't have changed a thing - except sharing the adventure with that special someone I still cared deeply for.

Planning a trip to a far-away exotic land, somewhere you've fantasized about over the years is a massive undertaking (FYI: Martini's help). I've always encouraged family and friends to do this at least once in their lives. It is important. Why? Because expanding one's horizons should be a part of personal life goals. It breaks the rut of routine. Not the monastic part. That's not for everyone because unless you're already practicing meditation and have a yearning for a spiritual quest, it's not a path I recommend. Two reasons jump to mind. One: you're going abroad, hyped-up for your trip, craving to experience everything your destination has to offer, which dovetails into reason two: slamming the brakes on the excitement that travel affords, for a month of serene meditative practice in an isolated yet beautiful jungle retreat is a hard thing to wrap your headspace around.

It is extremely healthy, even vital for the ego to be humbled by the sheer mass and kindness of people in a different land. Different languages, customs, mores and lifestyles can easily throw you for a loop, especially when *your* cultural norms don't matter. You want a western breakfast of eggs, bacon, hash browns with an extra side of cholesterol? Why the hell would you want that? You can get that at home anytime or go to a western chain hotel if you're jonesing hard. Don't be afraid of the dim sum, noodles, soups, mystery meats and fish, stews, fruits and vegetables available all around you. Get out of your comfort zone and open your senses and heart to what's local. For those of you worried about getting sick, look at it this way; All those people who eat, live and love in those far-away places? They're alive and thriving in numbers. If it was really dangerous to eat and drink there? They'd all be dead.

Travel planning - the flights, visas, locations, transportation, sim card, money exchange, accommodations, shots, all needed research and commitment. Is this the right place? Is there a better flight? How do I get around? Do they have toothpaste? Deodorant? Toilet paper? What about this, that and the other thing, while the brain spins into monkey-mind mode? That pesky monkey really gets in the way of making decisions. Thoughts racing along - nineteen trains running at different speeds simultaneously on twelve tracks with no conductors; try to be decisive with that running through your untrained and unfocused mind! Hence ... the monastery.

But that is the high-wire act of travel: we endure chaos because we believe deeply, possibly irrationally, that something extraordinary will happen. That we'll see ourselves clearly for once. A stranger from a world not our own might greet us with a soft smile, wave us over, and share a bowl of something impossibly fragrant and delicious, its steam curling into the air in welcome. And in that quiet lane, in a town whose name we can't pronounce no matter how hard we try? We'll carry that moment forever in our hearts. Those precious moments happen more often than you imagine.

To deeply connect with yourself, your resilience, your stamina, your empathy and compassion - that is all part of being someplace different. The willingness to observe through unfiltered eyes and heart, the beauty, both subtle and grand, of a foreign land where every sensory input ... the sights, smells, language, taste and sounds are completely different from what you know, is incredibly rewarding. You'll feel it in your heart and soul. That *"it"* feeling wells up inside as you grasp that you're actually inside a grand adventure.

Apathy. It's that slow erosion of wonder and lives inside us all. The need for *new* runs through all our veins, sometimes to ruinous effect. The familiar leads to a lack of awe at the predictable, gentle kindness of everyday life. Apathy is the soul crusher that makes our brains lazy, crazy and desperate for stimulation in any form. Why do you think TV, social media, casinos, movies, games, streaming services, live sports, and parties are so popular? It's because those take us away from the repetitive boredom of everyday life. It's that moment when you realize that waking up will lead to our routine that falls short of a James Bond life and simply give in to the unremarkable. It can be paralyzing. That's the dirty secret of comfort: it doesn't satisfy, it sedates. But what so many of us crave for is not a "same day." It's that "not same day" - where everything is new and different, wondrous and exciting, that drives me to explore beyond my comfort zone. It's why travel is healthy - it shatters apathy's hold over the soul.

⁂

I have had the fortunate opportunity to travel in my life and though it can be intimidating, the rewards far outweigh the uncertainties. It is those unnerving uncertainties, the unknowns that many people shoulder when planning their vacations. That's why all-inclusive resorts, where guests never leave the facility (*"of course I've been to Mexico - it's wonderful - you never have to leave the pool!"*) are so popular. That's not Mexico. It's your any-town town where everything is Mexican-themed. But those places are not Mexico in any way except geographically. And this is not endemic to Mexico. You can find those rube paradises everywhere the sun shines and the results are always the same. Hangovers, bloated waistlines, a T-shirt, logo hat and a phone full of food, drink and sunset pictures to show for it. You're lucky if you get out of those places without drunkenly signing up for a time-share.

Instead, go somewhere foreign. Immerse yourself in a culture completely different from your own, even if you're irrationally terrified at the mere prospect of setting down in a strange land. And, unless you're planning a sex-cation, you should do it with a romantic partner. It's much better to share those encounters with someone you love and enjoy traveling with, to experience whatever adventures come your way, together. Laugh at your mistakes, and believe me, you'll make a few. Revel in little victories like figuring out how to use the ticket machine for the subway together; discover what those golden fried balls sizzling away at the street cart are (hint: they're delicious!); learn how to politely say hello, goodbye, please, and thank you and how to order food and drink without being bossy or rude; how to hail a cab, or ride in a maniac-driven tuk tuk zipping through lanes of traffic, dodging bumpers and pedestrians by an inch.

What's the worst thing that can happen? You could get sick from the food or water, or you might get pick-pocketed, or you'll lose your passport or phone. In the real world these problems rarely happen. Be observant. Be careful how you carry yourself as you step out your hotel door and stop draping yourself in jewelry. That's setting yourself up as a target for the ne'er-do-wells of the world. Everywhere seems dangerous and terrifying with evils around every corner if you make yourself a target. You'll find that you don't need to flash your status around because the locals really don't care that you have a Gucci bag or a Rolex; at least not the folks you want to hang out with.

Those muggers hanging out in every shadowy doorway? Those dope fiends looking to jack you up? They're rife throughout travel stories and posts. We all hear dire warnings from the minority to whom bad things have happened to, more often than not because flashing gold, diamonds and a fat roll of cash in public was their preferred method of ego fulfillment. How often do you hear about or read stories from the vast number of travelers, the overwhelming majority I'll add, who had an amazing vacation and nothing dire happened on their trip? I didn't think so.

Travel, at its best, rearranges your molecules. It doesn't care about your itinerary. It's there to challenge, unmake, and reforge you. You'll get knocked off course, and if you're lucky, that's when things get good. When fear gives way to wonder with a healthy dose of humility thrown in for good measure, then add in some prudent measures for your personal well-being; when you share heartfelt laughs with strangers, and awe blooms inside of you as your eyes take in sights you thought you'd never see, then throw in some exhaustion-driven sleep - that's when you know you're on the path to adventure, come what may. Remember - adventure doesn't come looking for you - you must chase it, stumble into it, then welcome it with open arms and an open heart. Just don't forget to enjoy your ride.

CHAPTER 1. OF MONKS AND MEETINGS

'Gratitude opens the door to abundance.' - Zen Proverb

In my second year of college, I met a mystical monk from Nepal. I was studying at our off-campus house in Palo Alto, California when I heard voices coming up the walk to the front door. This was not unusual. We had a three-bedroom house (nicknamed "The Happy House") with a friends-are-always-welcome attitude. There were people coming and going at all hours of the day and night. Typical of many student houses back in my day.

I preferred to study in the living room when no one was about as there was more room to spread books, binders, pens, paper and other necessities of course work, on the decrepit coffee table and beer-stained couches.

It was a spring day, the weather was nice, and the front door was open allowing a warm breeze to flow through. In walked Jim, a tight friend with everyone in our household. He had a funny little fellow in tow dressed in deep maroon robes. Jim pointed at him, and said, "this is Namdak. He's a monk," and left it at that. A couple of pregnant seconds drifted by. I stood there, my mouth a little agape - as if that introduction explained everything.

Jim had spent time in India or Nepal (I can't remember which) at a meditation center and monastery, which we all thought kind of magical, ballsy and mystical at the same time. We were open to anyone coming around as long as they were "cool," and Jim, with his adamant ideas about music, food, art and spirituality was definitely in the cool camp, always marching to his own rhythm track.

Namdak had dark round Asian features and wore a smile that lit up the room. He reached out and took my proffered hand. I had no clue if that was a proper way to greet a monk. Do you shake hands? Bow? Genuflect? Jim introduced his companion a little further. Namdak was a Tibetan-in-exile Buddhist monk living in Nepal. He'd come to the Bay Area in advance, to act as the facilitator/fixer for a visiting Lama who would be teaching Dhamma classes and leading meditation sessions at a retreat house in the quaint coastal town of Capitola, just south of Santa Cruz. Both are located over the coastal range from what the world knows as Silicon Valley.

That monk had something about him; his kindly eyes radiated warmth and sincerity in ways that I had never encountered before. I literally felt them bore into me, mining into and comprehending the depths of my soul in an instant. It was visceral.

My roommates and I were close friends. We were happy-go-lucky lads. Serious students and working stiffs. We had a penchant for parties, girls, cooking, wine and cocktails, music, sports, outdoor adventures and more. We were typical college guys but with a twist. All of us had traveled and lived in various places around the world, with a broader understanding of what other cultures looked, felt and tasted like. Even with all the places I had traveled to and the wide range of people I had met in my life, I had no one to compare Namdak to. It was welcoming, if not a little unnerving to meet a monk in our living room. I should have tidied up.

Namdak left a lasting impression. One that has lingered over the years and though our face-to-face friendship was brief, I've never forgotten that smile, his inherent kindness and intuitive understanding of his surroundings and the people he encountered. To wit: the first time he met my roommate Eric, with nothing more than a brief introduction, Namdak began talking out of the blue about Burma and Thailand, temples and towns, from where Eric had recently returned. Eric had not said a word about his recent travels, nor had I. I asked Jim later and he said he hadn't mentioned Eric's travels either.

A few days after our initial meeting, I was toiling away on school assignments in the living room; books, binders and notebooks spread out everywhere. There was a light knock on the door. I was surprised to see Namdak standing there with his trademark smile and warm eyes, though this time he was alone and in lay clothes. His beautiful robes were nowhere to be seen. After greeting each other, a puzzled look on my face, I remembered my manners and invited him in, offering up tea. Yes, our college household was a little different in many ways. Over cups of Jasmine tea, he asked me in his broken English, if I "liked the Bao?" Puzzled, I asked him what he meant because phonetically it sounded like I was either supposed to bow to him, or he to me.

He began to laugh. He laughed at almost everything (unless it was mean-spirited, like when he came to watch an American football game on TV. We sometimes got a little over-enthusiastic with our commentary) and replied *"no"* with a slow-rising inflection that sounded like incredulity. "Bao - *buns*." I'd lived many years in San Francisco and eaten as much Asian cuisine as possible in that city. The dim sum "Bao" (in Nepalese they are called Momo) - are those soft white buns filled with sweet and spiced pork or fermented bean paste. As his explanation hit, lighting the dim bulb over my head, comprehension slid into place. I enthusiastically said yes! I loved those things. I first ate Hom Bao as a little boy at Wing Lee Bakery on Clement Street (that shop is still going strong). Bao are one of Chinese cuisine's perfect and delicious snacks.

He politely asked - or rather gently directed me - to return to my studies, then headed off to the kitchen without a glance backwards. A large olive-green rucksack, which was slung over his shoulder at all times, followed its master. I mused at this strange turn of events. He didn't seem the kind of guy who would rage out of the kitchen brandishing a butcher's cleaver. After all, when was the last time you heard of a Buddhist monk going on a rampage? I did as he asked and didn't give it another thought, returning to my sprawled papers and books.

Occasionally I heard cupboards and drawers opening, closing, a muttered word or two, a snippet of a hummed tune and the sound of something bubbling on the stove. I fielded random questions: where could he find this in the pantry, and did we have that? As you might surmise, we had a well-stocked kitchen.

It was after a stretch of uninterrupted studying that I had almost forgotten about the little monk in the kitchen, when he quietly came and sat by my side looking at what I was working on. He was so quiet, so stealthy that I hadn't noticed his approach until the cushion on the couch shifted as he sat down. He had a slight dusting of flour covering most of him and as I looked at him appraisingly, he smiled, placed his palms together in an upraised manner, and said, "now wait."

After fifteen minutes, Namdak rose and went to the kitchen, which was welcome as it was awkward trying to focus with a monk sitting next to me, observing me study and take notes. Try it sometime. It can be a little distracting. I got to a good wrap-up point and reckoned I was done for a while. I packed things away and went to join him in the kitchen.

I stood in the doorway in awe. Three towers, each with three levels of large Asian bamboo steamers were drafting steam on the kitchen table, each level filled with Bao. He'd made enough for a party. The kitchen was in a ruinous state. Flour and dough scraps all over the place, the cutting boards covered in Char Siu (Chinese BBQ pork) trimmings, a pot with a red sticky sauce dripping off the lip, little piles of cut wax paper, the sink piled high. I didn't care. The aromas coming off the steamers? Intoxicating. Obviously, he had come prepared - his rucksack, in a corner of the kitchen, lay there like a deflated balloon.

"Try one - but hot - be careful..." I vaguely remember hearing him say as I snatched one up. Too late. The blazing-hot filling of Char Siu oozed into my greedy maw. Molten pizza cheese, or in this case, sticky BBQ pork burn-blistered the roof of my mouth. It must have been the streaming tears and rapid, open-mouthed panting that caused him such concern. He grasped my arm looking at me with anxiety. However, the flavors and textures and the fluffiness of the buns were amazing, so I resumed eating as the pain subsided, and the Bao had cooled to a temperature a touch cooler than liquid bronze. I helped him clean up the kitchen. It took us an hour.

It was dusk as my housemates and friends drifted in and tried Namdak's Hom Bao. We unanimously offered him an open invitation. He could come over any time he wanted to, but he'd have to make more Bao. And with that, over the next month, he came around often. He even came to some of our regular weekend parties, which was a little awkward. Though he wasn't wearing his robes during those days, everyone had heard he was a bone fide monk. Having a sacred guy wandering about one of our parties added a unique texture to the mix. It's a truly unique thing to have a monk cook for you, let alone hang out at a college party, because while we were not Animal House, we weren't far off that mark.

At the time I didn't know that cooking was, for many monastic orders, a forbidden activity for monks. Life as a mendicant means that all food is donated by local farmers, or from the alms graced to monks and the monastery by the surrounding villagers and other generous donors. Lay Buddhist volunteers cook breakfast and/or lunch and that is the norm for most Buddhist orders. I didn't know that at the time, but I was still quite curious as to how this monk was able to make such incredible food. I found out later, during one of our chats, that his "mother," a woman assigned to raise him in secular matters outside of monastic training, was considered one of the best cooks in Kathmandu.

In my monastic family - the Dhammakaya order - we were not permitted to cook, even though I pleaded with my teachers on several occasions to allow me to help in the kitchen. I wanted to learn the secrets behind some of the amazing Thai staples. Instead, we had people from surrounding mountain villages who volunteered their time and energy every day to feed the Sangha (brotherhood of monks), twice a day. This (and the inability to play or listen to music) was a deal-killer for me when considering taking life vows. Cooking is one of my greatest pleasures. To make a healthy, complete meal for family and friends is one of my love languages. Cooking brings about its own meditative state and is an excellent vehicle for practicing mindfulness because really sharp knives, with fast and fine slice-and-dice prep will do that for you. Focus, Focus, Focus! Unless of course you don't value your fingers.

Namdak became somewhat of a fixture around the happy house and as our friends got to know him, they all sensed the same thing. Here was an unusual fellow (from our perspective) who was just really "with it," kind, and extraordinarily focused on his path. Each time he came around he would regale us with stories of life in Nepal, Thailand, Malaysia, Burma (now Myanmar) and India as a Tibetan on the lam. Or how his travels in service to his monastery took him to many exotic places. I began to realize that each chat was actually a lesson rife with parables and allegories of kindness and compassion, in humility, in humor, but always with a deep abiding respect for others.

One morning I was puttering around the house cleaning up. It was after mid-term exams when suddenly Namdak was standing in the kitchen looking through his rucksack. As if by magic, he was just there. He had told me a few days before that he had kidney problems and that he was out of his medicine. I asked if I could take him to a hospital or clinic to get a prescription, but he said that he needed a different kind of medicine. When I asked him what I could do, he hesitatingly asked if I would drive him up to the city, to Chinatown. He had heard of an herbalist that would have, he hoped, what he needed.

He had shown us so much kindness and brotherly love without a hint of judgment, even when witnessing first-hand some shall-we-say, rather debauch behavior during weekend-long parties that I agreed to drive him up to the city without any reservation whatsoever.

We headed north up the 101 Freeway to San Francisco on a beautiful sunny day. He opened up about his life, telling me that he had been orphaned as an infant. He didn't know what age he was when he lost his parents, or if his parents had simply consigned him to the monastery. He didn't know what date he was born or how old he really was. The local monastery raised him in the Buddhist tradition of spirituality and a lot of hard-core advanced education. I asked him if he spoke Chinese since we were headed to Chinatown where English is rarely used. He smiled and said, "Some dialects, OK," and then said, "I speak little bit Chinese, Japanese, Spanish, Italian, Portuguese, Russian and Korean. Oh, English too."

Mind blown, I asked where he learned all of these very different languages. "At my monastery and traveling," was his quiet, understated answer. I now knew that not only was he creative, intelligent, and the most Buddhist guy I'd ever met, (not that I'd met many) but that he was a polyglot. That takes some serious brain power!

Namdak laughed. "I'm terrible with maths," he said, like he was tossing me a lifeline, reminding me that even monks have their weak spots. I laughed with him and confessed I was mathematically hopeless, barely passing calculus and I'd accomplished that only because I spent an inordinate and irrational amount of time with a tutor.

We got to Union Square and made our way to the northeast corner where the Grant Street Dragon Gate stands leading into Chinatown. I began to look for (dare I say it) a parking space. It was the middle of the week and fairly early, so I prayed for good luck. We had been slowly circling for a while, plying the side streets of Chinatown and North Beach, and had circled back to Grant when a car pulled out a couple of hundred feet up. Perfect! Grant Street in Chinatown is a one-way so no one could drop a quick U-turn to claim the open space. The fact that parking opened up on Grant at all was a miracle. I eased my car in. As we got out, Namdak said, "Larry," smiled, and pointed up over his head. We had parked in front of the Chinese herbal medicine shop he needed. So, he possessed good parking juju as well? I mused that under no circumstances should we ever let this guy out of our sight, adopt him and make him stay with us forever.

Namdak and the proprietor, doctor, alchemist, herbalist, shaman, whatever, chattered along. Their serious discussions interspersed at times with occasional uproarious laughter. The store looked like a picture-perfect movie set depicting a brooding, ancient Asian herbal medicine shop. Glass jars from huge to tiny, stainless tins and bins packed with ingredients that I had no clue about, and bunches of dried flowers, herbs and roots either hanging or displayed in cascading bamboo baskets were everywhere. Each had a hand-printed sign in Chinese identifying what they contained, *if* you could read Chinese. An enormous antique iron and brass double-balance scale sat off the counter alongside four ancient, large stone pestle and mortar grinders that looked like they had been in service since the Xia Dynasty. A large glass jar of empty spansules sat on the back counter by a collection of worn tin funnels hanging at the ready.

After their lengthy discussion, the proprietor gathered minerals, spices, plants and roots from various containers about the shop, slowly and meticulously weighed and measured them out, then ground up two different recipes in separate mortars. Using a weird little machine and the tin funnels, he worked away until there were two large baggies of capsules. All the while the owner and Namdak chatted, a couple of times looking at me. I remember thinking how beautiful it is that across all our divisions, language, culture, continents and history, we still find ways to make life function together. Something deeper than difference is always at work beneath the surface. As we were walking out the door, the cheeky proprietor said with a grin in perfect English, "Thank you for your business. You'll feel better soon." Really? C'mon! I could have joined in the conversation and learned something! Namdak winked.

We grabbed a table at the Far East Café, a favorite Chinatown haunt of mine that I'd been eating at since I was a boy. It is a cavernous Chinese-American restaurant right across the street from the herbalist. As we ate, I asked Namdak what language they had been speaking. He replied, "Min mixed and Cantonese some" (he had a funny way of rearranging sentences.) "Chan is funny man and wouldn't believe I know Min. He tested me with riddle about chili farmers attacked with ants going up duan da, (I had to ask - pants), then rubbing their privates to stop biting. I told him the answer ... that's what so funny. It's old story in

Asia" he grinned, chop-sticking sticky and cloyingly-sweet-and-sour bell pepper and pineapple chunks into his mouth. I guess my raised eyebrows begged for an answer. "It's how dance start," he said as he winked and giggled.

A week later I was manning one of the BBQs in the backyard. We had three Weber dome grills that saw almost daily use. I felt Namdak's presence behind me. The guy was spooky, though in a good way. I remember wondering "how does he do that?!" Namdak was looking atypically sad. Gone was his smile. The twinkles in his eyes were still there but subdued. He was dressed in his traditional robes, something I had not seen since our first meeting. Those deep maroon robes were impeccable, draped with such calm perfection that I couldn't tell whether it was divine grace or decades of practice that kept them from falling off.

Surprised, I pulled what I was cooking off the grill and asked him what was going on as I was a little worried about my gentle friend. Namdak smiled - though not with his usual spark. He said it was time for him to begin the work that had brought him to the Bay Area. Namdak asked if I could drive him to Capitola the following day. I had a class scheduled but screw that. My friend, and someone who had become my confidant and unbeknownst to him, my mentor, needed help. Whatever he asked me, I would do without hesitation, without question. Some people earn that kind of trust without ever asking for it.

"Of course I will. It would be my honor, Namdak," I replied. I felt his mood and today, with more life experience, I know it was a feeling of empathy for my friend whose sadness was palpable and who was destined to leave us to perform his duties.

The next day dawned gloomy, and fog bound. I swung by the campus apartment he had been living at and loaded not one, but four large identical rucksacks into the car (so that's how he did it all!) and as we pulled away from the curb, I saw him look back, acute sadness painted his face. The smart, wise, funny fellow who had befriended us all was completely out of sorts.

I had to know. "Why are you so sad Namdak? I thought this was something that you loved; your life as a monk, your role in your monastery ..." I asked as I drove west along Page Mill Road toward the 280 freeway.

He took a moment and drew a few deep breaths while gazing straight ahead seemingly in reflection, then slowly replied, "In my living, I never experience of this freedom I live here. Now I assume duties I was assigned. I'm unsure how to feel, if returning to monk life is for me." He paused, took another deep breath, then said, "I blame you!" and with that he laughed his real laugh, his eyes-back-to-clear, focused joyous laugh. A tear worked its way down my cheek.

The drive over the hill was non-eventful though the subdued mood permeating my car was emotionally thick. We chatted about a lot of things. I told Namdak with intention that we would meet again somewhere, someday. He smiled at me and said, "I hope we do that. I want you come to stay at my monastery at Kathmandu."

Back in those days we didn't have cell phones or GPS maps, so I drove the hillside streets of Capitola until Namdak spotted what he was looking for. He pointed at a house up the hill on a perch overlooking the Pacific Ocean. Dozens of Tibetan "lung ta" (prayer flags) danced in the breeze, sending invocations out into the world. We pulled up, parking along the curb. I was helping him with his bags up the steps when he asked, "Could you come meet Rinpoche? I'd like if you do."

Walking into that house would change my life.

DUDJOM JIGDRAL YESHE DORJE

The house, up on a rise, had worn, wide wooden steps, the peeling dark red paint showing the constant barrage of airborne salt, wind, sun, fog and sand. They led up to a broad wrap-around deck in the same condition. By the door, there was a rack to put shoes, a large sand-filled stone bowl with incense sticks burning, and an old stone Buddha in the corner. Namdak opened the door and entered the house as I was removing my shoes. He paused, turned, and asked me to wait a moment. He left me on the porch with the rucksacks. I turned to gaze out at the expanse of Pacific Ocean, bathed in a layer of high fog, the prayer flags gently flapping in the damp salty breeze, while screeching gulls flew their arcing paths as they played with the wind. I was lost in a moment of quiet thought, when Namdak appeared and beckoned me inside. Other monks materialized, grabbed his sacks, then were gone like smoke.

"I make sure Lama wasn't already busy. I want him to meet you. He doesn't speak much good English, so I translate for questions or anything." I lingered in the entryway, uncertain and fidgeting - shifting on my heels, my hands wandering in search of some natural resting place that didn't exist. I felt ... vulnerable.

A few moments later an elderly monk dressed in fancier robes than Namdak's, still of the same deep maroon hue of their order, but with gold braided trim, came out of the front room and smiled at me. Namdak introduced him as Lama Dudjom Dorje, saying "he my boss" to which the elderly monk smiled and gently nodded. He had the same sparkling eyes that Namdak possessed that seemed to look right through and into my soul in an instant. He also had a weird presence, a peaceful aura, relaxed and perfectly matched to his kind smile. I thought, for the first time in my life, *"so that's what happiness looks like"*. His serenity was instantly recognizable.

I didn't know what to do or how to act so I offered him my hand to shake. His gentle two-handed grasp engulfed mine, accompanied by a broad smile. It was something I hadn't expected. There was genuine affection pouring out of this gentle man and without thinking, I bowed to him.

He smiled and said something, which Namdak translated. "Lama Dorje says you have nice manners, and he would to welcome you and offer blessing. If you have time, we could have tea together?"

What did I have to do? Nothing really. I had already skipped class for the day and only had the drive back up and over the hill to consider. I remember saying something to the effect that "I would be honored to stay for a while and have some tea with you." It came out more like "Um, OK, yeah, sure."

The Lama laughed and said something to Namdak, who disappeared down the hall. The Lama, my hand still in his, led me to the front room which had three large wood-cased windows gazing out to the ocean, a couple of low deep-red inlaid tables, some comfortable-looking low-slung chairs and fat pillow-seats on a huge Persian area rug. A large golden Buddha stood beside the fireplace surrounded by a makeshift shrine. There were lush, tall potted plants in every corner. Asian tapestries adorned the walls as a small stone and bamboo water fountain gurgled a delicate song hidden among the foliage. It was a light, comfortable, and tastefully decorated space.

He motioned for me to join him at one of the low tables, waving me towards a well-stuffed pillow. The Lama sat on the rug in classic lotus position, and it was then that I noticed, with the natural light streaming in from the broad windows, that he was older than I had initially thought. Was he 80? 90? I couldn't tell because his glow, his obvious happiness and peace kept his age masked, instead, portraying an elderly body filled with vim and vigor rather than aging frailness.

Namdak entered the room bearing a tray of small teacups alongside a clay teapot. I motioned for Namdak to sit next to me, to which he looked at his master, said something, then replied, "master Dorje to spend time with you first," as he poured us tea and quietly left the room.

What the hell was I going to do now? But then Lama Dorje quietly asked, in halting English, searching for the right words, "You are very fond of Namdak Lama, are you?"

I was a little startled for a moment, but replied, "Yes, I am. Namdak has become a true friend in the short time he's been around. He doesn't know but I look at him, not only as a friend and confidant, but a mentor too. He's taught me so much without knowing it. I've never met anyone like him, or you for that matter."

"He knows", the Lama chuckled and grinned. "He say you are guide too."

Wait! What? I was a little tongue-tied as I tried to put things together.

"My Namdak is very gifted when he meet people. He understand people quickly. You are reason he stayed; to learn from nice American. He doesn't think I know, but he was leaving our order and my service. He want to travel more. But something showed him, you and house friends; friendship, loyalty, kindness, changed his mind," Lama Dorje continued.

To this day I have no idea what that could have been. Was it something simple - one of our dumb jokes, or a shared meal, or the way we tried to care for our friends at all costs? Me and my roommates were close. We still are, for those left standing.

But to be an unwitting mentor to the young, though wise-beyond-his-years monk who radiated wisdom, left me feeling oddly foolish and somewhat unworthy. After all, what did I have to offer this bright, kind and generous young man from a distant land, except friendship without strings?

Lama Dorje picked up a small brass bell and gently rang it. Namdak came in, looking expectant. They spoke for a moment and then Namdak sat down on the cushion next to mine. I poured him some tea, even though he tried to shoo my hand away. I insisted, explaining that I was not here for him to wait upon, that he was my friend, that we were equals. He smiled and took the cup of tea gracefully.

At that moment, as the serenity of the tea was settling in, a woman in a flowing hippie dress, smelling strongly of patchouli, a lack of personal hygiene and garlic launched herself into the room, followed by another monk who looked flustered. She began rapidly prostrating herself on the floor and airily blurted, "Welcome, Rinpoche," with as much enthusiasm and fanfare as she could muster. Rinpoche? I had no idea what that meant.

Namdak quickly assumed his role as aide and now obviously the Lama's guardian. He rose and as she stood trying to move into our space, asked her politely though quietly, for her to join him out in the hall. When she made no effort to leave, instead moving even closer towards the Lama, he explained forcefully that she had come into a private ceremony, and she would be welcome to come back tomorrow. He was physically blocking her from advancing. Crest-fallen in face, her enthusiasm deflated, the woman glared at me, rose, spun around and left briskly with a bit of a huff. All that time, the Lama had said not one word of recognition but had simply focused on me.

"What was that all about?" I asked Namdak when he returned and settled himself back on his cushion.

Namdak did something oddly very western. He thumb-wagged towards the Lama with a grin and a giggle and said, "he is, as you say, big deal."

I had never considered that a monk could be famous, be a "big deal." I'd heard of the Dalai Lama, but I'd never heard of other famous monks and wanted to know more so I asked about the word she'd used. "What does Rinpoche mean?"

Namdak explained: "Rinpoche is reincarnated Buddhist master with life sometime go far back in time. My master full title is Kyabje Dudjom Rinpoche Jigdral Yeshe Dorje. I just call him boss-man, but when other monks around we use respectful title, Dudjom Rinpoche," Namdak replied in his typical it's-not-a-big-deal teaching style.

Namdak and I had never really delved too deeply into his calling, and at that time in my life, though I'd tried a little bit of meditation (there was this girl, you see), and a childhood acquaintance, I didn't know much. I really didn't know diddley-squat about Buddhism, reincarnation, karma or anything else that would enlighten me on the subject.

"So.... How old is he, are you?" I blurted out without thinking, embarrassed the second that came out of my mouth. I'm not known for filters. Lama Dorje laughed out loud. I mean he *really* laughed, rocking back and forth, his hands clapping with mirth. Once my ridiculous indiscretion and the laughter passed, I learned from a master Buddhist about reincarnation. Mind you, this is one of those elements of eastern philosophy that still doesn't sit solidly in my mind. I find it difficult to reconcile my western upbringing with thousands of years of Buddhist history and wisdom.

"It's not age," he said gently, it's something called lineage. We don't sign up for Rinpoche. It's who we are…"

I nodded like I understood. I didn't. The idea that someone could live again and again, training from childhood to become what they'd already been, twisted in my brain because I had never given reincarnation a second thought other than *"great; if reincarnation is real, I'm going to come back as a slug."*

"If we don't achieve enlightenment to break cycle of suffering, when we die, we are reborn. Other monks train to see signs that identify us. When they recognize a Rinpoche has been reborn, we start training again and spend new lifetime earning more merit and studying Dharma more. Some Rinpoche lineage go *many* generations," the Lama explained. All without irony.

I sat and pondered that for a little while as Namdak and his master talked. Namdak then gently grasped my hand and said that they had things to do as their schedule was really busy, but that Lama Dorje would like to perform a blessing for me. This time I said with conviction that it would be my honor to accept such a kind gift. I had no idea what a blessing entailed.

Namdak rose, left the room, then brought back some items I didn't recognize, placing them on the low table next to Lama Dorje. There was a beautiful lacquered water bowl and what looked like a small hand-held whisk broom, long white scarves, a two-sided brass object (it's called a Vajra; I had no clue what it was for), a strand of wooden beads and a beautifully etched brass bowl. Namdak lit some incense in the ornate brass bowl and nodded gravely to his master.

"Please, to sit here" Rinpoche asked and pointed to a cushion facing him. He gently took my hands, placed them together in what is known as a lotus prayer, and placed one of the white scarves over my wrists. He closed his eyes and began to chant and sing in a manner alien to me, as he used the various items that Namdak had placed on the table. He waved them above, or around me as he continued chanting. This was more involved than I had anticipated. I thought a quick bow and a pat on the shoulder with a sword would do it. My legs were cramping as the chanting continued, sometimes joined in by Namdak for what I assumed was the chorus or bridge. It was quite something to have two monks in their beautiful robes performing a ceremony that I had no clue about. I hoped it wasn't a fertility ceremony as I didn't need a pregnancy on my hands.

After a while as my knees screamed and my forearms and hands cramped (the ceremony had lasted almost an hour) both Namdak and the Lama's chanting and singing came to a crescendo as I was sprayed with water from the whisk for a third time, and then it was over. A white scarf was draped around my neck, the other pulled from my wrists and placed in my lap, and the circlet of wooden beads, called Mala, was gently draped over my wrists where the scarf had been.

"Please to remember us" the Lama said as we rose. He smiled at me with kindness and left the room. I bowed to him again as he departed though I don't think he saw. But then again, of course he did.

Namdak and I stood there for a moment. He then said, "That was blessing for health, peace, love and compassion. May you find the Buddha nature inside. It was very special blessing. I never seen him give anyone before. You very lucky Larry."

I did something I had not done before. I reached out and pulled him to me and embraced him in a hug, trying to impart as much brotherly love as I could. Namdak whispered something in my ear. I began to cry.

Namdak hadn't expected that hug. I found out many years later, relating the story to someone I've now forgotten, that hugging is not really a thing in Asian cultures unless you're family. Oh well, it felt right in the moment, and he felt like a real and true brother to me. He still does.

I never saw Namdak Lama or Dudjom Rinpoche again. That singular, surreal afternoon in Capitola came and went like a tide washing up something beautiful, strange, and sacred, then pulling it all back out to sea while I stood blinking on the shore.

About a year later, I drove back over the hill on a whim, some vague hope tugging at me like an old song I couldn't quite place. The house still stood, stoic against the salt air and fog, with a tangle of prayer flags fluttering like forgotten party streamers. Most had faded into pastel ghosts, but a few new vivid strands suggested that someone still cared or at least had recently. The old Buddha statue and the incense bowl were gone from the porch. That absence hit harder than I expected. I knocked on the weather-worn door, waited a long minute that felt longer, then knocked again. Nothing.

I made my way down to the tidy beachfront quay below, hoping someone might know something, anything. The town hadn't changed much: the same sun-bleached shop signs, the same scent of brine, burgers and saltwater taffy, the same vague hippy vibe that clung to everything like massage oil. I asked around, hoping that the monks had merely relocated to a bigger property. Only one woman working an ice cream counter remembered.

"Oh yeah, I remember them" she said, squinting into the fog of her memory. "Those foreign monks? Sweet guys. They didn't stick around for long. I think they moved on after a few months. I don't know where to." She paused, then added, "There's some tall European man up there now. He teaches meditation or something. He's a bit odd. Looks like he hasn't eaten in a while."

I laughed then, more than I should have, and felt tears sting my eyes. That's how life tends to go, doesn't it? One day you're sitting on the floor with a reincarnated lama who makes you feel like the universe is a little less lonely, and the next there's a stranger in a kaftan teaching breath-work to tech bros.

The people who change you don't always stick around for an encore. And maybe that's OK. Impermanence isn't just a Buddhist concept - it's a design feature of all our lives. A gift wrapped in grief. I didn't know enough back then to say thank you properly, and I still wish I'd made the effort to visit more while they were near. But even in their absence, they gave me something that stayed: a little more stillness. A little more kindness. A little more faith that, sometimes, meaning shows up uninvited and disappears without warning.

In the wake those monks created as they journeyed through, then past my life, I found myself paying closer attention - to myself, my choices, and the people around me. A new, different calm settled in. Not all the time, because living is still life rife with frustrations and anguish, and that awkward scaffolding that becoming an adult offers up as complications. It does that to everyone. But now and then I think back to that blessing ceremony and feel quiet gratitude rise up and wash over me; an introspective calmness that hadn't been there before. That blessing and what Namdak whispered had landed somewhere in my heart and soul, taking root.

It's strange how the moments that shape us rarely announce themselves. We stumble into them, distracted, unprepared, often unaware of their weight, or their impact, until much later. Some arrive wrapped in silence, others in laughter, or sorrow, or the quiet grace of someone who simply sees you. And if you're really lucky, a monk shows up at your door and makes you some Bao.

CHAPTER 2. LEAVE THE MONKEY, TAKE THE CANOLLI

A young novice monk asked his master, "May I send you email?"
"Yes," replied the master, "But no attachments please."

Have you ever been locked into something, playing music, sketching a flower, chopping shallots, or something as mundane and boring as sorting laundry - when the rest of the world simply vanished? Time gets slippery. Background noise fades. Your brain quiets down, and for a few golden minutes, you are entirely "*here*". Congratulations: you were meditating. And you didn't even have to light a single stick of sandalwood.

Many people envision that meditation requires sitting cross-legged in some softly lit serene cave chanting passages difficult to pronounce. But the truth is, meditation shows up in all kinds of disguises. Painting a landscape. Throwing a baseball. Writing code. Stirring risotto or brushing your teeth. If you're completely present, even for a fleeting breath of time, you've entered a meditative state, no robes or mantras required.

Back in the late 1970s, when I was a teenager, guitar in hand and a head full of Grateful Dead, Led Zeppelin and Beatles riffs, I started to notice something strange. There were moments, mid-practice, when I'd lose track of time. The music would pour out effortlessly, as if my fingers had taken over and my thoughts had gone away on vacation. It wasn't just playing - it was something deeper. The kind of focus that bypasses thinking altogether and goes straight to knowing. And when it ended, I'd snap back into normalcy and think, "What the hell was that?"

I didn't know it then, but I'd stumbled into a meditative state. No guru with a beard flowing down to his knees, no gongs and triangles - just a guitar and clarity. That sensation, that calm immersion in the *now*, became a kind of compass. I started chasing it. That elusive zone where mind, body, and song blur into something bigger, something unified. That's when I first believed in what I called The Flow: a current that pulls you into perfect alignment, when the noise drops out and the truth, whatever it is, starts to sing.

Pete Townshend of The Who has a great comment in the movie The Kids Are Alright, and though this is a bit of paraphrasing, it gets the point across:

CHAPTER 2: LEAVE THE MONKEY, TAKE THE CANOLI

"When I'm on the stage, I'm not in control of myself at all."

Pete Townshend may not be the first person who comes to mind when you think of meditation. Windmilling his arm across his guitar, jumping mid-air in tight white pants, smashing amps while the rest of The Who detonated behind him, it's not exactly the image conjured by words like "stillness" or "serenity" or "mindfulness". And yet, in those moments, Mr. Townshend was completely present. Fully immersed. The rest of existence had melted away. That, inconveniently for our incense-and-singing-bowl stereotypes, is a meditative state.

It's hard to reconcile the chaos of a Who concert with the soft-focus idea we often have of meditation. We picture crossed legs, hands in a mudra pose, a tranquil pond, the sound of subtle bamboo chimes. What we don't imagine is someone destroying a Rickenbacker in front of a screaming crowd. But the essence is the same: total attention, total absorption. No past, no future, simply now.

And if that doesn't shatter your peace-and-love bubble imagination, consider this: modern militaries around the world have embraced meditation - not for bliss or chasing enlightenment, but for clarity. For soldiers, the stakes are literal life and death. Mindfulness training is being used to sharpen focus, regulate emotion, and soften the long horrors of PTSD. It's not about being calm; it's about being awake.

For me, those rare, shimmering moments of mental and emotional clarity were elusive at best. Most of the time, my flow buddy was a flake. A no-show. Like a stoned roadie who forgot the gig. But when it did arrive, oh, it was everything. Floating bliss. That high of effortless harmony, where time collapses while awareness sharpens into something weightless. I didn't know how to summon it back then. No rituals, no road map - just the blind hope that it might show up if I practiced long enough or tuned just right. It was as if some minor deity who responded only to specific riffs mixed with moonlight would show up when he or she wanted to.

The feeling itself? Euphoric. As if the universe had decided to grant you a tiny taste of what it's like to operate at full human potential without sending a bill. It wasn't just technical ease or confidence; it was the sense that, for one miraculous moment, you were exactly where you were supposed to be. In sync. Awake. Humble and alive. Honestly, it felt so good I started wondering why I wasn't living in that space all the time. Why couldn't life always be like that? Enlightenment, but with a great backbeat.

And when my flow did show up? Everything felt so absurdly easy that I couldn't believe I'd ever struggled with the instrument I'd been playing since the first grade. As if all the years of practice were some elaborate setup for a cosmic joke: *"Oh, you mean it's supposed to feel like this?"*

At that point in my life, I knew exactly two things about meditation: one, it involved sitting very still, and two, it was practiced exclusively by unwashed Eastern mystics with silver beards, draped in bedsheets, perched on craggy Himalayan outcrops or in an incense-choked cave surrounded by golden statues and silence. Maybe at Shangri-La, assuming you could find the place without a Sherpa, yak and a vision quest.

Around that same time, my mother had some friends who were straight out of central casting for the 1970s Patchouli People's Parade. Their family VW good-times van looked like something the Partridge Family might've rejected for being *too* psychedelic; school-bus yellow, neon orange and purple cartoon flowers, peace signs, as if they were competing with the Merry Pranksters for who would get pulled over by the cops first. The mother wore actual flowers in her hair, and not ironically. On occasion, they'd drop their son Keith off at our place for a weekend sleepover while they disappeared to a "commune retreat," which my mom explained away with a shrug, like it was a totally normal thing that adults did, drive deep into the woods to chant and chase wisdom.

Keith, for his part, was smug about the whole situation. He'd been given a mantra by his parents' guru, which he told us about in the same tone one might use to announce their acceptance to Oxford. He told me he used it for his meditation practice, then promptly shut himself in my bedroom for half an hour, demanding total silence like a pimply bell-bottomed Dalai Lama.

I, meanwhile, lurked outside the door, baffled and increasingly annoyed. All I wanted to do was ride bikes, or skateboards, surf, or make loud noises with guitars. But no! Keith was *meditating*. Or so he claimed. For all I knew, he was in there talking to God or doing something unspeakable to my stuffed Teddy bear. I didn't know what a mantra was, but I was pretty sure it didn't require that much alone time and a locked door. I had a vivid imagination.

My friends and I gossiped and imagined stories about communes. I came to the lurid, though incorrect conclusion that Keith's parents and the "meditation" they went off to do, was all about naked, back-lit, sun-drenched bodies running freely through dappled glades and glens in slow-motion and the wild sex that everyone except me must be having in the meadows, the trees, the creek-side tall grass as mayflies danced in the sunbeams. My immature fantasies ran wild in a youthful body full of raging hormones. I didn't consider that there might be more to a spiritual lifestyle that many of those communities were seeking through Buddhist or Hindu-inspired exercises and even back then meditation. Yes - there were communes where the above happened - just not the one that Keith's parents went to. It was, I found out when I was invited to go, a Transcendental Meditation (known as TM) center. Talk about a major disappointment and shattered imagination!

I was young and dumb, living the California life, chasing that sunshine daydream of sandy beaches with glistening surf and the screech of the gulls, beautiful girls with their long blonde hair shining in the sun, cool cars with rock and roll slowly rolling by, all-night parties and the magical world of music, music, music. I didn't take much seriously and to that end, the whole hippie-lifestyle meditation thing seemed a little too much like the commune cult in my mind.

The Beatles with George Harrison leading the visible charge, thought it important enough to go to India, spend time with Maharishi Mahesh Yogi (the founder of the TM movement), showcase the power of meditation, and that spiritual growth was a healthy and noble pursuit. This was a global in-your-face prescription, an open invitation for self-love, mental health and peaceful coexistence. I was too cool for that school - or trying to be - so I scoffed and ignored what was inside me all along, something that I was trying to attain but didn't know it. That was a mistake. The hippies, like my mom's friends got it right.

People from every walk of life, in every nook and cranny upon the world, meditate. Some with great intention, others by accident. You might be surprised to learn you've meditated without even realizing it, perhaps while washing dishes or mowing the lawn, which isn't exactly the Himalayan peak most people associate with spiritual breakthrough. That's just a lack of understanding - or, as one of my teachers put it, "a knowledge gap you can fill without incense."

He explained that with enough mental training, meditation starts to slip quietly into everyday life. Not because you're lighting candles or chanting ancient passages, but because your mind has learned, through practice, how to drop into a calm, singular focus. You brush your teeth, and - bam - you're present. You take a shower, and suddenly it's the most grounded you've felt all day. You eat a slice of toast and become one with orange marmalade. And that's not a hard state of awareness to achieve.

It turns out, this kind of clarity ... that pure, undistracted focus, is far more powerful than our culture's beloved multitasking myth. Ever notice your computer slowing down when you have forty-seven tabs open, four apps running, as Spotify wrestles for bandwidth with a Zoom call? That's your brain on Tuesday. We've all got too many browser tabs open in our heads. And when those tabs start blinking and freezing, the monkey-mind kicks in.

In Buddhism, "monkey mind" is what happens when our thoughts swing wildly from one branch of distraction to the next, like a caffeinated chimp at a jungle rave. It's that inner chatterbox tossing banana peels across your mental floor, gleefully wrecking your peace. The result? A frantic, overstimulated mess of a mind that can't find the car keys or remember why it walked into the kitchen to open the refrigerator.

Left unchecked, monkey-mind doesn't just make you forget birthdays. It clutters your thinking, slows your cognitive gears to sludge, and fuels the spiral into anxiety - or worse, the apathetic fog of "what's the point?" where even basic tasks feel Herculean. That's the edge of depression, and for some, that's when the prescription pads come out, and a parade of mother's little helpers march in with promises of balance and better living through chemistry.

But here's the thing: that scattered mental mess? That's completely normal. Welcome to the club. You're not broken or alone. You're human. The good news is that your monkey-mind isn't a life sentence. With consistent meditation practice, even the clumsy, inconsistent kind we all start with, you can train your brain to stop swinging from vine to vine and just sit still for a second. That alone is miraculous.

Meditation isn't about perfection or performance, it's about practice. And about getting that damn monkey to stop pelting your brain with mangoes every time you try to focus.

So ... *what is meditation*? Big question. Simple answer. Or is it? Meditation, at its core, is the art of training the mind to focus - to rest gently in awareness rather than be dragged around by every darting-squirrel thought or emotional twitch. It can be done by concentrating on the breath, silently repeating a mantra, listening intently to a sound, or giving your relaxed gaze something completely unexciting to linger on, like a doorknob or that grain of rice you've been meaning to pick up off the carpet for two weeks. The goal isn't transcendence or enlightenment, (though those make nice marketing bullet points); it's about being present, clear, and quietly awake in your own busy mind.

What meditation is not - besides upright napping or getting baked - is the practice of emptying your mind into some blank, trance-like void where no thoughts exist. That's not meditation. That's fiction. The human brain doesn't work that way. Trying to force it into silence only amplifies the noise, like yelling at a toddler to be quiet while handing them drumsticks and some old pots and pans.

One of the great meditation masters of our age, Yongey Mingyur Rinpoche, a monk who runs the Tergar Osel Ling Monastery just outside Kathmandu, has a great sense of humor about this. When teaching group meditation, he uses a simple exercise to make that very point:

"OK. Relax. Take some deep breaths, slowly, in, out, and gently close your eyes. We are going to start our meditation by not thinking about pizza. Don't think about pizza ...Here we go ... "

A few minutes pass as the hall slips towards silence. Everyone is calm with eyes closed, sitting erect, hands in lap in earnest supplication to the moment. At that point, when everyone is showing off their perfectly poised meditation pose, Mingyur Rinpoche laughs, breaking the spell, and asks the participants, *"How many of you thought about pizza? Raise your hand."* And of course, every hand goes up. That's what your brain does and to deny it of its job is impossible.

"Meditation is easy," they say. And maybe it is, until our brains get involved (I know - oxymoron). Because if there's one thing we do well, it's over-complicating the hell out of everything that might otherwise be transparent. We obsess over the setup: Am I sitting the right way? Are my hands in the "Official Mudra Position"? Is my spine aligned with a celestial axis? Why are my shoulders up by my ears? Am I breathing too loud? Not loud enough? Should I pant rabidly like a hyena at a kill? Maybe that's the secret. And just like that, the calm, serene act of sitting still becomes a stress-inducing performance piece.

What meditation *can* do is train you to step back and observe your thoughts and emotions without getting yanked about by them. You let them float by without judgment or reaction. There is an age-old classic Buddhist analogy of a bright blue sky with puffy little clouds drifting by. Each cloud represents a thought. Meditation is laying back quietly on a cool grassy rise and watching those clouds pass without trying to lasso one, or panic when another looks like a thunderhead. That's the whole gig. Is that easy? Yes. And no.

As Jeremiah Tower, the famously demanding chef from Chez Panisse and Stars once said, *"Nothing is as complex as simplicity."* He wasn't talking about a perfectly poached egg.

There are countless meditation methods out there - some ancient, some modern, some suspiciously identical except for branding, theme music, and font choice. The important thing isn't the method; it's the mindset. And this is where a little healthy skepticism goes a long, long way.

Somewhere, always, in the patchouli-scented mainstream of feel-good spirituality, you'll find *That Guy*™ - the grinning guru who seems to vibe with your current existential crisis. And wouldn't you know it? He's holding the key to the kingdom of calm. "*My method*," he says, with a beatific smile and a man bun tight enough to warp judgment, "*is the one true way.*"

Spoiler #1: it's not. It's not even close.

Anyone who tells you all other paths are wrong is either deeply confused, dangerously arrogant, or selling enlightenment at a discount - but only if you click now. Usually, all three. That isn't a teacher. It's a sales funnel wearing mala beads (*he'll sell you an identical string for $49.99*).

Modern snake oil doesn't come in little brown bottles anymore. It comes in sleek social media videos, reels with acoustic guitar, sitar and drone footage, and hardcover books with subtitles like "Unlock Infinite Calm in Five Minutes a Day or Your Ego Back." Sometimes there's even a companion app. Or worse, a retreat. In Pasadena.

And let's not forget those crystal-peddling "influencers" who claim your third eye is blocked because your quartz isn't vibing with Venus. Or the Tony Robbins-type alpha shamans shouting you into transcendence, as if personal growth were a contact sport.

Spoiler #2: you can't scream someone into serenity.

The truth? Meditation has as many flavors as Bertie Bott's Every Flavor Beans. Every faith tradition that practices meditation, Buddhists, Hindus, Sufis, Janes, and even a few surprisingly limber atheists, has their own take. So, who's right?

That's for *you* to figure out. And that's where many people get stuck. You try one method - you light a candle while trying not to choke on the fistful of sage you lit afire, as you sit cross-legged, chanting something sounding vaguely Sanskrit - and instead of inner peace, you get a cramp and a brooding sense of disillusionment. "*I must be doing it wrong*," you think. Maybe you are. Or maybe that method simply isn't right for you.

I've been there. I tried a few techniques. I got deeply frustrated. I almost gave up. Then I did something radical: I cheated. I built my own system, borrowing what worked from different traditions and ignoring what didn't. A little Zen, a little Vipassana, a dash of Tibetan focus training, some Dhammakaya, and a whole lot of common sense, all stirred into a personalized soup of sanity. It works. For me. Your mileage may vary.

Because here's the thing: no one method is perfect for everyone, no teacher has all the answers, and any path that doesn't eventually lead you back to looking in your mirror and doing the actual work is a waste of time. Which brings us, of course, to the unholy trinity: dogma, religiosity, and the institutional juggernaut known as The Church... while in the other corner is the wily, untamed creature called spirituality.

Unlike stone tablets and top-down mandates of organized religion where rites, rituals, and eternal reward or punishment are doled out by a soul manager in the sky, the world of spirituality and meditation offers no such clean, authoritative blueprint. For many, that's disorienting, even scary. No instruction manual, no guaranteed results, no hotline to divine customer service. Just... you. Alone. With your mind. Good luck.

⁂

In cultural traditions where meditation is baked into daily life, yes, you'll often see colorful ceremonies with robes, chanting, incense, and enough gongs to start a prog-rock band. But when it comes to the actual practice of working with your own mind, the fluff falls away. There are no universal twelve-step plans to inner peace. And that's the rub. Meditation requires you to do something far scarier than obeying. It requires you to look inward. Honestly. Without flinching. That's why so many people bounce off of it. That hard work demands personal responsibility, the kind that can't be outsourced to a higher power or filed away after Sunday service.

And that's where religion sometimes wins. With its structured routines and divine delegation, it's easier to say a few prescribed words, ask forgiveness for flattening the neighbor's constantly yapping dog, and trust that someone upstairs is keeping score. But meditation isn't about scorekeeping. It's about letting go of the idea that anyone else is holding the clipboard in the first place.

It's said that we all carry Buddha-nature within us. Some just have to dig through more emotional drywall to get there. With meditation, the innate well of compassion toward others and ourselves slowly becomes accessible. It's not flashy. It's not easy. But it's real. And best of all, it doesn't require tithing or a confessional booth. Just you, your breath, and the uncomfortable, liberating truth that looking inward might be the most rebellious, healing thing you'll ever do.

That doesn't mean meditation is some glittering cure-all, a spiritual Band-Aid that never stings when ripped off. For some, especially those grappling with mental health challenges, it can actually be destabilizing, even dangerous. This isn't some recent concern cooked up by skeptics either. In India, over 1,500 years ago, Buddhist monks compiled The Dharmatrāta Meditation Scripture, documenting not only the benefits of meditation but also some of its psychological side effects. They described experiences we now associate with depression, anxiety, dissociation, even psychotic breaks, the mind folding in on itself instead of opening up.

These days, meditation is fully mainstream - no longer the domain of saffron robes and incense-scented rooms with guys named Garret leading chanting and getting it wrong. It's a certified wellness buzzword, a mental health darling, and the golden child of the self-improvement culture. Thanks to this surge, we now have "mindfulness", the Western re-brand that makes ancient wisdom sound like something you download on your smartwatch. Most beginners aim for fifteen or twenty minutes of daily practice, and the more committed may stretch that to an hour - at which point, for the uninitiated, starts to feel less like a soothing ritual and more like spiritual homework.

But here's the thing: meditation doesn't have to be a grand production. Once you've built up the habit, it can be done in quick bursts, what I call "micro-meditations." With enough practice, you can drop into that calm, focused state in under a minute, like rebooting your brain without logging out of life. A quick mind reset while brushing your teeth, standing in the shower, or staring blankly into your coffee can go a long way toward neutralizing the little irritants that would otherwise burrow under your skin and stay there all day.

In recent decades, the benefits, and yes, the occasional risks of meditation have been absorbed into modern scientific research. What's been learned is powerful: your mind is capable of incredible self-transformation. And that idea? That inner peace, resilience, clarity, even healing, it all might come from within, well, that doesn't sell many pills or therapy sessions. After all, if you realize you can cultivate compassion, self-worth, and mental strength from the inside out, Big Pharma and half the mental health industry are out of business. That's rough for them. But for you? Cheaper. And *way* more empowering.

Depending on where you look and who you ask, the documented physical health benefits of regular meditation range from the pleasantly surprising to the downright impressive: lower depression, reduced anxiety, stress relief, burnout mitigation, and even some documented cases of chronic pain reduction. But wait, there's more.

The psychological benefits are where it gets really interesting. Meditation has been shown to boost empathy, improve interoceptive awareness (that's science-speak for being able to feel what's happening inside your body without spiraling into WebMD self-diagnosis paranoia), and even foster self-transcendence, a term used for stepping outside the cramped quarters of your own ego long enough to see the big picture without judgment or emotional turbulence.

Some of the greatest minds of our age, people with actual, you know, hard-earned degrees, like actual bona fide qualifications have been poking at this whole "meditation thing" for a long time now.

Take Dr. Richard Davidson, for example (great name BTW.) He's the Professor of Psychiatry and Psychology at the University of Wisconsin-Madison, the founder of the Center for Healthy Minds, head honcho at the Healthy Minds Innovations project, and just to keep things light, a top-tier neuroscientist. You know, in case he gets bored. He sounds like someone who could host a TED Talk, do the dishes and pilot a spaceship through a meteor field at the same time.

Davidson and his team spent decades wiring up subjects including seasoned meditators like they were setting up a NASA launch, slapping neuro-sensors onto the shaved heads of monks. Real ones; no, really! His Holiness the Dalai Lama and Mingyur Rinpoche were just two of many seasoned meditators who were wired up - to watch what happens when you sit still and breathe with purpose. The results were wild. Whole regions of the brain usually lounging around like interns after a smoke break started lighting up like Times Square on New Year's Eve. Meanwhile, the parts of the brain that usually run your anxiety parade calmed down to a gentle hum. Meditation, it turns out, isn't just "woo," it's neuroscience with a side of magical reality.

And if that isn't enough to impress your inner skeptic, on February 4th, 2025, researchers at the Icahn School of Medicine at Mount Sinai dropped a little gem in PNAS (that's the Proceedings of the National Academy of Sciences, not an unfortunate acronym for something else). Their super-catchy paper titled "*Intracranial substrates of meditation-induced neuromodulation in the amygdala and hippocampus*" - a title that screams 'I want to read this all night long' - reported on intercranial EEGs planted *inside* people's heads (no monks were harmed as far as I know). They found easily measurable changes in the brain's emotional and memory centers when people meditated. Not imagined changes. Real, electrical, measurable changes. Think about that for a moment.

And those are just two examples from thousands of published, peer-reviewed, scientifically scrutinized papers. Papers that identified, tested and documented people who didn't just "feel calmer" after downloading a meditation app. They showed remarkable brain activity in regions normally reserved for other things. And that was witnessed by folks who know their amygdala from their abdomen, and they're proving that meditation isn't just legitimate, it's transformative.

But there is a dark side to all of this feel-good new age wisdom too. In 2021, a study published in Psychotherapy Research blew a hole through the glossy aura of the modern meditation movement. In a nationally representative sample, more than 10% of people reported what researchers diplomatically called "meditation-related adverse effects." Translation: anxiety, traumatic flashbacks, and emotional overwhelm ... some symptoms lasting for weeks. So much for inner peace.

Then came March of 2024, when investigative journalist Madison Marriage dropped a podcast series like a depth charge into the waters of the mindfulness world. Her exposé on Goenka-style Vipassana retreats - ten days of total silence coupled to ten hours of seated meditation each day - detailed real mental breakdowns, psychological trauma, and even suicides experienced by some attendees. While countless practitioners have emerged from these retreats radiant and deeply transformed, others have spiraled into serious distress. And from my personal experience meditating for over forty-plus years? I'll say it: ten hours a day of meditation of any kind is far too much time to be spelunking the caves of your own mind.

Sure, there are days when a meditation session feels like a warm bath for the soul. You want to linger, to explore, to see what that quiet spaciousness might teach you. But then there are sessions that feel like taking a wrong turn and ending up in the 8k meter kill zone of your psyche, where the lights are out and something's dripping in the corner. Forcing yourself to stay there out of some spiritual machismo isn't brave, it's harmful, I would even say stupid. I've had those moments too. Sessions that turned dark and jagged like a Carol Reed noir piece, where observing the mind like a passive witness wasn't calming, it was corrosive. And I've ended those sessions early. Not out of weakness, but out of wisdom.

Walking away isn't failure. It's self-knowledge. Knowing when to close the door on a session that isn't serving you is its own kind of practice, a different form of clarity. If you want to torture yourself, sit in the lotus position for an hour and see how long you last before you move.

Yes, for the vast majority, meditation is a beneficial, life-enhancing tool. But like anything powerful, it demands respect and moderation. It's not about cranking up the intensity until you break through. Sometimes, it's about knowing when to pause - when to give your mind a break before it turns on you with a blackjack.

I've developed a rule of thumb for my meditation sessions: keep it to about a half hour unless the session is flowing and you're tossing away guilt and shame like peanut shells at a ball game. If you're cruising your awareness train, then by all means, stay on board. But thirty minutes is plenty. Personally, I prefer midmorning sessions. Not too groggy, not too caffeinated. Just right. That sweet spot when my brain's alert enough to notice its own bullshit but still soft enough to be quieted. That's when I take a focused mental cool-down lap.

Pay attention the next time you finish washing dishes, writing an email, reorganizing your spice rack in order of cuisine relevance, and realize you have no idea how long you were at it. How do you feel? Peaceful? Productive? Or are you suddenly panicked that you've time-traveled again?

That moment when you shift from full immersion back into regular programming. That's gold. That's the point where you get to decide: Do I hold on to this calm clarity for a moment longer? Or do I slam headfirst into my to-do list like a coked-up male howler monkey let loose in a filing cabinet permeated with female howler estrogen?

Make no mistake, your monkey's always ready. He's hanging out just offstage, fingers twitching, eyes darting for an opportunity and ready to yank on your mental strangler vines the second you lose focus. But if you catch that transition, if you actually see it happen, you've already got a leg up. You can either take a breath and return to calm... or go joyriding through your cortex with your hyperactive inner primate. It's your call, but I recommend the former.

❧

I'll never forget the first time I hit what I can only describe as meditative gold. I was sitting on the bank of a lazy river, one of my favorite places to simply be. The air was warm, sweet and clean, bees and bugs were busy making their rounds, and everything was just... alive ... in that soft, summertime-is-easy way. As I settled into meditation, something shifted. Suddenly, I had control, a gentle steering of thought. My mind responded to the lightest touch, like a Formula 1 car going balls-out with Lewis Hamilton at the wheel. I could focus. I could release. I could parry and thrust. Thoughts floated by and I could identify and observe, then swipe them into the mental recycle bin, one by one, without a second thought.

And then I laughed.

I mean, I really laughed. A genuine from-my-core laugh. Because it felt so good, and because I was fully aware I had "*done it.*" It was that mythical state of flow and clarity everyone talks about. I was in it, living it in real time.

And with that laugh, the whole thing scattered like dandelion seeds to the wind. The moment broke. The birds kept singing, the bees kept buzzing, the river kept flowing, and I was left blinking at the sunlight, feeling euphoric, yet a little sad that I couldn't slip right back in. I was high on presence for the rest of the day. Of course, I thought, *I got this!* I didn't "got this" at all.

So that's the deal: meditation isn't about candles or caves or impressing your Tik Tok followers with your serene cushion pose. It's about paying attention - to your breath, a sound, a mantra, your unhinged mental zoo. Some days you get a moment of peace, a glimpse of that elusive Flow. Other days, it's just you and your monkey, chucking feces and old wooden blocks at your concentration. Either way, it's progress. It's you, trying.

That's why it's called practice.

CHAPTER 3. TAKE A WALK ON THE THAI SIDE

"Thailand was built on compassion." – Bhumibol Adulyadej

What can I possibly say about the place known as The Land of Smiles that hasn't already been wrapped in a travel guide paperback, filtered through some influencer's smoothie-fueled blog, or declared "life-changing" by a backpacker who rode an elephant and now sells himself as spiritually evolved? I don't know. But I'm going to give it a shot. With the help of journals, questionable memory, and a deep love for a place that's equal parts reverent, magical and ridiculous, hopefully you'll get a glimpse of the wonderful world that is Thailand.

Thailand. The Kingdom. The exotic. And yes, depending on where you point your sandals, the erotic. Thailand wasn't just my first step into Asia; it was a deep dive into a sensory kaleidoscope. A place where the normal, the sacred and the profane exist on the same block: monks gathering alms at dawn, a pharmacist helping a tourist get over Bangkok Belly, and neon-lit bars full of women offering questionable massages by nightfall. That cultural whiplash is part of its charm.

My obsession with Asia started early, fueled by a silver-on-black silk-sewn drama mask my father brought back from Korea, a war souvenir that hung on the wall like a haunted invitation to mystery. It stared at me through childhood, whispering tales of foreign lands, spicy, exotic food, and mysteries far beyond my experiences.

By the time I landed in Thailand, I'd already spent years marinating in San Francisco's heady Asian communities, and Seattle's International District, eating dim sum and noodles, wok fries and rice in every form known to man. I wasn't just chasing exoticism, I was chasing something honest, something real, and maybe a little unhinged. I wanted to eat the food, meet the people, and not be *that* tourist complaining that the Wi-Fi in paradise was too slow. And, thanks to my stubborn streak, I was determined to stay off the well-trod tourist conveyor belt.

So, why Thailand? Part research, part instinct, but primarily because I found a Theravāda Buddhist monastery that didn't look like a cult or a resort. I wanted the real deal. I wanted to live within the culture - not float above it with selfie stick in hand.

What I've learned from earlier travels to places around the world can easily be summed up: if you treat people with dignity, honor, respect and genuine curiosity, they'll meet you halfway with a smile and sometimes a steaming bowl of something that might change your life. Or kill you. Either way, it is memorable.

But where to start? At the beginning I suppose.

Before June 23rd, 1939AD, shrouded in mystery and history, the Kingdom of Thailand was known as the Kingdom of Siam, derived from various linguistic interpretations of Syam, or Xian ethnonyms. The region has been continuously inhabited for over 20,000 years give or take a few sacked kingdoms. The place is old, with a capital O. Archaeological evidence (granaries, drop pits, home remains, ritual ceramics, and fire pits) shows waves of civilizations - the Mon, the Khmer, the Lao, the Chinese (of whom the Tai are thought to be part of through linguistic roots), the Burmese - all leaving their fingerprints on the land, art, architecture, food, the peoples who integrated with one another, and language.

It has been recognized under a variety of names since it was the Kingdom of Sukhothai, founded in 1238AD, when the political structure shifted from a wealthy city servicing the rice and spice traders and silk route travelers, into a political entity under the rule of Si Inthrathit. Before that and stretching way back in time, the region, with shifting borders and allegiances depending on who sacked who that month, was known as the Kingdom of Funan which was the first mighty and omni-powerful Southeastern Asia kingdom, dating back into the 2nd Century BCE.

You feel it. Not just in the stones or statues or endless Wats with names that sound like arcane magic spells, but in the eyes of the people.

And yes, Thailand is the Land of Smiles. That's not just tourism board fluff. But those smiles? They're not all the same. There are at least thirteen officially recognized types of Thai smiles, from the "I'm genuinely happy to see you" broad grin to the "you just did something idiotic and I'm politely pretending otherwise" smirk. You learn to tell them apart if you hang around long enough, and if you make a complete mess of a Thai phrase in public, you'll earn a few of them at once.

Something about all those smiles to note. Because smiles (Yim) are used throughout Thai communicative expressions. It is a subtle system full of nuance and meaning that, unless you grow up within the culture, let's just say the differences can be easy to miss or misinterpret.

There's the teasing smile - mischievous and playful; the awkward smile - somewhat forced in an uncomfortable situation; the flirty smile when trying to catch someone's interest; the respectful smile showing admiration for the receiver; the discreet smile, used to shy away from intention; an embarrassed smile - we all know that one; the polite laughter smile - we all know this one too; the secretive smile - hiding message and meaning except to those in the know; the genuine smile, obviously heartfelt and joyous; the fake smile which I observed many times as rude tourists demanded something without courtesy or respect - also used a lot during haggling negotiations; the polite smile which is professional and formal; the apologetic smile showing regret; and last is the hesitant smile which is subtle, wary.

Of course, there are exceptions to the rule but everywhere I traveled, the vast majority of locals I ran into and the interactions I had were that beautiful and heart-warming real smile experience. If you're not a difficult tourist and please don't be that person, you'll almost always be greeted with Yim tak thaai - the genuine smile that lights up faces and rooms.

The Thai are funny, sharp, curious, and disarmingly charming. They will laugh with you as much as at you, which is honestly the best kind of laughter. Miscommunication becomes its own language - equal parts pantomime, Google Translate mishaps, and blind faith. There's something delightfully human about fumbling your way through a conversation with a smile and a shrug and ending up with a new friend over a shared plate of something delicious.

I love the tantalizing mystery that comes when traveling in a country where you don't speak the language. Thailand turned that mystery up to eleven. Every country I've visited where English wasn't the primary tongue has been a wild mix of hilarity and humility. But Thai? Thai took the cake, ate it, and then politely handed me back the plate.

The oral language is nuanced, tonal, sometimes brash, sometimes elegant - but to my untrained ear it might as well have been Romulan spinning riddles. With five tones that can change the meaning of a word entirely, one wrong pitch and instead of saying "hello," you just proposed marriage or asked if you could have sex with a lawnmower. Plus, there are twelve recognized regional dialects, mostly branching from Issan and Lanna cultures, so even if I did manage to say something correctly, odds were decent the listener would just smile politely and walk away very confused.

And the written script? It's mesmerizing: swirls, dots, loops, and curls that look like they were hand-drawn by a calligraphic octopus with a flair for the dramatic. Take ร้านอาหารทะเล - Thai for "seafood restaurant." Beautiful, right? It looks like a title, or a stanza in a poem or "get off my lawn!".

Reading signs, menus, labels - none of that was happening. Thai doesn't use Latin characters, and the structure is wildly different from English. There are also high, middle, and low script characters, which adds a bonus round to the confusion. Thai was, for me, the equivalent of a linguistic Mount Everest.

And yet, there's charm to it. Thai has this built-in structure. Case in point: "krab" and "kha," gendered polite particles you append to everything if you have any manners and grace. *Sawatdee krab* if you're male, *Sawatdee kha* if you're female, means 'Hello sir, or ma'am. Like verbal punctuation marks of courtesy. It's sweet, thoughtful, and a total minefield when your accent is bad enough to make every child within earshot giggle.

I didn't have months to embrace the language, and frankly, given my track record with foreign tongues, I needed years and a brain transplant to get even an inkling of comfort with so foreign a communication structure. So, I focused on the essentials: greetings, "thank you", "delicious", "I'm sorry", "may I have the check?" "where's the bathroom?", and a few noble attempts at "with great respect." The rest? Lost to the wind. My pronunciation was a wrecking ball, and people laughed at me. With repetition and some gentle corrections, I got better.

And when in doubt, there was always the magic trifecta: a real-time translation app, a friendly smile, and a willingness to act out whatever I needed with the gusto of a silent film actor on espresso.

Here's a real-life example: My first full day in Bangkok and already I was mosquito feed. Fresh off the plane, I smelled like fresh meat. I earned a few bites while lounging by the hotel pool and immediately activated my pre-departure plan. Secure high-powered, skin-melting bug spray with enough DEET to give a forest cancer. I didn't care if DEET had been banned in half the civilized world - it's either that or dengue fever or malaria, and I don't like jaw-locking fevers unless they come with dance numbers.

Off I went, first to the nearest 7-Eleven (it was twenty feet away), where everything was labeled with great detail in Thai. No bug spray leapt out at me, unless it was playing hide-and-seek in the anti-fungal section. I left with a pack of gum and ventured down the street until I found a giant hypermarket, the kind of place where you can buy a mop, durian, a model airplane kit and a motorcycle helmet all in one aisle.

After some wandering, I zeroed in on the long personal hygiene aisle. Shampoo, toothpaste, deodorant, hair dyes, false lashes, mystery creams, check. Mosquito death juice? Nowhere to be found. I wandered the aisles when I spotted a young man at the end stocking shelves and gave him my best, "I need bug spray, help me not die" look. He blinked. I blinked. He shrugged. Then, the universal sign for "I have no idea what you just said but wait here," he held up a finger and vanished.

Enter backup. He returned with a young woman who looked thrilled to be dragged into a foreigners' quest. I repeated my question. More blank stares. They looked at each other, then back at me. I could practically hear the sitcom laugh track in the background.

It was pantomime time.

I sprang into action: arms out, flapping wildly like a drunk pigeon, whining out a nasal zzzzzzzz as I wobbled in circles, then nosedived a finger toward my arm, jabbed it, then scratched furiously like I was hosting a flea circus. Those unfortunate store clerks stared for a heartbeat, then burst into full-throated laughter, nearly doubling over. It was the kind of laugh that makes your knees buckle. They beckoned me down the aisle. I'd just won charades for Team Mosquito-Bitten Tourist.

Moments later, I was inspecting two bug sprays as the young woman earnestly pointed to the percentages of DEET on the back label like a pharmacist. Victory.

As I was checking out, I heard more laughter. The same young woman was now re-enacting my mosquito interpretive dance for another store employee, pointing in my direction. They were howling. I waved, then bowed dramatically like it was final curtain on Broadway. International communication achievement unlocked with bonus humiliation points awarded. Now *that's* fantastic communication!

My point is you should at least try and make the effort with the local language. If you travel to a country where your native tongue is not dominant, it's your obligation to work with the local language as much as possible. The onus is not on the locals to learn your language and no, speaking your language **LOUDER** and S-L-O-W-E-R does not work. In fact, it proves to everyone around that you're an idiot.

There's a cinematic richness to the everyday scenery. The street vendors with their rainbow umbrellas looking like candy-colored mushrooms sprouting from the sidewalks. Motorcycles and scooters swarm like locusts, buzzing between cars, sidewalks, and wherever they can squeeze through. Power lines knot themselves in thick chaotic webs above the street like a giant forgot to finish a macramé project. Bright gold Buddhas gleam in roadside alcoves surrounded by offerings of incense, lotus bulbs, cigarettes (it would seem that Buddha was a pack-a-day guy), Fanta bottles with red straws sticking out. It would also seem that the divine also has a thing for sugary beverages.

Even the signage is loud and proud: shop names curling in looping Thai script, flashing lights that blink with urgency, welcome, or mystical foretelling - I couldn't always tell which. And then there's the constant background hum of life: sizzling oil, hawkers calling out, a radio playing Thai pop, a rooster crowing at a whiny dog and the ever-present whir of ceiling fans trying their best not to give up in the heat.

It's overwhelming in the best possible way - like walking through someone else's dream while mildly dehydrated.

The architecture in Thailand is a full-contact visual sport. It sprints from the ancient to the aggressively modern, from transcendent beauty to "who greenlit this crime against eyes?" - often on the same block. Your optic nerves need a seatbelt and a welder's helmet at times. And if you're a minimalist? Brace yourself. The Thai aesthetic does not shy away from color. In fact, it sprints toward it with open arms and a glitter cannon.

Take Bangkok's new obsession with building cladding. This fevered dream trend involves wrapping perfectly innocent, though plain-Jane boring concrete buildings in jagged, or flowing metallic exoskeletons anodized in acid-trip hues as a public service to those who felt their day wasn't visceral enough. These futuristic facades often look like a Transformer had a midlife crisis and crashed into a Home Depot. Not one of them was what you'd call "elegant," but sure, the concept had vibes. I hope the trend doesn't spread.

Then there's the traffic. Oh yes - the lunatic-fueled unhinged traffic!

Traffic, as a concept, is universal. It can be light, heavy, snarled, fast, slow, passable, or the kind of soul-sucking crawl that tests your patience. Everywhere in the world has traffic issues except Antarctica, although I suspect the penguins have their own waddling gridlock come mating season.

But Thailand... Thailand doesn't have traffic. Urban Thailand *is* traffic.

For the uninitiated, Thai drivers operate on the left side of the road like the Brits, Aussies, Kiwis, and the rest of the Commonwealth holdouts. But that's where the similarities end. Because in Thailand, driving on the left doesn't mean you *stay* on the left. Or in a lane. Or in any particular state of linear time. Thai traffic is a living, breathing organism governed less by rules and more by instincts, mood, cosmic forces, and a shared telepathic agreement that today's journey will defy Euclidean geometry.

It is, at any given moment, an interactive, high-stakes ballet of cars, motorcycles, tuk tuks, songthaews, trucks hauling everything and anything, buses that somehow weave effortlessly in and out of the flow, and the occasional rogue dog. The experience is like riding inside a 5,000-piece kaleidoscope operated by a rabid squid with a fondness for pachinko.

And yet - miraculously - it works. Mostly. Thai drivers seem to operate on some hive-mind logic, where split-second decisions are executed with such synchronized perfection that it's akin to performance art. No one uses their horns with anything approaching the relentless fury of, say, Mumbai, where honking is communication and punctuation. In Bangkok, it's all visual cues and peripheral awareness.

So, what is it that keeps traffic in every town and city all around the world flowing in an orderly manner? Laws. Those rules of the road that we all learn when we get our licenses no matter where we live. And then there's Thailand!

Where I live, as I am assuming where you live, there are rules of the road that we willingly follow, not wanting to either die or to cause death to someone else. Seems fair, right? Laws that were enacted to facilitate order and flow for the movement of vehicles, people and goods, no matter what those vehicles may be, are a good thing. Cars big and small, trucks enormous to tiny, adorable tuk tuks done up in garish regalia, scooters, mopeds and motorcycles, bicycles, tricycles, food and hand-drawn carts of infinite variety, all vying for space and progress. The objective being getting from point A to point B is usually the modus operandi, and it is through those agreed upon rules of the road that allow all modes of transportation to coexist and flow.

Yes - there are rules of the road in Thailand. You can tell because someone went through the trouble of painting lanes and installing traffic signs, lights, crosswalks and other manifestations of the desire for controlled movement. And to live to see tomorrow. And like everywhere, those signs are there to tell us how fast we can drive, where to stop, if you can turn, watch for pedestrians, etcetera. However, and this is just simple observation at work, it seems that once the driver/operators of any sort of vehicle in Thailand gets their license, every one of those rules gets downgraded to a minor list of suggestions, and inconvenient ones at that.

The roads in Thailand are a glorious symphony of frenetic energy - equal parts comedy, adrenaline rush, and vehicular roulette. Keep your wits about you or become a hood ornament. And it's not just the roads. Oh no. Sidewalks, alleys, restaurants, temple courtyards, and quite possibly living rooms all seem to be considered viable transit routes. Mind the cat and the toddler please.

Screw the coffee! Want a real wake-up call in Thailand? Try crossing a six-lane boulevard in Bangkok at rush hour without a walk signal. It's like playing Frogger, but with your life.

There's an art to crossing a busy road in Thailand. It's called *commitment* and the technique is all about the art of aggressive timing and concentration. Think ballet meets demolition derby.

Now, if you're a rational human being with a healthy fear of rolling metal objects, you'll be relieved to know that there are options that don't involve risking life and limb. Major boulevards often have pedestrian overpasses - bridges for your feet. Or, if you're lucky enough to be near a BTS SkyTrain or MRT subway station, you can use those as glorified over and underpasses, complete with the added benefit of snack bars and sometimes air con.

But sometimes... sometimes it's either more practical or just morbidly thrilling to cross at street level. Why? Because you're already sweaty, slightly delusional from the humidity, and deep down you want to feel intensely alive.

Thai drivers of cars and scooters are quite used to playing slalom games with pedestrians. Nobody blinks when a random human darts into traffic like a panicked squirrel. It's part of the ecosystem. That said, crossing a Thai road is not for the faint of heart. You will engage every neuron in your brain. Your fight-or-flight response will tap-dance on your frontal lobe. If you're not laser-focused, you'll end up part of the pavement and not in a poetic, travel-blog kind of way.

However, there's a method to your commitment. You observe the flow. Study it like a lioness eyeing a herd of Springbok for the slow and injured. Scooters and motorcycles are your primary threat - quick, agile, and slightly suicidal. Cars are next. Buses? They're too slow to kill you unless you really screw up.

Then comes the big moment: the gap. The holy grail of urban pedestrian warfare. Once you see it, you must commit. No hesitation. No second-guessing. If you bail halfway through, you're toast and so is the poor soul who is trying to avoid slamming into you.

Move it like you mean it. Straddle lane lines. Slipping through spaces your logical brain insists are too narrow. And here's the magic: once drivers see you're serious, they'll veer around you with all the grace of synchronized dance. For it is a dance. You do your part, they do theirs. Everyone lives another day.

But if you flinch? If you second-guess? That's when it goes sideways.

So yes, you could always use a crosswalk at the light or take the overhead walkway. But where's the story in that?

Then there are the markets. Not the sad, half-hearted kind we have in the U.S. You know, a parking lot with a couple of dozen stalls, some kale selling for $18 a bunch, a perfect enormous leek that'll set you back $20, a woman named Melinda the Magnificent selling lavender sachets and pseudo-wisdom, and *that* guy aggressively hawking raw honey out of a cooler. No. Thailand doesn't do markets like we do. Thailand lives markets. Breathes markets. Dreams in markets. Then wakes up and opens another market.

There's no way to measure the worth of Thailand's street markets in GDP points or sterile economic reports from my desk. But you feel it in the smoke, the shouting, the rhythm. But if you *had* to put a number on it, the country's informal markets - hawkers, night bazaars, roadside grills - quietly generate somewhere between $2 to $5 billion USD a year by estimate. That's not chump change. That's the lifeblood of neighborhoods, entire communities, the pulse of cities, the reason a kid in Chiang Rai gets dinner tonight. It's messy, it's vital and flows directly into the pockets of people. It's also more honest than the malls where that retail revenue drops first into the corporate coffers.

Day or night, the famed Thai street markets are an unrelenting assault of color, smell, sound, and capitalism. They are wild, glorious, and packed to the clouds with everything you could need, want, or never imagined existed. And for the most part, it's quality merchandise. Handcrafted leather goods and delicate jewelry, vibrant hand-made umbrellas, sacred amulets, hand-painted postcards, potted plants the size of young adults, hand-sewn clothes you'll never wear again, and food - so much food, sizzling and steaming from every corner like a street fair collided with a cooking show.

And yes, nestled between the artisanal and the edible lies the shady end of the souvenir spectrum: *the rayon elephant pants*. You know the ones. Soft. Billowy. Loud. Worn exclusively by tourists who left their shame back at the hostel. They're the unofficial uniform of "I went to Thailand and bought these ridiculous pants."

But my personal favorite? Black Velvet paintings. Yes, that medium is still going strong there. Right there in the middle of the market, beneath a canopy of string lights as smoke from the neighboring grilled squid stand floats through the crowd, a man is airbrushing a tangerine-orange Buddha onto crushed black velvet like it's 1969. Elvis, Jesus, clowns, tigers, ballerinas, temples. It's a full velvet revival and garish. I love it!

And then there's music. Every hundred feet or so, there's another band or solo act belting out tunes, some traditional Thai, some 90s Euro-pop, all slightly off-key but delivered with unshakable confidence and sincerity. The whole thing feels less like a shopping trip and more like a neighborhood block party designed by someone with synesthesia and an energy drink problem.

The market Prices? Ridiculously reasonable. So reasonable in fact that it blows my mind each and every time when tourists haggle like they're closing a multi-million-dollar real estate deal. Do you really need to knock 20 Baht off that handmade bracelet, Karen? That's .59 cents. Less than a pack of gum. Sure, you may get your petty thrill of winning *"the deal,"* but that 20 Baht actually means something to the vendor. It might pay for laundry soap or the tuk tuk ride home. You, meanwhile, will spend more on your next iced latte. Think about that the next time you try to low-ball the vendor.

OK yes, there is a different price for tourists. Of course there is. That is part of the dance. Locals get the secret handshake rate. You, the sunburned gringo in a tank top that says, "Pad Thai is my Spirit Animal," get the premium. And do you know what? That's fair. You are incredibly lucky to be there. Pay the .50 extra cents. Smile. Take your grilled banana leaf fish and your velvet Jesus home and feel good about the whole transaction. You will earn merits and experience less self-loathing later.

The markets, sprawling across a dozen city blocks or more are a sensory riot wrapped in string lights. Picture it: a near-endless grid of colorful booths and carts, each strung up with lights attached to anything that will stand still long enough - lampposts, rooftops, a meditating monk - casting a warm glow over the entire bazaar. It's like Christmas, but with noodles, fried insects and durian.

The air, thick with the mingling aromas of a hundred sizzling carts hawking everything from fried black scorpions to Michelin-rated bowls of noodles. There's Pad Krapow, curries, Pad Thai, Larb, Pad See Ew, fried rice and mango sticky rice, roti with bananas slathered in condensed milk, fresh-pressed fruit juices that punch you in the vitamin C receptors, and enough coffee and tea to caffeinate a military division.

The brilliance though of Thai market foods lays in portion size - small, smart, and engineered for grazing. No one is dishing out troughs of Pad Thai to share with your extended family. You *can* order that way, but no one does. This is snack-and-stride territory. You eat sitting down if you can find a seat at the ever-crowded courtyard tables, but more likely standing up, leaning against whatever is nearby. Railing, tree, possibly a surprised stranger, and then dive back in for round two, three, four and more, with no regrets.

At the Chiang Mai Saturday Night Market, in the walled old city, I succumbed to peer pressure and ate a large, glossy, black fried scorpion on a stick (*Scorpiops chiangmai*, if you're Googling for nightmares). A fellow traveler saw me taking photos of the skewered beasts and asked if I'd tried one. I had not. He hadn't either. We dared each other. Since I am not one to back down from a dare that involved eating what could pass for a Sith Lord's house pet. He ate his like it was popcorn. I, however, gag-crunched my way through the thing. Was it delicious? No. But it was crunchy in a disturbing yet satisfying kettle-chip-meets-spider-leg way. I do not recommend it for the flavor; scorpion is like spicy cardboard with a touch of past due-date crab and spam with an exoskeleton, but for the bragging rights? Priceless.

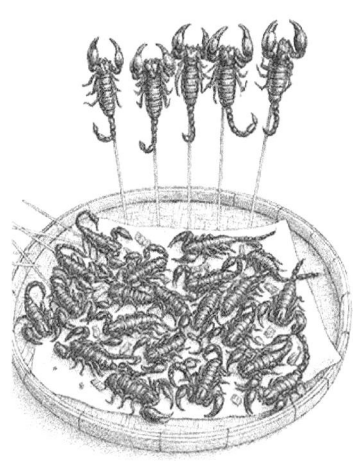

I rewarded my bravery with a bowl of Tom Yum Kung - a sweet-sour prawn soup steeped with lemongrass, galangal, and kaffir lime leaf. Three huge prawns. Eight ecstatic spoons of yummy. Barely over a dollar. Then came four bite-sized Sichuan pork chops, bone-in, dipped in chili oil and a spicy-sweet peanut sauce that should be declared a controlled substance. I wanted to get that sauce to go and put it on everything! The chop crusts were shatteringly crispy, the meat inside juicy, and the Sichuan peppers hit with their trademark floral zap that makes your mouth feel like it is simultaneously freezing and being electrocuted. Bliss. I wept a little.

For dessert, I had the single greatest mango I've ever eaten. An angel's cheek masquerading as fruit. Thai mangoes *do not* mess around. They are all sugar and perfume, and somehow always perfectly ripe, as if the mangoes themselves are in on the tourist seduction plot. Then, a solo cup of fresh-pressed high-mountain orange juice so tart-sweet and aggressively orange-y it felt like being mouth-mugged by a citrus grove.

The weirdest thing I tried hands down was chicken-and-tamarind cotton-candy floss. I still don't know whether I was eating food or applying for a dare-based reality show. The flavor hovered somewhere between "maybe I like this?" and "nope, that's poultry-flavored sticky air." Final verdict: hard leaning toward "never again," but I sort of respect its creativity.

All told, the total food expense on that first experience of the Chiang Mai Saturday night market. Under $10.

Walking is hands-down, my favorite way to explore. Slow, curious, and inefficient enough to feel virtuous. In Thailand, I averaged fifteen kilometers a day. Some days I would stroll an easy 5k. Other days I walked 25k then hobble into a massage parlor begging for mercy and two hours of mint-oil hand-crushed knot-kneading foot-rubbing bliss. Thankfully, foot massages are as common in Thailand as Starbucks are, well... everywhere, and far more affordable.

Locals in the neighborhoods where I stayed thought I was friendly and always game for a chat, but a bit ... off. They'd ask where I was going, as they eyed a tuk tuk or scooter cab to save me from myself. When I politely declined and patted my stomach explaining I was trying to burn the flab because I hate crunches, they would nod and smile. But I could hear the thought behind the smile: "Ah yes. Crazy American."

These observations are based on the cities, because once you're out in the hinterlands you get to where you want to go by whatever means you conjure up. I tried to use The Force but alas, I discovered I am not a Jedi. Sometimes you just got to hop on a bus or summon a Grab.

But it is only when walking deliberately yet aimlessly that you find the magic. Not the bougie city boulevards lined with global chains and knockoff luxury boutiques clawing at your wallet with "*special tourist prices!*" No, the real Thailand lives in the alleys. Clean, narrow, and humming with local life. They're the backstage pass to the city's personality. One minute you are squeezing past a noodle cart, the next you're browsing hand-stitched silk shirts in a shop the size of a walk-in closet, next to a weed shop with a name like "Thai High" or "Buddha Blazed." Coffee and tea joints tucked into what looks like someone's former living room, each one serving better drinks than any coffee chain on the planet. The alleys don't sell you the Thailand Experience™ - they *are* the experience.

One narrow alley I ducked into turned was downright lovely. Yes, lovely. Lined on both sides by tall, weather-worn four-story apartment buildings, their ornate wrought-iron balconies proudly displaying a colorful cast of laundry. It felt lived-in in the best way. Overhead, Bangkok's signature power line lunacy crisscrossed like a Pollock painting in wire, an unintentional art installation depicting modern life. At street level, it was all action: tiny shops, hole-in-the-wall eateries, and locals doing what locals do. I had wandered down Sukhumvit 21 because one of the front-desk guys at the place I was staying gave an impassioned, borderline-romance recommendation: an Indian joint he swore was the best in Bangkok. But what I found directly across the alley from it? Even better.

"High Tea by Pickaboo" was a lurid dreamscape of whimsy and storybook delirium. Adorable, creative, and piratically perfect in every way. The façade was a riot of flowing vines, hanging plants, and four giant upright book spines the formed the door-frame, each painted to look like something looted from a dusty British manor library. The actual door? Agatha Christie's "Murder on the Orient Express, and Other Hercule Poirot Mysteries". Three exaggerated keyhole windows - a nod to Alice in Wonderland - peer outward while the interior exploded with murals from Peter Pan, Gulliver's Travels, and various other escapist dreams. A teenager-sized purple rabbit clutching a pocket-watch guards the entrance - a Lewis Carroll bouncer - and a black-and-white zigzag floor straight out of Twin Peaks cut through the fantasy with enough edge to keep things even weirder. Even the stair risers were painted like classic book spines, because apparently nothing is safe from a literary makeover. Honestly, if the tea had been terrible, I wouldn't have cared. Places like that earn their keep on charm alone. As it turned out, their tea and snacks were as top-notch as their design obsession. *That's* why you wander down alleys. I went back two nights later for more tea, then to Hinata Izakaya (a casual Japanese pub with a million small food options and lots of sake) two doors down.

And that is just one of thousands of alleys - each with their own unique combo of weird awesomeness.

※

In Bangkok, my method was simple: pick a random station, either subway or SkyTrain, out on the edge of the transit map, somewhere that sounded unfamiliar, download the route to my phone, hop on the BTS or MRT, and ride until the tourists thinned out and the city started getting local. Then I'd stroll back. It was urban exploration meets cardio, with a high likelihood of getting semi-lost. More than once, I turned in slow confused circles like a dog trying to lie down in a too-small bed, hoping as a last resort that my phone would magically orient me.

That strategy required an early start, which meant joining the Bangkok commuter crush: shoulder to shoulder, packed tight as could be. Back in my San Francisco days, we commuters read the San Francisco Chronicle (a fine newspaper if ever there was one), the tall four-panel fold mastered so perfectly it looked choreographed. We would read headlines and columns, hold a coffee, our brief cases safely stashed between our feet, and swing around turns without stabbing anyone in the face. These days, glowing rectangles dominate. Phones, tablets, e-readers all cast blue light on expressionless faces. The historic smell of ink and newsprint has vanished, replaced with battery heat and the quiet anxiety of doomscrolling and candy-crush losses.

Comfortable, sturdy, well-made flip-flops are all you really need to conquer the cities, towns, and even countryside of Thailand. I swear by the high-end leather ones (I am partial to OluKai.) They are durable as hell, stylish enough to pass for "advanced smart casual," and built to survive a monsoon, a street noodle spill, an impromptu hike, or 25k in a day. They're the Swiss Army knife of footwear. Plus, when it's sweltering outside (read: *always*), you'll want that airflow.

Every Wat requires bare feet to enter shrines and surrounding buildings, and sneakers? Sneakers are the devil's device in this context. I've watched tourists contorting like drunk yogis, balancing on one foot while they perform the ritual of the double bunny ear. Meanwhile, I'm already inside, flops off, snapping photos of a 30-foot gold Buddha and taking time for a little triple-gem prayer.

If walking isn't your jam, fear not. Bangkok's transportation menu is as endless as it is eclectic. You've got multiple forms of busses, the subway (MRT), the SkyTrain (BTS), enough water-taxis to make Venice blush; everything from picturesque, fast and noisy longtail boats that are all captained by pirates, to sleek ferries that keep a tight schedule on the city's many rivers and canals. Tuk tuks, often brightly painted, buzz by like hornets, songthaews (utilitarian red trucks with benches in the back) shuttle locals and the brave-hearted alike. You can hail a cab, grab a Grab (Thailand's Uber, but cheaper and friendlier), or hop on the back of a scooter taxi and let someone else risk your life for you. Bicycles? Sure, if you're feeling bold and invincible. You can also hire a private driver through a half dozen apps, and if you hit it off, they'll drop their number into WhatsApp like a Tinder match with a Toyota. They will take you anywhere you want for a fair price and a good laugh. But if you stick to transport alone, you're just getting from A to B. And in between is where the weird, wonderful stuff is hiding; it's always halfway down that alley you didn't take.

One genuinely useful tip - yes, this one is actually useful and not just "drink bottled water" is about electricity. Thailand has figured out the universal wall socket. Their outlets are the ultimate in power deliverance: they'll accept any plug configuration you throw at them: US, UK, EU, OZ, you name it. As long as your device's power brick says something like "110v–230v" (it's the fine print you ignore until your phone catches fire), you're good to go - no adapter necessary.

Hair dryers and electric razors remain the divas of the electronics world. Those tend to fry faster than a spring roll in boiling oil so proceed with caution or just use the hotels. Still, it is not a bad idea to carry an adapter for peace of mind. But in practice? I didn't need one in Bangkok, Chiang Mai, Chiang Rai, or even on the far-flung island of Koh Chang. Even my monastery deep in the Thai backwoods where geckos ran the place had sockets to juice up my laptop.

CHAPTER 4. CHIANG MAI. MUCH ADO ABOUT SOMETHING

You only discover who you really are when the ground stops feeling familiar.

PART 1 - Pre-monastery

Repeat after me: "chee-AHNG-my."

That place, those people, the smells of exotic flora, the street food with its accompanying sound of woks working everywhere, tuk tuks and scooters buzzing by, the thump of sub-woofers at night drawing you into hippie and expat dens, pot and hash clouds wafting out doors and windows accompanied by bleary smiles and gestures of welcome; a dozen dialects being spoken, all looking for the good stuff no matter what that good stuff may be ... Chiang Mai is a wonderland assault on the senses. The multifaceted smiles that adorn almost every Thai face in greeting (and the red-faced tourists tortured by the heat, humidity and mosquitoes) ... There is so much to delight in that it gleefully overwhelmed me at times.

As the insanity and 1000-volt buzz of Bangkok ebbed into the background and my soul relaxed into evenflow, the chill atmosphere of Chiang Mai eased into the void vacated of the explosive sensory excess like a scented soft breeze. Yes, Bangkok is a rush and where Bangkok is like mainlining a thousand-bean extract of caffeine, Chiang Mai is the exhale, more hum than howl. Gooier, like the smiling vibe you get while gazing at a back-lit cloud sunset where the edges are afire with a dozen hues of gold, the inner rim fluffy cotton candy like a plumped-up feather pillow. It's got the kind of vibe where you wonder if you've joined a cult without realizing it.

Chiang Mai is Thailand's *"new city."* That is a delightful contradiction. It was founded sometime between 1294 and 1296. But what's a couple years when you're measuring things in centuries? For perspective, where I'm from, anything over one hundred years old gets a plaque and several preservation committees. In Thailand, a hundred years old is brand new.

Located 435 miles north of Bangkok in the mountainous plateau region called the highlands, it is the central governing seat of the larger Chiang Mai Province which boasts verdant valleys filled with picturesque agriculture, rivers, mountains, and National Parks. There are ten scattered around the province. The city itself is nestled in a broad, flat valley, surrounded by mountains to the north, east and west thus it has a very different feel from Bangkok. Chiang Mai, however, feels like fun. There's an atmosphere that feels expectant and vibrant. From the newest hip neighborhoods right into the heart of the ancient moat-surrounded old town, everything feels ready for action but without Bangkok's intensity blast to your cortex.

My first full day in Chiang Mai found me wandering the streets of the Nimman District from early to late morning. I was getting hungry when I stumbled upon the Hong Tauw Inn, on a high raised sidewalk along Nimmanhaemin Road. It was there that I enjoyed the best Tom Kha Gai and Poh Pia Tod I've ever eaten. The old restaurant had a small sign which read "Est. 1938". Guided by that alone I figured that they knew what they were doing.

Two split old wood-shutter doors and the window frames were painted an odd sea-foam blue green. A menu hung on a nail on one of the outer doors, an open sign hanging in the window. The interior glass door sported completely out-of-place ye-olde-English lettering showing hours of operations while the lintels above the windows and door had alternating blue and green stained-glass panels. Nothing made sense yet the place beckoned to me. It was still early, just past 11AM so the lunchtime crowd wouldn't start filtering in for a while. The dining room looked like it hadn't changed since Thailand was called Siam.

Two elderly, smiling women came out from behind an ornate carved teak screen to say "*Sawatdee, kah*" and seat me at a table. Music began to quietly draft through the front of house, which to my delighted surprise was classic jazz. Davis, Gordon, Hirt, Evans and Monk played in the background throughout my lunch. They seated me near a portable air-con unit which was welcome as the climate had gotten hot and sticky outside. I'd been exploring the hipster and digital nomad-infested Nimman neighborhood since dawn as the temperature and humidity steadily rose. It does that every day in Thailand.

The menu was a "greatest hits" of Thai cuisine and as much as I wanted to order everything on the twelve-page book of classics, I stuck to my guns and kept it light. I ordered soup, fried rolls and Thai milk tea knowing I'd be exploring later for dinner.

Tom Kha Gai is the perfect Thai soup. Made with coconut milk, lemongrass, galangal root, kaffir lime leaves, straw mushrooms, cilantro, green onions, fresh lime juice, mouse drop chili (those incendiary little Thai chilies also known as bird's eyes) and chicken, it's about as interesting a spoonful as you'll ever experience. Explosive in aromas and flavors with complexity and depth I'd never come across, yet it also possessed a delicate mouthfeel. It was a masterpiece in soup. Even my dining partner, a lone fly on the table, seemed in awe as if patiently waiting for an errant splatter to land near before making its move. We had a little chat to determine if he was in the end-of-life stage, but every time I asked his opinion, his wings flicked. Out of curiosity I put a small drop of broth near it. Jumping into action, he enjoyed my offering. To this day it is the only fly I've ever spent time with socially that wasn't a complete pain in the ass.

Next was Po Pia Tod, those heroin-addiction-like fried spring rolls. They were the color of a 24-karat wedding band. With no hint of oiliness, they were blazing hot and possessed a supernatural crunch that made me smile. The sheer mastery over oil, heat and timing was textbook perfect. Then there was the dipping sauce. Not the cloying cherry red corn-starch sludge we get back in the States. C'mon... when a sauce is so overly starched that it doesn't drizzle off the back of a spoon? This was the same flavor profile but with notes of hibiscus, preserved lemon peel and just a touch of vinegar to brighten what in my experience is usually a thick, sticky abomination. When the rolls were finished, I spooned the rest of the sauce into my mouth, it was that good.

I'd been studying a little Thai language for a few months and when one of the ladies saw me eating the sauce with a spoon (her look plainly asking if I was OK), I looked at her and said "aroi mak mak" which loosely translates to OMFG! OK, no it doesn't, but it does mean "this is amazeballs!" No, it doesn't mean that either. It literally means *"this is very delicious!"* though I prefer both of my translations. She laughed and smiled with one of those Thai smiles that is full of love.

Once I knew I'd be heading to Chiang Mai before the monastery I fell headfirst into the internet rabbit hole, deep-diving every detail about the city and province - especially the food. And like any internet quagmire, it was informative, though the lion's share of data skewed to wildly subjective opinion. I've learned that in the online food scene, a rock-and-roll-themed chain restaurant can get five stars for *"huge portions!"* while a mom-and-pop joint with transcendent traditional dishes gets dinged because *"they don't speak English,"* or *"the service was slow."* I reserve non-exclusive rights to use the middle finger for those inane reviews.

Back at my hotel, just a short walk down the block, I prepared for my upcoming monastery retreat: making lists, making sure I had documents and pick-up in place, while double-checking everything. I was still dragging around a roll-on full of jet lag, my brain was still noisy in semi-fog mode: overthinking everything, executing nothing. So, I did what any time-zone compromised traveler would do. I took a shower, a nap, then hit the streets in search of dinner.

Wandering with purposefully vague intention, I stepped out onto Nimmanhaemin Road, the main artery pulsing with life, neon and LEDs, while the occasional scent of something delicious tempted my resolve with every street cart and restaurant door I passed. I turned right and wandered down a few blocks. There it was: a Mickey D's. That's a hard pass, Ronald! I walked past markets, improvised art galleries on the sidewalk, banks, pharmacies, and assorted mystery shops, a huge beer garden bar, none of which summoned me with that magical traveler's call. I turned around and walked the other way.

On the corner of Nimman Soi 2 and Nimmanhaemin Road, just past the street where my hotel was nestled down from the main road, stood a brooding black building with the kind of swagger you'd expect from a Bond villain's bachelor pad. In bold, glowing white letters against the broad flat-black wall, it announced itself to the world: "Fresh Harvest Farm Butcher Steak," which, if nothing else, is a name that doesn't bury the lede. I was intrigued. Not just by the austere confidence of the building, but by the name itself, which sounded like it had been assembled by a marketing team craving beef while using Google Translate.

Out front, a dais displayed the menu like sacred text for carnivorous pilgrims. And oh, it delivered. If you're vegetarian or vegan, this was your cue to flee. This place wasn't just meat-forward; it was meat-centric. OK - they did have side salads and potatoes but that was an aside. Everything on that menu whispered sweet nothings to my inner caveman.

As I was mentally composing a sonnet to Wagyu, the restaurant's owner/maître d' appeared. Enter Jackie: Thai, stylish, confident, and brimming with the kind of entrepreneurial charisma that makes you want to buy whatever he's selling, even if it's a frozen chicken breast dressed up as poulet de Bresse.

Jackie introduced himself with a wai and a grin. With a blend of pride and salesmanship, he explained that he personally raised Wagyu cattle on two properties in Chonburi and Tak provinces. He assured me that he followed all the prescribed husbandry protocols specific to the breed. No shortcuts, no cheats. Just high-grade Thai Wagyu, born and bred with care, precision, and (presumably) Stella Blue and Morning Dew playing in the background while the cows were getting their daily massage.

"Wagyu" breaks down simply: Wa means Japanese, Gyu means cow - so yes, this ultra-fancy meat everyone's raving about is literally "Japanese Cow." But not just any cow. It refers most often to the Japanese Black breed, though there are three other variations under the Wagyu umbrella, all of them pampered like cattle royalty. Sometimes you'll see it marketed as Kobe beef, which is the same animal, but with the luxury pedigree of being raised in the Kobe region of Japan. It's the same principle that makes people shell out extra for "Copper River Salmon" from Alaska, "Napa Valley" Cabernet Sauvignon, or "Champagne" from France. Geography becomes status symbol. Thus, the term Kobe becomes a point of pride and a strong marketing tool guaranteeing authenticity and quality.

The tenderness and flavor of the highly marbled meat (intracellular fat laced between the muscles) makes for an outrageously flavorful and tender product. You might think that all that fat would come with a voucher for a free ambulance ride to the nearest cardiovascular clinic but the fat in the Wagyu breed is mono-unsaturated; in other words, it's the good fat that your body and brain needs without that bad LDL (low-density lipoprotein) cholesterol guaranteeing a prescription for statin drugs in your future.

Jackie wasn't just some local hustler with a nice shirt and a good story - he'd spent three years studying the art of Wagyu husbandry in Australia and Japan, then brought that hard-earned knowledge (and, impressively, some Japanese Black cows) back home.

Here's how it works at Fresh Harvest: the meat is pre-cut, weighed, vacuum-sealed, and tucked into a freezer like cryo-sleeping astronauts. Each package is labeled with cut, grade, thickness, and weight. You, the customer, get to play butcher-shop sommelier. You pick your steak and tell Jackie where on the scale of rare to well-done you want it cooked. Wagyu requires a different cooking style than your standard rib-eye or New York strip. I recommend medium-rare.

I selected an eight-ounce A5 rib-eye, gloriously marbled that was winking at me like an enthusiastic bar girl. Medium rare. Anything else is culinary malpractice. To round it out, I ordered mashed potatoes and a fresh green salad with herbs. An omnivore's trifecta.

Jackie's drink menu included wines of unknown quality alongside over a dozen local and rotating craft beers on tap. I ordered a brown ale, expecting a pint. Instead, a towering 60-ounce pitcher and an industrial-strength mug arrived, daring me. I'd missed either the fine print or the concept of restraint.

With time to kill and beer to conquer, I struck up a conversation with Jackie and a fellow diner from Singapore seated at the next table. What began as casual banter turned into a carnivore's round table: rib-eye versus strip, bone marrow roasting tips, braised shanks, the glories of offal, and coagulated blood. Nothing brings strangers together in a steakhouse like the poetry of meat.

Forty-five minutes later, post-defrost and fire-kissed to perfection, our plates arrived. Jackie faded off to charm other tables, and we got down to business. The steak was flawless! Rich, tender, the kind of meal that makes you briefly reconsider vegetarianism so you can feel smug about coming back from it.

Wagyu showcases a natural sweetness and buttery richness that seeps into the muscle fibers thanks to all that intricate marbling. As the fat hits high grill heat, it renders into the meat, amping up the umami into full-on mouth-symphony territory. This isn't serrated knife-cut chomp-and-swallow beef; it's melt-in-your-mouth, cut with a fork luxury. The marbling breaks down connective tissue, leaving you with a texture somewhere between cloud and silk.

Add to that a scoop of Robuchon-worthy mashed potatoes and a salad so herb-packed and fresh it could have moonlighted as aromatherapy.

I didn't finish the ale. I tried. But at one point the line between "dinner pairing" and "drunken regret" has to be drawn, especially right before monk life began.

The next morning, I stumbled out of my hotel early in search of caffeine. I ended up at an indie coffee shop called Blue, where the espresso is less "coffee" and more "Arabica jet fuel syrup." I ordered a quad-shot latte, which drew raised eyebrows either out of concern or quiet admiration, hard to tell. I should've reassured them that professionals monitor my blood pressure.

Vertical and jittery, I wandered deeper into the crosshatched lanes of the Nimman neighborhood in search of something solid to pair with the caffeinated euphoria buzzing through my bloodstream. That's when I found Manifreshto, a charming café tucked into Nimman Soi 5. Yes, that's the actual name and no, I don't know what it means either. Sounds like a deodorant for youthful testosterone-driven pimple boys. The outdoor balcony with its golden hardwood tables and hanging jungle of plants was pure Chiang Mai charm. I ordered the smoked salmon Benedict with asparagus, a fresh croissant, and a mango smoothie. Everything was perfect. The Hollandaise was silky, bright, buttery, and unbroken. Let me repeat that: unbroken. A small miracle worth documenting.

I made my way back to the beating heart of Nimman: the Maya Mall. Look, I don't like malls. I never have. But in Thailand, mega malls are temples. They're massive gleaming cathedrals of aspiration where each new mall seems designed to outdo the last in sheer extravagance. The Maya Mall had all the mall essentials: high-end trophy stores, a food court that would make an American mall weep in shame, electronics and sunglass kiosks, and a luxury grocery store called Rimping, where you can casually toss A-lobes of foie gras, live grouper, large tins of Ossetra caviar, and a $47 round of Époisses de Bourgogne into your basket as if you're grabbing milk.

I needed two essentials and figured the mall might deliver. It did not. Everything I found was either not right or priced as if I were shopping on Rodeo Drive, but without the celebrity sightings. I left empty-handed, reaffirmed in my belief that malls suck, even when they come with sushi-grade tuna and a Porsche showroom.

Chiang Mai has a vibrant Japanese expat community that had settled a century ago, which raised my expectations, because where there are Japanese expats, there is always excellent Japanese food - and not just tourist-trap teppanyaki where a chef flips shrimp into your mouth from the flat-top. I plunged into the digital underworld of foodie reviews and after wading through the usual slurry of hype and horror stories I found something promising: a recently opened restaurant called ShiShiTei, tucked along 21 Nimmanhaemin Road. Elegant, authentic, and just pretentious enough to suggest someone in the kitchen had trained under a sushi master perfecting one grain of rice at a time all while enduring a decade of emotional neglect. It would be my final culinary hurrah before heading off into the hills to commune with monks and mosquitoes.

I harbor a deep respect, an emotional attachment to sushi. So, in one of those "you only live once, and also I might not eat again for a month while meditating in a robe" moments, I decided this would be a perfect last supper. Though ShiShiTei was officially listed as a sukiyaki and shabu-shabu joint (but with A5 Wagyu), it was the sashimi reviews that made me sit up straighter. Comments gushed about the extraordinary quality, the kind of breathless awe usually reserved for epiphanies or standing at the rim of the Grand Canyon for the first time.

I've had the great fortune to eat world-class sushi many times in places where the rice temperature alone could inspire poetry. But ShiShiTei came in hot, kicked open the sliding door, and calmly obliterated every one of those memories with a quiet, confident "thanks for playing, now pack up your bamboo mats, hand over the Yanagiba, and show yourself out."

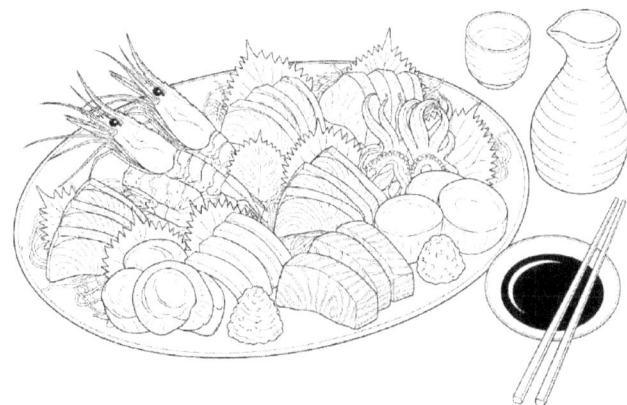

First up: the uni. Fifty grams of sea urchin gonads (yes, gonads) from the Hokkaido species *Heliocidaris crassispina*. These little ocean treasures were extracted from their intimidatingly spiny shells just moments before making their way to my table. They arrived with the kind of reverence normally reserved for newborn royalty. They were served with toasted sheets of nori (that's seaweed, for the sushi novices in the back), the dark green paper made from either *Pyropia yezoensis* or *Pyropia tenera*. There were also shiso leaves (*Perilla frutescens*), a member of the mint family *Lamiaceae* that tastes like what might happen if mint, basil, and a sweet summer breeze had a torrid love affair.

The uni was better than unreasonably good. They were like licking the soul of the ocean while being serenaded by a siren in a silk kimono. Fresh, creamy, briny perfection; pure tide pool. They didn't just melt in my mouth; they whispered sweet nothings on the way down.

Next was an appetizer that sounded like a jazz saxophonist from Okinawa: Gyutan Ponzu. Thin slices of marinated beef tongue (don't flinch - it's delicious), served in a shallow bowl with preserved lemon, fermented tobiko (*Parexocoetus brachypterus* flying fish roe, and the most impossibly thinly shredded Japanese cabbage I've ever seen. I'm really proficient with my knives and French mandoline but this was on another level! The whole thing was tied together by a house-made ponzu reduction; a tangy, umami-rich sauce anchored in yuzu, that punchy, aromatic Chinese citrus fruit that tastes like a grapefruit got its life together and had fun with the tiniest whisper of honey. Every bite was balance-incarnate: bright, savory, acidic, rich. The kind of flavor geometry that makes your tastebuds sit up straighter.

Then, the crescendo: the sashimi plate. A curated riot of oceanic treasures, sliced so precisely it was a work of art. As mentioned, while ShiShiTei markets itself as a high-end shabu-shabu destination, this place is also a church for fish purists. There's rice if you want it but notably, there was not a single nigiri choice on the menu. No fish-on-rice. Just the raw, unadorned truth. It was sushi stripped of its accessories; elegant and unapologetically perfect.

The Chutoro and Otoro - those buttery, transcendent cuts from distinct parts of bluefin tuna (*Thunnus orientalis*) - were clean and flawlessly delicious. But they were, against all odds, upstaged. First by the Ika (squid, or *calamarium*) which was so fresh it squeaked. It had that perfect snap between the teeth. Then came the Saba (mackerel, *Scombrini japonicus*), delicately smoked but un-brined, as if someone had whispered "campfire" to it from across the room. And though I initially rolled my eyes at the inclusion of Sake (salmon, *Salmonidae*) - the woo-woo prom queen of sushi menus - it humiliated every negative expectation I had. Fatty, velvety, fresh enough to convert the most hardened sashimi snob. I was briefly silenced.

The Hotate (scallops, *Pectinidae Aequipecten*) nearly floated off the plate. Ethereal is not hyperbole here. They were sweet, buttery and yielding, practically humming with oceanic delicacy, topped with little glistening bubbles of seawater foam like Poseidon's own garnish.

Last was Amaebi (large freshwater prawns, *Pandalus montagui*). Tender, translucent, delicate, but with a secret vendetta. Microscopic barbs, nestled along their carapace, exacted their revenge the moment I leaned in to do what one must

\- suck the juice and brain from the heads. It was primal, perfect and left my lips looking like I'd lost a fight with a microplane.

Is it rude to bleed for your food? Perhaps. I regret nothing.

Wasabi: That green chalky paste that comes with your supermarket sushi or the stuff slathered onto rolls at most sit-down bars? That's *not* wasabi. That's powdered horseradish, dyed an artificially Superfund-site green, bulked up with dried mustard and flavoring agents, and shaped into a sad impersonation of the real thing. That stuff we call wasabi is like calling Velveeta Camembert.

True wasabi, (*Wasabia japonica*), is a high-maintenance diva plant. It's a knobby, light jade-green rhizome grown in pristine, cold, slow-to-moderately moving fresh water in shallow gravel beds shaded from direct sunlight like a spa treatment for vegetables. It demands exacting temperature and humidity conditions, at just the right time, and throws tantrums if anything is even slightly off. Agriculturalists refer to it as the botanical equivalent of an opera soprano with a thousand clause contract. Unsurprisingly, it's staggeringly expensive and nearly impossible to grow at commercial scale, which is why most have only ever tasted the imposter.

But once you try real wasabi, the vast difference is obvious. Sure, it still has that sinus-clearing zing that wakes up parts of your skull you forgot existed, but beyond that it is subtle. Earthy, grassy, a little fruity, a little floral. There's complexity in that heat. It doesn't punch you in the face like the fake stuff; it leans in and whispers secrets. You don't need much, just a dab. And whatever you do, do not stir it into your soy sauce. Unless you *really* want to offend the chef.

At Shi Shi Tei, my sashimi arrived with a generous pillow of fresh wasabi - grated on a sharkskin board which is traditional and dramatic. By the end of the meal that beautiful green mound was gone.

Then there was the soy sauce, which deserves its own standing ovation.

Forget the little red-capped bottles we all know; serviceable, sure, but that's the vin ordinaire of the soy sauce world. The soy at ShiShiTei was a different beast entirely. It was deep, rich, almost creamy, with restrained saltiness, layered umami, and a molasses-charcoal whisper on the back palate. I pinky-dipped into the shallow bowl when no one was looking to taste it by itself. More than once. Many times. No shame!

Soy is not a sauce to drown your fish in. It's seasoning. An accent. If your fish needs to swim in soy sauce, something has gone terribly wrong. A good piece of sashimi requires just a kiss of soy if it needs any at all. True sushi master's will season your fish before it ever hits your plate, no further customization required. The result? Pure magic.

Seeing the rapture on my face somewhere between spiritual transcendence and food coma as I wiped my hands and face with a fresh, citrus-scented warm towel, my server appeared with a quiet smile and placed a scoop of rich, impossibly creamy matcha green tea ice cream beside a cup of shockingly exquisite green tea. "Compliments of the chef," she said, "for ordering well and eating like a Japanese gentleman." I almost teared up. Sometimes a lifetime of obsessive food nerd-dom actually pays off in the smallest, most gracious of ways.

And the punchline? When the bill came with the gold-capsule chilled Junmai Daiginjo sake and the kind of service that made me feel like a dignitary, it was... incredibly reasonable. Not cheap. But not gouge-your-eyes-out, this-must-be-a-mistake expensive. I've paid more for burgers, fries, a wedge salad and cocktails at a gastropub back home in Walla Walla. I left the restaurant full, glowing, slightly buzzed, and deeply grateful. Sometimes life doesn't just feed you, it throws in dessert, bows politely, and thanks you for showing up.

PART 2 - Post-monastery

"Traveling - it leaves you speechless, then turns you into a storyteller." - Ibn Battuta

Coming down out of the mountains and back into "civilization" was disorienting to put it mildly. My time up at iMonastery was extraordinarily purifying, peaceful, and addictive. The camaraderie forged among brothers clad in saffron, both my intake classmates and the resident monks was deep. Leaving it behind stirred a quiet melancholy I hadn't seen coming. But as the road carved down toward Chiang Mai, a ripple of excitement rose within. Lay life loomed ahead, electric, and unpredictable. I wasn't entirely sure if I was ready, but readiness felt beside the point. That path was now before me.

Most people don't realize how relentlessly exhausting decision-making is. The constant pressure: what to eat, what to wear, where to go, how to spend your day feels banal... until it's gone. Monastic life, by contrast, is structured and serene, pared to a clean daily rhythm. No errands. No emails. No brunch plans. No juggling warring clan factions. Now I was back in Chiang Mai, no longer cloaked in saffron, steering my own ship again. The sheer freedom of it was a heady mix of mortifying and thrilling.

If you looked closely, the evidence lingered. My head was freshly shaved (though thankfully, my eyebrows had begun their slow comeback), and I still had that quiet, post-monk glow. But technically, I was no longer a bhikkhu. In the Dhammakaya tradition, leaving monkhood involves a private disrobing. A ritual senior monks perform with grave solemnity. Few will do it; symbolically, it's killing a brother. Afterward, you shed the robes and return to civilian life.

Putting on "normal" clothes felt strange. Familiar, yes, but also vaguely illicit, like I'd stolen someone else's pants and was waiting to get caught. Something felt missing, like I'd left a piece of myself folded up with the robes.

Once disrobed, you vow to uphold the Five Precepts (or eight, if you're feeling extra devout) which are basic ethical guidelines for lay Buddhists:

1. Refrain from killing any living being,
2. Refrain from taking what isn't freely given,
3. Refrain from sexual misconduct,
4. Refrain from lying or spreading gossip,
5. Refrain from intoxicants that cloud the mind.

Unlike a monk's 227 rules, the layperson's five are simple, obvious, and entirely self-enforced. There are no Buddha-cops issuing tickets for mild gossip or a second glass of wine. And if you do kill someone, there are traditional channels for that sort of idiocy. Mostly, though, you just have to live with yourself. The precepts aren't about policing. They are a moral GPS, quietly recalculating when you veer off course.

In Thailand, ordaining as a monk, even temporarily, is considered an essential rite of passage for young men. It's deeply cultural and deeply respected. A man who has walked the path of the Dhamma, even briefly, brings pride to his family and earns personal insight that is seen as critical to becoming a good and worthy man.

When I returned to my Chiang Mai hotel, the staff greeted me not with polite professionalism, but with something closer to awe. They'd known I was ordaining, and now I was back, slightly changed, still monk-adjacent, still radiating that quiet monastic energy. I felt vaguely fraudulent, like I should be holding a lotus flower and blessing the elevator. But the staff were gracious to a fault, practically tripping over themselves to offer help, iced drinks, extra keys or anything I might dream of. In Thailand, it turns out, respect for monks lingers long after the robes come off.

After checking into my artfully comfortable room (each at the Nimman Mai Design is uniquely styled with just the right dose of boutique flair), I did the only logical thing before unpacking: I took a long, indulgent, civilization-grade hot shower. Yes, I'd had my usual monastery rinse that morning but that wasn't about hygiene. That was about transition. For the first time in a month, I could just stand there, letting steam rise and water cascade. No handheld wand flailing about, no sudden temperature shifts, no strategic negotiations with the spider kingdom.

Monastery showers, you see, came with what I began calling *arachnid negotiations*. Getting the water to a bearable temp required a delicate pas de deux with the dial, often while a frisky huntsman or golden orb weaver casually dropped down like it had notes. And the post-shower ritual? That's when they got bold. You're vulnerable, draped in nothing but a towel and a thin film of dignity, squeegeeing the stall per protocol and that's when they made their move. Let's just say I've learned the precise speed at which a man can squeegee with one hand, hold a towel with the other, and fend off an eight-legged incursion in real time.

So yes, that first spider-free, hot-water-that-stayed-hot shower was pure bliss. It lasted a while, I assure you.

I was staying at the Nimman Mai Design Hotel for a week before moving to another spot tucked within Chiang Mai's old city. I like to move around a bit when I travel. Different corners of a city offer different angles to the story. But at that particular moment, getting unpacked and semi-organized was priority one. Then I could wander out, find something good to munch on and start dreaming about what this next chapter - this unscripted, open-road phase - might reveal.

High on my list was visiting an ethical elephant sanctuary because if you're in Northern Thailand and don't hang out with elephants, did you even Chiang Mai? I've been fascinated by pachyderms since childhood. The closest I'd ever been to an elephant was behind zoo bars or, more dubiously, at a circus my parents took me to when I was very young. This, I hoped, would be different. Less sadness, more soul. Elephants are revered in Thai culture, and I wanted to meet them on their turf, no rides, no tricks, no spectacle.

I'd also made plans with my monk brothers to take a Thai cooking class before they departed the country. It felt like a fitting way to mark our reentry into the world: former monks in aprons rather than robes, fumbling our way through curry pastes and wok technique while trying not to unmake whatever karma and merits we'd just banked.

I had my marching orders, so I rolled up my sleeves and set about lining up the details.

The Nimmanhaemin neighborhood of Chiang Mai has an upbeat, manicured vibe about it that's palpable. Commonly shortened to "Nimman" by expats, digital nomads, and people who say "content creator" with a straight face, this northwest neighborhood wasn't always the buzzed-out, globally sourced, oat-milk-foamed haven it is today.

A couple of decades ago, Nimman was a sleepy, tree-lined neighborhood. Schools, kids playing in the street, dogs that actually belonged to someone, and neighbors who knew whose mom made the best som tam. Quiet. Familial. Unfussy. Then came the bulldozers of progress, humming with the promise of redevelopment. Just up the road from the airport, Nimman was targeted by government incentives and that mysterious engine known as *new money*. The neighborhood got the classic gentrification spit polish: humble homes gave way to condo towers with glass-front balconies no one uses, and rooftop pools built for social media cocktail hour, not swimming.

The transformation was swift. Within a decade, the neighborhood evolved from kids playing tag to startups playing venture capital poker. The local soi dog now wears a bandanna and has an Instagram following. Nimman today is a high-octane mishmash of lifestyle branding and postmodern indulgence. There are boutique hotels where the furniture is incredibly uncomfortable but looks fantastic in photos.

Restaurants? Yes. All of them. Lebanese mezze, Moroccan tajines, Hawaiian poke, Swedish fika, artisan Neapolitan pizza, Mexican taquerias, French, Italian, Russian, Issan and Lanna, Cambodian, Laotian and four places that will try to convince you they invented avocado toast. There are wine bars, beer gardens, whiskey dens, cocktail labs, and mocktail temples. At least one place serves drinks in over-sized light bulbs. And of course, there are the tattoo parlors, co-working spaces with neon signs that say things like "Rise & Grind," artisanal soap shops, and massage parlors where the receptionist is finishing a graduate thesis on AI ethics.

And then there's the coffee. My God, the coffee!

Small to large coffee shops lurk on every corner, like caffeinated hydras. You could sneeze and hit three espresso bars before your tissue hits the trashcan. There's more atmospheric pressure coming from all the La Marzoccos and La Pavonis than a space launch. The air is thick with the alchemy of fresh grounds and oat milk micro-foam, a vapor trail wafting down every alley. If you close your eyes, you can almost hear the gentle hiss of milk steaming and a man in a linen apron whispering, *"single origin."*

You could spend two weeks in Chiang Mai, visiting cafés three times a day, not sleeping and achieving a state of transcendental alertness usually reserved for hummingbirds or teenage coders with a case of energy drinks. And you wouldn't even scratch the surface. This is not so much a neighborhood as it is a caffeinated dreamscape created by hipsters with design degrees and trust funds.

And yet it works. Somehow. Nimman has mastered the art of chic chaos; a neighborhood where cultures mingle over soy cappuccinos and suddenly, you're talking about crypto with a Danish UX designer, a Russian mobster and a Brazilian yogi. It's ridiculous. It's beautiful.

But it wasn't just roasting coffee beans perfuming the air in Nimman. Mixed into that olfactory cocktail was another unmistakable note. Fresh sticky green and its louder cousin, skunk. Depending on the wind and time of day, the whole neighborhood could smell like a reggae festival or the parking lot of a Phish show. Passing pot shops, I was occasionally transported, not spiritually, but sensorily - back to the haze of youth, to Grateful Dead runs and brownies from the lot with suspiciously long-lasting effects.

Chiang Mai was deep in its "cannabis honeymoon" phase. Pot shops dotted the neighborhood like Starbucks in Seattle - each with punny names ("Buddha Blaze," "Thai High Club," "Monk Munchie") and laid-back patios straight out of a California boardwalk fantasy. You couldn't walk a hundred feet without someone waving you in with a joint and a grin. Everyone looked like they were having a great time, or at least a slow, thoughtful one.

That hasn't been my thing for years. I still enjoy the smell. There's something comforting about someone else's journey into oblivion but now I prefer altered states from good coffee, wine, unexpected kindness, or a well-executed foot massage. More than once, I was invited into circles of blissed-out twenty-somethings trading tokes and tales. Invitations came when someone spotted my weathered "Winterland 1978" shirt and figured I had stories (they weren't wrong). I'd smile, thank them, and decline with a polite "I've got somewhere to be," even if that "somewhere" was a noodle stall calling my name.

In hindsight, I should've shared a story or two. But I was chasing a different kind of high. Clarity, connection, whatever the opposite of a munchie-fueled binge is.

Not everyone in Chiang Mai - or Thailand more broadly - is thrilled with the "pot paradise" vibe. Many locals, especially near tourist-heavy spots, are less enchanted by dazed foreigners sparking up in public, outside temples, or, ultimate insult, right next to families enjoying a picnic. There's a fine line between freedom and being *that* guy, and some folks cross it with a joint in one hand and zero awareness in the other.

Cannabis may be legal for now but Thailand's relationship with weed waxes and wanes with every election. One government greenlights it; the next threatens to roll it back. Yet, with the genie out of the bong-shaped bottle, a full reversal seems unlikely. There's too much money, tourism, and jobs that politicians love to tally as wins almost as much as ribbon-cuttings and photo ops.

The shift has created a divide. On one side, those embracing the benefits: dispensaries, CBD cafes, "ganja-preneurs." On the other, locals don't want to feel like they're living inside a Sublime album. It's tension in the air, literally and figuratively.

Connectivity - that modern convenience that makes the world go round. Every coffee shop, café, bar, brewery, market, cat cafe, hotel, restaurant, fuel station, pharmacy and pot shop in Chiang Mai offers complimentary high-speed Wi-Fi. This is one of the key reasons Chiang Mai became ground zero for digital nomads long before the term was splashed across LinkedIn bios.

What's a digital nomad? If you've got a laptop with Wi-Fi, Bluetooth, a camera, a decent phone, earbuds, and just enough skill not to get fired via email, congrats. You can hang out in Thailand and pretend you're "consulting." With high-speed internet and enough bandwidth to link space stations, Chiang Mai is the OG Southeast Asian hotspot for caffeinated keyboard jockeys. You'll find them in cafés, pot shops, and bars sipping their third latte or first Singha, juggling Zoom calls, munching croissants, or sketching business funnels between hits from a gravity bong.

Now, co-working spaces abound. You can rent by the hour, the day, the week, or your entire visa window. Chiang Mai started the trend, but now you'll find these hot spots in about every Thai town from Chiang Rai to Koh Lanta.

Of course, not all storefronts cater to the entrepreneurial expat or wandering UX designer. Chiang Mai, like the rest of Thailand, is also home to three other ubiquitous business models: massage parlors (by the hundreds), pharmacies (you can score antibiotics like you're buying Tic Tacs, and you can get E.D. drugs while solving the problems from you last encounter that required the antibiotics in the first place), and the ever-present 7-Eleven.

Let's talk about 7-Eleven.

In the States, 7-Eleven stores are often depressing, flickering fluorescent outposts selling rubbery nachos with liquid plastic cheese and hot dogs that taste like the '90s. In Thailand, 7-Elevens are clean, well-lit, and everywhere. I mean everywhere. It's not unusual to find two on the same block; sometimes across from each other like a passive-aggressive turf war.

They're busy too. Locals and backpackers pop in for sundries, fresh fruit, dirt-cheap ham-and-cheese paninis (nicknamed toasties), or surprisingly decent cappuccinos. Most sell hard liquor. Some don't stock alcohol or cigarettes. Others offer chopped salads, bento boxes, or are shrine-like temples to sugary snacks. Franchise rules set core products, but owners have flexibility, so each 7-Eleven has its own personality. It's wild.

Even more surreal: in 2000AD, 7-Elevens were still rare in Thailand. The first opened in Bangkok in 1989, but since then they've metastasized like Mickey D's on a Red Bull binge. As of July 2024, there were just shy of 14,000 in the country. Fourteen. Thousand!

They've become so essential that travel sites like Agoda and Booking.com list "7-Eleven nearby" under hotel amenities right between "free toiletries," "WiFi," and "flat-screen TV." Because who needs a gym when salvation is a ham-and-cheese toastie away?

✻

Chiang Mai isn't small, but it still feels cozy, livable, and totally navigable, like a city that knows when to hold back. It scores high on lifestyle charts: safety, affordability, food, friendliness, digital infrastructure, coffee shop density, you name it. But there's one catch: the dreaded "smoke season." Every year, farmers across Thailand and neighbors Laos, Myanmar, and Cambodia torch spent rice and wheat fields to prep for the next crop. The result? A thick smoky fog that settles like an overstayed guest who chain-smoked and refused to crack a window. It's a tradeoff. Live in wonderland most of the year, but from February to April, invest in a good air purifier or a sudden interest in southern island life.

For most of the year, Chiang Mai is easy living with an upgrade. It's got everything: wet markets, street markets, hypermarkets, top-notch healthcare, sometimes polite drivers, and most critically restaurants ranging from "amazing noodle stall for 50 baht" to "yes, we sous-vide duck in angels' tears and press it through our presse à canard." Everyone I spoke to preferred Chiang Mai's "small-town" charm and accessibility over Bangkok's relentless sprawl and ambient intensity. Even those living in Bangkok. Chiang Mai isn't just livable. It's lovable.

Then there's the culture. Chiang Mai punches way above its weight. Ancient Wats with mind-bending architecture; centuries of history; museums people actually visit; rock, roll, and jazz clubs with fantastic musicians; film and theater festivals; a philharmonic orchestra and ballet if you're feeling fancy. Add a robust festival calendar, plenty of fine art galleries, and more street food than your digestive tract can handle. Chiang Mai is an amazing place to park your hat.

For sportsters, there's kayaking, rafting, hiking, spelunking, biking, climbing, zip-lining, pickleball, cricket, rugby, golf, and football pitches plus public parks and community sports grounds where locals and tourists alike work off their overindulgence-induced guilt and bellies.

After a week of savoring the stylish ease of the Nimman Mai Design Hotel, my time in that slick, espresso-scented neighborhood was up. I was ready for the change and to shift gears. My next hotel, which I had pre-booked back in the States, looked perfect on paper. A heritage building tucked away down a charming soi just a hundred feet down an alley from the famed Saturday Night Market Bazaar. Quaint. Affordable. Full of promise.

The outside of the small hotel was charming in that deceptive way bad decisions look in hindsight. Whitewashed walls, cute wooden balconies draped with flowering vines, the kind of place that whispers, "Trust me, I'm quaint." But that would turn out to be the absolute highlight of the property.

Check-in was my first red flag. My reservation had been switched to a room with two twin beds. I *never* book twin beds! I don't even think in twin beds. Strike one. The desk clerk, who claimed they didn't even have rooms with king beds, despite my printed reservation saying otherwise, shrugged and offered no explanation beyond his non-apology. Strike two. I then learned the elevator, listed on the booking site, was apparently a figment of someone's optimistic imagination. Up the stairs we went. Strike three.

He opened my room, and I was hit with the squalid aesthetic of George Orwell's "Down and Out in London and Paris." Spartan would be generous. Strike four. The clerk dropped my bags on the second twin bed that displayed no give though it was the only available surface. I asked politely if there might be a discount due to the false advertising. "No," he said. Just that. One syllable. Delivered with the charisma of an undercooked turnip. Strike five.

Then I checked the bathroom. The rotting plastic door (extruded to resemble putty-gray wood) groaned like it knew it was complicit. Inside, a giant cockroach scuttled up the wall and disappeared through a crack in the ceiling, probably to file a tenant complaint of its own. The bathroom was so small you had to sit on the toilet to shower, using a little nozzle protruding from the ceiling like some dark punchline. Strikes six and seven.

I sat on the bed. It had all the give of a butcher's block. Strike eight.

At that point I knew I wouldn't be staying for the full duration of my reservation. I was willing to tough it out for one night, but the moment I opened my laptop to find a better place to stay, the Wi-Fi limped along like it was running on a potato battery *(ok - so yeah - I am complaining that the WiFi wasn't fast)*. I couldn't even stream something to distract myself from the ambiance of despair. Strike nine. A full inning of strikes in fifteen minutes flat.

The weekly rate was cheap, yes. But so was the experience. I wrote it off, considered it a donation to the Ministry of Bad Choices, and began plotting my escape. This wasn't a hotel. It was a backpacker's hostel in disguise, and not even a good one.

Sometimes, when adversity strikes, the best move is to take a deep breath, admit your inner turmoil, and remember no one makes good decisions when hangry and traumatized by lousy plumbing. I gave myself five minutes. Sat cross-legged on the hard bed, took some intentioned breaths, and meditated right there in that sad little room smelling of mildew and crushed dreams.

I cranked up the laptop and left it to load up a booking site as I headed out past the recalcitrant clerk.

I strolled the immediate neighborhood and grabbed a bunch of delicious munchables from street carts (fried chicken that was outrageously perfect, cut up watermelon and pineapple, and a long-braise pork knuckle that was transcendent), wandered around a few art galleries and clothing shops then called the night good.

Upon my return to that disappointing hovel, and after a glacial load time and more buffering than a 2006 YouTube video, my laptop screen showed a new listing I hadn't seen before: Namton Boutique Hotel, located cross-town at 18 Samlarn Road. The photos looked promising. The location was central. And the rate? The deeply discounted deal felt suspiciously like karmic reward even though I was skeptical, while considering that bad luck and dicey choices rarely strike twice in a row.

I didn't hesitate. I pulled the trigger, booked the next six nights, and began drafting my break-up discussion to Hotel Cockroach.

I rose early with a plan. Though "woke" wasn't quite accurate. I hadn't really slept on that slab of hardwood masquerading as a bed. I'd walk across the old town at dawn to check out where I'd spend the next week. But first, a shower, if you could call it that. The bathroom situation was grim. I sat on the toilet under a feeble trickle of water, technically warmer than cold by a few degrees. Determined to get my money's worth, I used both sandpaper towels (yes, petty, no regrets), emptied the half-full shampoo and conditioner left by the previous prisoner, despite barely regrown stubble, and lathered up with a stranger's used bar of soap. A farewell shower of spite.

The walk to Namton took about twenty minutes, cutting through the old town's crisscross of lanes, alleys and temples. When I arrived, I smiled. The hotel was on a modest but lively road and to my delight, sat right next to the Gravity Café and Bistro, where I'd had a fantastic lunch after visiting Wat Phra Singh during my first spin through Chiang Mai. The Namton already had good juju.

Out front, the hotel had what I can only describe as a semi-ironic lounge setup: broad patio, low wicker tables, big, padded rattan chairs and couches atop bright green astroturf. There was a raised shrine where Buddha watched over the exterior and locals delivered offerings. It was charming in a way that made me chuckle, as if the designer said, *"Yeah, it's a little off, but hey, it works."*

To enter, you slide open a huge teak wood-and-glass door by hand, which looked like it might groan under its own weight but didn't. It glided open silently, like some secret passage in a very tasteful Lanna-inspired hideaway. Inside was a wonderful surprise: surrounding me was a high-ceiling Lanna-style courtyard with earthy stone flooring, dark polished wood, intricate beams and pillars, elegant statues, and genuinely striking art. Water gurgled through tiered ceramic pots overflowing with aquatic plants, the air perfumed with calm. If my last place screamed "post-war utility bunker," this whispered, *"your life just got much better."*

I walked across the cool courtyard tiles to the front desk, where a woman greeted me warmly. I introduced myself and explained the situation, softening the story like a diplomat caught between cultures. In Thailand, direct criticism or causing someone to lose face is a *major* faux pas, so I politely sidestepped naming names, pointing fingers, and airing my list of hostel horrors.

Her name was Sand. And when I gave her the barest sketch of my ordeal, her eyes widened in disbelief. I explained that while I was sure the other place was perfectly fine for other people, I needed something a little more... *me.*

She nodded with a kind of unspoken solidarity, tapped a few things into her computer, and then looked up with a smile that said, *"You're OK now."* I'd been upgraded, she said, to a top-floor room, thanks to the online deal and the length of my stay.

That sounded suspiciously like good karma cashing in early.

When I told her the address of the previous hotel and asked if they had a driver or shuttle that might help me retrieve my bags, her reaction was wordless but unmistakable. She knew. I didn't need to say anything else. Recognition flickered across her face like a knowing glance exchanged between survivors. She understood.

"We don't have a service like that, I'm sorry. I could order a Grab car if you'd like?"

"That would be fine" I replied, trying not to sound too deflated. I'd hoped for some more hospitality magic, but I figured I'd take what I could get.

Good timing and karma were clearly on my side. Just as Sand reached for the phone, a young man strolled in, clearly part of the hotel crew. He breezed past me and into the staff area, then hovered near Sand, glancing at the computer screen. They discussed my position in Thai, during which Sand looked at me and smiled.

"This is Gorge. He's not working today, but he said he can help you go get your bags, if that's okay?" Sand offered.

Was that okay? That was fantastic.

Gorge had the casual charisma of a guy who could charm his way out of a speeding ticket or pick up any beautiful woman he desired. "Let's go get your stuff," he said with an easy grin, reaching over the counter to shake my hand.

I told him I needed five minutes to cram things into my bag and check out, and that I'd meet him out front. The other place was in a tight little soi with no space to park, but he waved it off. "No problem. I'll circle until I see you."

We drove back to the unmentionable place, where I packed with the determination of someone fleeing a crime scene, and handed over the key to the grim desk clerk without fanfare. I said I was moving on. I didn't bother rehashing the extensive list of disappointments and there was no refund offered, nor apology given. Some places deserve the Irish goodbye.

When I rolled my bags out to the alley's edge, Gorge was pulling up like a knight clad in shining armor in his shiny SUV. They say timing is everything and, in this case, seeing Gorge's smile and a thumbs-up through the windshield felt like breathing crisp mountain air.

The Namton didn't have an elevator either, but by then I didn't care. Gorge hauled my bags up four flights of stairs like it was nothing. The staircases weren't simple, either. Each level had two 90-degree turns, like some dark teak-wood M.C. Escher design. But the climb was beautiful: wide, polished teak steps without a creak or groan to be heard, carved banisters, and at every landing, museum-quality art tucked into niches or hanging above antique Asian cabinets. Chandeliers dangled overhead, their crystals casting light diamonds as Tiffany sconces emitted a warm glow.

At the top landing, Gorge set my bags down beside a pair of paneled wooden doors, painted bold Chinese red, each panel adorned with hand-rendered natural scenes with ornate characters in greens, browns, blues, and gold. The kind of doors that felt less like a room entryway and more like a portal to a sanctuary.

The locking mechanism was fantastically analog: two vertical wooden handles, one on each door, with a carved wooden hasp that slid into both handles. The hasp had a hole at one end, just wide enough for a long-shank padlock, the kind you might use on a barn, or a secret garden gate. Gorge slid out the lock, slid the latch aside, and pulled the heavy doors open with a quiet creak, like he was letting me in on a secret.

I looked down the hallway and caught my breath. Through the open doors my room was stunning. The floor gleamed with rich, natural brown-red stone, radiating organic warmth under the lights. One side of the hallway was lined with full-length mirrors framed in carved teak: the other featured wood paneling inlaid with lighter-grained designs. Along that paneled wall rested a massive antique armoire and a heavy teak bench, standing like a sentry. Gorge placed my roll-on and daypack on the bench. They fit easily.

He led me into the room where a king-sized bed rested beneath a hand-painted wooden panel the size of a billboard. At its center, a recessed carved lotus was backlit by a warm romantic bulb. Reading lights flanked the headboard and were perfectly placed, perfectly restrained. The ceiling was subtly recessed, with broad wood beams hiding adjustable LED lights that bathed the room in a gentle amber glow.

Fridge? Check. Security safe? Check. Everything was immaculate.

The bathroom was just as impressive. A deep soaking tub sat on a tiled teak base, with a padded headrest and handheld shower wand. The cabinetry echoed the earthy tile palette, greens, blues, browns, straight from a rainforest dream. A raised copper sink rested on top of the counter, with modern Moen fixtures and a large ornately framed mirror that reminded me of home. The ceiling matched the bedroom's recessed beams and hidden lighting. Tasteful wooden shelving curved around the bath like thoughtful arms, ready to hold everything I'd need. The towels were thick, soft, and clean enough to make up for the last place ten times over, with actual face cloths, a rarity in my travels. Amenities were top-notch designer stuff.

More art greeted me: ceramic panels with extruded peacocks, turtles, and intricate inlays even in the bathroom. Back in the main room, a writing desk stood ready with pens, hotel stationery, and complimentary bug juice for outdoor adventures. On an antique dresser, a flat-screen TV perched neatly. Windows were shuttered with broad teak slats and heavy blackout curtains tucked to the sides.

I gave Gorge a tip, generous by Thai standards, for all of his help. He accepted it with the same grace and easy smile he'd shown from the start, then disappeared down the stairs, leaving me to settle in.

I unpacked slowly, gratefully, in full awareness of every movement and placement. Hanging clothes into the big armoire, smaller things into the dresser. Cash and passport in the safe and toiletries lined up neatly in the bathroom. Then

I sat down on the bed for the first time. It was perfect.

Firm, but with enough give to cradle you just right. A fluffy duvet sat folded at the foot, ready to wrap me into the kind of sleep I hadn't had last night. I placed my nighttime books on the bedside table, took a deep breath, and let a wave of relief wash over me.

Winding up in a really fantastic room has its benefits. Something I would come to appreciate the very next night. Was it something I ate? Probably. I'd grazed my way through local cafés and food carts over hours of exploring the neighborhood. Or maybe it was ice in a drink that hadn't been filtered, or a rogue mouthful of tap water while brushing my teeth. Hard to say.

In Thailand, it's called Bangkok Belly. In Mexico, Montezuma's Revenge. Every place has a catchy name for the gastrointestinal horror show that strikes unsuspecting tourists with equal opportunity vengeance. It starts with a little stomach grumble and ends in a full-scale coup by microscopic insurgents who've found a five-star resort in your gut.

And so *that* happened.

At first, just a little discomfort. Then waves of cramping, bloating, a fever that had me pendulum swinging between soaking sweats and teeth-chattering chills. My body, normally an amicable host, had declared martial law. I lay curled in bed, then shuttled repeatedly to the bathroom as my digestive system waged war on the interlopers and vice versa. I tried to trace my steps, analyze every bite and sip from the past day, but the source remained an enigma. It didn't matter. The invaders were in, and they weren't leaving without a fight.

I was trapped in a cycle of agony, vertical only for necessary water refills and moments of vital hygiene to feel vaguely human. Eventually, when the siege reached a temporary ceasefire, I brushed my teeth, washed my face again, and staggered downstairs to the front desk in search of salvation. I needed a pharmacy, and I needed it fast.

The staff at the Namton were exceptionally kind. I explained my situation as delicately as I could, no small feat considering the symptoms, and was gently told to return to my room. Someone would be up shortly. Perfect timing, because by the time I made it back upstairs, a far more aggressive assault had begun.

I was shivering under the covers, caught in the grip of an ice-cold fever attack, when I heard a voice at the door: "May I come in?" I muttered something between "*yes*" and "*dear God, help*," and in walked a staff member I didn't recognize, carrying a bag. It was from a local pharmacy.

He stocked the fridge with Gatorade, set aspirin and Imodium on the bedside table, and told me to rest. That was the last thing I heard before slipping into unconsciousness.

I awoke sometime later, now boiling hot, and made the now-familiar pilgrimage to the bathroom. As that next episode subsided, I downed some drugs, chugged a full Gatorade, then clicked on the TV, hoping for a little distraction from the soundtrack gurgling from my guts.

Only one English-language channel came through. And unfortunately, that channel was stuck in a loop of Tom Jones concerts.

Too weak to argue, I left Tom on, gyrating in his open polyester shirt, gold chains and glittering bell-bottoms, singing his heart out to an invisible audience. As I drifted in and out of fevered sleep, I was reminded all night that the style fads of the 70s were, in fact, an international fashion crime. Eventually, Tom took his final hip-thrusting bow as Tony Bennett took over crooning duties. Tony I could hang with.

The cycle continued: bed, bathroom, bed. But the Imodium was finally winning the war. Through it all, the Namton staff checked in every few hours with compassion. Cold washcloths dabbed my boiling forehead. Someone held my head steady while urging me to sip hot tea steeped in ginger.

Just before 4AM, two days later, I woke up clear-headed. My stomach was calm, my body had called off its internal riot, and for the first time in 36 hours I didn't feel like I was moments away from spontaneous combustion or that I was lying naked on an icy crag during the Holocene.

I immediately downed another Imodium tablet and chugged another full bottle of Gatorade in case those microscopic bastards were planning a desperate last-ditch offensive.

By eight, I was showered, shaved, weak but human again. Looking in the mirror at my newly slimmed-down self, I considered naming my new diet plan *The CM-Diet*™. The only real downside, aside from the gastrointestinal apocalypse, was that my belt no longer fit. I didn't have anything to punch a new hole, and my shorts had given up trying to stay on my hips. They puddled around my ankles unless I held them up like a Victorian damsel gathering her skirts before a fainting couch.

I can't, in good conscience, recommend that as a weight-loss regimen. But if you do find yourself in the unfortunate position of being stricken by Bangkok Belly, I highly recommend being stricken at the Namton Hotel. They treated me like family, nursed me through the worst of it, and saw me through to the other side with grace, kindness, and Gatorade.

The center of Chiang Mai - what's known as the Old Town - is a central ancient, walled city surrounded by an equally ancient moat. Surrounding that is the rest of Chiang Mai that grew outwards from the core. Within the center lives a bustling, near-constant party with a distinctly international flavor. There, hundreds of cafés, restaurants, bars, pubs, and street carts dish out cuisine and cocktails from every continent. Add in the multitude of pot shops and you've got a vice-filled wonderland for indulgent seekers.

But Chiang Mai isn't all sin-city. Amidst the nightlife and noodle stands are art galleries, flower shops, indie boutiques, and clothing stores (offering more than the ubiquitous elephant-print pants beloved only by tourists). There are fantastic bookstores (*my favorite is The Lost Bookshop on Ratchamanka Road, a multi-level oasis of new and used titles*). You'll also find hardware stores, scooter repair joints, pet shops, appliance and computer repair spots, and wet markets hawking everything from anchovies to zizania to mystery items I couldn't identify. Add clinics, hospitals, schools (from kindergarten to grad programs), and enough government offices to renew any visa or license, file for permits, etc., and you've got a self-contained city-state. You never actually have to leave the Old Town unless you want a different view.

One of my favorite moments in Thailand took place in Chiang Mai, on a soft December morning just after breakfast. It was early. 6AM. The city was still wiping sleep from its eyes. I'd slipped out into the breaking day with no particular destination, just that familiar pull to see what the morning had to say.

I've always loved getting out before the world wakes up no matter where I am. There's a kind of hush that hangs in the air when the light is still slanted and pure, and the day hasn't yet decided what kind of day it's going to be.

That's when you find the good stuff. Before it hides behind the hustle. Before it retreats into shopfronts and the daily routine of life lived. You wander the side streets and alleys not for direction, but for discovery. That's where magic lives. Not on the boulevards, but in the quiet corners that don't expect to be seen by travelers.

The day was beautiful. Cats and dogs were already out and about, some with their people, others on solitary patrol. Birds chirped their hearts out from the bushes and trees, and sleepy locals shuffled along with the soft smiles of people greeting the new day. I meandered wherever the alleys took me, simply soaking it all in, when I stumbled across a tidy little place called The Little Sunday Cafe. It was tucked on a quiet corner, Moonmuang Road, Lane 5, and Rachadamnoen 5 Alley, where small residential side streets intersect.

The place was straight out of a travel magazine: whitewashed walls, pale wood accents, a raised patio shaded by elegant umbrellas, and flowering pots spilling over with a sun-drenched riot of color. It was open. That was all the invitation

I needed.

One look at the menu confirmed it was owned by someone with serious restaurant chops. This wasn't some greasy hash-slinging dive. This was next level: omelets and Benedicts, waffles and pancakes, homemade muesli, yogurt, cured meats, fresh pastries, hard-core coffee from a gleaming la Marzocco espresso machine.

And yes, I know what you're thinking: You're in Thailand. Why the hell are you eating a Western breakfast? Fair observation. But sometimes, streets steer you into something you weren't expecting. I didn't seek it out; I just followed the rhythm of the roads and let my feet make the decisions. And there it was. A café tucked quietly into a sleepy corner.

That kind of stumble-upon-it moment isn't giving in to a craving. It felt like breakfast had been waiting there all along, arms folded, checking its wristwatch, wondering when I'd finally show up.

I ordered waffles with a gently scrambled egg on the side and seasonal fruit. I paired it with a quad-shot latte (subtlety is for Tuesdays) and a tall glass of Thai milk tea, which, I'll admit, has become one of my more reliable vices. Sweet and earthy. It tastes like vacation.

Before the server walked away, I hesitated for a beat, then asked the one question that would determine the fate of the meal.

"Do you have maple syrup?"

She smiled and nodded. "From Canada."

I smiled back with gratitude.

When my breakfast arrived, it was a work of art. The presentation was gorgeous, the waffles crisp yet fluffy, like someone had whispered sweet nothings into a cloud and the fruit could bring tears to your eyes. Thailand and New Zealand are the only places I've been where fruit consistently tastes like it's been blessed by Gods. The mango and passion fruit were ethereal. The dragon fruit - often a beautiful but tasteless dud back home - was juicy, floral, and sweet, like a lovechild between pear and watermelon. In the Pacific Northwest, the imported dragon fruit looks like a supermodel but tastes like plaster.

Full, grateful, and grinning, I thanked the staff and stepped back into the golden hush of morning. I wandered the alley where bougainvillea spilled over walls in electric pinks and purples, heading toward a main road. Shopkeepers were raising metal doors. The rhythmic *"shick shick shick"* of twig brooms echoed as sidewalks were swept. Hanging plants were getting their morning drink, rugs were being beaten senseless, while laundry gently flapped above the lanes and alleys. It was the choreography of Thai morning life.

As I approached the lane's end, a little black cat trotted up to me - tail high, eyes smiling.

All my life, animals have come to me. Not in that Disney-princess, bluebirds-on-the-fingertips sort of way. They pause, assess me with a head-tilt or a slow blink; sometimes they decide I'm safe enough to approach. It's one of those inexplicable personal oddities, like being the guy who always ends up sitting next to the talker on the plane. Only in this case, the talker is four-legged and furry.

I don't know why it happens. Maybe I give off the right energy; equal parts curiosity and restraint. Or maybe animals, like some people, just respond to someone who knows how to shut up and listen.

But in Thailand, as in Mexico, as in Spain, and other places around the world, the rules seem different. The strays here carry the memory of being ignored or mistreated. You can see it in the tension of their shoulders, the way they hesitate before stepping into the open, as if freedom might be a trap. Most cats and dogs glance at you with that universal expression of street-hardened skepticism: Don't even try it gringo. Then they bolt, tails low, paws silent, gone before your intention even finishes forming.

Still, I will try. I always try. I crouch down, soften my eyes, angle my body slightly, not directly facing, not threatening. I become low and still and non-threatening, offering what can only be described as a peace treaty in posture. And then I wait. For a flick of an ear. For the hesitation in their retreat. For a twitch that says maybe this guy isn't dangerous.

Because when it happens, when a dog circles back with its tail raised, or a cat dares a single brush of its side against your leg, it's being granted entry into a quiet, sacred place. A place where nothing is asked of you except gentleness.

That moment, brief as it is, always restores something in me. It makes me feel a little more grounded. A little more seen. A bit more humane. A little more okay.

It's not language, not really. It's something deeper. The mutual recognition that, at our best, we are simply bodies moving through the world trying not to harm each other. Trying, if we're lucky, to find small comforts in the presence of another living thing.

But that little one? She was different!

She came bounding toward me without hesitation, her sleek black tail held high like a flag of friendship. Her posture radiated trust, her body language open and unafraid. And those eyes, those smiling slow-blinking electric green, "*I love you, pet me now*" eyes melted me.

The end of the lane spilled onto Mun Mueang Road a half-block further on. It was unusually quiet that morning, no cars speeding by, no scooters screaming around corners like mechanical hornets. I found a small plastic stool someone had left out and sat down to enjoy a proper make-out session with the cat.

My cat, Dolores McGonagall, was back home, thousands of miles and oceans away. She and I were tight. Like, gazing into each other's eyes forever tight. So yes, I'd been craving cat time, and this little bugger, who even looked like Dolores with her sleek black fur and emerald eyes, showed up like a feline fix. I renamed her Dolores for the duration of our fling. Why not!

I should mention that I'm allergic to animals. Not in a cute, sniffly way, but in my-lungs-close-up-like-a-deflated-sack way. Still, it's never stopped me. I've always figured that with enough handwashing, discipline, antihistamines, and a solid sense of denial, I could love on animals and live to tell the tale. And here, in the early morning light of Chiang Mai, that theory was in full swing.

After about fifteen minutes of snuggling and purrs, the newly christened Dolores decided we were done, as cats do. With zero explanation or apology, she stretched and strutted off like we hadn't just shared a moment. Either back to her people or to destroy a bird.

I stood up, brushing fur off my shirt when I noticed a portly older man. He had to be in his nineties and had been watching me from the shadows of an open shop bay across the alley. His face was a weathered masterpiece of sun-worn deep-set creases that radiated wisdom, adorned by a Fu Manchu mustache and a goatee so theatrical it deserved its own casting agent. If Vincent Price and a temple guardian had a lovechild, this was him.

He didn't speak. He just stared at me, one eyebrow cocked in faint amusement, before motioning for me to come over. When I hesitated and began to move along - still not sure if I was being summoned for a sales pitch or not - he let out a soft, birdlike whistle and doubled down with an insistent "come here" wave.

I looked around, half expecting a trapdoor to drop me down into a Shianghai cell and crossed the alley. His shop was a Frankensteinian mashup between scooter rentals and laundry service. I knew that he knew exactly where everything was, even if no one else did. Half assembled bike parts hung from ceiling hooks next to drying sheets and shirts, and an oscillating fan that had given up all pretense of oscillating on axis.

I assumed he wanted to rent me a scooter and then, after I crashed, clean my bloody clothes at a generous discount. Very enterprising. I smiled and shook my head.

"I'm *not* renting a scooter," I said, pointing at one of his machines.

He ignored me completely, then walked over, gently took my arm like an insistent grandfather, and with a solemn urgency, said, "Come. Wash hands. Cat dirty. You rub face! Wash!" Which, to be fair, was entirely true.

Which, to be fair, was entirely true. I'd just let Chiang Mai's doppelganger of Dolores rub its mange and memory all over me, and now my face was beginning to itch like the prelude to an EpiPen scene.

Before I could protest, he was leading me - arm in hand to a deep basin in the back of his shop. He turned the water on, assessed the temperature with the back of his hand like a seasoned caregiver, and handed me a clean washcloth and a plastic bottle of liquid soap - that smelled like durian. I took a breath and lathered up like I was prepping for surgery.

As I scrubbed, he hovered nearby, nodding approvingly and muttering in a mix of Thai and English, telling me the cat was "very friendly," but "dirty. Always dirty. Must wash. Make you scratch sick."

It was surreal. One minute I was chasing nostalgia in feline form, the next I was being nannied by a nonagenarian scooter-laundry patriarch who took hygiene far more seriously than the local restaurants. The line between absurdity and kindness blurred in the best conceivable way.

Just as I was patting my cheeks dry and wondering what sort of Yelp review this whole thing would earn, the shouting began.

A woman roughly his age, though somehow with the energy of someone who'd just had her fifth cappuccino and many lifetimes of dealing with him, rounded the corner like a monsoon in house slippers. She stopped short when she saw me at the sink, her eyes narrowing in a perfect cartoon expression of exasperation. Then she turned on him with the theatrical precision of a woman who had performed this scene many times.

It was in Thai. Rapid-fire yet melodic, a series of tonal flourishes that sounded less like scolding and more like jazz, but the gist was clear. *I* was the problem, and *he* was the cause.

I froze mid-pat, dripping water onto the floor, unsure whether to bow, apologize, or fake a seizure. My impulse was to flee, dignity be damned, but before I could make a break for it, he stepped between us like a man both brave and entirely used to those arguments.

They went at it. He calm, she volcanic. He with soft, placating gestures and the occasional shrug, she with finger-pointing, arm waving, and a perfectly timed eyeroll that I felt. There were voices raised, yes, but there was also the unmistakable undercurrent of affection. This wasn't war. It was sport.

She glanced at me again, this time less like I was a threat and more like I was a stray cur who had wandered into her kitchen. I offered her a sheepish smile, and she gave me a long, slow blink that somehow managed to convey: "This is my life. This man. This nonsense."

Then she turned on her heels, muttering something under her breath. I'm pretty sure it wasn't a blessing.

He turned back to me, sighed with a weary kind of dignity, and motioned for me to finish washing up, as if nothing had happened at all. I obediently resumed scrubbing my face, hands, and arms like a TV surgeon, now on round three. He handed me a towel, soft, clean, and obviously a result of their laundry business prowess.

When I handed the towel back with a bow and a *"kop khun krab,"* he nodded solemnly and gently took my arm once more. He guided me to a pair of sun-bleached and cracked mismatched plastic chairs under the awning that shaded the front of their shop. The kind of chairs that had outlived conversations, monsoons, and a skirmish or two. We settled in.

He told me his name was Larry (his chosen Western name) offered before I could give mine. A strange symmetry. Two Larry's, from opposite ends of the world, seated side by side like some cosmic fable.

We sat and talked for over two hours. He wanted to know everything. My life in America, my travels, what I thought of Thailand, and still clinging to hope, whether I might be persuaded to rent a scooter. (Still no.) He told me his tales of traveling across Europe and Asia as a young man, journeys that were epic and still alive in his mind.

He told me he knew the streets of San Francisco because of Clint Eastwood and Steve McQueen. Dirty Harry and Bullitt, barreling their cars through impossible chases that thrilled him still. When I explained that those chase scenes were edited horseshit, that none of those streets actually connect. He laughed so hard he nearly fell off his chair. "I love Hollywood," he shouted out to the passing traffic. A woman watering plants out front of her shop across the way yelled at him, obviously having heard too much over the years.

When I admitted I wasn't a fan of khao soi he looked at me as though I'd insulted Buddha himself. He made me promise to keep trying until I found one that changed my mind. I asked if his wife made khao soi, gently fishing for a dinner invite. He chuckled and waved me off. "She cannot cook laundry, let alone food."

My plans I'd had for the morning were rescheduled under the gentle insistence of his company and a few cold post-breakfast beers. The age-old breakfast of philosophers. He was stunned when I told him I'd spent a month at a Buddhist monastery. "Why?" he asked, with genuine confusion. "So many pretty Thai wife for you!" I explained about the breakup. He nodded, not unkindly, then chuckled. "Good Thai wife help you forget that one."

His wife, meanwhile, sat behind the service counter, pretending not to listen. But every now and then I'd catch her glancing up, her expression somewhere between stern disapproval and long-suffering affection. The look of someone who's heard it all before but still finds a certain charm in the repetition. From time to time, her glare softened into something else - something almost like a smile. The kind that escapes before the ego traps it and shoves it back into a corner lest it be discovered.

I'll never forget that morning. Not because anything momentous happened but because something beautiful did. A door opened. A stranger decided, without hesitation or agenda (except to rent a scooter of course), to care for me. And in the span of a conversation, we were no longer strangers. What started as a random encounter at the end of an alley turned into one of those lovely moments of human connection that stays with you for life.

I got up to leave and walked to the back counter, thanking his wife, not just for the towel or the space or the patience, but for loaning me her husband for a little while.

She rolled her eyes in that global language that spoke of long-term relationships and the challenges that come from marrying souls, but there was a glimmer behind them too. A wink, quick and sly, that said she understood far more English than she let on. She gave me a little shooing wave with her fingers, gentle but unmistakable.

It was time to move on.

CHAPTER 5. WHEN I GET OFFA THIS MOUNTAIN, I KNOW WHERE I WANNA GO

Cooking is meditation with sharper tools. When your hands are busy, and your concentration is cruising at 100%, your brain gets to rest. You can't doomscroll while holding a knife!

What's the first thing my brother monks and I wanted to do when we got off the mountain? Chef it up. That might sound surprising coming from a bunch of freshly disrobed monks, but somewhere between meditation marathons and monastery chores, we'd discovered a shared passion for the kitchen.

Over our free afternoons, some of us would swap stories about pre-monk lives: meals and dinner parties, chili competitions, backyard steak and veggie BBQ's, and my love of making a deeply satisfying long-simmer Bolognese or pan-seared crispy-skinned steelhead with a miso/orange juice and soy glaze.

I imagined Josh, ever the aesthete, confessing a preference for champagne and caviar, claiming to have once paired vintage Dom with truffle popcorn at a screening of La Dolce Vita. I could easily see that. Emiliano, from Mexico City, talked about making mole from scratch and the deeply spiritual process of pressing tortillas by hand. I recalled the time I attempted to make Pad Thai and failed spectacularly. That went into the trash faster than junk mail.

The universe has a sense of humor: in Theravada Buddhism as I've mentioned, monks aren't allowed to cook. Ever. So, there we were, culinary romantics in robes, forbidden from touching a wok. The dhamma giveth, the dhamma taketh away.

As our time on the mountain wound down, the idea of meals beyond the (admittedly wonderful) monastery fare began to feel downright erotic in a food-porn sort of way. I floated an idea: we'd take a cooking class once we were back in Chiang Mai. Several guys lit up at the thought - laughing over hot woks, recreating the curries and noodles we'd loved, reclaiming our foodie identities. But like most post-retreat intentions, the fantasy faded. Our brotherhood scattered with the wind. Some went home. One went kayaking. One headed to Cambodia. Two flew south to the Dhammakaya center near Bangkok. In the end, there were only three of us who opted for a cooking school adventure: me, Josh, and Emiliano. Champagne, mole, and barbecue, reunited in an apron-clad act of karmic balance.

I was the first of our not-so-motley monk squad to leave the monastery. I checked out a couple of days early, partly for logistical reasons, partly because my soul had reached its dhamma quota. There's only so much introspection and robes I can take before I start fantasizing about sharp knives mincing garlic, profanity over a stubbed toe, and a spider-free shower. And I had a mission. A secular one: find a cooking class. But not just *any* cooking class.

I wasn't about to spend my afternoon chopping carrots while pretending we were on some culinary adventure. I didn't want an urban churn-and-burn operation where the ingredients are pre-measured, the aprons are social-media ready, and the big achievement is sautéing a few token dishes before posing next to a wok like you've earned a Michelin star. No thank you.

I wanted the real deal. Fire. Flavor. Power over protein and produce. A pestle and mortar workout. I also wanted a Thai chef who ran the kitchen like a battlefield commander. Something raw, hands-on, and just far enough off the tourist grid that would stick with me. Less selfie. More soul.

So, I did what I always do in these situations: I asked people. Specifically, strangers who looked like they could cook. Don't ask me how, I just know. There was the woman at a café with a cookbook open, taking notes. Obvious choice. Or locals in the veggie section choosing obscure produce (always a good sign), concierges with no skin in the game, and jackpot: two sweaty, soot-smudged chefs I found out back, basting suckling pigs and a goat on rotisseries while having smokes in the alley. Targets acquired. Interviews ensued.

The Chiang Mai Thai Farm Cooking School was the clear winner.

The office was vacant when I arrived. I rang the bell as instructed by a little laminated sign taped to the counter. Nothing. I rang again. Still nothing. Finally, a door in the back creaked open and out came a gruff, flushed woman dressed in clothes that looked better suited to mucking out a horse stall than managing a hospitality desk. She barked several unexpected words and phrases that caught me off guard.

Then she apologized. She'd been expecting someone else. She shifted into business mode and pulled out a ledger with all the warmth of a customs officer having a bad day. I mentioned that I was booking for myself and two others - my brother monks. Her eyebrow went up like I'd just told her I was signing up a trio of cloistered Capuchin friars for a Muay Thai class.

That kicked off what felt like a vetting interview. She peppered me with questions about our motivations, our experience, how serious we were. Which was... interesting. I didn't realize one needed credentials to chop ginger and peppers, julienne basil and sling a wok. Isn't that the point of signing up? You get to wield a knife and pretend you're in a food-travel docuseries while someone lectures about the importance of your mise-en-place?

When she asked if I had ever cooked before, it was clear she didn't think I could handle the class. Maybe it was the monk thing, or maybe I just looked like a guy more likely to burn water than slow-braise shanks. But I smiled and quietly explained that, back home, I cooked almost every night.

I was missing cooking - missing it deeply. It's long been one of my love languages, something I approached with reverence: equal parts awareness and indulgence. For me, it wasn't just about feeding people; it was about honoring ingredients, sharing love, and creating edible beauty. I cooked for family, friends, lovers, and neighbors, with wine in my glass and music in the air. For quiet dinners and raucous backyard parties alike. My favorite question on any given morning? "Hey honey, what are you craving?"

Sure, I love grilling a perfect grilled cheeseburger or hot dog. What red-blooded guy doesn't? (Vegans don't count.) But if you were craving something more elevated - say, creamy chanterelle risotto with fall-off-the-bone veal osso bucco, a silky French omelet, or homemade crepes stuffed with sautéed Dungeness crab and a whisper of citrus. I was your guy.

I've slow-braised boeuf bourguignon for nine hours, because that's how long it takes to taste like winter in a French farmhouse. I've roasted ribs to sticky perfection, crisped chicken skin to holy status, and simmered pho broth that could give you a mouthgasm. Duck à l'Orange? Easy. Beef Wellington so good Gordon Ramsay might sit down and say thank you.

Need prime rib-eyes seared to a crusted medium-rare, with roasted garlic and minted green beans? Mashed potatoes so rich that Joel Robuchon himself would nod? Naturally.

Shrimp fried rice, dim sum, yakisoba, wok-seared vegetables? Just point me to the kitchen and get out of my way.

In other words, yeah. I can cook. Not "follow a recipe" cook. *Cook* cook.

As I was blathering on, another staff member came out of the back and sat at a desk going over some paperwork.

We ended up talking about food for much longer than I wanted to. I hadn't eaten breakfast. I was famished and increasingly frustrated. At one point I asked about the knives we'd be using. I'm a stickler for sharp knives and mine are kept razor-sharp at all times. When you love to cook, your knives are your religion.

She handed me my receipt, turned on her heel, and disappeared back into her office without another word.

For a brief moment, I seriously considered canceling and finding a different school. But the reviews were so good - glowing, even. How could this be the vibe? Was it because I'd refused to pay via PayPal? The sketchy, unsecure link in the email they sent me to the "proceed to payment" screen had "identity theft" written all over it. No way was I going to feed my bank card into some unsecured black hole on the other side of the planet so it could end up on a spreadsheet in a hacker's group chat.

The farm provided transportation as part of the program so that all I had to worry about was being ready at my hotel upright, caffeinated, and waiting outside at the appointed time. Josh and Emiliano, my fellow recently civilianized brother monks converged at my hotel early that sunny morning. Our reunion sans robes and back in street clothes, was exuberant. Big hugs, big laughs, and strong coffees all around. We were ready to throw down in a Thai kitchen.

Our guide, Mod, was petite but fierce, sharp-eyed with the energy to run a kitchen or a presidential campaign. She took charge as we headed to Ruamchook Market, a locals-and-chef haunt at the city's edge, rarely touched by tourists.

At the stalls, Mod flipped into sensei mode: twelve varieties of rice - short, medium, long grain; red, white, black, yellow; regular and sticky - stacked like minimalist art. She explained when to use each, moisture retention, germ polishing, and how all that shapes texture and taste. Then came a chili masterclass. How to spot, handle, and survive the fire and a rundown of curry pastes: green, red, yellow, Panang, and Massaman.

Our assignment: make curry paste from scratch. We'd pick from a menu of options, gather ingredients at the farm, and grind our own paste using mortar and pestle the traditional way. I'd never done that before and was genuinely excited to learn.

I bought a little bag of freshly fried grasshoppers to share. And no, they're not gross. They're crunchy, nutty, a little sweet and savory, and if you're into hot French fries dipped into chocolate shakes? You'd love them! They are weirdly addictive. Stop with the faces, they pair beautifully with beer and watching the faces of the squeamish.

Re-caffeinated and munching on fried grasshoppers, we wound through narrow rural roads. Lush greenery stretched out. Banana, coconut, tamarind trees playing checkerboard with vegetable and fruit plots. Rural, local, and alive just outside the city.

The cooking school sat on a gated farm thirty minutes from Chiang Mai. It was lush, quiet, undeniably gorgeous. We piled out, still buzzing from the market, handed aprons and hats. The full tourist kit. Charming, kitschy, mildly humiliating.

The open-air dining area was rustic but inviting. Long wooden tables, hanging plants, with an occasional cat inspecting our feet. Nearby, the "classroom": a U-shaped setup that housed twelve cooking stations, each compact and organized with prep boards, stone mortars and pestles, bowls, utensils and high-BTU two-burner gas stoves - one for pots, one for woks. Clean, ready, whispering potential. Like a low-budget, high-passion cooking show.

Mod pointed me to a station with a gleaming cleaver. I tested the edge - sharp enough to earn respect or seal a cut with super glue. I nodded thanks, received a wai and a smile. I was good to go.

Before cooking, we toured the farm's manicured paths, more botanical garden than production space. Exotic fruit trees, hedgerows, and natural dividers created order without sacrificing beauty. Everything organic? A bonus I hadn't expected.

We passed veggie beds of onions, root vegetables, tiny pea-sized Thai eggplants, and larger green ping-pong-ball-like ones. Then rhizomes: dense rows of galangal and ginger. Edible flowers for flavor, garnish, and dye. Chili bushes in every stage of firepower. Groves of pandan, tamarind, kaffir lime; lush, efficient, deeply Thai.

Back at the stations, sleeves rolled, I tackled Tom Kha Gai - the creamy, herbaceous sour soup - and Gaeng Keow Wan, classic green curry. I knew Tom Kha well but wanted to deepen my connection with fresh ingredients harvested minutes before.

The soup came together joyfully. I plucked kaffir lime leaves - double-lobed like nature's quotation marks - from a tree nearby. Their fragrance made your shoulders drop in relaxation. Add galangal and crushed lemongrass, and the steam smelled like herbal balm for the soul.

Tom Kha Gai means boil, galangal, chicken. Back home, finding fresh galangal is impossible, ginger's a poor substitute. Here, I had the real deal. I took a nibble. That was a freakin' huge mistake!

A searing astringency exploded in my mouth, followed by earthy heat and carrot-like sweetness that smacked me in the face. My sinuses blew open like I'd snorted powdered wasabi. Josh and Emiliano looked alarmed as I red-facedly signaled I was fine while discreetly spitting the fibrous mess into my palm.

Mod checked out my galangal fiasco, offering a knowing smile and a bottle of water. "You don't eat galangal," she said gently. "It's just for flavor. We don't chew it once it's cooked." Noted. Unlike ginger, my usual cooking snack, galangal isn't nibble-friendly. Lesson learned - painfully. But now I understood the flavor spectrum that makes a Tom Kha Gai sing.

Once recovered, prep and cooking went smoothly, though Mod raised an eyebrow when she saw me finely slicing three bird's eye chilies instead of one or two. What can I say? I like spice.

I stirred, tasted, adjusted. Perfect Tom Kha Gai!

I was tempted to slurp the whole bowl, but curry paste awaited.

Learning to create curry paste from raw ingredients using just a stone mortar and pestle fascinated me. At home, I lean on store-bought pastes for convenience. But this? Old-school elbow grease, hand-crushing, pure passion. Yep, ladies, I'm one hell of a date.

I'd chosen green curry for Gaeng Keow Wan. Others made red, Panang, or Massaman. I wanted to try them all, but time's a cruel chef.

The air pulsed with rhythmic pok-pok-pok of pestles on mortars. Ginger, galangal, lemongrass, garlic, shallots, coriander root, holy basil, chilies, all pulverized into aromatic pastes. A spicy percussion section pounding a scent-heavy symphony.

Mod circled, checking consistency. When she nodded at my paste - which looked like a cookbook photo - I felt absurdly proud.

Then the fires were lit. I grabbed the wok.

I love a good wok and use them regularly. I know how to tame the beast, read its heat, stir, toss. But this setup made me giddy. The burner cradled a rounded wok base, fired by a double-ring gas element, delivering true *"wok hei,"* the legendary smoky sear that no other pan can create.

Back home the stovetops don't accommodate round-bottom woks so we have to settle for flats. They work but can't match the authentic sizzle when ingredients leap and kiss the blazing metal with a fresh sear.

When the pan hit white-hot, steel smoking in curls, I added oil. It shimmered and danced a perfect slippery seal. Then came the vegetables, chicken, prawns - each tossed in stages, seared, set aside, the wok reheated, flavors layered like a kitchen symphony. Woks sizzled and clanged all around, metal spatulas banging, flames roaring. Hot, loud, frenetic and absolutely glorious.

With our first two dishes done, everyone riding high on the aroma of victory, it was lunchtime. The farm staff had laid out platters of steamed jasmine rice obviously knowing some of us (me) had gone chili-crazy and needed a tamper.

We gathered, passing plates, trading notes, low-key hoping someone else's curry was worse than ours. I was proud. Tom Kha Gai and Gaeng Keow Wan, though I doubled the chili count. Green birds' eye for snap, red for sweet burn. Not "see-you-in-another-dimension" spicy, but not shy either.

No casualties, thankfully. Everyone who braved my creations confirmed: yes, edible, yes, hot enough for some introspection. One British guy mopped his forehead, declared it "brilliant," then promptly piled more rice on his plate. That's the rice's job: flavor sponge and fire extinguisher.

Capsaicin broke the ice. Compliments flew, spoons clinked, and dish swapping began. We'd met that morning, but now we were bonded. Sweat, spice, mortar-and-pestle camaraderie. Plates circled as we all tasted each other's masterpieces.

⁂

Mod kept an eye on me all day, especially when I was back at my station after the break, turning carrots into ultra-thin matchsticks for my third dish: fried spring rolls. Now, spring-roll filling usually calls for something delicate - like a Nakiri blade - more an ultra-thin cleaver than the butcher-sized weapon they'd handed me. One knife per station, though, so I made do with my gleaming cleaver. It was like trying to fillet an anchovy with a Katana.

She watched, eyes narrowing. Was that admiration? Approval? When I finished, she gave me a broad smile and a thumbs up. "Nice work!" she said, like I'd just pulled off a culinary miracle, not hacked away with a blade better suited for splitting beef spines.

Awkward? Sure. But fun, like driving a big truck in a tight parking lot - clumsy but satisfying. My matchsticks were a tad thinner than intended (I got carried away trying to wield my "one blade to rule them all"). But at least I didn't chop off any fingers which I consider solid progress, especially after the galangal debacle.

Back to spring rolls: I've always loved making them at home, but the wraps usually puffed up into third-degree blisters instead of crisp, golden perfection. Turns out I'd been doing it all wrong. First mistake: vegetable oil. Cheap and convenient, sure, but not the frying oil of champions. And don't ask about the oil temperature. I was cranking the heat so high my kitchen doubled as a smoke sauna. An oil thermometer should've been on my Christmas list years ago considering I have every other kitchen tool on the planet.

Mod, ever the patient teacher, found me hovering over my flaming pan with that worried look. "Too hot," she said, deadpan. "Drop the temp and give the rolls time to crisp without burning. 360° is where you want it."

At the school, they used peanut oil; not my usual choice given the saturated fat content, but Mod gave the thumbs-up for canola as a substitute if you keep temps in check. She also schooled me on fryer etiquette: don't crowd the pan, flip rolls when they hit that perfect golden glow, and ditch the paper towels. Use a wire rack instead so oil drains off and your rolls don't turn into soggy sad sacks.

So that's my spring roll redemption story: the right oil, the right temp, and some patience. Who knew crispy greatness hinged on so little? Obviously not me. Now if only I could stop them from erupting into mini oil geysers the first bite. It's still a wok in progress.

Last up was mango or banana with sticky rice and sweet coconut milk and is Thailand's answer to "what's for dessert?" This dish is so ubiquitous it's almost mandatory at every meal. When the chef wants to get fancy, they dye the rice a vibrant forget-me-not blue with butterfly pea flowers. The farm had fresh patches of those flowers, so our blue rice was the freshest and most eye-popping I've ever seen. And yes, it tasted as good as it looked.

By the time class ended, I was riding high on flames, cleavers, and culinary victory. But the ride back to town was subdued. Josh, Emiliano and I had bonded over dhamma up the mountain, then woks and herbs, sharing food and laughter, but reality was creeping in: goodbyes loomed.

༄

Back at the hotel, we decided to extend the day with a night market crawl. We rounded up other brothers now down from the mountain and hit the labyrinth of brightly lit carts. Laughter bounced in the humid air as we grazed like kings of the street. It was surreal and would be our last meal together, not as monks, but as travelers who'd shared much more. Bittersweet hung heavy in my heart.

One by one, they peeled off. A train here, flight there. Tan Jain Wei stuck around the longest before disappearing into the night. I stood amid the crowds on Wua Lai Walking Street, alone but full of gratitude for what we'd shared.

Back at the hotel, stuffed with food and swirling emotions, I poured myself a few fingers of Johnny Walker Black and opened my laptop to a streaming service. The first thing on the screen? Anthony Bourdain's *A Cook's Tour - Thailand* episode. How prescient. Instantly, I was transported into his world, following his journey through food and culture.

The departure of my friends was a brutal reminder: impermanence is a cruel, insightful bitch. Nothing stays the same forever. I drifted off to sleep, dreaming of my next adventure.

CHAPTER 6. ARE YOU HAPPY TO SEE ME? AN ELEPHANT IN THE ROOM

The elephant isn't performative majesty; it just is. The rest of us are left trying to remember what that kind of integrity feels like.

Elephants have been stomping around my imagination for as long as I can remember. Majestic, gentle, impossibly wise, I've always been fascinated with them. So, landing in a country where they're not just admired but revered felt a bit like stepping into a dream - one that was about to come true.

The elephants of Thailand are Asiatic elephants - *Elephas maximus indicus* if you're feeling Latiny - whose territory stretches across the Southeast Asian and Indian subcontinents. Over the centuries, they've done just about everything: built civilizations, waged wars, hauled logs and stones, carried royalty and peasants alike, and, more recently, performed embarrassing tricks for sunburned tourists who really should know better than to subjugate an animal to humiliation. That last bit is a hard truth.

For too long, elephants in Thailand were used in battle, labor and entertainment. But times they are a changin.' Slowly, but changing, nonetheless. These days, more and more of those living attractions are giving way to ethical husbandry and sanctuaries where the elephants are no longer expected to perform, paint, or pose for selfies. Instead, they get to do what they were dreaming of all along: eat, wander, nap, bathe, and commune with their family.

After a week exploring Chiang Mai, my monk brothers having vanished back into their mists after our cooking class, it was elephant time.

My goal was simple: find an interactive elephant experience that didn't feel like a labor camp or training ground for a circus. To my happy surprise, nearly everyone I asked pointed to the same place: an ethical sanctuary tucked deep in the jungle about two hours west of the city on the edge of a national park. It was called the Elephant Freedom Project, which sounded like a politically ambitious indie band.

I checked it out online. Glowing reviews, elephant rides, hooks, and circus tricks not allowed, and the kind of sustainability badges that usually involve bamboo fonts and phrases like "carbon-free footprint." Best of all, they emphasized education and respectful interaction, all under the watchful eye of a mahout - the lifelong elephant handler who knows their companion like family.

The ride to the sanctuary came courtesy of a pickup that looked like it had been designed by someone with a deep dislike for comfort and structural integrity. In the back: two metal benches with just enough padding to mock the concept of cushions, a roll cage out of necessity judging from the quarter-panels of the rig, and a fiberglass shell that rattled like it was held together with duct tape, zip ties and prayers.

Our driver was clearly auditioning for a Fast & Furious spinoff: Chiang Mai Drift. He took hairpin curves like he was trying to outrun gravity and test the limits of g-force survival, never once glancing back to check if we were still alive or even still in the bed of the truck. Out back, three of us were gripping the roll cage with the intensity of people who'd just learned the word "mausoleum".

The road got worse as we went. It got narrower, twistier, muddier, wetter, potholier, until we were bouncing up a rutted jungle trail at a steady sixty kilometers per hour. Sixty. In a pickup. On a dirt track. Was it fun? Sure - in an Eli Roth flick way.

At one point, I caught the other fellow muttering something that sounded suspiciously like a prayer, while his wife's expression said, "We paid for this?"

Meanwhile, I was clinging to that metal frame like a man desperate to not fly out the back. This was not transportation. This was a trust fall with a souped-up engine and a maniac at the wheel.

The sanctuary stretched across thirty square miles of rolling jungle and rivers, a lush refuge carved out by a wonderful alliance: the Thai National Parks Service, elephant-rescue activists, and the royal family itself. It wasn't a zoo, or a petting farm, or another social-media backdrop disguised as conservation. It was land set aside with intention - a living breathing expanse where elephants could simply exist doing their elephanty things.

Michael moved with the quiet ease of a man who'd swapped city noise for the hills' soft whispers. He told us there were six camps spread across the reserve, home to about two hundred rescued elephants. Each elephant had a mahout. Not a master, but a companion. Two hundred pairs, linked not by chains or commands, but by trust and care. No hooks, no tricks, no riders. This was no circus. This was respect.

Elephants, like people, carry more than just weight and wisdom - they carry moods, memories, emotional baggage. The sanctuary honored all of it. Only six visitors were allowed in the full-day program, twice a week. The rest of the time, the elephants did what elephants do best: eat, bathe, snooze under shade, wallow in mud spas, and exchange low-frequency gossip that no human could ever decode. Living their lives with no stress or spectacle.

Michael explained there was another section for those elephants comfortable with a bigger crowd, thirty visitors a day, carefully managed in shifts. But the ones I came to know preferred quiet company. I was grateful for that.

I didn't come here only for myself. Part of me came for my father. He and I didn't always see eye-to-eye on most things, we didn't even share a horizon. But elephants were different. Conservation, too. That was as close to sacred common ground as we had. My dad spoke of elephants the way he revered early Dixieland jazz and a curveball that broke just right for the strike. They were sacred to him, carved from a finer, forgotten world. He never got to see one up close before he passed in 2005. So, this day wasn't just mine. It was a kind of pilgrimage and a homage, paid in patience. A quiet offering in a place where giants still walk slowly, without apology. For once, the elephant in the room had room to breathe, to be seen, and maybe understood. I like to think my dad would have loved knowing that I would be up close and intimate with a pachyderm.

By the time we rattled to a stop, joints aching, brain sloshed from the full Space Mountain experience on rutted mountain roads, we were greeted with bottles of cold water and bundles of clothing that looked more ceremonial than comfortable. Shirt and pants woven in a distinct color pattern were the kind you might expect to see in a folkloric tapestry or a children's book about jungle tribes. The cut was... generous. Let's call it "one-size-fits-some." Mine fit like a cross between hospital scrubs and a sack race costume.

Michael explained, with the calm certainty of someone who had given this speech many times, that those uniforms weren't for our benefit. They were for the elephants. The pattern, he said, was familiar to them, worn daily by the handlers they knew and trusted. By donning the same outfit, we were signaling to these intelligent, emotionally complex animals that we were part of the tribe and not a threat.

Once suited up and resigned to our new fashion identities, we were led to a shaded area for orientation. What followed wasn't some breezy welcome chat. It was a sharply delivered, no-nonsense session just shy of an hour. No fluff. No pandering. The kind of briefing that makes you sit up straighter, not just because the benches were slabs of hardwood (they were), but because you could feel right away: this wasn't about petting elephants and snapping selfies. This was about respect. About understanding the animals and the very real responsibility that came with being near them. And the harm that could be done by getting it wrong.

We learned about the Asian elephant's life cycle, their social bonds, the layered meanings in their vocalizations and body language, ears, tails, trunks, eyes, every twitch a kind of Morse code. We were taught how to interact: where to stand, when to move, how to read the signals, and most critically, what *not* to do if we wanted to avoid getting pancaked.

Because elephants are huge. And strong. And far more agile than you'd expect. Majestic, yes. Gentle, often. But also fully capable of turning you into a lurid smear if startled or annoyed. And while I'm sure there are worse ways to go than being squashed by an elephant in the jungles of northern Thailand, I can't think of many that would be quite as memorable for your grieving friends. "Oh, you didn't hear? Yeah - Larry zigged when he should've zagged. Tragic. But what a way to go, huh? Mustard on that Hebrew National?"

After our elephant etiquette seminar, we graduated to vitamin prep. We sat around low wooden tables and assembled pachyderm vitamin packets by hand, filling banana leaf wraps with a mix of smashed bananas, tamarind, salt, and brown rice, pounded to a pulp with mortar and pestle. Each of us made two, and the mood was light, more kindergarten craft time than wilderness survival.

Then it was time for first contact.

We followed a narrow dirt path down to an open-sided covered corral which provided shade. Three elephants waited like seasoned greeters. Casual, curious, and clearly aware that the new guests had brought edible gifts. Their trunks lifted as we approached, like periscopes, swaying side to side to sniff the air. Their massive bodies swayed with a rhythm that felt ancient and measured, not impatient, but a kind of anticipation that portrayed something that I didn't understand. They looked us over with wise eyes, clearly sizing up which of us might be the easiest mark.

We were instructed to step forward and introduce ourselves using soft voices and gentle, fluid movements. Those trunks! They shot forward with laser precision. My first packet vanished in a blink, suctioned up and deposited mouthward in a single graceful motion that defied belief in its speed and dexterity. It startled a laugh out of me - part joy, part "what just happened?"

It turns out that speed and accuracy is standard. I asked if the elephants were extra hungry today or just showing off. Michael, our instructor, smiled: "They love their vitamins." Apparently, that level of enthusiasm is par for the course, and every visitor gets the same eager reception. The second packet was hoovered up just as quickly.

Once the packets were gone (each elephant gets six per day, meaning the sanctuary staff, visitors and mahouts prep around 1,200 daily) we moved on to the buffet phase: bucket after bucket of chopped sugar cane, bananas, corn on cobs along with the stalks. The elephants dove in. Trunks dipped and curled with balletic grace, plucking food from our hands with unfussy confidence. If we hadn't run out of produce, I'm convinced we'd still be there watching them grasp and chew with contented thunder.

I asked Michael about their diet. "Each elephant eats around 500 kilos a day," he said without drama, but with just enough poetic pause to incorporate that mass into our brain pan. That's over a thousand pounds of food per elephant every single day. I looked at the size of them again, at the powerful yet quiet dignity with which they moved and ate. Awesome!

Elephants bond with visitors, or don't. And if they don't bond with you, there's nothing you can do to earn their trust. Basically, you're *persona non grata* in the elephant kingdom at that point. They talk you see. In our case, the trio was a family: grandmother, mother, and granddaughter who were inseparable. Michael told us elephants live their whole lives wrapped in family ties, a kind of loyalty that puts humans to shame.

Grandma Ninee wasted no time staking her claim on me. I stood there rubbing between her eyes, right at the top of her trunk where her skin folded like thick leather, the humid jungle air buzzed with cicadas and birdcall. The scent of hot earth and crushed foliage mixed with the faint musk of the elephants themselves, a raw, powerful perfume of wildness.

I was in full open-heart, loving-kindness projection mode, whispering soft nonsense into her enormous floppy ear, the rough edges like worn velvet. You know - like we all do when we meet a new puppy for the first time? Yes - we all do it. Don't even think about denying it.

Then suddenly, her trunk - thick as my thigh but shockingly nimble - curled around me like a living rope, strong enough to snap thick bamboo in a flash, but surprisingly gentle. That grip pulled me closer, a silent but firm claim of affection. I kept rubbing her, my palm tracing the cracked, ridged texture of her skin while her trunk explored me like a curious cat, drifting slowly up and down, brushing past my chest and shoulders.

I thought she was searching for snacks until her handler from Myanmar, flashed a mischievous grin, whispered through our interpreter that Ninee wasn't just hungry - she was memorizing me: my scent, my feel, the whole package.

So, there I was: marked by a wild creature as hers. A pachyderm girlfriend. I was going to have to have a serious discussion with Dolores back in town.

The jungle seemed to hold its breath around us - the rustle of leaves, the distant chatter and cries of monkeys, the soft murmur of the river nearby - all fading into the background of this intimate moment. I kept up my end, whispering admiration and affection into her ear.

The next part of our day was a slow-motion jungle hike with our pachyderm gals - an hour or so of ambling through towering grasses and bamboo groves that hugged the riverbank. Yes, they were eating. Again.

Close enough to count the whiskers on their trunks, I watched them strip leaves from bamboo stalks as tall as five-story buildings. They'd bend them over, then let the natural snap-back deliver a leafy payload straight into their curled trunks - with the precision of a sushi master plucking a single grain of rice with chopsticks. There was no denying the grace of those trunks - delicate, deliberate, beautifully alive.

At some point I started wondering just how much bamboo these ladies could devour before the grove looked like a post-apocalyptic stick farm. I leaned toward Michael and asked about regrowth, sustainability, and whether we were witnessing the last stand of bamboo near camp.

He smiled and reassured me: this particular species was a botanical powerhouse, lining every river and stream across the sanctuary. Bamboo is the Energizer Bunny of the plant world - it starts growing back the instant it's nibbled or snapped, re-leafing fully within a week if left alone. The mahouts rotated the elephants' dining spots to keep the buffet fresh.

There we were. Seven humans following three lumbering, leaf-munching dynamos as they drifted from one stand to the next. The tall grass swayed. The river murmured. The jungle seemed to take a deep breath with us. Every now and then, Ninee glanced back to make sure I was still hanging out with her. For all their power, these girls had mastered the art of slow living, one bamboo stalk at a time.

There was one plant, something I had dismissed as a big weed that the youngest elephant, Josie, had a fondness for. We were ambling along a sandy riverbank path, the sun filtered through tall grass and drifting seed fluff, when she caught the scent or sight of it. With the precision of a surgeon and the single-minded focus of someone retrieving their favorite snack from the back of the fridge, she wrapped her trunk around the base, planted a front foot firmly beside the stem, and gave a practiced tug.

Up came the plant, root ball and all, clumps of dirt still clinging. But Josie wasn't about to eat mud. With the precision that looked shockingly human, she began slapping the root against her foot - thwack, thwack - like she was knocking dirt from a boot heel. Only when it was sufficiently clean did she curl it back toward her mouth and chomp it down with a quiet, leafy crunch. She repeated this a half dozen times, each with the same mechanical skill. You could tell this wasn't a fluke or flailing guesswork - she had done this before, and often. I wondered who had taught her that technique.

Another surprise for me was that neither her mother nor grandmother paid the plant any attention. They were more interested in bamboo, grass, and sugarcane. I asked Michael about that, and he shrugged with a smile: "They have preferences. Just like people."

Of course they do. Because they are people, in a way - just massive, leathery, soulful ones with amazing memories and a keener sense of smell than most of us. And apparently, very particular palates.

As we made our way back to the main camp, the heat of the day draped itself over us like a hot damp towel. Even the elephants seemed to move more slowly now, their great feet stirring little puffs of dust with each step, ears flapping in lazy rhythm with their gait. It was time for a midday rest. For them, and for us.

Us guests were led to an open-air stilt and bamboo longhouse perched on a gentle rise, its thatched roof shading a row of hammocks that swayed invitingly in the breeze. From there, we overlooked a vista so beautiful it looked staged: ancient, terraced rice fields, etched like green fingerprints above and across the valley floor, hemmed in by rolling forested hills that shimmered with heat and humidity. Everything pulsed gently - the light, the insects, the rustle of breeze in the banana leaves. The world didn't feel still but softened, like someone had smudged the canvas a little bit.

I stretched out in a hammock and let myself sink into quietude, the strong coarse fabric cradling me like a warm hand. Below, in the corral, our elephants settled down too, their massive shapes easing under the awning and into the shade. I heard it - that low, almost subsonic rumble, like distant thunder or a purr from a massive feline. It came from them. Michael, our guide, had mentioned earlier: a sound elephants make when they feel safe, content, completely at ease. It was their version of a lullaby; a reassurance passed between herd and heart.

They can also rumble as a warning or to communicate over vast distances but since those were unnecessary in their sanctuary setting, those were rarely issued.

That sound nestled somewhere deep inside me, and I smiled, half-lulled, half-lost in wonder, as the lines of the mountains softened and blurred and the green terraces melted into dream.

An hour into our rest, just when I was somewhere between dream and dhamma, a deep resonant gong sounded from somewhere in the jungle - one long, low, pulsing sound wave that seemed to vibrate through the valley itself. It rolled out over the rice fields like a distant thunderclap, stirring us hammock occupants from our midday daze. It was time for lunch. For us, *and* the ladies.

As we made our way back up toward the classroom area, the aromas of delicious things - earthy, salty, sweet - began to waft through the trees. Lunch had been laid out in big hotel pans and sheet trays beneath the open pavilion, and it was a spread fit for royalty or, in our case, slightly sun-dazed amateur elephant whisperers.

There was Thai fried chicken, its crackling skin flecked with crispy lemongrass, ginger and chili, impossibly juicy and, in my completely biased opinion, the best in the world (yes, I've said that before and will continue to repeat it until someone proves me wrong. Good luck with that!). Next to that, trays of Pad Thai glistened with tamarind sauce, mung bean sprouts, green onions, crushed peanuts, and stir-fried freshwater prawns. A tangled mass of morning glory shoots and garlic that smelled like it had just been yanked from the earth in another tray. Platters of fresh-cut pineapple and watermelon offered cool relief, and in a big red glass door refrigerator off to the side - like a reward for the day's good behavior, were ice-cold cans of Leo beer awaited takers.

We filled our plates and found seats at low tables scattered across the shaded space. The vibe was mellow and familial - shoeless feet tucked beneath us, soft laughter, the clink of forks, spoons, chopsticks and can snaps. Somewhere nearby, the handlers were feeding the elephants their lunch of mountains of bananas, sugar cane, and greens. We could hear their powerful muscles masticating the tough sugar cane with loud crunches as the fibrous, thick and tall grass gave up their sweet juice, punctuated every so often by the unmistakable trumpet of one of the girls.

Michael grinned the first time it happened. "That's a 'hurry up' and finish your meal trumpet," he said. "She's ready to play." I wondered just what playtime with an elephant would entail. I hoped rugby and wrestling were off the table.

We laughed, but there was something sweet about it too. It's a rare, beautiful and comforting thing to feel wanted by anyone, really. But especially by an elephant with a soft spot for your presence.

We lingered a bit, letting the sun drift across the sky, letting our food settle, letting the call of the jungle and the elephants pull us gently toward the afternoon.

After lunch and the final swig of lager had been drained, it was time to regroup at the corral for what Michael called "elephant spa hour." Mud bath and river playtime. Sounded delightful. For them. For us, it was going to be a lot messier.

As we waited for the handlers to finish prepping the riverbank area, I noticed a beat-up acoustic guitar hanging from a peg on one of the support beams of the corral. It only had five strings, all of them straining in slightly different emotional directions, but I couldn't resist. I picked it up, twisted a few of the tuners into something resembling EADGBE, without the first string (that would be the top, high E for you non-players out there), and started to strum out a few warm, open major chords. Simple stuff. Campfire stuff. Music made for open air and sun-soaked afternoons.

I wasn't really expecting a response - maybe a polite ear flap at best - but what happened next almost stopped me mid-verse. All three elephants turned toward me in unison. Their ears perked slightly. Trunks lifted. Heads began to sway gently in rhythm with the chords, as if they'd heard this song a hundred times before and were happy to be reunited with it. It was surreal. A tiny moment of connection carried on a breeze, a beat, a few half-tuned notes on a borrowed guitar.

I kept playing, letting the music drift up toward the treetops, watching as Ninee, Josie, and the middle elephant, whose name I never caught, moved in slow synchronicity - swaying, listening, maybe remembering. Josie even let out a low, rumbling purr, that same contented sound we'd heard during our hammock nap, deep and comforting like the hum of a distant double bass.

But as always, the day kept rolling forward, and spa time couldn't wait. I carefully hung the guitar back on its peg, and as I did, I swear I caught a look from two of the elephants that could only be described as... disappointed. Not angry. Not impatient. Just that soft, subtle vibe of "Hey, we were enjoying that."

Which, of course, made me want to play them a whole damn concert.

But instead, I gave a small bow and a smile, and we all turned toward the river, ready to get muddy and soaked and see what kind of joy the next act would bring.

In the human - and allegedly humane - world of compassion, things can occasionally tip over into the absurd. Case in point: there are animal-rights groups out there who insist that interactive mud baths with elephants are demeaning, exploitative, even abusive. They argue that any sanctuary allowing such behavior should be stripped of its "ethical" label. This, frankly, is nonsense. Sanctimonious, opportunistic, PR-chasing bullshit.

This kind of hyperbolic claim isn't about elephants. It's about airtime. It's about lobbing a provocative grenade into the discourse to snag a few headlines, push an agenda, or fundraise off the outrage machine. It's performance activism at its most cynical. And it's dangerous.

Let's be clear: there is nothing abusive about giving a rescued elephant a mud bath. These are not wild elephants being wrangled against their will. These are animals who have spent their entire lives with humans - often in exploitative conditions - and have been rescued, rehabilitated, and gently reintroduced to trust, care, and play. They have always received baths. Scrubs. Interaction. They know how to say no. Believe me. If an elephant doesn't want something, that something is not happening. These are five-ton, hyper-intelligent creatures with the power to flip an SUV and the self-awareness to hold a grudge for decades. If they didn't want that mud scrub, you'd know.

To deny them that joy, that bonding, that soothing contact because of a manufactured sense of human guilt isn't ethical. It's patronizing. It strips them of agency and ignores the reality of their lived experience.

So no, slinging handfuls of cool, silky mud, then rubbing it gently into their hide and onto an elephant's back and flanks while she rumbles contentedly and leans into your hand is not abuse. It's affection. It's trust. And it's earned.

And if you're into the shame/blame game and don't like the rebuke? Too bad. I'll happily put together a large and distinguished panel of *actual* experts in these matters to teach you some manners and maybe a little knowledge as to the true nature of things in the real world along the way.

That deep-tissue mud scrub we helped with - on their bellies, behind their ears, along their flanks - wasn't just accepted. It was adored. Ninee and her offspring leaned into it with unmistakable pleasure. Ninee especially threw her considerable weight into each stroke, gently but firmly pressing her massive body against me with every new handful of silky warm mud I rubbed into her leathery hide.

Her eyes stayed on me, soft and golden, and her trunk followed my every move with a kind of wordless choreography. At one point she gently prodded my hip, then nudged behind her ear with her trunk - clear as day: "Right here, please." A thousand pounds of muscle and memory, directing me through her personal spa routine with grace and patience.

There's something humbling, almost holy, about being that physically close, that trusted, by a creature who could crush you flat but instead chooses to nuzzle and lean and guide. I wasn't just washing an elephant. I was in service to her comfort, to her care, and it felt sacred in a way I hadn't expected.

When it came time to rinse off, we ambled down to the river, Ninee and I, hand in trunk. She curled the tip of her trunk delicately around my hand as we walked, like a child holding a parent's hand. At the water's edge, all three of them - grandmother, daughter, granddaughter - waded in and exploded into joy.

They frolicked. There's no other word for it. Trumpeting, rumbling, ears flapping wildly as they splashed and sprayed, dunked and danced in the cool water. One minute I was filling a bucket, the next I was drenched from head to toe by a trunk-cannon blast. We soaked each other in a glorious, muddy, watery melee of laughter and rumble-purring.

I was laughing like a crazed lunatic, fully unhinged in the best way as Ninee snuck up behind me and blasted half the river down my back. It was play, pure and unfiltered. An interspecies water fight where we all understood the rules, and no one cared who won. (BTW: trunks beat buckets every time.)

Dried off and a little sunburned, I stood at the end of the day in front of Ninee, the old matriarch who had for reasons known only to her mysterious elephant heart, chosen me as hers for the day. I looked into her eye - golden, calm, impossibly deep - and felt my own reflection vanish into something bigger than myself.

It's disarming, almost destabilizing, to meet the gaze of another being who is not human, who cannot speak your language, and yet somehow sees you. Not just the approved garb-clad tourist with mud in his ears, but you, stripped of all pretense, all noise. In that eye I felt understood and accepted in a way that most of us spend our whole lives chasing in the faces of our fellow humans.

I tried to send her everything. Every ounce of gratitude and reverence I could muster. I poured it out through my eyes, through some unseen channel between us that didn't need words. "Goodbye", I told her. "I love you. Thank you. I'm sorry we live in a world that hasn't always been kind to you. You deserved better".

She blinked slowly. Her great lashes fanned out like black feathers, and she leaned in, gently, as if to say, *I know*. It's alright. I remember the good ones.

And that was it. I started crying - not the discreet, noble kind, but the full, heaving, chest-caving sobs of someone who just realized something true and enormous about the world and themselves and the fragile, feral miracle of connection. I don't cry often. Not unless someone dies, someone says with purity "I love you" or a dog does something heartbreakingly noble in a movie. But this? This broke me wide open.

I probably won't see her again. Life doesn't work like that. But in the fantasy version of my future where I finally wise up and trade in deadlines for dawns, traffic for trees, I move to that sanctuary, volunteer full-time, and spend my days rubbing mud on beautiful elephant flanks while listening to them rumble out their wisdom like a jungle lullaby.

Elephants remember. It's not a myth. It's been studied, filmed, documented and proven time and again. They carry entire lifetimes of memory inside those regal heads, and they pass it on, family to family, generation to generation, like precious heirlooms. Michael had shown us photos of people who'd come back after years away, to be greeted with unmistakable joy and recognition by the elephant they once loved.

I hope that's me someday. I hope I'll be standing there with even more gray on my head and Ninee - older still, wiser still - will rumble low in her chest and walk straight toward me, wrapping her trunk around my hand, saying without words: I remember. I see you. Welcome home.

To connect with a creature so utterly different, and yet so precisely attuned to your heart, even just for a day - that's not a tourist experience. That's not something you write on a postcard.

That's holy.

That's the kind of thing that rewires you, as it has me.

Forever.

CHAPTER 7. WELCOME TO THE JUNGLE: NOTES FROM A FOREST MONASTERY

Gin khaow hrux yang?
Have you eaten ricc yet?

It's a strange thing to completely change one's life, if only for a while. With that at the forefront of my thoughts, after those first two nights in Bangkok, I boarded a plane and headed north to Chiang Mai. It pales in comparison in both size and frenetic energy to the capital. From Chiang Mai I would embark up to mountains high and the iMonastery facilities. I scheduled 3 nights in the northern city to get my bearings, dump the last of the jet-lag drag and truth be told, have a few cocktails and good meals before heading up to the monastery and what I assumed would be a month of deprivation. It had been a long journey literally and figuratively and I needed to live *me* before giving myself up to the experience of a wholly different world.

Questions constantly arose in my head: What the hell am I doing? Who am I to leave everything and everyone behind to search for something that might not even exist?

The only thing I knew for certain was that for the moment, I was standing at the edge of something elemental, something that might change me forever. But I wasn't sure whether it was going to be the kind of change that made me feel enlightened, or the kind that made me want to crawl back to the familiar hell I had escaped. Either way, I was going.

The day came to head up to the mountains when I found myself wide awake in the pitch-black darkness of early morning, wrestling with an unfamiliar wave of panic. Anxiety doesn't hit me often, but this was different. This was cold sweats and mental confusion. The restless, hedonistic part of me didn't want to go. Like the soldier in the Huey, landing on the beachhead in Apocalypse Now, screaming "I'm not going," the emotional ape in my head wanted nothing to do with the journey ahead as the unknown gripped me in its talons. And as much as I had prepared myself for that radical shift, I was being swallowed up by the very act of stepping into it. Could I really go through with it? Could I really leave behind what I thought I knew about myself, and dive into the unknown with a bunch of strangers and a philosophy I had yet to grasp?

Somewhere between the second beer and the sound of monks chanting in the distance, it hit me that I've never actually explained what a Buddha is. Which is a bit like writing about France without mentioning bread, butter and wine.

Before we go any further, it's worth untangling what the Buddhist philosophy is actually built around - and just as important, what it isn't. In Buddhism, there's no supreme being pulling strings from the clouds, no cosmic landlord waiting to tally your sins. The Buddha isn't a god. He's a human being who figured it out - the ultimate expression of what a person can be when every ounce of ignorance, craving, suffering and delusion has been burned away. He's *the* embodiment of a new paradigm of humanity.

The man we call "the Buddha," Siddhartha Gautama, just happens to be the most recent model off the enlightenment assembly line in our little corner of the universe. But he's not the only one. Buddhism holds that there have been thousands of Buddhas, scattered across thousands of realms, through as many ages as you can imagine. Our Buddha's story is simply the one closest to us in time and place - the one that echoes down temple halls and roadside shrines across the globe.

It's tempting to think of him as a saint or superhero, but he'd be the first to wave that off. He was a teacher. A guy who looked at the mess of human existence and decided to see if there was another way, a better way to live. Then, having found it, he left a trail of breadcrumbs called the Dhamma for the rest of us - if we care to follow them.

I wasn't packing my bags to become a Buddha, or even a particularly erudite student. But knowing who he was and what Siddhartha stood for made the leap ahead feel a little less like blind faith and a little more like... well, a calculated gamble. And I've always been a sucker for a long shot.

My decision had been made. All that was left was to spank my monkey into submission. I was in Thailand and needed to follow through, if only to see what I might find, or what might find me so in that light, at the monastery I would spend a month in deliberate contemplation - not of big universal questions - but of myself.

Was it selfish to walk away from everything - career, comfort, the easy apathy of routine - and vanish into stillness just to see what was left? Some folks thought so. Others called it brave, or noble. But it wasn't either. It was something more bare-boned than that. It was the need to strip life down to silence and see what truths crawled out when there was nowhere left to hide.

I wasn't out to find myself in some spiritual brochure kind of way. I wasn't seeking wisdom per se. I just wanted to know if I could look myself in the eye without flinching.

The truth, I figured, was already there, coiled up, quiet, waiting. All I had to do was stop dodging it. Look long enough, hard enough, and maybe I'd catch sight of it in what Elvis Costello calls "that deep, dark truthful mirror."

I was ready to do the work. To stare into the silence, into whatever abyss had been growing in my soul, and meet whoever was staring back. Maybe he'd have answers. Maybe not. Maybe he'd just shrug and hand me more questions. But at least this time, I'd know who I was talking to.

At the airport, I waited at the designated pickup spot, scanning faces for a flicker of recognition. It didn't take long for a man with a laminated sign with the iMonastery logo to find me. He looked me over with quiet curiosity - like he wasn't sure I was the right brand of lost soul - but I confirmed my name, and he checked me off the list just as other men began to gather around.

Fourteen strangers from fourteen separate lives, all heading toward the same unknown. We were going to need a bigger van. I hadn't expected such a crowd, but then again, I didn't know what to expect. My brain had been more theater than reason lately - one big monkey cranking the gears of my imagination station, conjuring scenarios that ranged from enlightening to absurd.

Still, as I watched the others gather - quiet, cautious, mostly avoiding eye contact - I started to feel less alone. That same apprehension was written on all their faces. No one was pretending they had anything figured out.

What surprised me more than the number of us was where we all came from. Germany, Denmark, Russia, Mexico, Australia, and Singapore - it felt like we'd all wandered out of separate rooms in the same strange dream, now bumping into each other in this holding pattern before whatever came next.

I ended up sharing a row in van number one with River from Australia and Josh from the States. The kind of polite surface-level banter you'd expect followed. "Where are you from?" "How long are you traveling?" "Hot enough for you?" - until it gradually shifted into the meatier stuff. The "why are you here" kind of talk. The stuff that makes a van ride feel like a confessional booth on wheels.

That's when it hit me - how different our reasons were for signing up. Each answer was extremely personal. It hadn't occurred to me until then that a single place could act like a lighthouse for so many drifting vessels, each with its own backstory and bruises.

Some of the guys were chasing peace. Others were clearly on the run - from jobs, heartbreaks, failures, addictions, maybe even themselves. Some sought wisdom. A few just needed the volume turned down for a while. And listening to all that made me realize there wasn't going to be a single path through this thing. No manual. No right way to show up. It was going to be as tangled and varied as the lives we'd each stepped away from.

I wasn't ready. Not really. But I *was* willing. And maybe that was enough for now. Somewhere in that willingness, I hoped to find something. A thread. A shift. A small light in the dark. Something real enough to carry home when this was all over.

The van ride up into the mountains was a two-hour journey, giving all of us time to reflect. After a while we all shifted towards quiet, delving into introspection. But there was something in the air, a kind of shared tension, as we were all about to shed skin and step into a new version of ourselves. None of us knew what that version would look like. All I knew was that the old me had to die, and I had to embrace that new reality and honor my evolution.

The landscape gradually shifted from towns to villages, then to hamlets, each one smaller, each one a little more forgotten to time. The road grew narrower, curving back and forth upon itself like a serpent as it rose into the mountains.

Just a month earlier, floods had ravaged the region. The rains had been the worst in decades and in many places, it looked like nature had thrown a tantrum, leaving behind scars. Deep red soil appeared as though the hillsides had been slashed by a giant dragon's claws, left in ruins to bleed out.

When we finally turned off the highway and onto the unpaved mountain road, the damage from the floods was even more savage. Slopes that had once been overgrown by lush jungle were now exposed; raw gaping wounds opened up the earth. Piles of trees and all the other flora that makes up those jungles lay in massive corpse heaps at the bottom of the slides, as if the mountains themselves had hemorrhaged during the season's fury. We made slow progress, inching past road crews with heavy machinery, their giant shovels and graders rearranging the earth, trying to rebuild road that had been ripped away by the torrents.

After two hours with all that anticipatory tension permeating the cabin, we finally arrived at what would be our home for the next month: iMonastery.

We arrived to what looked less like a spiritual gateway and more like a temporary event tent - some long tables, chairs, and the unmistakable scent of hand sanitizer. This was the check-in station, though once we finished intake it would become our designated dining space. Not inside the main hall mind you. That was for the real monks. We, the aspirants, had our own area off to the side of the dining hall. A humble reminder that we weren't quite in the club yet.

Intake was kind of like checking in to a seminar. Perfunctory and efficient. No one said much. You could feel the collective hum of inner monologues - equal parts curiosity, hesitation, and the occasional *"What the hell am I doing here?"*

I couldn't tell whether I felt excited or quietly duped by my own ambition. Was this the start of some grand journey? Or just another of life's cosmic jokes at my expense?

And yet, as I settled into intake at that compound nestled somewhere between the jungle and my unresolved psyche, the more I understood that the road to clarity isn't a straight line. It's riddled with potholes, both literal and metaphorical. And there I was, rolling straight into one, dragging a carry-on full of neuroses behind me.

The irony wasn't lost on me. I was just a middle-class guy from Washington State, showing up to a Buddhist monastery in northern Thailand, hoping to find something resembling truth.

But maybe that was the first thing I had to set down, the idea that this was about "finding" anything at all. Maybe it wasn't about what I was going to learn or fix or achieve. Maybe it was about what I would let go.

It was then that we met the monk in charge of intake: Luang Pi (Brother Monk) Phop. He was gruff, fast, and demanding, though all the while sporting a cheeky, subtle grin. The high-voltage demeanor came from a man who obviously had nothing left to prove. I've spent years honing my BS meter, and this guy? His body language was broadcasting loud and clear - his whole "tough monk" performance was an act. I don't know what my fellow neophytes picked up on, but I felt I had his number from the get go. He didn't need to be as rough as he came off, but it was easier to impose this persona on us from the start, set the tone and get us in line quicker. He had 14 not-monks to wrangle and process so while his method was brusque but efficient, it wasn't hard to see through.

Curious to see how deep his role might go, I subtly poked the bear and had a little fun at his expense. Not overtly - just a casual comment to see if he'd bite. And he did. His guard dropped faster than expected - smile first, wink second. He and I knew the jig was up though only a couple of others saw the crack. He did a quick pirouette from gruff competency to genuine warmth while still maintaining managerial efficiency. Phop wasn't as much about sternness as he was about getting results, and it was clear that beneath the brisk, "boss monk" persona, he was more than willing to share a laugh once he figured out that you could see through his armor.

I would come to rely on his sharp wit, rapid organizational skills and calm demeanor over the next few weeks. He wasn't just a mentor; he became one of my most trusted allies, and in the end, a genuine friend in my strange new monk world.

LP Phop assigned each of us a large lidded plastic bin - our new personal vaults that would reside in our tents - to be filled with only the bare essentials from our luggage: flashlights, bug spray, medications if necessary, and a smattering of personal items deemed compatible with monastic simplicity. I quietly slipped in a contraband copy of "The Year of Eating Dangerously" by Tom Parker Bowles, reasoning that even a monk-in-training deserves a little downtime from self-enlightenment. I mean c'mon - man cannot live on dhamma alone. The rest of our worldly baggage would be packed back into our travel bags, then locked away into storage until our reentry into the "real world."

Fortunately, I'd packed two sets of silk thermals, two sets of thick winter socks, and a fleece beanie - items that weighed almost nothing but delivered big when it came to keeping my soul from vacating my body at 3AM. They weren't exactly in the spirit of full renunciation, but I wasn't aiming for martyrdom.

One of the monks (he shall remain nameless to protect the semi-innocent as his advice was slyly off-script), who interviewed me via Zoom months earlier, strongly suggested I stash a few cold-weather comforts. He repeated that tip enough times for me to get the message: this was a very good idea.

A week into our residency, the temperature plunged into the low 40s Fahrenheit as rain set in for a week. Without those extras, I'd have spent the nights curled in a fetal position in my sleeping bag, teeth chattering, questioning the Four Noble Truths - and my own intelligence.

I don't need a French feather mattress though I enjoy those immensely. I'm not a Hilton monk. But I also don't believe in needless suffering dressed up as spiritual discipline. November in Thailand may be warm down in the cities, but up there, it felt like late October in southeastern Washington: soggy and cold. Enlightenment's great and all but I wasn't about to get hypothermia trying to find it.

Our assigned tents, modern nylon cocoons with rain tarps, sat on raised platforms beneath thatched roofs, propped up by sturdy steel beams. Each was separated by a patch of tropical gardens with just enough distance to suggest privacy.

The tents were generously sized - for a tent. In the center I could stand, but just barely. Still, it had ample room for my sleeping setup - a thick pad, an insulated mat underneath, real sheets, a serious sleeping bag, and a pillow that by some miracle, wasn't a sack of rocks. My plastic bin fit neatly in one corner, with just enough room left to toss laundry in another until it staged a mutiny.

Then came the parting. We said goodbye to our civilian clothes and travel gear with a longing I hadn't expected. For many, it didn't matter much. They'd be continuing in the Dhammakaya order or heading straight home. But me? I was setting out across Thailand for months when the program ended.

When the warehouse door shut behind us - locked tight for the month - it felt like more than luggage I was leaving behind.

Changing into our monastery-issued white T-shirts with the monklife logo and draw-string pants were less about tradition and more about reality crashing in. No more looking like a tourist. We were officially inducted into the monk army.

That first night a strange thing happened. We discovered that the ascetic life the monks led did not mean deprivation or starvation. Because we'd arrived a day before the program began, we were served dinner. A final evening meal. It was nothing short of a feast featuring traditional Thai dishes in abundance: curries, stir-fries, sticky rice, noodles, fruits, salads, vegetables, soups, with hot teas or espresso drinks, and ice cream or yogurt for dessert. It was all so incredibly... normal. And deliciously indulgent. But the next day the monastic schedule would begin. No more dinners. Only breakfast and lunch, prepared by lay Buddhist volunteers from the surrounding mountain villages.

After a brief tour and tutorial on where and how to scrub our plates in the washroom tucked behind the kitchen - a space that smelled of dish soap and wet mops, we were released to explore the grounds and settle in. The goal wasn't to make it feel like home (that ship had sailed), but to coax something vaguely homeish from a nylon tent and plastic bin.

I did a quick recon of the grounds, staked my claim in my tent with the optimism of someone pretending sleep would come easy, and stashed my toiletries in my assigned bin in the shower-and-shave building.

There were two communal bath houses. One for us, and another identical version for the full-time monks. Each structure had stone floors and six generous dark-stone walk-in shower stalls, each equipped with a modern toilet, shelving, and a thick lockable door for privacy. The only thing not included? Any sort of netting or barrier between the top of the stall and the jungle beyond. The roof was thatched and overhung, yet open to the elements on all sides, which meant every shower was shared with a broad range of arachnid biodiversity. Spiders of every shape, color and unnerving size hung out in the rafters, corners and on the walls. They weren't alone either. Other insect life took up residence, though the spiders did an admirable job managing those populations. Of course, that meant that our spiders kept getting bigger.

Along the center between the six shower stalls (three on both sides of the perimeter), ran a bank of six large sinks, again, three on each side, set into broad counter tops, each with a mirror above for shaving or, in my case, making eye contact with my reflection.

Laundry was fully accounted for: three modern washers, three dryers, and multiple clotheslines under the overhang out back. Backup supplies - soaps, razors, toothpaste, bug spray, and more were stocked in the supply closet, free for the taking when your personal stash ran out or when a spider laid claim to it. There wasn't back-up shampoo because, well .... monks.

All in all, the facilities were sophisticated, clean, modern, well-designed and well-considered. The kind of thoughtful practicality that whispered: *"we'll take care of the details; you take care of your mind"*.

I awoke to the jungle, high in the mountains of northern Thailand at iMonastery along the Luang River after a surprisingly deep and rest filled night. The jungle, boasting a staggering array of greens, yellows, browns, grays, with the occasional splash of reds, blues and pinks peeking out from the foliage, was dense and exotic. A mixture of deciduous broad-leaf and evergreen trees integrated into the grounds and surrounds. The banana trees were especially beautiful yet comical - their stereotypical broad-leafed form interwoven with palms, teaks, ficus, laurels, mango, frangipani, jackfruit, golden shower, trumpet bush, papaya, cannonball, fig, oleander, poinciana, bamboos, jasmine and pandan bushes hit my vision like a movie scene, only missing choppers with Wagner's Cry of the Valkyries blaring through the canopy. Many hardwood trees sported long wispy beards of moss and lichen, mocking the shiny clean-shaven heads of the monks, their trunks adorned with bromeliads and orchids residing in every joint and angle they could root in.

And thus, monk life began. The massive gong in front of the meditation hall tolled three deep sonorous notes beginning at 4:30AM sharp every morning, its reverberations rolling across the jungle like an ancient reminder that time, as we know it, doesn't give a damn about your sleep schedule. I set my alarm for 4am. I was fortunate - I'm a natural morning person - but 4AM is still 4AM and you're supposed to somehow feel spiritually uplifted at that early hour. The first few days weren't so bad. We hadn't been issued our sabong bottoms yet - those strange, pleated, folded sarong-like garments that require a degree of origami skill to tie just right. For those initial mornings, our drawstring cotton pants, and long sleeve heavy cotton T-shirts would have to do.

At 5AM, we met at the meditation hall for morning chanting. Yes, us monks love a good chant. Chanting is what you do in monasteries, even when you're tired, half-sleeping, and your knees feel like they might just snap from the pressure of holding you up on a hard floor at the hour of absolute quiet. The older monks make it seem effortless. Those chants are long. Sometimes, they stretch over forty-five minutes, the drone so rich and steady that it starts to feel like you're tapping into something ancient - something that predates your very comprehension of time. The words and ancient phrases in the Pali language, looped together in a melody so strange to western ears, it becomes strangely mesmerizing. But those first few mornings? We sounded like a bunch of choirboys coming out of an Ambien jag. The rhythm of it, the alien words, the strain in your feet, ankles and knees, nothing about it felt spiritual. It was physical discomfort disguised in a veil of deep meaning.

Chanting: It's not just for breakfast. There's evening chanting as well!

When I looked around, trying to check my classmates for some sign of shared misery, sure enough, there it was. The collective bleary-eyed deer-in-the-headlights look. We were all in this together, getting it wrong in imperfect harmony. I looked up at the enormous flat-screen TV - modern technology, thank you very much, for adding some digital flair to a sacred ritual where scrolling, beautifully rendered images of temples from across Southeast Asia graced the screen as our cue to chant along. We weren't exactly nailing the phonetics, but we gave it our best shot. We were like a group of seventh-grade band members trying to keep their instruments in tune during the first practice.

But eventually, something happened. A transformation. The chants started to seep in. The rhythm settled. The words and phrases, once unfamiliar, started to click. It was like my body and mind learned the cadence as mental muscle memory, and with it, the stories - ancient, sacred, and far older than anything I could ever wrap my head around - began to burrow their way into me. Slowly, almost imperceptibly, it became *our* chant, not just a chant. It became the rhythm and pulse of our early morning and evening meditations.

And here's the funny thing: no one talks about how much you'll miss it when you leave. No one warned me that I'd pine for those moments as we got better, and the chants started to flow their ancient stories up into the hills. Not the knees, not the cramping, but that eerie resonance of voices, all of us singing in the jungle. The sound of history flowing through you, and you can't get it back. Even now, sitting somewhere far from our meditation hall, I try to replicate it - chanting to an empty room with a YouTube prompt flowing beside me, hoping to feel that presence again, but it's simply not the same. The chants aren't something you can just pick up and play when you feel like it as I do with my guitars. You need the place, the time, the community. All of us. Together. That's when the magic happens, and you only realize how much you miss it once you've walked away.

CHAPTER 7 WELCOME TO THE JUNGLE: NOTES FROM A FOREST MONASTERY

Bhante - an honorific bestowed upon me the moment I arrived, not because of any spiritual wisdom or extraordinary feats of accomplishment, or that I could channel my inner Buddha better than you. It was due to my age. I was the eldest of our group, which, in the context of Asian and Buddhist culture, automatically demanded respect. The title itself was an uncomfortable surprise. In monastic, and indeed in Asian cultures, age affords you a bundle of privileges: I always went first at meals. I could, if I wished to, choose my chore assignments. And my accommodation, conveniently enough, was closest to the washhouse (with age comes bladder issues?). But the weightier expectation that comes with those invisible epaulets was to guide the others with my so-called "wisdom" and "awareness" even though I had no clue what those things looked like in a monastic context.

In my Western upbringing, respect is something you earn, not something that's handed to you like a participation trophy. So, being titled Bhante felt false, felt untrue. Like I was that asshole kid in school who turned in plagiarized homework and still managed to get an A, only here, my A came with ill-defined responsibilities that I hadn't exactly earned. I brought my consternation up with one of the teaching monks during a quiet moment. He explained, gently, that this is exactly why I was perfect for the role; my lack of desire to lead others is often what makes a good leader. I understood the psychology behind it - hell, I'd used it myself on others in the past.

But still, it felt like I had been handed the role of a wise elder without any preparation or expertise. I sighed, resigned, feeling completely unworthy of the weighty title that carried the expectations of wisdom, humility, and leadership. It felt like wearing someone else's shoes - too big, too wide and completely uncomfortable. As the days and weeks unfolded, I would find my role would prove me wrong. I wasn't a fraud. At least, not completely.

Sangha - a word that gets tossed around in lay Buddhist and monk circles like it's going out of style. What is it, really? It's the third of the triple gems (the first being the Buddha, the second, the dhamma) that we pay homage to. We chant the phrases and bow to the wisdom within with humble reverence. But here's the catch: it doesn't mean a group of meditators or like-minded folks sitting cross-legged on a beach trying to manifest peace in the world. Nope. Sangha is a group of monks, living together, sharing life as a monastic family. In the West, we've adopted it more loosely as a term for any gathering of meditators, but that's kind of like calling a baseball team a football team. Sure, they're both sports but that's where the similarities end - it's not quite accurate. But hey, Buddhists? We don't get bent out of shape and shake our heads over cultural appropriation. If you're going to mess it up, at least do it with good intentions, right?

After morning chanting, which, if I'm being honest, feels less like devotional practice and more like synchronized yawning when you haven't had coffee

- it was time for dhamma class. Or dharma class if you're feeling Sanskrity and spiritually accomplished before 6AM.

We filed into the meditation hall like schoolkids who'd accidentally enrolled in a philosophy seminar. The floor was hard, but we had zafus - (*meditation cushions*) and chairs, depending on how advanced your knees were in their rebellion. I tried sitting cross-legged for ten minutes before my lower body staged a full mutiny, and I defected to a chair with no shame whatsoever.

Our guiding monk, calm, warm, and somehow both awake and enlightened before breakfast, began walking us through the Four Noble Truths. He spoke slowly, like someone who knew that comprehension was a fragile bird, and we were all holding it wrong. There were diagrams. There were metaphors. There was the subtle panic of a room full of grown men pretending to understand concepts they were definitely going to Google once they got down off the mountain.

He told us why we were here, what we were supposed to be doing with our minds, and how to approach it all with patience and presence. I nodded along like a man deeply absorbing wisdom, but internally I was still trying to figure out whether "suffering" in the first Noble Truth was meant to include the chair.

By the end of that first class, I was pretty sure I'd learned something. Whether that was the first glimmer of enlightenment or just the urgent importance of lumbar support, I wasn't entirely sure. But I stayed upright and attentive, and that felt like progress.

Then came the first meditation session of the day. Let me tell you, the 5AM blush of a sky just beginning to wake up, while your back is doing its best to stay upright, rigid and relaxed at the same time on a rather thin zafu ... it's a hard combo. But we persevered in the name of sila (*morality*) and samadhi (*concentration*), until the clock mercifully hit 6:30AM.

And then came the chores.

Not symbolic chores. Not the kind where you sweep a single leaf in soft focus and call it spiritual redemption. I'm talking real monk work - thorough and deliberate and done in focused awareness. This wasn't the kind of place where a few broom sweeps earned you spiritual merit. No one was exempt, and nothing was beneath us. We cleaned and stocked the dining halls, swept and leaf-blasted every forest path as if we were preparing for visiting royalty, mopped the open-air platforms and pavilions scattered throughout the grounds, cleaned the meditation hall with reverence, and scrubbed toilets with a level of diligence that would've impressed any health inspector.

We sorted laundry, folded robes and cleaned the shower stalls while having personal boundary discussions with our spidery companions.

And yet, oddly, at least for me, it felt a little like home.

Not the place, but the rhythm. In my life back in the West, I'm that guy who finds peace and tranquility in order. I've always deep-cleaned everything in the house with presence. Cleaning windows, washing delicate Riedel wine stems, mopping floors, dusting furniture and tending to the yards - there was already a kind of private reverence in those acts, a mindfulness I hadn't thought to name.

So, monastery chores weren't a burden; they were a bridge. A quiet continuity. One unexpected thread tying a life of dinner parties and Pinot to one of quiet diligence up in a jungle compound.

At 7:30am, like clockwork, it was breakfast time. And let me tell you, after three hours of spiritual and physical labor, you start to wonder: Is this the real practice - or am I just here for the food? We weren't monks in a luxury resort. I mean yes, iMonastery is comfortable in all truly important ways. We were monks with a purpose. But damn, breakfast was delicious!

Breakfasts at the monastery were lavish by any standards, but considering the setting, they were downright luxurious. Long tables loaded with crock pots, hotel pans, steamers and cold platters were set up outside the dining hall on the long, covered veranda. We weren't ordained monks yet, so we didn't have the privilege of dining inside with the teaching monks, visiting dignitaries and our Abbot. Instead, we dined like the soon-to-be-monks we were, with all the humble reverence of an overstuffed brunch buffet.

Thanks to the kind graces of the lay volunteer cooks, we were treated to a grand spread of traditional Thai dishes with enough to feed even the most voracious appetites. There was always a soup or congee, fried and hard-boiled eggs, ham and sausage (yes - meat, but as long as we didn't kill it ourselves, we were fine. A loophole I could live with), rice or noodles, and daily smorgasbords of fresh fruits and green salads. We also had a large and very high-tech espresso machine which got more use than a beer garden trash can at a rock festival. That machine got so much use that I gave it a name - Monkzap, though I liked Dhammablaster better. And to make sure we were well-balanced, there were also cereals, instant ramens (the salted egg ramen was particularly vile), yogurts, chips, cookies, and a variety of other snacks - basically, the breakfast spread of a 4-star hotel that just so happens to be surrounded by jungle and bald heads.

Clean sweet mountain H2O - both hot and cold - was always available no matter the time, in massive urns, making sure that hydration was never an issue. Deprivation? Not in the slightest. In fact, one of our teaching monks laughed during our initial Q&A and mentioned that many program participants actually gain weight during their time there. We were encouraged to eat as much as we wanted, but leaving unfinished food on your plate to be thrown away is an offense to the monastic lifestyle as well as to the generous people who donated that food. The key was not to pile your plate high with everything thinking that was your only shot at breakfast or lunch. If you're still hungry during mealtimes, you could go back for more. No questions asked or guilt thrown your way.

At the head of our table, next to me, sat a rotating cast of our monk teachers, who would lead us in the pre-meal blessings of the triple gems and regale us with stories ranging from the deeply allegorical to those that seemed designed to remind us that spiritual lessons could come with a dash of humor. We blessed our food, the lay volunteers who cooked it, the facilities, and the generous strangers who donated food through the local alms exchange or just straight up gifts. Those were, indeed, gentle times - filled with camaraderie, reflection, and, of course, a fair amount of lighthearted ribbing. No one was immune to little practical jokes at their expense.

One morning, a brother monk, in his quest for sweetened condensed milk to add to his coffee, accidentally grabbed a bottle of salad dressing. Hey - Kewpie mayonnaise looks like condensed milk, OK? Unaware of his mistake, he poured it in, stirred it up, and took a few sips, only to discover his coffee was, well, not the rich, creamy concoction he was expecting. I made sure to bring this up at every available opportunity until the joke got decidedly cold - though I wasn't the only one. Just saying.

After breakfast, cleanup was a group effort reserved for us not-yet-monks - a humble, post-meal ritual we approached with whatever scraps of awareness we could gather between introspection and the creeping heat of the day. We washed dishes together swapping stories and discussing the dhamma. A kind of camaraderie emerged through the clatter of cups, bowls, plates and the squeak of rinsed utensils. When we were done, and everything tidied up, we were free.

Free to roam, free to think, or not think. Some wandered to the monastery library, others journaled in sunny corners, trying to make sense of whatever internal earthquakes had rumbled through them during morning meditation. Some of the guys made their way to the riverbank to sit in the sun and relax - an activity that I enjoyed as much as the snakes, leeches, and spiders, who, in the jungles of Thailand don't always RSVP. They just show up when you're not looking, more often than not simply to say hello. They all seemed to like us monks - until of course, they didn't. Those were moments I'd frankly rather not remember.

For those of us more socially inclined, the stoop of our tent platforms became the front porch of temporary brotherhood. We sat on the edge of the platforms, or on the steps, swapping stories, finding out more about each other, sometimes delving deeper into some serious life questions, cracking jokes, or just watching the jungle breathe around us together as we listened to birdsong and watched the huge golden orb spiders slaughter anything that was stupid enough to venture into their webs. It reminded me of Brooklyn in the summer, where stoops are confessionals and comedy clubs all in one.

Out here, though, we were stoop-dwelling monk hoodlums but with bug spray. And strangely, it worked.

The stillness, the talking, the odd mix of sacred routine and covering any open skin with DEET, it was becoming something like home, if only in that moment.

At 9:30AM, we returned to the meditation hall for Dhamma class - a half-hour more or less of teachings, followed by a full hour of meditation. Of all the sessions built into our daily rhythm, this mid-morning meditation was my favorite.

By then, the early-morning chill had lifted. The body had moved, the stomach was no longer bargaining for attention, and the mind - having already navigated breakfast, chores, and a bit of shared RnR, seemed more willing to cooperate. There was a kind of readiness in that hour, a quiet window when everything aligned to make stillness feel natural, rather than forced.

I often sank into those sessions with an ease that surprised me. Not because I was mastering anything, but because I was, perhaps for the first time, letting go of the need to. Insights didn't arrive with fireworks or fanfare, it came gently, like mist lifting off the trees. Just enough to see a little further inside.

And on most days, that was more than enough.

Afterward, it was time for lunch, our last meal of the day. The lunch spread was just as extravagant as breakfast but with more noodles and stir fry, meats and seafoods - no one was leaving hungry. After cleanup we had more free time until 2:00pm when it was back to Dhamma class and meditation until 4:00pm.

The midday breaks were lovely moments. A pocket in the monastery's clockwork day where time seemed to fan itself out like a lazy puppy in the sun. The mountain light took on a syrupy quality, pouring through the jungle canopy like rich golden waterfalls, catching on the dust motes and wings of hovering insects. A symphony of birdsong - less composed, more tumultuous - echoed from their jungle hideouts, with sudden bursts of rustling leaves and snapping twigs below announcing the unseen dramas of scurrying creatures. The jungle, dense and unruly, pressed right up to the monastery's edge like it was waiting for us to let our guard down.

The trees, shrubs, and flowering plants formed a tangle of unfamiliar shapes and hues, as if nature had been working from a palette and botany book I'd never seen. There was extraordinary beauty, yes - but a watchful allure, the kind that doesn't quite trust you. At times it felt like a pack of Velociraptors might burst out from the green wall, eyes glinting, ready to reclaim their territory and shred every robe-wearing intruder in sight. But aside from the monks - who often moved like ghosts - my co-inhabitants were the occasional squirrel, a few scrawny but streetwise temple dogs, and butterflies. Lots of butterflies. Outrageously colored, almost arrogant in their perfection, they flitted around the back veranda of our meditation hall where I'd sit to meditate, pausing just long enough to make me wonder if they were tiny surveillance drones sent by some celestial intelligence to make sure I wasn't slacking off.

Every moment felt like an immersion into the present. The troubles, fears, doubts, and sadness that had once seemed so pressing, faded away like distant memories. They were still there, lingering at the edge, but I was too busy soaking in the fresh mountain air, the view and the inner workings of my mind to care.

Then it was back to "free time," a loosely defined interval that promised rest or reflection but often translated into wandering the grounds with my journal and pen in hand with no particular plan. I would read or write, but more often than not I found myself wandering in slow loops, often connecting with a brother from the Sangha. Usually, this meant orbiting conversations about anything but monastic life - talk of past travels, future plans, food and cooking, art, music, or life milestones. The rest of the time I simply watched from a distance, trying to decipher the rhythms of the more seasoned practitioners, as if proximity might grant me a clue to their inner peace.

At 6:30pm we returned to the Meditation Hall. The evening session of evening chanting and meditation beneath the humming lights and serene gaze of Buddha, until 9:00pm. After that, it was a quiet shuffle to the wash house, where we brushed our teeth with ritualistic precision and washed the day off our faces in cold water. Then, back to our tents, zipping ourselves into our nylon sanctuaries like spiritual caterpillars, observing the strict 9:30pm curfew with reverence. Or maybe not.

Was I the only one using a flashlight under the blanket? Like some wayward Hogwarts student hiding from the Dursleys? Probably not, but I didn't pry. We were a chatty bunch, but asking about rule-bending felt like a violation of that unspoken "don't ask, don't tell" policy. I've always read at night. It's how I shut my brain down, but let's just say my reading list wasn't entirely approved curriculum. I'd borrowed a few dhamma texts from the monastery library to try and, you know, actually learn something about the world I'd ventured into. But my real bedside prize was The Story of Sushi by Trevor Corson (another book I'd smuggled into my bin), a gripping deep dive into the world of raw fish, seaweed, and obsessive culinary apprenticeships. Maybe not the most enlightenment-adjacent material, but it was exactly what I needed.

So, there I was, flashlight barely flickering under my blanket like some teenage delinquent in a tent, sneaking in a few pages before the charge or my eyelids gave out. Outside, the jungle was more than happy to do its part in lulling us toward sleep. The nocturnal soundtrack was a full-throated, cacophonic riot of chirps, buzzes, rustles, and the occasional haunting call from creatures who didn't want to be identified. It was chaotic, alive, and oddly comforting as if the whole jungle was saying, *"Don't worry, we're awake so you don't have to be."*

And that, my friends, was the schedule: rinse and repeat for a month.

On Thursdays, the schedule shifted. Instead of the usual mid-afternoon dhamma talk and meditation session, we'd gather down by the lazy little Luang "river" (which was, let's be honest, more of a stream with big rapid aspirations) on the thatched, open-air platform known as Sala 1. The Sala was a favorite hangout spot even on non-confessional days - a breezy perch with enough space for twenty monks to sit in a circle, plus a few cushioned wicker chairs and couches for reading, journaling, chatting or contemplating our spiritual progress while slowly roasting our upper bodies into the perfect shade of "Thai tan."

But on Thursdays, the Sala took on a new vibe: equal parts group therapy, Dharma-themed summer camp, and deeply sincere soul stripteases. Led by one or two of the teaching monks who'd show up with a prompt, like "When did you last feel truly seen?" or "Why are you here?" or "What are you still holding onto that no longer serves you?" We were invited, encouraged, gently pushed, or outright volunteered to speak our truths. It was the Buddhist version of a trust fall, minus the physical risk but with *way* more emotional exposure.

Since I barely knew those guys, and also because I've long since abandoned the illusion that protecting my ego does anyone any good, I went all in. I sliced my aortic soul wide open and let the guts spill out. Childhood hang-ups, identity crises, daddy issues, divorce, spiritual doubt, the full psychological mixtape - I held nothing back. One monk later called my approach "brave," but I think what he really meant was "unfiltered and mildly alarming." Still, something shifted after that. People followed suit. One by one, the masks dropped. We heard stories of heartbreak, addiction, lost faith, faith found, loneliness, longing, confusion, the whole shared human mess of it.

And in that open-air Sala, with the breeze from the Luang threading through the trees, we became more than just fellow monks observing precepts and sitting in a circle. We became something closer to brothers. When you bare your soul without flinching - and people don't turn away but nod that they've been there too - that's when real friendship happens. That's when you stop feeling like a spiritual tourist and start feeling like you belong.

It was the day after our first monk-chat-klatch Thursday when something happened that caught me completely off guard and changed my life. One of those rare things that slips quietly into you, settles in without fanfare, and stays lodged in your heart forever.

I was in the dining hall, taking a mid-afternoon break, nursing what could only be described as a fifteen-shot latte (monastic life didn't mean going without caffeine), and scribbling in my journal. The place was empty, a gentle, warm breeze drifted through the mesh walls as jungle sounds wafted in. That's when one of my fellow inductees approached and politely asked if he could join me.

Tan the Man. That's what I called him. He was a quiet guy or so I thought. From Singapore, wiry, muscled, tattooed, calm, with a kind of cool detachment that had made me assume he was just here for the meditative tan and some peace. I knew only one other thing about him: he worked as a dive master on a small, impossibly idyllic island somewhere I hadn't heard of.

He'd only opened up a crack during the group session the day before. But I had noticed something: when I was laying bare the raw, excruciating wreckage of my failed marriage, he was really listening. Not politely. Not out of obligation. But with a fierce, quiet empathy. His eyes had welled up. Just for a second. But I'd seen it.

He sat down and asked if we could talk. I slid my journal aside and said "yes, of course".

What followed was one of those rare, soul-to-soul conversations that rarely comes along in a lifetime. He shared his own story. Just as painful, just as wrecked. A parallel collapse. A different country, a different face, but the same ache. The same unraveling of love and passions for another. And in that moment, our pain braided itself together like two strands of rope finally finding tension and hold.

We talked. We cried. We cursed the circumstances that had flayed our hearts. We nodded at each other through the heartbreak, as if saying, *Yeah, man. I see you. I get it.* And in that raw, unguarded space, we became true brothers.

Tan the Man, this gentle, open-hearted, quietly extraordinary man, gave me something I didn't even know I was starving for: real, unvarnished human connection. No platitudes. No fixing. Just presence. Kindness. Empathy. Truth. A space where it was okay to be absolutely wrecked.

I looked at him differently after that. With deep gratitude. With respect. That afternoon stripped away more pain than weeks of meditation or counseling ever could. It was a lesson in compassion. I'll never forget how healing can come not through solitude, but through someone else simply saying, You're not alone! Me too.

We became fast friends. Still are. And even though we live a globe apart, whenever we catch up (WhatsApp is awesome for that), it's like flipping back to that table, like time politely stepped aside to let something important through. Our bond we forged in the quiet aftermath of his generosity still hums in the background, steady as ever.

Every time we talk, I find myself wishing we were side by side again. No robes. No river. Just two men with a cup of tea or a cold beer between us. That familiar hum returns - not the sound of enlightenment, but something better: the easy rhythm of two open hearts that once crawled out of the same abyss and somehow found each other on the ledge.

Call it wisdom. Or shared survival. Or just the rare comfort of knowing there's someone out there who saw you in your most stripped-down state and didn't look away.

Perks came with my role as Bhante. Most notably, I had the privilege and honor of recommending, instigating, and occasionally guiding my brothers in a variety of ways. As the eldest, I was supposed to offer wisdom and direction, but in truth, I was winging it. Playing the role of a leader who wasn't quite sure if that whole "guiding" thing was a passing phase or something I'd have to keep up until I got a real job. One thing I was sure of though: I had done a lot of research on Thailand before arriving, and not just the obligatory travel guide stuff. I dove deep into the festivals, the food, the culture, the history, the land and its people. This obsession paid off in ways I hadn't anticipated.

One festival in particular had snagged my attention: Yi Peng. The Festival of Lights. And wouldn't you know it? Chiang Mai is the center of Thailand for that celebration. The date was perfect. November 15th, 2024. Smack dab in the middle of our monastic time. By then we would be fully ordained monks. Fate sometimes shines brightly. I had heard about the Yi Peng festival from a monk back in the States who found out I would be near Chiang Mai in November and clued me in. I sought out images and videos of glowing lanterns (called *khom loi*) floating into the night sky as people released those beautiful airborne light rafts skyward, creating a magical sea of rising hopes and prayers. What I saw was visually stunning and spiritually enchanting. But of course, there was one catch: we were two hours up in the mountains in monk mode, with no opportunity for a night out on the town.

Naturally, I wanted to go. I mean, sure, "desire causes suffering" - that cycle of dukkha that we were all trying to break, but when you're sitting on a mountain of monkish duties and responsibilities, the idea of an epic light-filled celebration becomes an enticing form of suffering. So, I decided to go for it and leverage my Bhante role into something fun for all.

I sidled up to Luang Pi Phop - my mentor, my confidante, my soundingboard in things intellectually rebellious - with a question that shimmered with potential scandal: could we venture into town to witness that grand spectacle? The issues were many. Not least were geography, logistics and optics. Yi Peng would be lighting up Chiang Mai two hours away, while we were stashed deep in the hills like enlightenment trainees on lock-down wrapped in orange robes and spiderwebs, serenaded by the jungle's symphony. But what's life without a little scheming? A plan formed in my head. Hazy, half-baked, and potentially heretical. One that might lead us to a moonlit celebration filled with floating lanterns and spiritual symbolism ... or into a quiet lecture about attachment and frivolity. So, I kept my trap shut. Until I had a solid "yes," this little rebellion would stay hidden. If it turned out to be a "no," well, nobody had to know I'd plotted an adventure.

"Karawa krab, Luang Pi Phop. May I speak with you for a moment in private?" I asked.

"Of course Brother Laurence," he said, his eyes crinkling with warmth as we strolled along the sun-dappled path, the jungle quietly surrounding us. "What's on your mind?"

"I'd like to see if we could all to go to Yi Peng. I want to pay for vans to take us all there, as a Sangha," I explained.

Luang Pi Phop turned to me, his smile deepening, but there was a flicker of something thoughtful in his gaze.

"You are good Bhante. I am not sure if that can happen, but I'll discuss it with Luang Pi Narongchai at our next meeting," LP Phop said, a glint in his eyes.

I exhaled a little, hoping that my plan, with over a week's notice and my offer to cover the cost of two vans would be enough to convince the powers that be. After all, what better way to bond as a Sangha than sharing in something as beautifully Thai as Yi Peng? A true cultural experience for the monastery as a whole.

The days ticked by with all the urgency of a broken clock, and yet, not a word was spoken about my request. We fell into our routine, that familiar rhythm that felt increasingly like a veil between me and the world outside. I began to worry. Maybe Luang Pi Phop hadn't managed to bring it up with the Abbot after all. Maybe my well-intentioned plan to introduce some Thai cultural magic to our Sangha was just a well-meaning fantasy, doomed to dissolve into thin air.

As the suspense morphed into an insistent, nagging suspicion that my idea had quietly died in the jungle underbrush, I found myself pacing and mentally restless, like a monk on the brink of an existential crisis, or at least a really inconvenient bout of FOMO (fear of missing out). My monkey mind, that eternal trickster, had clocked in for overtime. It tossed banana peels of doubt across every promising thought. Maybe Luang Pi Phop was pretending I never asked. Maybe I'd crossed some invisible karmic line by even entertaining the idea. Maybe there was now a special chant dedicated solely to my lack of discipline.

I tried to meditate it away. I really did. I sat on my mat overlooking the stream, straight-backed and determined, silently repeating, "let it go... let it go... let go." But all I got in return was a technicolor slideshow of floating khom loi, candlelit rivers, and Thai boys and girls in silk releasing their lanterns with excitement that mocked my inner turmoil. Why was this such a big deal? I argued with myself. This is classic clinging. Textbook craving. You came here to release attachments, not go chasing fireworks like a Buddhist moth to flame.

And yet, wasn't joy also part of the path? Wasn't beauty a dhamma gate too? Hadn't the Buddha himself, at some point, cracked a smile?

By the end of it, I'd authored a full internal thesis justifying the spiritual merit of sneaking off to a festival. Chapter One: Impermanence of Lanterns. Chapter Two: Mindfulness in Motion. Chapter Three: Non-Attachment to Schedule. I was losing the plot, but in a philosophical way.

And still no word from Luang Pi Phop. Just me, pacing around, craving moral loopholes.

Finally, I couldn't take it anymore. I approached Luang Pi Phop, who was looking as unperturbed as ever, as if he hadn't been the star of my anxious thoughts for the past several days. It was like he had been avoiding me but that was just my monkey mind screwing with my mind.

"I don't want to bother you, but did you get the chance to discuss the festival with Luang Pi Narongchai?" I asked as we worked together to fold my jiwon into the perfect robe.

"Of course I did. You're being impatient," he said, laughing. "We are all going to go and Luang Pi Narongchai was touched by your leadership and willingness to sponsor the activity for everyone."

A wave of relief flooded through me - part joy, part thank-Gautama-I-didn't-get-expelled. It wasn't just that the festival was happening. It was that I hadn't caused some kind of robe-rustling disturbance in the Force by even asking for it. No raised eyebrows, no passive-aggressive proverbs slipped into morning chanting, no sudden double-latrine duty. Just... silence. Strategic, suspicious silence. They'd kept it under wraps. A surprise.

Oh, those playful monks. Cloaked in saffron, mystery and kindness, apparently capable of pulling off covert ops better than a CIA field team. For days they'd walked around serenely, like nothing was brewing, while secretly plotting a festival jailbreak. Somewhere between morning alms and evening meditation, a plan had been hatched, and I hadn't even noticed a sparkle in anyone's eyes.

I couldn't decide whether to bow in gratitude or accuse someone of gaslighting me with metta. Either way, we were going to Yi Peng. And now I had full spiritual clearance.

The festival was only two days away, cutting it pretty close, but it felt like an eternity had passed in my mind. I had successfully dragged a bit of the outside world into our monastery cocoon, and I was gleefully excited to see it all unfold.

"Would you like to make the announcement at meditation this afternoon?" Luang Pi Phop asked.

"If it's OK with you, I'd rather you or brother Srijug or Wut make the announcement. I would feel a little out of place," I replied.

I shifted my weight from one foot to the other, a little hesitant to take the spotlight in front of the Sangha even though I was technically the one behind the curtain pulling the strings.

Luang Pi Phop, slipped into his stern leadership role: "I don't think that's appropriate. It was your idea and desire to treat your brothers to one of our most important festivals, so it must be you who tells your brothers. Be the leader you're meant to be."

I sighed. "Alright, but will you be there?"

"Maybe." And with that he chuckled, his big grin leading the way as he left to attend to his always-busy schedule.

※

It was Wednesday, November 13th. As 2PM rolled around I made sure to arrive at the meditation hall early, strolling in with the deliberate serenity of someone who had news and was trying hard not to look like they were vibrating with excitement. I'd taken extra care with my robes, creased and wrapped with the kind of obsessive precision normally reserved for origami swans and sushi chefs. If I was going to be the bearer of glad tidings, I figured I might as well look like a man who had his spiritual (and sartorial) act together.

Call it vanity, call it mindfulness. Either way, I wasn't about to announce a sanctioned escape to one of the most dazzling festivals in Thailand looking like I'd just rolled out of bed.

To my surprise, Luang Pi Narongchai - our brilliant Abbot and head of our monastery - was already there, seated at the teaching desk with that same serene smile he always wore. I sometimes wondered if he slept with that expression on, like an enlightened Cheshire Cat. Up until then, his appearances had been rare as his time was spread thin across his vast responsibilities in the Dhammakaya order, so when he did show up, it meant something.

Once our Sangha had settled into place, mats aligned and backs straight, I led the incantation paying respect to the Buddha and our teaching monk. We then paid homage to the triple gems to start the afternoon session. Then, without missing a beat, Luang Pi Narongchai turned his smiling gaze toward me and said, "Your Bhante has something he would like to share with you."

I rose. "Um, hi, my name is Luang Pi Sattibalo and I'm an addict... of fun."

A few grins broke out, recognizing the classic 12-step program intro, others just enjoying the awkward charm of it. Either way, the ice was broken.

"Sooooo ... I hatched this mad plan, thinking we could all attend the Lantern Festival down in Chiang Mai. We all get to go on Friday," I announced.

Silence followed. Then a few smiles cracked open. Then came the clapping, hesitant at first, then growing louder. And finally, a chorus of "Thank you, Bhante!" rang out from some of my brothers.

I think it took a moment for it to register. *We were going to town.* We were actually going to witness one of the great spectacles that captures the attention of the world every year and we'd be fully monked-up in our robes, heads shaved and compassion flowing outwards like a tidal wave. Lanterns, lights, celebration. Bring it on!

After the extraordinary privilege of listening to a dhamma lecture from our Abbot and sharing a meditation session with him, one of those quietly powerful moments where the air smells sweeter, I stashed my mat and hurried to catch up with Luang Pi Narongchai as he glided toward the administration hall. And I do mean glide. The man didn't walk so much as float, like gravity was an optional setting he'd long since disabled. Robes flowing, his steps inaudible, serenity radiating off him like incense smoke. He didn't even turn around when I approached. He somehow knew it was me.

"Hello, Luang Pi Sattibalo," he said softly, using my monk name. (Yes, that's me. I know - it has a certain "ancient wisdom" ring to it.) "That was fun," he added. "The appreciation from our brothers was quite wonderful."

I chuckled, a little awkwardly. "I've never really known how to take a compliment, but yes... everyone was incredibly kind." Then, getting down to logistics: "I'll find Luang Pi Phop and head to the warehouse to grab cash for the vans. Just let me know how much it'll be, and I'll take care of it."

But he just gave me his classic Narongchai smile - equal parts compassion and knowing amusement. "You won't need to do that," he said. "We've decided the monastery will cover the costs for the trip."

I stopped cold, floored. "But I want to do this," I said, and I meant it. I wanted to give this experience as a gift. A thank-you. A memory.

"We know you do," he replied, his eyes warm and steady. "Which is exactly why it's our honor to do it for you, and for our brothers."

And just like that, I was wrecked. Gratitude welled up in my throat, sudden and humbling, stinging my eyes. I thanked him with every ounce of sincerity I could summon, overwhelmed by a simple truth I hadn't expected: real generosity doesn't just come from giving, it also lives in letting yourself receive.

I wandered down to the Luang and parked my butt on the grassy banks after a thorough snake, leech, and spider check (which, for the record, is not paranoia but a healthy respect for the local ecosystem gained from experience) and let myself just sit. I meditated not on breath or sound or posture or any of the usual inward stuff, but on generosity. The kind that gives without needing to be seen. The kind that asks nothing in return. The kind that reminded me that we're all carrying each other, whether we realize it or not.

I was gazing into the moving waters of the Luang with the kind of soft, half-lidded focus that comes only after a long sit, where the world is quiet and you start to feel more like a tree than a person. Simply there. Breathing. Still. I wasn't meditating anymore, not exactly. I was just being, eyeing the way light played on the surface and how the current carried tiny bits of leaf and story downstream.

I felt presence behind me. That subtle shift in the air, that sixth sense you develop when you've been living among people who walk like cats and open doors at the volume of a whisper.

I gently peeled myself out of that liminal headspace, half expecting I was about to be playfully shoved into the river by a gang of robe-clad merry pranksters. Fair enough I thought - I'd earned it. But instead of a splash, I felt hands reaching out - not to push, but to pull. A few arms slipped around my shoulder; a couple of warm pats landed on my back. Smiles, nods, murmured thank-yous. A gentle hug. Not big gestures but heartfelt ones.

My brothers - those fellow seekers, misfits, travelers in saffron - were thanking me for organizing the upcoming field trip. And in that moment, something opened up in me.

I felt... pride.

Which, as any monk will tell you, is a very naughty thing to do. I made a note to meditate on that later. After I finished enjoying that moment.

Because here's the thing: we don't always appreciate how much a quiet "thank you" matters, or how rare it is to feel seen and loved. But in that shared moment, there was no doctrine, no dogma. Only humans, stripped down to the basics - kindness, appreciation, and the unspoken bond of a group of men who'd chosen stillness over speed and reflection over reaction.

That little meandering river never looked more beautiful.

❦

It was Luang Pi Phop's time to shine. Planning, logistics and execution were the work he was born to do. Transportation had to be arranged. Local monasteries had to be notified of our intention to attend the festival, boundary ballet being what it is. The timing for the day, from city arrival to festival time, needed to be dialed in. And finally, rules had to be established. How we, as newly ordained monks, were expected to behave while out in public for the first time, *en masse*, in our robes.

Luang Pi Phop tackled it all with his usual vigor, energized by his checklists and the challenges.

The day before the festival was my birthday. A quiet one. The kind that creeps in unnoticed, like a cat through an open door. The idea of impermanence, of everything fading, everything shifting, etched itself deeper into my mind as the date rolled round. Another year passing while I was monked-up, wrapped in robes instead of party clothes, eating sticky rice instead of birthday cake. No calls from back home came through though I was allowed my phone just in case. No family gathering around a cluttered table. No wine, no toasts, no one setting the salmon en brochette on fire by accident.

Not that I needed a party. But come on. Where was my damned cake?

Still, the day was kind. I was sitting out on my stoop in a pool of mid-morning sunlight, watching my arachnid neighbor Boris - a golden orb-weaving spider who had taken up residence beside me - build yet another architectural masterpiece with unsettling speed and terrifying grace. I'd begun to swear I could hear him grow as he plotted world domination. Or maybe just lunch.

Then, Tan the Man strolled up.

He had a glimmer in his eye, the one that meant either mischief or tenderness, depending on how his breeze was blowing. Without a word, he handed me a small slip of paper, gave me a warm smile, and wandered off like it was nothing. Like he hadn't just delivered something that would live in my wallet for years to come.

I opened it. Inside was a letter of heartfelt kindness, a birthday blessing. Simple, spare, and so heartbreakingly sincere that I felt the air leave my lungs. It wasn't flowery. It didn't pretend everything was fine. It held up a mirror to the hard truths of life and love and time, and then wrapped them in something soft, something compassionate. Every one of those words rang true and glowed like burning coal.

I still have that note. Tucked safely away like a revered ancient scroll. A relic of human decency. A reminder that a true friend can speak volumes with a few honest lines.

What a guy.

What a blessing.

And that was my cake.

Friday had arrived! Yi Peng day. After our early morning chanting, meditation, chores, and breakfast, we were excused from our duties and instructed to assemble at the front of the monastery at 11:00AM. There, we would board two vans for the journey down to Chiang Mai and the Dhammakaya center on the grounds of Dhutangastan Lanna, where we would be treated to the Lantern Festival.

Excitement buzzed through the van as we wound our way down the mountain. I shared what little I knew about the festival with my brothers: Yi Peng, the Lantern Festival, is an annual celebration marking the end of the monsoon season - a time to thank the gods for the water that would, hopefully, lead to a bountiful harvest. Always held on a full moon night in mid-November, the festival's roots trace back to ancient India... and then vanish into the mysterious fog of history.

What I didn't know - what none of us knew (except the upper echelons of monastery leadership, who kept secrets like operatives in robes) - was that, as monks journeying down from a remote mountain monastery, we wouldn't only be spectators at the festival. We'd be honored guests. Visiting dignitaries. VIPs in saffron robes, minus the security detail, shortwave coms and mirrored shades.

That revelation was still somewhere on the horizon as we descended from our jungle retreat, stopping at one of Thailand's ubiquitous highway mega-stations - those strange commercial micro communities that dot the highways like oases of air-conditioning and neon convenience. These places are miraculous in their consistency: a sprawling gas station, a large spotless public restroom (always a relief), a 7-Eleven or Lawton's, an Amazon Café (no relation to Bezos), a fast-food chain or two and a few independent stalls selling things that smell incredible but are definitely not monk-approved.

Sometimes there was even a boutique peddling pastel streetwear - a baffling collection of cropped hoodies, rhinestone bucket hats, and graphic tees that no monk should ever be caught dead in. Or cremated in. Or reincarnated wearing.

As newly ordained monks we also weren't allowed to handle money. That meant even a bottle of water required a subtle game of charades and delegation. If you wanted something, say, a pack of menthol lozenges or a banana-flavored soy milk, you'd subtly point, or nod, or make a respectful gesture toward your item of choice, and then a senior monk would float over like your own personal spiritual concierge to make the purchase.

It was, in essence, a weird little dance. Renunciation meets retail. The dhamma meets Slurpee machine.

What really sent me, though, were the expressions on the store clerks' faces as the temple van doors swung open and an orange tidal wave poured into the aisles. We looked like a Buddhist flash mob. A synchronized formation of shaved heads and serene faces, moving slowly but with purpose, inspecting the snack shelves as if evaluating them for karmic consequences.

I noticed one young employee frozen mid-restock, her eyes wide, as a monk picked up a box of Pocky sticks and studied it like it might contain a hidden sutta. Another cashier looked torn between reverence and panic, bowing nervously at a monk who was deeply engaged in a contemplative squint at a shelf of seaweed snacks.

It was peak monastic surrealism.

❀

We arrived at the grounds, pulling onto a large grassy field. It was then that abject misery and suffering struck us like a playfully cruel spirit. We slowly made our way through the coned corridors, where bank after bank of street carts and food booths were set up, all of them cooking and selling everything you could ever desire to eat. There was a grilled steak cart - c'mon - that was just cruel! The aromas were intoxicating and tortuous at the same time because we were not allowed to purchase or eat any of those munchies. Our vans were led through one security barrier after another until we were parked as close as we could get, which happened to be two reserved spots at the front of the reserved parking area. Unfortunately for our noses and saliva glands, next to our vans were a fried chicken cart, a pad Thai cart and a fresh fried donuts cart, all in action, cooking up incredible smelling food, all of which we had to walk past and ignore as it was past 1:00PM, our cutoff time for eating. But those scrumptious items wouldn't be allowed anyway.

The first inkling of what was to come hit us the moment we stepped out of the vans. All around us, people stopped what they were doing, and bowed and offered wai's. Not casual nods - full, respectful bows, hands in prayer position, heads lowered. I reflexively bowed back to one smiling gentleman, only to have him look up at me in surprise, like I'd just tried to tip a statue.

Luang Pi Phop gently pulled me aside and whispered, "Brother, we don't bow back. Only to senior monks."

Well, that was awkward.

To my Western-raised brain, returning a bow felt like simple courtesy –an acknowledgment of connection and mutual respect. But I learned that in Thai Buddhist culture, laypeople bow to monks as a form of reverence, not as a social gesture. It's not about mutual exchange; it's about the chance to generate merits, which is something people take very seriously. My instinctive urge to level the playing field had, in a way, short-circuited his sacred offering.

Lesson learned: sometimes the kindest thing you can do is simply accept honor.

We were greeted by a group of warm, good-humored elderly senior monks who lived at the center. With gentle smiles and the kind of grace that made me feel like royalty instead of a sweaty foreign monk, they personally led us to a vast hall where cold water and iced fruit juices were laid out for us.

Thank goodness we were finally out of range of the food carts. Because earlier, as the smell of grilled meat and fried chicken wafted through the air, something deep and primal had stirred. Specifically, the image of a perfectly charred ribeye - the hardwood smoke, salted fat sizzling onto hot coals, each drip sending up a puff of flavor, which could break my willpower. It had invaded my sensory mind like a Trojan horse of hunger. I wasn't just craving steak. I was yearning for my domed BBQ back home like a lost lover.

After we'd refreshed from the drive, we were invited to tour a garden farther down the campus grounds. It had been transformed into a showcase of our Dhammakaya Foundation's outreach programs with the mountain village tribes. The goal: to shift these communities away from not only traditional opium production, but a newer, far more destructive scourge: methamphetamine.

Through education, regional grants and government subsidies, the foundation was teaching tribal members how to promote eco-tourism, monetize the beauty of their traditional arts and crafts, and cultivate high-value crops like coffee and tea. It was economic alchemy, turning poppies and poison into livelihood and pride.

The hill tribes had set up demonstration booths, each with polished signage, multilingual interpreters, and displays that told the stories of transformation. It was strikingly professional. Each section was a testament to resilience and reinvention. This wasn't just a feel-good PR campaign. It was real, positive, tangible change.

After a couple of hours wandering through that hopeful future, we returned to the main hall. We were invited to use the dedicated meditation space on the grounds. Many of us jumped at the chance. The hall was quiet, expansive, and bathed in the golden hush of late afternoon. I settled into a seated posture and before I knew it, an hour had passed like a single breath.

Then, a gentle voice pulled us back: one of our teaching monks informed us it was time to prepare for the evening ceremonies. None of us knew what that meant exactly, but dusk had settled over the garden like a velvet curtain, and the stage was clearly being set for something far beyond our expectations.

As it turned out, this was an even bigger deal than any of us had imagined.

Our host monks explained that the ceremony grounds were centered around a massive, tiered stupa where many monks - most of them novices, would perch for the duration of the ceremony. This was "monks on display" at a whole new level. They asked if we'd like to participate. Of course, we all said yes.

There were two options: one group would sit in padmasana, or lotus position on the stupa, candle jars in hand, holding meditative posture for several hours. The others would join a ceremonial parade, walking three slow, barefooted laps along an arced pathway that circled widely around the stupa and through rows of seats prepared for thousands of ticket-holding guests.

I chose walking meditation. As beautiful as the stupa option sounded, I knew my knees - and every joint below the waist - would've filed a formal protest. There's just not enough ibuprofen in the world to make lotus pose for hours seem like a good idea for me. I'm simply not built that way.

The grounds were nothing short of theatrical. Professional-grade lighting, a booming arena-blasting PA system, and music that could've been ripped straight from a Disney princess montage. I half-expected dwarves to march by with mining tools.

For the two hundred of us monks taking part in the walking procession, we were led along a hidden path behind the massive stupa and arranged into perfectly spaced, double-row lines. A monk with a flair for order, likely Luang Pi Phop's spiritual twin, handed each of us a candle. It came with a handle underneath and a glass bowl on top, shielding the flame from gusts. When the signal came, we began our slow, deliberate march.

As I rounded the corner of the stupa and stepped into full view of the crowd, I was hit by the scale of it all. Thousands of people, possibly tens of thousands, had filled the parade grounds. Every single one of them dressed in immaculate white, like a spiritual Coachella. These weren't just festivalgoers. They had paid serious money for those seats. They stood silently, reverently, lining the circular path, bowing as we passed, snapping photos and shooting video of our barefoot procession as if we were the main act.

As we walked, I allowed myself a sly glance at the stupa when there was a lull in the paparazzi-like masses. Every tier was occupied by monks in lotus position. Candles glowed in front of them like stars caught in amber. It was beautiful and undeniably cinematic. But also, I thanked Buddha I wasn't one of them. To this

126

day I have no idea what the three laps around the stupa symbolized, but I was more than content walking in mindful circles instead of locking my knees into eternal stillness.

Finally, our laps were completed. I was in dazzle mode, feeling a bit like a celebrity. I had slipped into a walking-meditation trance after the first round, when suddenly, we were done with our duties. That's one of the wonderful things about meditation - time becomes liquid.

Slipping behind the stupa and down a path that was hidden from the public's eye, we handed back our candles and retrieved our sandals. We were now free to enjoy the ceremony so I and some of my brothers who did the walk followed Luang Pi Wut around the back side of the public grounds to where I thought would be a decent viewpoint. I was wrong.

A massive, new, open-air marble temple loomed in front of us, clearly still under construction. Piles of construction debris and taped-off sections hinted it was months from completion. When we were led toward its wide stone steps, I assumed we'd made a wrong turn or were about to get in trouble for trespassing.

But without a word, Luang Pi Wut and Luang Pi Phop with smiles on their faces lifted the construction tape like bouncers at an exclusive club and ushered us up the grand staircase. The structure was dark but with the open walls and full-moon light filtering through, we could see well enough to climb without face-planting.

At the top, we stepped onto an enormous marble pavilion, its scale swallowing our footsteps. It was as big as the Parthenon. We were guided all the way to the far edge, where two long rows of chairs had been arranged for us. Some were already filled with my monastery's senior monks, along with a few unfamiliar faces. I guessed we're the monk-world equivalent of high society.

Sprawled out before and below us were thousands of festivalgoers, all organized into neat family groups, each group fussing with their lanterns, prepping for liftoff. The evening's emcee, perched somewhere in the arena with a mic and impeccable timing, kept the momentum flowing. There would be four synchronized launches, complete with blasting music worthy of a Broadway spectacle.

It was a monk's-eye view of something I had dared to imagine witnessing, let along being part of. And we hadn't even gotten to the main event yet.

My Aussie brother River and I shared an amazed and genuinely surprised smile as we were led to our seats. I sat next to Luang Pi Phop and put my arm around his shoulder. I looked at him with an incredible amount of admiration in my heart and said, "thank you so much for making this happen." He looked back at me, smiled and said, "it wasn't me - it was you who made this happen. We just took care of the details."

Then the crowd became unruly. Well, as unruly as a bunch of partying lay Buddhist could get. The MC was revving up the crowd - one that needed no encouragement - as she attempted to stave off their zeal for letting their first round of lanterns fly free into the warm night sky. She kept reminding the crowd, as the music built towards a crescendo, to wait for the countdown.

And then the first, and then another, then a dozen, then dozens of lanterns floated up like a spectral dream. It was a beautiful sight to behold. All the while that poor MC was desperately trying to control the situation, but to no avail. Her performance reminded me of Kevin Bacon in Animal House frantically pleading with the parade crowd, *"remain calm, all is well..."*

And then she gave up. Abandoning any hope of a stately, synchronized countdown, she blurted out "Fivefourthreetwoone!" Thousands of glowing lanterns lifted into the night sky at once, flooding our vision in a way that felt mythical. It was absurdly beautiful. I wasn't sure if it was just me sitting there on the elevated edge of the temple, slack-jawed, but every monk was silent, while those with seniority - meaning they had the privilege to carry about their smartphones - were filming like proud dads at a school play.

I've seen some truly beautiful things in my life. Natural wonders across the globe. The loving gaze and smile of my ex-wife, back when those things were still directed my way. My eyes have been blessed, bedazzled, and even brought to tears, happy ones, occasionally. But this? This festival of floating fire? It earned its place at the top of the list, possibly elbowing everything else off the podium. Despite the bass still thumping somewhere in the background, the entire crowd - who just moments earlier had erupted in wild cheers when a rogue dozen lanterns jumped the gun - now stood utterly silent. Faces tilted skyward, as thousands of hopes, prayers and resolutions drifted toward the heavens, glowing like earnest UFOs. And it happened again, then again, and again. Each liftoff did nothing to diminish the previous round's sense of awe.

Back in the van, heading home in the dark like some rogue monastic snack cartel, we rehashed the night while I not-so-stealthily passed around a large bag of contraband munchies I had cajoled Luang Pi Phop into purchasing for me on the sly. I had stashed away my cache - a bag brimming with Lindor truffles, Milky Ways, and gummies for the ride home. Technically off-limits. The result? A feeding frenzy worthy of Shark Week on cable TV.

Up front, Luang Pi Phop maintained his noble facade of moral high ground, eyes forward, pretending to meditate, presumably thinking about impermanence or road safety. But I caught him - the faintest curl of a smile sneaking across his lips. He knew. He approved. Or at least, he didn't disapprove enough to remonstrate us.

As we wound our way back into the hills, the black of night wrapped around the van like a soft robe. We occasionally spotted distant clusters of lanterns still rising skyward from little villages tucked away in the trees and folded into the mountains, still in mid-reverie. It was like watching the festival continue in whispers, long after the music had faded.

Josh sat next to me, my brother and fellow globetrotter. We'd shared many conversations, intellectual rabbit holes, and the kind of sibling telepathy forged through time and shared dysfunction. But now he was quiet, staring out into the night, somewhere far away in his head.

"So... what did you think?" I asked him quietly.

He turned slowly, with that big, beautiful, unmistakable Josh-smile, his eyes were a little glossy.

"It was the most beautiful thing I've ever seen anywhere on earth, in my life," he replied.

CHAPTER 7. WELCOME TO THE JUNGLE: NOTES FROM A FOREST MONASTERY

CHAPTER 8. HEADS SHAVED AND ORDINATION. A RADICAL SHIFT

As one famously neurotic bald man once said about confidence and the bald man... well, I'll let him keep the quote. But he wasn't wrong. If you're curious – look up Larry David's great line!

When you make the decision to participate in monastic life it's not something you stumble into like a yoga retreat with robes. It's a commitment. Real, deliberate, and definitely not half-assed. Part of that commitment is studying and adhering to the disciplined lifestyle you're about to live, including, at the very least, adhering to the Eight Precepts. And a part of that commitment is participating in all ceremonies with an open heart, a willing spirit, and ideally, without trying to sneak in snacks.

November 5, 2024 - Pravejya rehearsal day.

The first ceremony that demanded our full presence - not just physically, but soulfully - is the head-shaving ritual called Pravejya. In the West, we blandly refer to it as "tonsure," which sounds like something you'd get at a spa with cucumber water. But no, this isn't a casual spin in the barber's chair where you chat about Giants box scores and who they're trading next season. This is a rite of passage. A mundanā.

Pravejya, the day of mundanā, is thick with symbolism and ceremony. The literal translation means "to go forth," its historical lineage dating back to the Vedic writings and rituals. It marks the transition of an ordinary man into bhikkhu - a monk - and it begins with the *very* literal stripping away of ego. Your head is shaved. Your eyebrows too. And, of course, the regulation face-scrape. Everything goes. In the Buddhist view, facial and head hair are signs of vanity, and vanity has got no place under the Bodhi tree.

According to the Vinaya, the ancient rule book of the Buddhist canon, head-shaving isn't a one-time ego purge. It's a regular ritual, done on every new and full moon (Uposatha Day), which averages out to twice a month. Though, as I quickly learned, plenty of monks just go ahead and shave it all off every single day.

Bald is beautiful, and apparently, spiritually efficient.

We knew this day was coming. Most of us approached it with a mix of curiosity and mild dread. Especially our brother PeaceLove from California, whose magnificent golden dreadlocks had become something of a legend. If you've ever grown dreads, you understand. This wasn't just a haircut, it was a full-on sacrificial offering. His hair was a lifestyle, symbolic, and possibly had its own glossy magazine.

Another source of my personal unease? Eyebrows. Specifically, the unsettling rumor that once you shave them off after a certain age, they may never return, or worse, they might come back all wiry and chaotic, like an aged mad professor who's just seen something unspeakable in his particle accelerator. I didn't want that energy permanently affixed to my face.

And then there was the weather. It had been solid gray and rainy for the week. Not a dramatic monsoon, just a slow, moody drizzle - cool but not cold, persistent and wet enough to make the idea of bare feet in ceremonial smocks feel less sacred and more soggy.

The iRetreat complex, located across a small bridge that spanned the Luang River, around a couple bends and up the mud-slicked dirt road, was our sister complex to iMonastery and was for lay Buddhists to stay at, meditate and receive some dhamma wisdom without taking vows of monkhood. Much of iRetreat was still under construction. But the crown jewel of the facility was a stunning, open-sided pavilion with a soaring roof, had been completed in the nick of time, as if the universe demanded it be there for our big debut. It was beautiful. And our ceremony would be its grand opening act.

We climbed the gently sloping road, winding past vegetable patches and fruit trees, then up and back behind the pavilion to a makeshift, questionably engineered wooden staircase leading to a longhouse. It creaked ominously. Nails protruded at just the right height to snag a shin or a robe. A gentle reminder that enlightenment can still involve tetanus.

Once again, the Bhante role came calling, which meant I'd be leading the sangha.

Inside the pavilion, the setup was impressive: a large U-shaped arrangement of stations, seven on each side, with a long table at the bottom of the U for visiting dignitaries. Outside the U ring was set up for family and guests. Cushions, chairs, and benches all in place. The middle layer was occupied by low tables for our bowls and other ceremonial necessities. And the innermost ring was where we would sit, facing outward, awaiting our transformation. Behind our chairs, ample space had been left for the honored guest barbers, those joining in the privilege of shearing away our hair, one symbolic snip at a time. For them, it was a spiritual honor. For us, it was the beginning of something else entirely.

Down those treacherous stairs, then a hard left, followed by fourteen slick, grassy (and now quite swampy) steps, across a makeshift wooden walkway that flexed, bowed and groaned underfoot, and finally onto the stone pavilion floor. From there, we followed the arc of the elongated U starting from the right, continuing around until the U was filled and each of us landed behind our assigned seats. All of this was to be executed at a slow, dignified pace, timed to some rather enthusiastic music flowing through a PA system.

This was not a casual stroll. It was an exercise in choreographed poise: chin high, eyes forward, an expression of serene detachment on our faces (or our best attempt at one while sloshing through wet grass). We each carried a ceremonial platter - large, lacquered, and solemn - its contents arranged just so: banana leaves serving as an elegant placemat; trimming and shaving tools laid out on top. It was meant to project grace and gravitas. I was wet, anxious, and trying to ignore the fact that a leech had taken up residence on my person. A tiny, bloated Count Dracula happily gorged himself on my ankle.

Because the Pravejya ceremony is steeped in history and symbolism, we were encouraged to invite loved ones to witness it. I had no one to invite. Or maybe more truthfully, no one would come if I had.

Others did.

Their families showed up in full force. Mothers, fathers, partners, old friends flying in from New Zealand, Australia, Vietnam, the U.S., and Europe. They came with flowers, smiles, and tears. I stood to the side, watching it all unfold, feeling something like awe laced with ache. I hadn't realized how profound this moment would be. Not only for us, as we surrendered our hair, ego and names, but for those who came to witness our transformation.

When rehearsals finally wrapped, our teachers gave their approval. I got glowing marks for leadership, which inflated me just enough to imagine I might actually pull this thing off with dignity. My brothers and I made our way back down the muddy road to the monastery. I was eager to get that blood-sucking worm, who was now bloated, off my foot. I showered in the hottest water I could stand, changed into dry clothes, and joined the others for hot tea, cocoa, or coffee. We lounged and chatted, waiting for evening meditation and bed.

I woke the next morning to the patter of rain so relentless it sounded like it was trying to tunnel through the thatched roof. Thunder rolled in like a cosmic timpani section. Any hope for a mild, sunny ceremony evaporated. The day was dark, the air cool and wet. The road to the monastery was tough on a good day. That day it was borderline biblical.

After our morning obligations, back we trudged to iRetreat, where music and an emcee's warm-up chatter already filled the air. It was early, but the show was underway. There was no going back and no rain delay announced by Buddhist umpires. At least we had umbrellas.

Up in the jungle longhouse, perched high above the pavilion, we waited. We'd been issued our first ceremonial shirts - poncho-style tops in blue, red and black colors - paired with pale blue sabongs. We milled about, sipping hot tea, water, or sodas, nervous energy fizzing just under the surface. Monks flitted around us like high school prom chaperons, attentive and a little giddy; it was all somehow both sacred and completely human.

There was a strange vibe in the room. The usual talkers had gone quiet, pacing off alone. The introverts were suddenly chatty and aglow. It felt like we had all stepped into an alternate universe where everyone responded to stress by swapping personalities.

Some brothers took the ceremony with profound solemnity, their expressions reflecting the deep weight of tradition. Others seemed to treat it like a cultural excursion with spiritual flair. I sat somewhere in between. I felt the weight of it, this rite of passage, the ancient thread we were weaving into, but I also couldn't shake the surreal awareness that I'd be back in linen pants and eating from street carts in a few weeks. For all the ceremony's gravitas, I knew of only two of us who had plans to continue their monastic training beyond the month.

And yet... there was something about it. Leading these men felt epochal. Sacred. Temporary, yes. But very real.

Being Bhante, as I've said, came with certain privileges. Some small, some profound. This one stopped me in my tracks.

Luang Pi Phop, my indefatigable monk-mentor with the calm patience of a saint and the bounce of a Buddhist golden retriever, pulled me aside just before the ceremony. Because I was Bhante and had no family there, I was being granted a great honor: Phornsan Kamlang-ek herself would serve as my ceremonial mother.

This was not some symbolic gesture made for convenience. In Thai culture, the role of a mother - biological or ceremonial - is imbued with immense spiritual weight, especially during rites of passage. To be given a mother is to be given a lineage, a place, a kind of invisible scaffolding of belonging.

And I was being given Phornsan Kamlang-ek. The formidable matriarch behind the entire Monk Life Project. Alongside her husband, General Arthit, she had built this cross-continental initiative up from a disheveled organization, personally shaping the path that brought so many of us to this moment of transformation.

I nodded, mouth dry, heart pounding.

The others had their mothers or fathers, siblings and friends. I had Phornsan Kamlang-ek.

Which is kind of like showing up to the prom with the Queen of Thailand as your dance partner.

It was absurd. It was overwhelming.

And it was one of the greatest honors of my life.

My first thought? *"Doesn't she have more important things to do?"*

Apparently not. She would be with me through all three - yep, count 'em - three ceremonies.

It was time. I rose on the cue from Luang Pi Phop and led our group in orderly file to the launch spot at the top of the steps, trying to keep the rain from my eyes, waiting for the green light from central ops. Word came. Phop gave me his trademark grin and nod, and as I turned the corner and descended the steps, leading our stately little monk parade, I realized the pavilion was packed. I mean packed. Crammed wall-to-wall with people. I didn't have the foggiest idea where they had come from. iRetreat is in the middle of nowhere. I was half-convinced these people were forest spirits or mushroom fairies who had sprouted from the mud and mist, popping into existence in our small space in the world, because Chiang Mai is two hours away, and it had been raining for days - tadpole-sized drops, no less. I was curious as to their motivation and the determination of those observers to be with us during that sacred ceremony.

With subtle side-eye scanning (you know, the serene monk-like kind), I tried to keep my peaceful gaze intact while doing some quick math. Best I could tell, there were over 400 people present, many who had minimal, or no direct affiliation with iMonastery. They came to witness our transformation. And somehow that was both awe-inspiring and absolutely nerve-shredding.

Rarely in my life have I felt as relieved as I did when it became clear that I had led my Sangha without incident. No tripping, no slipping, no accidental flying lacquer platters and my slow stately pace had been pulled off with grace. As I took my seat at the head of the U, I allowed myself a deep breath. The hard part, I thought, was done. Now I could retreat into my own little bubble and just be a ceremonial monk for a while.

Then I turned, looked across the great divide past my chair, the low-slung table and to the other side, and locked eyes with Phornsan Kamlang-Ek, who was beaming at me with what can only be described as maternal pride.

And just like that, my nervous system rebooted back into DEFCON ONE.

The first ceremony after our grand entrance and seating was the public-participation hair snipping. Step right up folks and don't forget your scissors! My "person," the matriarch of the entire monastic order, kicked off the ritual by clipping a few strands of my hair, placing them gently on the banana-leaf placemat draped over the platter in my lap. We exchanged greetings, at which point she said something that blew my mind: *SHE* was honored to serve as my mother for the day. She said that quietly, kindly, and with sincerity I could feel. I tumbled into ease within seconds of her pronouncement.

After that brief moment, she moved on to the next monk-in-progress, as a new person approached me, smiling warmly, wielding sharp scissors.

Everyone had incredibly kind things to say, or, for those not fluent in English, offered big, beaming smiles that lit up their whole face. Or they would place a gentle hand on my shoulder in a manner that conveyed *"it's all going to be OK."* They'd lock eyes like I was the only soul in the universe, and then - snip! - off came another chunk of my ego.

Our California Rasta, dreadlocks dyed a golden sunburst, and our tall, affable Russian, whose flowing blond mane gave off strong Bee Gees circa 1978 vibes, were especially popular with the scissor-happy crowd.

Once the initial carnage had passed, and everyone who wanted a go had had their ceremonial snip, it was time for phase two: the full head shave. Only ordained monks are allowed to perform this next part of the ritual, which I found oddly comforting. At least I wouldn't end up the victim of some rogue Buddhist fangirl or boy reenacting a Sweeney Todd moment in the jungle. It's Thailand. Stranger things have happened.

As my new "mom" for the day sat across from me, we chatted quietly about life; how funny it is, how unpredictable it can be, how sometimes you wake up thinking it's a normal rainy day and end up bald in front of 400 strangers. Phornsan was gracious, deeply kind, and effortlessly present in that way powerful people sometimes are - like they've bent time to sit with you. For a fleeting moment, I felt like being Bhante wasn't just an odd cosmic joke. I felt deeply honored to fill that role and promised myself I would do it with grace through the rest of my tenure.

That's when I noticed the monk standing behind me with razor in hand wasn't just any monk. It was my monk: the Abbot, Venerable Narongchai Thanajayo. A man of razor-sharp intellect, warm humor, and a smile that could melt or incinerate depending on the context. His usual smile was radiant and generous, but I'd also seen his "did you really just say that?" version. A smile so dry it could start a brush fire.

I glanced up at him, just as he was poised for the ceremonial first scrape, and whispered, *"You've done this before, right?"* with a wink. Without missing a beat, he giggled - yes, my Abbot giggled - then placed a hand gently on my shoulder, and replied, *"Maybe."* A jokester with a razor. Perfect.

Dip in the water. Scrape. Dip. Scrape. Repeat.

As he shaved my head, bald for the first time since I emerged from the womb, my mom-for-the-day and I kept talking - about my life, her life, love, loss, change, the whole Pad Thai. I swear I could feel waves of energy pulsing off her like she was a benevolent force field. I had noticed that wherever she walked, people moved. Not out of fear, but reverence. The kind of reverence that says, "This woman probably knows where all the bodies are buried and has blessed each site personally."

By the time I was smooth as a cue ball and feeling like my scalp was made of industrial-grade micro-Velcro, it was time to lead our band of baldies back up the slick steps to the longhouse. There, more monks waited, ready to inspect for stray hairs. And just when we thought it was over, we got a treat: a nice, bracing splash of cold mountain water to rinse off nicks, cuts, and what little ego remained. I was lucky I escaped without bloodshed. Others looked like they'd headbutted a rose bush.

Khop khun kráb, venerable Narongchai! That's "thank you, sir" in Thai, though in that moment, I meant, "Thanks for not turning my scalp into a bloody battleground, sir."

We were instructed to change into new, pure white, front-button shirts that looked vaguely Indian - the next layer in our ceremonial cake - as the first stage of our transformation was complete. Much like a kurta shirt but shorter. We huddled around steaming cups of hot tea, trying to thaw out from the damp chill while waiting to be summoned for the next ceremonial phase of the day.

It was then, sipping tea and assessing the damage, that we collectively realized just how profoundly a face changes when it's stripped of hair and eyebrows. The effect was disorienting. Guys I'd been brushing teeth next to all week suddenly looked like strangers. There were some hard blinks and puzzled stares, the kind you give someone at a reunion when you're 70% sure they were in your class but 100% unsure if that's their original face.

That middle-stage of ceremony - the gifting of our saffron robes and alms bowls, would lead up to the culmination of our long, soggy day.

Monks are not allowed to buy their own robes or alms bowls. Those must be donated. This is one of the primary reasons you'll see donation boxes at Buddhist monasteries all over the world. Dressing a monk, it turns out, is expensive. Enlightenment might be free, but the dry cleaning isn't.

And then it was time. I gathered my newly minted cue-ball crew and led my Sangha down the slippery steps again as music blasted from the speakers, all the while the ever-cheerful emcee rattled off announcements about upcoming monastery events and ways to help, donate, or get involved with our community outreach programs. Honestly, she was having a blast. I'm pretty sure she could've sold raffle tickets and T-shirts and no one would've batted an eye.

We took our seats once more, sitting a little taller, a little prouder. We were only a day away from full ordination now. There was still some chanting to do to bring everyone into the right headspace, and so we dove in. Thankfully, we'd been rehearsing these chants for over a week, so memory kicked in and we entered that sweet fake-it-till-you-make-it zone, our mouths moving more or less in time with the syllables, our souls catching up as best they could.

Back at our assigned stations, our seats had vanished while we were up in the longhouse, sacrificed to the gods of Sacred Ceremony Setup. This was the most solemn part of the day: the moment our sponsors - "our people," or in my case, my newly adopted ceremonial "mom" - would present us with our robes. There were songs. There were speeches. There was a stately presentation by our Abbot and the head Abbot of the entire Dhammakaya order, all performed with the kind of precision usually reserved for royal coronations.

The robe package was elaborate: two Jiwon (one for everyday wear, and a second one for special occasions - because monks need formal wear too), our Sabong or lower wraps, a cloth belt, and the pièce de résistance, the golden sash that tied it all together. Think Buddhist haute couture, monk edition. We had been instructed to kneel in humble supplication: feet under bottoms, knees screaming in protest on the mat that really was not much of a mat, heads bowed, arms outstretched like supplicants in a Renaissance painting, palms up and ready to receive our robes.

As the speeches stretched on into eternity (or at least far enough to consider faking a fainting spell), the packages were finally, mercifully, placed onto our aching arms.

Then came the final act: the gifting of our alms bowls, or Patta. These beautifully crafted, enameled brass bowls came with their own saffron-colored cloth hammocks, the ultimate monk accessory. Thankfully, this part was brief. Once the bowls were placed in our hands, we were told to rise, our knees sending up tiny prayers of gratitude.

Ceremony concluded, I once again led my bald brethren up the slippery stairs to the longhouse, where seasoned monks helped us don our new saffron robes. Wrapped in orange for the first time, we descended once more into a crowd of tearful, proud faces. It felt... *monumental*.

Then came the paparazzi.

Suddenly, we were in a full-blown monk-themed photo shoot. Cameras everywhere directing us into every imaginable pose. Videographers captured all of it while trying to stay out of sightline of the dSLRs. We were herded, grouped, re-grouped. People we didn't know gushed with admiration. If this was what it felt like to be famous, I had serious empathy for Princess Diana and the tabloid betrayals that tried to destroy her. The symbolism of it all hit like a tidal wave: we were now public figures of a sort, stand-ins for purity and discipline. No pressure.

Back at the monastery, the mood shifted. You might expect celebration, camaraderie, or a rowdy late-night tea party of reliving epic moments and sharing spiritual epiphanies.

But none of that happened.

Instead, we quietly peeled off in different directions, like leaves blown loose from a branch. No goodbyes, no "see you at breakfast," not even a knowing nod. Just a slow, almost reverent dispersal into the jungle darkness.

Something had settled over us, not exhaustion exactly, though we were all bone tired. It was the weight of meaning. The ceremony had delivered a sort of finality that I felt inside, and now each of us had to sit with whatever had taken up residence.

I slipped into my tent. The silence outside was deafening and for the first time since I had arrived, I didn't feel isolated from the world.

ORDINATION DAY

I awoke at 3AM, an hour ahead of schedule and a full ninety minutes before the first gong. It was dark. Not just dark but mountainous monastic dark. Even the bathroom portico lights had been turned off, which made me wonder if our wise, all-knowing monks had intentionally killed the lights knowing we'd be too nervous to sleep. Those guys were mystical clairvoyants with the bedtime instincts of Victorian nannies.

We'd spent the past week preparing for this: memorizing two crucial lines we'd have to recite to our preceptor monk, ideally without butchering them into incomprehensible Pali gibberish. My monk name - "Sattibalo" - means "man of many abilities," which felt dishonest because memorization was not among my abilities. Not even a little.

November 7th - A day of transformation.

Did I mention it was cold? Colder than anything we'd felt yet up in our mountain hideaway. And of course, that day - when we'd be standing outside for much of it - it was the coldest day yet. It was also pouring, huge fat drops soaking everything in their earthbound path. That rain came with a chilled wrath that made me question every decision I'd made leading up to that day.

After our usual morning routines (plus bonus touch-up shaves for the baby-faced guys whose hair grows faster than gossip in a small town), we prepared for the biggest moment of our monastic lives. All other duties were suspended. Today, there was only one job: take the vows. Enter monkhood.

No more training wheels. No more powder-blue sabong and yellow sweatshirt. This was it. And despite the numbing rain, chilled feet, and a brain stubbornly refusing to recall Line Two of the Pali chant, I was ready.

As I wrote above, rote memorization is not, nor has it ever been, a talent I've possessed. In fact, the more important the memorization, the more my brain decides to throw a jazz riff into the mix - improvising with heart, sure, while withholding precision. I always get there, just not in the way instructors or solemn-faced preceptor monks might prefer. My brain is less "recitation engine" and more "interpretive monologue." Given time, I can deliver. Give me a few days? Absolutely not.

When they handed us the ordination study sheet, paragraph upon paragraph of ceremonial lines, chants, and call-and-response Pali, I experienced what can only be described as full-body academic panic. There were whole call and response scripts, stories, and verbal obstacle courses. And then there were the two key lines - my solo - to be performed directly to the preceptor monk. At a special hall. Miles away. In front of everyone. The make-or-break moment of the entire monastic rite, that's all. Again, no pressure.

We donned our robes. Or, more accurately, I attempted to assemble my robe ensemble like a blindfolded chimpanzee attacking an origami kit. Thankfully, Luang Pi Phop, my patient monk pal and now unofficial spiritual stylist, intervened before I could debut as a Picasso version of a monk. He gently pulled me aside and, with the quiet competence of a man who's done this hundreds of times, turned me into someone who looked like I belonged. I had nailed the Sabong and belt - the monk version of pants. But the Jiwon, the elaborate upper body wrap that had to be folded and draped just so? I was a complete disaster. Wrapping an enormous rectangular cloth around my torso with monastic elegance was not my strong suit.

At this point, it was too late to back out. I was "on the bus," as Cowboy Neil would say, and there you have it. You pay for your ticket; you take the ride.

Loaded into two vans, we drove through misty mountain villages and fields of waving rice, on our way to the ordination center - a 200-year-old ordination hall (so yeah - brand new) perched in the middle of a picturesque rice paddy, golden grains ripened around it like something out of a spiritual fairy tale as they shivered and shook with the onslaught of raindrops.

A crowd of over a hundred laypeople had already gathered. Word had clearly gotten out that fresh monk was in season. Thankfully, our monastery monks once again played wardrobe supervisor, adjusting our robes and wiping our brows, making sure we looked the part. If I learned anything on this journey, it's that the Thai paparazzi are deeply committed to capturing a perfectly robed monk. The camera cranes and umbrella-holding assistants made it feel more like a red-carpet procession than a sacred ritual.

It was time for me to be Bhante again, the ceremonial starter pistol. My role was to light incense and candles and place them at the altar outside of the ordination hall in specific order, without screwing up. This had to be executed perfectly, or we'd have to cancel the ceremony and come back another time. I didn't want to be that guy. Just me, a side pavilion full of monks, thirteen anxious fellow almost-monks, a full audience, and enough camera lenses to film a Marvel reboot. I managed my role without a hitch because while I may have the recitation memory capabilities of a steel I-beam, simple processes I can nail.

Then came the hard part. Inside the tiny, ornate, airless ordination hall - packed wall to wall with monks lining the walls - we'd each go through our ordination in groups of three. As Bhante, I was in the first group. Yay? Each round would take about thirty minutes of kneeling on wooden floors, backs straight, feet folded under our butts like some kind of medieval Pilates challenge, palms pressed in prayer, sweat beading down our backs. We'd respond in Pali, line by line, to our preceptor - a wise, ancient monk flown in like some ceremonial final boss, whom we'd never met.

We'd trained for this all week. The rhythm, the logic of it, had started to make sense. That is, until we hit the solo vows. The part where I, as Sattibalo, had to recite my part from memory, in front of everyone, and promise to uphold 227 precepts: to live cleanly, purely, honorably, intellectually, and spiritually.

It was time:

Preceptor: *Kinnamosi:*

    Aham bhante Sattibalo nāma. I would respond.

Preceptor: *Ko nāma te upajjhāyo:*

    Upajjahāyo no bhante āyasmā Kantedhammo nāma. That would be my second response.

Two short call-and-response lines (that happened to carry the weight of a supertanker.) That was all I needed to memorize. *You* could commit them to memory in minutes, even if only phonetically. But my brain doesn't work that way. If it hadn't been for one of my kind, understanding teaching monks gently guiding me through the ceremony (*and subtly mouthing the lines in my line of sight*), I might have been expelled from ordination. I need to understand - to feel the words, to grasp their meaning through translation - before they can lodge themselves in my mind and heart. But there was no direct translation available. I nearly blew it, squeaking out my lines like a terrified little mouse.

My dear brothers, who knew of my struggle with memorization, were sympathetic and supportive. I wish they'd laid on more pressure, cracked the whip a little, if only to get my brain to shape up and deliver. But they had their own lines to remember, their own tightrope to walk.

In the end, I got through it. Not an Oscar-worthy performance by any means, but it was enough to satisfy the Preceptor. As I rose, the weight of what I had just done crashed down on me like the Titanic hitting the ocean floor. I walked out, legs shaking from pain and tension, surrounded by doting monks shielding me with umbrellas. And then - just like that - I was outside again, under a slate-gray sky, with rain pouring down, cleansing me with grace.

As I reached for my sandals, I asked my fellow monks to keep their umbrellas for someone else. I didn't want protection. I wanted to feel it. I needed the earth to drench me in her tears, to mark this moment - raw, sacred, and real. I walked barefoot back toward the covered pavilion, toward the cameras and the crowd of well-wishers, who waited with alms and balms, knowing what we had just endured physically, emotionally, and spiritually.

The gathering after ordination had the texture of something ancient and sacred, something that didn't need words to explain itself. The air was thick with reverence, not just for tradition, but for the simple act of devotion that each person had come to honor. There was love in their eyes - unmistakable and unselfconscious. It poured out toward us like warmth from a hearth, steady and undeniable. Their joy was not for spectacle. It was for what we had become.

I felt the first dissonance of my new role, my new persona. As monks, we were not permitted to bow in recognition or respect. The gesture that had always been second nature passed back and forth with dignity. That was now reserved only for the laity. We could only receive it. It felt disrespectful and false to not mirror their humility, their generosity and love. I wanted to tell them, with the tilt of my head or a simple folding of hands, that I saw them, too. That I honored their presence, their hopes, their sacrifices, their prayers. But tradition asked for stillness instead of response. It asked that I wear the mantle of monkhood with a solemnity that didn't bend back.

As more groups entered the ordination hall to complete their ordination, the sky began to soften. The rain that had fallen hard all morning thinned to a mist, and the air turned thick with rising heat. I felt a growing urge to step away from the press of people, to carve out a moment of silence for myself - to listen inward. But that silence would have to wait. The crowd, now gathered under the covered portico, had waited through that soggy day to meet us. Their offerings - red good luck envelopes filled with baht (of which to a man, was donated back to the monastery for our children's education fund), wrapped gifts, pressed palms and whispered prayers - were as much a part of the ceremony as the ancient chants spoken inside the hall.

Among the gifts, each of us received a box of herbal balms, a quiet gesture of empathy from those who knew what the body suffers in stillness. I held court for a time, speaking when asked, blessing those who came forward, receiving all that was given.

Eventually, the tide of attention receded as the next group came out of the hall as monks. And in the hush that followed, I slipped away - not far, but just far enough to become no one again for a few minutes.

I opened the balm box and unscrewed the bottle marked "extra strong." The scent hit me - sharp, herbal, elemental - it was as if the land itself had sent it. I rubbed it into my knees, my thighs, the arches of my feet. The sting came first, then the warmth, and finally a slow, blooming relief that felt almost holy. Of all the things I had been handed that day, it was this - the simplest, humblest bottle - that felt most immediate, most merciful. I would donate the envelopes and the other gifts. But the small bottles, and the comfort they gave - those I would keep.

CHAPTER 9. ALMS ROUNDS - A BEGGAR IN THE WILDERNESS

Big gestures get applause. Small ones change people. Guess which one Buddha would've upvoted?

We were now fully ordained monks in the Dhammakaya order, and everything shifted. Some things subtly, others like the earth tilting a few degrees on its axis. Our interactions with our teachers changed, imperceptibly at first. The tone softened into mutual regard. The distance shortened. Where once there had been gentle guidance from above, there was now a back-and-forth, a give-and-take. The bows remained (monks bow to each other all the time), but so did a sense that we had stepped through a doorway into a different kind of brotherhood. One built on shared vows, robes, shared insight and silent moments that screamed loudly.

But the greatest change for me came with the knowledge that we would soon go on alms rounds - Dāna - in the mountain villages beyond our monastery grounds. Not through tidy streets with designated paths like city monks, where food is gifted as predictably as the sunrise. No. We would walk into the remote highlands, places so far-flung that some were nothing more than rumors hidden among rocky folds of mist and memory.

Among my newly ordained brothers, this practice stirred something uneasy. We spoke in low tones under the pomelo and teak trees, our saffron robes brushing dust as we paced and pondered. The idea of becoming beggars - because that is what the Pali word for monk truly means - left many of us uneasy, some even ashamed at the next step. We had grown up in lives where food came easy, where need was theoretical. We were the givers of canned goods and charitable checks, not the ones with open hands.

Now we were to walk into the lives of people who had so little and ask wordlessly for more.

To take rice from the hands of those who lived day by day, hand to mouth, felt backwards, morally crooked. It cut against everything we'd been taught to admire in ourselves: independence, contribution, the quiet nobility of not needing anything.

Some of us tried to reason our way through it. Maybe this was theater.

Maybe the villagers did it out of habit or obligation. Maybe they didn't really miss the food we took. After all, hadn't we eaten more than our share at the monastery already? Meals abundant, meticulously prepared, never once lacking.

Still, I couldn't shake the question: What right did I have to ask for more, from those who already had so little?

It was a deep philosophical reckoning; one we revisited often in our debates. None of us had ever begged for food. Not once. That thought alone ran against everything we'd been taught to admire. Self-sufficiency, contribution, control. To stand in front of another human being with an empty bowl and expect sustenance from their hands? It felt almost indecent. We didn't understand the impulse to give when one had so little to spare. It unsettled many of us.

Perhaps you've seen images, monks walking silently in single file at dawn, heads bowed in humility, feet bare, saffron robes fluttering faintly in the morning breeze. They move like smoke - quiet, steady, reverent - toward people who kneel or sit, waiting with rice, stews, bundles of noodles, fresh fruits and water. You see those images and think of peace. Grace. Harmony. I saw those images too and felt an existential dread.

It stuck in my craw like a bad dream: being the receiver in a world where I'd always been the one offering. I didn't feel worthy of that kind of generosity. More than that, I didn't feel it was necessary. These were people with little, feeding those of us who - truth be told - had so much already. Our meals at the monastery had been abundant. Plentiful. Sometimes even excessive. We'd never gone without. How could I, in good conscience, hold out my bowl?

What we hadn't yet grasped was the *root* of their giving. Despite our long debates and sincere efforts to understand both sides of the alms ritual, we were still missing something essential. Why give when it hurts to do so? Why offer up what might be needed for one's own child or aging parent?

Only later would I put two and two together and begin to understand that the food we received came not from surplus, but from sacrifice, and that this, perhaps, was the point. Our monastery was fed not only by local farmers, many of whom grew crops expressly for us, but also by donors from across Thailand and beyond. Some were former monks from our program, returned to the world but still tethered by memory and gratitude. Others gave anonymously - shipments of food and funds.

And it wasn't just for us. That abundance, so generously offered, often became surplus - surplus that allowed the monastery to extend its own alms outward: to struggling schools, to village clinics, to families in need. There was an interlinked ecosystem at play, a circle of giving where nobody held onto what they could pass along. And I had to ask myself: was I really at the bottom of that circle, or was I simply unused to standing still and holding my hands open?

Sometimes the offerings were meager and slim, other times astonishing in their generosity. I remember walking past the sorting tables near the kitchen, where enormous stacks of brand-new fleece blankets lay folded in crisp rows, still carrying the scent of the factory. They had arrived as a single anonymous donation and were already being prepared for re-donation to two mountain communities far beyond the last bend in the road, villages whose names didn't appear on maps. These were places so remote that the floods of September and October of 2024, had stranded them in darkness for weeks, with no power, little clean water, and only the fading hope that someone might still be thinking of them. The blankets would bring not just warmth, but proof that the world hadn't forgotten.

We, the newly minted monks, couldn't yet understand such acts of giving. We debated them in our hushed corners of reflection, trying to trace the motivations. Some suggested guilt - the karmic calculus of the privileged, paying spiritual dues with tangible goods. Others believed it to be obligation dressed up as virtue. But none of those explanations fully accounted for the softness of those blankets, the thoughtfulness of their timing, or the way they would be carried - on foot, in silence - into villages more sky than road.

That day would open up something in us. Slowly, and in different ways for each man, our understanding began to shift. What we thought we knew of generosity, of need, of giving and receiving, would melt and reshape itself. It wasn't about the food or the blankets or even the material exchange. It was about something far older and deeper than that, something quiet, humane, and universal.

We were beginning to understand that compassion, true compassion, doesn't measure the cost. It gives because it must, because it can, because to withhold would wound something sacred. In that unfolding, we too were changed.

※

Friday dawned cold - 39° Fahrenheit and raining. Not a mist or a drizzle, but big, fat, unhurried raindrops that seem to fall straight from the gut of the sky and go splat. It had only been two days since we'd taken our vows, formally entering the iMonastery fraternity as Luang Pi - brother monks in the Theravada tradition - and now we were to go on our first alms round. We would walk as real monks, honest-to-goodness, shaven-headed, robed mendicants, into the folds of the high mountain villages that clung to the hills like moss to stone.

It was still dark when we climbed into two Toyota pickups. The sky had just begun to smudge with light along the eastern ridge, dawn unspooling in threads. Our caravan crept slowly, quietly, up toward a village we would receive food from those who, by all Western logic, could least afford to give it.

Alms rounds are never random. They're not something you just throw together. These routes and visits are organized well in advance and negotiated between the elders of the monastery and those of each village. You don't show up, fifteen monks deep with bowls in hand, like door-to-door salesmen at sunrise, expecting a welcome committee and a pot of jasmine rice.

Those urban alms routes do not exist in the rural highlands. There are no plastic stools. No tidy queues of merit-seekers. No daily routes. The villagers need notice. They must wake up early, cook rice, prepare stews, gather fruit, bag up little care packages of chips or cookies, and pour juice or water into bottles to give. And of course, no one village can support the full weight of fifteen hungry monks every week. That kind of karmic enthusiasm would wipe out their pantries.

Going forward, we'd be sent out in smaller groups - four monks here, four monks there - sharing the load across the scattered hill communities. There's no sense in showing up like a Buddhist locust swarm.

Our first outing wasn't just about sustenance. Yes, we'd gather food for the communal tables back at iMonastery, but more than that, this was a lesson. A living, breathing tutorial in humility. A chance to see, for many of us, the first time in our lives, what generosity actually looks like when it isn't performative or tax-deductible.

Being Bhante, I was instructed - ordered, really - to ride inside the truck cab with the heat on, nestled behind the driver and Luang Pi Phop. The rest of my Sangha huddled under tarps in the bed of the trucks, shielding themselves from the wet and cold as best they could. I argued my position that I needed to be in the back with my Sangha. Leadership by example. And I meant it. I wanted to be with my brothers, cold and wet and equally miserable. But Luang Pi Wut, my teacher and friend, gave me a look, one that spoke volumes, immediately closing the argument as if slamming a book shut.

We had been carefully robed for the day, dressed like textbook monks, every fold and pleat just so. But the chill was real, and so was my fleece beanie, my thick socks stuffed into Birkenstocks, and the blanket I had smuggled into the truck like a guilty pleasure. I bundled into them while I could, knowing the time would soon come to shed the layers, physical and metaphysical, and step outside, into my role.

iMonastery is tucked into a small valley in the Thanon Thong Chai range, surrounded on all sides by mountains whose peaks snag clouds like prayer flags. We wound our way up muddy switchbacks, through mist and rain, to the village of Lochi, a place known for its highland rice and tea plantations. The road narrowed with each turn until it was hardly more than a ribbon of mud wide enough for a truck and a dog to pass each other without an argument.

Eventually we reached the top of Lochi, where the village elder had arranged for us to begin. Our trucks rolled into the broad, flat driveway of an ancient large teak-wood house, or barn. I couldn't determine what it was. The engines died and a thick blanketing silence fell like a curtain.

It was time to take off my beanie. Time to fold the blanket, remove the socks and sandals. Time to stop being a comfort-seeking Westerner and step into the quiet, ancient rhythm of the monks walk, high up on the mountain.

The first thing I noticed as I stepped down from the truck was that the air had changed. It was thicker up there. Sweet and saturated, like the forest had exhaled something thick just for us. The chill was still there, but it carried less bite, softened somehow by mist and altitude. And then, of course, my feet landed directly in a puddle of muddy, cold mountain water. That, and the wet nose of a village dog introducing itself to my rear end, brought me back from any lofty thoughts. One of dozens, it turned out. The dogs kept close, shadowing our group like shaggy silent sentinels. Not begging. Not barking. Just… there, shadowing our every step. I figured it must be the robes vibe. We didn't feed them. We didn't pet them. But they followed anyway. Maybe they sensed we were trying to be decent?

It was time. Time to cinch the invisible strap of monkish resolve, put on my metaphorical walking-meditation hat, and forget the rain soaking my jiwon. I had taken vows. I wore the robes. Now I had to walk the walk.

Each of us slung our Patta across our shoulders, the large black orb nestled in its sling. That's when I noticed, taped securely to the lid in large type, was a printed blessing we were to recite in unison to each almsgiver. A divine cheat sheet. In the other hand, we held umbrellas. I managed to hang onto mine for exactly two homes before I surrendered it back to our driver. Hard to balance an umbrella when you're lifting a bowl, while hanging onto the lid, to accept generosity from someone you feel unworthy to even look in the eye. I gave in to the drizzle. Moments later, the rain eased to a gentle mist. I'd like to think the universe gave me a nod for letting go and let karma weave her spell.

Seventeen newly minted monks, with our senior monk guides at the lead - lined up by height, though as Bhante, I was placed right behind Luang Pi Wut at the front of the line. Our feet found the steep muddy slope of the village road, more like a wide trail carved into the ridge. The place looked like it had grown up from the earth rather than being built. Houses of slatted wood rose on stilts, balanced like nesting birds on the edge of steep terraces. Tawdry plastic sheets flapped softly where windows might've been, if there was plastic at all. Many window portals were open and uncovered. Dogs, cats, pigs, ducks and chickens moved about like they owned the place, which, in a way, they did.

    The first dwelling we came to was two levels, the bottom, open space, a rudimentary slat board wall facing the street, with a dirt floor. Inside housed a scooter, a couple of bicycles, laundry hanging in the dark to the rear, and a large, ancient, blackened stone brazier where an equally ancient large metal cauldron hung over the fire on wooden crossbeam supports, cooking breakfast for the family. Upstairs were the living quarters, the slats again, spaced apart, so it must have been quite cold and damp at night. Animals roamed about, checking us out and alerting the neighborhood that those strange guys in robes were back.

    We stopped. Waited. Faced forward. The village exhaled around us. Then an elderly couple emerged with overfilled baskets, hands already pressed in wai. Their neighbors joined them. No announcements were made, no doorbells chimed, no cell phones rung - just a silent, understood rhythm. Sai Baht. The offering of food, of love, of memory.

One by one, we received gifts of sticky rice, fried pork rinds, bottles of water, packages of ramen, bags of stew, all placed with quiet hands into our bowls. Then came a moment I hadn't expected. The couple crouched low on their haunches, uncapped small bottles, and began to pour water slowly onto the earth while Luang Pi Wut began to chant. I learned later it was a ritual for the dead; a blessing for departed loved ones, the water, symbolic of a life poured forth, or the watering of future abundance. It was the kind of gesture Tolkien might've tucked into a forest ritual among elves. Yet here it was, real, muddy, sacred.

We chanted our awkward blessing, our taped cheat-sheets trembling as shaky hands in the mist tried to hold steady through the solemnity of the moment. We sounded like a drunken choir of tone-deaf monks, but the villagers smiled. Not in mockery. Not in pity. But in a kind of warm-hearted understanding, as if they were saying, *"You'll get it. In time."* And I believed them.

We continued. From primitive house to house. Some gave. Some didn't. All welcomed us.

Even as families bustled with their mornings - cooking, tending livestock, ushering children to school - they made space for us in their rhythm. They had prepared for this. Woken early. Cooked extra. Waited in the rain. Not because they had extra to give, but because they wanted to. Always with smiles that reached into our hearts.

The villagers obviously had no wealth that we westerners would identify as such. Many of them had disfigured feet from a lifetime of toiling in fields with no shoes. The hard labor life of subsistence farming was evident in the lines mapping lives on faces, while the dirt under their nails belonged there. And yet, their clothing was immaculate, clean and pressed as they crouched at their driveways in the rain.

What struck me most, after the fourth or fifth house, was the very real joy, the loving adoration and devotion that was evident in these people's eyes as they filled our bowls again and again with nourishment. I was taken aback. I was taken by surprise. I was flabbergasted. While some of the houses we stopped at were tidy and tightly built, some of them looked to be barely standing or to be able to withstand the slightest gust of wind - it was at those homes that the alms offerings seemed to be even more generous. Our drivers, who were quietly following in the trucks at a discrete distance, would come between our stops, with larger bins, to collect what had been given to us in our bowls.

I suddenly became acutely aware, as if a brightly lit diamond shot into my forehead, that I felt ashamed. Ashamed of my assumptions and my complete lack of understanding of what it meant to be rich. My assumptions that these people were poor, related entirely to *my* upbringing, *my* life, the expectations and definition of success - of what it meant to be wealthy in western society.

I was ashamed to think that these lives, these beautiful people, centered around an ancient stone brazier in a slat-board hovel, where the comforts of material wealth were completely absent, that that was poverty. I realized that my life, until recently, was an abomination of the human spirit. These people, living simply, were the richest, most soulful, beautiful humans I had ever encountered. They wanted for nothing. They didn't need a fancy house or cars, a wine cellar with Riedel glasses, steak or lobster or foie gras served on hand-painted Italian pottery to show their dinner guests how sophisticated they were. These seemingly simple people were wealthier in spirit and love, with a deep soulful sophistication, than anyone I'd ever met. You could see it in their eyes, their smiles, that they were more comfortable in their skins and lives than we were. It was an epiphany unlike anything I'd learned before and I was humbled to my very core.

That singular experience has forever changed the way I look at humanity. The vanity of excess that I had lived, not seeing it as such, was suddenly ugly; bereft of the soulful happiness that I was witnessing.

And in that moment, trudging along in our line of monks through a fog-wrapped village perched on the bones of the mountain, I realized that for the first time in a very long time, *I* wanted nothing. I just wanted to be worthy of the gift of being here. I felt light.

As we wound our way down, through the mountainside village, time after time, house after house, person after person gave with love, respect and humility, supporting their local monastery, with the hope that those gifts of nourishment would see us through our journey. All they asked for in return was a simple blessing to see them through *their* journey, their day and week ahead.

By the time we reached our final stop, a modest tea producer whose quiet generosity kept the monastery's tea tins full and steaming throughout the year, we were no longer the same monks who had climbed out of those trucks' hours earlier. Everything had shifted. You could feel it in the way we held our bowls, in the softened focus of our eyes, in the slower, more deliberate rhythm of our steps and breath. We arrived that morning as newcomers, freshly minted bhikkhus, cloaked in wet robes and good intentions. But we left as men changed, not by theory or scripture, but by sticky rice, rain, and the radiant dignity of people who gave until it hurt and smiled anyway.

This wasn't begging. Not even close. This was the ancient heartbeat of mutual understanding, a sacred barter of need and nourishment. We offered presence, assistance, community and blessings. They offered food, effort, and something less tangible. Something that shimmered, like the mist that clung to the ridge lines: grace? Or love in a more elemental form.

As we began loading up the trucks, my bowl lighter, but my heart considerably fuller, Luang Pi Phop caught my eye. His smile was a quiet lantern in the fog. He walked over to me, his steps unhurried, his robes swaying like the mist-wrapped branches of a cypress tree in a gentle breeze. He placed a hand on my shoulder, not to steady me, but to anchor something between us. His eyes, ageless and amused, searched mine for a flicker of recognition, and when he found it, he nodded once.

"Would you like to come with me on Tuesday?" he asked, the question soft but lit with purpose. "Smaller village. Three or four monks."

He already knew my answer, but I gave it to him anyway.

"I would be deeply honored."

The ride back to the monastery was quiet. It had started to rain again shortly after our last blessing recitation. I got back in the truck, glad for the blanket I had brought with me in the early hours of that cold morning. I used it to wipe first my tears, then my feet. I came to the realization that at some point during the 30-some-odd stops we had made at homes that I now looked upon with fondness, that I had forgotten that I was barefoot, sidestepping hungry leeches, walking through rivulets of cold mountain rainwater on steep, muddy lanes. As I wiped my feet down and dried them off, I was about to put my thick warm socks back on, then stopped, realizing I didn't need them anymore.

※

The following Tuesday, I joined Luang Pi Phop, Emiliano, and Peter for alms rounds to a much smaller village - one that could generously be called a hamlet. Again, it was dark, barely heading into the first inklings of pale dawn. We'd been on the main track for about a mile when our driver veered up a very steep path - one that could charitably be described as a goat track if the goat was drunk and didn't mind landslides. There was no sign, no trailhead, no indication that human beings had any business up there at all. It was one of those roads where the jungle closed behind you as the entrance disappears the moment you take it, as if the mountain itself was swallowing you up to keep its secrets.

We climbed slowly, steadily in the truck, the tires slipping now and then in the soft red mud, and I realized this wasn't a village in the usual sense. This was going to be a speck of a community, maybe a dozen rustic houses and a spirit shrine. When we finally reached the end of the track, we stepped out and began walking along a narrow ridge, the air thinner, cleaner, and brighter than it had any right to be. You could feel the altitude in your chest, and in your thoughts, both a little harder to hold onto.

Before we reached the first house, Luang Pi Phop stopped. He gently took my shoulders in his hands and with the grace of someone turning a dial to tune in a faint frequency, rotated me about forty degrees. "Look," he said softly, his eyes already reflecting what I hadn't yet seen.

There, across the wide, deep ravine, rising from a flat-topped mountain like something conjured from scripture, was a tree. Not just any tree! A colossus of the forest. It towered above every other living thing for miles. Gnarled and noble, its crown touched the waking sky, as the breadth of its canopy spread over everything else on that ridge-top, catching the first fire of morning. Blazing from behind like a golden halo, the sun began its climb creating a theatrical backlighting that Nolan only dreamt of. A few wisps of mist curled around its massive trunk like they knew they didn't belong higher. It was The Tree of Souls, not just from Avatar, but from every story ever told where something ancient, sacred, and alive waited for you to notice it.

My breath caught in my throat. I couldn't swallow. I couldn't speak.

"Amazing, isn't it," Luang Pi Phop said softly, his voice projecting a quiet and encompassing reverence. He sounded almost sorry, like he'd interrupted a prayer he didn't mean to overhear.

I nodded, unable to answer, because something in me had profoundly shifted. That tree wasn't just a tree. It was memory. It was history. It was power and it owned the wisdom of ages.

The grieving my soul had been tortured with was launched heart first into bass relief as I gazed upon its magnificence, while that hero of times past and present waited patiently across the ravine for all to understand. It had been there the whole time. Through it all. I couldn't look away as I burst into tears.

CHAPTER 10. CHIANG RAI AND THE GOLDEN TRIANGLE

I'm not who I was before the moon followed me across oceans. It's strange what changes when that same light hits us upon different ground.

Heading up to Chiang Rai, the northernmost province of Thailand, and home to the northernmost city of size. The provincial population hovers around 200,000, thus it is tiny compared to the urban hubs of Chiang Mai, Nakhon Ratchasima, Nonthaburi, or, of course, the behemoth Bangkok. Still, it punches above its weight historically: Chiang Rai was founded in 1262 as the seat of the Lan Na Kingdom, which makes it, like so many places in Southeast Asia, ancient enough to make American history an irrelevant footnote.

When I first started planning that leg of the journey, I didn't consider Chiang Rai all that much. I knew I'd swing through the area to check out the Golden Triangle, but my expectations were minimal. However, thanks mostly to the chorus of online tourist reviews declaring, "You only need a couple of days in Chiang Rai at the most; there's not much to do," - *that* made me wonder. In travel speak, that kind of disdain is often code for "I never got off the bus long enough to actually look around". That kind of clickbait dismissiveness piqued my curiosity. If most tourists say it's skippable, odds are good, it's the exact opposite. I delved a little deeper and what I discovered made me rethink everything. I decided I'd be spending at least a week there.

The best way to get from Chiang Mai to Chiang Rai - if you're not in the mood to rent a car or join the testosterone and adrenaline cult known as motor-biking - is a comfortable four-hour bus ride. I splurged the extra $2 for the V.I.P. bus, which came with reclining seats and air conditioning. The total fare for the ride was not "reasonably priced." It was downright cheap.

The journey was officially listed as 3.5 hours in duration, but thanks to a massive highway infrastructure project, a broad concrete snake on high-rise pylons being built on top of the old road, it's closer to four. This new elevated freeway was poised to bypass every small village and roadside noodle-and-snack shack in its path. I couldn't help but wonder what would happen to those micro-economies once the traffic sailed overhead. For now, though, the new highway looked like a public works mega-project powered entirely by human muscle and ingenuinity. It seemed like every able-bodied man, woman, and child in the province was out there mixing cement, hauling rebar, and building supports, none of it with the help of heavy machinery. It was surreal, impressive, and mildly terrifying all at once.

Chiang Rai Province is largely agricultural. Historically, that meant rice, tea, tobacco and, once upon a less-regulated time, opium poppies as far as the eye could see. That all changed decades ago when the government cracked down on poppy production and offered financial incentives and education programs to coax farmers into growing less narcotic crops. Today, roughly 70% of the region's population is part of what's called the "informal workforce," cultivating coffee, tea, pineapple, papaya, mango, jackfruit, rice, and wheat - with a nod to sustainable and environmentally sound practices. Which is adorable, considering the widespread use of spent crop burning. Between the smoke pouring out of northern Thailand and the bonus plumes drifting over from Laos, Cambodia, and Myanmar, the entire region turns into a post-apocalyptic smog machine come spring. Every year, the smoke sends thousands to the hospital and more than a few to the cemetary. Environmentally sound indeed.

My plan was delightfully vague: tramp around rice fields, tour tea plantations and find a waterfall or two to perch under in one of the region's many national parks. In other words, chill, relax, and let adventure do what it does best: sneak up unannounced.

The bonus? All those "you only need six hours to see Chiang Rai" reviews meant there would be fewer tourists clogging the paths and views. Anyone I did run into would be a traveler, not a tourist - a critical distinction. Travelers tend to carry curiosity and journals; tourists carry schedules and complaints.

But the reason I came this far north was the alluring temptation of the Golden Triangle. I wanted to stand at the nexus of three ancient countries - Thailand, Myanmar, and Laos - on a spit of Thai soil, and gaze across the Mekong as it heaved its brown muscle through the hills, carrying silt and centuries of the ghosts of millions of transactions both legal and otherwise.

Disembarking at the Chiang Rai bus terminal, roll-on in hand and daypack slung over one shoulder, I strolled away from the hawks, those savvy drivers aggressively stuffing gawking tourists and backpackers into seats at scalper prices. I needed a ride too, but I've learned a thing or two during my travels. You never grab a ride on the first go-round. That's when they smell fresh meat, circling like sharks about to launch into a frenzy.

I walked around the corner and made a tactical stop at the nearest 7-

Eleven. Gatorade. Snack. Curb. Smoke. I sat like a chess player waiting for the board to shift. My destination was a well-rated guesthouse, a few klicks away, not quite walking distance but doable if need be.

As predicted, the same tuk tuks and cabs that had just unloaded their human cargo returned for another round as the next buss-load emptied into the terminal. They were now circling back and pulling into the 7-Eleven for their own refueling: beer, pork rinds, smokes, and a lottery ticket for fantasy kicks.

One guy plopped down next to me with a smile that was 80% teeth and 20% "how much can I extract from you without triggering a diplomatic incident." He circled conversationally, then pounced. "You need a ride?"

"Sure," I said casually. "How much to Gita's Guesthouse?"

He quoted 150 baht, bless him. I laughed out loud and shook my head. "No thanks. I'll walk. It's only a few kilometers." I returned my gaze back to my phone, looking utterly unbothered.

He studied me like a math problem with a hidden trick, took a drag of his smoke and a long pull from his Tiger. "Okay," he said, dropping the price to 50 baht - the local's rate. I smiled, nodded, and we shook on it.

"You visiting family?" he asked as we stood.

"Why?"

"You act like local coming home," he said.

That made me laugh. I explained my strategy. He grinned wide and said, "You one of the good ones. Want a beer?"

And just like that, we were drinking lagers on the curb outside a 7-Eleven in northern Thailand like old pals. His name was Nom, and he turned out to be good company and a fun guy to hang with during my time in Chiang Rai.

Gita's Guesthouse, tucked along Kaoloi Soi 12, is technically a yoga retreat and though it's rated a modest three stars you'd never know it. Overflowing gardens, immaculate rooms, peace and quiet. The place had glowing reviews for being clean, central, and relaxing so I never understood the three star ratings, but it played well into my hands when making the reservation as my 8 nights in Chiang Rai would be uninterrupted with a relocation. I'm not exactly a yoga guy but I figured I might stretch into a class or two. At the very least, it looked like a perfect place to lay low and decompress. I would be slow traveling Chiang Rai so the idea of bouncing between accommodations like I did in bigger cities didn't appeal. Everything I wanted was within walking, biking, tuk tuk, scooter or Grab cab distance.

It was late in the afternoon, and I was feeling a little worn and frayed. My previous night in Chiang Mai may have included a little too much fun. After checking in and meeting the staff, I knew I'd be staying in for the night, post-dinner. Everyone at Gita's was warm and professional in that effortlessly Thai way that somehow makes you feel both pampered and humbled at once.

Room No. 7 was large and spotless. Spartan yet well-appointed. The bathroom boasted a large walk-in shower with excellent pressure and actual hot water, a true rarity in Southeast Asia, where "warmish" is usually as good as it gets. Realistically, that's all you need because it feels great compared to the heat and humidity that's your daily companion.

The room was modest, thoughtfully arranged, and, while the bed was therapeutically hard enough to realign a chiropractor, the place oozed quiet charm and no-nonsense comfort. Between the serenity, the creepers and flowers spilling over every available spot hanging on the grounds, and the friendliness of the staff, Gita's would definitely be a good base for the duration.

Once I unpacked, I wandered down the street and around the corner, an area I'd scoped out earlier from the back of Nom's emerald-city green, glitter-dusted tuk tuk. I'd spotted a clutch of neighborhood food carts just around the corner, drawing a crowd of locals which is always a green light. Dinner was stir-fried noodles with vegetables, a few perfectly crisped fried chicken legs and thighs, and a sack of mangoes, oranges, and a watermelon so heavy I carried it like a newborn. I ambled back to Gita's, ready to eat, stash, crash, and reset.

I flipped on the TV for some background noise with dinner, which quickly turned into entertainment in its own right. Thai soap operas are a psychedelic mess of glossy hair, sequined wardrobes, and melodrama so over-the-top, they make "Days of Our Lives" look like a stoic BBC documentary. Even without subtitles, I knew exactly what was happening: someone had stolen someone else's baby, poisoned a lover's soup, and was about to be run over by a pickup truck driven by their long-lost twin. I've long suspected these shows are Thailand's answer to Bollywood, and they're giving it a run for its rhinestone money.

I rose early to a fresh, sun-drenched morning, the grounds alive with birdsong. I enjoyed a healthy breakfast before heading out the door to explore. Chiang Rai is gorgeous. Broad tree-lined boulevards with sidewalks that aren't broken up at odd angles waiting for the unwary walker to twist an ankle. I stumbled across a painted path in blue, like a bike lane except for walkers, leading down a road lined with massive old trees, stately homes, a museum, a park and small businesses. The thoughtfulness of mapping out a well-defined path for the pedestrian was something I had not seen before in Thailand.

Chiang Rai is clean and tidy. Many of the houses I walked past made it clear there was serious pride in neighborhood and ownership. I made a two-hour circumnavigation of the area, going up this street, then another and another, taking note of the alleys from which the best smells wafted. Along one "major" artery I found a southern-style BBQ joint with a big hardwood pit out back. There were burgers and fries' shacks, noodles, soups, two fish restaurants and three pork fry places, a multitude of coffee shops and bakeries, of course a 7-Eleven. As an added bonus - a sushi bar that when I looked it up had rave reviews. My new neighborhood would do nicely.

I picked up a couple of munchies for the fridge back in my room and headed to the place down an alley where I first smelled the aroma of wood-smoke and saw a dozen glossy mahogany-red glazed ducks hung, ready for the cleaver. It was still early, around 9am, but it was packed with locals. Score! I pointed to the roast duck noodle soup on the picture menu. It was all in Thai, which meant that I had no idea how to pronounce what I wanted, and waited for transcendence in a bowl. I was not disappointed. A delicate yet deeply flavored ducky stock, the surface glistening with little floating bubbles of aromatic fat, a bed of thick, slippery rice noodles piled high, which raised the sliced duck above the soup, keeping the skin crunchy. Fantastic! A great breakfast and start to the day.

After duck and noodles, I stopped into a small coffee shop. I wasn't going to coffee up, but the speakers outside had the Ramones singing "*Gabba Gabba Hey*" - my kind of place. As I sat, sipping a ridiculously rich cappuccino, I watched local life stroll by. Mom's with strollers, older kids in their uniforms taking a snack break from school, the chef across the street sharpening his knives on a spinning stone; a fine wiry fellow with a deeply weathered face, his muscles taught like piano strings pulled a handcart loaded with vegetables, stopping every few yards as restaurateurs came out to refill their stocks for lunch and dinner crowds, everyone smiling, saying "Sawatdee kah" or "Sawatdee krab".

Finishing my java, I continued along my way for an hour, finding the Kok River (yeah, sure - insert joke here), more parks, a couple of schools with the gleeful sounds of recess-induced shouts of games and laughter merging into the sounds of lives being led. The small canals throughout the neighborhood where I was staying hosted bird life flitting in and out of the foliage.

I headed back to Gita's house for the afternoon. After a wonderful meditation session, I sat and read my newest bookstore find ("Lessons In Chemistry" by Bonnie Garmus) under a pergola that was covered with climbing vines and orchids. I whittled away a relaxed afternoon in peace.

As dusk fell, I headed out on foot to find the main drag - Phaholyothin Road - where the Saturday Night Bazaar lit the evening with magic. The night market had the reputation for high quality goods, featuring hand crafted clothing, leather and jewelry, local hill tribe crafts, a great food court, and quality art. It was about four kilometers down the way, but I'd already covered that ground that morning.

As I neared the market area, a busy lane with colorful hanging lanterns floating above the roadway, stretching down eight or ten blocks. Beautifully lit up, the main road had a festive atmosphere to it. Granted, Christmas was only a couple of weeks away and had been heartily embraced by commercial interests throughout Thailand, and yet the pictures I had scouted up on the web showed that even without a festive holiday season in full swing, the area was normally active and alight with shops open late from Thursday through Sunday, packed with people eating, drinking and shopping. An interesting thing to note about Chiang Rai with its much smaller tourism numbers is that this twenty-block zone of activity seemed to be mostly local-supported.

I found the night market, (that was easy) with its 4-block-long vibrant and fun walking street, lined on both sides with vendors. Those tied into side courtyards, also packed with vendors. Everything was lit up, the displays of goods beautifully put together with artful presentation. The quality of wares was evident. I took mental notes on items I'd pick up before leaving Chiang Rai and found my way through inner courtyards until I found the big food court with about 75 independent stalls according to my rapid count. It was time to crush the growling hole in my stomach and order up something delicious.

First up was a bowl of Malay-style goat's head soup (Sup kambing mamak) - something I had not come across so far in my travels. The owner must have liked me - or wanted to see if I'd flinch - because I got an eyeball, one of the prizes of this dish and usually reserved for someone special. It was better than delicious, it was sublime; a complex bowl of soup that hit all the right spots in flavor and body, masterfully cooked. The chef was eyeing me with her friends as I scooped up the eye, popped it into my mouth and gave her a thumbs up. She smiled and gave me a thumbs up back.

Next up was a Bahn Mi sandwich from a Vietnamese stall where I swear, they were pumping out the aroma of their baguettes with a hidden fan into the crowd. I had a Pavlovian response, immediately craving one. I ordered up a classic Bahn Mi with everything. The fantastic homemade liver pâté spread, pickled radish and onion, cucumber, green chili pepper, smoky marinate pork shoulder, fresh herbs and a bright dash of Maggi sauce made that sandwich sing. The crunch on that airy Vietnamese roll was ethereal, the fillings perfectly balanced and robust. After the first tester bite, I scarfed that sandwich down as if I hadn't eaten in a week.

After a little break I found a guy frying up small balls of dough with river prawn in them. They were lighter than air as I dipped them into a homemade red chili Sambal. Scorching sweet heat but with complex depth and flavor!

Last up was to search out some mango! Now I know you've had mango and what's not to love about mangoes. In Thailand I'm positive it's a crime to serve a bad mango. The mangoes in Thailand are the best I've ever eaten anywhere on the planet including in Mexico while sitting in the orchard where they were being plucked off the tree in front of me; those don't even come close to what Thailand grows. Dripping and pornographically sweet, creamy flesh with just the right texture. Simply pure candied, creamy mango dripping down your face and fingers with each bite. I tried to buy mangoes separately but the couple at the cart would only sell them with sticky rice, so I ordered two, and like I did several times before in Chiang Mai, when no one was looking, I tossed the rice with the sweetened condensed milk and devoured the mangoes on their own. I like rice, but I *love* the mangoes. I dream of them to this day.

Feeling full and ready for bed, I headed back out through the throng of people still shopping and haggling for goods along the pedestrian lane, to Phaholyothin Road, the one with the beautiful hanging lanterns. After a bit of good-natured jostling through the crowd, I made it to the main drag with the idea to head back the way I had come. But the voice in my head said "turn left, not right" instead. I listened and explored the blocks further along the way. What a series of glorious finds to behold.

A wine shop full of mystery brands; a raw silk shop where an older gentleman was hand-weaving scarves; an expat bar with a bunch of ruddy-faced dudes watching sports (I quickly passed that by); a smoke shop with big glass jars of loose-leaf tobaccos; a leather shop that smelled fantastic; a couple of massage parlors, an ice cream shop, a pharmacy and more.

It was there that I stumbled across a Chinese restaurant where, in the big pane window, cooks were pulling noodles by hand - one of the nirvana finds for foodies all over the globe. Then two doors down, an Indian restaurant where the aromas drifting out the door were magnificent, rich and complex. I knew I'd be spending time along this stretch of road until I had exhausted my options.

I was salivating but not hungry - an important distinction at all times but a very important line-in-the-sand in Thailand, where the smells alone could trigger lustful-addiction binge-eating like few other things can. But I'd already gorged myself at the food court, and I wasn't about to ruin a perfectly good future appetite by pushing it.

I turned to head back up the road, when a scooter came screaming down the sidewalk, clipped me like a bowling pin, and sent me sprawling. I didn't hear it coming. There had been too much ambient chaos - grilled meat sizzling, tuk-tuks buzzing by, a car honking like a wounded animal, music blaring from shops, somebody's baby crying close by, and that ever-present hum of every city alive at night.

What surprised me most wasn't the pain - I'd taken worse spills doing dumber things - but the pure, operatic rage that followed. Not from me. Not from the scooter driver, now laying dazed on the pavement next to the scooter, its wheels still spinning. No, the fury came from a tiny woman in a flowered dress who'd been lounging outside her massage parlor, cheerfully beckoning me in just a moment before.

She went full gladiator as she strode over like a general surveying a battlefield, and then - whap! - started smacking the helmeted rider's head like it was a percussion instrument. Every time the poor bastard tried to get up, she knocked him back down with the righteous fury of someone who's had more than enough.

I stepped in as my Buddha nature kicked into gear. I wasn't hurt, just scuffed up and slightly stunned, and the helmet-beating felt a bit... excessive. Massage-lady didn't see it that way. Even after I wedged myself between her and the scooter hooligan, she kept hollering past me like a street prophet with a grudge. Eventually, I got her to pause long enough for a truce. She grabbed my hands, inspected the scrapes like I was war-wounded and needed a field medic. Satisfied that I was mostly intact, she spun back to scream at the fallen rider some more.

That's when the rider stood up and removed *her* helmet.

"Oh God - Are you OK?" she asked, in perfectly crisp English, with a curious Thai-meets-Eton boarding-school accent you find in families with diplomatic passports.

I was immediately, and perhaps irresponsibly, smitten. She had long, silken black hair, a dazzling smile, and a look of genuine concern that made me feel like I'd just been hit by a very polite angel on two wheels.

Then scooter demon turned and shouted "MOM! *STOP!* It was an accident - the throttle stuck. I couldn't stop!" and pulled her still-screaming mother into a tight bear hug before the older woman could land another blow.

Mom. The woman beating her with a diminutive hand was her mother. The entire surreal crash then street brawl was suddenly cast in a much softer light. Maternal rage, Southeast Asian edition. It also meant mom spoke English just fine and had been screaming out earlier with Thai mom fury. Excellent. What a strange night!

Amanda - the scooter menace - apologized on loop, visibly mortified. She righted her scooter with an efficient flick onto its stand, then gently grabbed my wrist and guided me two doors down to the pharmacy where she unleashed a volley of rapid-fire Thai at the pharmacist. In under five minutes, my hand was cleaned, disinfected, and wrapped like I'd just finished a back-alley boxing match.

We returned to the scene of the crime. Amanda's mother sighed, tsked, and shook her head. A gesture that somehow managed to convey annoyance, affection, and at least three different kinds of disapproval at once. A universal mom move, language not required.

One minute we were on the sidewalk as Amanda apologized over and over again. The next thing I knew, we were inside a dim, cool cave of a bar soaked in Jamaican regalia. Posters of Marley, UB40, Yellowman and Steel Pulse, faded flags in red, green, and gold, hand-written graffiti from visitors past, all over the walls and ceiling, and a speaker system pumping Peter Tosh's "Don't Look Back" filled the air. They called it The Reggae Bar. No points for originality, but it worked.

Before I could orient myself, a large, ice-cold Leo appeared in front of me - remember kids: hydration is important, especially when it comes with a side of ice cubes and a shot of Thai rum. Then came the questions. Amanda. Nim, the bartender, a few local pool sharks with quick eyes and easy laughs and various other travelers who looked like they'd wandered in months ago and couldn't find their way out past the haze of ganja smoke. All of them wanted to know me. And what I was doing hand-in-hand with one of their favorite locals.

Where was I from? Did I like Chiang Rai? What had I seen?

I hated disappointing them. I'd just arrived the day before, but I was open to suggestions, which earned me another Leo. Then another shot of Thai rum slipped in, ninja-style. Then another. Then another. Somewhere in there, I think I learned someone's life story, lost a game of pool and I remember drawing the line at karaoke with a hard NO. But then again, with more rum and beer flowing, anything's possible. Even that.

Amanda was watching me the whole time. That smile, part mischief, part charm offensive, never left her face. She was alarmingly beautiful, dangerously witty, and unnervingly direct. Every time I looked her way, she was already looking back, like she was reading the next page of a book I hadn't written yet.

We became friends the way you sometimes do in places like this: quickly, without much pretense, with just enough rum to grease the connection. When she found out I was staying at Gita's, whose owner was an old friend of hers, she laughed. "I know how to find you," she said. "What room are you in?"

Over the next week, we became pool-playing, beer-drinking, rum-shooting co-conspirators. Through Amanda, I folded into the bar's unofficial traveler tribe. Swedes. A Palestinian whose best friend was Israeli. Ukrainians. Italians. A Kiwi who looked like he'd been shipwrecked for years. A couple of Canadians who swore a lot but meant well. Every single one of them turned out to be good people, curious, open, and absolutely floored when they found out I'd been a Buddhist monk up in the mountains.

They didn't believe me until I showed them photos: shaved head, robes, the whole monk-in-the-mountains package. Amanda burst out laughing, then kissed me full on the mouth. "*I've always wanted to kiss a monk!*" she said. That got a cheer from the peanut gallery and a free round from Nim.

The Reggae Bar became my nightly ritual. Days were for wandering, exploring, eating, pretending I was doing something meaningful. I mean I was - I was researching northern Thailand for this book after all. But the nights were for Leos, laughter, and conversations that didn't need to go anywhere. Chiang Rai was small. It had everything I wanted and more.

Even Nom Parawachitan, my tuk tuk buddy and unofficial night watchman, was a regular at the Reggae Bar. He never drank, not while on duty anyway, just sipped his soda water and swapped stories like a sober helmsman at a table of pirates. He took me under his wing without asking, the way older Thai men sometimes do when they've decided you're worth the trouble.

Nom filled in the gaps - history, rumors, the best places for real khao soi, the ones tourists never found. He made sure I got back to Gita's every night, often waving off my attempts to pay. The standard outsider fare was a flat 100 Baht or more, even for a ride barely longer than choking down a cigarette. I always gave him 40. It was the least I could do.

Somewhere along the way, I stopped feeling like an intruder. I wasn't local, not by any stretch, but I'd been absorbed into their orbit, invited in just enough to stop feeling like a traveler. A name, a barstool, a familiar face on the street. That's the closest thing to home you can ask for on the road.

The next day, after my visit to the White Temple (which, for the record, you'll find in the Wats Up Doc chapter), I retreated to my guesthouse for some high-level loafing back under the gazebo, book in hand and mind at ease.

But the night? I had plans. *Big ones.* It was noodle time.

I took a leisurely walk using a different path - one that was a little out the way - to explore other avenues and alleys. I was headed back to Phaholyothin Road to Lanzhou Noodles, where chefs were hand-pulling stretchy dough in the window. Talk about an excellent marketing strategy! If you've never had hand-pulled noodles, you're missing out on one of life's great edible miracles. Forget the instant ramen and mass-produced noodles you find in most restaurants that are made *en masse* at some factory sweat shop. This is high art in carb form.

Here's how it goes down: Start with a hunk of dough - fist-sized, thick as a banana. Grab an end in each hand and pull until your arms stretch wide, bounce it like a jump rope to keep the elasticity alive, then fold it, stretch it again. And repeat. Each pull and fold doubles the strands, each bounce coaxing the gluten gods to cooperate. You want them thin? Medium?ABde like a belt? It's all in the hands.

When the dough's been pulled to perfection, the chef rips off the ends like he's breaking apart edible shoelaces, fluffs the noodles like a magician revealing the trick, and drops the whole glorious mess into a wire basket and into alkaline water. Then: the cauldron lineup. Six massive pots, each with its own stock - beefy, porky, chicken, mushroom, a blend or veggie delight for those who disdain meat. Brothy, spicy, subtle. Customer's choice. Noodles into the bowl, wait a minute, then a ladle of molten heaven and your pick of meat and/or veggies.

Sounds easy? It's not. It takes years to pull noodles like that. More years to make the dough right. Even more to nail the stocks. This isn't fast food - it's kung fu with carbs and bones. Watching a noodle master do his thing from a few feet away turns dinner into theater. Lanzhou doesn't just serve food, they put on a show.

I ordered braised tripe and tongue salad. Delicious, yes, but deeply offensive to anyone raised on chicken tenders. While I waited for the main event, I soaked in the show, bowl after steaming bowl parading out of the kitchen to other, luckier mouths. It hurt. Not real heartbreak, but that childhood-grade ache. The Christmas Eve kind. The squirmy, irrational desperation of *please let it be my turn next*. Some feelings never outgrow us - they just throw on adult clothes and wait impishly for noodles.

Finally, it was my turn. My server arrived bearing a tray from heaven. On it, a bowl the size of a small basin, steam rising from broth glistening with flavor blobs of braised fat. Next to it, a plate of toppings that should have been gilded.

Fried pork shoulder. Braised beef short ribs. Wilted morning glory shoots. Scallions. A soy-marinated egg boiled to that sweet spot between jammy and firm. And chilies, red and green bird's-eyes, ready to torch your soul if you got cocky.

I looked at that table like a man seeing Nibbana in a bowl of soup.

She turned to go. I attacked it like an Olympic diver breaking the surface headfirst, no hesitation. My chopsticks and spoon were a blur, cartoonishly fast, and unapologetically noisy. Because yes, I've mastered the noble art of the noodle slurp - loud and proud. It's not just acceptable here. It's expected. It's how you say *"this is delicious"* when words are completely inadequate. And when food hits like that? Words are definitely inadequate.

The noodles were heavenly.

I'd gone with the normal size noodles - not too thin (those can overcook and dissolve into floppy starchy strands), not too wide (gut bomb territory). The right tender-to-chew ratio, a noodle Goldilocks would die for. The beef stock was a deep, soulful punch of flavor - rich, umami-heavy, a hug and a haymaker all at once. Instead of dropping the pork shoulder and ribs into the broth, I just gnawed on them directly like some caveman gourmand, dipping them into the broth for additional flavor bursts. The marinated egg and greens made it into the soup. Balance, right?

I was halfway through my bowl, completely entranced, when the waitress wandered over and asked if I wanted more soup or noodles. She told me they were free, just say the word. Of course, I said yes. I thought I'd get a little top-up. A tasteful encore. Wrong.

A whole second helping of noodles appeared. My stomach let out a foreboding groan. I stared at the bowl like a man staring up an 8,000-meter Himalayan peak, knowing he had only flip-flops and ego to get him to the top. I adjusted strategy: no longer a sprint, this was a slow, methodical noodle marathon.

An hour later, I tapped out. Not from lack of desire - just sheer physical inability. I couldn't do it. Even my food lust has a limit.

Things had slowed in the kitchen by then, so I waddled over to the pass and asked if I could film the chef pulling noodles. He grinned and asked, "You a Giants or A's fan?"

What. The. Hell?

He laughed. Said he'd grown up in both Shanghai and Oakland and claimed he could hear a San Francisco accent a mile away.

"Giants all the way, my man. And thanks for the noodles - they were perfect."

"C'mon! Billy Martin? McGwire? Canseco? The Catfish? Rickey Henderson?" Chef challenged.

"All legends, sure. But none of them touch Mays and McCovey. What about Will the Thrill? Best swing in baseball." I offered in retort.

There I was - 5,000 miles from home, stuffed to the gills with noodles, arguing baseball in a Chiang Rai noodle joint with a Chinese-American chef who'd memorized the '89 AL roster. The universe is strange and occasionally perfect.

"This conversation needs a beer or three." I asked him "What time are you off?"

"Ten minutes. Gotta brief the closers. Then I'm down - don't get many city kids in here."

Fifteen minutes later, Chu and I were at the Reggae Bar, trading stories over beers. Bay Area dive bars, playoff heartbreaks, noodle shop gossip. Football. Food. Life.

At one point, he asked me what my favorite restaurants in San Francisco were. I threw the question back at him. Back and forth we went, debating who had the best cioppino (Tadich's if you need to ask), Dungeness crab cakes, dumplings vs. taquerias and carnitas burritos, noodle broth hierarchies, and where to find the best late-night eats in the Mission. Eventually, I glanced at the clock on the wall.

It was 3:30AM.

The Reggae Bar, still buzzing, clearly didn't give a damn about the 2AM closing law.

When I asked Chu about his week, he said he was flying out later that afternoon. First to Shanghai to visit family, then to Lanzhou to spend a few weeks at the chain's flagship shop. The head chef was getting married, and there was no apprentice ready to step up. Timing's a bitch.

Still, before we parted ways, he leaned in, raised his bottle, and gave me the kind of sendoff that makes the world feel a little less large.

"Table 4's yours when you're back in town."

***

The next day, once the grogginess (OK - hangover) wore off, I grabbed one of the guesthouse's rickety bicycles and pedaled off toward the old clock tower, one of Chiang Rai's main attractions. It's big, ornate, and it's unapologetically gold. Blindingly gold. I checked that one off the list. I did see it again a couple nights later, lit up like Vegas-meets-Asian-overkill bling. There were hundreds of bats flitting around the glow, feasting on mosquitoes like it was an all-you-can-eat buffet. Following the balletic interplay of those bats was something special and something that everyone should see once in their life - it's quite an amazing show.

I was walking the bike along a sidewalk when I noticed a very narrow, grimy alley leading into what looked like a market. Curiosity won out. I locked the bike and followed the covered alley through the maze of stalls until it opened into a covered, sprawling wet market. This was Chiang Rai's culinary underbelly, and not a tourist in sight. This wasn't curated for Instagram; this was real. Fish, fowl, and meat were butchered on the spot. Vegetables and fruits - some familiar, some completely alien, piled high in a kaleidoscope of colors. The smell was strong. The energy was pure.

If I'd had access to a kitchen, I would've left with bags of protein and produce and whipped up a stir-fry. Instead, I sat down on a plastic stool in front of a food stall run by a young woman slinging bowls of noodles with greens and broth. Yes, more noodles - don't judge me. They're cheap, they're delicious, and they go with everything - especially hunger. I picked her stall out of the dozens slinging bowls and plates because three Thai police officers were eating there. Another travel tip: eat where the cops eat.

She didn't speak English, and my Thai was still limited to sub-toddler level, so I pointed at one officer's bowl and gave him a hopeful thumbs-up. He chuckled and, in broken English, asked where I was from. We managed a decent conversation in a language that was about 40% words and 60% facial expressions. The soup was fantastic. His buddies slid the condiment tray toward me and showed me how to customize the bowl like a local - fish sauce, vinegar with chilies, palm sugar, and crushed peanuts. I thanked them for their company and made my way back to the bike.

I rode around aimlessly, stopping to peek into a courtyard decorated like a North Pole Christmas explosion, fake snow, elves, reindeer, a Santa that looked like he had just survived a bar fight, and giant plastic candy canes marking off the path. Hallmark on mushrooms. Eventually, I found a peaceful park with a pond full of turtles, fish, egrets, and a fountain that shot water high into the sky like it was trying to pierce the heat itself. Taking a deep breath, I sat on the lawn and slipped into meditation.

That night I ventured back downtown and wound up forgetting dinner. Well, I didn't forget but I stopped in at the Reggae Bar ostensibly for a beer. And didn't leave until Nom dragged me out at 2AM where he unceremoniously dumped me at the gate to Gita's, laughing as he drove away. Oops! I meant to go grab a bite but Amanda and a few of her girlfriends showed up and that was the end of any other plans I may have thought up.

Mid-morning found me on the veranda with a huge bottle of fridge-chilled water, another Gatorade and more than a few aspirins rattling around in my system, I tried to ease into the day with anotherr book and some deep, contemplative self-pity. Something in the pages whispered that tonight called for Indian food.

Something rich, spicy, fortifying and healing. And luckily, I knew just where to find it. I texted Amanda who said she'd love to join me.

ACCHA Indian Restaurant was a block down from Lanzhou Noodles. I had spotted it during my initial night of wanderings, right before getting mowed down by Amanda. The aromas drifting from the ornately carved wooden doors were unbelievable.

I'd fallen in love with the incredible flavors of India's cuisine when I lived in London in the early 80s, playing in a punk band. At the time, the British culinary scene hadn't yet grown up. Marco Pierre White hadn't ushered in the modern wave of world-class British cuisine and Fergus Henderson wasn't even on the radar.

Back then, the best the UK had to offer were fish and chips (which, to be fair, were excellent) and steak and kidney pies (which sometimes weren't). Everything else was overpriced hotel fare or French and Italian spots I couldn't afford. But the Indian restaurants? My god, they were everywhere like taquerias in California. They were cheap, delicious, and smartly run with heavy meals served with loads of rice, lunch openings followed by a dinner service that ran late into the night to catch pub-goers stumbling out at 11PM with a buzz and a craving for a meal.

I got hooked. Hard. The spices, the sauces, I formed a lifelong bond with those dishes.

When I got back home to San Francisco, I went to my favorite bookstore on Clement Street to hunt down an Indian cookbook. The owner knew exactly what I needed and ordered me a couple by the legendary Madhur Jaffrey. A week later I picked them up, then spent months tracking down the right spices and teaching myself to make some of my favorite dishes from scratch. I even came up with a cast iron pan cheat for naan since I didn't have a tandoor. I still have those two well-worn books today.

Why am I telling you all this? Because I know Indian food. I know how it's supposed to smell, taste, and feel. When I stood outside ACCHA, with that heady aroma of cumin, coriander, cardamom, cinnamon, onion, garlic and ghee-brushed bread wafting out the door and glanced over the menu, I knew I'd found the real deal.

Surrounded by beautiful Indian design aesthetics, sitar music flowing softly through the room, Amanda and I got catch up about her life, which we hadn't delved into last night. Mainly because we had been busy drinking with her girlfriends. She'd been buried in work because one employee left and another got fired so the bar was a pressure-cooker blow off where personal issues dared not vent.

We poured over the menu together, but Amanda admitted she wasn't too familiar with Indian cuisine. I explained what each dish was but at one point she gave up.

"You order. I'll eat anything," she said, locking eyes with me, no blink, but a big smile. My pulse ticked up a notch. Game on.

The meal was spot-on perfect. We shared Madras lamb, tandoori chicken, a mushroom tikka masala, saffron basmati rice, and papadum with that glorious spread of spicy mango, hot eggplant, and mint chutneys. We added plain and onion naan, mango lassi, and a few cold Tiger beers. Every dish hit the mark. The curries were rich, complex, and spicy, just how I'd asked for it. Somehow, the naan stole the show: blistered and crispy on the outside, pillowy inside. The onion naan was even better, the allium sweetness coaxed out from slow sweating.

Ten stars. If the rating systems allowed it, I'd give eleven.

After dinner, of course, we wound up back at the Reggae Bar, where we ran into Pascal, a lovable Swiss lunatic on a quest to bicycle through the entirety of Asia. Many of the locals knew of the restaurant but had never eaten there. That changed quickly. After that night, ACCHA was going to be a regular stop for everyone in that circle. And deservedly so.

THE GOLDEN TRIANGLE

There are places in life that you know you'll never see again. When you have an idyll firmly planted in your brain, something that fired your imagination long ago, maybe in Boys' Life, High Times or National Geographic - and you finally get there, it is never quite the vision you cooked up, no matter how much YouTube deep-diving or measured hyperbolic research and study you do.

The Golden Triangle, for me, was one of those mystical places, almost a Shangri-la, a place steeped in so much mystery and history that it forces you to reckon with the truth that legend is borne from reality, with a vast time-frame in between, distorted and twisted, as fact flows into fiction.

The Mekong. The Dharma River. A legendary over 3,000-mile long river steeped in lore, rushing down from the high Himalayan Tibetan plateau, irrigating China, Laos, Thailand, Myanmar, Cambodia and Vietnam was, for me, such a place. It's more than a legend, more than a river. It's the aorta of a continent - the lifeblood for millions, generation after generation, living for the most part, deeply rural lives. Lives, where what we take for granted - continuous electricity, clean water, supermarkets and paved roads, as norms. Those social constructs that have no place, no voice in the daily reality for the generations of families for whom the Mekong has provided everything.

I was naive enough to believe that I would pull up to some remote Valhalla vista, see the countries, all of whom, in this region, produced, for a very long time, most of the world's opium, and gaze upon vast fields of colorful poppies swaying gently in the breeze. This imagined scene has not been true for over 40 years when Thailand, Laos and Burma (at the time) banned growing the flowers while also banning, under penalty of life in prison, or the merciful option, death, the production of opium. Myanmar is still in that dirty game (even though it's "illegal"), but crossing the border into Myanmar is a risky if not downright suicidal venture these days, especially as an American. Extra stupid points awarded if you're doing it just to get high.

I made it. I stood at the Thailand point under a huge golden Buddha, serenely gazing over the river, the Golden Triangle. I gazed upon the legend that is the Mekong and felt its history calling to me. I signed up for a longboat tour, climbed aboard, and drank ice-cold Lao Golden lagers with my new shipmates, as we cruised up and down the Mekong for a couple of hours, approaching Myanmar and then Laos at a discrete distance, while the tour operator narrated what we were looking at. All the while hip hop club music blared away over cheap scratchy speakers.

China (and one particularly money-mad, connected developer) along with the Laotian government, carved out a "special economic zone" across the musky and mighty Mekong. Rife with condo towers and casinos. The monstrosity across the river is ready, willing and able to take any rubes money - as long as you exchange your money for Chinese Yuan first. From the outside it all looked brand-spanking new, like the skyline of Miami or a shrunk-down Dubai. We were told that aside from the casinos, power was spotty, the food lousy at best, and services were almost non-existent. And when you really needed it? Like to transfer more money over from your Swiss bank account to pay your casino tab? The WiFi was almost always unavailable.

Myanmar, by contrast, boasted one dingy low-slung small casino on its riverbank, complete with camo-clad guards armed with huge military-grade automatic machine guns.

And then there's the legendary No Man's Island, agreeably owned by none, in the middle of the river between the three nations, where you can still sidle up and purchase opium if you dare. You have to purchase with gold due to IMF banking regulations geared at slowing the tide of drug money laundering in the region. Myanmar and No Man's Island are both off to the left as you look upriver, while Laos looms directly across the river from the Thailand side, its sparkling new skyline of high rise casinos and condo towers beckoning anyone dumb enough to believe in luck against a casino.

I was laughably naive to think I could go to Chiang Saen, slip into a dark storybook past of back-alley dens, pampered by the proprietor as I lay on a cot, a ceiling fan whirling above, chasing the dragon while gazing out, bleary, comfortably numb, upon the vast river that has fueled millions of lives for thousands of years, alongside my own pathetically immature foolish fantasy.

And yet, on the Thailand side, to which we were obliged to abide, was still, to a great extent, an innocent throwback. Sure, there was tourism development, but, and this is an important note, Thai style. Dozens of small stalls and shops selling tourist junk, T-shirts, elephant pants, and myriad small-bite food choices that all smell unfreaking believable! The Thais are smart. And they're not greedy. This seems to be interwoven into their DNA because unless you're an asshole with that big invisible sign saying "rip me off for being a rude tourist on the loose" you're golden. The idea of make a little, sell a little, and I don't need a Mercedes to be happy... the Thais call it Sabai and it's about as Buddhist as it comes.

The sun was going down, burnishing the Mekong bronze, the lights of the casinos across the river blazing to life. Humming The Stranglers "Golden Brown" to the world around me, I popped into the ever-present 7-Eleven, bought a pint of Johnny Walker Black, wandered back to the riverbank and sat on a log, listening to that timeless river flow by.

Because how many times in life do you get the chance to sip good scotch while gazing at a legend?

CHAPTER 11. PAD THAI AND OTHER GATEWAY DRUGS

Every meal is a love letter. The least you can do is read it with your mouth full.

Over the years and across many miles, many meals, I've learned a few things about food, and about myself through the glorious art of cooking. Yes, I said art. Not a task. Nor a chore. Not a life skill you begrudgingly pick up when your microwave dies. Cooking is an art form. One that reveals deep truths about humanity, or at the very least, why some people shouldn't be allowed near a spice rack.

Here's one of those universal truths: if you're just eating to live, you're doing it wrong. It doesn't matter how busy you are or how many unread emails are waiting for you. Food is a full-body sensory joyride - from aroma to flavor to texture to temperature. It's primal. It's sacred. And if you're shoveling sadness into your mouth while inserting a formula tweak in a spreadsheet on your phone, you might need an intervention. Feed yourself like you give a damn. Better yet, cook something that says I love you for someone else without having to say it out loud. And stop going to McBurgNugWrapAndZap! Seriously! That stuff will kill you with a side of regret and a garnish of colon cancer.

Thailand, blessedly, gets it. Thai people don't just love food, they worship it. And not just their own (though let's be honest, Thai cuisine owns its own celestial tier), but all food. These folks are culinary polytheists. You can be wandering a random soi in Bangkok and stumble across the best wood-fired pizza this side of Naples, a shockingly good shawarma joint, a killer ramen cart next to a French crepe wagon and someone deep-frying tarantulas because, hey, why not? I'm not saying you'll find traditional Inuit seal and roast puffin but give Bangkok six months and a craving and someone will figure it out.

This, of course, is not some uniquely Thai affliction. Plenty of cultures are just as food obsessed. Italians, for example, will go to war over who makes the best lasagna (it's whose grandmother is closest to the argument) and the French argue over who makes the best Cassoulet (It's always them). But the Thai people? They don't just love food; they worship at the altar with a kind of joyful all-in zeal that puts most foodies to shame. Cooking it, eating it, debating it, and sharing it, even if it's just a rickety sidewalk table and a plate of stir-fried something that would make a Michelin spy weep, they're in. You could be sitting alone, mid-noodle-slurp, and a local will wave you over like you're the long-lost cousin they've been waiting for. It happened to me more than once, and not just because I looked pitifully lonely.

And when you grasp that Thai food culture began over fourteen centuries ago and has been evolving ever since? Yeah, they've had time to work out the kinks. Your trendy fusion taco place that opened six months ago? The Thai solved that flavor and texture profile back in the fifteenth century. The taco place is merely catching up.

There's a saying in Thailand: "Thais eat eight times a day." They're not kidding and it's not an exaggeration. Those eight times a day? They're not full sit-down meals but more like a never-ending parade of delicious bits and bites in between life's other duties. A small bowl of something here, a fried nibble there, a bag of little sausages with shredded cabbage, Thai chilies, and lime tossed in for balance, and suddenly it's your seventh snack of the day and you're still going strong. They savor each bite like it's the last taste before the meteor hits.

You don't get bored eating like that. You settle into a few go-to cravings, but the real fun is in throwing out your culinary "*ewwwww*" gag reflex and diving headfirst into the unknown. And it's amazing what happens when most of what you feared to eat turns out to be delicious.

Over the course of a few months, I munched, slurped, and devoured my way through a sprawling buffet of Thai dishes, some familiar while others were completely new to me. A few didn't land (we'll get there), but several were revelations. And just when you think you've figured a dish out, boom, there's a regional variation that flips it on its head while still staying true to the heart and soul of the core recipe. Thai cuisine is like jazz: it riffs, it plays, it surprises.

THAI CUISINE GREATEST HITS

Let's begin with the one dish that even the most tragically unadventurous eater has heard of: *Pad Thai*, the international rock star of Thai cuisine, and the reason half the world thinks they've "done Thai food." You'll find it from Bangkok to Boise to Beaune, slung out of woks with wildly varying degrees of authenticity. When done right it's a masterclass in balance: the tart, semi-sweet tamarind sauce clings to silky rice noodles that have a toothsome bounce. Add a spritz of fresh lime, a mess of crunchy cold bean sprouts, green onions for brightness, and wonderful peanut nuggets bring the crunch.

You'll find Pad Thai loaded with wok-seared shrimp, chicken, or tofu for veg-heads. And while it may now be a global staple, Pad Thai has a strange history. Depending on who you ask, it was either A) invented in the 1930s as part of a national identity campaign - a unifying dish to rally around as Thailand tried to modernize and distinguish itself from Chinese influences - or B) it's actually Chinese, introduced by immigrants and slowly adapted to the Thai palate until it morphed into the dish we know today.

Both stories are true in the way history loves a paradox. The Chinese brought the rice noodles. But it was the uniquely Thai flair for sour-sweet-savory-bitter-spicy that made it sing. And here's the kicker: the rice noodles weren't just a culinary trend - they were a political and survival solution. Thailand was facing a rice shortage and grinding it into flour for noodles stretched the supply a lot farther than a pot of steamed jasmine ever could. Practical, patriotic, and delicious. That's Pad Thai for you.

Then there's *Gaeng Keow Wan* - green curry - which sounds innocent until it hits your tongue like a flamethrower disguised as a fragrant hug. This is the curry that smiles sweetly at you as it punches you in the esophagus. The base is a vibrant green curry paste, made from mouse-drop chilies (*lots of them*), galangal, lemongrass, kaffir lime zest and leaves, coriander stems and a host of other aggressive-yet-inviting aromatics. It's spicy, yes, but also bright, almost floral, and vegetal in that way only something this green and this unapologetically Thai can be.

Traditionally, it's made with fish balls. Bouncy, ocean-flavored spheres that are delightful once you stop overthinking the name. But like most Thai dishes, green curry plays well with just about any protein you throw at it - chicken, pork, beef, tofu, or shrimp if your cholesterol is too low. The heat, however, doesn't care who you are. It's coming for you.

One of the unsung heroes of this dish is the eggplant - not the kind your grandma slices into a tray of parmesan layers, but two Thai varieties that remind you the world is bigger than the produce section at Whole Foods. The tiny, bitter pea eggplants pop like caviar with a vegetal crunch, while the second one - the Thai green eggplant is firm and meaty, more squash than sponge. They both bring a texture that's utterly unique, like a stir-fry crashed a curry party.

And don't expect the usual rich stew-like body and texture here. Green curry is often thinner, more of a pour-it-over-your-rice affair than a stick-to-your-ribs consistency. Green curry is a dish that doesn't just flirt with your palate, it kicks down the door, leaving you sweating while smiling like an idiot, wondering if you should go back for seconds (*you should*.)

Tom Kha Kung (kung = shrimp) or *Tom Kha Gai* (gai = chicken) is Thailand's fragrant love letter to soup. Rich yet light at the same time, it has a wonderful balance between creamy coconut milk infused with lemongrass, kaffir lime leaves, lime juice, and the bold, earthy, peppery kick of galangal. Galangal, for the record, is not ginger, no matter how many Western recipe bloggers swear it's "basically the same." It isn't even close. Ginger is warm, floral and cozy; galangal is earthy, sharp and unapologetic. Tom Kha often uses straw or shitake mushrooms and if you're dining in a fusion-happy café in the West, you might also get bamboo shoots or water chestnuts tossed in.

The word Tom means "to boil," which is why all Thai soups start with Tom. Kha translates into galangal. This dish appears to have boiled its way into Thai culinary history sometime in the late 1800s, with the first known recipe showing up in an 1874AD cookbook. Trying to make an authentic version outside of Thailand, though is like trying to play a Mozart symphony with a kazoo and a YouTube tutorial. Kaffir lime leaves are elusive, galangal gets swapped out for ginger, and the balance - so integral to Thai cuisine - goes a bit sideways. Still, even a not-quite-right version of Tom Kha can transport you, if only briefly, to a place where soup is sacred and kaffir leaves are plentiful.

Continuing with soups, possibly the oldest dish in the Thai canon is *Tom Yum*. Emblematic of central Thai cuisine, this soup's history stretches back centuries, deep into the mists of culinary antiquity. It's such a cornerstone of Thai food culture that UNESCO recognized it as part of Thailand's Intangible Cultural Heritage. Not bad for what started as a peasant fish soup that was based off whatever the catch of the day was with veggies and herbs in a pot.

Tom Yum reflects centuries of ecological adaptation and that unmistakably Thai love for contrast: spicy, sour, salty, and sweet all dancing together in one bowl. How does it pull off that mouth-gratifying balancing act? With a lineup of flavor powerhouses: galangal, lemongrass, kaffir lime leaves, chilies, fish sauce, and tamarind in a fish-based broth, traditionally a clear one. Toss in whole-shell giant river prawns and a generous handful of fresh herbs, and you've got the historical blueprint for the dish.

But there are variations, not least being the modern addition of coconut milk for a creamy version. The creamy iteration is considered by traditionalists to be a bastardization of the heart and soul of the soup and is thus frowned upon by purists. However, that doesn't mean that changing things up now and again is wholly discounted.

Chefs use crab, fish, frogs, or eels, or a whatever-was-flopping-around-in-the-river-today mix. And somehow, all those ingredients in concert create a dish long believed to have natural antiviral and antibacterial properties. Galangal is a well-known anti-inflammatory, lemongrass an efficient detoxifying monster, and chilies? They set fire to your bloodstream in all the right ways. During flu season, Tom Yum becomes Thailand's unofficial cure-all. And I can vouch for that firsthand.

There was a beautiful Thai restaurant called Royal Thai, on a tree-shaded corner of Noe and Henry Streets in San Francisco's Castro District. I ate there once a month for years. The food was phenomenal, and the all-Thai staff were lovely people. One winter, I contracted pneumonia and was utterly wrecked. Somewhere between fevered delirium and a pharmacy's worth of meds, I realized I needed to eat. Unfortunately, everything sounded as appetizing as a pile of raw lentils.

Over the years I'd heard that hot, spicy and sour soups were good for illnesses, especially bronchial afflictions. That wisdom was born from the deeper knowledge of ancient Chinese herbal medicines. I asked my partner to pick up some Tom Kha Gai. I also requested that the chef crank up the heat. Once chef understood how sick I was, he made a judgment call: he swapped the Tom Kha for two orders of Thai-spicy Tom Yum, with instructions that I eat only that over the next two days and nights. So, I did.

I awoke the morning after the two-day soup prescription with a clear head, a clear chest, and while I still lacked energy, I no longer felt like I'd collapse just trying to make it to the bathroom to take a shower, something I hadn't managed in a week.

Was it the blazing Thai-spicy Tom Yum? Was it the drugs? Was it the bed rest? Probably all of the above in concert. But I like to think it was also something more: centuries of folklore and kitchen wisdom. Whether it was a soup-powered placebo effect or the real deal, I know one thing. It didn't hurt.

This next dish? Vegetarians and Vegans - you'll want to skip this part (your loss). It's all about crispy-skinned pork belly, known in Thailand as *Moo Krob*. It is wildly popular throughout Asia and in other parts of the world as well. Like in Mexico where chicharrónes are a ubiquitous snack everywhere you go. It's an ode to crispy, porky perfection and it's awesome! The origins of the method reside in the Guangdong province of southern China where it is known as siu yuk and is believed to have been perfected during the Qing Dynasty (which lasted a long time, from 1644 to 1912).

At some point, an amazing Chinese chef with a hell of a lot of time on his hands, found that if you put pork belly through a day-long process using multiple steps of cleaning, scoring, marinating and then boiling it in salt and vinegar, cooling, poking, basting, baking, cooling, drying, basting again, frying, cooling again, then re-baking; through this arduous process you wind up with an incredible pork wonderland of flavor and texture. Through this long and involved cook, the delight of moo krob comes forward: the contrasting textures bounce around in your mouth like a party. Ultra-crispy skin, followed by a silky layer of pork fat, then followed by a layer of sweet and tender pork meat.

Moo krob is used in a variety of ways (aside from shoveling it into your grateful mouth). Either as a stand-alone dish served with steamed rice and a dipping sauce or as an ingredient to other dishes, it is versatile in its application. Some vendors use it as the base for pad kra pao, or in a stir fry with Chinese broccoli (pad kana) in soups and curries. Its uses are as endless as it is delicious.

Larb - also found with the spelling Laab which is closer to its phonetic pronunciation, is the beloved culinary diplomat of Laos and is often touted as that country's national dish. Though it has long since crossed borders and planted flavorful flags across northern Thailand and throughout the rest of Asia under different guises, it remains very Laotian. This spicy, citrusy, savory minced meat salad has ancient roots in the Mekong River basin where food was less about plating and more about survival. Traditionally made with beef or pork, though chicken, duck, buffalo, mushrooms, or fermented fish may join the party, larb was a way of making use of every part of the animal; no waste, all flavor. The Laotian version is anchored in an Asian trio of fish sauce, lime juice, and toasted ground rice, giving it a bright and sour edge. But when the dish migrated south into Isaan - the northeastern region of Thailand - it took on bolder, spicier characteristics. Thai chefs began infusing it with assertive spice blends: cumin, clove, black pepper, cinnamon, prickly ash seeds - cousin to Sichuan peppercorn - and the occasional star anise thrown for licorice notes.

Texture is critical - this is not meat mush. Your protein choice is stir fried to a delightful crunch while roasted rice or puffed millet adds a nutty crunch, as crispy fried shallots play the role of salty confetti. Depending on where you're eating it (and how brave you're feeling), the dish may be enriched with coagulated cow or pork blood for depth and umami, though this component is often left out of raw versions to avoid, well, disaster. It's served either hot or cold, though always with a flurry of fresh herbs - mint, cilantro, and royal basil leading the charge - and accompanied by sticky rice, which acts as both utensil and fire extinguisher. And yes, larb can be spicy enough to make you rethink that first bite. But once the heat subsides, what lingers is complexity, history, and the unmistakable taste of a borderless dish that somehow manages to be both rustic and refined.

Pad Kra Pao (or *Krapow*) is Thailand's answer to the "*I need something fast, cheap, and delicious before I fall over*" culinary dilemma. A blistering-hot wok, some minced pork or chicken, a fistful of holy basil (which Americans often mislabel as

Thai basil - close, but no cigar), garlic, chilies, and a splash of soy and fish sauce, and boom - you've got Thailand's version of the burger, the taco, or the emergency slice of pizza. This dish is everywhere: from humble roadside carts to upscale food courts to your neighborhood Bangkok café with a cat on the counter. It's the national comfort food for people who are short on time but not on standards.

Historically, Pad Kra Pao didn't show up in Thai cookbooks until the mid-20th century, but it's firmly rooted in the country's wok-based stir-fry traditions introduced through Chinese culinary influence. The Thai spin came with the holy basil, kaphrao in Thai, which lends the dish its peppery, anise-tinged, borderline-electric aroma. Holy basil has a more medicinal kick than the milder sweet basil or the purplish Thai basil Americans are familiar with. That said, home cooks abroad can swap in Genovese basil, and while it's not quite the same, the high oil content gives it a similar aromatic punch.

The dish is served with steamed jasmine rice, not sticky rice, which is reserved more for the northern and northeastern regions. Pad Kra Pao is often crowned with a crispy-edged, runny-yolked fried egg (*kai dao*), because why stop when you can gild it with a creamy, eggy addition. It's traditionally eaten for lunch, the kind of thing you grab on your break and inhale in five minutes while sitting on a plastic stool in the shade of an umbrella on a busy sidewalk. But make no mistake - this humble stir-fry is a heavyweight, delivering heat, fat, umami, and herbal freshness in one deceptively simple plate.

Pad Pak Boong, or stir-fried morning glory, is one of Thailand's most beloved vegetable dishes - simple in preparation, but full of character. Known elsewhere as water spinach, morning glory is a leafy green with long, hollow stems and delicate leaves that create a satisfying contrast when cooked. The stems retain a light crunch, while the leaves wilt just enough to absorb the deeply savory flavors of the sauce. The dish is typically flash stir-fried in a very hot wok with a heap of minced garlic, fish sauce, oyster sauce, fermented soybean paste and ripe red Thai bird's eye chilies. The result is a savory, slightly sweet, and spicy profile that's bold without being overpowering.

While fresh morning glory is ideal, spinach can work in a pinch, though the texture and flavor won't quite match the original. Bird's eye chilies, which are increasingly available in markets in the U.S., add a clean, sharp heat. They dry well and can be stored and re-hydrated when needed, making them a useful addition to any pantry if you enjoy Thai cooking. Or simply want to light your mouth on fire.

For me, Pad Pak Boong became my favorite vegetarian dish, thanks to the interplay of texture and bold flavor. It's often served as a side but stands confidently on its own, especially when served with a scoop of jasmine rice. There's something deeply satisfying about its balance - the earthy, yet sweet greens, the salt and heat of the sauce, and the brightness of the chilies all working together in harmony. It's a reminder that sometimes the most unassuming dishes are the ones that stay with you longest.

Panang curry is one of Thailand's most distinctive curries - a gently spiced, deeply flavorful dish that brings together warmth, sweetness, and a subtle nutty richness. It belongs to the red curry family but sets itself apart with a generous use of ground peanuts, which lend both texture and a mellow, rounded flavor. The curry paste is an intricate blend, traditionally made with two kinds of dried chilies - fiery bird's eye and the milder, slightly sweet prik lueng, a type of Thai banana pepper. These are combined with galangal, lemongrass, lime zest, garlic, shallots, toasted coriander seeds and mortar-pounded stems, cumin, shrimp paste, and salt. Peanuts are pounded in with the rest, not just as a garnish but as a defining ingredient in the paste itself. Think curry with peanut butter.

Panang curry works with a wide range of proteins, including beef, pork, chicken, duck, lamb, or game meats, each absorbing the curry's rich profile in a slightly different way. What makes this dish especially unique is the absence of added stock or water, instead, coconut milk is used, giving the curry a thick, velvety consistency. Palm sugar adds a gentle sweetness, while fish sauce deepens the savory, umami notes. Finely sliced kaffir lime leaves are often stirred in toward the end, their exotic citrusy brightness balancing the richness of the sauce.

Served with jasmine rice, Panang curry is a satisfying meal, particularly when it leans into its natural heat. Despite its depth, it never feels heavy or overwhelming. Instead, it's a dish that reflects the careful layering and balance that defines Thai cuisine: spicy, creamy, aromatic, and deeply comforting.

Massaman curry is one of Thailand's most unique and quietly complex dishes - another gently spiced, slightly sweet curry that reflects a blend of Thai technique and its Muslim culinary heritage. The warm, golden color comes from turmeric and toasted spices, and unlike many of Thailand's fiery red or green curries, Massaman leans into a subtler aromatic profile. It's thought to have originated from Persian-influenced Muslim communities in southern Thailand, particularly through connections with neighboring Malaysia, and it has remained a fusion dish ever since - distinct from, but still very much a part of Thai cuisine.

The paste is built from the familiar Thai base - galangal, lemongrass, garlic, shallots, coriander seeds, shrimp paste, and bird's eye chilies - but what sets it apart are the additions that reflect its Muslim roots: cardamom, cinnamon, cloves, star anise, cumin, nutmeg, bay leaves, and mace. These ingredients aren't found in other Thai curries, and their inclusion gives Massaman its mellow warmth and slightly sweet, almost dessert-like undertone. Roasted peanuts are another key element, offering a soft crunch and a richness which complements the creamy coconut milk base.

Chicken is the most common protein used, and it pairs well with the gentle spices, but I tried a version made with duck that was exceptional - the slight gaminess of the meat played beautifully against the sweet sauce. Massaman is typically served with steamed jasmine rice, though it's also delicious with roti or naan.

Compared to the intensity of other Thai curries, Massaman is a welcome change of pace - comforting, nuanced, and deeply satisfying without overwhelming the palate with heat. It's a dish that invites you to slow down and savor each bite, a reminder that not all flavor needs to shout to be heard. It's also refreshing in the way it doesn't light your face on fire while the rest of your body erupts into a flop sweat.

Som Tum, the iconic green papaya salad, is a vibrant and refreshing dish with deep roots in Lao and northeastern Isaan cultures. Though it has since become a staple throughout Thailand and much of Southeast Asia, its origins again trace back to Laos, where it has been part of the culinary landscape since at least the mid-18th century. Over time, the dish has evolved and adapted to local tastes, with each country - and often each region - adding its own signature variation. In Thailand, Som Tum has taken on a special prominence, balancing bold flavors, brightness and fresh textures in a way that reflects the essence of Thai cuisine.

Som Tum is made from finely shredded green papaya, which has a crisp texture and a neutral flavor that absorbs the punchy dressing. The salad is prepared in a large stone mortar and pestle, allowing the ingredients to be lightly bruised together, releasing their juices and melding flavors. Common additions include garlic, bird's eye chilies, roasted peanuts, dried shrimp, cherry tomatoes, holy basil, long beans, and shredded green cabbage. The dressing is a carefully balanced combination of palm sugar, fish sauce, and lime juice, resulting in a dish that is simultaneously spicy, sweet, salty, and sour.

Som Tum is served alongside sticky rice, and it pairs well with grilled meats or simply eaten on its own. While its freshness is part of the appeal, it's the interplay of textures and temperatures - crunchy papaya, warm rice, cool herbs, that elevates it. Depending on the region and the chef, the heat level can range from mild to bracingly intense, defining what Thai-spicy means, but even at its spiciest, there's a clarity to the dish that keeps it light and invigorating. More than just a salad, Som Tum is a reflection of local ingredients, traditional preparation, and the enduring appeal of bold, harmonious flavor.

Poh Pia Tod, Thailand's crispy fried spring rolls, are a beloved street snack and appetizer found just about everywhere, from bustling night markets to restaurant menus worldwide. Light, golden, and satisfying, these crunchy parcels are typically eaten on the go or as a shared starter, offering a savory contrast to the bold, often spicy main dishes that follow. While the exact origin of the spring roll is difficult to pinpoint, culinary historians trace its beginnings to China's Tang Dynasty (618–907 AD), where early versions likely evolved from flat, fried scallion pancakes. Over time, this concept spread throughout Asia, adapting to local ingredients along the way.

In Thailand, Poh Pia refers specifically to the thin, delicate rice-flour wrappers used to encase the filling, distinct from the thicker, wheat-based wrappers used in Chinese rolls. Poh Pia Tod are typically vegetarian, filled with a mixture of finely shredded vegetables such as carrots, cabbage, onions, and mushrooms, often including black fungus for both flavor and texture. Most versions also feature glass noodles (bean thread noodles), which give the filling a soft, springy quality. While pork is sometimes added for richness, especially in home-cooked or regional variations, the vegetarian version remains the most common and widely enjoyed.

The beauty of Poh Pia Tod lies in their versatility. Each cook adds their own twist, whether by adjusting the vegetable mix, seasoning the filling differently, or pairing the rolls with a signature dipping sauce - sweet chili, tamarind, or even a vinegar-based blend for contrast. The widespread popularity of spring rolls across Asia has led to a variety of styles that are now associated with different cultures, from Vietnamese chả giò to Filipino lumpia. Yet despite their global reach, Thai-style spring rolls remain distinct in their balance of lightness and flavor.

Sai Krok Isan, the fermented pork and rice sausages of northeastern Thailand, are one of the country's most satisfying street food snacks. The small, round sausages - typically about the size of a little ping pong ball - are made with a blend of ground pork, cooked rice, garlic, salt, and regional spices, each vendor adding their own signature twist. What sets them apart, though, is the fermentation process: traditionally, the stuffed casings are left to open-air ferment for anywhere from one to a few days. This creates a gentle tanginess and a slightly funky, savory depth that pairs perfectly with the charred smokiness from hardwood grills.

The use of fermentation isn't just for flavor - it's also a time-honored method of preservation that's well-suited to hot climates. Today, Sai Krok Isan are found throughout Thailand, but they remain especially popular in the north and northeast where they originated. Whether you're wandering through a busy Bangkok night market or exploring a quiet village roadside stand, chances are good you'll come across a cart sizzling with rows of these juicy links.

They're typically served in sets of three to six on a skewer, accompanied by a handful of raw accompaniments meant to be eaten together in alternating bites: freshly sliced ginger, crunchy cabbage, and fiery bird's eye chilies. This combination creates a perfect contrast - cool and spicy, savory, crisp and chewy - and helps cut through the richness of the sausage. It's an experience meant to be eaten with your hands, with no pretense, just the joy of tangy earthy flavors enjoyed on the move.

You'll often find Sai Krok Isan alongside a variety of other Thai sausages - herbal, spicy, grilled, or smoked - allowing you to sample the full spectrum of Thailand's sausage culture. But there's something about the fermented complexity of

Sai Krok Isan that keeps you coming back: they're bold but balanced, humble but unforgettable, and as deeply tied to place as any dish can be.

Pad See Ew is one of Thailand's most beloved comfort foods - a smoky, savory stir-fried noodle dish made with wide, flat rice noodles that soak up flavor like a sponge. The name translates simply to "stir-fried with soy sauce," and that's what gives this dish its signature taste. At high heat, dark soy sauce caramelizes against the hot surface of the wok, creating telltale reduced and intensified flecks on the noodles, visual proof of the dish's rich, slightly sweet depth. It's typically made with Chinese broccoli or other sturdy greens, garlic, and a protein like chicken, pork, or tofu, though beef and shrimp are common as well.

The texture is a huge part of Pad See Ew's appeal. The broad rice noodles - similar to Chinese chow fun - are soft and silky but with just enough chew to hold their own against the crisp vegetables and seared protein. When done well, the dish achieves a balance between smoky, salty, and savory, with the soy sauce marrying the ingredients into something greater than the sum of its parts.

Though deeply Thai in its current expression, Pad See Ew also has Chinese roots. The method of stir-frying noodles in a hot wok originated in China and spread across Southeast Asia through centuries of migration and trade. In fact, many Thai noodle dishes owe a debt to Chinese cooking techniques, which were seamlessly woven into the local culinary tapestry. Versions of this dish, with regional tweaks, appear in Vietnam, Malaysia, Indonesia, and beyond, adapted to local ingredients and tastes.

In Thailand, Pad See Ew is an everyday staple, found at street carts, casual eateries, and in refined restaurants. It's quick to prepare, satisfyingly hearty, and endlessly adaptable. Whether grabbed on the go or served as part of a larger family meal, it's the kind of dish that manages to be both simple and deeply comforting, hitting all the right notes with just a few well-chosen ingredients.

Khao Pad, or Thai fried rice, is another humble but satisfying dish that stands apart from its Chinese and Japanese counterparts thanks to its use of jasmine rice and the unmistakable influence of Thai herbs and seasonings. The word khao means rice, and pad means stir-fried, but unlike many other Asian fried rice dishes that use either Basmati or other long-grain rices, Khao Pad is built on the delicate, aromatic foundation of jasmine rice, a variety native to Thailand which adds a subtle floral note and light fluffy texture even after stir-fried.

You'll find Khao Pad everywhere. From roadside stalls to family kitchens to casual restaurants, and it's endlessly customizable. The most traditional proteins are chicken, pork, or prawns, but you can ask for crab, tofu, or beef depending on your preference. Regardless of the protein, the dish includes egg, garlic, green onions, and tomatoes - the latter being something of a signature Thai addition, rarely found in other regional versions of fried rice. The tomato adds both color and a bright acidity that balances the saltier elements of the dish.

Seasonings are used with restraint but purpose: a splash of soy sauce, a touch of palm sugar, a dash of fish sauce (*nam pla*), and if you're in the mood for heat, Thai chili flakes or a spoonful of chili sauce. Everything is tossed together in a searing-hot wok - often in less than a minute, until the egg sets, the rice is slightly crisped.

It's served with traditional garnishes that provide a cooling contrast to the wok's smokey heat: slices of fresh cucumber, wedges of fresh tomato and lime, sprigs of cilantro and green onion, and often a small dish of phrik nam pla, the spicy-sour dipping sauce made from fish sauce, sliced Thai bird's eye chilies, lime juice, vinegar-marinated garlic, and shallots. This adds a sharp, tangy kick you can dial up or down depending on your taste. BTW: You should add a dash of phrik nam pla onto almost all Thai dishes because it will give a blast of authentic Thai flavors and it's always available on carts and restaurant tables.

While Khao Pad is a quick, unpretentious meal, there are elevated versions too. In one particularly memorable version I tried, the cook used preserved yuzu, much like North African preserved lemon, which gave the dish a citrus punch that lingered on the palate and completely changed the tone of the rice. It was bold, bright, thoroughly Thai, yet an excellent example of how even a modest dish like fried rice can surprise you.

Khao Niew is sticky rice. It is ubiquitous throughout Thailand and is much a culinary staple as it is a utensil. As mentioned before, it is known as glutinous rice though there is no gluten in it. It gets that description because it becomes a little sticky and chewy when cooked properly. This species has been cultivated in Thailand for centuries, especially in the north where to this day it is a staple of almost every meal.

Cooking sticky rice uses a different method from other grains. The rice is first soaked in water for several hours which softens the grains and makes them sticky. Then the rice is drained and steamed in a bamboo steamer called Khao Niew Krua. Once it is cooled and served, locals often use it as a scoop for curry dishes.

Khao Niew Mamuang - mango sticky rice - is Thailand's ubiquitous, beloved dessert. It's a simple yet indulgent combination of ripe mango slices served atop sticky rice that's been dressed in sweetened coconut or condensed milk. You'll find it on dessert menus, at street stalls, in night markets, and in home kitchens throughout the country. The dish is remarkably consistent no matter where you try it, and while recipes may vary slightly in sweetness or presentation, the core components are always the same: glutinous rice, sweet coconut milk, sugar, a pinch of salt to bring out the depth of the sweetness, and of course those perfectly ripe Thai mangoes.

The origins of mango sticky rice dates back to the late Ayutthaya period (roughly the 18th century), when tropical fruits like mango were first incorporated into desserts. Over time, this pairing of juicy fruit and chewy rice evolved into a quintessential warm weather treat, eaten especially during mango season (typically April to June), when the fruit is at its peak: golden, fragrant, and absurdly juicy.

Personally, while I can appreciate the cultural significance and texture contrast the dish provides, I never fully fell for the combination. I like sticky rice well enough, but for me, pairing it with mango and condensed coconut milk dulls the vibrant, sun-ripened sweetness of the fruit. More often than not, I'd find myself quietly nudging the rice aside once no one was looking, laser-focused on the mango, which was all I really came for. Still, the popularity of the dish speaks for itself, and when everything is in perfect balance, the slightly salty rice, the sweetness of the coconut milk and the juicy fruit, it's easy to see why it's such a crowd favorite.

Those are just a handful of the classic Thai dishes you'll encounter at nearly every Thai eatery around the world. From humble street carts and bustling food courts to elegant white-tablecloth restaurants. Whether you're wandering through the alleys of Chiang Mai or sitting down at your neighborhood spot back home, these dishes form the foundation of a cuisine that is vibrant, layered, and deeply rooted in both history and regional identity. Thai food is far more than the sum of its flavors. It's a reflection of the country's culture, geography, and spirit. I encourage anyone with a curious appetite to explore beyond the familiar staples, try something unexpected, and taste firsthand why Thai cuisine continues to be celebrated as one of the world's truly iconic culinary traditions.

But there are also a few so-called "classics" I don't care for, and of course, since food, like music and art is incredibly subjective, take the following with your own grains of salt. Chief among them, the much-touted northern Thai darling: *Khao Soi*. Heralded as the pride of Chiang Mai, this curry-based noodle soup is the region's culinary prom queen. I tried it before leaving the U.S., wanting to familiarize my pallet with a dish I'd never ordered, as part of my pre-departure research (i.e., eating my way through Thai takeout), and my first encounter was underwhelming to the point of offense. On paper, Khao Soi is interesting: silky noodles swimming in a complex, spiced coconut curry broth, topped with a crispy nest of fried noodles for a dramatic textural contrast. What could go wrong? *Everything*, apparently.

The version I tried back home was a crime against both soup and noodles. A gritty, under-seasoned curry sludge - courtesy of what must've been a Costco-sized jar of curry powder and a ladle of cornstarch - sat like a muddy swamp in the bowl. The wet noodles clumped together like overcooked tagliatelle that had not been stirred, while the fried noodles, meant to bring crunch and flair, had all the charisma of cardboard. The whole thing had the mouthfeel of regret and the flavor profile of apathy. It was a culinary disaster. I left the restaurant feeling betrayed and mildly angry at the chef, and the Yelp reviewers who gave it five stars.

Traveling through the Chiang Mai and Chiang Rai regions I figured I owed it to the culinary gods, or at least the northern Thai aunties, to try this legendary dish on its home turf. Maybe I'd just been duped by some hungover line cook in rural Washington. Maybe the real Khao Soi would redeem itself and rise gloriously from the ashes of my skepticism. I approached the experience like someone giving an ex a second chance: wary, side-eye engaged, bracing for disappointment but secretly hoping magic would strike. After all, this was northern Thailand's national treasure, their edible ambassador. Surely it had more to offer than gluey noodles and pasty curry-sludge sadness. I was ready for revelation and confirmation.

What was I looking for? Not much. Just a bowl with a broth that had depth and balance, something that didn't taste like curry powder dumped into canned stock by a cook on autopilot. I wanted noodles that weren't congealed into one unified lump by impatience, and topping noodles that could hold their crunch for more than a ceremonial dunk in the soup. That's the whole pitch, right? Silky meets crispy, rich meets bright.

Up in Chiang Rai, I made my way back to the back-alley restaurant, which was really a converted garage with plastic chairs and zero pretense. I'd stumbled on it earlier in the week, lured by a street-side A-board advertising duck noodle soup and the kind of intoxicating aromas that make your stomach negotiate with your feet. Tucked away a few blocks from my guesthouse and buried down an alley, the place had a thick chopping block so worn down from decades of duck and pork carnage, it was a countertop canvas of the restaurant's history. That first bowl of crispy duck noodle soup had been incredibly perfect - rich, layered, soulful and extremely ducky. This wasn't the kind of spot tourists wandered into. I was the only foreign face there and got a warm, almost amused smile from the cook, like I'd passed some kind of unspoken test. Packed with locals again, just like before, it checked all the right boxes. If any place was going to redeem Khao Soi, this had to be it.

My second time around, I ignored the sultry siren-song of the duck, which practically quacked from the kitchen, insisting I order it again. It nearly worked - my stomach was already clearing space. But I stood firm and ordered the Khao Soi. My theory? If this place could craft a duck soup with that kind of depth and precision, borderline transcendent, then surely they could nail anything on the menu, including the elusive Khao Soi.

And they did. They really did.

The broth was light but layered, complex without being muddy. The curry notes were warm and fragrant, floating above a clean, yet savory stock base, with whispers of galangal and mint that played delicately on the nose and the palate. It was lightly spiced, a minor miracle in a country where "mild" still means "have fun sweating through your soul."

The rice noodles? Silky, tender, and perfectly slippery, with just enough chew to keep things interesting. The crunchy noodles - hallelujah - actually crunched. No sad, soggy toppers here. Each bite snapped with texture. It was, by every metric, a perfect bowl of Khao Soi.

And yet... it didn't convert me.

As much as I admired the execution, I couldn't get behind curry as a soup poured over noodles. There's something about the combo that feels inherently off to me. Maybe it's a texture thing (which is odd since I adore Pho), or a flavor delivery issue. I don't know. I've repeatedly wracked my culinary mind and can't figure what about it doesn't work for me. All I can say is that even in its most elegant, balanced, technically flawless form, Khao Soi still didn't win me over.

As the old saying goes 'to each their own weird kinks.' OK - yes, I made that up. However, what I've come to accept, as a sommelier and through years of cooking and chasing tastes across continents - is that sensory pleasure is wildly, unapologetically subjective. If your happy place involves White Zinfandel paired with pickled herring with a sprinkle of chocolate shavings? Great! Go for it. We all have our culinary soft spots, and one person's comfort food is another's gag reflex.

So, while Khao Soi isn't for me, I get it. I can see the appeal, especially after a long night knocking back beers and shots until you start mistaking tuk tuks for unicorns. In that state? Yeah, bring on the salty, noodley, crunchy-curried bowl of belly-filling and alcohol-absorbing goodness. For my palate though, it'll always be the soup equivalent of a drunk dial: momentarily satisfying, deeply confusing, and better left out.

Pad Thai. The dish with a variability range as wide as the A23a iceberg. Most of the time, it's dirt cheap (we're talking a buck a plate) and does its job admirably: gut filler with a Mr. Peanut smile. I had plenty that were perfectly edible, even tasty, but I kept craving more. More texture, more contrast, hot noodles, refrigerator-cold sprouts, a sharper lime zing, noodles that didn't feel like they'd been merely the vehicle for sauce, and peanuts that delivered crunch.

Here's the thing. Pad Thai in Thailand feels like a menu obligation. The cooks make it because tourists expect it, not because they're dying to show off their wok skills. Meanwhile, back in the States? Pad Thai is treated like sacred culinary scripture. Most Thai restaurants there put real pride into it, and it shows. Ironically, the dish that made Thai food famous abroad often ends up being the most forgettable in its home base.

I discovered something else regarding Thai chefs and its cuisine. Presentation, or more specifically, the lack of presentation. That extra flourish, the artful plate design, the delicate sauce swirls and dots, the vertical food stack with microgreens adorning the peak like it's auditioning for Cirque du Soleil. At most of the places I ate, it was "here's your food, now eat." And hey, from street carts? Fair enough. You're getting a paper plate and a low stool (maybe) - nobody's expecting edible microgreen confetti.

But restaurants? Indoor restaurants with chairs that don't fold? Still, for the most part, no dice. Thai food is dished out like Grandma's been running the kitchen since '68 and she's got zero time for camera-ready nonsense. A scoop here, a ladle there, now move along. That of course is not true for all venues. I had some dishes that were both inspiring and beautiful, but that is not the norm. And no, I didn't take many social-media-ready pictures. Food is for eating.

Strangely, other cultures do a better job prettifying Thai food than the Thais do. In America we want our meals to not only be delicious, but to perform and entertain as well. We need drama with our dinner. We want our plates to look like they studied under both Eric Ripert and Jony Ive and graduated with honors.

The Thais, on the other hand? They don't seem to care what the dish looks like. It's food, not a freakin' Monet. You eat it, you don't hang it on a wall.

In the U.S. and in other cultures as well ... (ahem, France), we treat food like performance art. Dishes look like they were curated by a design team with mood boards. In Thailand? If the food's good (and it almost always is), don't stare at it. Shovel it into your face. Presentation is for people with time to burn and a social media addiction. Thai cooks aren't trying to impress your followers. They're feeding you. There's a difference.

And yet, despite their "don't-look-at-it-just-eat-it" culinary ethos, the Thais have a voracious appetite for cuisines from all over the world. They're global gourmands with no borders on their palates. Fancy an Argentinian steak the size of the table? So do they. Those places are packed. Sushi bars? Wall-to-wall with chopsticks flying. Italian joints? You better have a reservation and a bribe. The French restaurants? Fully booked, even if all you're getting is a thimble of duck foam on a smear of pomegranate disappointment.

One Tuesday morning I ventured out for a full English breakfast because nothing screams vacation like blood sausage and fried bread at 8AM. I'd seen a place hyped in a local foodie newsletter and showed up early, thinking I'd beat the rush. Nope. I waited 45 minutes behind a crowd of ravenous Thai customers all jonesing for beans on toast and broiled tomatoes.

And it's not just Irish breakfasts. American burger spots, Indian curry houses, real-deal Mexican taquerias, British fish and chips - these places are consistently packed. I once walked past a Russian restaurant (yes, *Russian*, not exactly known for lighting the culinary world on fire), and it was full on a Wednesday night. The menu? Borscht, mushrooms and boiled meat. And the Thai crowd? Smiling, laughing, devouring it like it was a holiday dinner. It wasn't. I checked. I don't know what kind of witchcraft was happening in that kitchen, but clearly someone cracked the code on cabbage and potato-based happiness.

That's the thing about Thailand, about food, about people, about life there. It's not about perfect presentation or Michelin-starred sommelier pairings. It's about joy. About nourishment. About eating something good while laughing with friends and family or sitting on a plastic stool by yourself, sweating through your shirt and wondering how a $1 bowl of noodles just made an ethereal deity come to life on your tastebuds.

Thais don't fuss over the abstract. They live in a deeply practical kind of grace. If the food is flavorful and balanced - it's good. If it makes you smile or sweat or sigh with pleasure, it's doing its job. No one here is posting selfies with their curry. They're too busy enjoying it.

And that taught me something. For all our Western obsession with perfection - plating, prestige, elevated experiences - we often miss the point. Food is supposed to feed you. It's supposed to root you in the now. It's a kind of mindfulness that doesn't come from a yoga mat or an app. It comes from a spoonful of something delicious and real, handed to you with a smile.

So, whether it's a mango that needs no rice, a Khao Soi that still doesn't win you over, or a braised Russian mushroom stew on a humid Thai night, what matters is that you showed up hungry with an eye towards exploration.

Show up. Taste. Honor what others love by trying a bite, even if it's not your thing. Because in the end, that exploration is the real feast.

CHAPTER 12. DÉJÀ CHIANG

*You don't compare countries; you just trade one set of absurdities for another.
The trick is deciding which flavor of chaos tastes better.*

Leaving Chiang Rai was emotional - it was much harder than I'd given even the slightest momentary thought to. Nom took me back to the bus station and as we hugged goodbye, I felt my throat tightening up. Settling into my seat, I gazed out the window with an unexpected longing to stay in Chiang Rai. Forever.

While I was excited to get back to Chiang Mai, Chiang Rai had stolen my heart from its sibling to the south. But I was on the bus and looking forward to seeing Chiang Mai again because by this point, I had gotten to know the place, some great people, restaurants, bars, cafes, galleries, bookstores and more. I knew what was where and how to get there. It had a feeling, a little like home, and that was one of the reasons I was going back, instead of straight south to Bangkok, to answer a question that had been bouncing around in my head. Could I Live in Chiang Mai?

I hear what you're thinking. You've been to Chiang Mai for a grand total of a couple of weeks and now you're thinking of pulling up stakes back home to plunk yourself down in a small city on the other side of the world, where you have a less than rudimentary grasp on speaking, and even fewer skills with the written language. I thought about that too and it was all a part of the matrix of could I, should I, why, and why not.

Chiang Mai is much like Bangkok but without the 24/7 sensory overload. It has a lively, youthful, international feel to it. With an incredible array of food and drink options, an artistic sensibility, a broad range of cultural activities, and delicious food for any palate. Add in that the location is fantastic (it has an airport and bus and train stations making ingress and egress easy), and everything you need to make a beautiful life in an exotic yet accessible place full of history and wonder? What's not to like! Was it a daydream that falls into the wishful-thinking category? Others have done it and done so successfully. They're called expats, and I was contemplating joining those ranks. Then again, as Groucho Marx quipped: "I wouldn't join a club that would have me as a member."

I've got a bad habit: gambling on last-minute travel deals. This meant that I hadn't booked a place in Chiang Mai until two nights before sliding out of Chiang Rai. Everything was either laughably expensive, somewhere I'd already stayed before, or was so aggressively boring that I'd rather bunk down in a shack at the edge of a rice paddy. One place popped up proudly touted itself as "perfect for large gatherings and families with a lot of children (which translates to 'huge parties and screaming kids.") Fantastic. Absolutely not! I'd rather share a bunk bed with a meth head. Then, one morning, a notification lit up my phone: a discount at the Banthai Village Hotel - a place I'd been low-key obsessing over since the first time I'd perused the listing.

I'd been stalking Banthai like it was a hot celebrity and though it was included in every travel app, they never budged on price. Now don't get me wrong - I'm not, as you may have gathered, opposed to spending money. When the urge hits, the quality is amazing, or I'm feeling stupidly reckless, I'll spend, within reason. But a great deal? That hits differently, especially when it's about where I'm going to lay my head down for the night. And there it was: a big, fat, enticing discount, valid for booking that day only. I pulled the trigger. My plans were wide open until late December when a friend would fly into Bangkok when we'd head south to Koh Chang in the Gulf of Thailand for the days and nights surrounding New Years Eve. There's nothing quite like spending a party weekend in the tropics with white-sand beaches and rum!

The Banthai Village Hotel, tucked east of Chiang Mai's old city in the Changklan neighborhood, sat conveniently close to the city's other famed night markets. It was showered with praise - not just from travel magazines and booking sites, but from everyone who'd bothered to leave a review. High marks across the board: staff, pool, breakfast, neighborhood, rooms, beds, bathrooms - you name it. Designed in the traditional Lanna style I'd come to love at the Namton, it featured dark wood, swing-latch doors, with open patios wrapped in lush gardens. I was eager to stay there and see what that corner of Chiang Mai had in store for my wandering feet.

As the countryside melted by outside the coach window, my mind spun back to the friends I'd made in Chiang Rai: Nim and Nom, Amanda and Gita, Pascal (the fanatical Swiss guy who thought life was meant to be lived on a bicycle), and Chu - the noodle master, who could out-drink a frat house if you put a bottle of scotch and a few Fernet shots in front of him. All them were really good people. Real people. All of them genuine and open, no drama and no bullshit. When (not if) I make it back to Thailand, Chiang Rai will be my first destination for an encore to catch up with them and explore more of the gorgeous pastoral countryside.

Rolling into Chiang Mai's bus terminal felt like getting prodded with a live high-voltage main right to the temple. After a week of easy-paced days and nights up north, the onslaught of traffic, noise and swarming people jacked my pulse through the roof. My Sabai level was high - too high, leaving me woefully unprepared to rejoin a bustling world. I knew I'd adjust, but Geebuz, that first jolt back into live-action chaos was like trying to run a 100-yard dash immediately after waking up from a nap.

Rush hour didn't help. It took forever to grab a cab but when I did the fun began. My driver - an older fellow with one long, stubborn, greasy strand of hair left on his scalp, tobacco-stained teeth and fingers the color of new-corpse yellow, wearing a massive gold chain weighed down with Buddhist medallions - he couldn't wait to show off his English skills. He said, "my English great" which it wasn't, though it was charming in a deranged lunatic way. I surrendered to the experience with grins, thumbs up and nods.

It was a comical ride bouncing along while his surreal monologue, a bizarre soundtrack of advertising slogans, random gospel lyrics and quotes from Gunsmoke, Dragnet and M*A*S*H raped my eardrums. He seemed especially fond of Hotlips Houllihan making lewd sounds as he recalled Frank Burns's lust, which was now obviously his. Sometimes you've got to let the madness flow and hope to hell it knows where it's going.

The Banthai Village Hotel was crammed into a labyrinth of alleys and ridiculously small, curved, high-walled lanes. Check-in was smooth and so professional that I wondered if they confused me with someone important. My ground floor room was under a deep, heavy overhang with a veranda choked with pillow-encrusted benches, comfortable chairs that whispered, *"you'll be sipping Johnny Walker Black on me later"*, and a small table complete with ashtray. The toilet-bowl cleaner blue color of the pool in front of the room was intriguing. Everything was surrounded by tropical trees and shrubbery that cast shadows in all directions. As the concierge finished the tour of the room and I stowed things away, I was ready for a discovery jaunt.

The front desk clerk handed me a clever map of the surrounding alleys and streets, a yellow highlighter showing the easiest ways to either escape to or from madness. I say clever because of where the Banthai was located. There were tricks to the immediate neighborhood and the map showed in detail how tiny twisting alleys connected up with a couple of major roads that, if one didn't know how to navigate, would be easy to get lost, go feral, to be found years later hiding out in the back room of a massage parlor. Not that being lost is a bad thing, but it might look bad if family flew over with a search and rescue team, found you knotted up in a ball in some dark corner in need of a shave, raving for more oil. Worse yet, once I left the hotel grounds with its Wi-Fi coverage, my phone's GPS couldn't find signal past one bar. The map would have to do.

Rather than head towards the familiar grounds of the historic old city, I went the opposite direction towards the closest night bazaar. When traveling without an agenda, I find it best to follow instinct. Within a block it became very apparent; this wasn't the rustic charm of the old city or Nimman's hipster zoo. This was the real, raw Chiang Mai - the part where locals hang out, sell pirated iPhones to each other in one corner, fake Channel bags in another, and get massages that make you good and strong long time.

Heading south down Loi Kroh Road towards the river, taking my time to duck into alleys, popping in to vintage everything shops, I had another syrupy espresso from a hand-pull machine older than me, and offered return greetings to all the friendly ladies sitting outside their massage studios. They are welcoming and even if you don't want a massage they are great to sit and have a chat with as they tend to know the ins and outs and all the social dirt of their neighborhood, plus they all have really dirty senses of humor. I stumbled upon the Fah Lanna Night Bazaar, a genius monstrosity where dozens of micro bars wrapped around pool tables. Each place had their bar girls ready to hustle anyone and everyone out of their traveler's stash in exchange for making them feel like the center of the universe - at least until they woke up the next morning with no wallet, phone or dignity left. It was fantastic!

I kept my wallet safely tucked away in my pants and came upon the O.M.G. Bar and Restaurant at the corner of Loi Kroh and Charoen Prathet. What attracted me was a classic Guinness pub sign hanging proudly above the corner. Capitulating to desire I went in and ordered a Guinness and a shot of Jamesons because life is short and I was way too sober at the moment, what with all the coffee. Inside was all football, rugby and a tournament sized pool table at the back with some likely lads taking a game so seriously that I figured it was a hustler's school. The menu read like an edible apology for colonialism - bangers and mash, fish and chips, steak and kidney pie with mash and liquor, sausage rolls, and every weekend they did up a classic English Sunday Roast that required a reservation.

Joy, the bartender, explained that her husband Stewart (a British fellow), owned the place and that the pool league boys in back were tournament pros and were so serious that it seemed national pride was at stake. Maybe it was because they usually won tournaments playing against other bars about town. There was a match coming up with another expat pub so tonight was ruthless practice with game after game being shot.

As friendly as everyone was, this was not what I was looking for. I had one more pint of Guinness, pinned the location to my maps app and wandered off to the Ping River to walk off the creeping buzz.

The riverbank still bore the scars of the 2024 floods. You could still see the high-water mark at the top of the pilings, where mangled plants were still warped around the base of the roadway on the underside of the bridge as a reminder of how fucked the place had been. The sheer volume of water during the calamity had broken over the banks and into the neighborhood. The folks at O.M.G. showed me where they had to rebuild - the entire lower half of the bar and kitchen. Mother nature can be a real bitch at times.

Heading back, I wandered around the bazaar looking at the stalls that were hiding behind the gauntlet of micro-bars. There was an eclectic mix of artisan jewelry and homey decoration items I had not seen at other markets.

I got enmeshed into a long chat with a Persian rug dealer named Zahir, who's shop displayed gorgeous hand-knotted rugs. I was very up front with him that I wasn't buying a thing as he tried to wrangle me into his beautifully appointed brick and mortar store. But there was one enormous area rug hanging on the far wall that had caught my eye, not only for its size but the extraordinary beauty of the piece. It was breath-taking and I wanted to know what something like that cost.

Zahir had the droll patience of a man who knew he was about to waste time talking to a traveler who had no intention of dropping big bucks on a rug. He humored me anyway. Once I explained my journey and total lack of intent of owning a landmark area rug, he dropped the sales pitch, and we sat and talked on the stoop of his shop as the bazaar across the street hustled.

Zahir and his family had immigrated from Iran three decades prior but many of his extended kin back in Tabriz were hand-knotting rugs at the highest level of quality and had been for generations. I learned about knots-per-square-inch (KPSI). I stopped jotting notes after a while and simply listened to his master class. He explained natural dyes they employed, and the gradients of silks, cottons and wool used and the art of hand-knotting rugs. He spoke with a reverence usually reserved for holy relics and first-release mint-condition Beatles albums. Once he got into knotting methods I was lost but still fascinated by his passion and in-depth knowledge of the craft. Finally, I asked what the piece on back the wall cost.

"Do you really want to know?"

"Yes though I know I'll be shocked into depression." I laughed.

"It is actually the finest piece we've ever had in the store. It took nine people four and a half years to make." Zahir explained.

"I take it that means it's exorbitant."

Zahir smiled. "Quite."

"Aaaaand? The suspense isn't killing me but I'm getting hungry." I laughed.

"How much would you say it's worth?"

"Man... I have no idea. The last really nice rug I bought was small and it was $400 American dollars. That was over thirty years ago," I continued.

"Let me explain - that piece is going to wind up in a museum someday. If someone were to buy that and we found out that pets would be playing on it, we would not sell it to them. Unless they paid full price in cash," he laughed.

"And?"

"Twenty-five and a half million Baht." Zahir took out his phone and did a quick calculation, showing me the exchange rate. "That would be about seven hundred and fifty thousand US dollars."

I laughed so hard I almost dry-heaved. "Yeah... wrap it up and I'll pop it into my carry-on." as I wiped a tear of confounded mirth from my eye.

We chatted more as I found him to be really great company, so I invited Zahir out to grab a bite to eat when he was finished. I helped him close up shop and when the last metal door was rolled down and locked, we headed down the long line of street carts lined up at the edge of the bazaar and shared a fantastic array of halal dishes. Chicken biryani, roti with quail eggs, lamb curry, a sensational rice pilaf, and watermelon smoothies.

Zahir had an early morning ahead of him so we parted ways as I went back down the alley, past the Planet Hollywood Chiang Mai (that would be a hard *no*), then into the part of the night bazaar where all the micro bars were. I thought a game of pool and a couple of drinks would be fun before heading back to the Banthai.

At the first bar I nursed an absinthe with ice water while secretly keeping score as the pool-hustling bar girls worked over a couple of drunk Dutch guys, taking their money and getting them to buy watered-down drinks, for which tourists pay double. I almost bought popcorn the show was so good.

Suddenly... a tiara-topped birthday girl bombshell blasted onto the scene with a dozen glitter, sparkle and sash-laden banshees in tow. Where I'm from, we call them "woo girls," as in high-volume "*woooooooo*" energy. The horror!

Being an unencumbered farang, I was immediately targeted like a gazelle by a lioness hunt party. Before I knew it, I was pulled from my stool, grinding against glittery strangers, taking shots of questionable provenance, and laughing at jokes I'm pretty sure were about me. Biology is a hell of a thing. Somewhere between the fourth bar and the third sloppy kiss, I pulled the "*I have to pee*" escape move, melted into the crowd like a sought-after criminal, and ghosted my way back to the Banthai. It was 4AM and I had glitter in my hair, along with the taste of regret and cheap whiskey lingering like bad cologne.

In Thailand, the pools are rarely heated. During the hellish blast of summer, that is exactly what you want: a teeth-chattering polar bear plunge to shock the heat stroke out of you. My morning plunge was a stupid attempt of carpe diem, making me instantly regret my decision to pursue instant resurrection. The sky had been a moribund gray for days; there wasn't a trace of radiant heat, and the water had turned into a cryo-chamber. Shrinkage and internal screaming profanities over, I pulled myself out, rushed back into my room and took a warm bath in the sunken Japanese Ofuro-styled tub, trying to convince my body that survival was still an option.

With no grand plans to shackle me, I wandered across the jungle patio to the breakfast buffet at the hotel. Yes - I know - never eat the hotel buffet - but the Banthai had a fantastic assortment of fresh fruits, croissants that looked perfect and homemade yogurts. I read and wrote the morning away on the patio couch with a pot of coffee the size of my torso, as I pondered what I would do with my remaining days in Chiang Mai. I decided to head down to the local hypermarket and pick up some chocolate, fruit, juices, some smuggled durian and other munchies to stock up the room.

Heading out in a new direction (*I didn't want to run into any lost wooo girls who got separated from the pack, still hunting for me from the night before*). I was about to enter a Big C market when WhatsApp lit up my phone. It was my monk brother Josh. Now let's be honest: we all have a list of people who we always answer the phone for. The rest we let go to voicemail purgatory or wait for the follow up text. Don't deny it; you do this too. I answered Josh's call immediately. He was in Japan excited about picking up Japanese kitchen knives, so he called me for advice. We chatted back and forth and I geeked out about Shun knives. I have a collection of razor-sharp beauties that slice through tomatoes, arteries, bone and stainless steel. They are relatively easy to keep razor sharp and if you're right-handed like me, they fit perfectly in your grasp because of the octagonal shape of the handles. Then we caught up on life in general. It was one of those calls where you hang up and the world seems a better place.

Groceries in tow, I headed back to Banthai to stow my goods, then decided it was a good day for a long stroll. I filled the fridge and slipped into my flops, dialed up a Grab and booked it to the zoo, way over on the far side of town from where my hotel sat. It was time to wander around Chiang Mai, find new streets, sniff out new discoveries and ponder my newest plans for Bangkok, which was coming at me faster than I had anticipated.

The Huai Kaeo Arboretum was a shady strolling park laden with native trees, shrubs and flowers, all neatly tended and marked with small signs. Rather than walk along row after row of Songthaew's and the incessant traffic belching fumes, going to and from the temple on the mountain top, the interior path through native trees and shrub species was peaceful, with big trees and hedgerows blocking out the din of the city. Eventually the arboretum path spit me out at the Angkaew Reservoir - a man-made lake busy with joggers, bikers and one strolling traveler stuffing mango slices in his face. There was a cart you see.

I came across a rugby match in full swing just in time to see a bunch of university kids murder each other in the scrum. Some shouts and possibly a few dislocated ribs later I moved along heading back to the main drag.

Coming across a building advertising "New Brain" I wondered if I should make an appointment. Mine was long out of warranty coverage so I kept moving. Further along I was tempted by a very attractive storefront that, once past the door, had scattered, disjointed array of Chinese-made clothing and fake "antique" Asian furniture, made of press board and child labor. The clothing was all cheap knockoffs though with very professional-looking brand-name labels. I almost applauded the effort of the scam. Man, the hustle never sleeps.

I crossed the road, dodged a few scooters trying to break the sound barrier and made my way towards the Maya. Buried beneath air-conditioned multi-levels of swag is Rimping, a high-end hypermarket. I used to haunt the place when I lived in the Nimman hood. The cut mangoes? Witchcraft! I grabbed another tray like an obsessed neurotic (though I did pick up watermelon and pineapple as well) and started a slow roll back into familiar territory.

Cutting southeast through the city's ancient spine, I passed by old haunts and shops that had become part of my Chiang Mai mental map.

Next stop: Lost Books. This is one of my favorite sanctuaries from the sun in the whole of Thailand. I needed something new for poolside reading. I swapped some travel stories with the clerk, Sangi. She and I had similar taste in genres and authors with the same zero-tolerance policy for literary fluff. I asked her for some off-beat recommendations and walked away with new tales in my bag.

From there, it was up the road to Gravity, where the crew greeted me back like an old friend. I ordered my usual - avocado toast with fresh pico de gallo, and a tall, iced latte. Jasmine, the unofficial soul of the place, had started on my java the moment she saw me strolling towards the door. We exchanged a smile and a wai; a quiet, though heartfelt exchange of mutual respect in a city that runs on it.

After refueling (and cooling down) I popped into the Nampton next door to say hi. Sand was running the show as usual, the human example of grace and quiet competence. Gorge floated in and out like a specter. We caught up - Chiang Rai tales about noodle joints, duck soups, that I still didn't like Khao Soi. I hadn't known, but Sand came from a small village to the north of Chiang Rai, so my journeys were familiar to her. When I told her about the hand-pulled noodle shop, she said she made it an almost sacramental commitment to eat there every time she went north. I tipped her off about the Indian joint further along the sidewalk without reservation, and explained that this was not pre-made, reheated tikka masala on a plate of overly spiced daal. Sand lit up like a sunrise, saying she would definitely hit it up as she was heading north to visit her family soon.

By the time I wandered back to Banthai Village, my stroll was just shy of 10k and 5pm. Perfect time to wash the sweat and dust off, then go hunting for dinner.

Tha Phae Road, is one of Chiang Mai's major arteries. It cuts east straight into the heart of the old city through the Tha Phae Gate - you know, the one that everyone takes pictures in front of that bronze plaque? Built in 1296AD, It's the epicenter and ultra-famous landmark of tourism in Chiang Mai. But the path to get there from the Banthai was convoluted and secretive. Instead of walking the long way round to major arteries, I walked around the back of the hotel, down a small alley covered by a long arbor covered with flowering vines, like some enchanted shortcut in a Miyazaki film. Past a couple of tiny family-run laundries, shirts and sheets flapping on their lines like prayer flags. Past Wat Buppharam, whose quiet monks and stray dogs barely register the foot traffic (except for one small monk who liked to hide under his robes on the rise of the courtyard stupa, until a visitor strolled by. Seeing a pile of orange robes on the stone steps attracted attention. I saw the little trickster, as visitors approached, pop up with a giggle. He was lousy at hide and seek but fantastic at surprising visitors. Within two minutes you're on Tha Phae - if you know the way. If you didn't know that alley was there it would take an extra fifteen minutes going around the long way. Like I said, clever map!

Tha Phae Road was a fantastic, busy mess, in a good way. A loaded mix of dive and upscale bars, some very good to meh restaurants, tourist shops of all sorts including a couple of really cool antique stores that while the merchandise was excellent, the attitude was all about taking the tourists money through aggressive sales. The road itself was crowned by twenty-four arching ornate structures covered in white lights at regular intervals; at night, these were ablaze with thousands of tiny bulbs making it into a makeshift runway for drunken backpackers and the occasional street food pilgrimage.

It was there, amidst the haze of sizzling coconut oil and a throng of sweaty humanity that I stumbled upon Pa Day - a Roti cart. Not the thick, puffy roti you half-heartedly tear through at your local Indian place. Nope! This was different. Those roti were ultra-thin, crepe-like miracles: crisp on the outside, tender chewy goodness inside, much like a croissant, and stuffed with your choice of savory or sweet fillings, depending on which flavor of gluttony you were after. The line was 15 deep on three sides - a chaotic ballet of greedy desperation. That's what happens when you're 5-year running Michelin-award street cart that sells roti for a dollar - you command a rapt audience.

I waited among the churning horde, carefully studying others order to figure out how, one: I could get one of these touted masterpieces of simplicity myself, and two: not appear to be an idiot when it was finally my turn. The ritual was simple: follow the trickle of bodies to the cart, grab a chit, check off your desired fillings (banana? Nutella? egg? cheese?), then scrawl your name at the top. Around the corner you hand over the chit and money to the gatekeeper along with a paltry amount of cash. Then you wait, jealously watching, as tray after tray of roti float past into someone else's grateful mitts.

Behind this chaos is one woman. One! A wrinkled, badass elderly woman who had to be in her 80s, cooking all of the orders. She manned the Roti Tawa (the traditional flat griddle that delivers that ethereal crispy exterior) armed with nothing but her bare hands and what must be asbestos-tipped fingers. No spatula, no tongs, no spoons. Just pure calloused mastery. She could cook four roti at a time, each one needing about five minutes to achieve that perfect golden crispy crust, get filled, folded, and flipped again for a crunchable seal, then handed to the ever-anxious customer.

Hovering around the pickup table, an ungodly level of palpable anticipation mixed with desperate patience permeated the crowd. Every time a tray went to someone else, you could see a soul die a little as the excitement in their eyes faded. Seeing the sagging deflation at the realization that that roti - the one you thought was finally yours, is handed to someone else; it's comically heartbreaking.

I ordered banana and Nutella and melted into the crowd to hang back and watch humanity waiting for their turn at a Michelin-rated roti. Travel tends to break down barriers. To wit: the two fellows I wound up next to in the crowd, our six eyes intently watching the progress of roti after roti being fried up, were friends traveling together. I never got their names, but one guy was Israeli, the other Syrian. They had met on the road in Nepal, then again in Cambodia. They became fast friends and were going traveling through India together when they left Thailand.

The world's a funny, wonderful place at times.

Finally, after forty-five long minutes and more emotional whiplash than a season of Lost, it was my turn. I said my goodbyes to my newfound roti brothers and went to stand vigil at the pickup table. Watching that old woman work, flipping roti after roti with fingers that should, by rights, have been vaporized years ago, I began to salivate.

And then it happened. My name, called out like a hymn. My tray was handed to me like a sacred offering. I dodged the desperate gazes to find a quiet spot down the sidewalk. I took my first bite.

Holy fucking Toledo!

How can something so simple be everything your mouth has ever desired? The whisker-thin crispy crust shattered under my teeth giving way to soft, steamy, chewy layers inside. Then the warm banana and molten Nutella hit, and for a brief moment, all was right with the world.

No wonder Michelin noticed. That little cart deserved credit and praise. My roti disappeared in seconds, leaving me with the desperate, guilty thought: I should get back in line. But the throng had doubled, and my appetite needed something more substantial.

I'd be back. Next time? I'd be ordering two. Minimum.

I had plans for the following day that required an up-and-at-it early morning so dinner would be an easy to-go Pad See Ew and Tom Kah Gai take out. I ate poolside on the patio and enjoyed my quiet meal serenaded by frog and cricket orgies hidden from voyeurs by the ponds and bushes around the courtyard. I had already had that outrageously great roti dessert for my first course and didn't want to spoil that memory hunting for anything else.

Being close to my last day in northern Thailand I decided to go on an adventure. A planned excursion run by a local company that put group packages together called Chiang Mai Mountain Biking and Kayaks. I had no desire to go mountain biking, instead opting for a different full day: caving at Chiang Dao in the morning, lunch at a monastery, then kayaking a lazy river - the Mae Ping - in the afternoon. I don't usually book group activities but I wanted to experience a lightweight outdoor sporting adventure, for which northern Thailand, especially the area surrounding Chiang Mai, is justifiably famous for.

CHAPTER 12 DÉJÀ CHIANG

Talking is humanity's favorite defense mechanism against introspection.

A truck picked me up at 7AM sharpish. I was rested, caffeinated and ready to roll. I was excited for the day - until we collected another passenger: a human Eeyore who proved to be ... let's just say she was difficult. She started complaining before her foot touched the truck's step (it was too high). If happiness and optimism were oxygen she would have suffocated long ago. In my head I gave her ten minutes before I started rooting for Darwinism and natural selection.

At the company headquarters, we got a standard *"don't die"* briefing on the do's and don'ts ... of not dying. That's where I met my salvation, Pip. South African from Cape Town. She was quick-witted, funny, and equally alarmed by the emotional black hole we were now orbiting. We quickly formed our two-person clique, essential for mutual emotional survival.

CCDD, or in long hand "Chatty Cathy Debbie Downer," was still prattling on - a word-vomit machine gun - about everything that would go wrong and how we were all going to suffer. Did she not pay attention to the "Do Not Die" lecture?

Our guides, Bor and Muth, were a jovial, joking duo while being pros at the same time. They clocked the group dynamic within moments, quarantining CCDD as if she were emotional Marburg. She didn't even realize what they were doing while she kept her doom and gloom verbal diarrhea running.

I used to kayak class 3 rivers back in California before I realized I didn't want to die. I wasn't great at whitewater kayaking but enjoyed it all the same and since I'm alive I guess I did OK. Class III runs require cockpit kayaks complete with float bags and a spray skirt plus handling the Eskimo-roll trick to flip upright if you went over, which I did. A lot. I got pretty good at the C hip-and-paddle snap out of pure necessity.

The boats supplied for our excursion were sealed, sit-on-top kayaks. The Mae Ping River was a sleepy Class 1 run of about nine kilometers where the greatest danger was sunburn. At its deepest through only a few stretches it might have reached six feet, so even if you did flip, you'd get wet and that was it.

But first: caves. The Chiang Dao Caves are a sprawling network of limestone tunnels, halls, caverns and claustrophobia located under Doi Chiang Dao, the third tallest mountain in Thailand. This cave system is located about 70 km north of Chiang Mai, the system stretches several kilometers into the mountain.

As we pulled into the parking lot we were greeted by a beautiful site; a peaceful little temple complex abutting the entrance to the cave system. Monks and local vendors were selling flowers, shrine offerings and food pellets for Koi which swarmed a pond at the entrance. The area was surrounded by lush jungle and towering cliffs lending a primordial feel to the place.

Once inside, an earthy, musty smell enveloped us like a blanket. The stalactites, stalagmites and frozen-in-time stone ripples of the floor were beautiful. Chambers echoed the sound of slow dripping water, continuing their gravity-induced building schedule. It was a living soundtrack played throughout the caverns as it had done for eons. There was a sacred feeling throughout the caves. Pip and I felt a sense of awe - as if time has completely stopped. CCDD was stumbling and complaining towards the rear but at this point I had created a mental block, so she wasn't as painful.

The caves were filled with dramatic stalactites, stalagmites, shimmering rock formations and bat guano. Illuminated with electric lights, the main trail is tourism paradise. Other zones require a guide with a lantern to explore, lending a mystical, magical and adventurous atmosphere. Several of the caverns housed ancient Buddha statues, shrines, and carvings, showing the site's long spiritual significance. It had an Indiana Jones vibe going for it which Pip and I enjoyed. Guess who didn't?

The air inside shifted from cool, to warm, and back to cool depending on elevation, but always a clammy humidity holding you in its invisible grasp. Many tunnels were narrow and winding, then opening into grand halls, two of which were magnificent, called Tham Phra Nawn ("Sleeping Buddha Cave") and Tham Seua Dao ("Cave of the Stars").

Our guides had hired a local to bring us into deeper sections further into the system. Those guides carry old school oil lanterns which cast eerie yellow glows and shadows on the paths as we followed them through tight crevices, at one point, crawling on our bellies to get through to a particularly fantastic grand auditorium. Darker and tighter, squeezing through small gaps and crawling like worms along the stone floor, we were rewarded by grottoes filled with glittering crystals, strange rock shapes and more tucked-away Buddha statues surrounded by flowers, incense and candle offerings.

Our guides were fun and knowledgeable, pointing out Kitti's hog-nosed bats, enormous Huntsman spiders and a snake called a cave-racer that finds bats absolutely delicious. They spotted the snake, a rarity, way up high above our heads on a small ledge, right next to where bats were sleeping off their nocturnal bugfest. How that serpent got up there I have no idea, but I did get a pretty good snapshot of it, while wondering how I'd react if it slipped off its perch thirty feet above our heads and landed on me. They are non-venomous but I assumed the worst, that it would fall, using its fangs as a climber would use an ice ax, to arrest its descent, spearing his teeth into my neck. We made our way past Nagini without incident.

CHAPTER 12. DÉJÀ CHIANG

Lunch was eaten through a simple exercise - ignoring the soundtrack of Eeyore complaining about something or other. The rice? The air? Her own, or everyone else's existence? Pip and I grabbed ice cold beers out of the refrigerator, which met with silent smiles of approval from both our guides and a disapproving scowl from CCDD who shook her head and told us how irresponsible we were because of the dangerous kayaking trip ahead of us. Pip and I laughed.

After lunch, it was on to kayaking. A second group joined up with us as we hit the river. Within about thirty seconds of launching, two people managed to capsize in what could generously be called a "minor riffle" that was about two feet deep. It was like watching baby deer try to walk for the first time.

Back at the shop during the "don't die" instructions, our guides had asked if any of us had prior experience with kayaks. I quietly told them of my time on the rivers flowing west from the Sierra Nevada range in California. They were happy because now there were three experienced boaters. Only Pip had spent any time in a kayak before. I was asked to be a part of the lead and to help out if someone was really inept.

Right at the start of the run was a class 1 tongue rapid which I gleefully paddled into. Having a paddle in my hands and riffles under my butt for the first time in ages was fantastic. Bouncing through the little waves and troughs, I eddied out at the end, turned and saw two of our group lose it into the water. This was going to be a long float!

With a couple of soaked boaters climbing back onto their crafts from thigh-deep water, we were on our way further down and around the bendy river. A few more tips and dunks happened but when people realized all that would happen was, they'd fall in the river up to their necks at the deepest points the fear factor lifted and our neophyte boaters gained a bit of confidence to tackle little curving riffles without further incident. This was certainly not the Grand Canyon, or even a class 2 paddle, so I was able to spin my boat around constantly to make sure no one was drowning and check out the flora and fauna along the banks of the not-so-mighty nor roaring Mae Ping.

Overhanging dark bamboo forests interspersed with tropical hardwoods, then broad, open fields and orchards growing all manner of grains, fruits and vegetables down to the riverside; each little eco-zone housed common kingfishers (*Alcedo atthis*), red-breasted parakeets (*Psittacula alexandri*), and great egrets (*Ardea alba*) who made their presence known as we rounded this then that bend, flapping noisily to escape our brightly colored flotilla. I enjoyed the egrets immensely as they took off slowly, like dinosauric airplanes.

The pace of the river started to pick up a little bit so I could finally have some fun playing in a standing wave, surfing the nose of the boat upstream. Rounding a bend we came across Wat Pha Lat, a jungle temple. Our guides explained that it was normally a secluded and very peaceful retreat that we would have stopped at, but because of the floods it had been damaged and was now awaiting funding to repair and rebuild sections that had been either damaged or swept away by the raging walls of water that swept down every river and stream as the monsoon season battered SE Asia. It was still very cool and a little King Kong-ish.

On the way back to town, we pulled into a village store where Pip and I picked up a few beers. I realized that this was CCDD's kryptonite and as Pip and I chatted, miracle of miracles - our third wheel settled into silence for the remainder of the trip seemingly at the end of her emotional torture. Why she ever signed up for the trip, I'll never know. Through it all, I still, to this day, wish her well and may she find her peace somehow.

Dropped off at Banthai at 7PM, I hung my river-damp swim trunks and t-shirt out to dry on the patio chairs. I was hungry. A quick shower later and I was out to find dinner. I had no idea what I was in the mood for, so I let my feet lead the way to delicious. I made my way down to Changklang Road and after rejecting a few cuisines I came across Yoshimune Izakaya, a Japanese place that was modern, chic and busy. By now you know I love sushi as well as grilled skin and guts on a skewer, so in I went and as luck would have it, there was one spot open at the sushi bar. It was meant to be. But they were out of sake - I mean really? How is that possible? Settling on a beer I ordered up some yakitori chicken livers, chicken skin, chicken hearts, fatty pork skewers that sizzled and dripped as they were handed over the counter, and grilled okra.

Then it was sushi time. Their list wasn't extensive, but they were doing something I hadn't seen before. Most of their nigiri sushi set was served "burned." They used a blow torch - the kind you'd see used by a guy in a full-face welder's helmet. I was sure you could hear the blast of pointed blue/white flames out on the street with the door closed. It was overkill but the results were delicious. The top surface of the fish took on a delicious light and oily char while the rest of the fish was still raw creating a juxtaposition of texture and flavor. I ordered whelk, unagi (eel), burned salmon with tartar, burned ebi (sweet freshwater shrimp) with lemon and low and behold, the special of the night was otoro - that ultra-fatty belly of blue fin tuna. That I asked for sashimi style, which got me a smile and a Daiskideso (love it) from the sushi chef.

The next day would be my last in Chiang Mai, so I figured I'd call it an early night. Or so I thought. I wandered back to Banthai using a different route, winding through the residential back alleys to catch a glimpse of local life powering down for the evening.

Just around the corner from the hotel's entrance, I stumbled across a micro-bar called Café Blanco, a name that made absolutely no sense, since nothing about the place was remotely white. There were six seats wedged around a 90-degree bar and three stools bolted to a narrow ledge out front. That was it. I was the odd man out, stepping into a scene that clearly hadn't been expecting company. The bartendress and her girlfriend looked momentarily stunned to see a foreigner wander in as it was clearly a locals-only joint, not flagged on any tourist map. Luckily, they had some excellent premium booze on the shelves and just enough English for banter, so we traded shots, beers, and bad DJ choices via the bar's communal iPad. They were fun, flirty, and saw me as a walking bar tab with decent manners.

Next door was "Billy's Italian Restaurant," a name that inspired about as much confidence in authentic cuisine as a guy named Vlad the Impaler opening a hot dog stand. I'd seen it online while scouting dinner options but skipped it on name alone. It was well-reviewed, but all the praise came from guys named Mike from Maryland and John from Brighton. Not a single Thai name in the bunch. That's a red flag dipped in marinara. Hard pass.

By 11PM, I figured it was best to quit while I was ahead. My room was less than a three-minute stumble away, and I had one last day to enjoy in Chiang Mai, preferably hangover-free.

The morning dawned bright and clear, already sweltering by 6:30AM. It promised to be a scorcher, so I declared it a me-day. Pool. Book. Bit of writing and a forty-second stroll to Wat Buppharam for some meditation time. I had some leftover snacks in the room and three fingers of Johnnie Walker Black to polish off, no point lugging it south when Bangkok sells liquor by the tanker-load.

I'd picked up The Sorcerer's Apprentices by Lisa Abend at the Lost Bookstore, a well-written peek behind the curtain at el Bulli, Ferran Adrià's mad-scientist restaurant on the Spanish coast. The book isn't flashy, but it's a solid slow-burn look at the staff who kept the machine running. It paired nicely with fruit, chocolate, and the thickly padded chaise lounge tucked under the overhang outside my room.

Still, I couldn't shake a craving: pho and bánh mì. I'd come up empty searching Vietnamese restaurants nearby, but just south, in the Miang Kham Village neighborhood was a place called Pâté Chiang Mai on Sridonchai Road. It was well-reviewed - and mostly by locals. The twist? It was halal, which meant no pork, a major curveball for Vietnamese staples that rely on the stuff. I was curious. How were they pulling off bánh mì without it?

Let's pause a moment to appreciate what a proper bánh mì really is. In my not-even-slightly-humble opinion, it's the greatest sandwich on Earth. The Vietnamese lifted the baguette from the French, then cranked it up: pâté, pickled daikon, carrots, cucumbers, grilled meat, chili slices, fresh herbs, and a splash of

Maggi. It's a party in your mouth with no intention of ending early, the kind of sandwich that disappears faster than dignity at an open bar.

So where did this sandwich sorcery come from?

In the mid-19th century, the French were doing their Indochina thing - imposing architecture, cuisine, territorial theft and colonial cruelty across Southeast Asia. Cambodia, Laos, Vietnam, parts of China - all "administered" under the tricolor. It was mostly a horror freak show, but a few culinary gems managed to slip through the blood-soaked bureaucracy.

The baguette stuck. And can you blame them? A well-made French baguette is a minor miracle. Crusty, chewy, aromatic, a loaf with swagger. The locals were hooked, and even regions that didn't traditionally grow wheat began experimenting with cultivation just to feed the demand. The influence didn't stop in Vietnam, either. Cambodia developed the num pang, and Laos brought forth the khao jee pâté.

Wheat. Here's the catch - wheat hates humidity, which is basically Southeast Asia's whole vibe. It took decades to get decent crops going with right place, right strain, try, fail, then finally success. Until then, wheat had to be imported - a journey of over 8,000 nautical miles from Marseilles, which made it impractical and very expensive. To stretch the milled wheat, Vietnamese bakers mixed in rice flour, creating, in that additions wake, a lighter, airier loaf.

Today, the Vietnamese have taken the art of the baguette to a heightened, albeit different space. Because of the heat, humidity and types of wheat grown in Vietnam, the baguette has undergone a transformation. Whereas the classic French baguette is an uneven lumpy, rustic long loaf with a serious thick, mandible-exercising crunchy crust and hole-filled interior of gluten-created chewy goodness, the Vietnamese version is much more uniform in shape, the crust is much thinner - yet also possesses a wonderful crunch - while the inside is soft and, well ... bready. And viola ... the Vietnamese baguette. The fillings are variable; the baguette is not.

I hoofed it down to Pâté Chiang Mai, hoping for greatness, or at least a competent impersonation. The place was a clean, casual hole-in-the-wall with Thai and Muslim families slurping noodles and devouring sandwiches. I slid into a two-top, scanned the menu, and faced my usual Thai-menu roulette. Fortunately, I'd picked up enough to know gai meant chicken. They'd subbed chicken liver pâté and char siu-style grilled chicken for the pork. Bold move. Worth a shot.

I ordered the house bánh mì gai and a pho bo (beef pho). I thought wistfully of my favorite pho spot in Seattle, a family-run joint in the Ballard neighborhood on 15th where the broth simmers for days and the tendon and tripe work medicinal magic on aging joints. But I knew better than to expect all that here. I asked the waitress if they had any of the good offal stuff. She smiled, shook her non-comprehending head. Out came the phone. I typed in my request. Another smile, a polite "no." Can't blame a guy for trying.

The sandwich and soup? Solid. A proper farewell meal, humble and hearty. Not a bad way to say goodbye to Chiang Mai.

The morning was gray and sullen, as if Chiang Mai itself had rolled in clouds just to see me off. It matched my mood - quiet, heavy, not ready to let go. I packed slowly, half-hoping some invisible hand might intervene with a reason to stay.

I didn't take the train. There's a masochistic romantic notion associated with overnight rail journeys. That is until you're reminded by the pervasive pain in your spine, knees and kidneys that it actually isn't all that romantic after all. For $39, I could fly south in just over an hour. An easy trade.

But northern Thailand had burrowed deep. Chiang Mai with its golden temples and alleyway surprises, with its gentle monk chants at dawn and bars hidden behind exotic potted plants. Chiang Rai, that quiet sibling with the wild imagination, its blue and white temples, its mythical tigers and improbable calm. These places had become more than pins on a map. They were chapters I didn't want to end. The friends I made, the flavors I chased, the quiet mornings and riotous nights - they're stitched now into the lining of who I am. Memory, imagination, and soul.

As the plane lifted, I pressed my forehead to the window, half hoping I could see one last glint of a temple spire or mountain silhouettes through the haze. Nothing. Just clouds. And a feeling I knew all too well: the ache of moving forward when parts of you linger behind.

CHAPTER 13. WATS UP DOC?

*You can visit temples anywhere in the world
but it helps if you shut up long enough to hear the echoes.*

What Is Wat? Let's begin with that question. It sounds simple but, like most things in life, a simple question often unfolds into something much deeper and layered - like an ogre. Got that Donkey?

Throughout the southeast Asian continent, the term "Wat" can refer to either a Buddhist temple or a monastery; the difference being that a monastery is where monks live, meditate, chant and study, whereas a temple does not have living quarters. The term is used widely throughout Thailand, Cambodia, Myanmar, Laos, and Sri Lanka, and sometimes loosely in the west. Wat indicates a Buddhist sacred site, a building, or multiple buildings. Today, the term Wat is also used for ancient temple ruins.

The most widespread and well-known use of the term "Wat" familiar to western culture is Angkor Wat - the sprawling twelfth-century temple complex in Cambodia whose name roughly translates to "Temple City." Fun fact: it's located just outside Siem Reap - a name that, with no small amount of historical awkwardness, means "Siam Defeated." Siam, being the former name of Thailand, and Thailand being the tourist base camp from which most people visit Cambodia. So yes, history has a long memory and a sharp tongue.

Every Wat is beautiful in its own way, the intricacy and details of the site, each with its own architectural variations, seem endless. Though there are variations from Wat to Wat, there is always an adherence to the central myths, themes and legends which comprise the stories of Buddhism, and often Hinduism as well.

The word itself, Wat, is derived from the Sanskrit vāṭa, meaning "enclosure," but in Thai it's evolved to signify far more: a place of refuge, of learning, of transformation. In the strictest sense, it translates to something like "city of temples" - and if that doesn't set your spiritual expectations sky-high, nothing will.

I found myself hopping from one Wat to another like a spiritual bar crawl. Each Wat is unique - a distinct fingerprint of cultural, spiritual, and artistic expression. Some are minimalist and serene, nestled in back alleys or up in the hills like secrets whispered from history. Others are maximalist psychedelic visions of intense color, gold leaf, mirror tiles, and serpentine staircases guarded by mythical creatures that look like they were designed during a multi-night ayahuasca jag.

And yet, for all their differences, there's a shared vocabulary that threads them together. The same core symbolism appears again and again: lotus flowers in bloom, fierce guardian deities staring down evil spirits, Nāga serpents slithering along balustrades, and Buddhas - so many Buddhas - gleaming gold, standing, sitting, reclining, meditating, teaching, smiling, frowning, and occasionally smirking like they know things you don't (*pssssst: they do!*)

The gold leaf adorning all those Buddha statues isn't decoration. It represents a mirror, depicting one's innate perfection. And those Buddha statues? They're hollow representing the absence of a solid, opaque self, telling of embodiment and the luminous transparency of being.

The stories told in those temples through murals, carvings, mosaics, woven textiles, written history and statuary, often are drawn not just from Buddhism, but Hinduism, ancient Thai folklore, and Chinese cosmology. Wat Arun, for instance, perched dramatically on the banks of the Chao Phraya River in Bangkok, is a dazzling mix of Buddhist reverence and cosmic multiculturalism, looking less like a temple and more like a porcelain spaceship built by enlightened aliens.

Temples in Thailand don't just tell you stories. They immerse you in them. They surround you with smells of incense, jasmine, and bergamot, the hypnotic thrum of chanting, the shimmer of heat rising from tiles and flagstones, the bark of a stray dog who's claimed the altar as his personal space. It's all part of the experience. Sacred, chaotic, layered, and alive.

TEMPLE ETIQUETTE: Do not be *that* tourist!

There are rules when visiting Wats, and before you roll your eyes, let me clarify: this isn't about blind conformity. It's about respect. Respect for the space, the monks who live and practice there, the teachings of the Buddha, and, not least, the thousands of years of tradition that shaped those sacred grounds. This is not hard folks! You don't have to be Buddhist to behave decently.

Fortunately, following those guidelines is not in any way like trying to master the mind-blowing details of say, quantum mechanics. Nearly every Wat makes it incredibly easy for visitors to comply as well. This is not a trick quiz from the culture police. The monks want you to visit, learn, and take it all in. They're not setting traps to catch you in a tank top.

Here are the basics: Shoulders and knees must be covered at all times. Hats and sunglasses removed once inside the buildings. Shoes come off before stepping into any sacred structure, especially the Ubosot and/or Wihan - those are the main assembly halls, the heart of the Wat where the most revered Buddha images are housed. Think of the Wihan as a spiritual living room, but for the entire cosmos, so maybe don't stroll in there like you're arriving at a beach-side barbecue. The Ubosot is even more holy - it's the ordination hall and often off-limits.

Turn the volume off on your phone. You don't have to turn it off or put it into airplane mode, just silence the thing. No one wants to sit in contemplation, gazing up at a large golden Buddha while listening to Tik Tok notifications and pings from text messages announcing your dinner plans. And speaking of sound, try to keep your voice low. You're not in a mall; you're in a living spiritual site.

Now for the behavioral part. No touching the Buddha statues. Not for luck, not for your social media feeds, not even if it "just feels right." Buddha is not calling on you to caress him. Those images and statues are sacred, not set pieces.

Photographing monks without their permission is a no-go. I know, they look amazing in their beautiful robes, but they're not extras in your travel documentary. Have some respect. Ask first. Always. I mean c'mon - that's just common sense. And you know what?' They'll almost always say yes.

Pointing is considered rude. If you want to bring attention to a particular point of interest to your traveling companions, do so with discretion. The soles of your feet are considered unclean, and it is offensive to aim the bottoms of your feet at any Buddha, monks, or other people. And it should go without saying, don't light up a cigarette, cigar, pipe, joint, your vape pen or a joint anywhere on the Wat grounds. I don't care if your vape pen smells like cinnamon and happy dreams. It's still disrespectful.

It was during my first swing through Chiang Mai, before heading up into the mountains to the iMonastery, and I had parked myself at Gravity Café and Bistro, a great place on the corner of Ratchamanka and Samlarn roads, where sweat and sanity all seemed to slide sideways by mid-afternoon. I'd been pounding the pavement, doing recon around Chiang Mai's old city, trying to map its charm and contradictions, and dripping what I came to call a full-bodied Thai-sweat. That's not a figure of speech. It's a real condition. A kind of 360-degree sweat halo that seeps from every pore, no matter how many electrolytes you try to drink to fight it. It's as if your sweat is sweating. The only cure is sunset, air-con, or surrender. The plus side? Your skin looks amazing!

As I sat there working through a sandwich and an iced lager, grateful to have found A/C and a moment of stillness, I reflected on the temple I'd just left. Wat Phra Singh Woramahawihan. Try saying that three times fast without sounding like you're summoning a Basilisk.

But the moment wasn't entirely serene. What I had just witnessed inside the temple grounds was the kind of bizarre tourist behavior that makes you want to fake your passport nationality if you're from the same land as the following character.

There she was. A woman whose accent betrayed some origin in Oceania - Australia, maybe New Zealand, hard to tell. Her voice, though, was unmistakable. Loud. Drawn out. The verbal equivalent of a highlighter pen with the end of sentences always on the rise. And she was angry. Full-on temple rage. Her problem? She'd been denied entrance to the Wihan - the main hall that houses the principal Buddha statue by a monk no less. A monk! Which, let's be honest, is probably the last person on earth you want to yell at if you care even remotely about your karmic scorecard.

Her outfit was, well ... not temple ready. She was decked out in a zebra-patterned miniskirt that screamed girls' night in Ibiza, glittery high heels, and a gold sequined tube top that looked like it had beamed in from 1968 and hadn't been kept in climate-controlled storage. The poor garment was clinging for dear life, waging a slow but inevitable war with gravity, and gravity - as always - was winning.

I assumed she couldn't read, because at the entrance to the grounds and at every possible sight-line, in multiple languages including English, and at the entrance to most buildings, she had, I'll assume, missed every one of the signs posted, that inappropriate attire is not acceptable and that visitors would be denied access if not covered. It's not like the dress code requires an evening jacket or a ball gown with pearls, or a head-to-toe niqab and abaya.

She stomped, hands on hips, and launched into a tirade about how she had paid her entrance fee, and therefore she had every right to go in and look at "the big gold Buddha, mate!" monk be damned. I watched the monk stand his ground, hands clasped in front of him, with the kind of serene patience I wish I could possess. His kindly and dignified silence, in response to the tirade being unleashed upon him, was quiet, unshakable, and completely ineffective against her cultural entitlement tsunami.

When her first parry didn't sway the monk, she attempted to argue for women's rights, and that she was her own person with rights, and she had yet more rights. The beauty of that stoic monk in the face of such nonsense was epic. He never flinched as her gesticulating arms and hands, used to pronounced effect to emphasize her points were like those tall blow-up dolls that wave people into businesses. He never acted condescending, or rude, not even a sneer on his lips showed. He was the personification of compassion and concern. Most likely for her mental well-being.

And yet, she kept going. Blah blah blah, as if self-expression via a bouncing sequin tube top was somehow a revolutionary act in the context of a 700-year-old religious sanctuary.

Her campaign to enter failing at every step, even as he gently gestured to a small building back towards the entrance of the grounds where she could borrow a shawl to cover her shoulders and a sari-like wrap to cover her knees. The temple could not have made compliance easier and yet, as the idiom goes, you can lead a horse to water, but you can't make it put on a free wrap.

Through it all, her man, bicep-boy, husband, boyfriend, or "personal trainer," stood by silently, arms crossed over his gym-built chest, nodded in loyal agreement. He sported a tragically thin and patchy pornstache and a thick gold chain that looked like it had been picked up at a dollar discount store. His presence seemed to say, "Yeah baby, you tell that monk! He'll get it at some point and then let you in!"

Sometimes, a sigh just sneaks out. Mine did. The absurdity of it all was both maddening and oddly mesmerizing, like being unable to tear your gaze away from a body-strewn crash site.

Finally, she'd had enough. When she realized she was not getting her way, she grabbed her fellow by the arm and stormed off towards the entrance. The monk was following them with his eyes, a sad look on his face. He was young, a lad in his early 20's if I had to guess. I walked over, greeting him with a wai - a bow with hands together - and apologized for the ways of the world and the rudeness of some of the humans who inhabit it. He looked at me with a look that I did not understand. It was one of sadness and frustration. He and I talked about what had just happened when he said something that surprised me. "Could you see the suffering she lives with?"

I was thinking more about the suffering her boy toy lived with, but the compassion that young monk showed for a person who had been berating him emphasized a very important lesson - that everyone is in pain to some degree, and lashing out was merely a symptom. Some people carry that pain with silence and grace. Others wear it like a zebra-print miniskirt and shout it into the world. But the pain is always there, bubbling just beneath the surface. I was dumbstruck and filled with admiration for that young man, who had just taken a verbal beating the likes of which I'd rarely witness in public.

Another thing which that visit to a Wat taught me, was on your first visit to a temple, if you are unfamiliar with the cosmology, the symbology, architecture, and iconography, it's a prudent idea to join a paid tour group. The docent-led tours are inexpensive and created specifically for foreigners who want to actually learn something. As you walk past tour groups, it is common to hear the docents' speaking languages from all over the world.

The downside is the tours can be large groups. That means a timed and regimented walk-through that doesn't leave space for musing and cruising. But you'll learn a lot about not only the Wat you're visiting, but the commonalities of Wat's you might visit in the future. There is a lot going on in the symmetry of the grounds, the architectural design flourishes and what each building is used for, making your next visit more informed, and to my mind, more informed means more enjoyable. Yeah - I'm woke. Sue me.

Wat architecture follows a remarkably consistent set of principles across almost all temples in Thailand. With few exceptions, each Wat is composed of two main sections: the PhutthaWat and the SangkhaWat. This division isn't just practical. It reflects the spiritual and communal functions of the monastery.

The PhutthaWat arena is dedicated to the Buddha and is typically open to the public. It's where laypeople come to make merit, light incense, and occasionally stare in wonder at a larger-than-life Buddha radiating serenity. While the architectural styles may vary from region to region, the layout and purpose of the buildings within the PhutthaWat are strikingly consistent. You'll almost always find a Viharn (the main worship hall), an Ubosot or bot (the ordination hall, often considered the most sacred space), a bell tower, and one or more Chedis.

In contrast, the SangkhaWat - the section of the temple where the monks live, eat, and sleep - is almost always closed to the general public. It includes living quarters, meditation spaces, study halls, libraries and sometimes small gardens or artfully secluded areas for walking meditation. It's the engine room of the monastery: quieter, more utilitarian, and distinctly less photogenic, unless you're into laundry lines and alms bowls.

Together, the PhutthaWat and SangkhaWat form the full spiritual and practical life of the Wat - a balance of devotion and discipline, public ritual and private practice. It's a layout that has endured for centuries.

The Chedi, also known as stupas are large bell-shaped domes which are often covered in gold leaf, gleaming in the sun like oversized trophies to devotion. At their core lies a relic chamber, typically housing remains or artifacts associated with the Buddha or revered monks. They are symbols of vertical transcendence.

There is always a Wihan - the often ornately decorated hall that contains large Buddha statues and artworks depicting the life of the Buddha. The Wihan is an assembly hall where monks and lay Buddhists, and the curious visitor, congregate to pay respects to the Buddha, hold ceremonies and more.

Some, though not all, Wats include an Ubosot, the ordination hall and the most sacred space in the monastery. The Ubosot is where a senior monk, trained in the detailed rituals of ordination, induct novices into monastic life. This hall is generally off-limits to the public. Only temple monks and the Upajjhāya (Preceptor) are permitted entry, underscoring its spiritual weight.

There is often but not always a Ho Rakhang - a bell tower used for waking the monks and to call them to ceremonies. If no bell tower is on the grounds, a large gong is used for the same purpose.

Often there is a structure called a Sala. These are in the form of a pavilion offering shade and a place to rest or meditate.

The structures in Wats across Thailand are like architectural cousins. They share a lot of similarities, as if all the temples were made by the same design team. Take the roofs for example. They cascade upward in neat tiers, like a layered cake, topped off with decorative bargeboards that run along the peak centerline of the roof. These bargeboards are often carved into intricate designs, attached to the projecting apex of the pitched roof, right in front of the gable. And those carvings usually feature Nāga, the snake deity that seems to show up everywhere, both in Buddhist and Hindu traditions. Seriously, if Nāga had a LinkedIn profile, he'd be the most connected deity in the world.

The Nāga is more than just a snazzy piece of decor though. Ancient mythology tells the story that after the Buddha attained enlightenment while meditating under the Bodhi tree, a torrential downpour commenced. A giant snake-like creature named Mucalinda appeared from the underworld and used its hoods to shield the Buddha from the rain. Now, that's what I call a good friend; a really big, scaly, multi-headed friend. Nāgas are most often found as the railings leading up temple steps, where they unfurl their giant serpent bodies, their heads at the entrance ready to give you a protective hiss blessing as you ascend.

And if Nāga doesn't quite do it for you, there's Garuda. This winged figure is the mount of the Hindu god Vishnu, its feathered wings spread out in elaborate designs, showcasing a mythical bird that's the spiritual equivalent of a rock star.

Both Nāga and Garuda are legends in Hindu and Buddhist iconography, often featured in local folk traditions as well. In some parts of the Himalayas, Nāgas aren't just for decorating. They're considered the divine rulers of the land.

The finials that stick out from the end corners of the bargeboards are called hang hong, and yes, that's their official name, even though that sounds like something you'd order for takeout while wondering if you should use a spoon or chopsticks. You'll usually find Nāga's head, turned upward and away from the building like it's gazing into the universe. And if you're lucky, you might encounter a Nāga with multiple heads. At Doi Suthep in Chiang Mai, each Nāga is adorned with nine - yes, nine - heads. That's a lot of facetime screen filler but hey, the more the merrier? Who doesn't need more protection these days?

At the central peak of the roof, you'll find the ornament known as the Chofa - or sky tassel - which predominately takes the form of Garuda's beak. Think of it as the crowning glory of the temple roof, completing the whole "sacred yet stylish" vibe. It's as if the roof had a feathered, mythical finishing touch, just to say, "This temple isn't just functional, it's also tres chic."

As one of the most sought-after attractions not just in Thailand but across much of Asia, Wats hold a magnetic pull for tourists. Which, of course, means they also tend to get very crowded. If you want a moment of peace with your spiritual self, or even just a photo without someone grin bombing your frame, you best show up early. Really early. Like before the tour buss crowds have finished their hotel buffet breakfast early.

I always found it a bit jarring to watch those enormous tour buses roll into temple parking lots like clockwork, expelling wide-eyed, sun-hatted tourists like a spiritual clown car. Most of them shuffle in clutching iced coffees in one hand and their phones in the other, capturing every gilded inch through their screens. Phones out, faces glazed over, recording everything - experiencing nothing. So much for awareness.

In Bangkok, Chiang Mai, and Chiang Rai there is no shortage of Wat marvels. Bangkok hosts some of the most symbolically important Wats in southeast Asia not only for their architecture but for their enshrined history. These are snippets because many of the Bangkok temples are discussed more in-depth later.

BANGKOK

WAT PHRA KAEW. DON'T EVEN THINK OF LITTERING!

Wat Phra Kaew, home of the fabled and fabulous Emerald Buddha, is located within the walled compound of the Grand Palace. Officially named Wat Phra Si Rattana Satsadaram, this is no roadside temple or dusty relic - it's the spiritual epicenter of a country that doesn't do anything halfway when it comes to devotion. The temple complex is among the most dazzling in the world, and for Thais, it is the most sacred of grounds.

At its heart is the Ubosot, the consecrated ordination hall, constructed to house a statue whose story reads like a Southeast Asian who-done-it history mystery. The Emerald Buddha - though technically not emerald, but a deep green jasper - was claimed from Laos by King Rama I in 1779 and relocated from Wat Arun to its current pedestal inside the Grand Palace. The statue had proven too sacred, too politically loaded, too cosmically significant to reside outside the king's watchful eye.

Visiting the Grand Palace is an experience that doesn't so much ask for reverence as insist upon it. It is a realm of paradox where opulence is a stratagem, designed to take you beyond the limits of your senses.

The grounds are immaculate in that only-in-royal-compounds kind of way: not a leaf out of place, not a tile out of line. I believe that weeds know they're not allowed. It's an alchemy of sacred geometry, opulent flourishes, and a steady breeze of awe. Stand anywhere, turn slowly, and you'll see a riot of rich colors and dazzling gold, uncountable spires adorning rooftops and Chedis, mosaic-tiled walls and halls shimmering everywhere like beetle wings, and statues frozen mid-blessing. It's not subtle.

The big draw is the Emerald Buddha which has a fascinating history behind it full of intrigue as all good spiritual and historical artifacts should be. From India where legend says it was carved, to Ceylon (Sri Lanka), to Burma (Myanmar) to the Kingdom of Cambodia, to the Kingdom of Laos, and finally to the Kingdom of Siam, the Emerald Buddha got to go on many adventures. According to myth, the Emerald Buddha was created in 43 BCE by a sage named Nagasena in the city of Pataliputra, India. Nagasena had help from the deities Vishnu and Indra, 500 years after Buddha attained Nirvana. Not bad - having a couple of heavy-duty deities to help you with your sacred craft project has got to make the job easier.

One account of how the Emerald Buddha, which had been lost to time, was re-discovered, tells the story that the statue wound up in a monastery in the Lan Na Kingdom through a succession of conquests (i.e. looting) and then royal lineage marriages as it was passed around Asia. In 1434AD as the story goes, a bolt of lightning struck the Chedi at Wat Pa Yia, or Bamboo Forest Monastery in Chiang Rai, revealing a stucco Buddha statue inside. The Buddha was brushed off and placed in the Abbot's residence. One day the Abbot noticed a chip of stucco on the nose had flaked off, revealing a green stone underneath. The Abbot ordered the stucco removed and once completed, they saw a small Buddha figure carved from the semi-precious green stone - jasper - which is a type of hard jade. After years of bouncing around through conquest and succession, it was brought to Bangkok to the temple of Wat Arun, where he resided until 1785AD when he was brought to his current home under great pomp and celebration.

Do not expect an imposing towering statue. The Emerald Buddha is a diminutive little fellow, sitting only 26 inches tall by 19 inches wide.

However - the Emerald Buddha has a really nice wardrobe that Yves St. Laurent would be envious of. During the summer season, he wears a stepped, pointed crown, a breast pendant, a sash, a necklace, bracelets - all royal attire. The garments and jewelry are made of gold, embedded with precious gems. During the rainy season he gets a headpiece of gold studded with sapphires and a gold-embossed monk's robe draped over his left shoulder. The winter season finds the Emerald Buddha adorned with yet another golden headpiece studded with diamonds and a jewel-fringed gold-mesh shawl draped over him. Nice attire and you get the King of Thailand as your personal valet. It's a good gig being the Emerald Buddha.

WAT ARUN: THE TEMPLE OF DAWN

Standing tall and proud on the right bank of the Chao Phraya - the big river that flows through the heat and heart of Bangkok, ancient Wat Arun stands tall against a skyline of modernity. This striking temple, standing proud at 282 feet tall, is a showcase of both architecture and art spanning centuries of political willpower and artistic vision.

I first saw Wat Arun from across the Chao Phraya River while I was having dinner with one of my monk brothers who was a Bangkok native. He had promised to take me out when I was back in Bangkok, to a restaurant which he said represented the best dining experience in the city featuring classic, though elevated Thai dishes. It was a warm clear night and across the river, Wat Arun, located on the opposite bank of the river, was lit up like something out of a fairy tale. Its centerpiece, a Khmer-style Prang (the tall central tower) glowed against a starry sky, its outer four prangs in perfect symmetry creating a vista that made my jaw drop with its power and beauty. I knew then that I'd cancel the plans I had made and head there the next day to check it out with my dear friend Chalermwan. Funny that I saw it at night because the translated name means "Temple of Dawn." Gotta love the irony.

The main pagoda had undergone many restorations over the centuries as the limestone and ceramic tiles used for construction and adornment are constantly being bombarded with heat, humidity, rain and more recently, smog, which creates acid rain, which loves to eat away at limestone. The most recent renovation began in 2013 and was finally completed in 2017.

Touring the magnificent temple grounds, going up the impossibly steep stone steps to the high walkway of the central prang, was incredible. You could feel the majestic history of the Wat all around you, permeating you.

Something I discovered that is quite unique about Wat Arun is that it was constructed not only with Buddhist principles in mind - the three levels represent primary existence on bottom, the heaven of fulfillment in the middle, and the seven realms of happiness up top, but Hindu and Chinese cosmology and symbology are represented in the motifs throughout the temple complex. The name Arun itself is derived from the Hindu deity Aruna - charioteer of the sun god Surya. This is not unusual in Thailand, where inclusiveness and the respect for other spiritual beliefs and religions are the norm rather than an uncomfortable exception.

WAT PHO. NO, NOT THE SOUP

Wat Phra Chetuphon Wimonmangkalaram Ratchaworamahawihan, or Wat Pho for those of us who simply cannot pronounce that name, is home to the world's largest reclining Buddha. It is the oldest Wat in Bangkok and home to the largest collection of Buddhas - over 1,000 - in Thailand. Building the Wat began in the 16th century, again by King Rama I. He was a busy guy and wanted a lot of merits, though it was King Rama III who in 1832AD had the reclining Buddha and temple commissioned and built, to further the good works of his grandfather.

The image of a reclining Buddha, head resting in hand as he lay dying during his eightieth year, yet completely at peace having shed fear long ago, is a popular motif throughout SE Asia. It symbolizes the Buddha entering Nibbana (Nirvana) thus ending the cycle of rebirth. The reclining Buddha at Wat Pho is the third largest in Thailand but the elegance of this statue has made it one of the most popular artistic expressions in the world and aside from the soles of his feet, is completely layered with gold leaf. Buddha's feet are equally impressive, inlaid with mother-of-pearl. Each foot displays 108 intricate, inlaid dioramas. Flowers, dancers, elephants, tigers, and altar accessories are engraved, as a kind of roadmap to discover the next Buddha to appear in this realm of existence.

He is quite a sight to behold. He's big. Not just big - he's huge! The Reclining Buddha is just shy of 151 feet long and forty-nine feet tall. Housed in Phra Buddha Saiyas Vihara, the hall itself is beautiful, adorned with complex murals on every surface and pillar.

The Wat Pho compound contains four great Chedi, ninety-one small Chedi, a large central shrine, spacious Viharas and pavilions and a museum. The ceramic-tile covered Chedis throughout the complex are all different in style and sizes, each one similar yet unique in its artistic expression. Large stone Chinese statues depicting deities and warriors are found throughout the grounds guarding the gates along the perimeter as sentinels at the inner gates.

But it's not just the gilded, enormous reclining Buddha, incredibly beautiful Chedi and art that surrounds you at every turn that makes Wat Pho special. While the Grand Palace grounds (just down the street) are immaculate, the grounds of Wat Pho are stunningly beautiful, serene, and magical. Each part of the complex has a unique aura to it. From elegant gardens filled with birdsong, to potted trees where one can spent time in contemplation, Wat Pho has a serenity and beauty beyond all other Wat's I visited throughout Thailand.

Wat Pho is also unique due to its historical foundation as a medical education institution which to this day is open to the public. It is also the birthplace of traditional Thai massage techniques, and as well as housing a traditional medical sciences and massage school, it has a Sala pavilion where visitors can get a Thai massage from masters of the art for a nominal donation.

But my favorite part of my visit were the school kids. Groups of students were wandering around with clipboards in their hands, approaching tourists with a questionnaire. They were adorable! I was approached by a group and enjoyed their questions. Who was I? Where was I from? Was this my first time to Thailand? What was I doing in Thailand? How long would I be there? Where else would I be going? What were my impressions? What do I do for a career? They were adorable and worked their English skills. They would ask me if they were saying something correctly. At the end of questioning from both groups, they asked to take pictures with me, so we hammed it up for selfies and then came the best part - they handed me small candies, handmade at their school.

CHIANG MAI

WAT PHRA THAT DOI SUTHEP

Often referred to simply as "Doi Suthep" it is also the name of the mountain atop where it is located. It is perched up high overlooking the city of Chiang Mai and is accessible by foot via a series of trails built through the forested mountains, bicycle (quite an uphill climb) scooter, motorcycle, car, bus, and the fleet of Songtaew. From the temple, the views of downtown Chiang Mai on a cloudless day are incredible.

But that mountain isn't just scenic - it's storied.

A monk named Sumanathera, as legend tells, had a vision. He was instructed to travel to Pang Cha to find a holy relic. He did and discovered what was said to be a shoulder bone of the Buddha. Mysterious powers surrounded the relic - it glowed, moved on its own, even duplicated itself. But when he brought it to King Dhammaraja of Sukhothai, nothing happened. No miracles. No divine light show. The king, unimpressed, told the monk to keep it.

Enter King Nu Naone, CEO of the Lanna Kingdom, who heard the tale and saw an opportunity. In 1368, Sumanathera traveled north to present the relic. This time, the relic snapped in two. The larger half was tied to the back of a white elephant - because if you're going to let fate decide something, might as well go full folklore - and the elephant was released into the wild. It climbed Doi Suthep, trumpeted three times, and then keeled over. Naturally this was interpreted as a divine sign, and construction of the temple began where the elephant died in 1383AD. Of course, it could have simply been the elephant dying of a freakin' heart attack from climbing the mountain, but we're talking mythology here.

The name Wat Phra That Doi Suthep is rich in layers. Phra denotes sacredness, That refers to a relic, and Wat is a temple - so yes, we're talking about a sacred temple built to house a relic of the Buddha himself. Legend holds that it rests in the center of the main chedi, just above the octagonal base and below the lotus-bud spire. Whether or not you believe the story, the reverence in the air is real.

Due to the Buddha's bone, Doi Suthep is one of the most sacred pilgrimage spots in Thailand and indeed throughout SE Asian countries. Chiang Mai, being the historic center of the Lan Na Kingdom, going back to the 14th century, makes this beautiful Wat something a little above and beyond your everyday temple.

Doi Suthep gets busy. Remarkably busy. One day an Aussie friend texted me at the same time that I was reaching out to her; both of us asked the other if we wanted to go up the mountain to visit the temple. It was meant to be, so with an assigned meeting place and time, we hooked up at the base of the mountain to grab a songtaew. She was fluent in Thai which made negotiating the price much easier, as those little red trucks charge much more per person if they are not fully loaded.

Up we went, passing numerous bicycle jockeys, power-peddling up the mountain in their peacock-colored spandex. Next to the parking area, flowing down the hill like a terraced vertical shopping mall, was a public market. Dozens of small stalls sold food, memorabilia, clothing, and of course touristy swag. But it was up the hill that intimidated me. I had seen the pictures, but the long stairs leading up to the monastery stretched to the sky creating its own horizon through the surrounding jungle.

Three hundred and six steps, flanked by enormous undulating Nāga serpents in green and gold, wound their way up - myth turned sculpture. I counted every single one of them. The stairs weren't just a physical climb. They were a rite of passage. By the time we reached the top our legs trembled under lactic revolt while our lungs begged for mercy. Our sweat had achieved full Woke-AF status.

We stepped into the inner grounds, and I had to stop for a second - this temple was almost unnervingly symmetrical, like someone had used a divine protractor to lay the place out. It was iPhone tight - all killer, no filler. It was Thailand's Father's Day, the national holiday celebrating the late King Bhumibol Adulyadej (Rama IX) and Wat Doi Suthep was decked out for the occasion. Paper lanterns by the hundreds, in every color, hung from the eaves. A thousand strands of prayer flags stretched up to the central stupa like a maypole. Monks threaded through the crowd, grinning like kids at a carnival. There was reverence, sure - but also joy, noise, and the gentle mayhem of a culture that knows how to throw a party for its King.

The layout of the temple is circular, designed for circumambulation - pilgrims walk clockwise around the golden chedi - of course I joined in; had to didn't I? We prayed and made offerings. Despite the crush of people, there was a rhythm to it all, like a living mandala.

Eventually though, the crowds wore me down as low-hanging clouds blocked the legendary view over the city. We wandered to the open-aired café perched over a lush ravine. We sipped lattes, watching birds rise and fall on the thermals, as if they too had come for a better perspective.

Bronwyn wanted to find brass bells for her house in Hobart, so we descended the Nāga staircase, thankfully easier in reverse, though hell on the knees, and wandered into a quieter market tucked off to the right. This was no rube tchotchke bazaar. This was the real deal. Antique wood carvings, hand-woven textiles, heirloom pottery, and in one glass case, an ancient and incredibly ornate Sak Yant bamboo tattoo kit nestled in a carved teak box. It was stunning. It made me want to tattoo myself. I still regret not buying it. Bronwyn had made her decision, mixing and matching bells from several different sets to achieve the style she was looking for.

WAT CHEDI LUANG VARAVIHARA. A LIVING WRECK

Wat Chedi Luang is located in the old town of the "new city" of Chiang Mai. Once home to the precious Emerald Buddha, construction of the huge stupa was initiated in the mid-1300's, though not completed until the mid-15th century. It was the largest building in the Lan Na Kingdom, standing at just under 270 feet, in the highlands of northern Thailand. It dwarfed all other structures and was visible to the entire region.

Sadly, in 1545AD, an enormous earthquake struck the region, toppling much of the upper temple. While it still looks like a crumbled ruin, the early 1990's saw the chedi partially restored. Japan and UNESCO provided financing, but the end results have been controversial. Many detractors say the restoration elements are not in the traditional style, losing historical Lanna architectural elements. Today, a copy of the Emerald Buddha, marking the 600th anniversary celebration, was installed in the reconstructed eastern niche. Made of black jade, it is worth spending time there to gaze upon.

Don't get me wrong. The history and antiquity of the stupa was magnificent, but it somehow felt more like a tourist attraction than a spiritual center.

That morning, I wandered the temple grounds, circling the ancient stupa beneath a canopy of shade trees. Wide stone benches lined the perimeter - perfect for sitting, squinting, and pretending to be deep in reflection. I gave it a shot. The place felt heavy with history, but oddly fractured. The new temple, all polished and pristine in modern Wat style, looked like it had been airlifted in from a theme park. It sat awkwardly beside the massive, crumbling brick stupa, the true anchor of the place. Less a companion than a visual contradiction.

Tucked deeper within the grounds lies one of the most curious, and frankly, unsettling, corners of Chiang Mai's spiritual legacy: the city pillar, the Inthakhin. Unlike the open grace of most temple spaces, this one hums with something darker, heavier. The pillar is housed in its own shrine, set apart like something not to be revered so much as contained. It's said to protect the city, but not all spirits guard with benevolent hands. Locals offer a quick wai as they pass - not in worship, but as a kind of spiritual insurance policy. A subtle, practiced gesture that says: I see you, I respect you, now please leave me the hell alone. Back home, founding a city involves paperwork and a bored clerk in a fluorescent-lit office. Here, it once required blood, bone, and an understanding that some forces don't play nice.

Only men are allowed to enter the city pillar shrine, a rule that struck me as both archaic and suspicious. According to legend, these pillars were once consecrated through human sacrifice. Young men, and sometimes pregnant women, the more "potent" the life taken, the stronger the spirit that would be bound to protect the city. No bones have ever been found, but then again, no one seems eager to dig. Some claim the practice lasted into the mid-19th century. Whether that's folklore designed to thrill, or history quietly and uneasily buried, the air around the shrine felt undeniably heavy, thick with old power and secrets best left undisturbed. That women are still barred from entering, even now, only deepens the unease.

But it wasn't until I was strolling past at night a few evenings later that the temple truly came alive. The stupa, lit from beneath on all four sides, glowed like a sentinel standing guard over the city, its ancient surface flickering with the ghosts of a million candlelit prayers. The air was still, reverent. Time felt suspended. And then, without warning, the sky dumped a biblical downpour. One moment I was marveling at sacred geometry bathed in golden light, the next I was soaked to the soul, slipping on stone. Nothing snaps you out of spiritual awe, quite like wet underwear.

WAT PHRA SINGH WORAMAHAWIHAN

This was the first Wat I spent time at during my travels through Thailand, which I've written about before, for Wat Phra Singh was the site where I witnessed the woman who didn't want to be encumbered by a covering for her shoulders and knees, causing quite a scene.

Wat Phra Singh is located in the old city center. The main entrance gate is guarded by Singhs (Chinese lions), which is a unique touch. Wat Phra Singh is located at the end of Rachadamnoen Road which runs east from the temple, via the ancient Tapae Gate, via direct line to the Ping River. Construction of the temple began in 1345AD and was originally intended to house the ashes of King Phayu's father. Now that's a loyal and dedicated son.

The crown jewel of the Wat Phra Singh complex is Wihan Lai Kham, a striking blend of teak and stucco built in the classic Lanna style, ornate, compact, and somehow managing to look both humble and royal at once. Inside sits Phra Buddha Sihing, Thailand's second most revered Buddha image, playing silver medalist to the Emerald Buddha in Bangkok. Though, let's be honest, the Emerald Buddha is roughly the size of a fat housecat and spends most of its time dressed like it's attending a royal garden party.

Phra Buddha Sihing's origin is shrouded in a haze of legend and possibly deliberate vagueness. Legend says it was sculpted in the image of Siddhartha Gautama himself - the Lion of the Shakya clan - a bold claim that conveniently can't be verified. The original? Long gone. Maybe looted during one of the many sackings of Chiang Mai, maybe "relocated" during a colonial moment of curiosity. Odds are it's sipping Tuscan light somewhere in the living room of a retired European diplomat, sandwiched between a stolen Khmer bas-relief and an infinity pool with excellent feng shui.

Historical accounts claim the statue originated at the Mahabodhi Temple in Bodh Gaya, India, passed through Sri Lanka (Ceylon), made its way to Nakhon Si Thammarat (Ligor), then to Ayutthaya, and finally arrived in Chiang Mai. That's quite a journey for a single artifact, and a tempting one for sticky-fingered pilgrims. Today, there are three contenders for the title of "authentic" Phra Buddha Sihing: the one in Chiang Mai, another in Wat Phra Mahathat, and the third housed in the Bangkok National Museum. None have been tested or authenticated, and just to keep things spicy, one of the heads mysteriously vanished in 1922. As one does.

I returned to Wat Phra Singh for a quieter, more contemplative experience: a monk chat. This daily activity allows visitors to sit with a monk, make a small donation, and discuss life's big questions, or just talk about your dog. The monk listens, offers thoughtful reflections, and concludes the session with a blessing. During the ceremony, he ties a knotted white cord around your wrist, a sai sin, while chanting a personalized benediction. Tradition holds that you should wear it until it falls off naturally. Mine was tied on October 30th, 2024, at precisely 11:11AM, and as I write this on July 22nd, 2025, it's still hanging on. That's either the sign of a truly powerful blessing... or incredibly good knot work. Possibly both.

CHIANG RAI

WAT RONG KHUN. TURN DOWN THE LIGHTS!

The White Temple. Yep, it's white! Gleaming white (dentists across the globe twist with envy at how white the place its!), it sparkle-dances across your retinas due to thousands of small mirror tiles set into every conceivable surface of this visually stunning ode to the Buddha's life journey. It's like someone took a giant scoop of snow, threw in a bunch of crystals, and said, "Let's build a temple!" On a bright, sunny day, I highly recommend a welders helmet - it's that white.

The juxtaposition between the blazing white structure, symbolizing the Buddha's purity, and the thousands upon thousands of reflective mirror tiles, symbolizing reflection and wisdom, makes a bold statement. The temple itself reflects the idea of reflection. Pretty clever, right? This constant mirroring is an invitation to think about our own inward spiritual journey towards enlightenment, a central theme in the Dhamma. It's all about self-examination, shedding desire, and purging the ego, so you can see your true nature, a kind of spiritual exfoliation.

Located fourteen kilometers to the south of Chiang Rai, unless you're in for a long walk (not recommended because its entrance is located off a broad highway) you'll need to hire a ride, but the good news is that every form of transportation in Chiang Rai will get you there. I called a grab cab to head out, figuring I'd find some way to get back to town once there.

One of the perks of having an internationally renowned artist at the helm of a project like this, who also has the funds to make it happen, is that the entrance fee is a mere 100 Baht (about $3 USD). It's a beautiful gesture, showing Chalermchai Kositpipat's commitment to making the temple accessible to everyone. Additional donations are welcome, but capped at 10,000 Baht (around $300), as he is adamant about not being beholden to any large donors - be they corporate or private. This is a rare move in the world of big-ticket cultural projects, where money often talks louder than the artist's vision. Kositpipat wants the temple to remain a personal creation, free from the strings of corporate or private interests. Level up, Chalermchai.

By the end of the 19th century, the original temple on this site had crumbled into near-oblivion. Chiang Rai, smaller and scrappier than its cousin Chiang Mai, didn't have the resources, or maybe just didn't have the interest, to save it. The Sangha aged, passed on, and the temple quietly collapsed into ruin. Fast forward to 1997: enter Chalermchai Kositpipat, a Chiang Rai native with international acclaim, a taste for the surreal, and, crucially, a very healthy bank account. He didn't restore the temple. He razed it, and from the rubble conjured something wildly new: a gleaming, otherworldly monument to Buddhism, Thai identity, and unfiltered artistic vision. And it worked. Today, Wat Rong Khun - the White Temple - pulls in tourists like moths to a mirrored lotus, easily the most visited site in the city.

The moment you step through the gates and onto the path toward the bridge, it hits you: this isn't just a temple, it's an art installation, a dark dreamscape, a warning. Chalermchai doesn't traffic in subtlety. His symbolism is bold, unflinching, and at times unsettling in exactly the way he intends.

The "Cycle of Rebirth" installation, which you cross en route to the main hall, doesn't ease you in. It grabs you. Hundreds of hands and anguished faces stretch upward on both sides of the bridge from a pit, clawing for something. Desire. Escape. Relief from suffering. Their neediness is palpable. The sheer volume of it makes the desperation almost unbearable. It's a stunning reversal: suffering rendered in purity. A reminder that unrestrained desire is the real hell, and that salvation isn't found in reaching for more, but in learning to let go. Heavy stuff!

At the foot of the bridge stand two Kinnaree, mythical beings from Buddhist lore with the upper body of a woman and the lower half of a giant bird. They're symbols of grace and beauty, but here they're more than decorative. They serve as gatekeepers, guiding visitors past the worst of human impulses: temptation, greed, desire. Their presence is serene but unblinking, like they've seen it all before and know most of us are still going to screw it up.

They reminded me of Rodin's Gates of Hell, not just in form, but in function. This is suffering and longing sculpted into stillness. It's not subtle, and it's not supposed to be. You don't walk away thinking about tourist trinkets. You walk away thinking about merit, rebirth, and the uneasy truth that most of our problems start with wanting too much.

One of the interesting things about the entire temple design is its allegorical story telling of the Buddhist path towards enlightenment. Each building as you cycle through the well-thought-out storyline takes you along the journey from rebirth to Nibbana, something unique from any other Wat I'd visited - a Wat, as a story-telling vehicle but ramped up to twenty.

WAT RONG SUEA TEN - BECAUSE WHO DOESN'T NEED A BLUE TEMPLE?

In Chiang Rai, having two iconic bold Wats was not enough. Now that they had the White Temple, in stark contrast to the Black House (Bâan Dam - a private art museum and temple), they needed another equally impressive temple in a new color as well, and they got one in the form of Wat Song Suea Ten, or Temple of the Dancing Tiger, in the Rim Kok neighborhood. Sporting a modern-design and painted a bold, striking cerulean blue, with a lot of gold to boot, Wat Rong Suea Ten is another very unique temple. Those crazy Chiang Rai kids!

Legend (okay, maybe not legend, but let's pretend) has it that one boozy karaoke night, the Chiang Rai community decided they needed another crown jewel temple. Something that would dazzle, disturb, and make grandma gasp. The call went out for designs that screamed "shock and awe." Enter Phuttha Kabkaew, aka Sala Nok, a protégé and contemporary of Chalermchai Kositpipat, the mastermind behind the White Temple. With white and black temples already taken, Sala Nok went bold: deep, electric sapphire blue, trimmed with gold so sharp it practically winks with attitude.

Completed in 2016, Wat Rong Suea Ten's central building is a showstopper, not just for its vivid colors but for the intricate, almost hypnotic detail covering every surface. And guarding the staircase? Two of the largest, most vivid multi-headed Nāga guardians I've ever seen, snarling like they mean business.

Wat Song Suea Ten is designed in the dramatic neo-traditional (read wild and wacky) style of Buddhist artistic expression, pioneered by Chalermchai, creating outrageous sculptures with bold psychedelic flourishes.

It was an early morning so pristine it practically begged for a heroic stroll. I slipped on my leather flip-flops, the ones that apparently qualify me as a local legend. No, really! Over a latte in Chiang Mai, a woman had paused mid-sip just to declare, "You're the American who walks everywhere in leather sandals?" That's right, folks - I've earned my street cred one step at a time in OluKai's.

I set out to conquer the six kilometers from Gita's Guesthouse to the Blue Temple with zero planning finesse. My route hugged a busy highway for most of the way, because why take the scenic route when you can smell exhaust and dodge speeding trucks! Still, the morning was cool, traffic sparse, and the sky that kind of blue that fools you into thinking, "This won't suck."

I came to the bridge spanning the Kok River, yes, the one begging for a bad joke. As I crossed, I was hit by a pastoral scene so perfectly southeast Asian it could've been plucked from a postcard or a daydream. The river stretched broad and calm, its banks punctuated by primitive wooden houses on stilts, weathered but sturdy, like old sailors standing watch. Small rice paddies patched the landscape, their neon-green shoots glowing in the morning light. White egrets stalked the shallows with dignity, while smaller birds darted and sang high in the trees.

A grassy spit jutted into the water - a perfect natural stage where half a dozen water buffalo grazed the tall grass, their slick black hides gleaming under the sun like lacquered sculptures. Flat-bottomed boats drifted lazily nearby, fishermen poling quietly, tossing fine seine nets in wide lazy arcs that rippled the mirror-smooth surface. The whole scene was so vividly alive it made me pause, blink twice, and remember why the hell I love this place.

Walking further I found the small side street leading me within a few hundred feet to a driveway into the parking lot of the Blue Temple. I was expecting something more akin to the white temple - with its broad, divided and landscaped driveway, tour busses, shops, and glittering signs pointing everywhere. This was much more to my liking. The Blue Temple was tucked away in a local neighborhood and if you didn't know it was there, or were not paying attention, it would be easy to pass by.

As I neared the parking area, I spotted Pascal perched on a bench, the Swiss bike-tourer with just enough madness to make you respect him. We had met the night before at the Reggae Bar in downtown Chiang Rai, where his stories of pedaling across Asia sounded like equal parts adventure and mild insanity. He was taking a breather for a few days, waiting on a friend to join him for the Thai leg of his journey.

Buried in his phone, he didn't notice me slide onto the bench beside him.

When he finally looked up, he did the classic double-take, like I'd suddenly materialized out of thin air. Then that broad grin spread across his face, lighting up with the unmistakable spark of recognition.

"Good morning. This is a surprise. How are you, How's your head from last night?"

We may have had more than a few beers and shots.

"I'm good - took a nice long walk to get the body working and sweat the drinks out. I thought I'd come up here and check out Song Suea Ten and all this ... blue," I said as I waved across the parking area at the temple compound where the deep sapphire theme was in full force.

I looked over at his bike, shocked that it looked like something you'd see in a postcard from some non-descript village in the Vietnam highlands, dating back a century.

"You rode that across the continent?"

Pascal laughed hard: "Hell no! My touring bike is getting worked on. I rented that from the hostel to get around for a few days."

"I was going to say - you're even tougher than you look, riding that thing around the world."

Pascal laughed. "It's awful. But I must keep peddling for muscle memory. The seat is torture!"

We chatted a little more, then said "see you at the bar tonight" as I rose and headed to the entrance of the Wat to check it out.

Australian, German, Spanish, French, Eastern European, Russian and a couple from Iceland - the early birds quietly marveling at the temple's unapologetic blaze of blue in the early morning sun. Inside, the murals were pure visual jazz. Against the deep cerulean walls, white and gold mythological scenes leap forward like three-dimensional visions. It was historical Buddhist storytelling on acid, and it worked.

If blue is your favorite color, then Wat Song Suea Ten is for you. Not only are the existing temple structures a deep, rich cerulean hue but the inside murals use the same color, making the depictions of elements of Buddhist myths and legends really pop. The method of using a dark background to make the lighter colors and whites pop out of a painting is not new. It's one of the original tricks of the trade. At Wat Song Suea Ten, it is used to incredible effect, making all the elements portraying the stories come to life vividly.

After wandering the temple grounds, taking it all in, I sat down with a cappuccino and realized I didn't need to retrace my highway death-march. A longer, quieter path back to Gita's appeared on my GPS. Glorious. I was just about to start off when a red-haired woman, about my age, bounced over with a sunny grin and a familiar accent.

"Where are you from, mate?"

"Washington State. You?" I replied.

"Ireland. County Cork. City proper."

"Oh!?!?!? Do you know the McLeary family?" I asked.

She shrieked. "They're my cousins!"

Turns out, Sionainn was going to walk back to town as her tuk-tuk driver had tried to swindle her, and being Irish, she let him know that was a very bad idea. Never, *EVER* mess with an Irish lass! I liked her instantly.

And just like that, Sionainn and I were off, two strangers ambling through the quiet residential streets of Chiang Rai.

The walk back was much better. We shared a fluffy croissant sandwich and some fried chicken, picked up some road beers at 7-Eleven (as one does when hanging with an Irish lass), and wound our way back toward town, trading travel tales, laughing, and comparing absurd hotel and restaurant reviews. When we reached the bridge over the Kok River, instead of heading up the stairs and onward, she tugged my hand and veered toward the riverbank.

"Let's stop a while," she said.

We cracked open our beers and sat in the grass, watching the egrets stalk the shallows as fish of an unknown type jumped at a hatch. Trading stories of heartbreaks, breakthroughs, and everything in between we both felt that traveler's connection. When I pointed out that her name, Sionainn, means "wise river," she looked at me in surprise.

"How do you know that?"

"Hey - just because I'm American doesn't mean I don't know stuff."

She laughed, her red hair catching the midday sun like a halo as she leaned down to me...

Time stopped.

Sometimes a temple visit changes your spiritual trajectory. Sometimes, it just changes your afternoon.

An hour disappeared, and with plans to meet up at the Reggae Bar that evening, Sionainn and I parted ways. Sometimes heading out early in the morning has unintended consequences and though Sionainn never came to the bar, I'll always remember that wonderful moment on the bank of the Kok river.

❦

WAT HUAY PLA KANG: A GIANT BUDDHA ... GODDESS?

Wat Huay Pla Kang can be seen for miles across Chiang Rai Province, its luminous figure rising above the rolling countryside like a celestial lighthouse. Locals and tourists alike call it "The Big Buddha," but that nickname's a bit off the mark. It isn't Buddha at all. She is Guan Yin, the Buddhist Goddess of Mercy, gazing out over vast pastoral fields and gentle rolling hills with a calm that feels personal, no matter where you stand.

The staff at Gita's Guesthouse arranged, per my request, a driver to take me out to Huay Pla Kang early in the morning. I wanted to catch the temple in that soft, golden light around 7:00AM. My ride showed up, and wouldn't you know it? It was Nom. My tuk-tuk friend. The same cheerful soul I'd met on arrival, the one I'd shared beers and laughs with on the curb at the 7-Eleven and later at the Reggae Bar.

We locked eyes, grinned, and shook hands like old friends reuniting after a war, or at least a few paragraphs. Then we were off on the 30-minute, 14-kilometer ride through Chiang Rai's lush rural countryside. On the way, Nom told me about growing up in Chiang Mai, how he and his buddies learned English from Hollywood movies and recorded late-night TV episodes. We pulled over for coffee and set the tone for what would be a damn fine morning.

Wat Huay Pla Kang is the realized vision of a single monk - Phop Chok Tissuwaso - who took what was once an ancient, very modest backwoods temple and transformed it into something extraordinary. It took him just four years. The man was clearly a force of nature.

Because it sits outside the city core, Huay Pla Kang is quieter than other Chiang Rai temples, though its popularity is growing fast. That morning, I had it almost entirely to myself. The silence was luxurious. Except for the birds - they were exulting in the new dawn - loudly.

Guan Yin herself sits perched on a high hill, then rises 259 feet tall above the hillcrest. She's about the height of a 25-story building, radiating a peaceful power that stops you in your tracks. Her gleaming white surface catches the light in a way that makes her seem both solid and otherworldly. One hundred and fourteen grand stone steps led to a massive, broad white stone foundation. Once at the top of the steps, for 40 baht (roughly $1), ride the elevator up through the interior to a viewing platform nestled behind her third eye. From there, the countryside spreads out like a painting, verdant, misty, eternal and very, very green.

Inside, everything is white. And I mean everything. Ornate dragons, delicate trees, deities of all sizes and shapes, each sculpted in stunning three-dimensional detail, like the inside of a dream carved from alabaster. The atmosphere is so hushed and clean it feels like walking inside a snowflake.

Next to Guan Yin sits the temple's second marvel: a nine-story pagoda that blends Chinese and Lanna Thai styles in a way that shouldn't work but somehow does. It's pyramid-shaped - less traditional than the rounded or squared silhouettes you usually see - and instead of Nāgas flanking the staircase, there are two brilliantly coiled, elaborate Chinese dragons. The whole structure is painted in firecracker red, imperial gold, jade green, and bright yellow, standing in dramatic contrast to the all-white serenity of Guan Yin next door.

The effect is stunning. The place shouldn't be peaceful - the bright and busy façade of the pagoda adds an energy in concert to the serenity of Guan Yin. Maybe because it was early or maybe because I was there with an open heart and a good cup of coffee in me. Maybe it was just Buddha magic.

The effect is unexpectedly stunning. By all rights, it should be visual nightmare. That riot of color and detail stacked next to Guan Yin's calm, minimalist grandeur? It ought to clash. But instead, the two play off each other like yin and yang. The pagoda doesn't disrupt the peace. It energizes it. Maybe it was the early hour. Maybe it was the rare alignment of caffeine, clear skies, and spiritual openness. Or maybe it was just good old-fashioned Buddha vibe, the kind that doesn't need to explain itself to tourists with opinions.

On the way back to town, I turned to Nom. "You busy after this? Or... hungry?"

Nom laughed, "I'm Thai. I'm always hungry."

I told him lunch was on me, but he started to politely refuse until I reminded him that his hire time wasn't over yet, and that I had no interest in seeing another temple or waterfall or tea plantation. I wanted food and conversation. He relented, smirking.

"McDonald's," he deadpanned.

I shot him a look. "Try again."

Nom: "I was kidding. I don't like McDonalds."

I liked Nom more every time we met.

CHAPTER 14. BANGKOK'S SIREN SONG

"Money can't buy you happiness, but it can buy you a ticket to Bangkok" - anonymous

That, my friend, is some straight-up no-BS sage advice. Bangkok. A city of massive scale, loaded with mysteries waiting to be revealed. It was my first stop in Thailand for two nights and I hated it. Hate is a strong word but at that point in my life, I felt it viscerally. I didn't know a soul, or where the good stuff was (*it winds up the good stuff surrounds you*) and I was in no mood for a place so charged, so intense, so vast and full of possibility, when all I wanted to do was run like a crazed man into the jungle, ripping off my clothes and live in a cave up in the hills never thinking of love again.

Returning south to that massive realm of possibility reminded me of what Levon Helm of *The Band* once said about New York in *The Last Waltz* - that some places don't welcome you so much test your nerve. They hand you a beating, you get your ass kicked, lick your wounds, and, if you're lucky, fall in love with the whole mess anyway.

That is exactly what happened to me. Up north, life had been chill, sabai - less bustle, more reflection, a quieter pace of discovery where the rules felt unspoken. But Bangkok? Bangkok doesn't whisper. Bangkok yells at the top of its lungs and doesn't care if you're ready for it. Since the monastery, I'd been hanging out in the slower rhythms of Chiang Mai, Chiang Rai and Chiang Saen. Up in the mountains I'd been sipping tea, eating jok and noodles and contemplating life's bigger questions alongside a small river. The transition south felt like jumping into the eye of a roaring whirlpool that had no bottom.

Cities thrill me, plain and simple. From nightlife to daylife, the cultural options a major metropolis offers are the best kind of education. Raw, chaotic, unbridled and unforgettable. They enlighten you in the ways of the world: artistically, culinarily, politically, socially, or just by teaching you how to cross a frenzied boulevard without dying. I've been lucky to soak up the gritty edges and elegance of cities like San Francisco and New York, London, Guadalajara, Paris, Barcelona, Aukland and more. Places that either invite you in or size you up. Some cities charm you slow; others throw elbows. I thought I knew the game - how to land, find the rhythm, learn the rules even when they weren't obvious. But Bangkok didn't play by rules. It didn't whisper or wink. It smacked my face, blasted the doors open and dared me to step through.

Until this trip, I'd never stepped foot onto the Asian continent and never seen, except in videos, anything like Bangkok. Mexico City, Mumbai or Ho Chi Minh come to mind as comps but for pure unabridged size and manic delirium, those first two nights in Bangkok filled my sails then shredded them. To say I didn't enjoy the experience would be incorrect, but I was also not in a state of mind to take advantage of that intense energy injection.

When I returned from northern Thailand, Bangkok was in full festive swing; Christmas lights and holiday music fought for dominance against the ever-present hum of traffic and life. I knew I was staying put for a while, enough time to see what Bangkok could teach me. I rented an apartment along the Chao Phraya River, away from the touristy intensity of Sukhumvit, Asoke, Thong Lo and Nana neighborhoods. The Sunreno Serviced Apartments was a far cry from the glitzy hotels downtown. It wasn't five-star luxurious, though it was very spaciously comfortable. But it had something better. Peace and quiet. A rare commodity in that city.

In the Bang Kho Laem district, life moves at a slower pace - for Bangkok. The clerk at the front desk gave me a skeptical look when I mentioned my long-term stay. She said most travelers weren't interested in that part of Bangkok. It wasn't glamorous, sexy or flashy, and there wasn't much to do except for Asiatique, the giant riverside shopping plaza across the street. But the Sunreno was tucked out-of-the-way quiet, and that was exactly what I needed. A place to settle in before diving headfirst into the madness.

I checked into Room #9, which wound up being a fully furnished, spacious apartment, one generously proportioned and boasting a decent, albeit poorly equipped kitchen, enough closet and cupboard space to stash a battalion's worth of gear, a broad writing desk, a comfy king-sized bed flanked by side tables with reading lamps, and a seating alcove with floor-to-ceiling windows that made me feel like I was in the middle of a voyeuristic city documentary. The only thing missing was a window telescope for a spy on the neighbors.

Add to that a balcony that was spacious and solid with two chairs and a small table.

The modern bathroom had a walk-in glass shower that would've made anyone with a love for steam feel right at home. The place was older, but had a perfunctory elegance, and with daily housekeeping, it felt more like a pied-à-terre than a temporary crash pad. I shot the bartender from Chiang Mai a quick thank-you text. He'd hooked me up in exchange for my teaching him how to make a proper Manhattan (his was, I'll graciously say, substandard). He had invited me behind the bar to teach him and in exchange, when he found out I was heading south, told me that his extended family owned the Sunreno. The swap was an excellent exchange of goodwill. He raved about my Manhattan.

I completely unpacked both bags, shoved my empty roll-on into a closet and my daypack into another, because I was going to pretend I wasn't living out of luggage for the next two weeks. I ironed my button-down shirts and multiple pairs of linen drawstring pants, yes, pants, because I had use for a higher level of sophistication at times where shorts and t-shirts just wouldn't do. Chores done, it was time for dinner and a drink. And that's where I made my first Bangkok-rookie mistake.

The doorman, Wing, was still sizing me up, and did what any well-intentioned hotel staff would do: he sent me across the street to Asiatique, the neighborhood's version of ground-floor retail therapy. I later learned that most short-stay guests spent every evening there, which should have been a red flag, but my curiosity got the best of me. After all, the Thai love these modern, upscale malls. So, like the agreeable guy I am, I thought, 'Hey, when in Bangkok, right?'

The driveway to Sunreno stretched twenty-five yards from the lobby door to Chareon Krung Road and at 6 PM, I thought I was about to embark on a leisurely stroll across the street. I walked out of the hotel's manicured drive, decorated with hanging wall vines and koi ponds, only to be greeted by the full force of Bangkok mayhem. Cars, buses and tuk tuks were gridlocked as far as the eye could see in both directions. You'd think you could just slip between the vehicles like some smooth, seasoned local, but no. Factor in innumerable scooters and motorcycles darting in and out of that parking lot of a thoroughfare, and you'd quickly end up in traction. Looking up and down the boulevard, I had the sinking feeling that every single vehicle in Bangkok was making a pilgrimage to Asiatique. I would have to use every last bit of my "How to Cross a Busy Street in Thailand" skill set to survive.

I made my move and made it across. With a broad grin and two enthusiastic thumbs up from the parking lot attendant manning Asiatique's parking lot exit (directly across from the Sunreno driveway entrance/exit), I felt like the king of the world. Since it was still early and he wasn't in full traffic-directing mode, I stopped for a chat. His name was Pravat and he was the human embodiment of Bangkok's energy as we looked upon the river of lights as it snaked toward retail paradise.

Pravat was from Mae Fa Luang in Chiang Rai province, and when I told him how much I loved that part of the country, how it had gotten under my skin, his face lit up like someone had just handed him a happy puppy. We stood there on the sidewalk swapping stories about what and where I'd eaten, where I'd wandered, and I told him how the people up north - his people - had made me feel not like a tourist but a family friend.

When I mentioned I'd spent several nights cruising the night bazaar, he grinned and asked if I'd bought anything. I lifted my shirt hem to show him the incredible woven leather belt I'd picked up, and his smile widened. "That's my brother's work," he said proudly. When I described the vendor - the round, easy-going guy with a laugh that could fill a room - Pravat pressed his hands together in delighted recognition. "That's my dada." He wanted to know how his father looked, and I gave him the honest truth: sharp, witty, healthy and kind. The kind of man who makes you feel like you've known him for years after just a few minutes.

We shared a cigarette, standing at the edge of Bangkok's chaos, and for a moment the city felt smaller. He leaned in at one point, lowering his voice, offering secrets to a friend: "I can get you anything you want, anything - what are you looking for?"

I smiled, pausing just long enough for him to wonder, before saying, "*Enlightenment.*"

He burst out laughing - a full, genuine laugh that probably still echoes in his memory, as it does mine, when he thinks about the guy with the belt from his father's stall. "You're on your own for that one farang!" he laughed.

"Asiatique, The Riverfront" - the name's a mouthful, like the place itself. What stands now as one of Bangkok's glitziest nighttime destinations once served a very different purpose. Long before it was boutiques and booze gardens, it was maritime hustle. Back in 1887, the East Asiatic Company, a Danish trading and shipping outfit, chose that 12-acre patch on a broad bend of the Chao Phraya River as its Southeast Asia base. And it wasn't just piers and warehouses. It was an integrated ecosystem.

This was a working port. Every trade tied to the shipping and fishing industries had a stake in the operation. Rope-makers spun their lines by hand. Sail-makers stitched broad canvas through monsoon seasons. Woodworkers and blacksmiths hammered, sawed, and forged the boats that needed building while fixing those they'd already put to sea. The daily catch came in like clockwork and funneled out again just as fast - wholesalers, hawkers, families with carts, all part of the buzz. It was loud, dirty, necessary work. It fed and funded the neighborhood and beyond for decades.

But by the mid-20th century, the tide was turning. In 1947, the company began its slow decline and withdrawal. Global shipping was changing, Bangkok's industrial shoreline was moving downstream, and the East Asiatic dockyards were left to rot as everything does in tropical heat and humidity. What followed was decades of decline: vacant buildings, rusted cranes, broken windows, weeds growing tall, splitting cracks wide into the asphalt, then silence where there once was industry. Suan Lum Night Bazaar briefly revived the area, a flash of life with its night markets and cheap thrills, but that packed up and moved on by the late 2000s.

Then came the developers.

The plan: repurpose the bones of industry into a new kind of commerce - shopping, spectacle, gluttony, consumption. They razed most of the outbuildings but left the larger warehouses standing. Those were gutted and polished into raw-brick and beam showcases full of restaurants and bars. Where workshops once clanged with hammers, and the voices of thousands of workers filled the air, new grid-blocks sprang up. Neon and fairy light-lit warrens designed to host small-stall businesses. Open-air mall meets Instagram trap. The concept worked.

When Asiatique opened in late 2012, much of it had already been leased. Sexy buzz sells. Designed as an upscale twilight/night market. Most vendors opened up around 4PM. Come nightfall it glows. Strings of lights everywhere, sculpted, landscaped walkways, colorful awnings floating above with multicolored lanterns and upside-down umbrellas creating a magical over-world, the air heavy with grilled meats, curry, seafood, soap and perfume as riverside breezes soften the crush of people. So many people! It really is a sight.

The north end of the complex is home to maintenance sheds and the prime space parking lot, right next to a towering white Ferris wheel, the kind with enclosed gondolas and spokes lit up like a carnival prize. Its center glows with a neon green logo of Chang Brewery, a reminder that even your sense of wonder comes branded. There's also a carousel with ornate horses and a haunted house ride. The playground is padded and landscaped like a miniature park.

The real business though, happens in the middle: over 200 restaurants, 1,500 vendors, and a tragically comical array of ways to spend money. Everything from silk scarves to street massages, fish pedicures (you dunk your feet into a tank of voracious little fish as they eat away all the dead skin from your shins down) to high-end cocktails. Want some British darts? Sure. Need a 75,000 Baht La Pavoni plumbed four-head espresso machine? Got that! Would you like to take home a large iguana or an endangered parrot? Be my guest.

Big C has a huge hypermarket conveniently located close to the main road. Pharmacies tuck into corners. Leather goods, candles, incense, tourist t-shirts, junky tchotchke, handmade soaps, custom perfumes, every kind and shape of Buddha from plastic to gold, and enough women's clothing and accessories to fill several western department stores. If it fits in a suitcase, and even if it doesn't, they sell it. It's dazzling. And expensive. Prices are geared toward camera-toting rubes, ahem, visitors, and Thais with fun money out for an evening in "Old Bangkok" without the grit.

And it's only getting bigger. Soon it'll include the Jurassic World Immersive Experience. Expect more crowds. And dinosaurs. Lots of screeching dinosaurs. Which of course means lots of screeching humans, just to kick the din up a bit.

My first night, I took it in quickly. Not for fun, not yet. I was scoping out my surroundings. I made mental notes: which stalls were near the exit, which pharmacies looked stocked, where I might find this, that or the other thing. By 6:45PM, it was swarming. I ducked out a side exit and took a left on Chareon Krung Road, the air thick with street heat and exhaust fumes.

The first place I spotted was a brick-and-mortar place with a sidewalk side hustle out front fifty feet from Asiatique's back gate with fryers and steamer stations out front. Dim sum menus were slapped onto folding tables. The kind of place that promises nothing but might just surprise you. And they had Xiao Long Bao - soup dumplings - one of my culinary crack addictions.

It was called Xingxing Mala, and despite the promising setup, the food didn't quite hit. The dumplings were ... fine, the Pad Thai utterly forgettable. The lychees with mango ice cream, though? That was the real deal. Fragrant, cold, tropically fruity and just what I needed.

As I ate, something curious caught my eye. Across the road, to the north side of the Sunreno driveway, scooters kept slipping in and out of impossibly narrow passageways between buildings. Like ants vanishing into cracks in the sidewalk, their sudden reappearances piqued my curiosity. When I finished my meal, I decided to follow one of those slipstreams and see where it led.

I stepped into a world I hadn't expected. The tight canal streets twisted and wound, snaking back behind the main drag like secret capillaries of the city. The homes here were built on stilts, perched above the water, their wooden and stucco structures held up by beams and dreams. Footbridges spanned the small canals, like delicate veins leading to doorways that seemed as though they belonged to another time, slightly crooked, but utterly charming. The "roads" were raised concrete walkways, elevated above the canal, just wide enough to let two and a half scooters pass or a wide hand cart squeeze by a cat.

On either side, lush planters overflowed with greenery and flowers while small flickering lights cast pools of warmth on wet stone. The occasional curl of cooking smoke rose lazily from windows, mingling with the scent of meats, garlic, basil and chili, the aromas weaving through narrow passageways. It was quiet here, the sounds of the bustling main road replaced with the murmur of voices drifting from inside small homes. It was local and real. A kind of intimacy that Asiatique, with its bright lights and endless tourists, could never offer.

I wandered, letting my feet lead me down winding alleys and quiet pathways, hoping to find some tucked-away two-seat bar or a family-run noodle shop with a fridge full of cold lager. But no luck. Instead, I found halal carts, the scent of freshly baked bread wafting through the air, clinging to the humidity like an old friend. But drink? Nowhere to be found. That was ... a little frustrating.

Three hours later, sore and tired, but satisfied with my urban adventure, I stumbled back onto a main road and made my way back toward the river, the echo of the clack of woks and scooters plying the narrow lanes still buzzing in my ears like faint mosquitos. There's a certain satisfaction in getting lost like that - no destination, no expectations - just city life revealing itself to you in the quietest, most unexpected ways.

I was getting to the end of a very long day. I still wanted a drink to celebrate my first night back in Bangkok. Reluctantly, I headed back into Asiatique for a tourist cocktail. There were half a dozen quay-side open-air restaurants with bars, all of them upscale with prices to match. I settled on a place called The Crystal Grill House which was architecturally and situationally beautiful. An ovate bar encased in a stylish black steel beam and glass building. It was the main entry to identical structures that ran along the riverfront connected via offset landscaped and underlit paths. The vibe lent a romantic aura to the place. It looked much better than the restaurant down the way. I'll leave the choice to you, but when I see a place with a name like a bad marketing campaign and a cartoon dancing happy fish welcoming you in? Run in any direction except towards the door!

The maître d', bartenders, and waitstaff at The Crystal Grill House were dressed to impress in crisp black-and-white attire, every crease sharp enough to slice a lime. I was doubly pleased to see that their well gin happened to be my favorite (Bombay Sapphire in case you're curious), always a promising sign. I ordered a martini. No nonsense, no gimmicks. Simply a proper, just-off-dry gin martini. I watched, with quiet satisfaction as my BT stirred, textbook-perfect pour into a chilled martini stem. He knew what he was doing. That's rarer than it should be.

Now, if you'll allow a brief aside on the subject of the martini, because someone needs to say it. I feel that someone should be me.

The martini is not just a cocktail. It is *the* cocktail. Elegant in design, austere in composition, and, when done right, delicately symphonic in flavor. But here's the thing. Real martinis require vermouth. Dry vermouth. A whisper of it, yes - an eighth of an ounce will do - but it must be there. Without it, you're not drinking a martini. You're drinking an under-dressed gin shot.

And let's settle this while we're here: Martinis are made with gin. Not vodka. *Gin*. This is not up for debate. Ordering a vodka martini is like asking a string quartet to play without the strings.

Don't try to impress your date or confuse your bartender with some hackneyed line like, "*Just wave the vermouth over the glass*" or "*show it a picture of vermouth.*" That shtick's as tired as it is misguided. If you're afraid of flavor, order water.

As for garnishes - green olives with pimento? Absolutely. Lemon twist? A strong, respectful yes. Even both, if you're bold and balanced. But any other stuffing - garlic, blue cheese, chili, anchovies - gets you a one-way ticket to martini purgatory. Dirty martini? No. Just... no. That's not complex. That's brine and misinformation and the ruination of good gin.

And if you sidle up next to me and order something called an Appletini - or anything that ends in -tini that isn't an actual martini - I will move, with disdain. I don't care if you're buying. The rise of the "*-tini" trend has done more to erode the elegance and dignity of the martini than Prohibition ever did.

Oh, and stemless martini glasses? That's not innovation. That's heresy. If you can't commit to the stem, you don't deserve the drink. Rant over.

❦

The Crystal Grill House staff were friendly, courteous and professional as I watched tickets being filled, as waitstaff whisked them away to the other structures along the waterfront. Customers were dining large on white tablecloths, gray velvet-upholstered high-back chairs and crystal stemware. My martini was perfect. My martini was New York expensive. I stuck to one, knowing I'd need to find a different bar away from Asiatique, but for that first night after walking canal streets in that maze neighborhood for hours, it was magical, as I sat and sipped while Bing and Frank's Christmas classics piped through a hidden sound system.

I moved outside to a seat along the river rail, gazing upon the cranked-up nightlife plying the river in all forms of big and small party boats. Dance hall beats blasted while colored LED's kept time with the pump of the thump that cranked out from each boat, while the glittering big-city skyline framing the river pierced the night sky. Sometimes cliché is authentic - it was sublime.

CHAPTER 14. BANGKOK'S SIREN SONG

I woke early from a solid sleep, had some perfunctory instant coffee (replace with real coffee went first on the shopping list), got some journaling in, then realized halfway through a sentence that I was hungry as hell. With a full kitchen in my apartment, it made sense to stock up. First: breakfast. Second: Big C hypermarket.

Chareon Krung Road to the right was already buzzing its early morning get up and go. I didn't know the neighborhood at all, so it was time to explore. I passed a dozen street carts already doing brisk business, queues of locals fueling their morning. I took notes on who was cooking what and grabbed a bag of khanom krok –crispy fried coconut milk cakes as breakfast dessert - munching as I wandered.

I expected to have to hunt for something gentle enough to coax, not shock, my stomach awake because nothing says "good morning" like a whole fried fish slathered in fermented hot chili paste. Lunch, yes. Breakfast, no! But less than three hundred yards down the sidewalk, I saw it. Like the angel of breakfast had descended, whispered "*This way my child,*" and nudged me toward salvation.

Tuang Dim Sum didn't just appear - it beckoned. Like a new friend who knew exactly what I needed and didn't make a big deal about it.

It was a cavernous yet covered open-air setup with around a hundred four-top tables, many of them already filled with happy faces chopsticking edible packets of deliciousness with glee. The open kitchen was cruising like a machine firing on all cylinders, a dozen cooks - led by Chef Yip, who looked to be well into his seventies, hustling over flat-tops, steamers and woks. I'd found my place.

Har gow, hom bao, xiā jiǎo, char siu, xiao long bao, shāo mài, chǐ zhī pái gǔ, chūn juǎn, jiǔ cài jiǎo zi, and cōng yóu bǐng. Don't get hung up on the phonetic Chinese. These are the steamed and fried dim sum classics you already know and love. Each table had two order sheets on clipboards (one for food, one for drinks) and a cup of blunt pencils. Holders for chopsticks and soup spoons and a tray of fiery condiments. I filled in my sheets with more options than space inside my body, nodded to a server-come-buss-boy, and ten minutes later, breakfast bliss landed in front of me. Was it the best dim sum ever? No. Was it solid, satisfying, and fast? Hell yes. And the cold, honey-sweetened Chinese herbal tea was fantastic. I'd found my spot for the mornings I didn't want to eat in my apartment.

I'd come prepared with reusable shopping bags so after breakfast I waddled to the Big C hypermarket - conveniently located just inside the Asiatique grounds. I sidestepped Starbucks with the same energy I reserve for potholes and pyramid schemes - marveling at the miracle of how something so omnipresent could feel so devoid of soul. I stocked up on fresh-pressed fruit juices, cream and northern Thai Arabica coffee beans, yogurts, granola, mangoes and watermelon, croissants, sweet French Normandy butter (the best butter in the world - really, *it is*!), strawberry jam, and Belgian chocolate (the true breakfast essential). Groceries in bags, I headed back to the apartment and loaded the fridge and pantry.

I decided to find a park with a bench and bring my latest bookstore find. This was going to be one of those rare, deliciously indulgent days where time bowed out and nothing was important. A simple love letter to myself.

As I was putting things away, something clicked: the night before, while winding through the canal alleys, I noticed a curious absence - no bars but lots of micro-bakeries. But there were mosques. Many of them. And just like that, it all made sense. Muslim neighborhood. Halal food carts. No alcohol. No wonder I hadn't spotted a single local bar tucked into the maze. Damn! Sometimes I'm little slow on the uptake, OK?

Green spaces were not showing up on my phone map, but a five-star hotel with a residential tower known for exemplary luxury sat a mile down the road, perched by the riverside. With a reputation for world-class-everything and impeccable discretion, I knew exactly what I was walking into and I was more than ready to take advantage of the situation. I changed into olive linen slacks that whispered when I walked, slipped on my elegant yet practical coffee-brown leather flip flops, and buttoned up a soft cream silk shirt that flows like water and catches the light just so. The look was deliberate: casual-luxury, the kind of ensemble that says, "Yes, I belong here and yes, I tip in cash."

At the hotel's roadside entrance, I spotted a semi-hidden path leading away from the drive, up to a grand, jungle-landscaped entrance. Ten feet in and I'd left the city behind. Up and away upon broad stone steps that meandered through a literal urban jungle, at its terminus a gracious doorman opened a twenty-foot door without a word. I wandered in, unnoticed and unbothered. Inside was marble, silk, huge teakwood furniture and quiet wealth. After wandering the main floor checking out the over-sized grandeur, gazing into Fendi, Dior and Hermes shops, then into an art gallery which led me past cascading ponds and toward the riverside patio. I paused to study a few modern pieces. Not my taste but as the saying goes - if it doesn't make sense, it's probably art.

The gardens stretched along the river, with private shaded nooks tucked between palm fronds and tropical blooms. I found one with a perfect view of the Chao Phraya, half-shadowed, serenaded by birdsong.

CHAPTER 14 BANGKOK'S SIREN SONG

I cracked open David Sedaris's "Barrel Fever", a collection of terrifyingly sarcastic essays. The server stopped by. I ordered a quad-shot latte and cucumber-infused sparkling water. A few minutes later, a cart rolled quietly up to my little alcove. The barista plugged into a hidden outlet buried in the shrubbery. A linen-covered side table was laid out, and soon enough, a steaming latte appeared next to me in heavy porcelain. I sipped. Read. Listened. Watched, as the slow river traffic drifted by - barge boats collecting dislodged aquatic plant rafts, long-tail river taxis roaring by, enormous, long flotillas of barges laden with rice, guided by tugs, as the tour boats honked for space.

I melted into stillness. Nothing to do. Nothing wanted or needed. It was a lovely day.

Back at the apartment later that afternoon, I took a long, luxurious shower, letting the warm water wash away the residue of the day. The kind of shower that stretched time and cleared my head. It wasn't until I was toweling off that I thought about what I'd do for dinner. No plan. No map. I walked out the door, turned left instead of right, and let fate give me directions for the evening.

The neighborhood had shifted with the hour. What had been sleepy, quiet storefronts earlier were now alive with light and life. The air smelled different - richer, heavier, laced with the scent of street food, marijuana, and coffee, mingling with the faintest breeze. Asiatique was waking up, the river of lights stretching farther than the night before, and the city felt like it was just about to burst into a Broadway spectacle.

And then - I saw them.

As Jerry sang in Scarlet Begonia's, sometimes a guiding light shows up in very strange places. It's all about the lens you look through.

At a fresh fruit shop that looked like it had been arranged by an artist with a keen eye for color and shape, balance and perspective, a rainbow of tropical fruit beckoned. But at the very heart of the display, resting like precious jewels amidst the glistening melons and mangoes, papayas, pineapples and rambutan, was the queen of all fruits: Mangosteen.

They were on my bucket list before I ever left the States. And. There. They. Were!

Deep purple orbs, the size of tangerines, glossy like fresh black plum skin, radiated a floral, Chinese five spice-and honeyed wildflower sweet perfume that hit me like a delicate kiss. I stopped dead in my tracks. I'm pretty sure I looked half-witted. Possibly drooling. This was fruit transcendence personified. And I wanted them!

A woman appeared from inside the shop - Chalermwan (which I learned later meant "celebrated beauty," a name she wore as effortlessly as the glowing smile on her face). I was too caught up in the vibrant piles of fruit and the serene, hypnotic way she moved to pin down her name the first time, but I asked again just to make sure I could come to a close approximation as it was literally foreign to my ears. *"Chal - erm - wan,"* she repeated slowly so my brain could catch up. I told her my name which she nailed the first time. What a great first impression, eh?

She pointed to the mangosteens, her eyes questioning mine, then spoke in rapid Thai, her voice, melodic. Whether she was inviting me to indulge or daring me to pick the best one, like a game, I didn't know, but I stepped closer like that little waif Oliver asking for more. Her English was halting. I was acting like an idiot. She was covered head to toe in the dusty dirty detritus of a busy fruit stall, but her laughing eyes and smile were enough for me to stammer out a *"Sawatdee krab,"* which made her eyes brighten. And smile. And that smile was radiant.

She was dirty. She wasn't just radiant. She was stunning. Her physical presence caught me off guard, but what really knocked me back was how present she was, how she owned every inch of space between us. It felt like there was no one else on the street.

I fumbled with my translator app, the weight of the mangosteen and my deep yearning for it on full display. She looked at me with obvious bemusement as I clumsily confessed the depth of my desire for her mangosteens, and when she laughed, it was warm and unhurried, an invitation into something simple.

Without another word, she snapped open a lockblade knife with the precision of someone who had honed that motion a thousand times. She tapped the flat of the blade against firm purple skins like a jeweler inspecting rough stones.

She cut with practiced ease, revealing the secret inside: gleaming ivory-white segments of fruit, as pale and luminous as moonlight. With the grace of someone handing over a precious heirloom, she passed me the mangosteen on a napkin, her smile lingering just long enough to leave a trace of warmth.

"Seed very bitter. Not bite eat," she warned with a smile, making the warning sound as ancient and wise as an old proverb.

I took my first nibble of mangosteen.

Holy F'ing Toledo! Bliss. An otherworldly juicy blast of bliss. The taste was a revelation - lychee, banana, peach, cantaloupe... but more. Something floral, ethereal, delicate. Like someone had captured the essence of a garden in full bloom and made it edible. The texture was soft, lush and seductive. I probably looked stoned, euphoric, maybe deranged. But it was the kind of bliss that comes only once in a lifetime. Like losing one's virginity.

She was watching me, eyes giving me a thorough once-over with a look that said she was considering calling for help; or maybe it was amusement and... something else. "You like!" she said, her voice dancing with playfulness, as though the entire world's worth of pleasure had just been passed between us in that one moment.

I bowed as gracefully as I could, murmuring "*Khob khun krab*" like it was some kind of incantation, a prayer of thanks. I tried to hand her some Baht notes. She shook her head and gently pushed my hand away.

Watching me devour that mangosteen, looking at me like I was a junkyard dog that had just discovered pleasure for the first time, was apparently payment enough.

Then she asked me, via her phone, if I was a chef.

I typed back: Not a chef. Just obsessed with beautiful things throughout the world. "But I do cook ... a lot".

She nodded thoughtfully but didn't speak. There was a pause between us, a flicker in her gaze that lingered a beat longer than I anticipated. It was almost too much to look at her, such was her beauty. I shyly averted my gaze from hers, though I really didn't want to.

As I turned to walk away, I saw her eyes following me, her face still illuminated by that radiant smile. I was still smiling too. And I couldn't tear my eyes away from hers. But damn, I couldn't help it. She was as disarmingly sweet as she was stunningly pretty, and I wasn't ready to leave that moment just yet. I stopped and stepped back to her.

I typed I'd return after dinner to pick up a few more if she was still open. She nodded but didn't speak. As I walked into the Shabu Shabu place next door, I turned to look back and caught her eyes still following me. Her face lit up. I couldn't describe what that was, just that it was something that hadn't been there before.

Inside, the clatter and steam of the Japanese-style hotpot joint was its own kind of music. Shabu Shabu, translates to "swish swish." It's what happens when dinner meets a party-atmosphere symphonic performance. You pick your raw ingredients from a checklist menu, and when your choices come, drop them into bubbling broth (I'd opted for the mild and hell-broth side-by-side combo) and play conductor with a pair of metal chopsticks. Swish. Dip. Eat. Repeat. Sauces range from subtle to incendiary, so you get to customize each bite like a choose-your-own-adventure ending. It's hands-on eating at its finest. An edible meditation, or maybe just the right kind of distraction when your brain's still back outside thinking about fruit, eyes and smiles and the wordless things that sometimes pass between strangers.

Dinner was delicious. A shabu shabu place located in "my" new neighborhood? The area was growing on me fast.

After that satisfying munch festival I returned next door. Through a heroic mixture of bad Thai (me), bad English (her), enthusiastic pantomime, and frantic pointing at fruit, phones, and occasionally each other, Chalermwan and I resumed our mangosteen summit. At one point I obviously botched some pronunciation so badly that she was doubled over, dripping tears from laughter. Her laugh was infectious. I wondered if I had just asked her if I could have a hot-lava massage. After we settled down, she advised me to hide the mangosteens in a bag before returning "home" because hotels didn't allow them in rooms, not for any durian-style stench crimes, but because the rinds bleed a vicious, inky purple that could stain jet-black things purple. "Like black magic," she said, and I lost it.

Then came the freezer warning. "Don't freezer. Make crystal mush," she said with a grave little shake of her head, followed by a squished face that somehow managed to be both tragic and adorable. Clearly, this was wisdom earned through personal tragedy. I didn't even know crystal mush was a thing.

I studied her then, not just the fruit, not just her broken Thaiglish, but her spark. I asked why she was into mangosteen? She leaned in a little, eyes twinkling, and in a quiet conspiratorial voice said, "Make man strong." I laughed and typed, "everything in Asia makes man strong." But I also wondered, was that flirtation?

245

Or simply age-old wisdom being passed along.

Taking a deep breath to regain my inner cool, I asked how long the mangosteens would be around. By way of explanation, I let her know I was staying at the Sunreno just down the sidewalk for a couple of weeks. She tapped out her reply, it was the beginning of the season. They'd be available for a while. I reached for a few that, to my untrained eyes, looked like food-porn centerfolds - glossy, plump, indecently perfect. But before I could bag them, she *tsk'd* me, gently took my hand, shook her head, and returned them to the pyramid. Out came the blade again, snap, using the precise flange-tapping method she'd used before. She selected four I'd dismissed as a little too rough, a little too off-camera. "These good. Eat tonight or morning," she said. I nodded, trusting the fruit whisperer.

The next morning, they were gone. Devoured with Greek yogurt and granola, each segment an indulgent high and sigh. I cut them open carefully into a thick wad of paper towels, just as she warned. No evidence. Just bliss. And something had clicked between us, soft as fruit flesh, but unmistakably real.

That day was uneventful; unless you count the six and a half hours I spent navigating the bureaucratic theme park known as the Thai Government Immigration Bureau. Add a ninety-minute commute each way on public transport, standing, of course, wedged between students, commuters and a fellow who smelled like showers were for the weak, and you've got yourself a full-day field trip into the heart of existential anxiety.

The process had all the charm and logic of a DMV office run by Kafka after many shots of vodka. You take a number. Which gets you some forms. Hand those over. Get copies of said forms. Then wait for the privilege of being given another number. Which entitles you to stand in a different line where someone glances at your forms, stamps a thing or three, and then directs you - wordlessly - to a third line with another number, which empties into a cavernous seating area with no signage, rhyme, or reason. An endless wait on plastic seats, along with hundreds of your favorite non-friends as we all watched the red LED number counter seem to move backwards into eternity.

The paperwork itself felt like an exercise in creative guessing. Forms that didn't match what was on the website, fields that assumed you had a local Thai phone number, a local address with a landlord who answers the phone, and psychic knowledge of how your passport photo should be cropped. I had five copies of everything, which of course meant I was missing the sixth copy no one tells you about until it's your turn.

And then came the deeply spiritual one-hour lunch break, announced not by a chime or bell or even warned about, but by the sudden disappearance of every official in the building as if the Rapture had selectively claimed only the bureaucrats. Myself and a thousand confused foreigners still clutching number slips for different lines were herded outside by security like mildly bewildered livestock, milling around in the humid purgatory of a parking lot, all asking each other the same question in different languages: "*Is this normal?*"

Yes. It is. I endured that bureaucratic mess for the privilege of staying thirty more days. And I get it. Over the years so many people have overstayed their welcome and their visa that steps had to be taken to stem the tide of paradise seekers who don't have a plan. Many of them are still there, likely living in the hills around Pai or purposely lost in the vastness of Bangkok's endless neighborhoods.

There was no enlightenment. There was no joy. But there was a moment - around hour three when I stopped resisting and fretting and oozed my way into acceptance. That I would die in this line, passport in skeleton hand, my face frozen in a polite grimace was a distinct possibility. But then, a miracle. My number showed up on the red LED scroll with a booth number. I almost had an orgasm. I emerged an hour later, wallet lighter, dehydrated and soul-thinned, but triumphant. A fresh stamp in my passport legally permitted me to bask another month in paradise. The ride back was brutal.

Dusk found me freshly armed with a new passport stamp and a half-baked sense of accomplishment from the bureaucratic slog. I made my way to Chalermwan's fruit store. The day had drained me, but there was something about the pull of her presence, the easy unhurried rhythm of our exchanges, the twinkle in her eyes, and the promise of fresh fruit that kept me moving forward. I was both hungry and thirsty, and fruit has the magical talent to satisfy both at once, plus, it was about as far removed from the sterile government building, I had spent the day in as I could get.

As I walked up, feeling broken, Chalermwan's face broke into a wide smile. But then she paused as she looked me over, her brows furrowing slightly. I looked like I had been through a war zone - face pale, even with a tropical tan, body and mind stiff from the long hours of waiting and the monotony of forms and stamps. She asked me something in Thai, her voice laced with concern. I gave her the rundown of my day via translate, showed her my new stamp, exaggerating the boredom for comedic effect, and as she laughed, her whole face lit up in that warm, genuine way that made me feel like I was more than just a customer. She placed her hand on mine and said, "It ok. Let go. Let it laugh."

"I need to stock my fridge with fruit but I'd like you to choose for me" I explained, though I certainly had additional motives for being there in her space.

She said something that I didn't understand as her eyes sparkled with amusement. She picked out an assortment of fruits with a skill that was both practical and poetic. A ridiculously juicy pineapple, a candy-sweet sprite melon, ultra-creamy fat bananas, tart mountain oranges, a watermelon with rind so taut I thought it might explode into a red splatter that might look like a kill zone if I looked at it wrong, and, naturally, more mangosteens. She was more than a fruit vendor; she was an artist at work.

She asked if I had a knife. I said yes via the translator - I had a knife in my room, but it was so dull that it was as useful as a screen door on a submarine. Chalermwan gave me one of those little laughs that was utterly charming, then disappeared with my fruit into the shop. In about a minute, she returned with the fruits sliced and bagged. Evidence that she had done this a thousand times.

She handed me the big bag of fruit. I could feel the weight of it in my hands, the promise of sweetness within. Then a delightful surprise: along with the hefty bag was a slip of paper, on which she had written her number. I looked at it, then her, and raised an eyebrow in surprise. How wonderfully old-school!

I stood there gazing at that slip of paper. That gesture was something rare and delicate. It wasn't just a number. It was an invitation, an offering in blue ink. And something about it - the simplicity, the directness - cut through the static in my brain like a razor. She stared into my eyes challenging me. Challenge accepted. I hadn't felt this kind of pull in a long time. No chase, no pretense. A simple connection. Was there something there beyond mere fascination? Time would tell.

With an almost frantic clarity, so as to not let this moment slip me by, I put the bag of fruit aside on the edge of a table and punched her number into WhatsApp, then sent her a quick text with my name and number. The sound of her phone pinging was the perfect confirmation of the spark growing between us.

Her smile widened as she looked back at me, clearly pleased, and I could almost feel her relief at the small but significant gesture of exchange. I felt it too. She opened up WhatsApp, found my text, snapped a pic of my bedraggled face to add it to my new profile. I looked like a half-awake zombie that desperately needed a shower and shave.

We texted back and forth deep into the early morning hours, revealing more about ourselves than either of us had intended. It was one of those late-night conversations where filters slip away and the usual guardedness between new acquaintances fades, replaced by a very real desire to know more. We found ourselves sharing things we hadn't planned, but that divulged naturally, as if we'd been talking for years instead of just hours. Each message felt like a piece of a puzzle we were composing - together.

There were no grand gestures, no overtly probing questions about each other's pasts. Simply honest and casual exchanges about each other, food, music, art, nature, the little quirks of each other's lives; tidbits you'd share over coffee. It was honest in that breathable, comfortable way that comes after the first walls come down, leaving the kind of conversation that feels more like a release than an effort.

As night crept towards morning, I felt the pull of sleep weighing on me, but I didn't want to end the conversation. Neither did she. We wrapped things up with a video chat, the glow of our screens illuminating the wee hours before dawn. It was intimate. Just the sound of her voice through the tinny phone speaker had the quiet power to make everything else feel unimportant.

"We meet at dim sum, yes?" she asked, her smile lingering as she moved a stray strand of hair from her face. "I no work until three."

I agreed without hesitation. The thought of seeing her again and getting to spend time with her in only a few hours, continuing up that cresting wave which seemed so effortless, yet unexpectedly profound, felt not only right, but vital.

And then, she did something that made my heart flutter for a micro-second. With that playful smile of hers, she leaned into the phone, closer to her camera and asked, "What we do after breakfast?"

The question hung there for a moment, heavy with potential, and I found myself searching her eyes for something more. Was it flirtation? We were already there. Was it curiosity to know more? To see how I would react to a loaded question? A playful spark testing the waters? Whatever it was, it made my heart race, and for the first time in a long time, I felt that flutter of possibility.

The entirety of our union felt effortless, as if we were stepping into something that was already meant to be. There was no pretense, no weighing of expectations or false starts. It just was. And that's the way it's supposed to be when an unexpected connection lands in your life.

We had a date!

And it wasn't the kind of date shaped by walled rituals and tentative expectations. There weren't any heavy build-ups or awkward pauses. It was two people connecting in the simplest, the most natural way.

Dim sum with Chalermwan was absolutely delightful. Our morning was filled with charming surprises and laughter. She was impressed with my chopstick skill. I've been using chopsticks since I was a little boy and had enough experience to be a decent contender in any contest. Her expertise, however, was in the obscure, in the dim sum secrets that menus dared not whisper to anyone outside the sanctum sanctorum. She ordered dishes that weren't listed, the cooks whipping them up just for us. One standout blew my mind and has kept me awake some nights ever since trying (and failing) to find the name of it. It was a whipped scallop and chive mousse ball, dipped in corn starch and rice flour, then fried to golden perfection. Ethereal is the only word I can think of. An amazing thin layer of crunch, followed by a creamy molten mousse of scallop and chive yumminess. I wondered if there was some kind of divine culinary intervention throwing us together.

Over breakfast, Chalermwan confessed that she had watched me the day before, sitting and eating alone, confidently navigating the sea of dim sum as if I were born with chopsticks in my hand. She said she wondered why I was on my own and then teased me about how much I ordered. There was something about the way she spoke and the way her warmth radiated out of her when she brazenly locked her eyes with mine, like she saw me in a way no one else had, with curiosity and something a little mischievous.

I asked her more about herself. When she told me she had family in San Francisco and wanted so badly to go there but could never afford the trip, I felt a sudden but unmistakable pang of empathy. I felt her. Her longing. It was sad, how her voice had a quiet powerful ache as she talked about that dream, a desire that wasn't only about a trip, but about something deeper - about wanting to escape, to see the world beyond what she knew. I'd never felt such a deep longing pouring out from anyone before. She wasn't just dreaming about San Francisco; she was dreaming about possibilities, freedom, and the hope of visiting someplace so far out of reach.

We shared stories of our lives: my California adventures and that I had spent over thirty years not only living in but exploring every inch of San Francisco. I talked about the rhythm of the fog rolling through the Golden Gate and how it slowly flooded the park as it flowed eastward towards the Haight. How the sonorous horns bellowed from vessels on the bay, invisible through the surface-bonded clouds, as the clang and dings of cable cars pierced those mists. The way the city changed from dawn to dusk and the way every street had its own character. Her eyes lit up as I described the broad sky over the Richmond District at sunset, how the ocean breeze smelled like cool salt and far away ports, and how you could walk down Columbus Avenue, hear a hundred different languages, but somehow it still felt like home.

Her dreams of seeing the Golden Gate Bridge, Ocean Beach, Fisherman's Wharf and Chinatown were vivid, so full of life and detail that I could see them through her eyes. She spoke of the bustling streets of my city, the food, the culture, the feeling of standing in the middle of San Francisco - a city that has been a symbol of freedom and reinvention for so many people. And then she mentioned the one place that surprised me. It felt more like a metaphor for everything she longed for: the view from the top of Twin Peaks.

"That the one," she said with quiet certainty. "That where I go when I see San Francisco. I want to stand on top, see all of it, like I make it."

I wanted to tell her of the many times that my friends and I used to go up there at night, getting high and gaze down upon the blazing yellow spear of Market Street glowing bright at night from the Castro to the Ferry Building, but I thought better of it. No need to bring up a past that had very little to do with who I was now. Yet.

We switched gears as I told her about my adventure, walking through the khlong (canal) neighborhood behind the hotel. She smiled and told me that she lived there. We made a deal. She'd show me around her neighborhood, the canal streets I'd become fascinated with, and I'd tell her about San Francisco in more minute detail so she could live its fog, its hills, its food, its sights, smells and sounds in her imagination. It would be fair trade, culture to culture. And frankly, to spend more time with her, any exchange would be welcomed.

The morning was beautiful with clear skies. It was the kind of day that promises good things ahead. It was still early enough that the heat hadn't started to creep upwards as it relentlessly does in Thailand. We walked through winding lanes and alleys, some so tall and narrow I could feel them sucking in their gut to let us pass. The homes were small, tidy, well lived in. Most had colorful gardens spilling out from every nook and cranny. Hanging planters along eaves and lush micro-gardens choked full of edible plants. It was so lush that I half-expected the vegetables and herbs to jump into a salad bowl.

Chalermwan guided me through it all, pointing out little touches of personality of each home, explaining what made the area so special. All the while we exchanged brief touches; an arm gently held while a finger coyly pointed at something to showcase an example of something culturally important, or eyes locked on each other for more than passing glances as questions bounced back and forth.

We strolled until she stopped at a little bridge, gesturing to a cozy, picturesque garden-covered house. "This where I live. Would you see inside?" she asked, as she tugged at my hand, the invitation hanging like an unspoken prayer come true.

There was no way I would - or could - say no. Invitations like that aren't about hospitality; they're about trust. About being offered a keyhole view into someone's life, unfiltered and uncurated. You don't turn down that kind of generosity. Not if you have even an ounce of sense, or any reverence for the beauty of being granted admission to something sacred.

My heart was thudding, loud enough that I knew she could hear it echoing in the small space between us. It pulsed in my neck, in my temples and wrists, like my whole body had switched to broadcast mode. Was she doing the same? Or was I the only one caught in this electric quiet?

We stood there for a long breath, side by side in the hush of her home, surrounded by the elegant dignity of her personal space. There was something unspoken in the way she had opened the door not just to her home, but to the personal corners of her life. No fanfare, no grand gesture - just quiet permission. And in that silence, I slowly turned in place, taking it all in. The subtlety of lived-in comfort as morning light filtered through small louvered windows, and the unmistakable sense that every object had been touched by time and placed with care. There wasn't a single modern electronic in sight - no TV, no iPad, no computer, no phone, no cords ... nothing but home. It was beautiful.

In the far corner of the main room which served as sitting, reading, open space, nestled against a teak wall tinged by the rich patina of age stood a small shrine. An elegant, timeworn stone Buddha seated in serenity on a carved teak table, surrounded by offerings. It was clear this wasn't for display. It was devotion. An ongoing, living relationship.

I shyly asked if we could take a moment together to pay homage to the Triple Gem. I had never led any of the incantations which I had come to love at my monastery. But I felt a strong urge to do so then and there. It was as if Buddha was asking me to step into a role I had walked away from - if only to feel that reverence again. She turned to me with a smile that was surprised yet gentle, quiet, warm, and full of understanding. She whispered "yes".

She moved gracefully, retrieving three joss sticks from a tall white and blue porcelain jar. The smoke began to rise in slow swirling threads, curling like dream prayers toward the ceiling. We knelt together on her deep Persian rug, the hush around us, its own form of music. I opened my phone to the Pali verses I had come to know and cherish, and in that small moment - knees on her floor, palms together, heart gently thudding in my chest - I led the incantation:

Namô Tassa Bhagavatô Arahatô Sammâ-Sambuddhassa

Namô Tassa Bhagavatô Arahatô Sammâ-Sambuddhassa

Namô Tassa Bhagavatô Arahatô Sammâ-Sambuddhassa

Iti pi so Bhagavâ-Araham Sammâ-sambuddho.

Vijjâ-carana sampanno Sugato Lokavidû Anuttarro

Purisa-damma-sârathi Satthâ deva-manussânam

Buddho Bhagavâti

Svâkkhato Bhagavatâ Dhammo Sanditthiko Akâliko Ehi-passiko Opanâyiko

Paccattam veditabbo viññuhiti.

Supati-panno Bhagavato sâvaka sangho, Ujupati-panno Bhagavato sâvaka sangho.

Ñâya-patipanno Bhagavato sâvaka sangho. Sâmici-patipanno Bhagavato sâvaka sangho

Yadidam cattâri purisa yugâni attha-purisa-puggalâ Esa Bhagavato sâvaka sangho.

Âhu-neyyo, pâhu-neyyo, Dakkhi-neyyo,añjalikaraniyo, anuttaram puññakkhetam lokassâti

The cadence of the words, like the verses of a favorite song, flowed lightly through the room, mingling with the sweet fragrance of incense. Our bows of supplication to the Buddha, the Dhamma and the Sangha were real and so personal that I felt a shiver run through me. The walls seemed to exhale around us as the ancient sacred syllables danced with the motes in the sunlight. Outside, I could hear the soft hum of the neighborhood, the splash of something in the canal, neighbors chatting, a rooster crying out a second morning. But inside, time stood still.

I could feel her beside me – not just physically, but in that deeper way, when two people are fully present in a shared moment. I didn't dare look over. I didn't want to break the spell. We had stepped into something older than both of us, something tender and true, stitched from reverence, shared silence and sincerity.

We sat there, knees still on the rug, hands now resting lightly in our laps. The stillness that followed wasn't empty, it was full. A sacred kind of full. And in that fullness, something had shifted. Something both beautiful and quietly thrilling.

She leaned into, then onto me. "Only people I like use name Charlee. I want you that" Chalermwan whispered into my ear, her voice barely louder than the breath that carried it. A shiver went through me – not from the air, which was warm and still, but from the closeness, the care and intention enveloped in her words.

"Too, you say name funny," she added with a soft giggle, the kind that made it impossible not to laugh in return.

"I know I do – I'll get it, but you'll need to give my tongue a lot of practice and time to wrap around *Chal - erm - wan*," I said slowly, deliberately, carefully.

I turned to find her searching eyes – wide, glimmering, half amused, half serious – and in that look was something unmistakable. It wasn't just affection. It was exploration. It was the tipping point between something casual and something that could no longer pretend not to be. That look must have been dancing in my eyes too because we stared into each other for a very long time.

I didn't know what I was supposed to do next. But I knew what I wanted. And for once, the wanting didn't come with panic or second-guessing. Just a steady, quiet clarity.

❦

We continued wandering deeper into the web of alleyways, each turn revealing another quiet corner of her world. In exchange, I painted San Francisco into her imagination as vividly as I could, describing the moody fog ghosting through the hills, the clang, ding and rattle of cable cars echoing off Victorian façades, the neighborhoods, the smell of marine brine, the aroma of sourdough, the bars and clubs of every flavor and hue, the museums, the parks, the book stores where the beat masters read and wrote and restaurants that had invented dishes the world now loves. Her eyes lit up, drinking it all in like a bedtime story she'd been waiting her whole life to hear.

Our phones, loyal but often hilariously inept interpreters, became bridges between our vocabularies. Mistranslations led to eruptions of laughter. We fumbled through phrases, turning communication into play, trading words like treasures. I taught her how to say, "Mission burrito," and she tried to get me to say "gra prao moo kai dao" (holy basil pork stir fry with fried egg) without sounding like a drunk tourist. I failed spectacularly. She erupted in a shoulder-shaking bout of laughter.

When I told her that "aroi" (delicious) was my favorite go-to Thai word, she laughed so hard she had to lean on the wall to keep upright. "That fit you," she managed between breaths, wiping tears from her eyes, her smile softening as her gaze, again, lingered on me a little longer than before.

Later, back at her home, the universe blissfully slowed things down. We sat cross-legged on thick outdoor pillows in her shaded garden, green tea steaming gently in our cups. Around us, dozens of hanging and potted aromatic herbs, flowers and succulents soaked up the rising heat and humidity, the air fragrant with lemongrass and basil, frangipani, roses and a hint of sweet banana. Hundreds of bees buzzed lazily, unhurried; they knew there was plenty of pollen for all. Birds sang to each other from the rooftops and hiding spots as the neighborhood hummed with the thick warmth of midday.

Time stretched. The kind of quietude you don't notice until you're wrapped in it, settled into place around us - light, kind, alive.

Chalermwan had a busy afternoon ahead. As we parted ways, she described the quickest route out of the canals back to the Sunreno. As I walked away from fantasy, I kept glancing back, burning the route, the memory of her and our morning into my mind; to capture those moments, the warmth in her smile, the fun Thai lilt of her voice lingering in my ears. I saw her eyes and smile following me, and though I couldn't hear her thoughts, the unspoken words between us peeled out loud and clear.

Emotionally charged, feeling alive, I made my way back through the labyrinth of alleys, now looking at this odd neighborhood with new eyes, imagining the lives led inside each home. The floating lightness of the day, the heat in the air, and the weight of emotional connection settled into me.

There was a tenderness in the way the sun peeked into the alleys casting shadows across the walls and streets, and on the quiet ache in my chest, born on the wings of hope, as the busy world continued its consistent march forward without mercy. There was a flicker of something else: unspoken yet but palpable, like that feeling before a rising storm when everything holds its breath. A stillness that promised, despite the world's chaos, that something was encroaching on the horizon.

During our meanderings I had asked Chalermwan for a recommendation. A local Thai restaurant or bar where only locals go. If restaurant, it must also make good cocktails. Hopefully, somewhere in the neighborhood. I described my futile quest the night before, and how I had, out of "necessity" ended up trolling the glitzy, overtly tourist-priced paradise of Asiatique for a cocktail, which she found hysterically amusing. "We not drink there" she admonished.

She lit up again, visibly excited to share her world, and told me about a place nearby that she said was excellent. However, there was a catch: it was owned by her cousin. "So, you're saying you're biased?" I teased, explaining the concept through the translator. She laughed, admitting yes, but insisted it was worth the visit.

I joked that she'd make a killing as a marketer with that kind of pitch. But she remained adamant that the restaurant was genuinely popular with locals, especially chefs (she had already learned how to pique my interest. Clever girl!). When she said that, my interest soared. After all, where do chefs eat? The coolest places with staff that know their craft. I've learned that there's no better recommendation than that of a local who knows where chefs eat. Chalermwan was becoming more intriguing by the second.

The afternoon passed quietly, though my slow exploration of the shops and service businesses on my return route to the Sunreno turned out to be a smart move. I knew where to find the essentials, which is always a good thing when you plant yourself in a new neighborhood. I spent the rest of the afternoon meditating, then writing, the steady rhythm of the pen moving effortlessly across the paper providing sanctuary from the blazing hot and humid world outside, then taking a well-earned nap. It was the kind of nap where you wake up feeling disoriented, but in that pleasant "am I high?" feeling, like you've been wandering in another dimension.

On my way to dinner, I stopped by Charlee's fruit stand to offer a hand; she and her workers were busy selling fruit by the bagful. I strolled up and asked if she wanted help. I wasn't asking for a job per se but truly wanted to be of use to her. She shoved me away - playfully, - saying, "You be in way." As I started to turn away, she grabbed my wrists and pulled me in, and planting a lingering, gentle kiss on my cheek. Then, with a grin and a theatrical shove, she pushed me out the door. I turned in the doorway. Our eyes locked. I winked. She smiled. I bowed. She spun, then turned her head, blew an air kiss, and with one last flick of her hand, shooed me down the sidewalk. I heard laughter. As I turned back - but stupidly kept walking - I caught one of her workers giggling beside her just before I stumbled straight into a light post. I didn't care.

Walking down the sidewalk, my cheek burned brightly from that kiss as a sweet warmth spread through me. The world had tuned softer as my core temperature rose. Bangkok was becoming more than inviting. Her curtains were being pulled back, and I was eager to catch the show. I prayed my world was about to change in a profound way, not because it needed to, but because I wanted it to. What I had been privy too so far was way beyond command.

The evening air was cooler but that shift did little to ease the heat lingering on my cheek. As I strolled, I wondered if I was worthy of affection. It was vulnerable but necessary, musings that hit like fleeting clouds. My monkey was having a field day. It was something that felt both foreign and familiar. In that moment, I didn't need an answer, but the question was important and the feeling of it, that loving magnetic pull developing between us left me in a quandary and broached the question, *"Am I Worthy?"* That bounced around in my head like a superball on cocaine.

⁕

The restaurant was a tasteful interpretive cross between Lanna and semi-Victorian architecture on Chan Road, just a short walk beyond the maze of canals and alleys I'd gotten lost in. The exterior was white with clean, elegant lines that gave it a mashup Thai-European vibe. The conservatory and exterior Edison-bulb strings had the place dressed up with eye candy. But it was inside where the magic really unfolded.

Victorian details were everywhere. High beamed white ceilings, crystal chandeliers, and tall, narrow windows draped in sheer gauze softened the edges. Dark wood furniture anchored the space, complemented by framed photos tucked into every nook and wall panel. Upholstered chairs and benches bore a mix of sophisticated fabrics, while the floors told their own story: aged deep red wide-plank teak in the dining rooms, and a crisp black, white, and gray diamond tile in the adjoining bar and snack café. White served as a quiet backdrop, letting every other design element shine.

Bursts of color added depth and charm. Royal and teal blues broke up the visual field, while brass sconces cast warm pools of light along walls and walkways. Tasteful Persian rugs grounded the spaces with pattern and softness. The result was a place that felt both grand and intimate - spacious and bright yet layered with warmth and character. It was unlike anything I'd seen in Thailand but felt deeply familiar. The place may have been local, but it showcased the owner's taste and obvious experience abroad.

My bartender, I'll call him Jaks, was a funny, gregarious fellow and was almost fluent in English. I asked for a martini. He was a pro. First, he asked what gin I preferred, how much dry vermouth I wanted, and whether I preferred olives or a twist. He asked all the right questions. I didn't bother with my martini lecture. With the precision of someone who knows their craft, he proceeded to stir up a perfect martini.

I had Thai-spicy yellow curry soup with pickled bamboo and sea bass, with incredibly fluffy jasmine rice. Jaks asked how I'd found his restaurant. I told him about the beautiful woman who had befriended me, Chalermwan. She recommended the place, saying her cousin owned it. He smiled knowingly, then said, "*Ahhhh ha*, so you're the farang she don't stop texting about," giving me a lingering once-over and a wink while polishing wine stems.

I raised an eyebrow. "You must be her cousin? I didn't know I'd made that much of an impression that she'd be texting everyone."

"Oh, you have," he continued, still polishing. I noticed him paying attention to me in an investigatory manner. "She talks about you like you're already part of the family. She calls you keeper, gentleman and smart. She likes you."

I chuckled, a little taken aback. "Well, she's got the gentleman part wrong," I teased. "She's a bit ahead of herself, don't you think? We only just met. We barely know each other. So far."

Jaks replied with a shrug. "Charlee doesn't waste time with stupid boys. They all after her. She says no every time." He finished his polishing with a flourish, clearly pleased with his work as he held a glittering stem up to the light. "You are different in her eye. Something about you she likes a lot. Even though you are white guy," he laughed.

I felt my cheeks warm, though I tried to play it cool, taking a long drag off my martini. "I'll try not to disappoint. She's really special."

Jaks only smiled, his eyes glinting with amusement.

It was a strange thing, hearing those words. I felt the weight of that conversation like an x-ray blanket Confidence settled into me the way an unexpected compliment hits you pure. And yet, the feeling that the evening was setting something into motion felt rooted. Whatever it was, I was already caught up in it and all too happy to take the ride.

"Um... not to pry into territory that may be sensitive, but Jaks - she's beautiful, kind, intuitive, smart in more ways than just her mind, and she's so friendly. I thought she just wanted to sell more fruit but we've moved way beyond that." I took the last sip of my martini. "She doesn't have a dangerously jealous husband in jail somewhere?" I knew the answer but thought I'd double-check ... just in case.

Jaks let out a hearty laugh, clearly enjoying my curiosity. "No one's good enough for her," he said, his voice full of affection for Charlee. "She's independent. The last boyfriend - we didn't like him - he got tossed into the canal a couple of years ago. He was cheating on her with her BFF. She's a jiu jitsu black belt, if you don't know. Flipped him right over the rail."

I blinked, trying to process what he'd just said. He smiled and shook his head, reliving the memory, chuckling to himself as he turned to make drinks for another customer, leaving me sitting there, empty martini on the bar, a little stunned.

Note to self: *Do not piss off Chalermwan!*

I texted Charlee, thanking her for the great recommendation and saying I was very fond of her cousin. I almost jokingly added that I couldn't swim (I can) but decided better of it.

A moment later, Jaks slid a second martini my way with a wink. "On the house," he said with a grin. Then, sticking out his fist for a bump, he added, "Before you go, unlock your phone for me."

It seemed to be a Thai thing that states "I'm now in your world and you're in mine" thing, so I unlocked and handed him my phone. He typed his digits in, handed it back with a grin, and gave me a fake stern warning look. "Don't make me have to come get you out of trouble. But just in case, there's my number."

I raised an eyebrow, then laughed. "Wouldn't dream of it." Then again, Thailand has so many ways to get into trouble. It's always good to have an ace up your sleeve!

Jaks returned to his work, leaving me with a wondrous sense of having made a genuine friend, or a protective ally, possibly both.

That night, we got more than a bit tipsy. Jaks, off the clock and already two martinis deep, leaned in with a trouble-making grin.

"So... I text Charlee to come by and hang out... she's closing up right ... about ... now." he asked looking at his phone, clearly enjoying the idea of playing matchmaker.

I, on my third martini, waved him off with a laugh. "Are you nuts? I'm buzzed. The last thing I need is your cousin walking here sober while I'm contemplating a fourth martini! She'd take me back to her place just to flip me into the water!"

We both burst out laughing, the sound of it filling the bar as the night wound down.

He slapped me on the shoulder. "Yeah, good call bro," he said with a grin.

It felt like the beginning of something, though I wasn't quite sure what. But I had the distinct feeling that if I ever did find myself on the wrong side of Chalermwan's good graces, I could count on her cousin to have my back... or at least to make sure I didn't drown in a back alley khlong.

I awoke just as the sky was showing off its blush, and admittedly, I was a little rough. My head was a battlefield, and my body was protesting the mere idea of being anywhere near a gym. But I dragged myself there anyway, determined to sweat out the previous evening's indulgences. After an hour of pouring martinis out of every pore on a bike and treadmill and silently swearing through the sweat that I should've stopped at two, my phone pinged.

It was Chalermwan.

Her message read: "My cousin in love you. Now we marry so you family." It was followed by a winking, crazy-faced emoji.

I grinned, my hangover momentarily forgotten, and replied "Well, I suppose it's not every day a man gets a marriage proposal that's so efficient and perfunctory. OK." Followed by a kiss emoji. It took her a while to translate but she followed up with LOL.

We met for dim sum again, our now-sacred ritual of steamer baskets and not so subtle glances. She suggested a walk through Lumphini Park - Bangkok's green heart - and just like that, the day unfolded with the quiet ease of something meant to be. Lumphini had already made my short list, but coming from her, it became something more. A shared plan, not just a personal wish. By now, I trusted her completely. She'd already proven herself a guide of the highest order - equal parts instinct and elegance, with a knack for knowing exactly what I didn't know

I needed.

"I'm in your capable hands," I told her, "Order whatever you like. Don't worry, I'm not squeamish about eating anything."

She grinned a bit evilly, I thought. I could tell she was going to test the waters. I loved it and was excited for whatever came to the table. I listened carefully as she launched into a rapid-fire conversation with a server. Her Thai flowed, while I, a mere spectator, nodded and smiled, looking like I understood more than I actually did, or anything at all for that matter. I think I caught *har* and *mai* at some point but that was all. The server nodded, rapidly jotting notes on the back of the order sheet. He had that rapt attention of someone cramming for a final exam.

Thirty minutes later (she'd ordered a lot), a parade of dishes arrived, each one more daring than the last. Tripe in fermented bean sauce, beef tendon bao, ox heart shiu mai, skewered chicken livers and skin, ox kidneys with fermented cabbage wrapped in sticky rice, fish balls cooked over open coals, and those mysterious scallop mousse magic bombs that were now etched in my sense memory. There were a few recognizable crowd pleasers for good measure, though they seemed a little out of place amidst the more adventurous offerings.

Sitting there, surrounded by dishes that were both foreign and familiar, I couldn't help but laugh at the absurdity of it all - being in Bangkok, with a woman who was turning my world upside down in the most delightful way who had a palate and stomach that matched mine. I would face her challenge and was looking forward to it all.

I was hooked. On the food. On her. On this sleepy corner of Bangkok. On all of it.

If I could only get the aroma of Juniper from all that gin out of my nose, I would have been at a level of Sabai I have rarely known.

The tripe had been slow-braised then wok-fried with fermented bean paste, rich and punchy with just the right chew and squeak. Tendon Bao? Fantastic! The hearts were grilled, then rubbed with spiced charcoal before being shoveled into shiu mai. Earthy, smokey and tender. The chicken livers came yakitori-style, alternating with crispy skin and basted in a shimmering, rich chicken-stock glaze. Freakin' delicious. The fish balls? Boiled in stock, then roasted over hardwood with a miso paste brush down until silky. This wasn't dim sum. This was art.

She asked if I wanted to try brain. I tapped out. Not at the thought of brain. I've had it before and it was delicious. But because I was running out of room and was craving their crispy chive pancakes (I'd had them on my first morning and my mouth did backflips), which were nothing short of perfection - paper-thin, fried to a golden crisp that burst apart like edible glass with each bite. Chef Yip's crew was clearly serious about their craft.

I grinned, trying to determine her motivation. "So… were you trying to freak me out with all the guts and gore?"

Chalermwan, with her mischievous playfulness in top gear, gave me a sly smile. "Seeing if adventure you are. I don't like brain but see if you go that way."

I raised an eyebrow, understanding that she was discovering me. Time to turn the table around. "So, Charlee … Do you like sushi? Sashimi?" That was the first time I called her by her short name. She caught it like an all-star shagging a deep fly ball at the top of the wall.

She smiled as her eyes lit up, then she squeaked with excitement. "I *love* sushi! But no family go with me. They say no taste."

Oh, this was going to be delicious. I chuckled, already plotting revenge with the glee of a villain in a fish market. I could almost hear her gasps of incredulous awe as I unveiled my world of sushi: fermented roe sacks, marinated raw quail eggs atop salmon roe, briny sea urchin with crab fat, buttery monkfish liver, and if the gods of the questionable were smiling, some oozy, aged delicacy that looked like it had crawled out of the ocean and given up mid-evolution. It wasn't going to be dinner. It was going to be theater. All I had to do was find the stage.

But, for now, we continued to eat, laughing and sharing our stories one dish at a time. The food, while wonderful, was only the backdrop to the real adventure unfolding.

It was time. Time to show how I was floating, how everything felt suspended, percolating in that thrilling space between us.

As we rose, I reached for her. My hand found hers as I gently pulled her into me. I stared into her eyes as the world around us faded. I kissed her. Not on her cheek.

It was gentle, but it was everything. Subtle, like a whisper, but charged with something that neither of us needed to articulate. Time stood still, holding us suspended in that instant.

We never broke eye contact. My eyes held a thousand whirling emotions, too many to pin down, while hers smiled back softly, approving, knowing. And in that exchange, I felt that marvelous flash when you know that the most powerful moments don't need words.

After breakfast, and our hurried exit to avoid remonstration, we made our way down the sidewalk to the bus stop. Chalermwan took my hand and playfully began to skip by my side. It was a silly, beautiful gesture of easy playfulness, one that caught me slightly off guard. Public affection isn't something you see often in Thailand, especially with older generations around, and though it was welcome, I hadn't expected it.

But something about that hand-in-hand moment... everything shifted. I slowed my pace, glanced at her, and for another second within a few minutes, the world blurred around us. Her sheer natural beauty shocked me again. She wasn't just beautiful - she was mesmerizing, a gathering of grace and warmth. I dissolved in the simplicity of her touch and the sincerity of her gaze.

We didn't need words to express what was happening between us; the quiet smiles we exchanged, the way we gazed into each other for longer than usual. It shouted volumes with a quiet whisper.

We hopped on the belching, funky faded-red No. 1 bus. That bus was so decrepit that it rode at an unnatural angle and plied the road with open doors and had a personality that could almost talk. I nicknamed him 'Mater.' A mile up the road we hopped off. I relished the freedom of those open-door buses. I was already grinning, waiting for the next part of our adventure. We rode up the escalator at Saphan Taksin BTS station. As we alit upon the station platform, she tugged me toward the ticket booth, but I had other plans. I tugged her back and made a bee-line for the automated machine, touching the screen to flip it to English, reading the instructions, then punching in the details for our stop, Sala Daeng. She watched me as I slid the exact coins into the slot and grabbed our tokens.

She observed my self-reliant handiwork, shot me a grin and snatched her token out of my hand. "I could've do that, but you smart," she teased, skipping ahead, her laughter the sound of a melody I wanted to replay over and over.

The train was jam packed when the doors slid open, but we squeezed in just before the doors slid shut behind us. She turned to face me and leaned into my chest, wrapping her arms around me. I gladly reciprocated. It didn't matter that there were people crammed in all around us; at that moment, there was only the gentle sway of the train, the feel of her warm breath piercing my shirt, her scent flooding my senses.

Though passengers exited at each stop, creating space around us, we stayed just like that. It felt natural. It felt wonderful. I could feel something flicker in me, something I thought I'd lost forever. The kind of love that's beautiful and terrifying all at once; that makes you hold on and never let go. I'd felt it before and knew that feeling all too well. But sometimes those brutal tsunami waves don't let you surf, they just grind you up and spit you out. I prayed that that wouldn't happen again.

We held hands as we exited the station closest to the park entrance. Though I'd never do that casually, this wasn't casual - for either of us. But it was all so young, so fresh. I asked myself how could this be more than rampaging hormones and the desire for new? Was that even possible?

Directly in front of the exit was an optometrist glasses shop when an idea hit me. I'd been meaning to get new prescription readers for a while. In the U.S., even with insurance, they were ridiculously overpriced for cheap frames and plastic lenses and took a week to get. You want good frames and glass in the US? Better take out a loan! That's how pathetic the health care industry has become back home.

I turned to Chalermwan and asked if she'd mind stopping in with me. I made it clear that it could wait but she said, "Mìmī payhā," - "no problem" – showing me the translation on her phone. We stepped inside the well-appointed optometrists shop to see if the rumors were true. Any kind of health care in Thailand? Professional, reliable, affordable and fast.

Thirty minutes later, after a thorough eye exam from an optometrist who'd gotten his degree from SUNY College of Optometry in New York (according to the diploma on the wall), and after choosing a pair of really nice frames, I was told my glasses would be ready in twenty minutes.

Wait! what? Did I hear that correctly? Hand-ground corrective real glass lenses in under an hour? Well, I'll be damned!

We were headed across the way to Lumphini Park, so I told them we'd be back in a couple of hours. To this day, it's the best $48 I've ever spent.

Lumphini Park is a sprawling green reprieve in the middle of Bangkok's consistent chaos - 142-acres of green calm surrounded by a riot of glass-and-steel ambition. It has everything a proper city central park should offer: towering deciduous and evergreen trees that look like they've been grandfathered in from some dignified era; larger than life statues depicting heroes of uncertain political or military provenance, manicured lawns that invite you to walk on them, playgrounds where children practice their gleeful dominance and mischief games, fountains, tennis courts, and a man-made lake so precise it practically begs you to pull out brushes and paint the damned thing.

There were rowboats and fiberglass pedal-swans to rent, if your idea of romance comes with a side of cardio. Benches dotted the paths and lakeside like quiet invitations to stop pretending you're there for exercise. There's a public pool, a sports complex, and because no utopia is complete without paradox, a view of the city's multi-hued and shaped skyline pressed in from every side. The walls of bespoke crushing deadlines.

By late morning, the sun had burned off any pretense of comfort. The air had begun to thicken into something tactile - that tropical air you can wear. The various park entrances were gated with tall, ornate wrought-iron fences, tipped with gilt, the kind that makes a casual stroll feel vaguely ceremonial. We entered, stepping onto a broad promenade which led us into the park's interior.

We reached the path that circled the lake, a paved loop shared by joggers, cyclists, rollerbladers, confused tourists walking while pouring over a phone map, and the two of us. Those stately old trees arched overhead, blotted out some of the sun's merciless beams, granting patches of shade that gave comfort like a shaded chaise on a hot beach.

Chalermwan reached for my hand again as we began leisurely walking along the path, the lake beside us glinted like a mirror in the sun.

I led her over to a shaded bench by the water, the kind of spot where retirees come to feed pigeons, to reflect on life choices and those they've lost. Once seated, I turned to her with the cautious diplomacy and asked, "Isn't public affection frowned upon here?" I tapped that into my phone, posing a variety of angles of the question.

Charlee read my phone, then met my gaze with a smoldering intensity, holding it just long enough to make me squirm. Then, without a word, she started rapid typing into her phone, because nothing says modern intimacy like typing your deepest truths and desires into a silicon, metal and glass computer.

She showed me her screen: "*I don't care!*". Her thumbs flew on her phone keyboard as she laid out her argument. The old ways weren't for her. She was her own person and would do what she pleased. Followed by a verbal, "You please me."

Before I could craft a thoughtful response she stood up. I followed suit, assuming the conversation was over. Instead, she turned into me, placed both hands on my chest, and gently pushed me back down onto the bench.

Then she straddled my lap and wrapped her arms around me.

I had roughly a second to process this new development before she looked into my eyes again and said, in her adorable "Thaiglish," "I never thought I like farang, but you different. I like. A lot."

And just like that, we kissed.

It was a smoldering, slow, love-filled kiss so deliberate that intention couldn't be mistaken - even by me. It wasn't so much an explosive lust launch, more a thoughtful ignition. It was a kiss that didn't ask permission from the culture, or the park, the pigeons, or the joggers pretending not to notice us. Sometimes you just have to toss tradition out the window and let the moment rewrite the rules. We absorbed pure emotional connection from each other through that kiss.

After catching our breath, smiling at each other in mutual appreciation and staring into our abyss, one we were both longing to dive into, we rose and strolled hand in hand, not caring about anything else except each other.

We came upon an attractive arched bridge that spanned two sections of the lake. A handful of elderly locals were tossing pellets into the water, their movements slow and deliberate, like they'd been doing this for decades, maybe longer.

The lake surface boiled. Fat carp, catfish, and tilapia surged up from the depths, their backs breaking the surface in a competitive scramble for the food. There was no delicate nibbling. The fish were massive. They moved through the water like aquatic wrecking balls, their bodies bloated from easy handouts, looking like stuffed caricatures of themselves.

It was a tumultuous mess. The surface surged with wriggling bodies, fins and tails slapping, mouths opening and closing in an unholy chorus of fishy gluttony. The whole scene had a primal absurdity to it.

We watched the aquatic madness unfold. Chalermwan laughed, shaking her head at the spectacle, and I couldn't help but think "this is the kind of place I could get used to as I slip towards dotage." A glimpse of the old, odd, unstoppable rhythm of life was very comfortable.

The lake was quite large, but I couldn't shake the thought: where the hell do all those fish go when no one's feeding them? Their sheer numbers seemed to outstrip the lake's capacity to house them, at least to my eyes. I mean, it couldn't be that deep, could it?

We continued on our way, walking slowly, my arm over her shoulder, hers around my waist as if we had been together for years. Around the far side of the water, we each pointed out points of fascination and laughed at the squirrel wars as they chased each other around, up and down trees. We came upon a classic white gazebo perched on a small rise, thrusting out into the lake like a beacon for romance and making choices. At the entrance, a bold red sign caught my eye:

Warning: Water Monitor Lizards

The list of disclaimers for *Varanus salvator* was impressive:

a) They're fast.

b) They're aggressive.

c) The park is not liable if you get too close and end up as a snack. (Translation: don't be stupid!)

I chuckled at the absurdity because where I'm from, dangerous wild animals don't roam freely around public parks in the middle of a city, with a sign shrugging it off like it's both an inconvenience and an attraction. But then Chalermwan, with the quiet seriousness, pressed her finger to my lips. "*Shhhhh.*"

She pulled me gently over to the railing on the far inside curve of the gazebo, her expression unreadable, then pointed down.

There, not ten feet away, was a beast. A water monitor. It was easily seven feet long, its keeled, scaly body gleaming in the sunlight like an ancient creature out of a paleontology textbook. Its long blue forked tongue flicked in and out, tasting the air, assessing us with the kind of cold calculation reserved by those that have been around for millions of years. I swear I could hear the Jurassic Park theme music drafting from somewhere else in the park.

A chill ran up my spine and caught myself instinctively taking a half-step back, pulling Charlee back with me. The thing looked like it could rip through a human with all the effort it takes to draw a breath.

I glanced at Chalermwan. She met my gaze, and we both burst into nervous giggles. It wasn't that lighthearted kind of laugh that means "this is funny if not a little bit creepy." No, it was more a nervous "well, hell, what now? Thar be monsters here!" kind of laugh - the kind that happens when you realize you're suddenly not the top of the food chain anymore and imminent danger is close by.

We held each other's hands tighter, as though that might somehow make the lizard rethink its lunch plans. I'm sure it only sparked "*ooooh, look, a twofer*" lust in that lizard brain.

Luckily, the water monitor was down there, and we were up in the relative safety of the enclosed gazebo. Why would a large, fast, aggressive predator be allowed to wander freely around a public park? Thailand, in its infinite wonderful weirdness, had struck again.

Then Chalermwan, who had been glancing about, pointed off to the right. There, beneath a low overhanging branch about thirty feet away, another monitor was lounging. Smaller, not by much, but still intimidating. It locked eyes on us, as if to say, "*I'm not hungry yet, but you're looking pretty tasty.*"

I scanned the area for possible defensive weapons, anything that could fend off a rampaging lizard. A thick branch on the ground? A stray rake left by park crew? Maybe a small child that had been left behind (preferably one that could run a little slower than us)? A trash can full of leftovers to toss as a distraction? I was grasping at straws, but my flip-flops were hardly up to the task of outrunning any creature with a pulse, much less a cold-blooded speed demon. Charlee was in better shape with her running shoes.

I'm an honorable fellow and like any chivalrous guy, should things go sideways, I'd be the one to get mauled by those Godzillas. Sure. I'd earn a scar or two and some nurse's sympathy to go with my gallantry though the idea of spending the rest of my life with a prosthetic limb was not all that enticing.

Still in the gazebo, I pulled out my phone and researched the creature. Fun fact: Water monitors can sprint up to twenty-eight miles an hour in short bursts up to forty yards, which was much faster than either of us in our flip-flops or sneakers. The thought of that made the annoyance of the mosquitoes feel far less urgent. Another fun fact: they are carnivorous. There went my hope of gathering up some greens and throwing them in the sprinting lizards' path, just in case, you know, he was in the mood for fiber.

Then I noticed that they weren't just lurking, they were circling. The occasional hiss as one got too close to another seemed much louder than it really was. I realized that the only thing between us and a potential animal kingdom takeover was the high railing made of wood. Another fun fact: Their jaws are strong enough to crush small to medium diameter bones. You put two and two together and see how your comfort zone is.

We quickly and quietly exited the gazebo from the only entrance, which faced away from the lake and the menacing lizards. That felt prudent. About fifty feet out, as we rounded a shady bend, an even bigger lizard greeted us. Massive and silver, it hauled itself out of the water just to our right with a fat thrashing tilapia in its jaws. The scene was straight out of some nightmare nature film, only this time, we were in the documentary. The lizard ignored us, intent on its sashimi lunch. It slithered under a tree, looking pleased with itself as any predatory reptile could with lunch in its jaws.

Just when I thought it would actually be kind of cool to get closer and watch a water monitor destroy a fish and that the worst was over, a bigger monitor appeared. The intent on an easy snatch-and-run lunch evident as he assertively went right to the kill. "Blackie" was the biggest lizard we'd seen yet, easily eight feet or more snout to tail end - and they got into it - snapping jaws, hissing, swirling tails, fighting over the fish like a couple of drunks brawling over the last swig off the jug.

It was a fast-moving game of "who's gonna get lunch first," only the players were straight-up terrifying. The monitors were fast. Way faster than I'd expected. They were a blur of scales, teeth, tails and aggressive posturing, twisting and spinning, biting and writhing, all in the kind of frenzied lizard wrestling match that seemed to go on forever. It wasn't graceful or elegant. It was raw, primal, and fast in a way that made me think twice about getting closer to shoot a better video.

Blackie won out, the tilapia now in its jaws, as the silver beast retreated into the water, disappearing with the beaten demeanor of a creature who knew it had lost the game.

We didn't stick around to watch the aftermath, beating a hasty retreat up the path, hearts pounding, grateful that the lizards were too busy with each other to care about what kind of meat we might be. We walked away from the lake, breathing intentionally, slowly lowering our guards. It wasn't until we were a few hundred yards out of lizard territory - away from the lake - that I felt a sense of normalcy return. I wrapped my arm tightly around Charlee's waist. She looked at me with a smile. The smile of feeling safe, secure and with a new bond forged through unexpected adventure and shared experience.

We headed back toward the main gate, making our way along Si Lom Road to the eyeglass shop. I picked up my new specs and they were perfect. They fit me better and had an incredible precision of focus - much better than my previous very expensive pair. I relaxed into myself which was no small miracle considering the amount of primal stress we'd been under moments before.

I asked the young woman at the desk if she knew there were dinosaurs just across the road in the park. She smiled and said they were cute. Cute? WTF? She obviously needed new glasses too.

Despite the persistent low-voltage adrenal hum still buzzing from our close encounter with creatures that could dismantle a human without breaking a lizard sweat (do lizards sweat?), I felt... sabai. Relaxed. Maybe it was the glasses. Maybe it was just the relief of leaving the lizard kingdom behind. No. It was Charlee by my side willingly participating in and around my life, as I was with hers, with her relaxed mood that spoke volumes about the meaning of comfort. But it was mutual. An emotional and unspoken give and take. It was a beautiful marriage of compatibility that we were both enjoying.

✽

It was early afternoon when I was struck by a sudden and insistent craving for a cheeseburger. It wasn't something I expected to miss in Thailand, but there it was. I asked Chalermwan if she'd ever had a cheeseburger. She said yes, but it wasn't quite what she'd imagined, and not all that great. It didn't please her. But I did. Ha! Larry 1, cheeseburger zip! I'm proud that I outscored a cheeseburger.

However, I have a strict rule. Rarely will I succumb to fast food or chain restaurants where the menus are creatively vibrant, but the ingredients are mere commodities to be foisted onto whoever schleps through door. It's a rare exception that I'll break it; that happens on road trips where family-owned joints just off a highway are as hard to find as a live dodo. But living in a place, in a community? No. I treat those fast-food chains as if they're serving up Ebola in a bun with a side with the fries.

However, sometimes, hunger makes you do things you wouldn't normally do. And that cheeseburger craving, as irrational as it was, felt necessary. I almost caved, such was my craving.

Along the sidewalk just down from us was a burger joint. One of those fast-food places that, in a pinch, will satisfy an olfactory lust for a flame-broiled cheeseburger. The scent of flaming beef was drafting out onto the street like a siren song. The dirty trick that cued up my craving. But I refused to go down that road. I saw the vent from the kitchen hoods above the street-side door. Bastards.

I pulled up a map app on my phone and found a locally owned burger joint a few blocks away instead. We strolled hand in hand to 25 Degrees Burger Bar instead of caving to the gravitational pull of KingMcJackCrack. The burger? Better than average, made with locally sourced ingredients. It was exactly what I needed to scratch that itch - though the brioche bun, while a nice touch, was a little on the sweet side.

Chalermwan, however, was... unimpressed.

How could this be? How could I consider a future with someone who doesn't enjoy a cheeseburger? That's like saying you believe in but hate Santa Claus.

"Burgers not your thing Charlee?" I teased her with fake exasperation.

She gave me a non-committal shrug. "Too much at same time," she said, as I reached over to gently wipe a dab of ketchup from the corner of her mouth. She smiled. Then dipped her finger in more ketchup and dabbed it back to the same corner so I would do that again. Vixen!

Burgers are America's, and now one of the world's answers to a gnawing stomach, in close contention with pizza, hot dogs, noodles and street tacos for what scratches that itch better. And, of course, with burgers come fries. As if we needed more. Charlee didn't like how everything was crammed into one ridiculously huge bite, and I understood. Some burgers are stacked so high it's like trying to bite into a mattress.

It's a trend for sure, bigger is better, the towering burger as a skyscraper of self-importance in a sesame-seed bun. But let's be honest: it's not necessary. These days, many people don't eat until they're simply satisfied, they eat until they can't breathe. Which induces that gut-bomb effect. As I've aged, I've come to admire cultures that lean toward smaller portions. No monstrous plates that leave you in a coma because let's face it: nothing kills a dinner date or party vibe faster than collapsing onto a couch after a heavy meal, brain fogged, body bloated, praying for a pillow and the mercy of unconsciousness, while trying to maintain eye contact and pretend you're still capable of lucid conversation.

After lunch Charlee needed to head back to her store. I had watched how hard she worked and when she's there (she has two employees that help out and cover her off days) and even when she's not at the store, she's placing orders, paying invoices, planning deliveries to restaurant and private customers, or pre-planning for upcoming harvests. This time I wasn't about to let her brush me off with a wave and a smile. I tagged along leaving her with no exit strategy. I made it obvious that there wouldn't be an out for Charlee today.

She tried. She *really* tried to talk me out of spending my afternoon and evening bagging sales and replenishing displays. I listened, then ignored her pleads with a firm but gentle "no way José" (I had to explain that phrase to her) and told her that whatever she needed, except for me to leave her side, that I would gladly take care of it, leaving her to help her customers. She said, "you traveling - why you work?" I explained that I simply wanted to be with her, to help, no matter what she had to do. She sighed. She smiled. She kissed my hands. She relented.

While she unlocked, still shaking her head at my insistence, I rolled up and opened up. We jumped into tasks together, pulling out display tables, setting them up, side by side. I shadowed and mirrored her every move to make sure my help was up to her exacting standards. I'd noticed the layout before, so it was fast, efficient, and smooth. She glanced at me once or twice but didn't say a word, just let me be part of her flow.

Inside, we started hauling fruit bins and trays from the walk-in cooler. I was reaching up for a box of pineapples when she turned and launched herself into my arms with far more force than I was prepared for. In fact, I wasn't prepared for any kind of sudden shifting momentum at all.

She wrapped herself around me like a boa constrictor, and as I stumbled to catch her, we toppled backward to the floor in a tangle of limbs and laughter. We landed hard - but laughing - and before I could fully register what was happening, she kissed me. Not a shy nor demure kiss. That kiss was deep and magnetic; a breath-stealing libido-surging kiss.

And then: strawberries. A whole box of them, falling from the shelf above, showered us with fat red fruit. The strawberries tumbled on and around us like a juicy red confetti cannon. Thank goodness there was another flat.

We broke apart, laughing harder, the moment suspended in fructose and beautiful absurdity.

She grabbed my wrists and pinned me down, her silken hair fanning around my head as she smiled her crazy beautiful smile; I wasn't fighting in the least.

"You work free!" she said, grinning. "Or... maybe kisses?"

"Definitely kisses," I said without hesitation. I'd take that pay rate all day long.

The afternoon and evening flew by, her stock of everything running low by 9PM, making the breakdown a breeze by 10. We strolled hand-in-hand down the sidewalk toward the Sunreno, but as she turned to give me a kiss goodnight and continue on her way, I took her hand and pulled her along with me towards the hotel.

Charlee pulled back and gave me a questioning look. I felt her hesitation, but I was not out to force myself on her. Not even close to my intention. I'd be lying if I said I didn't want her to spend the night, but not without her willingness. To ease her mind, I smiled and said, "Only a nightcap."

"What is nightcap?"

"It's when you really like someone, and you don't want the night to end. You don't want them to go, so you invite them in for one drink and that's it" I answered. "I'm inviting you in for a drink so we can talk face to face and not have to text another night away."

"You not want me to go? I not want you go, too …" She came to the decision I was hoping for. "Yes - nightcap."

Then I panicked. I had not thought this through. All I had on hand was bottled water, some fresh pressed watermelon juice, some ice, and a bottle of Johnny Walker Black in the freezer. JWB was plentiful and inexpensive in Thailand, so I kept a pint in the freezer for sipping before bedtime reading most nights. I had no idea if she liked scotch, and I could run around the corner and in one minute get anything she desired at the 7-Eleven, but we were already in the elevator, hands entwined, and there was no turning back.

Charlee took in the apartment with intent, scanning the space as she cataloged details. I was grateful for my borderline compulsive OCD tidiness. Her place was homey and comfortably immaculate, and I didn't want to come off like a guy who lived out of a suitcase with a pile of dirty laundry tossed in the corner. She came back from the restroom nodding. "You stay so clean and neat. I like shower" she said with approval.

I poured two small tumblers (OK, they were hotel water glasses, but hey - you got to make do with what you have. Do you think I am a barbarian and that we were going to drink from the bottle?) and handed one to her. I asked if it was OK as she sipped the Scotch. "I order sometimes if I go out," she said. I asked where she liked to go, but she just shrugged. "I don't know. I go out only a little." That surprised me. She was so beautiful I figured she would be out on dates a lot. But my conversation with Jaks caught up to my brain.

As an aside, I've always wondered how women navigate a night out without spending most of it dodging creeps and half-baked pickup lines. It has to be demeaning and exhausting. Her answer made sense.

I refilled us with heavier pours and led the way out onto the balcony. Tomorrow would be her first night off, so I asked if she had any plans.

She looked directly at me. "House clean. Wash clothing. Water plants. Make love."

"What was that?" I asked.

Chalermwan locked eyes with me, and for a long beat, we simply held each other's gaze. She didn't say a word. The world had paused, just for us, as our dynamic shifted. Seismically. Without breaking our gaze, she placed her glass down gently on the table, and in one graceful, fluid motion, climbed onto my lap. There was something about the way she moved; confident, feline, playful, the balcony felt electric.

We didn't speak. The moment was still so fragile yet full to the brim with the wonder of anticipation.

I woke to the low glow of early dawn filtering through the curtains, casting its soft light over everything. My eyes slowly opened, and there she was - Chalermwan, asleep beside me. Her face, relaxed in peace and slumber, a delicate smile adorned her beautiful features. I studied her forever, taking in the sight of her - the rise and fall of her breast, the gentle curve of her lips, the way her raven-black hair, silken to the touch, spilled across the pillow in sensuous waves. In two days, she'd managed to become a part of my life, as if she had always been there, just waiting for our moment to arrive.

I let out a quiet sigh of gratitude filled with genuine happiness and placed the gentlest of kisses on her brow. Careful to not disturb her, I slid out of bed. The air was cool making my skin prickle as I padded softly across the room to the kitchen. I put the kettle on for coffee as I found myself lost in thought, replaying the past hours, trying to figure out how everything in my life had recently shifted into such a beautiful rhythm. The simple truth, though, was that in the quiet of the night, I had found something I hadn't expected: a connection so raw and so real, it was impossible to define, let alone ignore. And I certainly didn't want to listen to the "caution, crossing ahead" warning careening in my skull. I needed to run screaming like a banshee into the maelstrom come wreck or ruin.

I glanced back at the bed, where she still slept peacefully. The morning light caught the outline of her figure, the snow-white sheet covering her lower body and for a second, it felt like time didn't matter anymore. I smiled, feeling the moment.

I moved through the apartment like a ghost, careful not to wake Charlee, assembling breakfast with deliberate care: two bowls of Greek yogurt layered with granola and fresh fruit (of course there was mangosteen), coffee pressed and steaming, two cups warming in hot water on the counter, cream and sugar waiting in quiet alignment. It wasn't much, but it was honest. And it was healthy to boot. Bonus round awarded!

I was placing spoons down when I felt arms wrap around me, soft and sure, and lips press against the back of my neck. I breathed deeply and sighed a smile of complete contentment, then giggled. She whispered, "what?" "That better be you Charlee!" I quietly replied. She laughed. I closed my eyes and let that moment root itself, her warmth, the silence, the hum of something beautiful. I reached down and held her arms around me, anchoring us both in a kind of quiet, fragile bliss. She whispered. Soft and sweet:

"สวัสดีตอนเช้าคนรักที่ยอดเยี่ยมของฉัน!" If you're a voyeur, look it up.

We enjoyed our early breakfast on the balcony, the growing hum of the city rising like background music, an overlay to something more intimate. I asked if I could take her to The Grand Palace and the Phra Ubosot to see the Emerald Buddha. I was sure she had been there but imagining her reaction to the opulence and history, how she would laugh or whisper something private made me smile. She reminded me of her chores, laundry to wash and hang, a garden full of flowers and herbs to water, and a house to clean. "You go," she said gently, "be tourist man. You love that. You write everything for me."

I nodded, trying not to show the pain in my gut that landed before my second cup of coffee. I tried to cancel my day then and there. I knew that as amazing as the Grand Palace and Emerald Buddha would be, the experience would pale without her. And I reminded her that I had dinner plans that night with one of my monk brothers.

We both felt it. The slowing of the runaway freight train that had, for the past couple of days, barreled through our lives as if it urgently had somewhere to be and there were no stops in between. It didn't stop but the brakes hissed and squealed as it slowed to a saner pace. Neither of us wanted to ride the brakes because riding the high of where we were, the here and now of us felt like magic. We both wanted that runaway crazy bliss. Alas, reality came, knocked on the door, then barged right in without permission.

We cleaned up breakfast together, a comfortable rhythm forming between us. Then, before I could stop her, she spotted the full bag of laundry I'd stashed by the door and scooped it up like it was her mission. "I take," she said with a grin, kissed me quick then darted away leaving her musical laugh hanging in the air, and was halfway out the door before I could protest.

She couldn't get far though because the elevators were key-card controlled. I chased her down, catching up as she stood waiting in the hallway, knowing I'd have to escort her down. Smart girl yet again. We rode in silence, standing close, the moment stretching thin and fragile.

Sadness crept in quietly, like smoke seeping under a door. I let it come. Let it wash over me, just to feel what it was made of. This wasn't just flirtation or the intoxicating haze of newness. It had weight. And depth. And it left me needing her in all the best ways. It was in that brief descent, as the elevator hummed its low song and Bangkok glinted in the morning light beyond the glass, that I knew: this wasn't infatuation. We were much more.

I stopped at the front desk and asked for another key card. I started to introduce Chalermwan to the woman at the front desk when suddenly they started talking coldly in Thai. I asked if everything was OK. Charlee refused to answer as she took the key, turned abruptly and walked away. I looked at the clerk who had a sour look on her face and said firmly "we're going to have a talk when I get back and I expect your boss to be here."

I trotted after Chalermwan and caught up quickly in the middle of the drive.

"What happened back there?" I asked.

"Jinwa say I took her boyfriend. But that happened in school. Long time ago."

"So, you did steal her boyfriend?"

"Yes. But he took me from other too," she replied.

"And is that who you flipped into the canal?"

Charlee stopped short. I'm pretty sure I had just gotten Jakkapan in trouble. Silence.

"No. That other stupid man." she replied.

I reached for her and held her tight, simply holding her close. "Is it OK if I text you all day and evening? I want to share everything I see and do with you" I whispered in her ear.

"If you not, I not talk to you!" she said with a mock scowl, folding her arms in between us in exaggerated protest. It was the kind of pout that made me want to promise her the moon just to see her smile again.

"We can't have that now. I'll share my day and evening everything, I promise. I already miss you." as I wrapped her in my arms.

That stopped her. She softened, eyes searching for mine. We kissed slowly, unhurriedly. I liked this breaking the rules more and more.

There's this thing Chalermwan does when she's truly happy - when the joy bubbles up so fast it can't help but spill out. She rises onto the balls of her feet and gives the tiniest bounce, like her heart's lifting her before she even knows it. It's subtle, like a secret only her joy knows. But I see it. Every time. It's pure, unfiltered delight, like watching a dappled sunbeam try to stay still. And God help me; it's so freaking cute it hurts.

She was bouncing on her balls, in my arms at the end of our kiss, her smile back in place.

Then she turned, my laundry bag slung over her shoulder, a light bounce in her step already cutting a path down the drive. I walked her to the road and stayed rooted to the spot at the end of the driveway, watching her grow smaller in the distance as my heart grew larger until she was just another part of the city.

I didn't raise my voice with the front desk clerk, but I didn't leave a shred of ambiguity either. Calm, direct, and unapologetically clear: Chalermwan would be coming and going from my apartment whenever she pleased. That wasn't up for discussion. I wasn't asking permission - I was drawing a line around her dignity.

The manager, standing nearby, looked like she might object, but I held her gaze. I wasn't about to let anyone reduce Chalermwan to a stereotype - especially not in her own neighborhood, where people should've known better. After a momentary pause, the manager broke the silence. She stated there was no issue. Then, with a sharp glance, she made sure her desk clerk knew who made the final call.

At 6:45AM the big wheels of Bangkok's daily grind were already turning. Figuring out how to get from the Sunreno to the Grand Palace was a puzzle. At this early stage in Bangkok, my understanding of the public transit system was barely above "lost and blind newborn." My research felt like I was trying to solve a Rubik's Cube missing half its stickers while in R.E.M. stage, and possibly drunk. There was no clean BTS or MRT route from my neighborhood to the Grand Palace, just a mess of transfers and enough cross-town gymnastics to qualify for the Thai Olympic team.

So, I did the only sensible thing: I scrapped the strategy, waved down a cab, and let laziness wear the crown. Occam's razor, once again, saving the day with blunt-force elegance. Was it the cheapest choice? No. But pretending I understood the city's labyrinthine routes at this point was an exercise in futility. I'd learn but this was not that day. Maps and alternatives went out the window faster than a lit butt. The roads were starting to hum with early-morning life. Bankers, lawyers, coders and consultants and number crunchers - all chasing a few extra Baht riding that Bangkok hustle. Their energy mirrored the rising burn of the city's movement: packed buses, weaving scooters, barking tuk tuks, and taxis like mine - gritty, grounded, and just as much a part of the hustle as anyone in a suit.

Twenty-five minutes later, I was unceremoniously dumped at the corner of Na Phra Lan and Maha Rat roads, near the river. My cabbie barely slowed down. He was already eyeing a U-turn back to the business district, chasing every fare he could before the business bell rang.

The morning air wasn't pleasant. It held that specific humid breath promising the coming heat, while the sun, still low and merciful, spilled its hesitant golden light across the pavement. My feet found the long stretch of Na Phra Lan Road - a grand boulevard pulsing with the low undeniable rhythm of the city beginning to stir. Beneath my flops, this broad stretch felt less inert stone and more like living history, and the sheer, improbable reality of being right there, felt like a jolt - a perfect convergence of geography, gut feeling, and something approaching jaw-dropping awe as the looming walls of the Grand Palace stood sentinel duty on my right.

It took a millisecond to grasp the undeniable truth: I wasn't charting undiscovered territory. The early birds, like me, were already there, a serpentine belt of anticipation coiling its way toward the entrance. It was still stupid early, the heat tropical humidity already clingy was making its presence ever more insistent as we stood shoulder-to-shoulder, engaged in our own quiet, impatient dance - a collective human tide drawn by the same irresistible current. History, the sheer, glittering weight of the Emerald Buddha's mystique, that universal yearning to witness something so genuinely grand that words invariably fumble over it - we were all here for the culture, the education, the pilgrimage.

FYI: the price of admission at the Grand Palace can land like an upper cut. It's easy to get used to the norm quickly: the ludicrously low ten, twenty or fifty Baht charged for entry into ancient temples tucked away along Sois and boulevards, wonders that ask for barely a pittance to see grandeur. One hundred Bhat approaches audacious. But five hundred? A solid fifteen US dollars? By Thai standards, that's exorbitant, the cost of a dozen excellent street meals. Yet, standing there, inside the gates looking at the sheer scale and majesty of the Palace grounds sprawling before you, and considering everything that ticket actually gives you, that initial sting begins to dissipate. It starts to feel, if not exactly cheap, then justified in a way that few tourist attractions anywhere manage.

Because it's not just a ticket to walk around the Grand Palace grounds. It's a full-blown, slightly overwhelming package. They hand you a full color six-panel map - vibrant, meticulously detailed, loaded with narrative that attempts to guide you through every glittering temple, statue, towering stupa, royal hall and sacred relic jammed into the compound. There are stacks of glossy pamphlets in twenty different tongues detailing the aesthetics, the history stretching centuries, the cultural weight of everything within. It's a self-guided deep dive, whether you wanted one or not. *And* they offer free guided tours in ten languages inside, a tempting prospect for many.

The unexpected bonus, the cherry on top of that pricey entry fee? An included ticket to the Royal Theater for a performance of traditional Thai dance, drama, and music. My mind immediately went there: finish soaking in the soul-adjusting monumental sights throughout the grounds, learn a hell of a lot about their world, then slip into air-conditioned oblivion for an hour or so to watch ancient stories unfold on stage? Absolutely enticing.

Right then though, the immediate task was simply absorbing the staggering magnitude of what stood before and around me. This wasn't just another historical site; this was one of Thailand's keystones - a place where centuries of history, layered mythology, profound philosophy, royalty and staggering art had collided with force, congealing into a dazzling, complex reality of gold, meticulously carved stone and wood, with craftsmanship born from dynasties. This, I grasped within moments, was the living, breathing son of Ayutthaya.

Stepping through the gate, I hung a sharp right - didn't really have a choice as that's where security pointed and pavement led. Wow - instant pay off. It wasn't just 'a sight'; it was eight of them, the elaborate towers known as Phra Asada Maha Chedi, rising like silent sentinels, each one uniquely ornate and magnificently covered in design attributes that would make the most audacious glittering disco dress blush in shame. They towered against the morning sky. Each one stood magnificent and undeniably present, less like architecture and more like a solid, irrefutable monument to something vast and greater than the sum of their collective grandeur - the kind of thing that silences the monkey chatter for way more than a minute.

As I walked the grounds, the air grew warmer. My thumbs were working overtime on the phone. Texting Charlee. Because of course I was. But something was off. Not outright grumpy, maybe, but definitely... a little snippy? A noticeable cloud hung over her usual unrelenting sunshine, and I could feel it through the pixels, the shift in tone. I did what any lover would do: I playfully grilled her, poking and prodding with questions until she finally fessed up. The truth, simple and human in its honesty: she missed me. She'd rather be with me, sharing the rising heat and the unfolding spectacle than stuck in her routine back home. Even though, she added with bluntness that only someone who's lived here, someone who has lived with this history, can wield, she'd "been there, seen that, got the t-shirt."

My immediate, reflexive and honest response? "I'll cut it short. See you in an hour!" A beat passed, the silence of the text thread louder than the murmurs of the crowd. Then her reply came, sharp and clear, cutting through the digital space with force: "NO! I sorry. You explore. See my country. I wish I was with you!" A simple directive, yes, but laced with longing and generosity that instantly reframed the moment, anchoring me right back in the privilege of walking those grounds, seeing it through my eyes as she intended. I sent her a love heart.

The Grand Palace. Official address for the King and Queen since the late 18th century - 1782AD, if you're keeping score, is a hell of a lot of history to pack into one place. And it wears that regal reputation like a glittering cloak. 218,000 square meters, a sprawl that feels less like a compound and more like its own incredibly opulent city-state - a stunning blend of history, working government offices (because the machinery of state doesn't stop for tourists), and sheer, unadulterated majesty. It's the kind of place where you could realistically wander for days, get utterly lost in the maze of temples and courtyards, and know you've missed half the story, maybe more. Every tucked-away corner, every intricate temple, every stone building seemed to hum forgotten conversations and the weighty tales they've collected over centuries.

The royal residences are impressive, the throne hall dripping with historical significance, the coronation hall undeniably grand. The central temple - the Phra Ubosot - is the embodiment and empowerment of the King's moral and spiritual authority. But these structures don't actually hold the charged current. Nope. The undisputed heavyweight champ, the real star attraction on everyone's lips is the Emerald Buddha. And listening to the buzz, reading the guidebooks, seeing the crowds funnel towards his temple, you'd build him up in your head. Wouldn't you? You'd picture some glowing, towering figure, maybe eighty or a hundred feet tall, the kind of presence that could stop traffic just by existing. Instead? He's a modest, almost unassuming little fellow. Seriously.

Tucked away inside the Phra Ubosot temple like a precious, undersized secret, he's revered by millions of people across the globe who hold profound devotion for that diminutive green figure perched up high. And yet, his physical presence doesn't demand attention with his size. He's quiet. You have to look for him, seek him out amidst the opulence. It's the devotion he inspires, the history he's lived; it's the belief surrounding him that makes him massive, not his actual dimensions. It's a hell of a cosmic joke.

Every year, millions come to gaze up at that jade-colored little fellow. That means you stand in line. Packed with the devout alongside the merely curious - devotees rubbing shoulders with tourists, a quintessential cross-section of humanity drawn by history and reverence, all desiring a glimpse. Once you're finally inside, unless you manage to find a spot to sink down onto the massive rug for a moment of prayer or quiet introspection away from the throng, it's a pretty brief window. You get maybe a few minutes tops, to stand there in a state of awe before you're nudged along, ushered to make space for the next wave. Like cattle being processed, but for spiritual illumination. You don't get to just linger, unpack your spiritual bags, and set up camp. Time doesn't slow down there; it accelerates, pushing you forward, perhaps because the presence of an iconic symbol this deeply revered, this historically weighted, is simply too potent to absorb for too long anyway. Or maybe they simply need to move the line.

As hallowed and royal ground which are also a major global draw, the grounds aren't just well-kept; it's manicured to within an inch of its life, spotless and polished to a degree that feels absurdly immaculate. There's an undeniable, almost unsettling precision in every corner - a careful, near-obsessive perfection that borders on performance art. You walk through feeling like you're exploring history and that you've stepped into an artist's hyper-real impossible dream, where everything is arranged just so, down to the precise way the sunlight decides to hit a specific patch of gold leaf. It's beautiful, yes, breathtakingly so, but it demands a careful respect that feels... deliberate, like you're meant to admire the sheer effort of maintaining this level of flawlessness.

What really hit me first, what grabbed me by the eyeballs and refused to let go, are the relentless surfaces. Mosaic tiling, intricate inlays, shimmering mirrors - they don't just decorate; they cover almost every single vertical inch, transforming each building from an inert structure into a living, breathing, shouting piece of art. Forget subtle narratives; each building tells its story through an incredibly overwhelming interplay of colors. The structures themselves - gleaming greens that look freshly washed every hour, impossibly deep blues that defy naming, rich, ripe oranges, and yellows so vibrant they feel like they're physically vibrating - they don't just sit there; they dance together in a dizzying assault on the senses, cranking the volume up on the visual world, making everything feel undeniably, almost aggressively, more alive. And setting it all off are those classic, cascading red, green and yellow roofs, tumbling down in that unmistakable Thai architectural style, looking less like construction and more like something meticulously brushed onto a canvas, straight out of some Technicolor painting.

Some of the structures are also adorned with mind-bending ceramic work, particularly the stupas - the ones that aren't covered with gold. Those are wrapped in multicolored, intricate mosaics.

Everywhere you look, you're met with Nāga, the multi-headed snake beings from Hindu mythology. These creatures, symbolizing both the underworld and divine power, climb up the sides of buildings, hang out on the roofs, and down stair railings, their tile-coated bodies coiling around stupas guarding secrets from the past while protecting today and tomorrow. And then there are the rising flower gardens, which show scenes from the Buddha's life and teachings, adding another layer to the surreal beauty to the place.

After a while though, the overwhelming richness of it all started to blur into a surging, psychedelic blitz. The colors, the patterns, the textures - they're all breathtaking, but it becomes exhausting. It's the visual equivalent of eating an Escoffier-inspired fifty-course feast in one sitting - each bite, each turn of the eye, revealed something magnificent, but by the time you've taken it all in, your senses are stuffed. It's a kind of visual overindulgence that's hard to digest, but undeniably magnificent all the same.

As I wandered through the grounds, I realized that this wasn't simply a collection of grand buildings and sacred temples. The place is teeming with mythical guardians of all shapes and sizes. The full range of netherworld creatures has found a home here: dragons coil around pillars, their sinuous bodies creating an eerie sense of motion in the still air. Garudas spread their wings in grand displays, their fierce eyes never leaving their guardianship over the realm. Shishi, lion-dog beasts known for their magical powers to ward off evil spirits are present. Everywhere I looked, spiritual protectors were etched, sculpted, or painted.

The six pairs of giant Chinese Yaksha guardians standing guard at various gateways around the compound caught my attention more than anything else. Those figures are a curious contradiction in an otherwise serene landscape. With their fierce stance, snarling expressions, warrior demeanor and elaborate armor, they seem out of place in a space so brimming with calm and holiness. They are the kind of creatures that look like they'd leap from their stone bases if given half a chance just to lob your head off for even thinking impure thoughts. However, Yaksha aren't harbingers of doom. They're benevolent nature spirits, assigned to guard precious things, in this case, the temples and royal grounds. Still, their intensity adds a layer of tension to the otherwise tranquil atmosphere.

Each Yaksha is unique - carved with striking details that bring their personalities to life in ways that are simultaneously intimidating and fascinating. They're beautiful, their terrifying visage and attitude formidable. I found myself wishing there was more to learn about each one - what legends they embody. But in a way, that mystery added to their allure.

One of the more surprising features on the grounds was an incredibly detailed replica of Angkor Wat. Though perfectly to scale, it is much smaller than its Cambodian twin, but that doesn't make it any less impressive. The craftsmanship is astonishing - every intricate carving, every delicate stone relief, seems to come to life despite the more compact size. While it's far too small to walk through like the original, it still holds an air of grandeur that stops short of feeling like a toy or a miniature. I couldn't help but admire the effort that went into making such a precise replica, with every detail preserved.

And just to really pile on the value after that initial sticker shock - the entry ticket also buys you passage into several museums within the complex, which are packed with incredible art works spanning the centuries of Thailand's vibrant, complex history. Add all that up, the sheer scale, the dazzling detail, the multi-hued layers of history and faith, plus the access to those collections, and yeah, that once-shocking entrance fee starts looking like one hell of a bargain after all.

Just a heads-up though, because despite the timeless history and spiritual, weighty grandeur, the grounds have a schedule, and they stick to it like a royal wedding plan: they lock it down at 3:30 PM sharp every single day. And by "sharp," they mean it. Strictly adhered to. So, if you want more than a hurried, sweaty sprint past glittering things as they usher you towards the exit, plan accordingly.

I'd been tethered to my phone all morning, locked in a steady stream of texts with Chalermwan, sharing anything and everything my experience was giving to me. It was the kind of conversation that felt impossible to put down for more than a minute, each ping pulling me back in, a constant, quiet current flowing between two points across the city. Eventually, the screen lit up with a message that had just the right mix of genuine affection and playful exasperation: it read "Okay, okay! Tell me everything tonight when we have an eternity in the stars to catch up."

I sent her a "?" because her text was amazing.

"I use your translator app ;)" she replied.

I burst out laughing, even more smitten.

Then came the three words. *Those* three words. Simple, direct, and they crash landed in my soul making everything else fade away, reducing the Grand Palace, the crowds, the heat - all of it - to background noise. *I love you.* Those simple words, appeared on screen amidst the chatter of a Tuesday morning in Bangkok, landed with an intensity that sent me to another dimension. For a split second, I felt the irresistible pull to type impulsive, reckless anythings that would have me abandoning all plans, wheeling around, and rushing straight back to her; to the calm loving connection waiting there.

Instead, standing there in the middle of the Grand Palace grounds, a world away, yet connected by cell towers, I paused. Smiled to myself. And sent back what felt, to me, like the only honest reply in that wonderful moment where profound emotion collided with the day's itinerary. "Alright," I typed. "Sounds like a plan.

Just so you know, I'm off to Chinatown in a minute to eat my way through guts and gore."

I waited. And waited .... and waited. No reply.

"Teasing! *I love you too!!! I have fallen deeply, incredibly in love with you!*"

"But I am hitting up Chinatown too ;)"

Unsurprisingly she didn't reply to that one. We'd both thrown solid love round-houses that had landed fair and square. Then again, what do you even say to that - a declaration of love immediately followed by plans involving offal? As I tucked the phone away - silenced for now, its glow extinguished in my pocket - the die was well and truly cast. My feet were already carrying me towards the tuk tuks and the glorious insanity of Bangkok's Chinatown, its alleys and side street labyrinths promising my next hit of sensory overload.

Adventure was waiting. Chinatown! Not just the aromas, the sizzling mystery meats, and the bubbling pots of who-knows-what, all those visceral, delicious unknowns, were destination enough on their own for a man with an appetite. No. The real, underlying current that made it sing lay in the knowledge that these stories, these tastes, those tastes, sights and sounds would wend their way back to her. To be shared, laughed over, and lived again. Together.

I hopped into a tuk tuk (it was fire-engine red with yellow flames painted down the sides - I mean, really - how could I NOT choose that one!), committing to my favorite exhilarating transport. My driver was a maniac behind the tiller, threading the needle through impossible gaps, weaving through traffic like he was delivering a hell hound late for his date with the devil. The ten minutes it took to get to Chinatown felt like a white-knuckle eternity compressed into a peaking psychedelic rush, but I was more than fine with it. The day was pitching perfect, hot enough to remind me I was gloriously alive, vibrating with the city's energy. And my heart? It was impossibly full, buzzing with childlike wonder - a feeling stirred by Chalermwan's last text, that jolt of pure connection. But it was also charged up by the undeniable pulse of Bangkok itself, a place that constantly throws the improbable and the profound into your path.

He peeled off the main drag, ducking down a narrow back lane, the kind of almost-invisible alleyway that only locals or the truly lost find - the preferred method of arrival into the belly of the beast. It wasn't long before he slammed to a stop.

Yaowarat Market loomed ahead. Not simply a market, but an old-school, no-nonsense food lover's entire neighborhood paradise. I'd been fantasizing about that visit since the moment I'd landed in Thailand. It's legendary for its insane selection of street foods. It has everything - and I do mean *everything!* From the everyday you-can-get-that-anywhere, to dozens of roasted or fried insects, to snakes and frogs, alongside a hundred types of dumplings, to sizzling stir-fried and deep fried you-name-it, to curries, soups, stews, mystery meats, fish of infinite variety served in just as many ways, to noodles, organs and ice creams. All of it offered at prices so inexpensive that it felt criminal to participate and purchase. I couldn't wait to dive in.

First stop was an unassuming stall radiating big heat and serious aromas. I pointed, ordered. A bowl of low mein arrived, topped generously with a whole crab *and* its fatty roe with a slab of seared foie gras.. It wasn't just good; it was a bite of unadulterated heaven - rich, buttery, and salty, the subtle mineral tang from the roe cutting through the richness of everything else, the noodles beneath masterfully tossed to achieve perfect texture and bite. It was 100 Bhat. It was the kind of dish that makes you pause, chew slowly, and genuinely question every other noodle bowl you've ever encountered on the planet. Next up, wok-fried dumplings - pork, shrimp, oyster, and oxblood. They were all crispy on the outside, and each one was a unique masterpiece. They were, simply put, perfect. Blisteringly hot, and utterly, completely, complexly satisfying. Each bite a small delicious validation of the journey, a taste of the adventure I came looking for.

Then, almost on cue, as if the sheer culinary density of the place had conjured them into existence: Chinese fried pork choplets a la Szechuan (the same kind I'd found up in Chaing Mai), stacked high, crisp and gloriously golden. I don't even know what they're called but since I'd tried them up north - let's just say, that like a junkie chasing after that first high? I needed them!

I wasn't done yet. Not even close. The true exploration, the glorious descent into the market's labyrinth, had only just begun. Moving in deeper, my eyes locked onto skewers. Seared water buffalo heart, kidneys and stomach on sticks that had been braised in some delicious stock of unknown origin, then flash seared over glowing hardwood. Unapologetically charred in a few places, glistening under the lights, utterly, undeniably tantalizing. Yes, please. They were all tender, yielding easily to the bite. A perfect balance of savory depth and bold, elemental flavor that felt utterly right skewered street-side.

Clearly not on any sort of sensible health kick - nor did I plan to start - I dove headfirst into another Chinatown staple: chicken livers, skin and gizzards. Grilled over hot coals until smoky and slightly crisp on the edges, they were served simply, dusted with a sprinkle of soy and black pepper. And yeah, they had enough grease clinging to them to make them feel sinfully decadent. This wasn't clean eating; this was honest, delicious, unadulterated street food. But no, naturally, the culinary mission still wasn't complete. The market's pull was relentless, demanding full immersion.

There was grilled tarantula. I'd eaten them before in Mexico and they are surprisingly delicious. Like a cross between crab and scallop. That was another 'yes, please' as I nibbled on legs that gave way with a fantastic crunch. So much better than scorpion!

And there was durian. The infamous spiky fruit, legendary across the region for a reason. Durian hits your nostrils like a physical blow. It smells like a butcher's cracked scrap trashcan left baking in the blazing summer sun, maybe with some old jock straps thrown in for good measure. It is, objectively, an assault on the nostrils, a pungent warning. But - and this is the crucial, faith-requiring part - if you're willing to push through that formidable olfactory barrier, if you commit, it tastes like something else entirely. Something sweet, profoundly custardy, bordering on the divine. A creamy, unctuous richness that coats the tongue with vanilla cheesecake, almonds with a whipped drizzle of caramel on top. I dug in with a small plastic spoon, the flesh spreading across my tongue in all its complex, undeniably funky glory. There is simply nothing else remotely like it on earth. And it's glorious!

I ate my way through the market, passing between stalls where food vendors hawked everything from grilled fish and prawns to meats that would make most Westerners balk. But that was my kind of heaven. Noise, aromas, textures and flavors all tangled up in one place.

I pulled myself away from the food zone to wander into the maze of alleyways. The internal warren of Chinatown is famous for its endless blocks and alleys of vendors selling hard goods - anything and everything, from cheap electronics to knock-off designer bags and luggage, old-school trinkets you didn't know you needed until you saw them. Like a Godzilla butane lighter - you press his dorsal fin down and fire blows out from his jaws! Completely awesome! The alleys seemed to stretch on forever, each one packed with more sellers, more sights, and more of that pulse that makes every Chinatown feel alive at all hours of the day and night.

Wandering deeper into the labyrinth, I began to get "it". The neighborhood was organized like an urban jungle, each section a distinct ecosystem. One alley was a mecca for luggage, piled high with everything from basic carry-ons to fancy heavy leather bags on wheels. Another block was a shrine to women's shoes - heels, flats, sandals, boots, cfm and bdsm and everything in between. If you wanted to look fashionable in a Bangkok alley, there was your runway.

Then there was the cookware section, where I could have spent the rest of the day just staring at the treasure trove of woks, cleavers and other blades, bamboo steamers in a dozen sizes, induction and gas burners, strainers, drainers and spiders. There was every Asian kitchen tool I could imagine. I found myself longing to buy an entire kitchen's worth of tools. They made me wish I were living in

Bangkok with a full kitchen to play in.

Instead, I opted for a 12-pack of beautiful hand-milled ebony chopsticks with silver inlay bands. Not a bad souvenir. Practical but with enough elegance to make them feel special and memorable. It was in that moment that the real luxury of Chinatown struck me - it wasn't the shiny goods or the endless choices, but the experience itself. That's the filling.

A few more turns, a few more alleys and I found myself in a sprawling block devoted to fungus, herbs, chilies, spices, and legumes. It felt like stepping into the very heart of a medicinal garden, many ingredients I'd never seen before in my life. Mushrooms in untold varieties, herbs in every color, fresh and dried that could cure ailments I didn't even know I had (WebMD's got nothing on a Chinatown fungus and herbal shop), spices that were so fresh the aroma almost caught in the throat, and piles of chilies so vibrant they practically burned my nostrils being near them. It was a jungle of smells, a riot of color, and an assault on the senses in the best way possible.

The next alley was a parade of toys. Everything from plastic dinosaurs, cars, balls and dolls to knock-off versions of whatever toy was trending on infomercials. Then, the knock-off luxury brands, bags, watches, sunglasses, underwear, all in various stages of being "authentic." But it wasn't just the merchandise that caught my attention; it was the energy. It all came together in a raging symphony of blatant consumerism.

But no matter how many distractions there were, I kept coming back to the thing: the food.

It was everywhere. The aroma of sizzling meat, the sharp tang of soy, fish sauce and garlic, the sweet sugary scent of freshly fried desserts wafting through the air. Each alley seemed to have its own specialty. Grilled skewers, fried rice, wok seared veggies, dim sum, sweets, meats on sticks, duck on rice. It was sensory overload in the best possible way, and I couldn't help but keep eating, tasting, and savoring bite after bite, knowing that this was a rare opportunity to get lost in the rampant indulgence of a food lover's paradise.

Heading back from the glorious, greasy trenches of Chinatown, the immediate, undeniable need was a shower and a change of clothes. Dinner with Sam, my monk brother, was the next appointment on the books, a welcome bit of grounding after the day's sensory overload, and I was looking forward to catching up. But there was something else, something quieter but far more pressing, sitting squarely in my heart.

Drawn by an utterly necessary impulse, I picked up three bouquets of vibrant tropical flowers - a riot of fragrant blooms, variegated leaves and stalks of a dozen hues.

On the blessedly air-conditioned MRT ride back across the city (Chinatown to Saphan Taksin was easy), amidst the drone of the train and the shuffle of passengers, I carefully rearranged them, combining the disparate elements into one riotously large bouquet, layering scent and stem with the focused intensity of a painter loading a brush, each placement an unspoken message.

The flower arranging project on that crowded commuter train drew a few curious smiles from fellow passengers - a small, shared moment of unexpected humanity in the daily grind. A wonderfully flamboyant ladyboy gave me a big thumbs up, dramatically batting her eyelashes and asking in a perfect, exaggerated female voice if they were for her. We shared a genuine laugh, the kind that cuts through language barriers and dissolves the day's edges. She grabbed the seat next to me when it opened up. Grinning, she leaned in conspiratorially and told me the girl receiving them was incredibly lucky as she helped me slip stems and petals into perfect position. My response came instantly, heartfelt and true, without a second of hesitation: "No," I said, holding the vibrant blooms, "I am the lucky one." And in that moment, surrounded by strangers but connected by that simple exchange and the intention in my hands, I knew it was the simple, undeniable truth.

Back above ground, emerging from the urban circulatory system, I flagged down a cab. The mission shifted gears: shed the sweat and smells of the day's explorations and prep for the evening's different connection. It was a fast shower, a rapid shave, then putting on a white Brooks Brothers button-down shirt, pairing it with my olive linen drawstring pants. The goal: elegant and presentable, certainly. Ready for dinner, yes. But more importantly, feeling a quiet, hopeful readiness for whatever came later. First though, I had flowers to deliver.

I stepped out of the Sunreno driveway and cautiously made my way along the sidewalk towards Chalermwan's shop. My eyes found her, radiant in the late afternoon sunlight. She slipped into her store with a customer, swallowed up by the daily rhythm of her business. That was my cue. Moving with a stealth that felt both necessary and absolutely absurd, like I was planting classified documents instead of flowers, I crept up the last few feet and gently laid the riotous bouquet across the top of our fruit, those deep purple mangosteens. Mission accomplished. I ducked back, melting into a shadowy alcove two doors down - out of sight but positioned to catch the moment her eyes landed on the unexpected gift.

From my hiding spot in the shadows, a nervous voyeur, I watched as she emerged from the shop. She handed off two bulging bags of fruit, and another satisfied customer was sent on their way. She turned back toward the stall, towards the mangosteens and the improbable splash of color interrupting the neatly stacked produce and stopped dead. The pause was wonderful, a flicker of confusion, then recognition bloomed across her face. And in a heartbeat, she scooped them up, pulling the huge bundle into her arms, clutching the bouquet tightly to her chest. A smile erupted across her face, sudden and brilliant, a genuine burst of unrestrained joy that could've powered half the city grid. She bounced on her feet, spun around, turning in every direction, scanning the sidewalk, searching faces, looking for the culprit.

The moment her back was turned I made my move, abandoning my lookout, covering the short distance across the pavement that suddenly felt vast. Reaching her before she could turn, I wrapped my arms around her from behind, pulling her back against me. I buried my face in her neck, breathing her in, feeling the impossible rightness of being close after the day's distance. I kissed her neck softly, over and over, a quiet, desperate, thankful reaffirmation that needed no words, not yet.

"I'm madly in love with you," I whispered into her ear, the words raw and entirely true, a confession offered only to her in the midst of the indifferent street bustle. And then, the simple human truth that underpinned everything, the weight of the day's miles and moments: *"And I missed you so much it hurt."* The entirety of that ache of separation felt throughout the morning and afternoon, released in a singular moment on that busy sidewalk.

She dropped the flowers. Just let them fall, a sudden colorful splash on the pavement by her feet. She leaned back into me, completely relaxed against my embrace, a perfect counterweight to my own racing heart. Her hands rose, finding their place, cupping my head, holding me against her skin against the unstoppable rhythm of her life on that street. I released her just enough to gently turn her around, pulling her fully into the moment. In that second, on that busy sidewalk, amidst the noise and the heat and the indifferent flow of the city - the vendors calling out, the tuk-tuks roaring past - not kissing wasn't an option. We melted into each other right there, a sudden, quiet, still point in the turning world, breathing each other in, eyes open, locked - seeing only each other, the rest of Bangkok a blurred, irrelevant backdrop.

I couldn't give a damn who saw. The faces that might have turned, the whispers that might have followed - none of it. All of that faded away, inane noise against the undeniable, magnetic truth of the connection binding us. I found my name for it. Purity.

We lingered a while after our sidewalk tryst, still caught in the afterglow, chatting softly. I asked her if she'd wait for me tonight. Without hesitation, she said yes. With reluctance, I peeled myself away. I needed to get across town to meet Sam for dinner. On the way out, I stopped at the Sunreno to let Wing, the doorman, know that Chalermwan would be staying in my apartment that evening. He assured me she'd be treated like royalty and that the manager had cleared the way - that she was not only expected, but to be treated with utmost respect. That settled, I flagged another cab and headed to the restaurant Sam claimed was the best Thai food in all of Bangkok. I was excited for the meal, but even more for the company.

Sam and I had talked Thai food during downtime at iMonastery. Over long afternoons we'd swap stories about food and restaurants. He'd get this soft look in his eyes when he described his favorite dishes - like he was seeing home through taste memory and enjoyed relating the details for me. At some point, we made a promise to each other: when I got back to Bangkok, we'd meet for dinner at a place he and his family swore by: Horsamut. Tucked away at 8 Tha Kham Alley, right alongside the river. If you ever find yourself in Bangkok, *go*. It's got style, location, great food and drink and is a fantastic romantic setting for date nights. But do yourself a favor and make a reservation. It's required.

My driver did his best cabbie magician moves, coaxing a path through Bangkok's Friday night traffic, ducking down alleys so narrow I could've reached out with a fingertip and gotten a manicure along the walls. We finally pulled into a discreet driveway that sloped down toward the water. There, a cement and steel structure stood. The sharp angles softened by trailing vines, light spilling from hidden spotlights above and below. It was clearly upscale, in that understated, "if you have to ask the price" kind of way. The other diners looked like they had stylists on speed dial and had just left a *GQ* cover shoot. The moment I mentioned I was meeting Sam, the hostess snapped into action, leading me upstairs to the open air dining deck and the best table in the house. Polished wood, hard stone accents, large tropical foliage and soft lighting set the mood for a sleek and modern restaurant. Sam sat waiting, smiling. He was looking forward to our reunion as much as I was.

He stood to greet me, and for a second, it didn't feel like we were in a restaurant at all. It felt like we were in a pocket of time, borrowed from a life we no longer lived. Our monk robes were gone but the monklife still resided within though we were worlds apart from our days at the monastery. We hugged like brothers, and I felt something in my chest go soft.

But even as I sat down, even as the waiter placed chilled towels in our hands and poured sparkling water as if we were royalty, a part of me was already rushing back to our apartment. Yeah - it was now *our* apartment.

Chalermwan was there. Waiting.

I'd asked her to wait. She immediately said yes, knowing this night was important. But it was a wrench for both of us. I wanted to hold on to every second with Sam. That would probably the last time we'd sit across from each other like this, not as monks or laymen, but as two men who'd met somewhere remote, bonded by faith and found kinship. And yet, I could feel the hours slipping, the weight of time stacked on both ends. I felt duplicitous and yet so fond of Sam that I didn't want that part of the night to end either.

To this day, I've never had better Thai food. No contest. From the first bite to the last, it felt less like eating and more like being serenaded by Thai flavors, textures and temperature with elevated presentation that I had not encountered at any other restaurant. The cavalcade of food flowed: giant river prawns were seared just enough to retain their sweetness; Pad Thai so fantastic it felt like a tribute to the noodle gods. The tuna tartar was absurdly good - clean, spicy, citrus-bright, and yet the flavor of fresh ahi shined through all the fanfare. The tartar came with a black and white baked rice cracker that was as beautiful as it was tasty and functional. The pork and shrimp dumplings were delicate as silk yet deeply satisfying. Then the stuffed squid - it practically dissolved under my fork! Even the rice - sticky and fried - tasted like it had been touched by some ancient culinary spirit. Each dish was a masterclass. Thai cuisine, yes - but transfigured and upgraded. Familiar, but re imagined with grace married to power. It felt reverential.

Sam and I caught up over the feast, slowly and easily, as if we'd done this every week for the last ten years. We talked about life after robes - his filled with family obligations, work demands, the friction and flow of Bangkok's daily rhythm. He didn't complain. He just said it like it was, in that calm, even voice of his that always made the world seem a little more manageable. I chipped in with some life skills and business advice, earned over years of dealing with the same workflow hassles he was dealing with. I think I helped. Sam certainly seemed to take what I said to heart. And all the while - that food! Wow!

I excused myself and wandered down to the restroom. When I came back up and stepped onto the deck level, I stopped dead. I hadn't looked out when I arrived. I'd been caught up in the joy of seeing Sam again, the swift ushering to the table, the anticipation of the food. But now, as I crested the last step and glanced out past the railing, a vision hit me square in the chest.

Wat Arun. Lit in full nighttime glory, it stood across the river like a power dream made of glowing stone. Its central prang towered upward, etched in brash relief and golden light against the ink-black sky. It didn't shimmer. It radiated. It emitted other-worldly power. A silent radiance that didn't ask to be admired but demanded admiration. Power and presence. For a moment, I couldn't move. I just stood there, breathless. That stillness you spend years trying to cultivate on a cushion? I felt it in an instant. That vision? It's still my screen saver on my phone.

I knew at that moment: I'd be back tomorrow. No question! Unless Charlee had other ideas. Then Wat Arun would simply have to wait because there was no way in hell I'd spend another day without her.

Sam dropped me off at the Sunreno. There was no ceremony to our goodbye. Just warmth. A long look, a real hug, and a knowing silence that said everything: This might be the last time. And that's okay. That's life. No promises. Just gratitude. But I know when I go back, I'll be taking Sam out to dinner. Someplace outrageous. Someplace I had found.

※

It wasn't late, but it wasn't early either, the clock sliding just past 11PM, when I cracked open the apartment door as quietly as I could and slipped inside. I moved silently, thinking Chalermwan might already be asleep.

We'd exchanged a few texts throughout the night. I'd tried to reassure her, promised I wouldn't be long, told her to make herself at home. I gave her the Wi-Fi password, the code to the safe, everything short of a notarized affidavit. Still, there had been that note of something. Curiosity tinged with unease. Her messages had a gentle edge: Who is Sam? Monk? Friend? Or something else?

I snapped a picture. Me and Sam at the table, mid-laugh, faces soft in the candlelight, plates half-empty, joy unmistakable. I sent it without commentary and let the image speak for itself. That photo? It's still one of my favorites out of thousands. Because it's not just a picture of dinner with a friend; it's a portrait of brotherly love and respect. Of two men who knew what the other had been through and honored that friendship through a fine meal in an amazing place.

※

What I walked into when I opened the door wasn't the dim hush of sleep. It was something else entirely.

The bedroom was aglow. Pillar candles flickered casting shadows that moved gently with the A/C's rhythm. The bouquet I'd left her earlier had been dismantled, its components distributed in glass vases, drinking glasses, jars, and bowls. Everywhere I looked, there was color and care. The room smelled like frangipani, jasmine and Charlee. Sweet, humid, alive. It was quiet, but not empty. It was walking into promise.

And there she was - Chalermwan - reclined on the bed faced towards the door on her side, radiant, ethereal, draped in the most beautiful lingerie I'd ever seen. The candlelight turned her skin to glowing amber, her presence quiet yet commanding. She didn't speak. She didn't blink. Her eyes met mine and held them, steady and sure. Then, with the smallest curl of her finger, she beckoned me forward. No drama, just a wordless invitation to come home.

Later, beside her in the hush and flicker of the room, I lay, barely awake. Her breathing was soft, sweet and steady against my shoulder, her hand resting lightly over my chest, grounding me in something I'd been missing. I blearily stared up at the ceiling, at the slow-moving shadows, and tried to take stock of how quickly everything had changed. Just weeks ago, I was wrapped in saffron robes in the jungle, rising to chants and the disciplined, scheduled monastic life. Days shaped by peace, structure, intention.

Now this. Bangkok buzzed outside the window. My belly was full of fire and flavor. Candlelight danced on the walls. And Charlee. Her warmth, her grace, her easy musical laugh filled me to the brim. The contrast should have been jarring, but it wasn't. It felt like continuum. Like I hadn't abandoned the monk but had absorbed him and carried him into a new kind of reverence.

Bangkok had cracked me open with a rib splitter. Not with spectacle, though there was plenty of that. But with small moments, disarming collisions of pure and honest intimacy and surprises in many guises. It wasn't just the temples, the food, or the frenetic poetry of the city in all its glory. It was, most of all, the people. The moments in between. Those threads of human connection that wove through everything else and made the heat, the noise, the uncertainty all worth it. I didn't hate the city anymore. Not even close. I was falling for it, hard, piece by insane piece.

Tomorrow, I'd return to Wat Arun. This time with Chalermwan by my side, if she'd have me. We'd see it in daylight, walk its stone terraces, trace the silhouette that had burned its way into memory and fantasy from across the river. After that? Who knew. Thailand was wide open before me. One footstep at a time. One breath, one dish, one connection at a time. But only if Charlee was by my side.

BANGKOK'S SIREN SONG, PART 2

Coffee steamed in our mugs on side tables, the early morning light glowed softly through the curtains. I turned to Charlee, curled against me in the sheets.

"I was thinking about going to Wat Arun today," I said, passing her my phone. "This was the view from Horsamut last night."

She took it from me, eyes widening as she scrolled through the photos, especially the one of the temple lit up like a holy beacon across the river.

"Wow," she whispered. "So beautiful."

"It really was." "I'd love to go see it up close with you, if you're up for it. But if you've got things to do - or just feel like laying low - I'm not going anywhere. Everything feels empty without you."

She smiled, handed the phone back, and nuzzled a little closer.

"Yes. I love to go," she said. "Arun is very special. Other things wait."

"Dim sum or breakfast in bed?" I offered.

We stayed in bed far longer than planned, tangled up in each other's heart and souls until the sound of housekeeping working next door was a reminder that time still existed. We shared a quick shower, dressed in record time, and stepped out into Bangkok, ready for whatever came next.

In terms of central location? Forget it. Bang Kho Laem isn't close to anything unless you count the river, a handful of local hardware, beauty supplies, mani/pedi boutiques, auto dealerships, scooter repair, pharmacy shops, and families of stray dogs with generational roots in the neighborhood. It's not on the tourist radar (aside from the Asiatique night market), and that's exactly why I'd fallen for it. The pace. The people. The life.

I attacked online transit maps like a SEAL commander prepping a hostage rescue, as I plotted a route to Wat Arun. The temple was miles away and across the river, a not-so simple journey that my 'system' transformed into an urban triathlon: Number 1 bus to BTS to Gold Line, to some yet-to-be-identified bus, and finally, a walk. From my untrained, warped vantage point, this labyrinth seemed... efficient. Did I consult Charlee? Wing the doorman? Anyone with a shred of common sense? No. I had a system. Flawed as hell, yes, but it was my system. Besides, a couple of hours traversing the public transport quagmire promised glimpses of parts of Bangkok resolutely un-curated for tourist consumption.

Having cracked the Da Vinci code of Bangkok's tangled transit we fueled up with dim sum and cold tea at our favorite spot. Thirty minutes later, we were back on Chareon Krung Road, hopping the No. 1 bus towards Saphan Taksin station. Across the Chao Phraya we went, the single stop to Krung Thonburi, then transferred to the Gold Line SkyTrain. We rode that to its end-of-the-line, Khlong San Station, before spilling out onto the street to flag down a bus that was headed in a general northly direction, paralleling the riverbank. The goal was simple: close enough to walk but get a real walk in too. I wanted asphalt under my flops, a chance to see what life looked like on that side of the water, away from the tourist glare. Chalermwan slipped comfortable, yet stylish flats on without a hint of complaint about the couple of miles we might stroll.

And then, the shocking part: it actually worked. My convoluted, multimodal transit plan unfolded exactly as conceived. By the time our feet hit the pavement on the edge of the Khlong San district, the mid-morning sun was already doing its best to roast us like chestnuts. Through it all, Chalermwan hadn't said a word of complaint about our odyssey. No head shakes in disbelief. Not even a subtle eyeroll. Just her knowing smile, the kind that suggests she was deep in calculation: was this slightly deranged farang she was falling in love with brilliantly resourceful, completely unhinged, or some perplexing, adorable blend of the two (her words, not mine)? Regardless of her internal verdict, we walked hand-in-hand, the heat a shared experience, laughing at nothing and everything, simply together, admiring the vibrant, messy beauty unfolding around us.

Our walk meandered first along Somdet Chao Phraya Road. We passed under the AH123 overpass and turned to the right, entering a quiet family neighborhood, the kind where life spills into the street without apology. Bikes leaned lazily against gates, colorful laundry billowed on lines overhead, somewhere, a radio playing luk thung as cats eyed our passing with suspicion. From open doorways, the rhythmic clatter of woks and skillets, replete with aromatics of garlic, onion, oyster and soy sauces, ginger and basil filled the air, provided the neighborhood's authentic life symphony.

The narrow streets and alleys eventually spilled us out not at our intended destination, but at the foot of something unexpected (yep - should have studied the map more): a vast, gleaming white stupa rising into the blue sky like an alabaster sail. It stopped us in our tracks with a sudden, breathtaking awe. It was Wat Prayurawongsawat Worawihan. The sign I saw was in beautiful, frustratingly illegible Thai script. For all the guidance it offered me, it might as well have been scrawled by a Martian with a calligraphy fetish. Charlee came to my rescue with translation but in that moment, all that registered was the stillness. A profound quiet that catches in your chest, delivering a humbling lesson in the meaning of peaceful existence.

We wandered the grounds, a lovely pocket of temple calm, maintained with a level of care and devotion that bespoke of the love the residence monks had for their home. Broad-stone paths, warm beneath our feet, led around the great white stupa. It stood sentinel, radiating light with an almost arrogant serenity, as if it knew exactly how photogenic it was. The only movement came from a few locals and monks performing quiet rituals - lighting joss sticks and kneeling before a gilded Buddha tucked into a wall niche. The air itself felt sacred, with the sweet perfume of jasmine and sunshine. Even the ubiquitous birds that love to hang around the temples seemed to have dialed down their volume, offering softened versions of their hit songs like they too had taken a vow of reverence. For a few minutes, basking in that stillness, I was utterly convinced we'd somehow tripped into a hidden Shangri-la, granted a peek behind the curtain by some cosmic lottery. Which, of course, was pure, unadulterated baloney. A quick check via the map later confirmed it wasn't a secret at all; it was a well-known destination. We hadn't discovered the undiscoverable; we'd just shown up unfashionably early.

Something about the symmetry, the white-on-white palette, the elegant grounds tickled the back of my mind. I knew this place, or at least, I'd seen it before. Then it clicked: The King and I. Rodgers and Hammerstein came ghosting in from some long-dormant neurons, dragging silk gowns and stage fog into the fore. I turned to Charlee and leaned in, unable to stop myself. In a voice better suited for a solo shower performance than sacred ground, I murmur-sang the only line I could remember: *"Getting to know you... getting to know all about you ..."*

She gave me a look of mock horror, her hands clasping her cheeks, eyes wide. "You sing so bad," she laughed.

She reached out and grabbed my face and kissed me. Just enough to jolt me out of Broadway and back into Bangkok.

Exiting the grounds, we ducked down a covered alley, letting the rhythm of the neighborhood and our curiosity steer us. Thetsaban Sai 1 Road gave way to Soi Wat Kanlaya, then to more narrow alleys, then narrower still, cutting through the guts of a working neighborhood. No landmarks, no signs I could decipher. Just the quiet thrum of local life: barefooted toddlers chasing each other, a woman sweeping her stoop with a twig broom, buckets of water sluicing down a worn path from a doorway, an old fellow ironing shirts and pants in his doorway.

Then, as if it had risen from the ground through a magic veil, Wat Kalayanamit Woramahawihan appeared.

You won't find it on most of the popular tourist maps (*see-eight-Wats-in-a-day* maps), which is a blessing. Despite being one of the most important temples in Thailand, it remains a place for locals. Not spectacle, but sanctuary. Its reputation runs deep in the city, deep within Buddhism, rooted in community life with ancient daily rituals that have been performed for longer than living memory can account.

Built two centuries ago by a nobleman who offered his fortune and land to King Rama III, Wat Kalayanamit was never meant to dazzle. It was meant to serve. The monks there are teachers, not simply practitioners. Schoolchildren still file through its gates each morning. Families come seeking blessings, lighting incense with the same quiet gestures their great-grandparents once made.

A massive Buddha - Phra Buddha Trai Rattananayok - sits at the heart of it all, towering over fifty feet tall, presiding over the temple like a figure who's seen everything and still manages a faint, knowing smile. The locals believe his presence brings peace and luck. I felt like he was seeing into and through me, which was a little unnerving considering the thoughts I was thinking about Charlee at that moment. She was backlit by the sun. My mind embraced her in every way.

There's a giant bell beside the main hall, weathered from centuries of use, the enameled paint chipped or faded away in many places. If you ring it, they say, fortune will follow. We rang it. Several times.

But what struck me most wasn't the Buddha or the bell - it was the silence. Not the absence of sound, but the kind of stillness you only notice after stepping out of the noise. It was even quieter than the previous temple. The soundwaves felt muffled like we were wearing noise-canceling headphones. I wasn't the only one to notice - Charlee pointed it out first.

The temple grounds are an unusual blend with traditional Thai rooftops, their tiered elegance rising above, and traditional Wat design motifs but intermingled with Chinese guardian statues, pagodas, dragons coiled in stone, an odd square Chedi, and curved gables trimmed in porcelain mosaics. The grounds feel as if they're folded in on itself, dense with iconography all pointing inward.

We were in the Wihan offering our thanks to Buddha. I had been slyly watching Charlee through our explorations, reveling in her by my side, her serenity, her presence, watching her explorations while deeply enjoying her quiet yet playful companionship. I leaned in and whispered my thoughts into her ear. She pinched my arm, her eyes lighting up with loving fire paired with that dazzling smile I now knew so well. Charlee, wisely, drifted off on her own, drawn toward the intricate murals stretching from floorboards to rafters, to explore the epic tales the temple wore as its skin.

I settled in with some monks for a chat, joined in with a chant, and received a blessing. The monk leading the chant was about my age, his voice low and steady, and for a moment, everything else faded away. I was back in the mountains. My heart filled with joy.

No photos. No commentary. Just breath and incense. When I rose, I felt calm, peaceful and grateful. I bowed a deeply sincere wai to the monks, then turned to see Charlee watching me with what seemed like admiration. She clasped her hands in front of her, then bowed to me with a look I hadn't seen from her before, raw and quietly fierce.

I remembered the line from The Lord of the Rings. I reached out, holding her hands in mine. Our eyes met, and I whispered into her ear, "You, my dear Chalermwan, bow to no one. Especially to me. I am not worthy of that kind of reverence."

She gazed back at me, tears spilling free. I pulled her close, holding her tight as her body shook through those tears.

Round about 2:30PM, we finally arrived at Wat Arun Ratchawararam Ratchawaramahawihan. Go for it - you know you want to try and say it. Take your time. It's OK.

The place was packed!

One thing I found oddly amusing: at larger Wats there is a cottage industry that's sprung up. Renting traditional, historically accurate Siamese outfits to visitors has become a thing. For a fee, locals and tourists alike can slip into period-perfect costumes - shoes not included. It's somewhat comical to see couples dressed to the nines in glowing colorful royal garb from the Sukothai or Ayutthaya eras, only to spoil the illusion with Chuck Taylor high tops and Nike Airs. They pose for pictures like Hollywood extras, often hiring professional photographers who hover on-site to capture that perfect moment.

The first time I saw this, I thought there must be some special event or festival. But no. This spectacle is just another everyday occurrence at Wat Arun and at several other temples I visited. Holy meets moly with a side of visual treats.

There we were. Me, in linen slacks and a short-sleeve button-down doing my best impression of "respectably and respectfully neutral." Charlee was beside me in a flowing long dress, elegant and understated, with a delicate silk wrap she'd brought to cover her shoulders. Around us swirled a living pageant, wide-eyed with selfie sticks, and Thais decked out in ornate period costumes, like extras on the set of a historical epic. Brocade jackets called khrui, bejeweled hairpins, chong kraben loincloths and golden sashes gleamed in the afternoon sun. The effect was stunning and intensely surreal. For the first time in ages, I wished for a little hallucinogenic buzz to go with the visuals that swirled around us.

It was clear that for many Thais, this wasn't cosplay or novelty. It was pride, a chance to connect with their deep heritage, to step into something ancestral and walk in it for an afternoon. But me? A farang with an understated (and now somewhat damp) shirt and a shaky grasp of cultural nuance? I had no clue.

Charlee nudged me. "You want to wear Siam clothes?"

I paused, weighing it. I could already imagine the ill-fitted silk tugging awkwardly at my shoulders, while camera-happy tourists snapped away, and locals giving me that look - half bemused, half resigned.

"Honestly?" I said, turning to her. "I don't think that's right. It would feel like I was wearing someone else's skin. Like... trying on something sacred because it looks cool for Facebook."

She nodded questioningly, quietly, then pulled out her phone. I watched as her thumbs flew across the screen, searching for something. It took her a while but she found what she was looking for and held the screen up to me.

"Cultural appropriation?"

I blinked, stunned. "Wow," I said with pure admiration, "You're really getting good at that."

But inside, I was thinking. Thinking about that line - somewhere between thick and thin - between appreciation and appropriation, and how slippery it can be. Especially when you're a guest in someone else's world.

Humility and respect felt right; knowing when something isn't yours no matter how beautiful, how audacious, felt better. It felt more honest to politely decline. That awareness - clumsy, evolving, full of good intentions but with occasional missteps was becoming part of my journey.

I did, however, seriously consider buying one of those outfits for Halloween back in the States. No one could top that!

After strolling Wat Arun's paths and pavilions, we climbed the intimidating, almost vertical steps of the prang itself. (Yes, you actually get to do this. Climbing an ancient, revered national treasure is totally acceptable in Thailand. In America, you'd be standing two hundred feet back wearing a VR headset.) We made a slow, spiritual lap around the mid-tier trying to decipher all that we were looking at. I was so engrossed in the sheer fact that I was standing on and in a living piece of Thai and Khmer history that it was emotionally overwhelming.

After a treacherous descent, (those worn stone steps are about eighteen inches tall and only ten inches deep) we wandered into the small but wonderfully engaging museum, spending time to cool down while reading the history of Wat Arun and its place in the Thai cultural assembly. Then we wandered more.

We found a quiet, shaded alcove beneath a bower, heavy with old, twisted white wisteria in full bloom. An elderly monk sat beneath the cascading blossoms, wearing a look that suggested either deep meditation or mild boredom. It turned out to be the latter.

His eyes lit up as we approached, and before I knew it, we were deep in conversation. His English was careful but clear, his enthusiasm for the temple's history and its modern role was contagious. We talked for quite a while, covering everything from Wat Arun's place in education and community life, to its architectural quirks and foreign influences, to the biography of its founding abbot.

"Somdet Phra Wannarat," he told me, his voice steady. "He helped make this temple what it is today. After Ayutthaya fell, and the new capital moved here, it was he who guided the restoration during Rama II's time."

I nodded, taking it in. I'd read plaques in the museum and Wikipedia before, but something about hearing it from him - under those blossoms, on temple grounds - made it stick.

"He was a wise man," the monk said, smiling faintly. "He knew beauty and discipline must go together. That is why this temple is strong."

I noticed Charlee shifting, subtly at first, then with the unmistakable signs of wanderlust. A gentle pivot here. A composed glance at her make-believe watch. The polite half-smile of someone saying, "Fascinating, truly, but I might chew off my own arm if we don't move soon."

I began wrapping things up, grateful to our impromptu teacher and mildly panicked by the thought of Charlee reaching terminal boredom. We bowed, smiled, and made our exit with all the grace of people pretending not to be making an exit.

That gentle monk smiled and winked like he'd seen it a hundred times before. How is it monks always seem to know everything?

We wandered the perimeter of the temple grounds, tracing neatly trimmed paths and lush landscaping, pointing things out quietly as we went, until the path curved toward the river.

And there it was.

Right in front of me.

A ferry dock.

Unloading a fresh horde of camera-toting pilgrims.

I blinked, half-expecting it to vanish in a puff of irony.

You have got to be fucking kidding me!

I walked over to the ticket counter in disbelief.

"Where does this go?" I lamely asked.

"Saphan Taksin. Last stop," the woman said, barely glancing up. "Forty baht."

I stood there, dumbfounded, the village idiot, staring at her like she'd offered to beam me up, Scotty-style, for the price of a coffee.

Saphan Taksin. The dock was a mile from our apartment.

The very place we'd started from (the BTS was above the ferry terminal!), which I had turned into the launchpad for a convoluted pilgrimage. I'd invented an odyssey, threading alleyways, hopping trains and busses, and over-complicating every stretch like a man on a personal quest to avoid convenience at all costs.

All the while, a ferry boat had been sitting right there, on the river, waving its little ferry flag and laughing at my deeply committed incompetence.

I turned to Charlee. She'd clearly pieced together what was flying through my head and was doing her best - nobly, heroically - not to laugh.

But her torso and shoulders betrayed her. They were jiggling with the effort of containment as her face was scrunched up, desperately trying not to crack.

"Well," I said, exhaling the laugh before it fully formed, "this is what I get for not asking you about anything."

She nodded solemnly, biting her lip desperately trying to not burst out in laughter like a saint, while her eyes sparkled and twinkled with moisture with exactly the kind of incredulous joy that comes from seeing someone walk headlong into their own lesson. And love them even more for it.

She nodded, still suppressing outright laughter, then slipped her hand into mine.

"But adventure, right?" she said breathlessly, stifling her obvious strain.

She took a deep, exaggerated breath, giggled, then sang *"Getting to know you..."* pitch-perfect. Better than I ever could. Then exploded into full-body laughter as I burst out in hysterics at my foolish self. We held each other through that uproarious moment, adoring each other.

We grabbed a bench port-side on the upper deck, tucked in close, the river breeze teasing at Charlee's wrap, the sun making her jet-black hair glow like obsidian as she leaned her head against my shoulder with the kind of relaxed affection that makes you forget you ever had doubts about anything.

The city floated by. Ornate temple spires jutted skyward, their gold leaf flickering in the sunlight like scattered treasure. Low-slung shops and houses lined the banks, peeling paint telling stories of decades, maybe a century or two survived. Riverside restaurants both established and makeshift, their tables full. Laundry fluttered from balconies as prayer flags fluttered alongside. Families perched on wooden docks, fishing poles and net lines in hand, chatting with the ease of lifelong neighbors.

The river teemed with an inconceivable array of watercraft. Longtail boats cutting wakes like brushstrokes, gleaming speedboats slicing the river's surface, slow-moving ferries creaking as they bobbed, long barges hauling their loads, and artfully paddled sampans and reụ̄x khlong balancing loads of fruit, flowers, vegetables, the vendors shouted greetings to each other. Their movements felt choreographed, a ballet danced by time and the river itself, turning a commute into a fairy tale boating magazine cover come to life.

Charlee pointed out landmarks now and then with calm certainty. "Over there, best mango sticky rice in city," she said, nodding toward a faded store festooned with yellow marigolds. "And that little place?" I asked. She grimaced, "No. We not eat there. *Baaaad.* Food make sick for days." Her voice carried the easy authority of someone who'd grown up just upstream, knowing the river's secrets and hazards.

The ferry stopped at every pier, four in our direction; a river bus plying its route. Locals hopped on and off with the practiced ease of people who didn't have to decode four transit systems to get there. Lobster-headed tourists shuffled behind, clutching GoPro's and half-empty water bottles, caught somewhere between dehydration and amazement. Their eyes darted from temple to phone to vista, looking awestruck while overheating.

And there we were, nestled into it all, letting the city unfold at river speed. Twenty-five minutes later, we pulled up at the Saphan Taksin dock, just a five-minute tuk tuk ride from the apartment. And that's with heavy traffic.

It felt like a minor triumph. I'd led us on a needlessly convoluted odyssey only to land right back where we started; wiser, sweatier, and definitely a bit foot-sore.

As we stepped off the boat, I turned to Charlee, trying to sound casual but fully aware I'd just orchestrated the Great Bangkok Detour of 2024. "So," I asked, "what did you think of my grand route plan?"

She grinned wide and genuine. "You fun," she said. "I like time to seeing you discover."

There it was. Affection laced with amusement.

Here's a PSA for those of you determined to follow my footsteps:

The commercial ferries, fast commuter barges, water taxis, and sleek longboats tearing through Bangkok's rivers and khlongs have a rhythm all their own. Equal parts insanity and choreography. Out on the water, there's a left-of-way etiquette that's observable, but when it comes to loading and unloading passengers? That's a whole different beast. It's madness disguised as a moving, breathing art installation!

Unlike the safety-first, composed and regulated docking procedures you see on public ferry services from Venice to Seattle, in Bangkok, boats don't tie up in any traditional sense. Instead, a crew member leaps off the boat as it approaches the dock, holding the mooring line with a kind of graceful urgency, acting as a human anchor. Does that crewman tie off to a cleat? Why would you when you'll be there for less than a minute. The boat might still be moving, but that doesn't matter.

The captain, with a level of expertise that is as skillful as it is poetic, deftly maneuvers his vessel to hover an inch from the dock, rapidly applying quick bursts of forward and reverse thrust, wakes and currents be damned. Meanwhile, the human anchor is barking out the station name like a drill sergeant: "Get on! Get off! Move it pal!" But in Thai.

All of this unfolds in a New York minute. Passengers board and disembark with the urgency of a subway crush at rush hour. The boat never quite stops; it slows just enough for bodies to hop on and off before it roars back to life for the next dock. At the last possible moment, the crewman springs back aboard, and they're off again. It's a well-rehearsed dance, repeated over and over throughout the day. I found myself watching that dance with a mix of awe and disbelief.

After getting comfortable using the rivers and klongs as a faster and more efficient way to travel the length and breadth of Bangkok, I came to appreciate the art of this rapid ingress/egress process. It's like crossing a busy street. Swift, committed action is required, or you'll find yourself in the drink. One false step, one momentary lapse of focus, and you could end up swimming alongside the boat. And believe me, the crew and fellow passengers will be rolling in hysterics (though they'll also be quick to save your soggy butt). It's messy and utterly thrilling and in its own way - a gritty performance piece staged on water.

I had a plan. Quietly, carefully, sneakily hatched the day before and orchestrated over the course of our day's wanderings, because what better time to scheme and implement than during well-timed bathroom breaks?

Back at our apartment, I turned to Charlee and asked with mock gravity, "My dear Chalermwan... May I take you out on the town tonight? Dinner and dancing? If you'll have me?"

Her lips curved into her enigmatic Mona Lisa smile, eyes flickering with curiosity and a teasing hint of mischief.

"I love to."

"Then you'll need to dress up."

She cocked her head, her fingers playfully tracing my chest, asking, "What you wear?"

I showed her my carefully selected ensemble. Grey silk slacks, a cream silk shirt with a whisper of pattern, and black closed-toe shoes, fresh out of the box and required for one of the places I'd scoped out.

She kissed me - long, soft, and deliberate - then wordlessly, she turned and slipped out the door. Her footsteps were light, a dance of their own, echoing the quiet promise in the air.

Now that she had her own key, our comings and goings no longer required planning or timing. It was a small but potent signal. An unspoken commitment wrapped in trust, and something I welcomed. She did too.

About an hour later, after a shower and some manscaping, I was just finishing dressing when I heard the door open.

There she was, standing in the doorway like a vision plucked straight from a dream.

Her black pencil dress, fringed with lace, hugged every curve as if it had been stitched just for her, her matching heels clicking softly against the floor. Her makeup was subtle, nearly invisible, simply enhancing her natural elegance that needed no adornment.

A micron-thin gold chain traced her graceful neckline, a single black pearl dangling delicately, matched perfectly to the earrings she wore.

Her presence shifted the air in the room. Everything felt warmer, brighter, alive. I couldn't breathe.

She didn't say a word as she crossed the room, unblinking and intense.

Her gaze never left mine as she reached out, taking the bottle of cologne from my grasp. Our fingers brushed - just a feather-light touch - but it sent a shiver straight down my spine.

Slowly, deliberately, she dabbed the scent behind my ears and then on my wrists, each movement measured and intimate, honestly, almost too much for my heart to handle. It was one of the sexiest things I've ever encountered in my entire life.

I stood there, utterly dumbfounded, caught between reverence and desire, struggling to string words together.

Finally, I managed, "*Wow!*" How's *that* for slick?

Charlee broke the spell, a playful smile on her face as she twirled on her heel.

"You like dress?" she teased, as if daring me to say otherwise.

I swallowed, trying to regain some composure, but it didn't come.

"You ... are ... absolutely dazzling. I like your dress, but I love who's in it much more."

A delicate blush flushed her cheeks.

It was more than just a compliment. I couldn't fully express my thoughts in that moment, but there was a lot of substance behind it. I stood there, soaking her in, realizing no words could quite capture how she made me feel.

Dinner reservations had been secured the day before as I hatched my plan between mouthfuls of delicious things in Chinatown. Sushi Masato, an Omakase sushi bar boasting a Michelin star, helmed by Maestro Masato Shimizu, a culinary rock star who'd paid his dues in kitchens across the globe before opening his own spot back home in Bangkok.

I'd stumbled on it after some deep online digging, drawn in by rave reviews and knew it was perfect. It was how I wanted to introduce Charlee into my sushi world. Not just as a karmic payback for the dim sum guts-and-gore marathon, but because watching Charlee enjoy a night out on the town? That would be my real prize.

With plans set, my pulse racing, I ordered a Grab. Masato was tucked away in the Sukhumvit/Thong Lo borderlands - an area of Bangkok known for hidden foodie's destinations.

We arrived at the entrance to the alley where the restaurant was hidden away, and... let's just say it wasn't quite the polished atmosphere I'd envisioned. The pavement was slick and glistening from a recent wash down, the wet surface catching streetlights and neon from other small alley businesses in fractured reflections - like a noir film set, but without the Hollywood budget. Shadows pooled in the corners, the air thick with a mix of exhaust, and the lingering ghost of last night's party.

It looked sketchy. As if Henry Chinaski should be slouched nearby on a battered five-gallon bucket, writing a poem, nursing a drink, begging a smoke. Definitely nothing like the glossy, upscale vibe you'd expect from a Michelin-starred fish destination.

But we pressed on, arm-in-arm, weaving carefully down the narrow alleyway. Eyes peeled, scanning for a sign and any potential trouble. I know I've said Bangkok is safe, even in the alleys, but stupid can strike anywhere, and I had precious Charlee on my arm.

Just as I was about to question the wisdom of hanging in the alley and double-check the GPS, Charlee gently squeezed my arm and pointed. There it was. A barely-there, unassuming façade, a wall of drying-oxblood-red and graying wooden slats, framed by stark flat-black beams. It didn't exactly scream "restaurant." More like "forgotten samurai outpost."

The only clue that this was no ordinary entryway was subtle. A dimly lit alcove tucked into that dark wall that had a ground lantern faintly glowing. A small brass plaque, etched with delicate Japanese characters, caught the faint glow of hidden lighting - one that had to be burning at a mere three watts. It was affixed next to a recessed blonde wooden door that looked as if it belonged more in a Zen temple than a semi-seedy Bangkok backstreet.

We slipped into the alcove. I reached for the handle, but before I could grasp it, the door slid open with a whisper.

A hostess greeted us with a warm welcoming smile that cut through the alley's shadows. She led us forward into a world that transformed the dread outside into refinement: elegant, with an air of quiet excitement, which made my pulse quicken. we'd stepped through a hidden doorway into something precious and I was hungry!

The ground floor was a visually thoughtful interplay of deep burgundy leather banquette four-tops flanking pale wood tables, grounded by a cool cement-gray aisle that cut confidently through the space. It exuded understated elegance, quietly confident, never overreaching. But our hostess didn't pause there. She led us past the hum of conversation and the clinking of ceramic, and up a discreet staircase to the third floor.

The L-shaped sushi bar dominated the room like a stage set for something ceremonial. Every seat was taken, every face rapt, every eye following the fluid motions of the chef's knife flicks, perfect cuts, concentrated coordination. It was mesmerizing. But I had reserved something a little more off-script.

At the far end of the upper room, tucked away from prying eyes was a two-seat alcove bar. It was intimate without being claustrophobic, sophisticated without pretense. A romantic hideaway in a temple of fish. The lighting was low and warm, bouncing softly off dark lacquered wood and the delicate grain of the countertop. It felt like a secret waiting to be unwrapped. In short - it was a very sexy space.

And waiting for us (pre-arranged because I'd perused their menus) was Masumi Sanka Junmai Ginjo sake. It glistened under the soft light, as rare and quietly dazzling as Chalermwan herself. Two green Kiriko sake cups, cut glass with a striking geometric pattern, rested at our places like jewelry.

She turned to me with a look I was starting to recognize: half curiosity, half silent praise. Then she smiled, slow and knowing, and I felt my chest loosen and my shoulders relax. Anticipation. Awe. Gratitude.

As we waited for the first morsels, I could feel the warm energy of the room enveloping us. The air hummed with quiet chatter drifting in from the main room, but here, it was just us, tucked away in our own intimate little world. Our fingers playfully intertwined as we chatted quietly about this and that, meaningless yet deeply meaningful at the same time.

Edomae-inspired Omakase-style dining is all about trust. No menu, no choices to make. The chef orchestrates the experience, sending out dish after dish of carefully crafted delights. Each bite was art, not just food. The tai (snapper) was as fresh as the deep sea, the monkfish liver was rich and indulgent, and the uni - sweet, umami and briny in concert. Then there were razor clams and oysters, skate and barramundi, otoro, Atlantic cod, wagyu beef tartar and more. Small dishes kept coming, each one more beautiful than the last.

But what truly made the experience unforgettable was watching Charlee. Each beautiful new kozara placed in front of her made her eyes light up, her smile spread wider with every bite. Her little gasps as she drank in the flavors, the textures, savoring each one slowly, delicately were pure magic. I found myself mesmerized by the joy on her face. I didn't even need to taste the food myself to know how extraordinary it was. Her reaction told me everything I needed to know.

As the last plate from the creative butterscotch macadamia roll was cleared away, I ordered a post-dinner plum wine to share. It was deep indigo and sun-kissed plum sweet. Charlee took a tentative sip, and her entire face up with that playful, adorable surprise I'd come to adore. She glanced around, making sure no one was watching, then leaned in, pressing her lips to mine in a kiss that tasted just as sweet as the wine.

Time stood still. The bustling restaurant, the passing thoughts - they all faded away, leaving only the two of us, wrapped in that perfect moment. Her kiss was slow, soulful, and full of quiet intensity that spoke volumes without a word.

It was one of those moments you don't want to end, where time feels irrelevant, and all that matters is the connection between two people.

Turns out, I'd chosen well. Sushi Masato wasn't just good - it was rated the best sushi spot in all of Bangkok by Samurai Gourmet. I hadn't known that when I booked it.

Back in a Grab, we rolled through the rollicking streets of Bangkok, the night air thick with anticipation, as we headed to Havana Social - a swanky, vintage cocktail bar and dance club that swept you through a wormhole to 1940s pre-revolution Cuba. I've never been to Cuba, but Havana Social? In that dark, sultry corner of Bangkok? It was the closest I could imagine to what I'd heard in stories and seen in pictures.

Because it's hip, because it's hidden, and because Bangkok loves a bit of theatrical flair with its cocktails, there's a catch to getting in. Outside, mounted like a relic from another century, was an old-school push-button payphone. Clunky, silent, covered in stickers and graffiti, yet suspiciously well-maintained. The entrance? Sealed. Unless, of course, you knew the code.

I'm not going to spill it here. Where's the fun in that? Let's just say if you've got half a brain, a smartphone, and a taste for mystery, you'll suss it out. I punched it in like I was a genius; the lock clicked, and with all the swagger I could muster, I held the door open for Charlee.

She slipped past me, eyes sparkling. The door closed behind us with a hushed thunk, and we were through the looking glass.

The ambiance oozed old-world Latin swank that was intentionally aged to perfection. Rich red wooden walls and distressed pillars abounded; patterned Spanish tiles intermingled with wide plank flooring; an old-world bar back that was stocked with ultra-premium liquors from around the world; the bar top lined with green glass and brass library lamps; antique wooden tables, trunks with old wooden seats and deep upholstered couches; it all beckoned a sultry invitation to indulge in something deeper than a drink.

We were hit with an intoxicating wave of Latin-rhythm energy. A DJ was working the pulse of Cuban and world beats that swirled the air. The horns, that sexy Cubano percussion, a slinky piano in stride, and the smooth undertone of the upright bass oozed musical sexuality. The various nooks and crannies were bathed in sepia-toned light; it was all alive with the buzz of conversation punctuated by laughter, clinking glasses, and the occasional burst of horns and congas. This wasn't just a bar; it was a time capsule, a place where the past had come to life. I could already feel our heat rising as the music teased. I had a suspicion that the dancing would be something else entirely - erotic, sensual, and as steamy as Havana's legendary summer nights.

Charlee, cuddled into my side. I could sense the excitement in her, the eagerness to move, to lose herself in the rhythm of the night. There was a magnetic pull between us, an unspoken understanding that this night was going to be one for the books.

I asked her what she'd like to drink, and she gave a little shrug. "I don't know drinks" she said, soft and sincere, with just enough shyness to make her statement disarming. It was one of those sweet moments that slips inside and stays there. We found a low-slung couch tucked around the corner from the bar, the kind that insists closeness. We sank into cushions as timbale rhythms washed over us, crisp, eclectic and erotic. I leaned in, close enough to share her breath, and started gently probing her palate: citrus or sweet, bold or floral, herbal or spicy? After a little playful back-and-forth, mint emerged as her winner. Fresh, cool, just enough bite to keep things refreshing. Like her.

Just as our conversation slipped into soft companionable silence - the kind where the eyes do all the talking - a server appeared with uncanny timing. I ordered a mojito for Chalermwan: muddled mint, fresh-squeezed lime, cane sugar, and a generous pour of white rum. Summer in a glass. For myself, I went with one of their signatures: the Ricardo Robson. Añejo rum, hibiscus grenadine, orange and lime squeezed to within an inch of disintegration and a ribbon of honey to smooth it all out. It tasted like a slow dance in a Havana back alley. We locked eyes again as the server disappeared, and for a beat, the only rhythm was the bassline and the unspoken what's-next hanging in the air.

Charlee wasn't much of a drinker, aside from an occasional sipping scotch we'd share in quiet moments back "home" so I offered a quiet heads-up. "That one's sneaky," I said, nodding toward her mojito. "It tastes like vacation but hits like a freight train running over a tuk tuk at full speed." No judgment, no warning lights, just the voice of experience trying to keep the night on its rails. She gave a little smile and a nod, curious and game. Trusting me to steer the ship.

She lit up at the first sip - sweet, crisp, minty, alive with lime - and before long her glass was more than halfway gone. The band was still tuning up, but the energy in the room had already shifted, rising like a warm tide, bubbling with promise.

I leaned back with my own drink, watching her over the rim with a grin I couldn't hide, the look of a man who'd just pulled off the perfect surprise. This was exactly what I'd hoped for: an evening to breathe, to laugh, to let the world fall away and sink a little deeper into her spell.

When she reached for her glass again, there was a playful flash of resolve in her eyes. Playful, focused, almost defiant. I laughed out loud. The look said it all: I'm chugging this glorious thing, and no one's stopping me.

"Easy there honey."

"It delicious! I love this. Why me honey?" Charlee asked.

"Because you are so sweet. It's one of those names people use when they're in love with each other. A quiet intimacy called a 'term of endearment.' Like a nickname love invents."

I reached out, offered my hand. "Come on baby. Let's dance before the rum really kicks in."

And could she dance!

Charlee moved like she'd been poured into the music. Graceful, fluid, charged, dangerous. There was nothing timid about it. Her every motion was alive with raw sensuality and that quiet, smoldering confidence some women seem to carry like a second skin. She didn't dance so much as command. And everyone noticed. How could they not?

The world fell away. The clink of glasses, the buzz of voices, even the band, all of it blurred, dimmed, until it was just her and the music... with me, caught in her orbit, along for the ride. Every flick of her wrist, the perfectly timed snap of fingers, every slow deliberate turn, every smoldering glance she threw over her shoulder was magnetic - pulling me in, pinning me there.

Me? I'm not going to lie. I dance like a man avoiding a hive of red ants swarming over a bear trap. My moves are about 30% earnest flailing, 69% blind optimism and 1% grace. Somewhere between "wounded marionette" and "overly enthusiastic drunk uncle at a wedding." I make up for it, however, with a complete lack of concern for what other people think, throwing self-conscious embarrassment out with the bath water. But with Charlee, it didn't matter. She lit me up from the inside and made me feel like the only man in the room, like rhythm was something we made up between us.

We'd been dancing for over an hour - her, radiant and unleashed, fully in her element; me, trying not to look like a winded oaf with two left feet. But I kept up, more or less. The sweat and tempo finally caught up with me, and I leaned in, kissed her cheek, breathless. *"Water,"* I gasped. She smiled and nodded, eyes glowing, hips already answering the next wave of sound.

I returned to the periphery with two bottles of sparkling water, but Charlee wasn't thinking about hydration. The music owned her, the magic coursed through her soul. She moved as current through a wire, pure voltage. Every beat sparked something new in her, something wild and beautiful. Other dancers started orbiting her, drawn in by her sheer force, like moths to flame.

And then, just like that, the spell broke.

He was tall, ridiculously handsome, dressed to kill and overconfident. The kind of man used to assuming the answer is always yes. He slid in fast, hands low, presumptive. He didn't ask. He grabbed. Fingers clamped well below her waist, yanking her toward him like she was something owed and owned.

Big mistake!

In one fast fluid motion, Charlee spun low, precise, devastating. She shifted her weight, dropped her center of gravity, and used his own momentum against him. One second, he was grabbing ass; the next, he was eating floor. Hard. She had him in some kind of lock. His wrist bent at an unnatural angle, her grip like steel, pressing into a nerve that made him gasp out something between agony and a plea for mercy.

She didn't bother with words. No lecture. No yelling. No performance. Just a fierce, storm-lit glare as she let go and walked away, her body still humming with rhythm, her eyes now lit with fire of a different kind.

I was stunned, yet also wonderfully terrified by how fast it all happened. One second, he was grabbing her ass as if she were chattel, the next he was gasping on the floor like he'd been zapped with a taser. She barely blinked. No drama, no shaken breath - not even a stray wisp of hair out of place - just a storm unleashing its fury, then passing through.

And yet - I knew. I knew that beneath that composure was a truth every woman carries: that moment when a man decides he's entitled to take and claim. It's not flirtation. It's ego, arrogance, stupidity, immaturity, and uninvited lust dressed up like cheap gold-plated charm. Mama should've bitch-slapped some manners into those testosterone gorillas when she had the chance to teach the word respect.

Charlee simply happened to have a better skill set to handle that kind of Y-chromosome bullshit. Most women don't have that luxury. And watching her reclaim her space with such calm surgical precision, made something deep in me flare. Pride and a deep, aching admiration. But there was also a slow burning rage at the fact that she even had to.

We found a quieter spot at the far end of the bar, away from the pulsing crowd, and sipped the last of our second round. The night's edge softened, cooling like embers after a fire.

I leaned in close, voice low and a little sheepish. "I'm so sorry, honey. Dancing's such a raw, sensual thing - especially when you move like that. And... well, you being you, you're always going to draw attention, wanted or otherwise."

She tilted her head gazing at me, the smoldering flame still there but cooling, eyes steady and voice soft but sure. "This why I don't go out. Always men want what I not give. But you... you like me when I'm dirty at shop. We have us. They don't have this," as she raised my hand to her lips and gave it a gentle kiss.

I glanced at her and admitted, "I shouldn't have left you there on the floor. It was an open invitation and that will never happen again" I promised.

She smiled, that quiet confidence still sparkling in her eyes. "You sorry? I stay to dance. Nothing wrong. We go... let's find quiet place. I want to show off."

※

I didn't understand what she meant by "show off," but I wasn't about to argue. Outside, a cabbie waited for a fare. He belonged to the night's rhythm. I showed him a screenshot of the Speakeasy Rooftop Bar, the romantic refuge I'd picked for a nightcap, where soft lights and the city skyline promised a gentler pulse.

Our driver moved through Bangkok's streets with effortless ease, away from the heat of the floor, from the tension that had filled the air. Sitting beside Charlee in the back seat, my arm holding her sympathetically, protectively, through some deep breaths I felt the knot in my stomach begin to slack.

The city sprawled beneath us. As we stepped into the elevator, it was like stepping into a different world where the night slowed, where the raw edges softened, and where something quieter but no less intense stirred. The space between us narrowed, not just with distance from what had been, but with something new, something unspoken and alive. My admiration for her had escalated into the stratosphere.

The rooftop was everything I'd hoped for. A star-studded velvet sky above, and around us, the skyline of the Sukhumvit, rising and shimmering; a canyon of glass and light. We weren't looking at the city. We were in it, suspended among towers that blinked and burned against the night. The air was thick with soft techno and frangipani. I'll easily admit that it was an ego stroke walking in beside a woman like Chalermwan. She had beauty, yes, but also presence - quiet and self-assured.

Heads turned. Every last one.

We were led to a glass-topped table along the balcony rail, where the sprawl of Bangkok shimmered all around us. I pulled out her chair because yes, I believe in being a gentleman. She sat, laced her fingers in mine, and looked up at me with that glint, the one that short-circuited my brain every time.

"Kiss me," she said.

I leaned across the table. I did.

When I finally pulled back, breathless and grinning, I asked, "Okay... what was that all about?"

She didn't hesitate. "This place is fancy. Men bring bar girls. Bar girls not kiss. No allowed to kiss. Now everybody know - we together. I not bar girl. Not just sexy-sexy."

I smiled, touched to the core by her pride and ownership of the situation, of me. She had clearly understood the moment we walked across the deck a social secret that I had not grasped. "*Ahhh*. I understand."

I rose and reached for her hand, guiding her up with tenderness. As she rose, I pulled her into me, full-length and unguarded, our bodies fitted together. We'd been designed that way. She folded into my embrace, arms winding tight around my back..

We didn't move to music. We swayed to something deeper - an invisible rhythm that belonged only to us. The rooftop faded into the periphery. It was just her heartbeat and mine, syncing in some ancient, private tempo.

After a long breathless pause, I eased back just enough to cradle her face in my hands. My thumbs brushed her cheeks, memorizing the moment. Then I kissed her soft and slow, with every morsel of care and love I had in me. Not to possess, not to impress, just to let her feel how entirely I saw her. Rhett and Scarlett had nothing on that kiss!

When I finally opened my eyes, hers were already waiting, lit from within, misted and bright. A silent *yes* in their depths.

We took our seats and waited. And waited some more. Then more.

Whatever doubts might've lingered in the shadows evaporated with that kiss. Anyone still foolish enough to label her a bar girl would've had to deal with me. I would've seriously considered throwing them off the rooftop. How very Buddhist of me I know. But let's be real: Charlee would've done it first. Faster and with better form. I'd just be the guy apologizing to the waitstaff while she adjusted her dress and walked away without a hair out of place.

Out of the corner of my eye, I noticed the bartender watching us, his mouth set in a thin, disapproving line. I wasn't about to apologize for loving her out loud.

We hadn't even been approached by a server yet. I raised my hand to flag one down, but Charlee grasped my hand and lowered it. "Please, honey, sit."

She looked at me with a sly glint. "My turn," she said, and in two syllables, she flipped the energy of the place.

She walked - no, she commanded her way across the rooftop to the dour barman, who now had the look of someone who knows they're in trouble. I was going to enjoy the hell out of what was coming his way.

Her movement was slow, unapologetic, deliberate. The kind of walk that changes a room's temperature. A sashay like silk over fire that exuded pure sexuality. Every eye turned, every conversation paused. She was the show now.

She spoke with the bartender for over a minute, calm and composed, as I watched him obviously backpedaling and apologizing. She turned then returned with that same ease, gliding back to our table. Charlee knew exactly what she was doing. The subtle grin she slyly sent my way as she sat said it all: *Watch this.*

As if some invisible cord had been cut, the tension around us released. Service snapped into high gear. Servers emerged from the shadows like second line dancers. Sparkling water arrived then poured into tall glasses with ice, a glass vase with fresh jasmine and orchids, placed at the center of our table. A bowl of water with floating tealights placed next to the vase underlit the flowers and our faces. And then came the pièce de resistance - a chilled bottle of Bollinger Rosé, carried with ceremony and respect. A soft pop, a cascade of bubbles into tall flutes, then the bottle nestled into a pewter ice bucket beside us.

"Whoa, honey, this is fantastic!" I said, my eyes wide. "How did you pull this off?"

Charlee didn't miss a beat. "I say you husband and true love and stop fuck us round!" she said, with a gleam in her eye and zero remorse. Then she burst into that musical laugh of hers. "I also say you Hollywood big shot." She giggled again, absolutely delighted with herself.

I laughed hard with her. When I finally caught my composure, I lovingly reprimanded her. "Charlee, honey, we don't need to fib. Let's just be who we are and let the world catch up to us. But seriously... thank you. This is incredible. *You* are incredible!" I gestured toward the bottle, still faintly hissing in its cradle of ice. "How did you know I love champagne? Have we talked about wine? I can't remember."

She shrugged, modest but proud. "I not know. I say best they have. Must be good. I already pay."

I blinked. "That was very sweet of you honey, but... I know what this costs pretty much everywhere in the world. You shouldn't have ... "

Charlee cut me off then waved my concern away. "You pay all the time. My turn now. Wait ... *How you know price?*" Her gears churned, and as always, she was incredibly quick on uptake. She'd caught what I had said. "How you know champagne?"

There was curiosity in her voice now, genuine and intrigued. I paused to let some tension build. She took my hand in hers. "*How you know?*" She asked again, demanding a response. I leaned in and offered some of what I hadn't yet shared. I mean, you have to keep some intrigue right?

"I worked in the wine industry for many years. Vineyards, operations management, production, retail with my own shop - you name it, I did it. I'm also a certified sommelier. This," I raised my flute, "is kind of my thing."

She tilted her head, amused, a bemused smile boring into me. "Why you not tell me before? What is somelay?"

"We've been kind of ... busy," I said smiling. "And you never asked."

She laughed, shaking her head. "Anything else I not know?" There went my plan to hold onto some secrets for later divulgence.

I sipped, then launched into a story. I told her how champagne is made, how the color of rosé comes from limited red grape skin contact during fermentation (called *saignée*), and which of Bollinger's estate vineyards in Aÿ, Tauxières and Verzenay likely produced the grapes in our glasses.

When I mentioned I was also a musician, she laughed. "Not way!" Again - freakin' adorable!

"Way," I laughed. "Guitar, mostly but some bass too. I also learned some engineering and production along the way. Played in a lot of bands over the years."

She paused, eyeing me with scrutiny. A wonderful gap in conversation that highlights how comfortable we were with each other. Then she leaned in, eyes searching mine. "Why you pick me?"

I didn't hesitate. "No, you picked me." So there!

She grinned. "I like you like my fruit. Mangosteen. Then you so nice and funny and flirt ... the way you eat my fruit with... passion? You make me like you."

I chuckled thinking about her statement. "I didn't flirt - you did," (she rolled her eyes in playful denial). "I was attracted to you then, simply because you were so kind to me. You took your time to teach, feed me, and then refused money for the fruit you cut open simply to allow me to experience mangosteen. That really struck me - and reinforced my admiration for Thai people. It still does. That's more important to me than anything. Kindness. Intelligence. Generosity. Caring and compassion. And I loved your laugh. It's... musical. Let's see - there's also your smiling eyes, your quick mind ... and the fact that I find you drop-dead gorgeous doesn't hurt in the least."

She made a pouty face. "But I dirty and not dressed nice!" she said in mock protest.

I reached for her hand. "Your smile lit me up. I saw you through the grime. It was easy - because you're you."

She blinked and suddenly tears slipped down her cheeks. She reached across the table and gripped my hands tight. A server hurried over and gently asked if she was alright.

Charlee turned, smiling through tears. "I love him so much!" she said, laughing again as more tears poured forth, beaming at me with an expression I'll carry with me for the rest of my life.

We stayed there long after the bottle ran dry, talking, laughing, falling deeper into what we were building. When I finally asked, quietly, if she wanted to come back to the apartment for a nightcap, she shook her head no.

My heart dropped for a moment until she took both my hands and whispered, "You come to bâan ... um, home? I make nightcap for you."

Relief flooded in. "Yes, yes" I said. "A thousand times yes. I would love to!"

We cabbed back to the Sunreno. As we rode the elevator she asked if I'd stay the night. Of course I said yes, but I needed to grab a few things. While I puttered around loading my daypack, she poured a small glass of black liquor - something viscous, herbal, sharp, cloyingly sweet, that she had smuggled into my fridge at some point. I asked her what it was to which she put a finger gently to my lips, said "*shhhh*", leaned in next to my ear and whispered, "make you strong!" But she made me stronger than strong. She was more than enough for that.

I packed only essentials. I glanced over to see her silhouetted at the window, framed in moonlight.

I walked to her, wrapped my arms around her waist, and pulled her gently back against me. She leaned into me, head against mine, as I nuzzled her ear and inhaled her scent - she was warm, floral, and unmistakably her.

When we reached her place, she asked me to wait outside in the garden. "Some minute," she said, and closed the door with a teasing smile. I settled on a cushion for a micro-meditation as frogs croaked nearby in the canal. A scooter buzzed by, followed by a drunk local tottering his way back home. Crickets chirped from all around as a breeze rustled the trees overhead. The world felt still, held.

Then, softly: "You come in now Larry."

I rose from the cushion and turned. The door cracked open. Inside, candlelight flickered across the walls, and I could smell incense as the smoke swirled gently out the door from the small altar in the corner. Everything smelled of cedarwood smoke, flowers and her. It was, quite simply, magical.

The door closed behind me. A latch. A lock. A click.

And there she stood. Dressed the same as the day she was born.

The futon was freshly made. Pillows fluffed and sheet turned down. Pillar candles glowed. Her home was alive with warmth and intention. My breath caught as I gazed at her.

I sank down onto the bed, body and mind giving in to her, to the night.

I looked up at her and teased, "I thought you said we were going to have a nightcap Charlee?"

She closed the gap between us, straddled my lap, wrapped her arms around me, forehead to forehead, then whispered into my ear.

"I am nightcap... honey."

BANGKOK'S SIREN SONG, PART 3

Bangkok is a city where food isn't just a part of life, it *is* life. With 180 Michelin-rated restaurants (from crystal-chandeliered temples of gastronomy to roadside carts with cracked plastic stools and a line of people sweating through their clothes) add to that, 320,000 unrated restaurants and a half-million street carts: the sheer number of options could bring a hungry person either to joyful tears or choice paralysis. Those numbers are not an exaggeration - they're fact.

But with all those chefs and cooks, moms, pops, aunties and uncles manning fryolators and woks feeding the city, a question arises: where do they get all that stuff? The answer, nine times out of ten, is Khlong Toei Market.

Sprawling across 14 acres like a crazed foodie's dream come true, the live meats (almost anything on four hooves), feathered things that quack, cluck and squawk, flapping fins and scaly tails, creepy crawlers and everything that grows in, on, above, below or anywhere near dirt, Khlong Toei is the largest wet market in Thailand - and among the biggest in the world. It's open 24 hours a day, 365 days a year, which means no matter when you show up - pre-dawn, mid-day, post-dinner, or mid-insomnia - you'll stumble into a high-octane ballet of buying, chopping, hauling, bagging, yelling, selling and the occasional chicken trying to make a run for it. It's not a place so much as an ecosystem: part trading floor, part slaughterhouse, part jungle bazaar, part bowl-of-something-yummy binge. And if you stand still too long, someone will either sell you a massive fistful of basil or run over your foot with a cart full of jackfruit.

But the true magic of Khlong Toei is its unswerving devotion to seasonality. If it's not in season, it's not there. No plastic tubs of sad-looking blueberries flown in from who-knows-where. No asparagus in October unless it's somehow Thai-grown and looking smug about it. This is radical freshness, dictated by sun, soil, and sea. And that's a beautiful thing: it forces you to eat now, in tune with the land. Which is how humans were meant to eat before we started vacuum-sealing and cryo-freezing everything and calling it progress.

If you've never been to a "wet market," the term might sound suspiciously like a horror movie setting. In a way, it kind of is. The phrase, coined in 1970s Singapore, was meant to distinguish the live markets from the sterile, pre-wrapped, shrink-filmed supermarkets that were beginning to pop up and gain popularity. "Wet" refers to the floor, which is perpetually slick with melted ice, sloshed water, and the occasional fish scale or goat hoof. It's part slaughterhouse, part bloody slip-and-slide.

Think of it as a visceral, full-contact shopping experience. The aroma? A dizzying cocktail of lemongrass, garlic and onions, blood, brine, and two-stroke oil. It hits you like a slap to the nasal passages but weirdly, you grow to love that slap quickly. Thank you sir, may have another!

But what really dazzles is the range of products available. This is not your pretty air-conditioned Whole Foods experience. You'll find seafood wriggling with life, chickens and ducks shooting you the stink-eye from inside bamboo and metal cages, and cuts of meat that would send your local butcher into either lust or cardiac arrest. You'll see vendors expertly shaving green papayas into translucent ribbons or hacking coconuts with machetes that double as thumb-removal devices, and entire families shelling shrimp at lightning speed while gossiping and slurping Tom Kha from a bag with a straw.

And the fruits ... and the vegetables - from sweet to savory - piles upon piles of alien-looking things, leaves the size of umbrellas, chilies that come in a hundred shades of red, green, purple, yellow with silent warnings, and herbs so fragrant they could jerk you awake from a dead faint. Need something obscure? Try fermented crab paste, banana blossoms, or frog. Yes, frog. Available skinned or still hopping, depending on how brave you're feeling and how you're preparing.

At Khlong Toie, waste is a dirty word. Everything moves fast, everything has a use, and everyone knows what they're doing. It's not chaos - it's choreography. A blood-slick, basil-scented, strangely beautiful dance that doesn't stop.

This also isn't just a market for curious tourists snapping photos of fish heads. Michelin-starred chefs, curry-slinging street vendors, and grandmas making dinner for the family all shop there. Because if you want the best, that is where you go. And because Khlong Toei never stops, it always has surprises - an unfamiliar mushroom one day, a fish with neon fins the next. It's a living, breathing tribute to what Thailand grows, raises, and catches. And if you know how to look (and don't mind getting a little wet), you'll find the soul of Thai cuisine right here, somewhere between a bucket of live clams and a pig's head.

The morning slipped in quietly, the light soft and golden, like a hand slowly brushing back a curtain. At some point, Charlee must have risen to blow out the candles, but I hadn't noticed - not with the spell she'd cast over the room, and over me. Sleep came easy beside her, like a sweet-scented promise kept. The kind of calm that finds you only when you've stopped chasing it.

As my mind began to stir, tucked against her warmth, I knew exactly what I wanted to do with the day. But waking her? Not a chance. That would've been a crime against beauty. I shifted just enough to pull her closer, arms wrapping around her like a shield against time. I let myself settle, breathing in the scent of her hair and breath, and slipped into a quiet meditation that wasn't about mantras, but something more present in the here and now.

I must have dozed off again because the next thing I felt was a kiss that had no end pressed gently to my cheek, a whisper of a touch that pulled me back from the edge of dreams. I smiled without opening my eyes, and drew her in, our bodies aligning instinctively, like puzzle pieces that had waited years to find each other.

"Good morning beautiful," I murmured, my voice still thick with sleep.

"Good morning... honey," she whispered back, her voice like sweet tea.

"Khlong Toei market?" I quietly asked, gently brushing her hair from her face.

"Mm-hmm," she hummed into my chest, nodding a subtle yes without letting go.

And that was all the planning the day needed.

There were still times when we had to lean on our phone translators, but Chalermwan was quick - sharp in a way that made me wonder if she was secretly grading me. She soaked up every English word I tossed her way with the focus of a scholar and the delight of someone solving unfathomable mysteries. Meanwhile, I continued to trip over Thai tonal inflections like a one-legged guy in a jitterbug dance contest. Still, she never lost patience, gently correcting me with that soft smile that let me know I'd butchered something, probably hilariously.

She often asked me to speak only in English - "I want to hear more words," she'd say - and whenever something didn't make sense, she'd stop me and ask. I loved that. There was no rush or embarrassment or timidity. Just our quiet little workshops of language and laughter we built between kisses and coffee.

After a long, lazy morning wrapped in each other's arms, we swapped stories, the ones that matter. The ones about who we were before now. Our loves, our losses, our irrational hatreds. I confessed mine: advertising, politicians, hypocrisy, lies and fascists. Not necessarily in that order. Though I made sure to clarify that I didn't actually hate anyone. I just reserved the right to be selectively exasperated.

I was sure the neighbors were beginning to wonder about the random bursts of laughter spilling out of Chalermwan's little bâan. Let them wonder. Behind that wooden door, we were busy sketching the outlines of our own private language, part dictionary, part inside joke, part tender confessions. It was made up of mismatched words and the kind of laughter that takes its time. A language built slowly, joyfully, without needing to be fluent.

We got to the market just shy of 10AM. I thought I knew what to expect. I'd been to many wet markets. I'd braced myself for mayhem, for noise, for the kind of glorious disarray and volume that's usually confined to children's birthday parties with a whole lot of sugar. But really ... nothing could've prepared me for the sheer intensity of choreographed crazy that engulfed us from every angle. If gravity suddenly gave up the ghost, the scene would've gone full 360° - a swirling ecosystem of food, bodies, and barely-contained anarchy. I felt like a feather in a tornado. In a really good way.

Every stall was in full swing, doing brisk business at a pace that would make a stock exchange floor during a buying frenzy green with envy. There was no pause, no lull, no observable system to the current of humanity surging all around us. Maybe a supercomputer, given a few years and an unhealthy caffeine dependency, could detect a pattern. I could not.

We parked ourselves near the poultry section, me with a bowl of Pho and Charlee with something that looked like larb but had more red and green chilies in it than the baskets a few aisles over. The ambiance was somewhere between "industrial raw" and "don't breathe through your nose." Still, the Pho was delicious - balanced, wonderfully spiced and comforting and loaded with all the things I like, and you don't, which made the squawking and occasional flapping behind us feel like just another flavor note. I wouldn't recommend dining next to the poultry section for appetite stimulation, unless your idea of a light lunch includes side-eyeing a chicken that might still be considering its options and nasal-clearing waves of ammonia. But I was way too intrigued by the surrounding circus to care.

"I want to cook for you tonight, it's why I wanted to come to the market," I told Charlee, already envisioning myself attempting haute cuisine in her kitchen, which was about the size of a coat closet and powered by prayer. "May I?" As if she had any real chance of stopping me.

"You can cook for me?" she replied, eyes lighting up with a kind of wide-eyed excitement usually reserved for street magicians or really expensive Jimmy Choos.

"Absolutely, I'd be honored," I said, beaming (yet sweating inside because I'd never checked to see if her kitchen actually had a stove. It was all based on assumption.) "And it looks like everything we could possibly need is right here, no matter what you desire." I gestured toward the glorious madness of Khlong Toei. "All we have to do is go hunting. Worst case, we improvise with one pot and a prayer. So, what can I make you for dinner tonight?"

She winked conspiratorially, "Spaghetti and meatballs" she said, absolutely deadpan. No irony. No hesitation. No local influence. Full Lady and the Tramp energy.

Oh shit.

Of all the dishes in all the stalls in all of Khlong Toei, she had to walk into mine.

Now, I'm perfectly fine - and more than capable - when it comes to making fresh pasta. I've done that plenty of times. But I always had the help of the Kitchen-Aid stand mixer and my trusty Marcato Atlas hand-cranked pasta machine, which were currently collecting dust far away on a different continent.

I'd seen Barilla boxes in Bangkok supermarkets. If worse came to worse, dried pasta was an option. But I had visions of doing it all from scratch, start to finish, a culinary love letter if you will. Still, I needed a compromise.

"How about lasagna?"

"What is lasana?" she asked, adorably butchering the word like it was dead weight.

"Repeat after me: lah-Zon-ya." I teased.

She nailed it - pitch perfect, then blinked back at me, waiting for the explanation.

"Think spaghetti and meatballs... but better. It's layered with a lot of yummy things in between pasta sheets. And instead of hand-cutting noodles, I can roll out big sheets," (As I wondered where the hell in Bangkok I was going to find 00 flour, semolina, and a Sangiovese-based red wine that was drinkable.)

She gave me a look like I'd just sprouted a third arm out of my forehead.

"Do you trust me?" I asked.

Chalermwan giving me a direct stare-down, took my hands in hers, without breaking eye-contact the way she loves to do, said with emphasis: "*I do.*"

I desperately tried to match her fierce gaze: "Ummmmmm... okay then."

I tried not to think too hard about those two little words in another context, yet a part of me heard her obvious intentions loud and clear.

Not surprisingly, procuring the basics in that market was a piece of cake. I asked Charlee if she would translate and request tasting samples as we roamed and browsed, and within an hour of lazy strolling (though an hour filled with foodie lust and wonder), pointing, and the occasional "what the hell is that?" our hands were full of small bags.

The tomatoes tasted like tomatoes should - juicy, sweet, umami, and supernaturally tomatoee. I found a plump and pungent head of dark red garlic with big, meaty cloves, a couple of firm yellow onions, two ultra tight shallots that I could smell from ten feet away, and a bag of fresh wild greens tossed together to my specs. Charlee translated like a pro, while casually flexing her growing command of English, all the while corralling vendors like she owned the joint. They paid attention to her. Everyone does.

Then came the mushrooms. God! The mushrooms! I wanted them all but settled on one perfect maitake and three ginormous porcini that could have been fungi porn stars. Every bit of produce and fungi looked like a food magazine editor had styled it.

Herbs and spices? Fresh bay leaf, mint, oregano, thyme, marjoram and basil bagged. Dried fennel seeds and crushed red pepper? Got 'em. Half a dozen free range organic eggs? Tossed in. I checked the eggs by asking for one. Egg-man handed one over for inspection. I cracked it, split the shell, opened it up to reveal a deep orange yolk with a perfectly clear albumin. He looked at me with that obvious glare that says, "you know I'm charging you for that, right?" I slurped it down and paid seven. Charlee grimaced; I snickered. Egg man grinned. I asked her about salt, pepper, and sugar. She had those at home. And everything was organic, but nobody made a fuss about it or jacked the price using "organic" as leverage. It just was.

Total damage so far? Just shy of eight bucks.

With a little guidance from mushroom-man, we navigated to the meat section and found the butcher he recommended. I asked for ¾ lb of beef and ½ lb of pork, freshly ground to order. Of course it was. Why wouldn't it be? And then he hand mixed it for me at Charlee's request (I had filled her in on how it would be used. I was seriously beginning to think she knew *way* more about cooking than she led me to believe.)

Now came the tricky part: Italian imports. If I couldn't find the right ingredients, this dish would fall apart faster than a bad first date. An idea hit. I pulled out my phone and texted Jaks.

"Hey brother - I'm in a jam and need help!"

"Where are you? I'll come to you. Are you OK? Need a lawyer?" Jacks replied.

"Oh shit - sorry! I didn't mean to sound the alarm. We're at Khlong Toei and I'm cooking for Charlee tonight. Can I borrow some restaurant gear? If not that's totally cool too."

My phone rang immediately.

"As you American's say - ASSHOLE! You scared me farang! So, what are you cooking? What do you need?" Jacks asked.

"I'm making fresh pasta sheets into lasagna. Do you know what that is?"

Jakkapan paused - loudly paused: "Dude! C'mon ... That hurts! Who are you talking to? What do you need?"

I rattled off my wish list but then came the million-Baht question: Where the hell in Bangkok could I find a legit Italian wholesale supply store? Not a shelf of overpriced, thin balsamic; past-prime but still expensive EVOO; and dried-out pasta at a high-end supermarket. Where was the real deal to be had? The kind of place that smells like Parmesan, shipping crates, artichokes, gun and olive oil. Ideally somewhere close so I wouldn't be schlepping produce across town in traffic that moves like coagulated blood.

He texted me a pin. I opened the map and grinned. Only a few blocks away. Perfect.

Check and check. While I was busy confirming directions, Jaks said he'd snag everything I needed from the restaurant, then followed it up with a second message: "They have flours, oils, cheeses, canned Italian stuff, whatever you want."

The place he sent me to wasn't just a specialty store, it was the Italian importer and distributor that supplied nearly every Italian restaurant in Bangkok and plenty beyond.

Without skipping a beat, Jakkapan texted again:

"I'll call them. Tell them it's all for me. They take care of you. Just sign and pay me back."

Just like that, the backdoor to Bangkok's Italian underground swung open. All I had to do now was show up and pretend like I belonged. And of course step gingerly over any bodies that may be in the way.

I hated to leave the market. There was still so much to ogle, sniff, and impulse-buy (yes I'll take those 4 lobes of sweetbreads, Khop Khun Krab!) - but duty called. Homemade pasta and lasagna layers are no quick task and I wanted to knock Charlee sideways with this meal, simply to prove I wasn't kidding when I said I could cook. Making everything from scratch is time-consuming and messy, and there was no time to lose if I wanted to keep the juggernaut rolling.

All this time Charlee was holding onto my arm, eyeing me, genuinely fascinated. "You keep all that in head?" she asked.

"Uh, yeah, and so much more" I said, half-smiling. "It's not all that great. Most days, and many nights, I can't shut it off. That's why I meditate so much."

She looked at me with a sympathetic gaze and squeezed me gently.

We hopped into a tuk tuk with a driver named Mini, who had a wild accent that sounded like Bangkok meets East-end London. "Where to, guv'na?" with a wai. I told him the name of the importer and asked if he'd wait while we gathered goodies. I promised I'd make it worth his time. He grinned, cranked up some Thai disco pop from the '80s and flipped on the rotating LED light bars, gave us a salute over his shoulder and we were off.

Inside, things moved fast. Jaks's call had paved the way like an all-access VIP pass at a stadium concert. The staff was all business - no upselling, no small talk, no bullshit. Just brisk, efficient professionalism. I was handed both fresh and dried goods sheets and a checklist. I ran down the supplies I needed, handed it over and within ten minutes, it was boxed and bagged. All I had to do was sign the receipt. I asked for the itemized Baht breakdown so I could pay Jaks' tab off.

I walked out with kilo bags (the smallest they carried) of both 00 and semolina flours, a 500ml bottle of ultra-premium first cold-pressed extra virgin olive oil (the kind that makes you question your perceptions of grocery store oil forever), a tub of fresh ricotta, a wedge of parmesan, a two pack of low-moisture mozzarella, a 250ml bottle of 18-year aged balsamic vinegar, and tomato paste and sauce? "What kind you want?" the man asked. They had everything San Marzano: crushed, sauce, whole peeled, sliced, diced, roasted, toasted, pastes, double-concentrates. It was like standing in the Italian goods aisle in heaven.

I was in business.

Walking out of there with two boxes of products that would've made any Nonna in North Beach drop her cane and shout mamma mia. The gods of gastronomy had smiled on me. I had everything I needed to make lasagna from scratch with no compromises or shortcuts. If I fucked this up, that would be on me as it wasn't going to be because I didn't have the right ingredients.

As if fate itself had decided to make my life easier, I had asked about wine and the staff at the wholesaler. He handed me the address to a wine shop that was conveniently down the block and around a corner. Thank you, universe. Charlee typed the details into her phone and turned to Mini, our tuk tuk driver, who had been quietly eyeing my haul like I was smuggling contraband.

Charlee said something in Thai to him. I had no clue what she said but his gaze changed.

Mini, looking back at the pile of produce, meats, pasta, flour, and cheeses that would've made even the most jaded food snob's heart skip a beat, then looked at me, gave me a crooked smile and a thumbs up.

At the Wine Pro Bangkok I got lucky. Again. Behind the counter, the clerk spoke flawless English. A little too flawless. It was almost like she was in the middle of a sommelier cosplay, only there was no time for games. I needed wine, and I needed it fast.

"Pasta with red sauce?" she asked as soon as I started talking what grapes, profiles, bodies and alcohol percentages I was looking for. I was impressed! And if you really knew me? That's a hard thing to accomplish in the wine world. She wasn't wasting time with small talk.

"Nice deduction! I'm looking for two bottles, both Sangio based. I need a sauce and slurp wine and then a knock-your-socks-off sex-in-a-bottle Brunello. I'd love it if you have an older vintage."

Charlee blushed at my description.

"Nice! That's easy. I have a couple of ideas, but you'll have to choose the vintage on the Luce; I have nine years available."

By the counter was a vertical open-faced cooler with cheeses, olives, charcuterie and butter. Next to that was a wicker basket loaded with Italian loaves of bread. I leaned down to smell.

"Those came in an hour ago. Still warm!"

I reached out to touch one and indeed it was lightly warm.

After a few more back-and-forths, I picked out a 2016 Luce Brunello di Montalcino as the heavy hitter, and a 2019 Tenuta di Arceno Chianti Classico for cooking and casual slurping. Then my eye caught a 500ml bottle of Oremus 5-Puttonyos Tokaji (look it up - don't be lazy!) that I couldn't resist for dessert. I also grabbed a couple wedges of freshly creamed butter and a crusty loaf of bread. This wasn't just about sustenance, it was about crafting an experience. The sauce needed to taste like Saint Lawrence had personally descended to stir the pot, which meant garlic bread was non-negotiable. And the wine? It ought to have our taste buds doing backflips.

Mini pulled his tuk tuk up into the closest alley to Charlee's lane and helped us carry everything to her walkway. There were eight bags and three boxes to haul, so the help was more than welcomed. I asked him how much we owed for the fare. He'd driven us all over the place, waited until we needed him. He was efficient, fast, fun, funny, and looked out for us. His taste in music was questionable, but Charlee had been bopping along to the tunes and was absolutely adorable with her cheeky little seated dance moves so as bad as the music was to my ears, I loved it.

Mini told me the ridiculously reasonable fare - about $12. I doubled it. He tried to refuse, because Thais are like that. I looked to Charlee for backup, whispering in her ear to help me seal the deal. She read him the riot act in such a kind way and with that devastating smile of hers, that when he finally agreed, he asked for my phone, typed his number into WhatsApp, and said, "Mate - anytime you need ride call me."

Respect. Honor. Generosity of heart and soul going both ways makes for some lifetime friendships. Mini and I still chat from time to time. I was invited to his son's wedding but couldn't make it. That made me sad because nothing says welcome to the family like an invitation into their personal history.

Mini took off, while I hauled everything into her place. Only then did I notice the stack of gear off to the side of the front door. Jaks had come through. The guy knew how to deliver.

I texted Jaks immediately: "So... you must really want to test me out? Can the farang cook?"

"No. I just didn't want the old man getting hurt carrying my gear from the restaurant." Followed by an emoji raspberry face.

"I'll make sure to include 'special sauce' in your portion." Followed by tears-laughing emoji.

In the restaurant world, *special sauce* is a loaded term. It could mean anything from biologically creative to truly disgusting. I'm not that chef. But the threat? Real. Anyone who's worked in kitchens for long enough knows: if you piss off the chef or the line cooks, the consequences can be dire. Ever seen those young, tattooed, angry cooks in the back? Think long and hard before sending that plate back for a "little tweak" because you didn't like the way the sauce was seasoned. You ordered it, you eat it.

When I cook anything beyond a simple dish I disappear. Like, full-on ghost mode. My head ducks down low, practically wedged in my own backside, and all that escapes is the relentless chop chop of knife on board, pre-measuring and combining ingredients so they flow in order into whatever the dish requires. Focused is an insult to how dialed-in I get. I'm not just cooking; I'm in the trenches, waging culinary war with onions, garlic, peppers and whatever else needs slicing, dicing and julienning. There might be some mild swearing because, honestly, what's a kitchen without a little salty language? But mostly, I don't look up. I don't ask or answer questions. I'm on a mission.

So, just before I dove in, I took Charlee's hands in mine and gave her the heads-up: "Look honey, I'm about to check out for a bit. Please don't worry or be sad, I'm not ignoring you. This is just how I make sure dinner ends up in a place in your memory and brings you joy every time you think about it."

She looked at me with that knowing smile, the kind that makes me think she's plotting something - probably how to steal the last piece - and said, "Then do it. I'm here... if you *need* me." She put in that emphasis. Just saying.

Buddha! That woman slays me with her double entendres. I'd come to realize she does it on purpose.

I completely annihilated Charlee's small tabletop and counter in no time, smothering every inch with a carpet of flour, egg yolks, salt and water to conjure up a proper pasta dough. I was used to my trusty shortcut-enabling stand mixer back home. Kneading that stiff, stubborn mixture into a smooth, glossy ball of dough for a full ten minutes? My forearms burned like I'd been arm-wrestling a grizzly bear, but I was way too deep in the zone to care. This was sacred territory, and I wasn't about to quit.

Then reality hit me. I'd forgotten plastic wrap in my shopping flurry. Damn! There was no way to let the dough rest and hydrate properly. Cue up my first kitchen crisis with foreboding music.

"Charlee, do you have any plastic wrap?" I called out, hoping she knew what I was talking about and not realizing she'd been right next to me the whole time, silently observing my every move.

She blinked once, then twice, gave me that slow, knowing smile like she was both amused and slightly concerned, and vanished out the front door.

Five painfully long minutes later as I cleaned up, she returned triumphantly with a roll of plastic wrap, looking like she'd just finished a marathon - hair wild, cheeks flushed. I leaned over and gave her a quick peck on the cheek in thanks. She was nothing short of a hero.

I wrapped that dough as if it was precious cargo and placed it gently into her little fridge while I moved on to prep the rest of the ingredients. The sauce was the heart and soul of this whole operation, and I was dead set on making it so good it'd bring everyone and anyone to their knees sobbing with joy.

I poured a generous glug of EVOO into the pot, cranked the heat just shy of medium-high, and tossed in the diced onions, garlic, and shallots. The kitchen began to thicken with that intoxicating aroma - sweet, sharp, and mouthwatering. I let the onions and garlic base sweat for a few minutes, giving the fragrance time to take over the cramped space like some old-world magic.

When the onions turned soft and translucent, I added a small splash of water - a classic old-school trick to coax the alliums to break down gently without scorching. I stirred it in, watching for the transformation to unfold like magic.

Then came the tomato paste. I gently worked that into the mix until the base turned a deep, rich brick red - thick and promising. Next, I dumped in the canned Cento San Marzano tomatoes, saving the fresh ones for layering in the lasagna. Layers of flavors is what lasagna is all about - separate then merged in each bite. Kind of like a burger but ... well ... better. I threw in a couple of bay leaves, a pinch of sugar to balance the acids like a sneaky friend, a thick slab of butter (my personal non-traditional twist, because life's too short), and a half dozen drops of balsamic vinegar - the dark, tangy umami acidic note that rounds out the whole thing.

As it simmered, the kitchen filled with the warm, nostalgic scent of a Sunday family dinner; the kind of smell that burrows deep in your memory, makes your stomach ache in the best way, and leaves you counting the seconds until you get to taste it.

I asked Charlee to pull the dough out of the fridge so it could warm up to room temperature because if you're new to fresh pasta, cold dough is a damned nightmare to roll out. You try to stretch it, and it fights you back like a stubborn ex refusing to let go.

While the dough was loosening up, I shifted gears to the meats. I grabbed the sauté pan, cranked the heat, and dumped the ground beef and pork mixture. I seasoned it simply, because you want that meaty flavor layer to shine through - salt, cracked black pepper, fennel seeds for that hint of sweet anise, a good pinch of red pepper flakes to remind everyone who's boss, and oregano for the herbal backbone. The sizzle sang its satisfying song as the meat went through its Maillard reaction, transforming from pale and raw to that rich, caramelized goodness that promises depth.

I skimmed off the excess fat with practiced ease, set the meat aside, and let out a little nod of approval. Things were moving along exactly the way they should.

Then, Charlee with purely good intention, reached for the pan, heading toward the sink to clean it. Without thinking - hell, without thinking at all - I barked, "NO." Just that one word, sharp and sudden, like a slap in a quiet room.

The instant it left my mouth, I felt it - a hundred-pound dumbbell of regret dropping straight onto my chest. Her face froze, that flicker of shock and hurt flashing in her eyes. I'd just punched her emotionally. The question was clear: Did I mean to be that cruel?

In that moment, I realized with brutal clarity I was a goddamn idiot.

I stopped cold. Took a slow, steadying breath. That wasn't me. I used to get unreasonably angry due to situations that hurt me to the core. Not anymore. Those days were gone.

Without hesitation, I reached out, pulled her into a tight, desperate embrace, like trying to patch the cracks in my own stupid heart, and now hers. "Oh honey - I'm so sorry, that came out all wrong," I whispered, each word heavy with regret.

I held her tight, quietly explaining how the flavors from the thin sheen of remaining meat fat and enriched protein sugars would deepen the mushrooms as they cooked. But the words felt thin, inadequate and irrelevant against the space I'd just carved between us.

Then I slunk down to my knees at her feet, looking up, hoping she'd see the raw honesty in my eyes. "Please, forgive me, I am soooo sorry!" I whispered, barely above breath, praying she'd find it in her heart.

She looked down at me for a moment that seemed an eternity, her face undecipherable, then smacked the top of my head - but with unmistakable warmth - and there was a smirk lurking in her eyes. The kind that said 'Don't ever do that again, idiot'.

"I told you; I disappear when I cook," I said, voice thick and lumpy, still carrying the weight of my apology. "I'm truly embarrassed, and I'm sorry I hurt you, Charlee."

She rolled her eyes just enough to let me know she was teasing, but there was still that razor-sharp edge in her tone. "*You finish sauce yet?*"

I rose, still ashamed and dove back in, chopping the mushrooms I'd cleaned earlier with renewed focus. This time, it wasn't just about ticking off a to-do list - it was about the moment, about her, about me, about what really mattered.

The mushrooms hit the pan with a beautiful sizzle and started to brown as they soaked up those meaty molecules like sponges. Once they released their water and had reduced down, they went into another bowl ready for use. The growing stack of components was shaping up, but I could still feel that moment -

my stupid, thoughtless mistake, the rawness - hanging thickly in the kitchen air, a reminder that no matter how good the food, you can't forget what matters most.

The sauce - gravy, if you want to get proper Brooklyn Italian about it - needed time. Time to marry, to meld into that full-bodied knock-you-on-your-ass kind of glory. There was no rushing that. You respect it. I let it simmer.

Meanwhile, I turned to cleanup. Cooking's a dance, a constant rhythm. Even when you're standing still, something's moving and if you're standing still? You're screwing up something that needs doing. Plain and simple.

The sauce bubbled and hummed like a living thing. I grabbed the Chianti, poured a couple of cups in, wanting the sauce to have that complex velvety backdrop, like Phil Lesh's bass line holding everything together. Oregano, marjoram, thyme, basil, salt, pepper, let it all mingle, like old friends who haven't seen each other in too long, swapping stories and settling back into the groove. Then a low simmer for at least an hour. Time was my ally again.

Charlee glanced over at the remaining pile of groceries lounging in the bag on the floor and asked what she could do next. Her eyes landed on the cheese - mozzarella to shred, Parmesan to break up. She didn't have a big grater; that's just not a thing in most Thai kitchens (her tiny one was meant for ginger and garlic, not mountains of cheese). Her kitchen was minimalist, stripped to the essentials and nothing more.

I took a long, deliberate gulp of wine, trying to find my way back to the calm, easy rhythm we'd had just a couple of hours before until I shattered us to pieces.

So, we rolled up our sleeves and hand-shredded the cheese together. Slow, methodical. It wasn't fast or fancy, but sometimes the slow, clumsy way is the only way and sometimes the best. As we worked, I felt her inch closer, like a magnet pulling two pieces of metal together. By the time the last shred fell into the bowl, we were hip to hip, caught in a quiet little bubble where everything else melted away.

I reached for her. She reached for me. I pulled her into me and broke down.

"I never, ever meant to hurt you, the thought that I hurt you hurts me so badly I just don't know what to say to make us better," I whispered between shaky breaths and tears slipping down my cheeks. She held me tight, steadying me, grounding me until I could get my shit together.

When she finally pulled away, embarrassment burned hot in my chest. I couldn't meet her eyes. I'd been a total dick. We both knew it, no need to say it.

Then she cupped my chin, gently lifting my face to hers. We held each other's gaze, silent but loud with everything unsaid. And with the quiet tenderness of someone who's been there before - who knows what love really means - she reached up and wiped my tears away.

And then she kissed me.

Not the kind of kiss from a movie, or lovers caught up in a moment. This was the kind of kiss that sees you; flaws, pain, and all, and stays anyway.

I lost it again, tears exploding from my eyes.

After a few deep breaths, tight hugs, and several splashes of cold water, and a reassuring embrace and nod that we'd be OK, I got back to work.

Garlic bread was calling: peeling cloves, chopping herbs, ready to make her tiny oven earn its keep.

I coyly asked Charlee if she'd mind cleaning the greens. At that point I didn't feel I had the right to ask anything of her other than more forgiveness. She didn't miss a beat though and giggled, slipping over to my side like she'd been waiting for this cue. She swung open the fridge and pulled out a bowl that stopped me cold. A gorgeous riot of fresh salad, laden with herbs and flowers from her garden. It wasn't just food; it was a damn masterpiece. She'd even found use for the mint I'd bought, though I didn't know why.

Simple things made stunning. She'd taken a basic greens salad and turned it into a work of art and right then, I saw her differently. Not just the woman I was cooking for, the woman I'd fallen head over heels in love with, but a partner who sees the beauty in the small stuff, who cares enough to make every detail matter. She shifted in my mind from lover and admired friend into a bubble of incredible, special, talented and resourceful.

"Baby, when did you do that?"

"You were busy make sauce. I make the salad. I make salad every day. You are good cook. You work fast. You clean when you make a mess. You are really good."

I blushed. No - really - I did! "I didn't want you to get stuck with the cleaning. I try and keep a tidy workspace when I'm in the kitchen. It's easier to get everything done. I hope you don't think I forgot you."

Charlee came over, grabbed my head in her hands and kissed me with passion. "You forget me now?" her musical laugh filling the space between us, the sparkles lighting up her eyes as we looked at each other.

I took a long series of deep breaths. I held her hands and brought them to my lips, kissing them tenderly. "Thank you for the salad, but much more importantly, your forgiveness."

She laughed her music, smiled at me, took her hands from mine, placed them on my shoulders, gently urging me to turn around. I did. She swatted my ass, then leaned into my ear and whispered loving things I'll never forget.

I took a deep breath, took a gulp of Chianti, and turned to her: "Now it really gets messy!" as I wiped down her small table, dusted it with flour again, unwrapped the pasta dough and dusted the rolling pin. Jakkapan had done me right, lending a marble pin that stays cool when working with dough.

I started rolling out the pasta dough, slowly, steady, evenly, knowing damn well I was in for a fight. Fresh pasta is a diva - moody, temperamental, and stubborn as hell. You've got to move fast before it dries out, or it'll snap back at you. No machines here. No safety nets. Just me, a dusted rolling pin, a dusting of flour on the counter, and whatever muscle memory I'd cobbled together over years of pretending I knew what I was doing.

The dough protested, stubborn and thick in spots, threatening to split in others until I showed Charlee how to lightly dust the wet spots as I worked. I pushed harder, coaxed it thinner, rolled it out as evenly as I could. It was a dance - delicate but demanding, a battle of wills between us and that tough dough. I nicknamed it Cagney just for a laugh. And something clicked, as Cagney went from persnickety to perfect and I got that blast of satisfaction that comes from making something out of nothing that you realize is going to work out just fine.

By the time I had my stack of imperfectly perfect pasta sheets, my forearms were screaming, my hands, pants, shirt and brain coated in flour, and my mind buzzing with anticipation. This was no store-bought nonsense - this was the real deal, ready to become the backbone of a lasagna worth fighting over.

Just as I finished the pasta sheets ... that's when my chef voice in my head screamed the next kitchen crisis: THE PAN, YOU IDIOT! I'd forgotten to prep the baking pan - no oil, no herbs, no gravy, nothing. Disaster No. 3 loomed like a health inspector showing up with his clip board during the lunch rush at a greasy dive.

I put the roller into the sink, sprinted to the counter, and saved my ass just in time. A slick of olive oil coating all surfaces by hand, a quick dusting of herbs, just a hint of salt and a ladle of gravy to coat the bottom - pan ready. Crisis averted. Back to the dough. Sigh some relief.

That moment? That was the kitchen equivalent of seeing your soufflé collapse just as the love of your life walks in for that first romantic, long-awaited, home-cooked, candle-lit dinner. You panic, you hustle, and if you're lucky, you don't ruin the damn thing.

The first sheets of pasta slid into the bottom of the pan like the calm before the storm. I pulled the sauce off the stove - it had reached the perfect point between "almost perfect" and "I can't wait another minute" - and grabbed the bowl of seasoned beef and pork, spreading it out in a thin, even layer over that pasta foundation.

And then - boom - it was rapid-fire assembly time.

Pasta layer. Sauce. Meat layer. Sauce that. Pasta layer. Drizzle of olive oil. Mushroom layer. No sauce. Pasta layer. Chopped fresh tomatoes drizzled with olive oil and herbs. Sauce it. Pasta layer. Ricotta mixed with a fresh hit of herbs and a sultry drizzle of balsamic. No sauce. Pasta layer again, sauce, then a generous crown of mozzarella. I gave everything a final dusting of herbs from on high, like a chef blessing the whole operation, then slid it in the preheated 275f oven (135c).

Baking fresh pasta lasagna is no joke because the pasta itself cooks faster than the fillings and the dried boxed stuff. You've got to drop the heat way down and let it go slow to get the balance of cooked pasta and heated layers of filling in equilibrium. Otherwise, the pasta turns to mush and the whole thing falls apart in a sad, gooey mess. At this stage in the battle, I was not about to let that happen.

Charlee had never seen anything like this before. Her experience with Italian food boiled down to the occasional spaghetti and meatballs and squash ravioli once a long time ago. She'd fallen hard for both dishes at some Thai-Italian joint that probably wouldn't recognize lasagna if it smacked it in the face. But here she was, as I wrestled that beast together from scratch, the kitchen filling with an aroma so rich and savory it needed no further introduction.

Her eyes widened as the scent curled through the air - warm, comforting, and unapologetically America Italian. This wasn't some quick-fix dinner. This was the kind of food that makes you pause, lean in, and believe for just a moment that everything's going to be okay.

I moved on to the baguette, slicing it lengthwise and peeling it open like a razor clam. I make it a rule to prep bread early, because if I don't, I'll forget it, then rush it, which at some point the oven will start to billow black smoke announcing that I'd screwed the bread - again. And after many years I still haven't figured out a use for totally burned bread (though I don't think anyone else has either therefore I don't feel quite so alone in that department,) so I've trained myself to pay way more attention to bread.

Charlee, for all her interest in the lasagna, looked a little nervous, like she was waiting for me to ruin something else (aside from our relationship), but I was in my element now and things were cruising smoothly.

I took a breath and shifted gears. Dinner was under control, the kitchen finally settled into a now-we-wait rhythm, so we drifted into sips of wine and easy conversation about the beautiful, edible plants growing in Charlee's garden. The kind of effortless chatter that fills the quiet cracks in a good evening, like the soft background music you don't really notice but wouldn't want to live without.

We kept topping off our small glasses of Chianti and before long the bottle was empty. It was better than decent and had enough backbone to keep the conversation flowing. The only hitch? Chianti, even the Classico style sometimes comes with a tart, bright berry acid edge, which I love. Charlee didn't care for it.

I leaned into her playfully and asked her to open the bottle of Luce. She gave me a look like I'd asked her to perform brain surgery on me while I was in the middle of cooking.

"You've never opened wine before?"

"No. I watched you open the other one. It looks hard." (she was starting to get her English tenses verbs and nouns right with a little coaching.)

"No problem. It's actually pretty easy" I reassured her.

She held the bottle of Luce like it might explode if she looked at it wrong. Which was funny because the glass they used could have shattered titanium it was so heavy.

"It looks... complicated?" An excellent use of a word we worked with just that morning.

"It's not. Just a little cut, a twist and pull. I'll show you."

I stood behind her, my head resting on her shoulder, her hands in mine. I placed the corkscrew I picked up at the wine shop into her hand and walked her through it, step by step. Cut the foil and remove. Center the screw into the cork and push to seat the tip. Twist it in evenly until the first hinge tooth can grip the lip. Pinch and lever the cork up to the first hinge. Release. Twist the screw in deeper, and pinch the first hinge again, but this time to the cork. Seat the bottom tooth against the lip, then slowly but firmly leverage the rest of the cork out. I placed my hands over hers as she worked, guiding but not taking over.

"The trick is to feel it, not fight it. Like coaxing something out of hiding."

"Like you?" she said, glancing sideways, a sly grin blooming at the edges of her mouth.

I laughed. "Exactly. Except I come out grumpy and covered in flour."

She gave the final pull, and the cork popped free with a soft sound, like a sigh. Her eyes lit up with surprise - equal parts pride and delight.

"I opened it. Look, Larry, it's perfect!" she exclaimed with pride of ownership. I noticed this particular moment vividly because it was the first time she crafted perfect, concise sentences. I kissed her cheek. She bounced on the balls of her feet.

She held the bottle up like a trophy. I asked her to pour us two small sips, to try it, while letting the rest of that big Brunello beast breathe.

We clinked glasses, quietly this time. No big toasts. Just that kind of soft, mutual understanding that things were gently falling back into place.

I smelled the cork and she asked why. I explained to her about TCA, (2,4,6-trichloroanisole) commonly known as cork-taint, which can permeate and ruin a bottle of wine. The cork smelled clean. We tasted our sips and her eyes bugged out.

"Oh .... *That is aroi!*" she exclaimed, grinning at me.

"Now ... we wait," I said, explaining how bigger wines with age on them need a little time to oxygenate.

I checked the oven, and it was like seeing an old friend. The lasagna was almost there, but I had to finish strong. There wasn't a broiler in Charlee's little oven, so I cranked that bastard to max heat and prayed. Ten minutes later (timed by one of the four kitchen timer apps on my phone), perfection: bubbling cheese with mahogany brown patches, crispy pasta edges curling around the rim like they were trying to escape from lasagna prison. I pulled it out, silently cursing the burn on my fingers as I juggled the pan with two thin and damp kitchen towels, but it was worth it. The aroma wafted up like a slow-motion nasal orgasm, announcing that dinner was now a work of art. I tossed a fist full of crumbled parmesan on top and let that melt into the mix.

The bread was now in the oven. A different timer set for eleven minutes. Now it was time to team up with Charlee and make the kitchen disappear. I moved like a Red Bull-fueled teenaged plongeur, wiping counters, cleaning cooking gear, grabbing plates until I saw three settings at the table. Not two. Now when did she do that? I didn't ask, just marveled.

Who else was coming? A friend? Mom? Or worse, dad? I didn't ask, but I did take another courage-sip of wine.

I fork-whisked together a quick olive oil, balsamic, salt, pepper, lemon zest and herb dressing for the salad when a knock on the door broke the magic of just the two of us. I reached for Charlee, held her tight, kissed her fiercely, then whispered "*I love you Chalermwan!*"

She smiled and spun away and went to answer the door as the timer dinged - announcing a perfectly crisped baguette. I pulled it from the oven, the two halves splayed open like a book waiting to be read. No way was I letting this garlic bread fall victim to overthinking or showmanship or bad timing as a guest showed up at the door.

Here's the quick rinse technique for great garlic bread: a fat clove of raw garlic per side, sanded down generously on the crumb, followed by a slow drizzle of good olive oil. Then a thin smear of premium butter to carry all that flavor and temper the acid in both the garlic and the oil. A scattering of salt, a buckshot scatter of fresh chopped herbs, and back into the oven for just a few more minutes. The result? Crusty, garlicky perfection. Like a good handshake - firm and confident.

※

It was Jaks at the door, looking like he'd just sprinted out of the restaurant. He'd pulled one of his guys off the line to cover the bar so he could taste my concoction. Charlee had been sending him pictures throughout the entire process - which I didn't realize she'd been doing. She showed me one later of me covered in flour, but with a stack of pasta sheets (the comment I later learned after she converted it from Thai for me was, 'Watch my honey cook in my little bâan - he is amazing' - with a love heart emoji.) I'd never been so flattered. As I plated food, I felt like a proud parent sending their kid off to school - nervous, hopeful, and secretly convinced they were the smartest one there.

The lasagna? Perfect.

The bread? Perfect.

The salad? Bright and alive. And more than perfect.

The wine? A goddamned lovely miracle here in a cozy little bâan in Bangkok.

Charlee was first. I watched her face change after that first bite - eyes widening, breath catching. She said something in Thai that sounded suspiciously like "*Oh God.*" It was the kind of sound I wanted to bottle and keep in my pocket for every bad day that might come in the future. She didn't need to say a word, but she did anyway, turning to me with a look that dared me to blink: "Xerdxrxy" (scrumptious), as she drew that word out like taffy. The Thai equivalent of a

Michelin star. Then came the garlic bread. The wine. And the look she gave me - part wonder, part admiration, all heart.

And me being me, I had to tamp down my ego before it started puffing up like over-proofed dough. Arrogance is a trait I'd recently fought hard into the trashcan at the curb, but pride? Pride's harder to shake when it's staring back at you from across the table full of love and grinning with a mouth full of lasagna.

Jaks, though, was a different story. The man ate in total silence; each bite studied like it held deep answers. He looked at it. Lifted the edges peering under the hood. No small talk, no polite filler, just quiet focus. When he finally looked up, I knew something was coming. And when it did, it penetrated like a bullet.

"This! This is the best Italian food, the best lasagna I've ever had. Where did you learn this?"

I smiled, not giving away the satisfaction that was bubbling up in my chest. When a solid restauranteur gives you high praise it's hard to not shout up at the stars in glee. "Does it matter?" I said, pretending to brush it off. But inside? I was thinking: "It was hard as hell to pull off, but hell yeah, I nailed it."

"My mom was a really great cook - especially the deep French classics. But she was pretty good with America-Italian standards too. She was very patient with me in the kitchen when she figured out that I was having fun helping her. Over the years, it's been a mix of places, people, and practice. I worked in a few restaurants as a kid, and I cooked at home nearly every night and never shied away from a challenge. I learned by doing - cookbooks, trial and error, watching, tasting, studying, the usual" I said casually, as if that was everyone's path.

"You ever want to open an Italian restaurant in Bangkok or Chiang Mai? I can make that happen. And that's a serious offer on the table here and now."

"You do know how old I am, right?" I emphasized old.

I chuckled, but I meant it. "Look Jaks, thank you. Seriously. That's an incredible compliment and I am deeply honored. But this is a young person's game, you know that. I know the financials, the staffing chaos, fluctuating food costs, the day you have a critic come in and the fucking oven dies, or the health board shows up and there's a dead rat in the dried goods that wasn't there that morning while at the same time the walk-in compressor craps out, as the dishwasher OD's in the bathroom with a needle in his arm. Add to that the burnout hours. I know myself - if I had to cook the same dishes every night, I'd end up hating something I really love."

Jaks burst into laughter "Yeah - those days happen. I get it bro. But this? This is next level. Better than anything I've had anywhere. And I love Italian food. The bread's perfect. And this wine? Best I've ever tasted."

I looked at Charlee. She'd been quietly listening, her eyes tracking every word. She reached across the table, took my hand in hers, and said softly, "This is the best meal I taste ever. Khop khun ma kah."

"You're very welcome honey. But your help - your belief and patience with me - made this possible. Without you…"

And then my voice caught. My thoughts did too. There it was. Unspoken, but real. The lump in my throat said the rest. I gulped deep breaths so that I wouldn't burst into tears again.

Chalermwan and I decided to stay in that evening, despite Jakkapan's insistence that we come by the restaurant for a cocktail, or ten. I sent him off with a few generous slabs of lasagna to share, making him swear he wouldn't hoard them all for himself. He grumbled, but promised halfheartedly, which was probably the best I was going to get.

With dinner cleaned up, we strolled back to the apartment so I could swap out a few things and put away the laundry Charlee had so thoughtfully washed for me. I'd get her back for that as I tried to figure out some kind, generous way to repay her. And no - dinner didn't count because I was going to do that anyway.

Back at the Sunreno, we puttered. I knocked out a few small chores while she tidied. We gathered up the fruits, yogurt, and granola from the fridge, packed a clean change of clothes for me, then noticed a small note from housekeeping - a simple smiley face drawn next to one of the flower vases from two nights ago. Charlee gathered up the flowers and candles to take back to her place while I packed my day pack with essentials.

Back at Charlee's bâan, I opened the Tokaji, the Hungarian dessert wine that I had slipped into the mix at the last minute. Again, her reaction was priceless as was the wine. Small sips, eyes wide in delight, she looked at me and said "apricot, nutty and cooked honey." She nailed it.

I'd mentioned early on, as we were still unraveling each other during texts and chats, that a friend, I'll call her Malaya, would be flying into Bangkok on the 29th. We'd planned to head south for New Year's Eve, and I made it clear - Malaya was just a friend. Charlee understood, but there was a subtle tension beneath her calm, a quiet unease hanging in the air like a shadow waiting to fall. As the date crept closer, I found myself excited for the adventure, yet dreading the trip without her. Yet Charlee, ever steady, reassured me the timing and logistics just wouldn't work - her family would insist she be with them for their traditional end-of-year rites. She asked if I could cancel and come for New Years at her family vacation home in Lam Mae Phim in the Rayong Province, a popular beach resort town. It was close to where I'd be anyway? I desperately wanted to but knew I couldn't. At least for that year.

That night, the heat pressed heavily in on Chalermwan's small house. No air conditioning, just fine mesh screens letting in the night's symphony - frogs croaking, crickets chirping, insects buzzing, all in their primal mating serenade. We lay together in that warm stillness, sharing secrets, dreams, and wishes, bathed in the flickering glow of a single pillar candle.

Time slipped by unnoticed, the night bleeding slowly into dawn. I wasn't tired. Instead, I felt alive, strangely peaceful and utterly awake. I turned to Charlee and asked, voice barely above a whisper, "What do you want to do today honey?"

Her smile was soft, her certainty absolute as she raised her palm gently to my cheek: "We are already doing. This. I love this. Just this."

Then, the floodgates burst open. Tears came raw, uncontrollable, and cleansing. We held each other tight, bodies trembling as the flood spilled over; love, grief, fear, relief, and release all crashing at once. It was a torrent of emotion I didn't know I needed, a catharsis that even the monastery's intellectual clarity had never offered. And knowing she shared this same sacred vulnerability? Maybe this was what love really meant. I thought I had known love before, but this - this was something so much deeper.

I gazed into her dark almond eyes and whispered without hesitation, "I am deeply and irrevocably in love with you, Chalermwan."

"I am the same with you Larry," she breathed back.

We drifted off in each other's arms, not from exhaustion, but from the quiet settling of souls laid bare.

When we awoke, the heat had intensified, sweat clinging to skin as we roused slowly. We pulled ourselves together and walked back to the Sunreno, sharing a long, slow cool shower that washed away the night's remnants - both physical and emotional. Refreshed, we ventured out to our favorite dim sum spot. As I began to fill out the order sheet like a seasoned local, Chef Yip appeared, pushing a cart piled high with steamers and plates of our favorites. His grin was wide, thumbs raised in salute. I rose, bowed deeply, offering respect and honor to a friend who'd become family. He patted my shoulder with warmth that said, "You're one of us now." I was falling in love with Bangkok even more.

The rest of the morning drifted along like a slow Serge Chaloff tune. Easy, unhurried, and wrapped up in each other's arms. First at the Sunreno, then over at Charlee's place, where the world outside was politely told to fuck off. We didn't want to be anywhere or with anyone else.

The weight of last night's feast still hung around us like a fat cat refusing to move off the bed. We spent time cuddling, laughing and testing each other's resolve to not get out of bed.

I asked Charlee if she fancied something lighter for dinner. "You cook or we go out?" she asked. After a delicate dance of negotiation (which, honestly, was me waving a white flag - I wanted noodles, again), we settled on home-cooked fish, veggies, rice, and a crisp garden salad. I knew her kitchen by now and wanted something simple but elegant. A classic French beurre blanc with delicate white fish sounded perfect... though I was going to lighten it up a bit. Then the real challenge: find a flaky, delicate white fish.

I scribbled a shorthand shopping list into my phone and planned a trip to Big C at Asiatique. They usually had what I needed, or at least close enough to improvise. I was ready for whatever culinary curveballs might come my way.

We had risen and I started to move about and tidy things up, with bigger plans for a total space shakedown. Charlee, however, had other plans. Cleaning was put on hold. Passion punched in for its shift.

Three hours, two near-injuries, and one broken hair tie later, we took another shower - laughing at our tangled mess of limbs, trying to rinse off and reclaim some shred of public decency.

We set out for Big C, a little wobbly, slightly disheveled, and with the kind of goofy, "we-shouldn't-be-out-in-public-like-this" look that surely gave the produce section something juicy to gossip about.

First order of business: match the beurre blanc's buttery hug with a fish that could stand up to it but keep things light and elegant. We hit the fish counter and bingo. Barramundi! A beautiful fish that's hard to find in the States, has a delicate, buttery, slightly sweet flesh that begged to be treated like black cod's cooler cousin. Fat, fresh, with eyes so clear and scales so shiny it looked like it had just walked off the set of a Cosmo seafood shoot.

Thanks to Charlee's expert translations and a few wildly enthusiastic hand gestures from me, the fishmonger sliced off two perfect fillets clean as a whistle, free of spine and ribs. I asked for the head and skeleton too. The poor fish guy blinked at me like I'd just proposed marriage to his daughter. Which surprised me.

I smiled and explained I was making a fumét, because nothing says "serious chef" like turning the heads and bones into liquid gold. He had no idea what I was on about (which surprised me again) but bless him, he handed over a couple extra heads and spines from previous monger duties, gratis. Apparently, I'd saved him from tossing those into the bin, so no harm, no foul. Fishy karma points awarded.

Cooking rice in fish stock in Thailand might very well be like lighting incense with a blowtorch - technically possible but guaranteed to raise eyebrows. Here, rice is sacred: almost always served plain, proud, and unsullied, like it just stepped out of a temple. Sure, there are variations, but rice is expected to either play a supporting role or be the star of the show itself. I, however, had other plans. A little French flair? Try full-on Bocuse. And when you've got the chops, why not use them?

We moved on to produce. I snagged a bag of fat shallots like I was planning a hostile takeover of a Parisian bistro (beurre blanc is butter and shallot based.) An onion, a fennel bulb, a leek, some celery, tarragon and parsley and I was good for the sauce and the fumét. Then I saw thick green stalks of asparagus, smugly erect, begging to be steamed, wrapped in porky goodness, and eaten with inappropriate noises. I grabbed them. That created the need for melty cheese. I found a tidy little brick of Fontina hidden among some Brie rounds. Prosciutto, too, because I may be in Bangkok, but my stomach speaks fluent Italian as well as French. So yeah - I was going continental instead of sticking solely to Frenchy sensibilities.

Charlee, meanwhile, had cozied up, hugging a fat bag of morning glory like it was a long-lost friend. I wondered if I should be jealous, she was so enthralled. I mean, it was perfect, but hey! I'm right here! She, of the perfect gleaming smile said she'd whip up pad pak boong - that holy grail of stir-fried greens that I love so much. Of course, that meant we needed more garlic because Jakkapan, the lovable yet sneaky scamp, had run off with our last cloves (*I would have too*) of the good red stuff from Khlong Toei market. We needed reinforcements.

More butter was a no-brainer. The garlic bread and sneaky addition into the red sauce meant we were running low, and beurre blanc doesn't make itself without a *LOT* of butter - it is French, after all. We grabbed roughage and a firm cucumber for the salad, a couple lemons for a sparkly drizzle, and two bottles of Mâcon Villages chardonnay - important because it is stainless steel finished (unoaked) which works better for sauces and as a bright foil against all that butter. Why two? Do you really have to ask?

Cart full. Hearts full. Appetite rabid. It was time to cook but this one was going to be much easier than the night before.

It was mid-afternoon. The day had ripened into something sticky and swollen, thick with heat, haze, and a smoggy soup of toxins that clung to our skin and crawled into our lungs. Bangkok was sweating and so was I. My chest and throat had that old familiar tightening, a subtle reminder that while I only sometimes dealt with asthma, my blood pressure was a more consistent bastard and days like that were bad for both.

Charlee though had it worse. A congenital heart condition had been her lifelong companion, a quiet predator she'd learned to live with. Our medicine rituals had become a kind of macabre bonding routine - two people clicking open pill bottles like bartenders lining up shots. Mornings and nights, we swallowed our scripts with the kind of dark gallows humor Bukowski might've written if he'd been even slightly in love and less drunk.

Charlee suggested a massage parlor within easy walking distance for later in the evening, that had a sauna and a wonderful soaking tub. I was hugging her and saying "yes, yes, yes" before she finished the sentence. "Yes, to everything! Except the happy ending." She laughed, play punched my arm, leaned in close, and whispered with a nibble on my earlobe, "I'm your happy ending, and you don't forget it."

No ma'am! I could never, nor would I ever dream of forgetting that!

Spa reservations made and plans set! Thank Buddha I hadn't returned the restaurant equipment yet. I needed a big pot for the fumét, and the sauté pan for the fish. Amazing company with someone you truly adore then a killer dinner, then a long steam, a soak, and a massage? Hell yes! That's how you do self-care when the world outside is trying to kill you.

Back at Charlee's, glasses of chilled Chardonnay at hand, prep got underway. I had one of those quiet, immensely wonderful moments when you realize you've hit a groove with someone. We'd gone from friends, to lovers, to more than lovers, to side-by-side line cooks without missing a beat.

I explained the game plan - how it would all come together - and she jumped right in, fine dicing shallots like a sous chef on coke who'd done this a thousand times before. She was incredibly fast, precise and efficient. My jaw dropped. Then she sliced the Fontina into perfect little batons just as I described. She then launched into prepping the morning glory and I saw it again. She fine-diced six cloves of garlic in less than a minute, like she was auditioning for a cable cooking series. Every dice was perfect, tiny. I looked at her, down at the garlic, then back up at her. She winked with a big smile but said nothing. I'd been played. I've never been so happy to have been played in my entire life. I laughed at my naivety then carried on gently shaking my head side to side in wonder.

She held up the chef's blade that Jaks had lent me. "Nice knife," she grinned, spun and bounced on her balls.

Definitely. Played! It was obvious that she had withheld some secrets of her past from me too. We'd be talking about that later. In between kisses.

Meanwhile, I got down to business with the fish heads and bones. No time for a long romantic cold soak here. This was speed dating for stock. Multiple cold-water rinses kept the concept - clean and efficient - enough to get rid of most impurities. Into the pot they went with some sautéed aromatics that I'd started a little while before. Once the heads and bones were nestled in, I hit them with a generous pour of Chardonnay. Once to temp, in went just enough cold water to barely cover the mess - bones, skulls, veggies and herbs - and the flame came back up, but slow and low, to coax out every ounce of oceanic soul.

After prepping out all the remaining ingredients I skimmed the surface of the stock, gazed into the pot to see a beautiful clear broth, ready for use.

Pro tip: Never allow any stock to come anywhere near a boil. Stocks should cook just above a discernible delicate simmer. If your stock boils? It'll be horrible. Throw it out and start again.

Charlee breezed through the salad like she was born with a paring knife in one hand, a Champagne vinaigrette in her sippy cup. Clean, fast, methodical. She worked with a kind of quiet grace that only comes from cooking under pressure. That turned me on. She'd already rocked the wok, the morning glory and garlic stir fry with oyster sauce and chilies was done in a flash, in a bowl waiting to reheat for plating.

I got the rice going in the fumét and moved on to the next task. Everything was cruising. We moved together like a well-oiled machine... if that machine occasionally bumped hips and flirted over the cutting board.

Charlee asked about the asparagus dish, so I walked her through it in broad strokes to see how she handled it. She nailed it. No questions, no flinching. She dove in like a pro. I fell in love with her all over again.

Done right, it's the kind of side dish that makes your main course jealous. It's perfect with fish. Hell, it's perfect with anything except Cap'n Crunch.

I used the oven to roast the asparagus, fontina and prosciutto wraps. Normally I'd serve that with Hollandaise sauce but the beurre blanc would be pulling double duty.

The beurre blanc came together fast, if not exactly textbook. Without a fine mesh chinois to push it through or a stick blender, the sauce had a rustic charm - let's call it artisanally lumpy. I whipped the hell out of it to get it close to smooth, but no amount of elbow grease beats pushing a sauce through tight mesh. No matter. I leaned into a French shrug and called it a day.

Butter went in the pan with a splash of olive oil to keep it from burning, and the Barramundi got its moment. Light dusting of flour and salt - no heavy-handed seasoning needed, just enough to kiss the surface - and into the pan it went. High heat. Crunchy crispy skin. Cook on only one side and let residual heat do the rest. When you hear the sizzle, you're on the right path. But the real trick is patience - do not move the fillets. If you move them prematurely the skin will be soggy and peel away, rather than crisp. Avoid the temptation to take a peek underneath! When you shake the pan and the fillets slide on their own? Then they're done and you have to pull them off heat immediately. They're still cooking!

The morning glory had been perfectly timed with a reheat in the oven next to the asparagus. I hadn't noticed she'd taken care of that. I'd come to realize she moves with stealth in the kitchen,) so it was on the plates at the same time as the asparagus.

Charlee beat me to the punch, cracking the second bottle of wine without hesitation, like she'd been raised by somms. Quick. Clean. Surgical. Damn! That woman picked up anything and everything so quickly it was marvelous.

First bite - magic. The kind of flavor that makes you close your eyes and reconsider your relationship with rice. Then a kiss - the kind that rewires your heartbeat and makes the cluttered kitchen vanish. One of those moments when time folds in on itself and you're not sure if you're in a Bangkok kitchen or floating somewhere above it.

"Do you cook like this every night?" she asked, fork paused midair with asparagus.

"Pretty much. I love to cook. I love to eat clean, fresh. And I always take care of the people I love." I looked her dead in the eyes and let that truth land. No blink. No retreat. Just the quiet, vulnerable clink of a sentence that meant exactly what it sounded like.

She laughed. I smiled. The night leaned in a little closer.

Without the shopping trip, dinner had taken an hour to pull off. Efficient, sensual and deeply satisfying.

Life was pretty fucking great!

Yin Yang "The Original Massage & Spa" sat on the corner of Chareon Krung 72/4 Alley, a short jaunt from Ramada Inn. Our reservations were for 8PM.

Dinner was done and the dishes rinsed, so we curled up for quiet snuggles and tales before heading out.

At 7:30 we set off, though it would only take a few minutes to get there. But who wants to march down the main road when you can meander through a maze of canal alleys hand-in-hand? We stepped out into that smog-thick Bangkok night towards a lung-clearing steam and a massage that promised new skin and easier breathing.

In one particularly lovely stretch - flowerpots, faded murals, laundry hanging like prayer flags - an elderly woman spotted us. She smiled, all sweet and wrinkled, until she zeroed in on our clasped hands. Her smile collapsed into a scowl. Then came rapid-fire Thai, in a tone that didn't require translation. A scolding, absolutely. Possibly a curse.

Charlee lit up. I'd never seen her get her hackles up before (unless martial arts was involved and even then she was so even-keeled I wondered if she had some magical control over rage), but she spun on her heel like she'd been waiting her whole life to be heckled by this woman. After giving the old gal a verbal beating, she turned, wrapped herself around me, and kissed me full-on. No tongue spared.

The woman screamed at us. Charlee laughed.

"She's always nosy. Gossips about all people," Charlee said as we sauntered past what I could only assume was the local Ministry of Moral Outrage. "Now she will really have something to say."

We laughed. That woman probably put a hex on us as she shook from moral outrage.

Inside, Yin Yang greeted us with soft lights and quiet music. The day had cooled, though it was still smoky and humid, the kind of weather that makes your pores feel dirty and your T-shirt think about up and leaving mid-stride.

If you've never been to Thailand, you're missing out, not just for the beaches or the food or the temples that look like Buddha hired a top-notch jewelry designer, but for the massages. Oh, the massages! The classic Thai massage though? Be warned. If you've ever made an enemy of your chiropractor, Thai massage will finish what they started. Those practitioners will bend you like a pipe cleaner and smile while they do it.

In the moment, it feels like you're being used as a demo in a medieval torture museum. Afterward, you'll float out with a blissed-out grin and no memory of your name. Personally? I prefer the essential oil deep tissue massage. It's less human origami and more melting into a puddle of semi-conscious goo.

We checked in and filled out the usual spa paperwork: What hurts? What shouldn't be touched? In the States, that's legal CYA to make lawyers and insurance agents sleep better. In Thailand, the questionnaire is simply good manners.

We sat down as two cups of warm sweet herbal tea appeared in front of us like magic. We'd signed up for the full spa couple's treatment: sauna, soaking tub, and side-by-side massages.

The sauna was wrapped in stone, the air thick with cedar and slow, herbal heat. When the door closed behind us, the world narrowed. A hush settled in. Everything inside was slippery. The bench, the air, our bodies. We moved carefully, blindly, groping through the haze. Slipping. Tangling. Not out of urgency, but alignment. It wasn't just lust - okay, not *only* - it was something warmer. Closer. That low, golden frequency when time loosens its grip and the moment leans in.

We emerged fifteen minutes later, flushed and glistening, two dumplings just lifted from a steamer. Outside the sauna, the world felt too sharp. Too defined. The tub waited, dark, steaming, still.

After the jolt of a cold rinse, we eased in. The water received us. Flower petals floated on the surface, drifting into lazy eddies. Her knee brushed mine beneath the surface. A soft, passing touch. Then her hand found mine. That was enough. More than.

We said nothing. Just water and breath. Heat and quiet. I leaned into her, nuzzled the warm hollow of her neck, and breathed her in deeply, gratefully. My lungs had opened. I remembered what it felt like to *breathe*.

When we stepped into the massage room, it was like entering a temple designed by a candle hoarder with excellent taste. Dark wood, soft fabrics, and that spa smell; a mix of leather, freshly washed cotton, lavender, tea, and rose hips.

We lay side by side, freshly steamed, boneless. I reached across the gap and touched her fingers. She touched back. Just a glance, a breath, a little *I'm here*.

The masseuses entered. Ghosts with warm hands. They poured warmed oil over us as if they were anointing royalty and got to work. Slow, strong, certain strokes that pulled toxins out of me with each pass. Toxins flowed out of my pores, but it felt deeper than that. Stress I didn't even know I was carrying got coaxed out and gently dismissed.

Charlee sighed. One of those deep full-body sighs announcing pleasure and release. I could hear she was smiling. I could feel it.

When our massages ended, we didn't move. Not out of sleepiness - though we were drunk on calm - but because it felt like getting up would snap the spell. We stayed still. Fingers twined, breathing in tandem, candlelight flickering across oil-slick skin.

Eventually, we sat up. Slowly. Surfacing from a dream we weren't ready to leave. I wondered why we shouldn't book another massage. We slipped into the robes they'd left out for us - soft and thick, smelling of wildflowers. Charlee's hair curled at the temples, damp and lovely, like a watercolor sketch of herself. She looked undone in the best possible way.

The spa was silent. As if it had quietly closed up shop after giving us exactly what we needed. We padded barefoot down the hallway, past closed rooms. Cold, sweet hibiscus tea and fresh cut mango awaited us in the lobby.

Outside, Bangkok hadn't stopped though it had the decency to dim the lights. The night air pressed close, thick with heat and something sweeter - sandalwood and jasmine. We didn't rush. The city could wait. We walked slow, as if the night owed us something.

Shops flickered. Motorbikes buzzed past like mosquitoes on Red Bull. Paper lanterns swung overhead, glowing like promises no one planned to keep. But all of that was backdrop. Set dressing. There was only her hand in mine. The whisper of her hip brushing mine when the sidewalk narrowed. The hush between our footsteps, where a thousand things could've been said but didn't need to be.

It wasn't silence. It was trust. It was the kind of quiet that only happens when the world fades out, and the only thing left is the person walking beside you and the heat still rising from the pavement. We didn't say a word. Didn't have to. The night was ours. And we knew enough not to ruin it by talking.

Morning came. It was our last full day and night together for a while. Chalermwan and I would have to simmer down and survive on text bubbles and WhatsApp video chats but for now? I was hoarding every millisecond with her.

I would be heading to Koh Chang with my friend Malaya. A trip I'd been excited about for weeks. A tropical island, a new adventure, and a chance to reconnect in a completely different part of the world. But leaving Charlee behind for New Year's felt like a gut-wrenching betrayal. A feeling I'm intimately familiar with.

Kind. Understanding. Soulful, insightful and wise. No - not me. I was a roiling mess. Chalermwan embodied everything good, pure and true in this world and I'd fallen into love, tumbled and spun into her cloudy bliss. I hadn't planned to meet someone during my travels. In fact, when leaving my monastery I had made a quiet, serious vow to myself to avoid the temptations that reel you in if you, like me, haunt nightlife adventure and have a romantic soul.

But Charlee wasn't some late-night detour. She wasn't a hookup or an escape. She came at me like weather - unpredictable, undeniable, unstoppable. A tsunami of presence and intention. Her love didn't coax me out of hiding. It tore my walls down and flayed me naked.

I would be checking out of the Sunreno with no plan for where I'd land once I looped back to Bangkok. Something would present itself. It always did. Some unexpected, slightly-too-perfect place with A/C that hummed just right and a balcony with a view of everyday life. A big part of me wanted to return to "our" neighborhood - to retrace the steps we'd worn into the sidewalk like initials in wet cement. But another part craved a last two-week hurrah in the Sukhumvit. I wanted the crazy. I wanted the neon overload and the overwhelming tide of possibility. I wanted to lose myself in it, just to see what might be waiting on the other side. And I wanted Charlee to join me, even though she had her life and responsibilities there in Bang Kho Laem.

She wanted me to move into her place and a part of me screamed yes, yes, yes. I seriously considered that, and what that would mean - because if I did, there was a distinct possibility I would never leave Thailand. Not an idea I was averse to.

But that was later. For now, we stayed in bed.

We talked. Not the kind of talk you do to fill space, but the real kind. The kind that peels back layers, which wanders through the past and plans toward a future that feels half-possible, half-fantasy. We talked about what this was, this love that had rapidly grown between us like some impossibly tightly wrapped bud ready to burst into an even more beautiful blossom. And all the while, we stayed close drifting deeper into each other with urgency and reverence. That ache, that sweet craving that comes when you know everything's about to change.

Eventually, reality slipped its fingers in. Our stomachs growled in unison, equal parts biology and metaphor. That kind of hunger isn't just physical. It's a reminder that you're alive, that you're tethered to the world again. And when you're in sync with someone - truly in rhythm - it's uncanny how the sine waves line up.

We looked at each other and simultaneously, without discussion, in perfect symmetry, we vetoed dim sum. The psychic timing of it undid me. My eyes welled. So did hers. That's when you know you're surfing the same swell. When decisions arrive wordlessly, effortlessly, simultaneously. When connection doesn't feel like work, it feels gently divined.

We wandered along Chareon Krung until a little café oddly named Fresh Milk Family pulled us in with the scent of strong coffee and something sweet in the air. We enjoyed overtly excellent syrupy java so fruit-forward it didn't need sugar; the flaky croissants that exploded with every bite, and fresh fruits glistening, colorful - so perfect that the plates looked like still-life paintings rendered by a master from the past.

I asked Charlee about her family's New Year traditions. Something gentle in her expression shifted, like a door creaking open to let history slip in.

"All us who can gather? Is that the right word? Do you understand? We cook all the time and learn what has happened in the family lives. I stay at my family house with brother, sister, cousins and sometimes for some strays ... like you. Except we can not sleep together or sexy time." She looked at me, her eyes darting all over my face, smirked, then smiled then started to laugh. And laugh more.

"What is going on in that beautiful head of yours?" I inquired. She couldn't stop laughing.

When she finally surfaced, fanning the air in front of her face with a menu card, she explained: "You - YOU. Yāy Saengdao will never stop asking you every detail of your life ... ever!" And with that she started laughing again. "You are in for long time with me and Yāy!"

It hit me with the subtlety of a big bag of pig iron falling on my head. Like most people on the planet, at any given time ... they come with family. I had been so happily enshrouded in our own private universe that in the beginning, when we were telling all about who we were and where we came from, I had only given that obvious fact a cursory mental glance before returning to us, to the here and now. I'd have to endure a proper grilling. A macro to micro-examination of a journalists salient big five questions. Who, what, when, where, why ... all of it and more.

This cold splash of reality flew through my brain in a millisecond. I looked at Chalermwan kissed her and ran out the door.   No, I didn't.

I didn't consider that option for even a second. I looked at her, cupped her face gently, kissed her deeply, and said, "I want to meet Yāy Saengdao. Your mom, your dad, your brother and sister, your cousins - every single one of them. I want to sit with them, listen to their stories, help chop vegetables, do the dishes, and earn whatever trust needs earning. Anyone who wants a piece of me can have it because they're part of *you*. Bring it on."

I paused, took a breath, and added, "But if your grandma grills me so deep that I start speaking in tongues, I'm holding you personally responsible."

Charlee exploded into that full-face smile of hers, so radiant it could melt Antarctica. Her tears came fast, no hesitation, no shame. She threw her arms around me like she was anchoring herself to something real in a world that sometimes tilts too hard. Her grip was fierce though not desperate. She rocked me slowly, like we were the only two people left on the whole damned planet. And then, in a whisper that fluttered with intensity, she pressed her lips close to my ear and kept saying, again and again, like a mantra she didn't want to end:

"I love you, Larry... I love you, Larry..."

This wasn't just "I love you."

This was *"I LOVE YOU!"* - shouted to the heavens between heartbeats. It wasn't performative. It wasn't rehearsed or planned.

It was pure instinct. Raw, unbridled truth. Her truth.

I didn't need to respond. Charlee already knew how I felt about her. I'd shouted it from rooftops. I'd whispered it into her ear in the quietest corners of the night, and again in the middle of crowded Bangkok streets. She'd seen me at my worst and glimpsed what might be my best, like Sinatra sung, "the best is yet to come" - and somehow, impossibly, she had embraced it all. The heights, the wreckage, and all my tangled contradictory mess in between.

But this moment? This was hers. Her time to offer something unfiltered, soul-deep, and sacred. I felt her need for this. And I had no reason, no right, to interrupt that outpouring. I stayed quiet, still, and let her words fall over me like a blessing.

Inside, I was screaming the same truth back at her. My own love, my own wild declaration was building behind my ribs like a choir waiting on its cue. But it would have to wait. My words would come later. Hers deserved airtime.

We'd made quite the scene in that little café, so we tipped well and made a quiet exit before we were either politely asked to leave or dramatically escorted out by some medal-winning Muay Thai champion wielding a long blade as in the days of old and a glare that could stop traffic.

The rest of the day had no schedule, and that was exactly what we wanted. We weren't chasing sights or checking boxes. We just needed to *be*. And more than that - we needed to be tangled up in each other.

Indoors felt too small for what we were carrying. Too quiet for the pulse between us. We kept walking. My arm slung over her shoulder, hers wrapped tight around my waist - our bodies stitched together like a banner. We weren't subtle. We didn't want to be. This was claiming in motion. A loud, burning parade of possession. I wanted to wear Charlee like a second skin, to breathe her in, to make a meal of every step beside her.

The world could stare. Let it. I'd stopped flinching at happiness.

But today wasn't about me. It was about her. What she wanted. What might make her laugh, tilt her head back and flash that radiant, wrecking-ball smile that left me soft every time. I asked her to take the reins.

"Show me something you want to do," I said. "Anywhere in Bangkok - or hell, beyond. As long as we're doing it together."

In hindsight, that may have been a tactical error.

Transportation was on the table in all its chaotic Bangkok glory: cab, tuk tuk, Grab, BTS, MRT - maybe all of the above, plus a longtail boat, a Sherpa and a yak. But this time, I wasn't going to micromanage like the neurotic farang I can occasionally be. She could handle it. Charlee was organized, graceful, and unfazed by the urban mayhem, whereas I had the transportational instincts of a blindfolded chicken in a rotating wind tunnel. I handed her the route, the lead, the day. I had transformed into a man who'd finally stopped trying to pretend he knew what he was doing.

"I want to ride roller coasters with you!" she said, grinning as she dug her fingers into my ribs.

Charlee had recently discovered that I am absurdly ticklish. Not just giggly - full-blown, can't-breathe, gasping-for-mercy, arms-flailing ticklish. And she *loved* it. She wielded her discovery like a benevolent tyrant with a new magic wand. All it took was a twitch of her fingers and I'd dissolve into a helpless puddle of laughter and defeat.

The cruel irony? She wasn't ticklish. Not at all. I tried everything - sneak attacks, soft brushes, the old feather-on-the-foot trick. Nothing. She'd just look at me with that serene little smile, like, *"Really? That's all you've got?"*

Okay, it did do something. Just not the squirming, shrieking, fall-off-the-bed response I was going for.

But that story... well, let's just say that's not a story for you.

I hadn't seen anything resembling a roller coaster in Bangkok. Not a single amusement park, traveling fair, or neon-drenched tilt-a-whirl with a raucous calliope blaring away in all my wanderings to date. No spinning teacups in parking lots. Nothing. If there were thrill rides in the city, they were playing a damn good game of hide-and-seek. And yet, Bangkok is so huge that you could hide another country in a corner.

But I had no doubt Charlee knew exactly where to find one.

Because Thais love fun. It's not just a pastime here - it's a personality trait, a national undercurrent. It's in the way they eat, the way they laugh, the way they greet you with a smile that says let's not take this too seriously. "Sanuk" - the Thai word for fun - is more than just a vibe; it's a principle. If something isn't *sanuk*, what's the point?

But "fun" in Thailand isn't always about noise and spectacle. It's sometimes quieter. A shared dessert on a curb. A pickup volleyball game in an alleyway. Singing badly - but with heart - at a karaoke joint down some winding soi. Kids splashing strangers with buckets and massive super-soakers during Songkran. Aunties gossiping in a circle while shelling shrimp. Life here is laced with playfulness and connection.

But here's the deeper truth, one that marks a beautiful and enormous cultural divide: in Thailand, even the simplest, most ordinary activity can be sanuk if one is sabai enough to recognize it. That is, relaxed, present, and open to delight. If you look at the world through grateful, unfiltered eyes, the kind that understand that simply waking up in the morning is a cause for heartfelt celebration, then joy becomes a built-in feature of life, not a reward you have to earn.

It's neither performance nor loudly displayed. It's in the spirit of being with others. Of laughing easily. Of honoring the moment for what it is. It's a beautiful thing. You should try it on for size. It always fits perfectly.

So, if Charlee wanted to ride the rails, she wasn't just talking about adrenaline. She was inviting me into simply another prismatic facet of her flavor of sanuk. Into the part of Thai culture that takes your hand, spins you around, and says, come on, let's laugh at this whole ridiculous thing together.

I was 100% in.

"And my darling, where would we do that?" I asked, trying to sound casual though I was buzzing with curiosity.

"Siam Amazing! It's cute and fun. Take a while to go there but we laugh a lot. I promise."

We hurried back to her bâan, where she swapped out her sandals for sneakers and slipped into clothes clearly made for, as she put it, "getting into trouble." Then came her stern orders, delivered with perfect theatrical flair: Bring swim trunks. Bring a second T-shirt. No questions. No negotiations. Fun was going to be serious business.

"Yes ma'am," I said with an overly theatrical salute.

My backside got a swat for cheek, though she had that lovelook in her eyes as she delivered my punishment.

Today was going to be playful. Equal. And I had the privilege of a peek into her inner child - on her terms. I'd been invited to join her party and honestly, there was nowhere else I wanted to be. Even if I did projectile vomit on the pendulous pirate ship. She'd just have to duck!

We made record time back and forth to and from the Sunreno. A Grab car was summoned with a few app taps and since it was only four minutes away, our prep was quick - presto chango.

We retraced our steps to the alley entrance along Chareon Krung Road. By the time we arrived, our Grab was already waiting like a patient accomplice. We hopped in, the city rushing past in a blur of neon and chatter as I felt the heat of anticipation.

An amusement park. The last time I'd been to one was back in 2001, when my daughter had turned five, wide-eyed at Disneyland. This would be a whole different kind of day.

Siam Amazing had all the rides. You know the ones: they spin you this way, twirl you that way, and twist you sideways until your stomach threatens mutiny. There were rides that shot you straight up into the sky, dropped you like a stone into some merciless chasm, then jerked you left, right, and every diagonal direction that made your insides slam into your spine. Oblong loops and obtuse angles, right-angle drops followed by immediate left turns, flips that flipped us upside down and inside out like a bodily physics experiment gone horribly wrong. They were all there, each one a siren call daring us to lose breakfast.

The air buzzed and pulsed with old-school carnival cacophony: the relentless whine of motors winding up, safety bars snapping shut with a metallic clack, and the shrieks and laughter, half terror, half delirious joy, as riders rocketed past. Neon blinked and spun in dizzying patterns that turned my head to jelly, competing with the heavy, scent of stir-fried dishes that was a completely bizarre menu of offering in the buffet hall. Sadly there were none of the traditional carnival goodies that I grew up with like sweet funnel cakes melting in syrupy goo, caramel popcorn sticking to fingers, and the sickly-sweet tang of cotton candy dissolving on the tongue as spun sugar clouds collapsed into a sticky mess. Then again, that's probably for the best as I would have definitely lost my stomach.

My heart pounded in my chest like it was trying to escape, my breath caught in a nervous hitch. I could feel bile rise. Not from fear, but in the pure, unfiltered craziness of it all, the overload of noise, color, and motion rattling my nerves like a blender on high speed. Charlee, meanwhile, was all grins, the fire in her eyes, an impish spark that said bring it on. She wanted to conquer every single one of those hellish contraptions.

And despite my brain screaming abort mission, my body somehow tightened with excitement. Because if I was going down, I was going down right alongside her - stomach churning, laughter bubbling, hands gripping each other for dear life.

Once Charlee had gotten her adrenaline fix from being spun, flipped, and catapulted we decided to skip lunch and change into pool gear. Siam Amazing, in case you didn't know, is home to the world's largest wave pool. That's not hyperbole - it's a bona fide Guinness World Record holder, as proudly advertised on a sign near the entrance. And it lives up to the hype. It's less "wave pool" and more "inland tsunami generator." Mostly it's the sheer size of the pool, though the machine-generated waves were also more than substantial.

Fun fact: in order to generate the waves, the engineering behind the motion displaces 500,000 gallons of water, then thrusts it up and out with a force that's unbelievable. The details are intense, but the results are awesome!

Teens shrieked with delight as water came rolling toward them like Poseidon was out to make sure that everyone was thoroughly soaked. Floats were launched skyward. Towards the shallower edge, toddlers clung to their parents like adorable little barnacles. Kids rode the crests, limbs flailing, shouting over the roar of water and each other. It was a symphony of splashing, laughing, and the occasional whistle from a lifeguard who looked one tantrum away from quitting.

Beyond that was the lazy river - lazy in name only. Yes, it looped gently around rocks and palms, but with the number of kids dive-bombing off inner tubes and Charlee's sneak-attack, dunking me from behind, "relaxing" was not on the menu. It was like trying to meditate inside a water park-themed rave.

And then there were the slides. Towering structures painted in every shade of neon anxiety with long supersonic-speed building trenches, while others spiraled into corkscrews, sudden drops, and dark tubes of watery doom. Some slides were open-air serpents, letting you see every gut-wrenching twist before you hit them. Others were fully enclosed blackout tunnels that shot you down at Mach speed, spinning you through blind curves before ejecting you into a pool like a human bullet.

And yes, each slide came with a complimentary high-pressure chlorinated sinus douche - nature's way of reminding you that fun sometimes comes with a head cleansing.

Charlee was in her element, all gleeful shrieks and slippery hugs, dragging me from slide to slide with an energy that could have powered the city. I barely kept up, but I didn't care. This was her domain, her sanuk, and I'd been handed an executive pass.

Soaked, sun-drunk, slightly bruised, and with water lodged somewhere in my middle ear, I realized I hadn't laughed this hard or felt that light in years.

We climbed into the back of the Grab car, mostly dry at that point, sun-dazed, smelling of chlorine. Charlee's disheveled hair - usually elegantly kept - had gone full aquatic rebel, curling wildly in the humidity. She looked beautiful. She always did. But this was a different kind of beautiful - joy-wrecked, carefree, au natural and completely at peace.

She curled up next to me like a content cat, her head tucked beneath my chin, one arm slung across my chest. Her hand found mine without looking, our fingers lacing together in that quiet, instinctive way that couples do. The cab rolled forward, Bangkok's traffic humming around us, but inside the car everything slowed to a honeyed crawl.

Neither of us said much. We didn't need to. Her body was warm against mine, our laughter still echoing in the space between us. She let out a long, happy sigh that could've doubled as a lullaby.

"Did you have fun?" I asked, brushing strands of hair from her forehead.

She nodded without lifting her head. "Mmmhmm. My cheeks hurt by smiling too much. But I had fun because I got to ride with you."

She pulled my arm tighter around her and murmured, "You good man, darling. You not scared of crazy Thai girl."

"No, ma'am," I said, pressing a kiss to the top of her head. "I'm absolutely terrified. But I'm in too deep now."

She giggled, half-asleep already, and I could feel her whole body relax the way someone does when they feel completely safe and secure. That felt like something. No, that felt like everything.

Outside the window, Bangkok shimmered in the late afternoon haze, temples glowing gold, scooters weaving like fish in a current, street vendors stirred woks and fried delicious things with hypnotic rhythm. The city pulsed with life, as always. But in that backseat, we had carved out a little pocket of stillness.

We headed back to our neighborhood clean up, maybe nap, maybe not. I didn't know what the rest of the day would bring, and for the first time in a long time, I didn't feel the need to plan it because I already had everything I needed, tucked under my arm, fast asleep.

※

I hated to wake her, but we were back at the alley along Chareon Krung. Charlee had really conked out and I had reveled in every second, holding her to me, feeling her slumbering breath spread across my chest.

"Honey ... we're back home," as I gently pushed more errant strands of hair away from her face and gently caressed her awake. "Big shower or little shower?"

"Mmmmmmmmmm .... big shower, honey," as she drifted back into this world.

I asked the driver to U-turn and take us a hundred yards to the apartment instead.

After a long, luxurious hot shower, the kind that clears your head and peels the day off your skin, we were wide awake again, refreshed and recharged. It felt like time to refill the slate, not wipe it clean exactly, but layer something softer over the adrenaline and wild ride of the afternoon. I wanted something slower now, something a little more sedate, but still carrying the brightness of Charlee's mood forward. She was glowing, crackling with renewed energy. I didn't want to dim that.

She looked surprised when I took her hand and led her across the street to Asiatique. But first, I made a point to detour past her store where her employee was doing a brisk and competent job of keeping things running, so we could use the actual crosswalk. You know, the kind with a traffic light and painted lines, where cars are legally obligated to stop instead of speeding up to test your reflexes. I know. Wild concept. Where's the fun of not playing real-life Donkey Kong with your vital organs?

There was something I wanted to do that paired to the surreal Siam Amazing-themed day. We walked arms looped around each other, as I steered us toward the enormous Ferris wheel at the north end of the mall. Asiatique Sky. It's the largest Ferris wheel in Bangkok, in all of Thailand, and one of those where you sit inside a fully enclosed gondola instead of dangling your legs like bait in a carnival seat.

I got our tickets, and we climbed into our own little capsule to ride the sky. The ticket gives you about an hour, enough time for everyone to enjoy a turn at the top. Charlee was delighted and to my surprise, she'd never ridden it before.

We settled into our floating tiny house, just the two of us, pressed close together as we rose steadily into the dusk. The city fell away beneath us in slow motion. Lights sparkled into life across the river while the Chao Phraya shimmered in the twilight, restless and tarnished silver. And up there, wrapped in the quiet hum of the wheel and the soft rustle of Charlee's breath beside me? Bliss!

After a few slow revolutions, it was our turn at the top. I'd like to say we behaved ourselves. We didn't. But I'll leave the specifics to your imagination - feel free to fill in the blank pages however you see fit.

I assumed there must be cameras in those gondolas. Not that we got any barked orders over a speaker while we were up there; no flashing lights or "sir, this is a family attraction" announcements, but when we stepped off at ground level, the attendant gave us a look like the weary expression of someone who's seen one too many rom-coms play out on his shift.

We weren't the first, and I'm confident we won't be the last to kiss in the sky. So, we shrugged, laughed, and walked off into the night like two teenagers who'd just gotten away with something small but wonderful.

Over the course of late-night conversations, between temple visits, strolls, snacks, dinner planning, and everything in between, I'd learned something surprising: Charlee had never tried Indian food (I had overly-exaggerated a gasp, which earned me a playful slap on my ass). Not once. That felt like a culinary oversight of near-criminal proportions. And since we were both ravenous, running on nothing but Siam Amazing, Ferris wheel adrenaline, and warm fuzzies, I figured we could kill two cravings with one meal.

I did a little research and found a spot just up Charoen Krung Road that had rave reviews. Yes, I know. Never trust online reviews. That's why I had a backup plan. I texted Jaks to get the local verdict.

"Yeah bro - it's excellent. I've got some pals from Pakistan, and this is one of two places in BKK they go. It's not fancy, but it's solid."

That was good enough for me. When someone with Pakistani friends signs off on the butter chicken, you pay attention.

Plus, I had a little post-dinner surprise in mind. Something quiet. Something us.

That didn't mean we were going to head out looking like we'd just rolled off the back of a tuk-tuk and rolled in the street. I had plans for after dinner, so we made a quick stop at Charlee's place to get her changed into something a little more... intentional.

After a shower, with the evening breeze starting to lift off the river, I helped her pick out an outfit. Subtly, of course. I didn't spill the beans about the post-dinner surprise, but I did steer her toward an elegant, smoky gray ankle-length dress that flowed when she walked. A shimmering black-silk tie-it-up belt and soft cream wrap with her black flats completed the look. Effortless, but quietly stunning.

Charlee didn't have an extensive wardrobe per se, there simply wasn't room for extravagant clothing options (and that really wasn't her personality anyway.) Her collection was more a curated arsenal of well-chosen pieces. Smart, versatile things that could be mixed and matched for anything from a street market lunch to an unexpected night out with a touch of magic.

She trusted my judgment. Or maybe she just liked the way I was ogling her in that dress. Either way, it was perfect.

Masala of India wasn't exactly going to win any design awards, unless there's a category for odd color choices and fluorescent lighting that was having issues with continuity, but if the food was even half as good as promised, I didn't care. I wasn't looking for ambiance. I was looking for something rich, warm, deeply spiced and authentic. Something that could wrap us up for our last night together before the week pulled us in different directions.

We stepped into Masala of India, which was only about half-full, though that wasn't hard to achieve since the place had a grand total of eight tables. Charlee told me to handle the ordering, and since she had a known affection for those incendiary little mouse-drop chilies, I knew spice tolerance wouldn't be an issue.

I went classic: butter chicken, lamb vindaloo, spinach daal, butter naan, papadum, saffron rice, and mango lassi.

As we waited, Charlee launched a full-scale charm offensive to get me to reveal where we were headed after dinner. It was a relentless campaign of feminine mischief and coquettish ploys. I loved every second of it.

"Darling," I said, desperately trying to hold my ground, "try as you might - and you're getting dangerously close to picking the lock - isn't it better to unwrap a surprise than go snooping in the closet?"

She pouted. Total sham. We both knew it. Then she launched a full-on offensive. Batting lashes and smiling eyes. Then coy sideways glances. When she whispered seductive promises about later activities, she ... almost ... had ... me! But I reeled it in at the last possible second before losing my resolve. "Not going to work, baby," I laughed, though she almost had me with that last bribe.

Thankfully, the service was quick, and soon the papadum and its entourage of chutneys arrived alongside the mango lassi. She snapped off a crisp shard, dipped it in the pudina chutney, and took a bite. I could watch that woman discover new flavors all day, every day.

"Oh, Larry... mī rā s̄ klmklxm!" she beamed, using one of the many Thai expressions for 'delicious.'

"And that's just the appetizer! Just wait, honey, Indian food is a revelation."

By the time we had finished those crispy, thin, fried lentil crackers and chutneys, the main dishes started to roll our way.

Every bite was a discovery. While Thailand is rightfully famous for its curries, Indian cuisine operates in an entirely different flavor universe. Less herby, more warming spice. Like being hugged by a spice cabinet that's read The Bhagavad Gita.

The butter chicken was perfect - tender, creamy, subtle tomato whispers in a spicy, buttery curry base that felt like it had been slow-danced into existence. I'd asked for that one with light heat, knowing full well that the vindaloo was going to light our skulls on fire.

The naan was perfect. Pillowy and golden with just the right char and chew, while the saffron rice had that braggart grain-by-grain fluffiness that only true rice masters can pull off.

One thing I have always appreciated about good Indian dishes is portion control. The chefs know how deep, how rich and how over-taxing their dishes are. It's very rare to go to a quality Indian restaurant and get loaded up with bulk. Instead, portions, while not small, are smart. Just enough for two, or three at a stretch. Which means that you don't waddle out of their restaurants, but you always leave completely satisfied.

There's also something deeper at work in Indian cuisine. The philosophy of balance. Many spice-forward food cultures understand this. There are warm spices and cool spices, and they don't just affect your palate, they affect your dreams. Literally. Warm spices like cardamom, clove, cumin, and cinnamon can send your brain into vivid, psychedelic, technicolor territory. Cool spices like fennel, coriander, and mint help you rest. It's real. It's studied. But tonight? We were riding the warm spice train, straight into the sensory jungle of the Indian subcontinent.

Fast forward to empty plates and we were out the door. I'd had Charlee wear flats for a good reason. We were walking to our evening spot. It wasn't far but it required some main drag strolling.

Remember that swanky hotel along the river I'd infiltrated for my morning reading session? That same property has a bar - the BKK Social Club, that was like everything else in the place, high-end, sleek, and damned impressive. It had been ranked by every professional alcohol and booze rag out there, including a top ten spot on the Best Bars in Asia list for 2024. That's right - not just Bangkok, not just Thailand. Asia. And if that wasn't enough, it held the #12 spot on the World's Best Bars list. That's dope!

As we rounded into the pathway leading to the hotel, Charlee squeezed my arm and asked quietly, as if not to disturb the plants, if it was okay that we were going there. I slowed, turned to face her, cupped her stunning face, and kissed her the way true lovers kiss. I assured her we'd be ushered in without a hitch, and we were. She giggled, "You are good with surprises! I love you."

That path looked completely different at night. By day it had a lush, shaded, hidden-oasis vibe. At night it was full of romantic-jungle dreamscape. As we strolled hand-in-hand, another gatekeeper gave us the once-over and silently swung open that twenty-foot door as if we were expected without a second glance.

These days, every bar on Earth aside from your cousin's moonshine shack has a "signature cocktail" menu. It's mandatory now, like exit signs on the highway. Some are decent. Some, genuinely sublime. But a few are crimes against ethanol, dreamed up by overzealous mixologists with too much flair and not enough judgment.

Thankfully, BKK Social Club's menu had only a couple of Frankencocktails. The rest? Solid contenders.

Charlee, as she'd said at Havana Social, wasn't steeped in cocktail culture. She asked for a mojito, but I dangled a suggestion. Maybe she'd like to explore a little more? There's a whole universe of flavor, texture, and layered surprises behind the bar. Falling into a habit too early in the game felt like a shame (says the guy who orders Sapphire martinis almost exclusively.)

She gave me the stare, cold as Lucca Brazzi with a job to take care of, to determine if I was blocking her, choosing for her, or merely using the moment to nudge her towards a new discovery. Sometimes Charlee's visual interrogations bordered on seat-squirming, nerve-wracking, patience-testing blissful agony. Unless I win. Then she breaks and bursts out laughing, breaking the spell. We'd started to fall into that game almost from the start, and it wound up a battle of "who'll break first." She usually won because staring at her natural beauty was like looking into a flawless 20 carat diamond set into highly polished platinum in clear mid-day sunlight - sometimes there was just too much stunning to hold onto.

But that night, I won. I was determined to not go down ... *again*.

"Teach me?" she finally said, laughing.

"It would be my honor, darling."

We eased into the rhythm that had fast become ours. A playful, teasing back-and-forth, full of careful listening. Instead of asking her about specific flavors, I asked her how she felt. Right now. This moment. And wouldn't you know it? She opened a new door: light, aromatic, floral, refreshing, strong. Sound familiar?

With her firmly on Team Martini, I shifted to my second favorite: a bourbon Manhattan. And yes, before you purists get all frothy, I know it's traditionally rye. I just prefer bourbon. Like I said, to each their own.

And then came the bar fight. Not the barroom brawl kind.

The first question out of our eager-beaver waiter was vodka or gin. Bzzzzt! Thank you for playing! At least he asked. And the fact that he asked with vodka leading the charge? Epic fail.

I was polite. I was politic. I explained exactly how to make a martini for Charlee without the lecture because we were here to enjoy each other, not for me to put on airs and my teachers cap. She'd already heard it during one our late-night rambling "getting to know you" chats. I don't even remember how I'd been coaxed into that Martini riff as Charlee is not a bartender about to fuck up a classic and needing course correction. She simply wanted a drink.

Somewhere between the olives, cherries and candlelight, we wandered into that late-evening zone where conversation drips slow and sultry, like AAA-grade maple syrup over naughty intentions. We'd already shared the meal, now came the dessert course: glances, low laughs, and the kind of teasing that hinted at pleasures still to come. The way she traced her finger around the rim of her glass made later abundantly clear.

We talked until the other customers had left and the bartenders started wiping things down with that quiet urgency that says please leave, but politely, with a side of ignoring our presence until it was absolutely necessary to turn out the lights. They knew what they were witnessing. Some moments deserve the long run.

Charlee and I were shoulder to shoulder in the low amber light, the table in front of us holding the remnants of our last two cocktails, both half-drunk and half-forgotten. It had become a space for our hands to clasp, fingertips and palms, gestures and touch.

"I want to go with you," she said, her voice low, threading through quiet jazz. "When you leave, I want to go."

God. That hit hard. That kind of truth was delivered without drama or plea. Just fact. Her eyes didn't flinch when she said it, and her voice didn't ask for anything more than honesty in return.

"I know you do," I said. "And I want you by my side every moment for the rest of my life. But right now... it's messy. There's stuff back home I need to settle. I'll be camped up in a spare bedroom at a friends house. It will be winter. Like *real* winter. Ten degrees and snow and ice that doesn't quit."

She smiled, soft and almost amused. "You think I care about snow? You keep me warm."

"No," I laughed. "I think you care about being comfortable and with me. And not introduced to my life back in America through a back door I didn't even choose. Though now, I'm so glad that all happened. I know we've talked about it, but she and I shared so much, except of course what she refused to share - and that's the stuff that hurt the most. Funny how she never understood, though I tried to make her see without throwing it her face, that her actions are what kept me angry for so long."

Her fingers found mine. Her eyes found mine. She didn't squeeze. Just held.

"I'll never do those things to you, and I can wait. But don't make me wait long. I love you and want us. I want this!"

That undid me a little. I'm not sure what face I made but it must've betrayed something because she leaned forward and kissed me. Not a "shut up" kiss, not a "save me" kiss. Just contact. Lips to lips. Saying "I'm here".

"We'll get there," I said as I pulled back from the edge of emotional meltdown. "We just need to do it right. And that means me handling things back home, so I can come back to you clear. Clean. Free. Without baggage banging around behind me."

"I will help you unpack," she said, her radiant smile that could level cities.

We stayed like that, entangled in words and plans and what-if's, until the last call had long since passed and the lights dimmed lower than they should have been. The bar staff gave us space. There are moments that deserve protection.

She asked what it would be like. My town, my people. I told her honestly. That my friends were amazing people and if I loved her, they would love her as they got to know her and deciphered her Thaiglish. But that she wouldn't need to win anyone over. Not them. And we could tell the rest of my past to go take a long jump off a short pier.

"Just be you," I said. "That will be more than enough."

At some point we stood. Slowly, like waking from a dream you don't want to end. We said deeply sincere thank yous to the staff for honoring our space with such polite discretion and stepped back out into the night air, soft and cool, sweetened with jasmine in the Bangkok dark.

There were still hours left ahead of us. But that conversation - that sliver of real - was the beginning of the rest of my life.

Back in her cozy little bâan, we didn't make love. We didn't say anything more because nothing more needed to be said. We offered up our blessings, together this time, to the triple gems, lit some candles and simply lay side by side, together, gazing into each other's eyes. Sometimes smiling gently. Sometimes a tear would trickle down a cheek, honoring the purity of what we'd found, out of the blue, organically, holistically, spiritually. We both felt it. We both knew it was real and pure and beautiful and completely unexpected. Neither of "us" was looked for, hoped for, dreamed of or up. We just were two people from different sides of the world who had met over a pile of mangosteens and fell for each other in ways that only happen in stories. Thank Buddha our story was real.

I awoke cramped and sore. We had fallen asleep holding each other so tightly it seemed we were trying to merge into one being. Neither of had moved a millimeter during slumber but now I had to. Buddha knows I didn't want to. As I willed my locked limbs and muscles to slowly move, Charlee stirred, breathed deeply into my chest and pulled me tighter to her. If I had to live with physical pain to experience that kind of love, acceptance, adoration? Fuck it! I had a bottle of naproxen and another of ibuprofen in my kit bag. I'd dose up later.

The day of sadness was upon us. I didn't need to be at the airport until midnight to pick up Malaya, so I'd planned the whole day in advance: get a haircut (my heroic follicles had made a healthy comeback from the scalping), restock the pantry and fridge, shop for some board shorts and industrial-strength SPF, and tidy up the apartment so Malaya would have an easy crash pad when she landed. A full schedule, locked in weeks ago.

I scrapped every bit of it.

This. Right. Here. Charlee, warm and sleeping in my arms, was far more important than any damn haircut or new swim trunks. The apartment was already spotless. Malaya would be arriving so late we'd barely be awake by the time we got to the apartment, and we were only staying one extra night before hopping a flight to Koh Chang anyway. I'd buy shorts on the island and unlike a tacky "I 🩶 BANGKOK" tee, they'd be a better souvenir.

Decision made, and since we still hadn't moved, I pulled Charlee in tighter. She stirred as I whispered, "I'm canceling all my plans today until I absolutely have to leave at eleven-thirty tonight."

There are moments when morning breath just doesn't matter. That was one of them. That was the poster child for "we should probably brush our teeth first but screw it, kiss me anyway." She didn't care either.

Morning drifted into mid-morning, and we caught up on what we'd put on pause. Sweet, eye-to-eye, breath-to-breath, slow, unhurried. But beneath it all hung that quiet sadness, like the June fog that blankets San Francisco. We knew what was coming. We talked and decided, together, to pretend - for a little while longer - that time didn't exist. That this was all there was. That love could stretch the hours into a lifetime.

Eventually, hunger pulled us from bed. We skipped dim sum again and stopped at her fruit shop instead, loading up on mangoes, mangosteens, papaya, pineapple, and a Hami melon so sweet it made my teeth ache. We hit 7-Eleven for sparkling waters, yogurt and protein bars and went back to her place.

We spent the rest of the day living like we'd always done this.

I helped her hand-wash the laundry and hang it out to dry. We watered the garden and fed the plants. I took out the trash to the communal bins at the end of her lane. I scrubbed her little bathroom until it gleamed, restocking everything from her stash of toiletries tucked in a trunk in her bedroom. Then I cleaned her kitchen from top to bottom, and made it sparkle like new.

I packed up the small collection of clothes I'd left at her place. She loved to wear my Grateful Dead Winterland '67 t-shirt, especially when the shutters were open. I hadn't washed it yet. It still held both of us. I tucked it under her pillow, a little time capsule for while I was away.

Meanwhile, Charlee placed her store orders, paid some invoices, and arranged for a cousin to pick her up for the family's New Year celebration. Her movements were efficient, practiced, but I could tell her heart wasn't in it. Neither was mine.

It was domestic bliss in its purest form. Quiet. Ordinary. Sacred. I wanted it to never end.

She turned. She looked at me. Tears were streaming down her face. I pulled her into a tight never-letting-go embrace until her sobs ebbed. I couldn't, wouldn't stop kissing her brow.

As the fear and sadness faded to an undercurrent, she grabbed her phone and instructed her staff to man the store. She would not be in today.

CHAPTER 15. KOH CHANG: FLIP THE NEW YEAR SURFING THE ISLAND VIBE

*Through the sunset of hope, Like the shapes of a dream,
What paradise islands of glory gleam! - Percy Bysshe Shelley*

There's something primal, even prehistoric, in our brains that lights up when we lay eyes on that classic tropical postcard: white sand so powdery it squeaks underfoot, coconut palms leaning like they've had one too many and are posing for a rum ad, sea grapes huddled near the edge of the dune, and that impossible, iridescent blue water that looks like it was poured straight out of an Adobe gradient tool. It's a hardwire vision to hijack our modern, overclocked minds. One glimpse and suddenly the fantasy switch flips: quit the job, hurl the phone into the surf, and move into a bamboo hut with Ginger. Gilligan's our harmlessly clueless neighbor, ukulele music drifts lazily on the breeze, and a deeply tanned local keeps appearing with bottomless piña coladas, icy lagers and the catch of the day on a banana leaf.

Tropical islands like Koh Chang know exactly what they're doing. They've weaponized leisure. They seduce you with simplicity. Your brain, accustomed to stress and schedules, gets chloroformed by salt air and fried bananas and wakes up believing this - *this* - is how life is meant to be lived. You find yourself seriously weighing life decisions based on hammock angle, depth of beach chair recline, and whether flip-flops are necessary at all.

And in that suspended haze of sun and sea, for a few blessed moments, you don't just fantasize about a simpler life. You live it.

Gauguin heard that call loud and clear and followed it all the way to Tahiti - paintbrush in one hand, delusion in the other. He paid for his libertine lifestyle with regret and syphilis, dying in paradise an embittered curmudgeon, ignoring the beauty, embracing his madness.

For me, the call came in the form of Koh Chang - Elephant Island - named after its headland which, from the right angle (and maybe a cocktail or five), looks vaguely like an elephant. Real elephants? Yes, a few. Imported, of course, for the tourists. Wild elephants haven't called this place home in a very long time, if they ever did.

That was where I spent the flip from 2024 to 2025 - a deliberate escape from Bangkok's concrete energy and neon noise. I didn't want the new year to catch me in the tangle of tuk-tuks and techno beats.

Malaya: friend, international traveler and fellow avoidance-pro of city-wide parties, was flying in to join me. A marathon of fireworks, endless shots and drinks, the screaming *Wooooooooooooooooo*'s wasn't her idea of a great evening either. Yeah - great - you can count down from ten. Welcome to the party, baccalaureate. We both wanted something quieter. A softer entry into the new year.

In my younger days, New Year's Eve meant the Grateful Dead's winter run. San Francisco or Oakland, depending on the year. Five shows in six nights, and the new year always began with a hangover that lasted until mid-January. I've aged out of that particular ritual and had done so in the late 1980s. These days, a gentle countdown somewhere warm and semi-conscious sounded just about right.

I handed off the planning to Malaya, no questions asked. She's the kind of traveler who can navigate immigration lines and ferry schedules like she's playing a casual game of Tetris, so it seemed smart to step aside and let her do her thing. My only job was to set up base camp in Bangkok; a comfortable landing pad where she could shake off the jet lag before we made the move south.

I hadn't mentioned anything about Charlee to Malaya. Charlee and I wouldn't be together on New Years, so it didn't seem necessary. Since Malaya and I weren't romantically involved, there was no reason to complicate things.

By early December, our inboxes were filling up with back-and-forth lists: "How about this?" "What about that?" - each message a negotiation toward someplace that wasn't a human traffic jam with a beach. We both knew what we didn't want: Phuket, Koh Samui, Pattaya, any of the usual suspects. Gorgeous, yes. But come New Year's Eve, they turn into neon and day-glow-soaked frat parties with sand. Thousands of tourists all chasing the same *"authentic"* island experience, hooting into the night like it's their first time drinking from a bucket. No thanks.

I opened her latest email in early December: Koh Chang, Trat Province. A quieter island tucked into the eastern curve of the Bay of Thailand, close to Cambodia and far from the blow-up flamingo scene.

The main island is the anchor of Mu Koh Chang National Park, established in 1982 as a maritime preserve covering a 52-island archipelago, scattered like green coins floating atop tropical blue water. Technically, the park designation for the big island was mostly symbolic - more a gesture than a guarantee - but I wasn't about to split hairs.

Everything I read told me it was still lush, still wild in places, and, most importantly, still free of the kind of infrastructure that turns paradise into parking lot. No major cities, no superclubs with DJ foam parties, no five-star resorts with "authentic cultural shows". However, there are towns with restaurants, pot shops, bars and DJ clubs dotted along the eastern coast of the island, but in microscopic ratios compared to the other tourist spots.

My deep sadness that Charlee would not be with me had been tempered by her own enthusiasm for my adventure, long planned before we met. Don't get me wrong, we were pining for each other in the worst way, not only for the intimacy that had blossomed, but for the genuine friendship that goes along with anything real.

Koh Chang however sounded exactly like what we were after. A tropical island that doubles as a national park? Yes, please. Snorkeling and jungle hikes, warm gulf water you can float in all day, seafood dinners eaten barefoot, umbrella drinks that arrive slightly too strong, and long, slow naps on feather-soft sand. The plan was coming together, and my optimism was cautiously creeping toward excitement.

December 28th, just past 12:30AM, I was outside Suvarnabhumi Airport, waiting for Malaya to clear customs. The air was warm and thick, like the city hadn't exhaled the remnant heat of the day yet. I didn't want her navigating a cab alone after all the effort she'd put into planning our adventure, so I waited out front, loitering near the cluster of private drivers in dark slacks and white shirts. The drivers and I shared a few laughs, swapping half-English jokes and pretending not to sweat.

Finally. At 1:15AM, she emerged from the sliding glass doors, backpack slung, carry-on rolling behind and smile intact. We slid into the waiting car and headed back to the Sunreno. The upside of landing in the dead of night? No traffic. During daylight, Bangkok's highways swell with enough cars to make seventeen miles feel like sixty. At this hour, the city slipped past the windows, silent and dark.

We would have a nap till dawn and then one full day/night in Bangkok before heading right back to the airport for the 45-minute flight to Trat. From there, we'd arranged door-to-door transport: someone would meet us at the airport, drive onto the ferry, and deliver us to the hotel on Koh Chang. The whole journey from Bangkok to beach would take about six hours. Manageable, especially with someone else behind the wheel.

I'd made a conscious decision to stop Googling everything. No more photos, or TripAdvisor rabbit holes. I wanted to arrive with fresh eyes, no script, no expectations. Just the simple thrill of stepping onto a new island and letting it hit me in real time.

❦

Our full day in Bangkok turned out to be a good one. I spent most of it texting back and forth with Charlee, keeping the thread going while Malaya and I played tourist. We hopped on the Chao Phraya ferry and let it carry us downriver, sightseeing like pros. See? I *can* learn! We wandered through the exhibits at the National Museum, took in the reclining Buddha at Wat Pho, and spent the rest of the afternoon bouncing around town eating, drinking, and half-distracted by the anticipation of sand and saline just over the horizon.

That night, we made the responsible decision to have an early dinner and crash early. No big bar night, just sleep so we could face the morning without stress or rushing. We dined at an Irish pub (I was craving Guinness) that was nothing special, but the stout was fantastic. I'd been at the Sunreno Hotel for eleven days. I'd made friends and explored the local surrounds. Both doormen, Wing and Chaipak had turned into allies and advisors. They'd been endlessly kind, always ready with directions, local wisdom, and Thai language coaching. Of course, there was Charlee and Jakkapan too - and it was a wrench to leave them behind. The Sunreno had become familiar, like Martin's recliner in Frasier - not glamorous, but solid and strangely hard to leave.

But new horizons were calling, so after some genuinely heartfelt goodbyes and a few awkward Thai phrases, we loaded into an early morning cab and said adios to Bangkok for a week.

It was odd though. Aside from the obvious and desperate need to stay and remain with Charlee, I felt Bangkok slipping her tentacles around me, grasping, sucking, whispering, *"Where the hell do you think you're going? We're not done here yet - not by a long shot!"*

❦

The little prop plane was packed, every seat taken, but thankfully the flight was merely a hop. The taxi to takeoff in Bangkok was longer than the air time itself. As we began our descent, the view outside was already leaning hard into tropical fantasy. Patches of green jungle, swaths of fields growing yummy things, and not a single glossy high-rise in sight.

Trat Airport was exactly what I hoped it would be: tiny, rustic, and blessedly free of anything resembling a security checkpoint. There was a dog giving us the once-over, but I wasn't sure if that counted as he looked like he was trying to find a place to pee rather than search anyone for contraband. A single two-lane runway, a cabana-style terminal no bigger than a 7-Eleven, and the kind of relaxed atmosphere that made you wonder if anyone here had even heard of the word "security protocol."

We climbed down the steps from the plane onto the tarmac and boarded one of those open-air buses you usually see at amusement parks - each bench seat with its own side entry - for the grand one-minute ride to the terminal. Our bags showed up a few minutes later in the bed of a pickup truck, where a genial fellow unloaded them by hand onto a shaded patio. Security consisted of walking through an open doorway into the parking lot. Outside, a driver stood holding a handwritten sign with my name on it.

That's how you land in paradise.

The ride to the ferry terminal took half an hour, winding through rural backroads that felt a world apart from Bangkok's sprawl. Out the van window, we watched the land roll past in a patchwork of agricultural plots: pineapple fields with their spiky blue-green punk hairdos, papaya trees leaning under their heavy fruit, stretches of neon yellow-green sugar cane, mango, rubber, and dense teak plantations. Everything was green and quietly industrious.

Every so often we passed a roadside stall or an isolated shop. Hand-painted signs, plastic chairs out front, the roar of an old refrigerator compressor audible over the sound of the tires on cracked asphalt. We passed clusters of greenhouses too, tucked back behind thickets of palms, and though the van's windows were only slightly ajar, the unmistakable scent of skunk crept in. Someone was growing something pungent in bulk out there.

There was no doubt we were off the beaten track. This wasn't glossy-brochure Thailand. No Trat area tours, no billboards for elephant rides, no golden arches or red and white striped chicken buckets. Just farmland and jungle and the slow steady pulse of a place unbothered by time.

Pulling up to the ferry dock felt like entering some forgotten outpost. The parking lot was a messy sprawl of dirt, gravel, and crumbling asphalt, patched and re-patched until the concept of "paved" was more philosophical than practical. It was packed with cars and trucks and no fewer than twenty of those silver Toyota Commuter vans you see everywhere in Thailand, little human cargo ships, each one crammed with sun-seekers and island dreamers.

The dock itself looked like it had been through a war, or simply decades of tropical wear and salted neglect. Rusted steel beams, block and tackle that looked like it would collapse with the weight of a crate of mangoes, bent railings, concrete that appeared to have been chewed up by a giant. Nothing about it inspired confidence, and neither did the ferries, which floated low in the water with the kind of weary dignity usually reserved for old men playing chess in a park.

Still, this was clearly a well-traveled route. Tourists, travelers and locals alike streamed aboard without hesitation, chatting, snapping photos, buying last-minute snacks. I tried not to think about the structural integrity of the vessel or the possibility of its rusted siblings already decorating the seafloor. Instead, I chalked it up to Southeast Asian providence: if the ferry hadn't sunk yesterday, odds were good it wouldn't sink today. I had a quiet chat with my inner Buddha and left the rest to chance.

Koh Chang. Visible from the opposing dock, slowly swelled larger as our ferry, which I had dubbed the S.S. OMG, chugged and sputtered its way across the Bay of Thailand. The vessel belched diesel fumes like it had a five-pack-a-day habit and was just trying to make it to retirement without any major incidents. It wasn't the kind of boat you'd bet money on in rough seas, but the gulf was calm, the sky was clear, and I was trusting in the magic of repeated success.

Up on deck was a blender bar selling fresh fruit smoothies. I ordered watermelon, Malaya got mango, and we leaned on the railing, sipping our drinks, watching the island grow larger and more beautiful by the minute. There's something about drinking a cold smoothie on a warm sea that briefly makes you believe you've figured some parts of life out.

Despite the S.S. OMG's tendency to wheeze and groan like an asthmatic lawnmower on its last legs, the trip felt more reassuring with every nautical mile.

By the time we neared the dock on the opposite shore, I had mostly stopped wondering how long I could tread water if we sunk.

When we finally pulled in and the ferry creaked into the dock, I felt a wave of honest-to-god relief wash over me. My neck unknotted, my shoulders released their death grip on my ears, and I let out a breath I didn't realize I'd been holding. We'd made it. Koh Chang was real, and we were there.

The other passengers in our van were all headed to White Sand Beach, the busiest tourist enclave on the island, a place known for its tourist bars, smallish late-night dance clubs, beach chairs, and general overabundance of … things. As they were being dropped off, two by two, I realized we'd be the last to go. Kai Bae was farther down the island's curving spine, tucked along the less congested southeast coast. That suited me just fine. It meant we'd get a rolling introduction to Koh Chang; an informal windshield tour of a place I'd never set foot on.

We curved up, down and around the narrow coastal road that twisted through pockets of jungle, then opened up to sudden, breath-catching sea views. Corrugated metal shacks gave way to palm-thatched cafés, then shops with handwritten signs. Every so often a dog trotted casually across the road just to make sure we weren't speeding. It was the kind of drive that required no conversation except the occasional "Whoa, look at that," as the island revealed itself in bits and pieces.

Malaya had booked us into the Kai Bae Beach Grand View, a not-so-modest spot with a prime location. I'd only given it the briefest of once-overs online when she sent the reservation, just enough to confirm it wasn't a hostel with a thatched roof and bunk beds made from driftwood. But otherwise, I'd kept myself willfully in the dark. I wanted this whole thing - Koh Chang, the beach, the bungalow, the sunsets - to arrive fresh and unfiltered. No predefined expectations, no mental Pinterest board. Just the real thing, as it came to me on its own terms.

Somewhere along the way, in a dip between jungle and cliff, I spotted a macaque monkey perched on the shoulder of the road, looking for all the world like a local, bored with the tourist traffic. He sat there casually, legs splayed, head bobbing back and forth like he was refereeing a tennis match. I'd never seen a monkey in the wild before, and that little scene, equal parts National Geographic and neighborhood gossip, cracked me up. It was a moment of pure, goofy delight, and I found myself hoping we'd see more simian spectators along the way. Maybe have a chat about roadside etiquette over a banana or two.

We dropped off our fellow van-mates at hotels, guesthouses, and modest resorts scattered around White Sand Beach. Then, with the last of them waved off, our van pointed its nose southward towards the smaller town of Kai Bae.

As we rounded the final bend, the landscape opened up in a way that made both of us lean forward, silent. There it was. Kai Bae Beach Grand View. Whoever named it hadn't been exaggerating. The hotel sat right above sand and surf, with an unobstructed, cinematic view of three offshore islands lounging in the turquoise waters like cats napping on a vast blue blanket. Sunlight shimmered on the bay, refracting off the water in that way that makes you forget about luggage, logistics, or the need for shoes. My breath caught. I felt the primal urge to ditch everything and just bolt for the surf, fully clothed, like some semi-rational castaway. I kept my cool. Barely.

After a smooth check-in at the open-air lobby, we were led past a spacious deck with a massive infinity pool overlooking the gulf. As we turned up a small path our beachfront bungalow was the first in line. The "bungalow," though, was a little more substantial than the word conjures. It was a new, modern design - sleek, clean, and perfectly integrated into the surrounding lush tropical landscape abutting the structure. Made of thick cement, it sported a soft hue of marshmallow, and was shaped like a long, tall half-tunnel. It was set back mere feet from a low beachfront bulkhead.

The concierge unlocked the door with a flourish. The front door opened directly onto a long vista, drawing your eye past the bathroom and open closet and long desk to the right (with a resident gecko chirping and checking out the new occupants - nice, we inherited a pet!) I smiled. Inside was long and airy, flooded with sunlight, impeccably clean, and sparkling with the kind of freshness you only get in a well-looked-after place. The space was open, with the layout perfectly designed to take advantage of the bay and island views. Past the "bedroom", a large glassed-in sitting area was at the far end. A floor-to-ceiling sliding glass wall framed the view, opening directly onto a small, manicured lawn atop the bulkhead, just large enough for two lounge chairs and a small table.

Seven cement steps led from the lawn down to the sand, framed by coconut palms, frangipani, naupaka, and pandanus. The afternoon sea was at its peak low tide, stretching out across the bay like an unbroken sheet of calm turquoise. Seabirds wove through the air and waded at the water's edge, while guests floated on rubber rafts or paddled kayaks, the occasional sailboarder cutting through the bay further out. Beyond them, a couple of pleasure cruisers slid slowly by, their passengers soaking in the tropical views. Despite the idyllic scene, it didn't feel overcrowded. Maybe fifty people total were scattered along the broad, lengthy beach, all enjoying the surf and sand in peaceful harmony. It was a picture-perfect postcard of tropical paradise.

After we'd explored the well-appointed room and its luxurious, very modern bathroom, decked out with top-notch amenities, we couldn't resist. I swapped into trunks, Malaya slipped into her swimsuit, and without so much as a glance at our bags, we made our way straight for the water. The sun was soft now, casting a golden sheen over everything as we waded out, which at low tide stretched seemingly to Hua Hin. We walked - and walked - until the water was deep enough to rise to our chests.

I paused, looked back toward the shore, and took in the scene. That perfect, poster-worthy vision of a tropical paradise, the kind you see in brochures, all azure waters and palms. It made me grin. Without another thought, I dove into the warm salt water, feeling it rush over me with glee. It had been years since I'd been in any ocean, and I reveled in briny liquid bliss. I'd be taking Charlee back there for sure!

We swam another hundred yards out to a buoy, the water slightly cool yet clear, the kind that makes you forget about everything else.

On the swim back in, I passed through a school of needlefish, their silver bodies flashing like lightning, each darting in perfect synchronicity. Just behind them, a school of cuttlefish, silent, ghostly, were on the hunt. I watched them in silent awe, half-expecting a Sir David Attenborough narration to cut through the air. It felt almost absurd, the perfect slice of nature happening just under the surface.

We rinsed off and got dressed, we tackled the essentials, unpacking the bare minimum, pretending to be motivated to do domestic, then made our way to the beachfront bar, just past the main lobby. Of course we did. We slid onto stools at the outside polished wood rail facing the bay, the sun now beginning to dip lower, painting the sky with the first streaks of pink and gold. We settled in, leisurely depleting their beer and scotch selections, as we caught up, sharing laughs and savoring the view. The world felt like it had slowed.

Several drinks in and not wanting to be boorish newbie tourists who overdid it within their first hour, it was time for dinner.

We strolled north on the beach to see what our dining options were because when you're in a tropical paradise there's always bars and restaurants on the beach. We stumbled upon KB Restaurant and Bar a half mile up. It was one of those large, open-air setups, a little too brightly lit with colored LED lights everywhere, draped and intertwined with a suspicious amount of holiday tinsel hanging down from and around every fixture and the bar. It felt like someone had taken a couple of party stores, thrown them into a blender, and shot the results into the bar from a t-shirt canon.

Normally, this would've been a red flag, the kind that makes you want to spin on your heels and leave immediately. But it was mid-evening on the New Years holiday weekend, and from what we had been told, most of the party crowd had already migrated north to White Sand. That's where the live music and wild revelry were, with bars and clubs jumping and jiving into the early hours of the morning.

As we waited, the sound of the surf crashing just thirty feet away made up the soundtrack to our meal. Calming, rhythmic, the kind of backdrop you only get when you're lucky enough to be on the beach at the right moment.

Dinner done and a few more drinks in us, we headed back to our bungalow, strolling slowly along the moonlit beach. The tide was still low, the sand firm and cool beneath our feet, rippled like corduroy from the receding waves. The occasional bit of driftwood or shell caught the light, but otherwise it was just the soft hush of the ocean, walking quietly in that shared silence that settles in when there's nothing left to plan.

Back at Number 8, we left the beach-side glass doors ajar to let in the sounds of the sea in, that gentle lapping of waves on shore, rhythmic and hypnotic, nature's lullaby. The air was warm with a hint of salt, and the ceiling fan spun just enough to stir it around the room. A surefire way to drift off to sleep. And sure enough, within minutes, we were both out cold, carried off to dreamland to the rhythm of the tide.

I awoke to sunshine pouring through the glass and the loud slap of waves crashing onto the shore. For a moment, I had no idea where I was and where was Charlee? Everything came pouring back into focus as the roar of surf and blinding tropical light cleared up more of the fog in my head. I shuffled over to the sliding glass wall, still bleary, to see what high tide had dragged in.

Not much, as it turned out. Just a lone coconut bobbing aimlessly in the current like it had missed its cue in some island-themed stage play. The gulf waters lapped up upon the third step. The waves weren't large, but with the waterline that close, they amplified into a surprisingly loud soundscape. Less gentle background music, more like a front row at a hippie drum circle.

I watched the coconut get sucked sideways at a ridiculous speed, carried by a surprisingly aggressive riptide surging south. It spun once, like it was waving goodbye, then was gone. Morning swim? No. Not unless I wanted to end up halfway out into the middle of the Gulf of Thailand before breakfast.

The day had started hot and heavy, humid enough to steam the glass if the doors hadn't already been cracked. It wasn't even mid-morning, and I could already feel the promise of a full-body, pore-cleansing sweat coming on. Tropical paradise, yes, but the kind that doesn't let you forget your body's still got work to do. I chugged a body full of water to give my glands something to work with.

Malaya spent the morning working on her laptop, juggling business emails and family calls via Zoom so I parked myself in a lounge chair on the grassy patio determined to match the color of steamed crabs. The surf played against the beach like a metronome. Charlee and I texted back and forth until her ride showed up.

She loved the pics I sent and we promised to catch up as soon as she was safe at her family home. The waves continued to sync to the rhythm of the book I was reading. Bill Bryson's "Dirt: Adventures in Lyon as a Chef in Training". A few hours drifted by in a loop of swimming against a strong current, sunning, and flipping pages. Eventually, I dried off, threw on a shirt, and decided to explore Kai Bae town while Malaya took care of obligations.

⁂

I strolled up and down the main road, taking in the usual island town suspects. Restaurants with laminated menus, bars pumping Bob Marley remixes, weed dispensaries, a handful of dive providers and of course, the ubiquitous 7-Eleven. There were also a few small goods shops crammed with knockoff Crocs, T-shirts, and mosquito repellent. The novelty wore off after about thirty minutes.

Then I spotted something that made me do a double take: a Mexican restaurant called el Barrio Koh Chang. Right there, in that sleepy village clinging to the edge of the Gulf of Thailand. Back home, the words "Mexican restaurant" often translates to "Tex-Mex purgatory." Tortilla chips with all the taste and texture of overcooked pasta made from gap foam, insipid salsa, canned refried frijoles, and lumbering combo platters drenched in orange cheese and pools of oil. And don't forget the margarita slushies in colors not found in nature.

Curious, I looked up the place online and was surprised to find a long list of reviews that rated El Barrio as not only the best restaurant on the island, but it was repeatedly mentioned as authentic Mexican cuisine. That earned it a second glance. I peered past dense tropical foliage and the open-air patio. Inside, it was beautifully designed. A warm, jungle-like atmosphere with terracotta pots, what looked like genuine Talavera tile, and wall-covering hand-painted murals of Día de los Muertos scenes that actually seemed authentic rather than kitsch. I was intrigued.

Sitting at the bar, piles of paperwork spread out in front of him, making phone calls and writing checks, was the owner. He had that multitasking, mildly intense energy of someone keeping a thriving small business running in a place where supplies come by boat, elephant, or divine intervention.

I grabbed a seat on the corner, out of his way, and glanced through the menu with cautious optimism, expecting a list of usual suspects with exotic-sounding names slapped onto tourist-friendly plates. But this wasn't that. The menu was lifted straight from the kitchens of Oaxaca, Puebla, and Jalisco. Ceviche made fresh, house-made tortillas, champiqueso, tacos al pastor, pescado a la diabla; real-deal Mexican food, the kind you don't find without someone's abuela in the kitchen. I was more than intrigued. I was hopeful.

I ordered the ceviche, chips and salsa, a pour of añejo tequila and an ice-cold Tecaté.

The fellow at the bar wrapped up his invoices and supplier calls, tucked away his papers and checkbook, and walked over. He asked how everything was and where I was from, an opener that was more curious than canned.

His name was Julien, and he was from Mexico. He'd learned to cook at his mother's side - mi madre, siempre - then honed his skills in professional kitchens across Mexico before heading to France to stage and cook.

I told him about my travels through Mexico over the years - my admiration for its layered culture, bold art, and food that speaks in paragraphs, not just flavors. We shared a few laughs about travel stories that only seasoned wanderers of the width and breadth in Mexico, and late-night street taco stands could appreciate.

Soon we were deep into conversation, riffing like two culinary nerds over mole sauces, regional ceviche variations, Pacific coast seafood, the magic of a perfect street taco using blue maize, and the virtues of really good tequila and mezcal. It was the kind of talk that makes you forget where you are until you look up, realize you're in a Mexican jungle restaurant on an island surrounded by the Gulf of Thailand, and remember how weirdly wonderful the world can be.

My food arrived, and with my first bite I knew: el Barrio was the real deal. No shortcuts, no lazy approximations - just honest, carefully crafted food that can only come from someone who knows what it's supposed to taste like.

The ceviche was fantastic, served cold, which on a hot, humid day is one of the most refreshing things you can eat. The crisp texture and clean flavors of freshly caught white fish and shrimp shone through, balanced with a zip of onion and just enough lime to let the citric acid do its alchemy. A splashy mix of tomato and creamy avocado, finished with a tight blast of cilantro. It was, simply, a perfect ceviche.

Fried tortilla chips came with four house-made salsas, each one a small triumph: a smoky chipotle, a fiery roasted tomato and red pepper, a tart tomatillo green, and a creamy queso dip. Spot-on authentic, all of them. Thank Quetzalcoatl! This was food I'd been missing though didn't realize it until those sense memories came flooding back - transporting me across oceans to coastal villages and dark cantinas.

There were details there. Attention to ingredients, preparation, and presentation, but more than that, there was soul. You don't get those kinds of flavor profiles unless you've lived the food, unless it's tattooed into your sense memory from childhood.

Julien was fun, gregarious, and full of island stories. Over the course of our chat, I learned about the local scene and the history of his restaurant. I ordered another tequila. Julien, being the kind of host who knows how to make people feel like regulars on their first visit, poured me a shot of his passion-fruit infused tequila on the house. It was bright, smooth, and sneakily strong.

If el Barrio was in my neighborhood? I'd be a regular!

Texting Charlee with my review and pictures, she was excited to go back with me. She'd never been to Koh Chang or tried Mexican cuisine. I was her recon.

I boogied back to the bungalow to report my discovery. Malaya reminded me of her less-than-enthusiastic love of Mexican cuisine, even after I explained that el Barrio was the real deal, a genuine gem, regardless of geography. She smiled dubiously and returned to her work, though not before we wandered over to the hotel desk to book a snorkeling trip to the smaller islands in the National Park for January 1st.

A quiet night was on order. We grabbed pizza because it was easy, then picked up some extra munchies and a bottle of SangSom Thai rum from a local curio shop that somehow managed to get everything just right. We lingered at the beach bar until closing, then made our way back to the bungalow for a swim.

The night sky was alive. Stars blazed across the endless expanse above as I floated on my back in the warm water. A ghostly bioluminescence gleam flickered from millions of tiny dinoflagellates along the surf line, as if they were trying to outshine the blazing stars above them. Far out in the gulf, a few blazing lights marked the position of squid boats working the night shift for tomorrow's market. It was quiet - just the soft, barely-there rippling of the surf as I drifted with the gentle current before I hit the shore; Charlee and I texted our deep love and sweet dreams to each other for the night. I headed to bed as that same soft surf sound dispatched me into dreamland.

New Year's Eve Day dawned. Malaya and I settled into a relaxed morning, deciding a hearty breakfast was in order. We walked the eight minutes into town on a quiet, balmy morning, strolling through the small streets and alleys, only to find a ghost town. We forgot it was New Year's Eve day. Hey - gimme a break - I was on vacation within a vacation! Plus, I had other things on my mind.

Places that would normally be bustling with breakfast crowds were deserted, shuttered, as families took the morning off to unwind before the inevitable onslaught of the evening's holiday-fueled festivities. Eventually, we stumbled upon a small, funky resort at the tip of a tranquil inlet. We indulged in their buffet breakfast, which hit the spot perfectly: fried chicken, eggs, wok-fried local fish, fresh fruit, pastries, salad, noodles, jok, juice, and coffee.

While we were digging in, I struck up a conversation with a traveler who was wearing a travel-worn New Zealand silver fern t-shirt. He was from Austria and had been solo traveling around Asia for the past year. One of the perks of visiting remote places is that the people you meet are usually fellow travelers, not tourists. They've done their homework and, like you, are seeking out places away from the crowds and the tourist traps. Zachary was a seasoned traveler, having roamed across the globe, so it was interesting to hear his impressions of Koh Chang.

"It's nice to see this place now, before it gets overrun," he said, sounding very much like Arnold S.

Travel + Leisure had recently anointed Koh Chang the number two tropical island paradise vacation spot in the world - the Maldives taking first place - effectively dropping KC onto the global tourist map with a glittering pin. As Oscar Wilde wrote, "Yet each man kills the thing he loves". There goes the neighborhood. Then again, I'm sure the island locals say that to themselves every time a vanload of tourists tumbles out onto the street.

Breakfast complete, Malaya and I set off along the sandy paths behind the resort, crossing a small, tastefully adorned Japanese-style arched bridge that spanned the narrow inlet. It was picturesque. Vibrantly painted family fishing boats lined the banks, moored with taut lines that hinted at rest rather than readiness. No one was heading out; not with New Year's Eve celebrations looming. The air was still; the only sounds coming from the exotic birds calling out from the trees, and the faint swish of distant surf.

New Year's Eve: Showered and dressed for an evening out, we were back at the beachfront bar for sunset. A few beers and a bourbon later, we bore witness to the sun as it dipped below the island-studded horizon. It was clocking out to avoid the coming madness.

We headed into Kai Bae, now throbbing with life - locals celebrating the holiday while travelers pretended not to be tourists, all elbowing through the same narrow two-lane main drag. Scooters wove through traffic while pedestrians mistakenly clogged the road, tuk tuks lit up with LED lights as the punch of subwoofers added to the cacophony with theatrical urgency. Songtaews loaded with partiers rolled by like mobile karaoke booths. The whole scene had the barely controlled madness of a street fair thrown together by someone with a head injury, a love of neon and a booming hip hop soundtrack.

Every bar, shop, and restaurant had flung its doors wide open, music blaring, glowing with light, trying to outdo each other in some unspoken arms race of festivity. It was as if the entire village had been plugged into a mega-generator and told to "vibe."

Malaya, who is Filipino and adores SE Asian seafood dishes, had gotten a recommendation for a Thai place called Bâan KaiBae Seafood - family-owned, of course, though to be fair, every square meter of Kai Bae was family owned. We found it quickly, the one with a boat out front absolutely packed to the gunwales with ice and today's catch. The fish and seafood laid out like runway models at a scaled and shelled casting call. We were ushered to the first available table and handed menus.

Up front, manning the flat-top, woks and pans the size of hubcaps, was a one-woman war zone. Grandma - barefoot, planted squarely on the cement floor like a general defending her stronghold was at the helm. She didn't so much cook as command, issuing orders in rapid Thai while flipping fish, frying and woking delectables from the boat, and somehow keeping mental tabs on sizzling pans, all while dancing back and forth to the flat top which was giving off heat waves like a mirage in the Sahara.

The family operation hummed around her like a beehive - scurrying children, grandchildren, nieces and nephews and servers running food, taking orders, and absorbing her withering glances if anyone dared move too slowly. She looked like she hadn't stepped away from her post since the Clinton administration. The woman ran that restaurant with the tactical precision of a field marshal and the dead-eyed intensity of someone who's seen things. Many things.

We ordered like people who hadn't eaten in a week. The logic was sound: the bungalow had a refrigerator, and leftovers are future victories. So, with full confidence and only a whisper of shame, we deep dove full bore on the menu.

There were prawns the size of a toddler's forearm, genetically destined for the flat-top, their long antennae curling like confused punctuation. A whole red snapper got the nod for the fryer, along with clams and scallops headed for a wok baptism in chili and holy basil. We added fried spring rolls and a heap of stir-fried morning glory - because what's a New Year's meal without swamp greens? Garlic-fried chicken something-or-other made the cut, mostly because it smelled amazing at the next table, and a mountain of fried rice came along for ballast.

Our server, a polite teenage boy with the demeanor of someone used to Western over-ordering, blinked as the list grew longer. He nodded, scribbled, and took the bloated ticket to Grandma. She read it, squinted toward our table like she was trying to decide if we were serious, stupid or just cruel, then muttered something sharp - probably along the lines of "amateurs" - and cranked the flames under the woks. The prawns hit the flat-top with a hiss. She shook her head the whole time, but her hands and feet never stopped moving.

Over the next two hours, we annihilated every dish like we were on an epic food-eating contest. I noticed Grandma, from time to time, peeking at us with what could only be described as a look of begrudging admiration. It's not every day someone tackles a menu like a locust swarm on a rampage.

As the last bite of fried rice disappeared and I leaned back, stuffed to the brim, Malaya got a spark of inspiration. "I want to meet her," she declared, pointing at Grandma, who was finally sitting down at a table next to her cooking station, fanning herself like she'd just won the Iron Chef battle against Morimoto.

Malaya approached with grace, admiration and warmth knowing full well she was about to steal a moment offering thanks for the meal. Grandma's eyes, which had been as blank as a monk in deep meditation cracked into her biggest smile. She scooted over on the bench, patted the seat, and motioned for Malaya to join her like they'd been old pals all along. There it was: the shift from kitchen general to family matriarch. The mood lifted, and I was handed Malaya's phone to capture the moment held within that meet-and-greet moment.

I snapped a few photos as they exchanged jokes in broken Tagalog and English, both of them laughing - though I suspected Grandma's laughter was 80% relief from a grueling night of cooking and 20% the joy of people who were so happily full they couldn't stand up.

Photo duties done, I wandered outside, digesting both the food and the local vibe, which was a strange mix of people milling about in festive New Year's gear while tuk tuks revved past like they were auditioning for the Fast & Furious franchise.

Walking back towards the hotel we passed a non-touristy open-front bar with rock-n-roll pouring into the street as booze poured into shot glasses. While the Jol Muy Bar had a blender, that was a place for shooting shots not sipping daiquiris. It reminded me of the Reggae Bar up in Chiang Rai but with a grittier vibe, and as there was a pool table in back, we decided to shoot a game and enjoy the party vibe.

Sometimes things don't turn out as intended. One game turned into five with beers and shots of whiskey accompanied each round. The owner and his wife played doubles with us, boys against girls, and though I'm not a very good player, sometimes the angles lined up and we beat the ladies three out of five. It was 11:15pm and I wanted to see the new year turn its page on the beach but Malaya wanted to stay and explore the town in party mode so we split up.

I called Charlee and we had lovely video chat time bawling our eyes out to each other over our screens - the pain of separation was lurid and desperate even though we'd promised each other we'd be mature about it all and wait until we were together again before losing it all over again. I got to see her mom and dad who waved graciously and then quickly bowed out, and Yāy popped in, looked at me on Charlee's screen, looked back at Charlee, then started firing off what I could only assume were "what the hell is going on here?" questions. We kissed our cameras goodnight, wishing each other a truly happy new year. When I hung up I'd never felt so alone.

⁂

The Thai have a fondness for getting a buzz on, and in Thailand, there are infinite ways to accomplish that. Spiritually, chemically, organically - there's no shortage of paths to altered states. With that in mind, there's a particular kind of fungi available if you're patient enough and ask the right questions of the right people.

I learned those nuances in Bangkok. I had ended up alone at a small, unassuming street-cart sidewalk table for dinner. I found myself within a party of five, as two couples - plates in hand - looked for somewhere to sit. The tables were packed, so I invited them to join me. I don't remember how we ended up talking about magic mushrooms but there we were, scarfing down plates of deliciousness, deep in a conversation about fungi. I was schooled in the art of finding what I was after by asking the right questions in the right way.

Once you know where to go, how to behave, and, most importantly, how to ask, let's just say, if you're looking for *it*, you can get *that*. In my case, it was Psilocybin - magic mushrooms to micro-dose, clear out some mental cobwebs, and have a little fun as the year flipped over. The conversation raised a few eyebrows when I mentioned my monk days, but once I explained my prior life in San Francisco, they all nodded knowingly and filled in the gaps. A little shock was there, sure, but also some understanding. They pointed me in the right direction.

What seemed, upon initial inspection to have the same visual, aromatic, flavor and texture as the shrooms back home, I thought to myself, sure - I'll have some trippy fun as the year turns over and giggle for a few hours. I know what these are ... and here we go. At least that's what I thought. Oops! One little gram chewed up and washed down with an iced beer. Thirty minutes later; BLAMMO. I felt like I was in an existential wrestling match with the universe.

So! Completely! Different! Wave after wave, ebb and flow, hour after hour of intensity, like a roller coaster in the dark, where the earth is constantly shifting beneath you. One moment, you think you're on the descent to normalcy, the next you're getting catapulted back upstairs towards some height of feeling and insight, only to plummet back down into the void. Friendly ghosts, dragons, and clowns took turns riding shotgun on my journey, their presence flickering in and out like some bizarre R. Crumb comic come to life. Every time I thought the ride was over, I was pulled into deeper, more alien territory, somewhere unknown, but welcoming, as if the mushrooms were opening doors to realms I had never even considered.

And with each trip through the carnival ride, I realized: this was not the same mushroom I had known before. The old acquaintance I thought I'd recognized from the clues, was, in fact, an entirely different beast. Familiar elements -

the spiraling, the intensity, the flickering lights and fits of giggles - but magnified, more potent, and with a depth that felt almost ancient. It was a lot to handle, like being told the truth about something you thought you understood, only to discover that the truth itself had no end.

There was nothing gentle about it like I'd expected. This wasn't nostalgia or a simple trip. It was something else entirely, a force that moved through me with the kind of purpose that made the world feel smaller, yet infinitely bigger, all at once.

It was New Year's Eve, and I was planted in the wrap-around rattan chair on the grassy patio outside the bungalow, sipping Thai rum, riding a time-warping fungal wave on that dark Kai Bae beach. It was 11:30PM, December 31st, 2024. The beach in front of me was empty, peaceful, suspended in that quiet, anticipatory breath before the world turned over.

I slipped in my wireless earbuds. Miraculous little things, considering that thirty years ago this kind of untethered technology would've seemed like witchcraft. I queued up the Grateful Dead's 1982 New Year's Eve show from the Oakland Auditorium. No hesitation. Off came the clothes. I padded naked down the sand, still warm from the day's sun, and waded out into the Gulf of Thailand.

Skinny-dipping in that velvet bath of saltwater, under an inky tropical sky, I felt like a blinking, half-lucid constellation myself. Small, suspended, somehow both ancient and brand new. At ten to midnight, fireworks began popping off lazily from both ends of the bay. Someone somewhere was lighting fuses with a beer in hand. Within minutes, the amateur sparks gave way to full-scale industrial artillery, blasting enormous fire-blooms across the night, flooding my vision from north to south.

Jerry leaned into his solo on "Midnight Hour", Wilson Pickett's anthem pulsing through my head, while streaks of color exploded in every direction. I howled with laughter, alone and elated, spinning in place like some salt-encrusted lunatic conducting a private ceremony to say farewell to a strange, magnificent, bewildering year.

Goodbye, 2024. You didn't go quietly - but damn if you didn't leave a mark. The highs were epic, the lows devastating.

It was early as I gazed out the glass wall of our room, the dawning of the new year revealed a cloud-covered sky and choppy, white-capped seas. This was less-than-ideal given that we were going snorkeling. Not the relaxing, glassy-sea serene day we'd had in mind. We had booked an all-day snorkeling tour with Mr.

Khai's dive operation through our hotel, which would depart for the southern islands within the maritime National Park from Bang Bao Pier, on the southwestern coast of Koh Chang. The plan on paper was to cruise a two-and-a-half-hour boat ride down to islands and reefs. Now it would be two-and-a-half hours of churning through chop, spray splashing over every crest. Absolutely nothing about that sounded appealing.

It was clear that the universe had a sick sense of humor. The kind of humor that insists you start your new year drenched in sea spray while your stomach has a quiet but firm conversation with gravity.

The tour company, of course, made sure we felt the full brunt of this adventure. They sent an open-air Toyota pickup truck with bench seats along the sides in the bed to pick us up at the hotel. The truck was packed to capacity with a mix of hungover and bedraggled souls. It was 8:00am and we were on the road south, heading toward the dock. From talking to some locals about our plan, I knew the road to the pier was hillier and twistier than the one we'd taken to Kai Bae.

A relentless wind blew through everything, amplifying the remnants of last night's shrooms and rum shots. It was shaping up to be a day to remember.

Bang Bao was the quintessential isolated fishing port, the kind of place you picture when you imagine life on the water. Boats of all shapes and sizes, from the sleek charter yachts to humble net-casters to work-worn commercial vessels, were moored side by side, each one showcasing their unique story of saltwater and toil. Nets draped over rails, like yesterday's laundry, swayed in the wind. Everything smelled of brine, seaweed, and the ocean's bounty.

The village, built on stilts over the water, was the kind of place you'd find on a blog. The market stalls promising fresh fish, fruits, veggies and trinkets, looked as if they'd been plucked right out of a picture book. The sort of place where everyone knew each other, where a shared community rhythm set the pace. But, of course, we arrived on New Year's Day, forgetting that even fishing villages have the decency to pause when the year turns. Most of the vendors were either home nursing hangovers, still drinking or simply enjoying the holiday with some well-earned time off. Yep - 90% of the stalls were empty and shuttered tight.

Still, the docks had their charm as salty air carried the music of ocean, the soundtrack to the lengthy stroll to get to our vessel. We were tantalized by the promise of the Islands ahead. Koh Yak, Koh Loan, Koh Mapring - each one a tiny islet with reefs to explore. But the real oddball on the itinerary was Hat San Jao, a beach known for its peculiar shrine, adorned with hundreds of ceramic chicken statues. That was something I couldn't pass up. I don't know why but it seemed kooky enough to warrant time. Maybe it was the remnants of too many weird off-beat encounters that had made me appreciate the quirky side of the world, but I was already picturing the photos I'd take. If there's one thing I knew, it was that oddities like that don't show up every day.

Reaching our boat at the far end of Bang Bao Pier, it felt farther than it was. A slow, quiet walk along the cement spine that stretched a kilometer and a half into the harbor. The usual clatter and energy of the market was nowhere to be found. It felt like the whole place had exhaled, as if the celebrations of the night before were still echoing faintly in the rafters.

There was one woman tending her stall, sweeping lazily and rearranging a few things with the half-hearted rhythm of someone easing into the day. I asked her if it was always this sleepy. She gave a small laugh, shaking her head. "Holiday," she said simply. "Still sleeping. Maybe still drinking." Her smile was thin, not unkind, but with weariness you sometimes see in people who keep things running while the rest of the world continues to make bad decisions.

She brightened as she encouraged us to come back after the boat trip, gesturing toward her shop filled with all the usual offerings - elephant pants, knock off brand sunglasses, keychains, kitschy t-shirts, fat-bellied Buddhas with a waving arm, and beach gear. It was all there, waiting for someone with a little leftover celebration money and nowhere else to be. I nodded and said we'd return after snorkeling. I wasn't sure if we actually would. I meant it in the way you sometimes mean things when you want to leave goodwill behind, even if your feet are already moving on.

She followed my gaze out to the sea. Even inside the shelter of the harbor, the water was restless. She gave a small frown and then said softly, "Be careful." It wasn't dramatic, just a simple gesture - one human passing concern to another. I thanked her, and for a moment I felt the tug of quiet obligation. Maybe we would stop by on the way back after all.

At the end of that long pier there was a stubby classic red and white lighthouse that wouldn't be out of place on a rugged New England coastline. It was as picturesque as you could want - straight out of central casting for "Seaside Village at Dawn." Requisite photos taken, we walked back fifty yards or so to where many of the dive and snorkeling boats were moored, most of them tied two-deep like they were spooning.

With the help of a sunbaked swarthy-looking crew (though all of them to a man had that Thai warmth with smiles plastered to their faces), we climbed onto the first boat, passed through, then onto the second.

Ours was a large wooden vessel, the main deck outfitted with booth-style benches facing each other, and a main cabin set squarely in the middle. Down the center ran a tall, narrow table - useful for lunch or communal seasickness, depending on the day. Today might very well be the latter.

Up a narrow ladder at the bow, the upper deck had reclined wooden seats facing forward, shaded by a circus-tent awning that looked like it had been through a few monsoons but still did the trick. It was a wacky boat - tall, with curved high-rising chines and every inch slathered in red, gold and green paint as if someone had handed the job to a candy-cane enthusiast on Adderall. Overhead rails on the main deck were strung with a hundred orange life vests, swaying slightly as the boat rocked in the swell, a not-so-subtle reminder of why they were there.

The boat was two-thirds full, with seventy passengers and ten crewmen aboard. As we made our way past the breakwater jetty, we immediately felt rougher seas and knew it was going to be a long ride. Thank goodness I don't get seasick! As we entered deeper water it got rougher with the white-capped crests continuously spraying over the gunwales.

The clouds blew through, giving way to a sunny day. Two and a half hours of stomach-churning nautical travel later, we arrived at the small islands on the east side of Koh Rung. We had to stop in and pay the National Park fee and though I wanted to get in the water, sitting in the lee of the island allowed for some of the amusement park perpetual motion to die down a bit.

Our first snorkeling stop was in the lee of Koh Yak, which is listed as an island but that's being more than charitable. It was more of a rocky outcrop, rising fifteen feet above sea level, about the size of a convenience store parking lot.

Fins, mask, and snorkel on, I made a not-very-graceful descent down the ladder and slipped into the water. I swam toward the rocks only to find the choppy sea turning snorkeling into more of a washing machine rinse cycle. The sea kept flooding my tube as I was tossed about like laundry. I flippered back to the boat to grab a life vest! I was floating and didn't have to think about anything except keeping my face down and letting the ocean bounce me about like a cork.

A few kicks got me up near the rocks where the surge calmed slightly, and when I looked down, I was suddenly hungry. The ledges below were covered in black sea urchins. Thousands of them. Uni. All I needed was a knife and some sake, and I'd have had myself a five-star sashimi lunch. But, alas, National Park. No harvesting allowed.

There were a few colorful fish darting around, though "schools" might be too generous. More like post-class math club groups, five or ten at most. A couple of black and green angelfish hovered about, but this wasn't exactly a reef teeming with life. Still, I floated and watched what was there until I noticed most of the other passengers heading back to the boat. On to the next "island."

Koh Loan was a bit larger, with a crescent arc that cradled us against the chop. It offered more protection, and better snorkeling. We had a little longer here, so I swam back and forth, between both horns, checking out the marine life along the way. It was livelier - more species, more movement. Schools of little cleaner wrasse flitted about, happily nibbling at any exposed skin they could find. These are the same fish used in those foot spa tanks, where tourists dangle their feet and let the fish exfoliate all the dead skin off - an all-organic pedicure.

On big reefs, cleaner wrasse set up what are essentially underwater spas - "cleaning stations" where larger species like grouper, turtles, rays and sharks come to get a good scrub. There's an observable détente in place: you clean me up, polish between my teeth, get the parasites off my gills - and I won't eat you. A kind of mutual respect forged in the name of hygiene.

I was out for quite a while cruising back and forth along the rock face of Koh Loan enjoying the trigger fish, banner fish, clown fish, cleaner wrasse, a giant grouper, an orange grouper, a porcupine fish, a small moray eel hanging in a crevice eyeing me back, anemones and starfish covered the floor and rock faces. Though it was still choppy water, I was much happier with the fauna, so the time passed without me paying too much attention to how long I was swimming about. I hadn't come across any other swimmers for a while, so I poked my head up to see where everyone was. But when I looked at where the boat had been .... *It was gone*. I watched as the ass-end sailed away. I up-righted myself to tread water, ripped the mask down, frantically waived my arm and began shouting as I saw smoke billowing out the stack up top.

After a few minutes of me treading water and waving, I began to wonder about climbing up the rocks to live as a castaway, except there wasn't even a coconut palm on the island. Fish by hand? Learn to be a savage? It rained enough that I could find a natural rock cistern and Buddha knows I love sushi. As my monkey mind rapidly spun through my options, the boat began to pivot on its axis and slowly reverse its course backwards, closer to Koh Rung but still within the lee side of the island. I realized they were repositioning the craft to take over a mooring buoy a few spots closer to the island. I took some deep breaths and slowly closed my eyes, slipping into meditation mode as I bobbed and calmed myself down.

After I got my mask and snorkel back in place I swam over to the boat, still a little shaken. When I got to the ladder I looked up to see a dark broad smiling face and crazy unkempt hair of one of the crew beaming down at me, extending his hand to help me aboard. As I gained the deck and took off the flippers, he laughed and said, "you know man - we could see your vest and fins and we haven't lost a paying customer in over a week!" Very fucking funny! I took off the rest of the gear and sat on a bench in the sun and closed my eyes, letting the rays bake the salt into my skin. I was getting my heart-rate back to normal when he reappeared with a small bottle of rum. I took a long swig, handed it back and said thanks as he retreated, snickering, still finding his joke funny. I sat in the sunniest place I could find, letting the rays and the rum do their job.

Koh Mapring was the last little outcrop on the day's snorkeling circuit before we'd tie up to a floating pontoon dock and head ashore to explore the mysterious chicken shrine. Again, calling Koh Mapring an "island" felt generous - it was really more of a lumpy pile of rocks with aspirations. But because of its proximity to the much larger Koh Rong, the swim was short, the water was calm, and the fish population was, at least in relative terms, abundant. It was the easiest swim of the day and made for a pleasant snorkel.

I drifted over small groups of reef fish darting around, colorful and curious. Still, I kept hoping for a bit more magic - maybe a curious cuttlefish flashing its ever-shifting alien camouflage, or a shy reef shark gliding past like a shadow. Even a mellow turtle would've done. Turtles make excellent snorkeling companions when they're feeling social, swimming slowly and allowing you to track beside them like a loyal sidekick. But no dice. Just the usual suspects I'd seen at the previous stops. After a while, I gave up the search, kicked gently to shore, and plopped down on the sand. I lay there, head cocked sideways trying to drain the sea from my ears, sun warming my back, trying to recalibrate my expectations. It had been a good day but not the kind of ocean communion I've felt in the Cook Islands or around St. John in the Caribbean, where the reef wraps around you like a warm embrace and the fish seem to accept you as one of their own. This was not that. Still, the rum helped.

The beach at Koh Rong was easy on the eyes: soft sand, filtered sunlight, a sense of hush. The so-called chicken shrine, however, was... well, let's call it modest. A squat little structure about the size of a backyard playhouse had been recently given a thick coat of paint - the only thing holding its cracked plaster together. A miniature wrought-iron fence that was both battered and rusted protected an "interesting" outdoor display of ceramic poultry. Maybe a hundred small statues of chickens clustered inside and on the stoop, as if waiting for instructions. And that was it. I tilted my head, gave it a once-over, and thought: huh?!

The boat ride back was uneventful in the way that only a drawn-out, sunbaked slog across wind-chopped seas can be. We set sail around 2:00PM, embarking on what was billed as a two-hour tour, which felt oddly familiar and vaguely ominous. After a day of middling snorkeling and an offbeat visit to a shrine of ceramic chickens, I was more than ready to call it a day.

The seas were still stirred up and white-capped, and the boat pitched and rolled like carnival ride. Every crest brought a fresh spray and the dull ache of anticipation - of land, of stillness. It wasn't rough enough to be dramatic, just irritating enough to make you count the minutes to mooring up. Time bent and stretched in a way that only happens when your swimsuit is clammy, your stomach is unsettled, and there's nowhere to go but wherever that thing is taking you.

By the time the pier crept back into view I had aged. Not much, but just enough to need a cold drink, and a long walk far away from anything that floats.

As we docked, I was looking forward to a hot shower and the reassuring steadiness of land underfoot. We strolled back along the long pier through the stilt village, and though a few more vendors had opened up since morning, it still wasn't bustling. We passed by the woman's stall only to find it shuttered and silent - she'd packed up and gone home for the day. Maybe she hadn't expected us to survive.

Malaya and I wanted to stay at Bang Bao for dinner at one of the seafood restaurants on the dock as they were all supposed to be excellent, but we had to make our way back up the road to meet our songtaew for the return ride to Kai Bae Grand View. So, fresh fish and sunset beers on stilts would have to wait for another trip.

Our ride was parked a kilometer up the road past the end of the pier. We climbed in the back with the other sun-dazed passengers and started the winding journey back, weaving through the outskirts of the village. After a ten-minute drive we pulled into a small roadside resort to let some folks off. A few cars were parked in the lot, but everyone - guests, staff, even the driver - were looking up into the trees across the road.

There, on the crossbar of a power pole, a trio of silvered langur monkeys lounged like furry electricians on a coffee break. They were watching the people who were watching them, and the whole thing felt quietly surreal. A little roadside mutual admiration society. We only stayed for a few minutes before rolling on, but it was worth the pause to see those mellow-eyed creatures just hanging out, as if that was a scheduled performance.

But as we pulled back onto the road, disaster! We tucked in behind a very slow and extremely smelly trash truck. It reeked of diesel, summer heated outhouse and rotting fish - an olfactory cocktail that hit us like a brick wall. The road twisted and climbed through the hills, with blind turns every hundred feet or so, making it impossible to pass.

There we were: trapped in a diesel-scented wake of Hades-inspired decay, gagging and gasping with every breath. The truck belched fumes. Our driver stayed close behind, inching forward at every curve hoping a view would open up with enough distance and freedom to pass the disgusting leader, now trailing a long line of vehicles behind.

After what felt like an eternity in a mobile version of the underworld, the garbage truck finally pulled to the side, the long, patient line of cars that had stacked up behind us all darting past him, everyone's face, green with nausea. I must say that I might be considerate of the driver. And just in time, too, as my ability to suppress my gag reflex was hanging by a very thin thread.

Finally able to breathe again, we made it back to our place and took long, hot showers - not just to get the salt crust off, but to try and erase the stench of that trash truck, which may still hold the title for foulest thing I've ever smelled.

Clean and refreshed, with a hearty swig of rum (I actually gargled the stuff) to help wash away the lingering memory, we headed into town. Passing the beach bar, we figured it would be a waste of perfectly good steps not to pop in for a few libations and recap the day.

We agreed that on a calm, hot day with glassy seas and tranquil dive spots, the whole experience would've hit differently. But while you can schedule a dive, you can't schedule the weather. Such is life.

We turned south along the beach, strolling through the mid-tide's warm shallows, because just past the end of the property was an open-air bar-restaurant called Porns. (Yes, *really*.) Malaya had spotted it during one of her swims and wanted to check it out, so off we went to see what the place was all about.

It was the kind of beach spot you hope to stumble across: thick, worn teak poles and floorboards, a thatched roof that had entire communities of geckos eating the bugs that would otherwise be swarming, and a breezy, nothing-to-prove *very* rustic charm. We grabbed a corner table right at the edge, where wavelets lapped at the rock bulkhead below our feet.

Fried chicken, fried spring rolls, and a few seared giant prawns showed up alongside a couple of cold beers. Our late lunch was nothing short of fantastic. There's something about the way the Thais fry chicken that's just magic - no thick batter, no grease bomb, just a whisper of crisp, crackly skin and perfect seasoning. It puts every fast-food chain you've ever known to absolute shame.

But something was amiss. I hadn't heard back from Charlee since last night. Hungover? She wasn't much of a drinker, so I doubted that. Probably just busy with family grilling her over her farang entanglement. Still. Something wasn't feeling right.

We got back from Porns and headed towards town, but not before a stop at the beach bar. After a second round, I convinced Malaya to join me for dinner at el Barrio. Even though she doesn't prefer Mexican food, my rave reviews encouraged her to relent, come meet Julien and enjoy some ceviche and tequila. We wrapped things up and headed into town and as soon as she walked into el Barrio and saw the murals and real Mexican terracotta plates and bowls, and Talavera tiles she was impressed. The place was packed, every table full of partying vacationers oohing and aahing over the food and margaritas. Julian gave me an enthusiastic welcome back and told us to wait at the bar until a table opened up.

Malaya is fluent in Spanish, so she and Julien started chatting away, swapping stories as she shared pics on her phone from her recent trip to Mexico City. I got me some satisfaction! She admitted el Barrio's was true to Mexico. The food and drink were great, as she ate more of my ceviche. I had one of her tacos and it was fantastic. The fresh tortillas and salsas also made her think twice, which made the effort worthwhile. Wrapping up, Julien gave us more shots of his fruit-infused tequila as we said fond farewells. Someday when I go back to Koh Chang, I will definitely be heading back to el Barrio.

We strolled along the main street for a little while then headed back to the pool bar. As is often the case, the ambiance was different with a different clientele than on New Years Eve. We still had fun with the owner and his wife but there were some other patrons who were very loud and obnoxious that were driving us both crazy. After only two games we decided to call it a night and bid our farewells, then headed back to our bungalow for our last night on Koh Chang.

More silence from Charlee. I reached out to Jaks. They must have been on a family outing.

The return trip from Koh Chang wasn't nearly as quick as our flight down. Malaya had been fast and efficient arranging the getaway - booked us a smooth 45-minute hop south on Bangkok Airways. But coming back? Different story. The post New Year crush had emptied the skies of return seats, so we booked a van through Koh Chang Transport. Door-to-door, they said. What they didn't say was: nine hours of slow-motion endurance, from beach-side bliss back to city blitz, ending at the Courtyard Marriott on Sukhumvit Soi 21.

You'd think a nine-hour van ride would be the choice of the desperate or uninformed. But no - it was the only option, and we weren't alone. The van was packed. Every seat was filled including the one up front normally reserved for an extra employee with GPS. Couples, solo travelers, we were all headed to different corners of the city but yoked to a shared itinerary: drop-offs dictated by luck and geography.

If it had been just us? Six hours.

That would have been easy.

But it wasn't just us.

And of course, we were last.

Still, the journey wasn't without its merits. As the van rolled north from Trat, past sleepy villages, the landscape began to shift. The air grew earthier. Tourists thinned out. And through the van windows, Thailand revealed something quieter, older, more lived in, more honest.

We drove through Chanthaburi, with its endless fruit orchards, big open barns and roadside tables sagging under piles of durian, rambutan, longkong, and mangosteen. Entire families worked the land as barefoot kids chased chickens, workers packed boxes for distribution, grandmothers squatting in the shade of broad banana leaves while fathers sharpened machetes under bamboo lean-tos. Life wasn't social media ready there. It was simply lived with the daily pace of agriculture.

Then came Chon Buri: rice paddies, coconut groves, banana plantations, everything growing, growing, growing. Green stretched on with the light of insistence - bright, unbothered, unrepentant or pretentious. This was Thailand stripped of gloss. No welcome drinks. No monks posing reluctantly for reels. No foreigners trying to out-Zen each other in elephant pants. Just people. Farming. Living. Minding their water buffalo. Waiting for the rains. It was the kind of beauty that doesn't care if you notice.

We passed into Samut Prakan next, approaching Bangkok's orbit but still anchored to the old ways: canals crisscrossing, stilted wooden homes, pandan thickets swallowing fence lines, temple spires rising gently behind banana tree clusters. Fishermen mended nets roadside, same as it ever was. And I found myself leaning into the window more and more, craving the ordinariness of it all. I wasn't ready to be plugged back in.

I was also profoundly relieved no one in the van had plans to be dropped in Pattaya. That town of neon sins and crumpled expats is a different kind of real - a sweaty desperate dream where the music never stops, the beer is always cheap, and pre-paid heartbreak is part of the package. It's a place for losing track of time - and sometimes yourself.

CHAPTER 16. SILENCE. THE LOUDEST SCREAM

Finally! I got hold of Jakkapan. By then, I was frantic - pacing, sweating, muttering to myself like a man on the edge. My phone was hot and slippery in my hand from all the unanswered texts, the redial loop of desperation. Charlee had gone dark. No replies, no emojis, no voice notes. It was like she'd vanished from the earth.

Jakkapan was more than a connection. He was kin. Her cousin, yes, but also my unlikely brother in arms. We'd bonded instantly, the way men sometimes do when love is involved, and you can both see it. He knew I adored her. He respected it. Encouraged it. He did the same for her.

That night I cooked for her - lasagna from scratch, handmade pasta, garlic bread that could make you believe in faith –Jaks had dropped everything to help. Lent me knives, his gear, hooked me up with his supplier, and came over to taste the final product. He'd offered to bankroll a restaurant if I'd let him. "Thong Lo," he said, "hip, perfect for a farang with talent." I told him no. I was too old for that grind, but I thanked him with a hug - one he returned like I was family.

So when Charlee disappeared - just vanished - I turned to him. Hammered him with calls. Ten. Twelve. Fifteen. Each one sinking deeper into dread.

When he finally picked up, I didn't say hello. I didn't breathe.

"What's going on, Jaks?" My voice was cracked glass. "Where's Charlee? Why the hell won't she text me back? Why haven't you?"

Silence.

"Is she okay?"

More silence.

Then - slowly, carefully, like each word was killing him - he said:

"Larry, brother... I don't know how to say this. So I just say it. She died last night. At the family home."

I felt the ground shift.

"She wasn't feeling good the day before," he said, his voice starting to tremble. "We thought it was nothing. That she was just depressed and missing you. Then... her heart stopped in her sleep. We didn't know until morning."

And then came the sound of a man unraveling. Jaks– stoic, steady, martini-perfect Jaks - sobbing through the phone like a child. I heard the moment his breath broke, the way grief snatches dignity from the strongest.

But I was already gone.

My knees buckled. I collapsed onto the floor, hand still clutched around the phone, forehead pressed to tile. My whole body was shaking. My vision tunneled. I wanted to scream, to throw something, to claw my way out of this waking hell. But I didn't move. I just lay there, staring, gasping, drowning in a silence so loud it roared in my skull.

No no no no no no no no - FUCK NO!

This wasn't happening. Not to her. Not to us. We had a love that people dream about. We had plans. We had everything. She had just texted me. Told me she loved me. Told me she missed me. Told me she was counting the seconds until we were back in each other's arms.

What do you do when the one who anchored you simply stops existing?

What do you do when love - real, rare, ridiculous love - is snatched away in the middle of a perfect sentence?

You don't move. You don't eat. You don't breathe properly. You live in a nightmare you can't wake up from, and the worst part is - you don't want to wake up. Because waking up means it's real.

Everything meant nothing to me now. I was a sad reflection of myself and one that until now, I wouldn't share. It was all too painful to even think about.

Silence.

Silence forevermore.

CHAPTER 17. IT'S A BANGKOK BOOMERANG

The best plan in a new city is no plan at all. Just keep moving until the universe buys you a drink – for every city is a test of patience and curiosity. The map's just a rumor; the real story's written in footsteps.

Night falls. The streets fill up, but I am empty. The heat had finally loosened its grip, but the weight of everything, thoughts, doubts, shifting moods and memories all hung on like a second skin. So, I walked. One more walk through that electric tangle of life. Commerce, seduction, and the sacred. There was no plan. Just feet moving forward, searching for something that doesn't have a name.

Street vendors shouted like auctioneers of the absurd. Oil hissed and popped as fish cakes turn golden. A wisp of jasmine-sweet incense curled up from a spirit house wedged between a pharmacy and a 7-Eleven. Life doesn't pause, not even for reflection.

A teenage girl laughed, posing with grilled squid. A cabbie nodded respectfully to a monk. Two farangs argued over which BTS stop to take. A scooter driver scowled at a stray dog trying to steal his food. The city hummed with cackled calls, just like always.

But I'm not the same. Everything's shifted. I didn't feel the need to respond, to analyze, to judge or even to pay all that much attention to the details. The city still roared, but I didn't roar back.

I knew what loss felt like. It's happened too many times of late. I didn't need it lit up in neon.

Bangkok hadn't changed. OK - it had only been a week since I was there, but odder things happen in the universe all the time. It was still the same electric sprawl, the same soundscape of scooters, tuk tuks, cars and bars, street vendors, pop and techno music, temple bells, and kitchen clatter. The same humidity that makes your shirt cling to your back and your thoughts drip sideways. But I had changed. I'd been left behind. I couldn't get back.

Charlee wasn't there.

She would not be waiting for me on the corner with a beautiful smile and a bag of fruit.

She wouldn't be teasing me about my farang Thai or grabbing my hand to pull me into a cool alley for exploration and a kiss.

She was simply not there.

There is a strange silence, a disconnect, in losing someone so special. No funeral, no flowers, no goodbye. Just a city that no longer included her.

I didn't cry. I didn't know how to, nor was I ready to allow that crushing weight land full force into my soul. Grief didn't come in cinematic waves with a fainting couch - it was a fog. Dense. Lingering. Impenetrable. It filled up my mind's rooms and darkened alleyways. The tuk tuks, sidewalks and noodle stalls where I used to feel light and fun? Everything still existed exactly where I left it, except my joy had fled.

We checked into the Marriott for two nights which was like Marriott's anywhere - perfectly groomed professionalism, top-notch amenities and service but with a complete lack of soul. The bed was comfortable as hell though.

After we stowed luggage in the room, I walked to the 7-Eleven down the block out of habit and bought a bottle of SangSom rum and a beer I didn't want and sat on the sidewalk watching the traffic flow along. I realized I was waiting for Chalermwan anyway. Not because I expected her to appear - but because I didn't know what else to do.

Malaya would be heading back to the States after those two nights. I'd be moving down the Asok to a quieter place I'd booked for the week. It was my second to last week in Thailand, though it felt like I was already gone - part ghost, part man, floating through the city with the strange sensation that time had both collapsed and stretched beyond recognition. All I wanted was to lie down and disappear into that netherworld where dreams don't follow rules, and maybe - if the stars were kind - Charlee would visit me there. I needed her to step through the veil, brush my cheek with her soft fingers, and whisper that none of this was final. That we would find each other again in the stardust, where memory bends and form dissolves. That kind of longing isn't romantic; it's what happens when grief refuses to leave.

But that was depression talking. That was the soft siren call of deeply wishful thinking dressed up in cosmic metaphors. It wasn't the here and now. Life, in its ceaseless momentum, doesn't pause for heartbreak nor does it consult our dreams before marching forward. So I took a breath and made a quiet vow. Not the kind you declare to the sky, but the kind you repeat under your breath like a mantra until it starts to take hold. I would try to see things with eyes unclouded by the fog of despair. I would live out my remaining days in Thailand with presence and a shattered soul. And I knew, without needing signs or symbols, that Charlee would have insisted on that. It was not just what she would have wanted - it was what she would have demanded of me. Because love, at its most honest, doesn't let you go under.

So it was time to get my shit together, or at least fake that I was still human and humane. Survival by performance. I'd done that before. Recently.

Malaya was ready to hit the ground running. She hadn't been to Bangkok in twenty years aside from the layover before we hit Koh Chang and was wide-eyed with that tourist energy that assumes the city's been waiting to unfold itself like a blooming lotus or some other poetic nonsense.

She wanted Thailand to open a path before her. Meanwhile, I was trying to find my legs - emotionally, spiritually, physically - just figuring out which way was up. I nodded and played along with the role I'd been dealt. It's strange how quickly you can slide into being someone else's guide when your own compass is spinning. I didn't have answers. Hell, I barely had clean laundry. But I could point out a great noodle shop or steer us toward a temple and pretend I was there in the moment.

Malaya wanted to see one of the grand Wats, so I picked Wat Pho. Officially named Wat Phra Chetuphon, it's one of the oldest and most storied temples in Bangkok, let alone Thailand, dating back to the 16th century. It was later expanded by King Rama I as part of his grand restoration of Thai culture. Wat Pho is best known for the Viharn Phranorn hall that houses the massive reclining Buddha, depicting his passage into nirvana. Fifteen meters high and forty-six meters long, covered in gold leaf, his feet inlaid with mother-of-pearl symbology, featuring the 108 characteristics (lakshanas) representing the perfections that led to his enlightenment.

But beyond the tourist-thronged statue hall, the grounds of Wat Pho hold a quieter power: courtyards lined with Chinese stone guardians, halls echoing with centuries of chants, and it's the birthplace of Thai massage which is still practiced in the shaded alcoves and available to all comers for a modest fee.

The grounds of Wat Pho are a riot of serene order. Neatly swept stone pavilions, courtyards and paths wind through manicured landscapes and bodhi trees. Everywhere, towering chedis that look like jeweled beehives, obviously built by obsessive-compulsive artisans. Everywhere you turn, there's something gilded, tiled, ceramic covered. Row upon row of golden Buddhas smile at you, while staring into a middle distance like an enlightened philosophers club. The air was perfumed with incense while the soft chiming of bells swaying in the breeze added to the musical score. Even the cats that lived on campus seemed to move with a kind of sacred dignity, except the ones stretched out on sun-warmed stone because they've already attained Nirvana. Those are the ones waiting for you to catch up.

Our time at Wat Pho was wonderful - more than I expected, really. In spite of everything I was carrying, I managed to enjoy it. As I slowly wandered around I found a quiet corner tucked away behind one of the smaller chedis, where an old bodhi tree cast dappled shadows across a small courtyard. It was the kind of spot you stumble into rather than seek out, like it chose you as you wonder if it's OK to be there. I sat down beneath the broad branches, closed my eyes, and let the world fall away for a while.

The stillness didn't solve anything. It didn't erase the devastating ache that flared whenever I thought about Charlee. But it did something else - something quieter. It let me sit with the pain without needing to embrace or fight it. There, beneath a descendant of the same kind of tree the Buddha had sat under, I felt a thin sliver of peace slide in. No grand epiphany. Just the ability to hold the grief without it hardening into resentment or outrage at the cosmic unfairness of it all. Charlee was gone. The world kept turning. The bells kept gently chiming in the distance, while a soft breeze danced with the bodhi leaves like a whispered reassurance: this too, this is part of it all.

If you ever find yourself in Bangkok, Wat Pho should be the first temple you visit. Don't overthink it. Just go. There's something about that Wat that gets under your skin in the best way. The grounds are stunning: elegant without being showy, expansive yet intimate. Even with tourists drifting through, selfie sticks in hand, oblivious to everything outside their viewfinder, the place holds its tranquility without trying. You feel it in your bones - like the temple is gently breathing all around you and you are part of that breath. Wat Pho has one foot planted deep in the ancient world, and the other stepping calmly into the present. It doesn't need to impress you - it just is. And that is a most impressive thing.

From Wat Pho, we headed to the Bangkok National Museum, just across from Thong Sanam Luang. It feels a bit like scholarly perfection and sprawl. Like someone opened up the attic of that 4,000-year-old civilization. It's the kind of museum that rewards the slow walker and the curious mind.

I love museums. The younger edition of me didn't because my mom would drag my sister and me through every museum within a hundred-mile radius, no matter where we were. At the time, I was more interested in the gift shops and escape routes. But in hindsight, those long, slow walks past ancient artifacts, galleries full of the masters' brush strokes, marble masterpieces and faded dioramas were priceless. I wouldn't have half the curiosity or perspective I value now without those experiences and memories.

The Bangkok National Museum is a place that rewards that kind of long-view appreciation. Much like the Smithsonian, it's not a single institution but a sprawling, encyclopedic collection of collections. Housed in what was once the Wang Na Palace grounds, it charts the story of Thailand from the earliest Sukothai kingdoms through the Ayutthaya dynasty, the rise of Bangkok, and into the modern era. It's too much to absorb in one visit - or ten or more. Still, even a cursory walk-through is enough to flood the imagination with wonder: ancient stone Buddhas, royal war and funereal chariots, shadow puppets, calligraphy masters' works, and weaponry, all whispering fragments of a much larger tale. It's overwhelming in the best way. A place that invites you to keep coming back, to listen deeply to the stories of an entire people.

We took our time drifting from gallery to gallery, building to building, trying to take in the sheer scope of it all. It felt like a living archive of Thailand's soul - layered, intricate, and deeply human. We toured slowly, out of quiet respect, without a plan, as each hall and room offered something unexpected and deeply moving.

Once we'd overdosed on historical eye-candy - gilded Buddhas, ancient scrolls, and enough ceremonial weaponry to start a new dynasty - we flagged down a tuk tuk and bounced our way toward Chinatown. Malaya was on a mission to find red lanterns for the Lunar New Year back home and even though I'd already spent a fair amount of time there, I decided to go along for the ride to watch her take in the excesses of Chinatown. Also, because I suspected she might need someone to carry things. Did I want to go back to the hotel and curl up in a ball? Yes.

As I've already written, Bangkok's Chinatown is not so much a neighborhood as a full-contact-sport sensory experience on a grand scale. We wandered through the maze of alleys that seemed to fold in on themselves - lanterns strung overhead like constellations, the scent of roast duck and two-stroke blue smoke in the air, while shopkeepers barked out prices with the urgency of auctioneers. Every turn offered some new marvel or mystery. It was, as always, chaos with character.

We found a noodle joint wedged deep inside one of Chinatown's endless food alleys - the kind of place with low worn benches and rickety tables, fluorescent lighting, and ineffective fans that swiveled just enough to remind you how hot you still were. There was no English menu, just photos, age-faded into abstraction under plastic and a server who sized us up, decided we were harmless, and took our orders the second we pointed at anything.

The noodles were perfect - springy, rich with pork broth, topped with a medium-boiled egg that collapsed at the touch of a chopstick. We shared a plate of dumplings that arrived suspiciously fast, and some golden-fried spring rolls that made up in crunch what they lacked in mastery. It wasn't elegant, but it was honest. The kind of meal that resets your brain and reminds you why dive food beats five-star dining nine times out of ten. Plus, their roasted chili oil was incredible!

Back on Koh Chang I had realized I needed to deal with the slow creep of stuff I'd accumulated through my travels - books from the monastery, more from the Lost Bookstore in Chiang Mai that hadn't been left behind somewhere, plus a more than a few garments I hadn't worn since the humidity made cotton a liability. Malaya, blessed with executive airline status and extra baggage allowance, offered to mule a load home for me. All I had to do was find a bag that didn't scream "emergency laundry day." I didn't haggle. The prices were more than reasonable. I settled on a heavy-duty expandable, nylon bag with a handle and wheels that seemed trustworthy.

One book I treasure above all others that needed to get home safely was a gift from the monks at iMonastery. It's called the Pali-English Chanting Book: A Handbook of Buddhist Chants, Translated from Pali, Sanskrit and Thai. Now there's a riveting title for you, eh? It's big. It's heavy. It smells faintly of incense and jungle mold. No, it's not topping any bestseller lists. The NYT doesn't even know it exists, nor will you find it stacked in airport bookstores next to the novelettes or celebrity memoirs. But for me, it's sacred. A living relic. A reminder of the time I spent in the mountains with those extraordinary monks, my brothers, my teachers, my friends, in meditation, education, chores and meals. Mosquito warfare aside, my monastery, and the lessons I took from those amazing men needed a memento and this was a beautiful piece that was perfect in every way. It's a reminder that I was there. That I had sat, I had listened, I learned, I tried. That I mattered to them enough for them to give me this before I left. And in my world? That's best seller material.

We kept wandering through Chinatown, slowly angling toward Rama IV Road in pursuit of both crispy-skinned duck and some perfect red lanterns. Not elusive in terms of quantity - lanterns were everywhere. Hanging from wires, storefronts and street carts. But Malaya was holding out for a specific kind of lantern magic. Right size, right shape, right shop.

We strolled by stall after stall, store after store, each display louder than the last. Rows of lanterns, the riot of red so intense it was psychedelic. Finally, just when I thought she might give up, she stopped. One shop along the boulevard had a range of sizes that fit the bill.

Inside was a riot of color and form - paper, silk, glass, tassels, lucky charms and amulets, and every shade of red known to humankind. But what caught me wasn't the lanterns. Sitting on a low stool at a wooden table sat a fellow, bent slightly forward, his hands gliding over long gold sashes. He moved with practiced calm, dipping a fat brush into a bowl of red ink and sweeping out calligraphy so fluid, so impossibly elegant, I nearly forgot to breathe.

I asked - awkwardly, with gestures and respect - if I could stay and observe. After a round of translation and some quiet smiles, he nodded. I stood there for fifteen minutes, maybe more, watching him create something I couldn't read but could still feel.

Malaya, lanterns in hand - collapsed flat like obedient little origami soldiers, had drifted behind, pulled into the orbit of storefronts. She browsed as I wandered ahead in slow motion, up the sidewalk as the city bustled around me. My personal fog bank was back. I had been trying to enjoy everything around me but the brave face I had worn was cracking.

༄

It was a hot, thick and sticky Bangkok afternoon. Chinatown was humming like it always does - bikes and scooters darting between cars and through impossibly narrow alleys packed with people, as hawkers called out their daily wares, the scent of grilled meats and hot fry oil hanging heavy in the air. I had found a stretch of railing along the roadside to lean against, a bit of shade and stillness in the crazy, while Malaya did her thing. She'd catch up.

It was during that break that I witnessed something that made me stop in my tracks and think deeply - about culture, about humanity, about who we really are as a species.

I was leaning on a metal barricade on the edge of Rama IV Road, the kind meant to keep pedestrians alive and scooters mostly in their lane. It was one of those small pauses that feels bigger than it is. Just me, the heat radiating off the concrete, and the low hum of a city that never fully powers down. I looked at the ever-entertaining traffic slalom by - tuk tuks, taxis, busses and trucks, and scooters stacked with improbable cargo - Bangkok's constant mechanical parade.

I reached out to Charlee in the quiet way I had started to do. Just a simple hello. I told her I missed her. No grand gestures, no skyward speeches. Just standing there, taking it all in, and letting the moment hold us both for a beat.

Beside me sat an older Thai woman, perched on a short blue plastic stool - the kind you see stacked alongside restaurants or tucked around noodle carts. We exchanged the usual pleasantries: a wai and a heartfelt Sawatdee krab and kha. A smile. A nod. A shared moment of quiet amid the thrum, together, from different worlds on a random curb in Chinatown.

We watched the world go by and occasionally point something out to each other - a street vendor with an overstuffed cart, a tourist struggling with a map, a tuk tuk badly in need of a tune-up, smoke belching behind it like a rooster tail - and chuckle, inviting the other into our observations. Her English was stripped-down basic, but her sabai was fluent and infectious. We shared a kind of unspoken friendship born of mutual amusement in the same place.

Then she gasped and grabbed my hand. Her Thai was rapid and her other hand pointing even faster. I had no idea what she was saying.

Across the boulevard - six lanes wide, which in Thailand translates to ten, a living river of motion and madness - an elderly man had collapsed at a bus stop. His body crumpled awkwardly, slumped half on and half off the bench, his head and shoulder twisted at an unnatural, awful angle.

And then, without hesitation, people around him moved. Not away, but to him.

At least ten strangers rushed in. No one looked around. No one pulled out a phone. No one waited for someone else to take the lead. They just moved, as if called by the same silent bell.

A few crouched in front of him, steadying his body, gently lifting him upright like he was something breakable. One held an umbrella above his head to shield him from the punishing sun. Another began fanning him with a folded newspaper. Someone else brushed the dust from his shirt with the kind of tenderness you might reserve for a father, or a friend, or someone you love.

They were standing in traffic. Bangkok traffic. But the city - usually relentless, loud, kinetic - somehow softened around them. The river of engines and exhaust curled away, as if it, too, understood this moment was not to be interrupted.

I ran across the alley to the corner shop, grabbed two bottles of cold water, and then crossed that arterial chaos one lane at a time, holding up my hand like I was Moses on a crosswalk. My heart was pounding like a war drum, but I felt pulled - tethered - to something larger than adrenaline or fear.

When I reached the circle of care surrounding the man, I tried to hand a bottle to a guy who had taken charge in the quiet way that real leaders do. He looked up, met my eyes, and said, gently but firmly, "No... no water. Ambulance coming. Bad for heat collapse." I didn't know that.

And just like that, I was no longer needed. I stood there for a moment, unsure, watching the man on the bench slowly come back into himself. People crouched beside him, smiling, reassuring. Holding presence like it was sacred.

Then I turned and crossed back to the other side. And as I stood by the railing again, hands still clutching the unopened bottles, I realized I was crying. Quietly, unexpectedly. Because I had just witnessed a moment of pure humanity - unvarnished and holy - in the middle of Bangkok traffic.

No one had asked, "What's in it for me?"

No one hesitated.

No one walked away or doubted what to do.

In a world that often feels atomized and armored, each of us scrolling, rushing, isolating behind invisible walls, this was something older. Deeper. A flicker of the ancient truth that we're not separate. That beneath the noise and the posturing, we *know* each other.

Ten strangers heard the same silent signal and answered without speaking. They just moved. As if remembering, all at once, that we belong to each other.

There was no spotlight. No hero. Just a brief, blinding reminder that compassion isn't taught. It's remembered. That there's a current running through us, beneath identity, language, and nation, and sometimes it surges to the surface, unbidden.

That's what culture really is: the collective shape of our instincts when no one's watching. That's what hope is too. The idea that no matter how far apart we drift, the signal still gets through.

There *is* goodness. There *is* love. It's not always loud, and it's rarely perfect. But it's there. And when we stop long enough, when we *see* each other clearly, we remember what and who we are.

Very early the next morning, Malaya headed to the airport for her long journey home, her red lanterns packed flat, colorful companions to her luggage. I shifted gears and locations, moving into the Asoke Residence Apartments at the end of Sukhumvit 21 Road, which truth be told was way more of an alley than road. It's a solid, no-nonsense spot within easy strolling distance over the Asok Montri Road bridge to the Asok Pier along Khlong Saen Saep. There, Khlong ferries whisk you up and down to other neighborhoods. And it was just a couple blocks from the Petchaburi BTS station. A practical choice. Central, quiet enough, with good bones and easy access to the veins of the city.

While the apartments were older, it was a welcomed change from the top-notch, yet sterile bubble of the Marriott - less polished, more lived-in, more Thai. My new place had the kind of character that only comes with age: wide rooms with tiled floors, worn but clean. A large, well-appointed bathroom with fixtures that worked just fine; and closets and drawers that promised permanence, or at least the illusion of it.

At the end of the alley sat a 7-Eleven, predictably open at all hours, and every afternoon, the sidewalks and alley entrance came alive with street vendors hawking grilled, skewered sausages, sliced and iced fruit, and steaming bags of noodles and soups. The neighborhood had all the essential comforts, wrapped in a now-familiar Bangkok mix.

But then the door closed.

Now alone, I unpacked without ceremony, without excitement for adventures to come. I hung pants and shirts up, unfolded T's and shorts into drawers with a sort of dull efficiency, as if completing a task would hold off the silence. I set up the bathroom. I opened my notebook. I put my pen to paper. The pages stared back, blank but not unkind, like a friend who doesn't know what to say. I tried again, but the words wouldn't come. My hands were still. Then everything rushed in.

With the distractions gone - no monks, no tourists, no planning ludicrous routes on public transportation, no errands or temples or jokes to share - the weight I'd kept at bay came crashing in like a gigantic wave I'd foolishly thought I'd outrun. It flattened me.

I didn't eat. I didn't go out. I lay there in the quiet hum of the AC, feeling myself disappear. The solitude was cavernous. I wasn't just lonely - I was unraveling. My heart ached for Charlee, for the serene rhythm of chants, saffron robes and something - someone - holy to hold onto. I needed a Wat. I needed monks with calm voices and kind eyes. I needed Buddha's silence to be louder than mine.

I searched maps online. Desperately. But for the first time since setting my feet down in Thailand, there wasn't a temple within immediate walking distance. Not even a small neighborhood shrine tucked behind a house or hidden under a Bodhi tree. Just concrete, traffic, and alleys that lit no spark to my imagination.

And then the silence changed. It became a crushing presence - a heavy, unyielding thing compressing me from all sides. My world grew smaller. My chest tighter. And when the sun went down that night, I begged it to take me with it as I cried myself to sleep.

Fitful sleep? No. Not even close. It was more like a series of short, fractured naps - each one hijacked by my monkey, swinging in circles, banging cymbals, shrieking reminders of everything I didn't want to think about. I tossed, I turned, I cursed the ceiling, I cursed the silence, I cursed myself.

I screamed at the universe for its insolence and audacity to say that I, like Icarus, had flown too high and was now paying the price. Dylan muttered somewhere in the background that it was all just a simple twist of fate. I tried to meditate. There was nothing there. Whatever inner tools I'd honed up at my monastery and on cushions in Wats had gone AWOL - leaving me to white-knuckle my grief alone.

By the time the sun rose, I was ragged. Eyes dry. Lips cracked. Dehydrated, disoriented, and emotionally threadbare. I was desperate for water but didn't give a shit. I took two melatonin with a stingy sip and waited for unconsciousness to do what mindfulness could not: smack my monkey into silence.

When I came to, it was 7PM. The timer had turned off the A/C and the room was thick with heat. My mouth was cotton. I could barely swallow. Hell, I could barely breathe. I lay there, half-lucid, until I finally had a not-so-friendly come-to-Buddha with myself - some primal, exhausted internal bootcamp sergeant dragging me upright.

I stumbled into the open shower stall, turned the tap full blast, and collapsed on the cool stone floor, curling into a ball under the stream. For half an hour

I lay there, not washing so much as hoping to dissolve - just let the shower carry me down the drain like so much wasted potential.

Eventually, hunger crawled in - not real starvation, but the kind that makes your stomach yawn wide enough to consider chewing off a limb. Problem was, I had no hoisin, no prik nam som, no noodles, no appetite for anything. Just emptiness.

Reluctantly, I pulled on clothes and slipped out. At the end of the alley, the street carts were doing their usual dance, but the fruit repulsed me. My throat clenched the moment I saw it. A single mangosteen brought Charlee crashing back; her face, her eyes, her hands, the sweet way she offered me that first one. I couldn't bear it. I couldn't look.

Instead, I went into the 7-Eleven and bought a fifth of SangSom rum, again. Outside, I loaded up with three kinds of grilled sausages, a tofu Pad Thai, and some nameless soup that was either divine or garbage. I didn't care.

The next morning, I woke up on the floor. Hungover. Sore. At least I'd dragged a pillow down with me. The bottle wasn't empty, but close enough. Two empty water bottles sat beside me; evidence that at some point, my better judgment made a brief cameo.

Was I better? No. But I was no longer willingly sinking.

I dragged myself to the shower, sat cross-legged on the wet stone floor, let the steam permeate, and started to breathe. Slowly. Deeply. Not forcing anything. Letting the pain be there but not win.

And then, for the first time in days, I felt something shift. The tiniest opening. The beginning of letting go. I slipped into meditation - not gracefully, but honestly. I breathed through the sharp-edged ache. I saw the impermanence of it all. I forgave myself, just enough to stay alive. My monkey slunk back to his cage, and I kept him there twiddling his thumbs in boredom.

And I stayed there, in the steam, in the stillness, having a long-overdue conversation with the one person I couldn't escape.

Anicca. That's the Pali word for impermanence - one of the core tenets of Buddhism. But really, it shows up in every tradition, East or West. As George Harrison sang, "All things must pass." Or, to put it a little more bluntly: that shit ain't never gonna stay the same. It just doesn't. That's at the very heart of Dukkha - suffering. That tension is the result of holding on when everything else is slipping through your fingers.

And so it was that I cleared my head to some degree. I reached out and reminded Charlee I loved her - again - and started to piece myself back together, just enough to walk out the door and not fantasize about a jet falling from the sky to crush me into sweet, painless oblivion. The cracks were still there, but they were taped together for now. Whether Elmer's or Gorilla, time would tell. I had no illusions that I wouldn't get tumbled and dashed upon more jagged rocks as waves of grief slammed into me, but today? Today I could breathe again.

It's hard being someone who loves, feels and empathizes so deeply and there are many times that I've envied those who skate through their lives feeling nothing more than a mild endorphin buzz from attraction and commitment - who've never been caught in the undertow, never wrecked by the tidal wave. But that's not me. I feel it all. Deeply. I always have. And it's been my ruin on more than several occasions.

But today, it was time to move forward - and leave the past where it belonged.

I found the hotel gym and beat the hell out of myself for two hours. I focused on every pedal stroke, every rep, every endless climb on the elliptical. Each breath was a small exorcism, forcing my body to sweat out the last of that bottle.

A quick outdoor shower and a cannonball into the empty pool snapped me back to life. I felt alive enough, at least, to start making decisions again. For myself.

And - sadly - for only myself.

Another wave of grief hit me with that realization. I didn't fight it. I leaned into it; let it roll over me. I even thanked it, quietly, for letting me see her again. Just for a moment.

And like the snap of a finger, that wave rolled on by - but this time, it left me standing.

Dressed, and finally in control of at least some of my mental faculties, it was time to go out and eat something substantial - get some strength back.

I was craving Indian. That cuisine always manages to put a smile on my face. The bold, unapologetic flavors and spices that know who they are. But I wasn't in the mood for the overly simplified, same-same fare that so many places churn out. I wanted something off the beaten path. The kind of place where the locals eat, Thai and Indian alike. If no farang had ever set foot inside? Even better.

I chatted with the young guys working at the front desk at the Asoke

Residence Apartments - always cheerful, and always eager to help. I told them about my quest.

Without hesitation, one of them lit up.

"Bombay Masala," he said. "About fifteen minutes down Sukhumvit 21, if you're on crutches. It's close and the best I've ever had including my mom's cooking." He was Indian and I feared for his well-being if his mother ever heard that come out of his mouth.

I mentioned this place earlier when describing High Tea Pickaboo, but it deserves a deeper dive.

Small, unassuming, and tucked near the end of that narrow alley, Bombay Masala was exactly the kind of place I'd hoped for. The big open roll-up door created an open bay for food. I walked in and saw eight tables. That was it. Three had been pulled together and was occupied by a group of Indian guys playing backgammon between bites of food that smelled like home, if your home was somewhere between Delhi and a fantastic mango chutney-perfumed dream.

They greeted me with polite nods, as did the gentleman behind the counter. I took a seat and opened the menu. Sure, it was the usual greatest hits - chicken tikka masala, saag paneer, garlic naan - but something told me the food would be far better than average.

Maybe it was the confidence of the backgammon players.

Maybe it was the warm air, thick with cardamom, cumin, turmeric, ghee, and a subtle undercurrent of surprise that said: "What's the solo white guy doing here? I thought we were hidden away enough to dodge the tourists."

There's something charismatic about the Indian lilt layered over English. It's one of those accents I've always found both musical and utterly charming. One of the guys at the front counter had that wonderful hybrid - Indian cadence with an "educated-in-Britain" polish. It was as melodic as it was professional, and I could've listened to him read a grocery list and been completely content.

We chatted while I placed my order: Tandoori Chicken, Mutton Masala (hot, hot, hot, please), Biryani Rice, Daal Tadka, some plain naan, and of course, a mango lassi, a drink I could never grow bored with. He wanted to know if I stumbled into his restaurant or if it was online or ... how did I discover his place. I told him about the guys at Asoke. He may have been a master poker-faced guy, but it really didn't seem to ring any bells. That gave me comfort, knowing that the kid wasn't the guy's nephew, or son, shilling the place out of loyalty.

Here's the thing: I'm someone who gets bored. Plain and simple. I get bored with complex things, and I get bored with simple things. It's one of the reasons

I've changed careers a few times in my life. That restlessness? It doesn't discriminate. It crops up in my professional life though most predictably, at the dinner table. Even when I've cooked something fantastic-plate-licking delicious, it rarely gets a second night of glory. Leftovers sit lonely and unloved on a back shelf while I crave something new, something different, something that surprises. It's also why I love to cook. Every dish is a new canvas. A new chance to not be bored.

So when I say I could drink mango lassi every day and never get tired of it, that's saying something. It's creamy, tart, sweet, tropical, floral - like a hug and a vacation all at once. I suppose, in theory, I could grow tired of it. But in that moment, sitting in that tiny restaurant tucked away at the far end of an alley in Bangkok, surrounded by backgammon-playing locals and the scent of pan-toasted spices, it tasted like home and escape at the same time.

I was sitting at a table waiting for the food to arrive, scrolling through book-o-face, the digital junk food monster, when one of the guys at the backgammon table asked if I would please join them. I smiled and told him I'd be honored, but only if they were willing to teach me a little backgammon.

Now, full disclosure: that was cheating. Not *cheating* cheating, but the kind of strategic undersell that would've made my old MIT-graduate friend and backgammon mentor Mark beam with pride. See, I've been playing backgammon since high school, taught by a man who believed the doubling cube was a spiritual instrument and who never played a game without money on the line, even if it was just enough to buy a cup of coffee. I had lost many nickels, a few dimes, and way too many quarters before learning how to stop bleeding losses and start seeing the game like a math equation dressed up as a gentleman's pastime. Eventually, I got good. Good enough to beat almost anyone who didn't spend their Saturdays reading probability theory and dice roll odds for fun.

There I was, humble bragging my way into a seat, acting like I wasn't about to sandbag the table. They welcomed me with warmth. I settled in, grateful not just for the game, but for the moment - unexpected spontaneous company.

And just like that, I was no longer alone. At least physically.

They made room for me at their table without hesitation, shuffling chairs and clearing space with the easy grace of people who've known each other a long time - and are happy to fold a new soul into the mix. Someone poured me a glass of pungent, sweet mint tea, the kind that smells like memory and tastes like childhood if you were lucky enough to grow up in a household where someone simmered things slowly with care.

They peppered me with questions between sips and chuckles. Where have you been? What are you doing in Bangkok? How did you end up here of all places? And as I told them the core of it - my monastic journey, my romantic disaster, my strange impulse to chase both silence and sensation - they listened with a kind of focused attention that caught me off guard. Not just polite curiosity, but something more. Genuine wonder, maybe, or the rare moment where someone hears you without trying to fix you.

One of the men, whose Sikh beard was magnificent enough to deserve its own wing in a museum, leaned in and asked me more about iMonastery. He'd been considering the program, he said, but kept finding reasons to delay. I shared all I could: the schedule, the calming hush of the jungle, the deep, sacred peace of it - and the hellish beauty of confronting your own nonsense without distraction. His friends gave him the look of *"We've told you to do this, brother,"* and nodded their support.

I told him he'd be more than welcome in our sangha. He responded with a low, seated bow and a warm, deliberate, *"Dhanwaad Ji."*

I had to ask what it meant.

Literally, it translates to *"Thank you, with respect, sir."*

But in spirit, it runs deeper - it's a phrase layered with humility, reverence, and a kind of quiet honor. A bow not just of body, but of heart.

My food started to arrive, dish by fragrant, glorious dish. The mutton masala, spiced to the flop-sweat-inducing level I had begged for, smelled like everything I needed. It hit the table like an old friend: bold, warm, unapologetically alive. I was already plotting how to build a tandoor back in the States, as if the flavors might follow me home and anchor something that felt lost.

The staff set the dishes at my original table, but the guys waved me over with the urgency of co-conspirators. They'd already eaten, they said it was time to induct me into their sacred backgammon circle.

I asked if money was involved, and that drew the kind of laughs that start low and ripple outward.

"Of course," one of them said, grinning. "But don't worry. We won't let you lose too much. Just enough to earn your seat. And the next round of tea? That's on you."

And just like that, surrounded by strangers who were rapidly becoming something else entirely, I felt it. Some small, defiant flicker of aliveness stirring beneath the grief. It didn't erase anything. It didn't fix the gaping hole where Charlee used to live. But it gave me a moment. A moment where I wasn't drowning. A moment where the world, in all its messy, spicy, laughing humanity, reached a hand into the dark and reminded me: *You're still here.*

"Alright," I said, "let's play. What could go wrong?"

We laughed - really laughed - as our voices bounced off the alley walls and scattered into the night. Laughter like that doesn't just echo - it lifts. It stitches. It fills in the cracks, if only for a while.

By my fourth straight win, their suspicion was thick enough to cut with a dull knife. My pile of 10-baht coins had grown impressively high. Silver trophies for a man playing the long con of pretending he didn't know what he was doing.

Eventually, I came clean. I fessed up to years of practice, tournaments, late-night games in smoke-filled rooms. I dropped the act and placed the coins back in their hands, trying to look appropriately contrite.

To make amends, I ordered another pot of that glorious mint tea, steeped in sugar, forgiveness, and the kind of laughter that floats, light and golden, above the heaviest things we carry.

Because sometimes, healing doesn't look like closure. Sometimes it just looks like strangers, a board game, and a cup of tea strong enough to remind you that life, in all its stubborn beauty, goes on.

The last I heard from Arvind, he'd decided to apply for the iMonastery program and was buzzing with excitement to dive into the calm and beautiful life of a monastic.

The food? Amazing. Better than any other Indian meal I'd eaten in Thailand - let alone Bangkok - let alone anywhere else except in London all those years ago. My taste buds were still tingling from the bold spices and smoky tandoori when I tucked the leftovers into a few containers and started the wander back to the apartment to stash them in the fridge.

❦

By now, the city had settled into its nighttime flow. I walked back and was almost to the end when I noticed something I'd completely missed in the daylight because let's face it, I was living in a fog and tunnel vision was my only means of keeping myself fed. A framed sign, out along the side of the alley just two doors down from my lobby. And another sign, mounted on a wall, now glowing softly with green back lighting: WYWS Cocktails. I had no clue as to what WYWS meant but I sure as hell knew the other word.

The building itself was tall and narrow, unassuming to the point of invisibility. Somehow, in my haze of basic survival - eat, sleep, try to stay alive though it wasn't a priority at the time - I'd completely overlooked it.

I brought my food upstairs to the fifth floor first. Indian food is wonderfully aromatic. Rich, inviting, and complex, but also potent, and I didn't want to risk offending the bar patrons by bringing that smell into a shared space. What kind of place was WYWS?. A dingy dive? A hidden gem? I ganja den/cocktail bar hidden away to avoid detection? I had no idea, so better safe than sorry.

I made my way back down and stepped inside WYWS and suddenly, I was somewhere else entirely.

Walking into WYWS, I boarded a Pullman dining car from the golden age of rail travel. You know the ones - luxurious, sleek, and meticulously crafted with rich detail and swank everywhere you looked. The Pullman Company revolutionized train travel in the late 19th and early 20th centuries, turning cramped, noisy carriages into rolling palaces on wheels. Their dining and bar cars weren't just about function; they were theaters of elegance, with polished wood, rich paneling, plush leather seats, gleaming brass fixtures, and dimmed, amber-hued lights designed to coax relaxation and conversation.

WYWS embodied all that grandeur. Intimate seating areas lined with soft leather that whispered stories of clandestine meetings and midnight rendezvous, walls slatted in dark, gleaming wood that tipped its hat to history. The lighting was warm and low, casting a golden haze over gleaming bottles and crystal glassware, like the place was preserving an era when cocktails were an art form and bartenders were alchemists.

It wasn't just a bar. It was a time machine. A secret lounge that felt poised on the edge of some glorious cinematic scene. I could almost hear the faint echo of swing jazz drifting in from an invisible Victrola and the soft clatter of the pill bouncing to its destination on a roulette wheel hidden away behind an Asian screen. Actually, the soundtrack was modern pop hip hop, but jazz really would have been more appropriate considering the stage setting.

For a moment, I wasn't a weary, heart-broken traveler chomping on leftovers in a Bangkok apartment while laughing at the exaggerated, emotive acting of a Thai soap opera plot twist (was she pregnant with her ex-boyfriend's evil twin's child or just faking a coma again?). I was someone who had stepped into a hidden world - one where stories weren't streamed, they were sipped - where smoky cocktails birthed memory and myth, and the past and present folded into each other like a bartender folding citrus peel over a flame.

I quickly abandoned my martini strategy. I mean, you now know I love a perfect martini - but this wasn't the time or place for one. This bar was clearly a temple for the cocktail devout. A martini here would be like ordering plain toast at a patisserie in Paris - technically acceptable, but deeply disrespectful.

WYWS was not a dive bar. This place was a cocktail laboratory. The bar back was a shrine to craftsmanship: rows of homemade bitters and tinctures in dropper bottles, vintage labels on obscure liqueurs, and enough high-end spirits to create anything and everything you might dream up. There was even a towering chrome citrus press that looked like it could juice a grapefruit and forge a horseshoe at the same time.

And the bartenders? Ert and Tee? Immaculate. Starched white shirts, black vests, neat bow ties. They moved with the calm, fluid choreography of men who had nothing to prove and everything to perfect. No juggling bottles or fire-breathing gimmicks here, just quiet confidence, glancing precision, and the occasional nod of approval when a lemon twist, having just been flamed, landed just right.

I watched them work, pulling oddities from lowboy coolers, adding a whisper of this, a vapor of that. Whatever these drinks were, they weren't just cocktails. They were compositions. Liquid sonatas. Beautiful concoctions in coupe glasses.

So, I did what any slightly cocky cocktail lover would do when presented with a master behind the bar: I ordered the hardest drink I knew.

"I'll have a Sazerac, but I'd like it with cognac instead of rye" I said casually, like I wasn't throwing down a gauntlet wrapped in an absinthe rinse.

The Sazerac is no joke. It's the drink that demands you know what the hell you're doing. The original New Orleans cocktail. A balancing act of cognac (if you're going for the true original), sugar, Peychaud's and Angostura bitters, and just the right ghostly swirl of absinthe - get one note wrong, and it's a wreck. Too sweet, and it's cough syrup. Too boozy, and you're chewing firewood. Skip the lemon twist? You're dead to me.

If they flinched, I didn't see it. Tee, the bartender at my end, gave a single approving nod, like I'd passed some kind of test, then reached for the ingredients with the calm assurance of someone who'd been waiting for a Sazerac request all night. He didn't consult a book or ask his coworker anything. I'd thought, this was going to be tough, Tee shrugged it off with that "what else ya got" attitude that says, "dude, I've made thousands of these."

And it was perfect!

A hidden gem cocktail bar thirty feet down from the lobby of my apartment? I knew where my nights would end while I stayed in this end of town, but that night? I really didn't need a repeat hangover command performance, so I did the one-and-done, warning Tee that I'd see them the next night.

I woke early after a decent night's sleep, but good enough. What I needed was some temple time. I dug a little deeper into the map and came up with Wat Uthai Tharam, a quiet spot about a mile and a half away, tucked off Kamphaeng Phet 7 Road. I decided to walk it, and I'm glad I did.

As soon as I crossed over the Khlong Saen Saep, the atmosphere shifted. The Bangkok I stepped into wasn't the glossy travel-brochure version. It wasn't tuk-tuk touts or smoothie stands or temples selling incense to tourists. This was a working neighborhood as corporate office blocks stood shoulder to shoulder with government buildings, high-rise condo and apartment towers, and mid-rise schools.

BMWs and Benzes claimed the parking lots close to the doors (must be the managers) alongside every Asian car manufacturer model filling up the rest of the spaces. Secretaries in a hurry and staff with office badges bound into the building entrances, coffee in one hand, phone in the other. There was motion everywhere - people darting and dashing, tight on time, already mentally seated at their desks.

It was real. No charm, no filtered glow. Just people going about the business of their lives. It had that unvarnished hum of routine, and maybe because of that - because there was no pretense - I loved it.

I strolled the commuter-hustling roadways until I came upon the temple grounds. Wat Uthai Tharam wasn't one of the showpiece temples pinned on tourist maps or circled in guidebooks. No vendors out front. No couples posing barefoot for their YouTube channel. Just a quiet stillness behind a modest entrance. It was beautiful, but in a way that didn't ask for attention. There was no pageantry here. Just an open gate and lovely gold trim. A place built for practice, not performance. That suited me just fine.

I wandered through the modest grounds, letting the sounds and stillness wash over me - the lazy sweep of a broom on stone tiles, the distant thud of a wooden mallet echoing from somewhere deeper in the compound where construction was continuing to evolve. The sky had gone a soft pale gray, the kind of color that made everything beneath it feel warmer, more rooted. It matched my mood.

I came upon a young monk. Old enough not to be a novice, but not yet old enough to shave. Except for his head of course. It was shiny and fresh, like he'd been newly unwrapped. He was full-on Thai with a shy smile and exactly one English word in his arsenal: "hello."

We stood there awkwardly for a moment, two humans with completely different operating systems. But the translator app on my phone came out of retirement and, through slow, careful exchanges, he learned what I was after: time with a monk for a chat. Someone who might be open to a conversation about impermanence and the loss that was gnawing at me inside out - about the big stuff.

He nodded once, then padded off barefoot at a purposeful pace. I followed, unsure if I was about to meet a teacher or handed a broom.

He was sitting on a low stone wall looking upon the progress of temple building, robes neatly arranged, with the kind of stillness that looked practiced. There was an exchange between the young and old. He rose and motioned for me to follow. We entered the wihan and sat down, lotus-style in an out-of-the-way corner. My hips, knees and ankles all filed complaints after the first three minutes.

We talked for hours.

Not in a formal way. It was gentle. Curious. The kind of talk that meandered but never strayed. As we spoke, I soon found a rhythm through my tale of woe. Pauses, glances, small hand gestures, a shared laugh at how clumsy language can be when trying to name things that are already slipping through your fingers.

He didn't preach. He didn't correct. What he offered was mental cleansing: Empathy. Big, quiet, generous empathy. He listened like he already knew everything I hadn't said yet. And like any good psychiatrist, he let me come into my answers by myself. Which always hit hardest.

When I left, I felt lighter - not because I'd offloaded anything, but because something in me had been seen. That's not something you can schedule on a travel itinerary.

But I also stumbled upon an observation: Monks would make excellent poker players.

✦

That night, after a light bite of salad from the 7-Eleven, and a leftover tandoori chicken quarter, the dinner that says 'I can't be bothered to do anything else', I made my way the grueling two doors down the alley to WYWS. I was looking for something easy, something familiar, something that didn't involve me spiraling through my memory banks at top speed. I pulled up a seat and started chatting with Ert and Tee, who were in good spirits.

"I don't know," I said, waving at the menu like it had personally wronged me. "Call an audible. Surprise me with something delicious that will lift the spirits of the downtrodden." That may have been misunderstood, and I didn't bother to explain, as they looked at each other and shrugged.

My mood wasn't sour. But that heartache - that low, persistent ache was hanging around, muttering reminders about Charlee's health. I'd known she had a serious issue with her heart. We had darkly joked about us imploding together while popping our pills in the AM and PM. Even after my long sit with the monk, I couldn't quite shake the feeling. Guilt flared now and again, like hot oil in a pan: I should've been there. I should've known. I should've carried her to the hospital or called the emergency line the second her tone shifted from bright to dim.

Instead, I sat there, on my second whimsical cocktail, some unnamed sorcery Tee had whipped up involving gin, calamansi, and what tasted suspiciously like flower petals and angel's tears.

The bar wasn't crowded. It was too early for that. A couple sat at a table at one end, deep in the kind of conversation that either leads to marriage or a long solo walk home. A group of four in a booth at the other end laughed. And me? I was right in the middle along the empty bar, Switzerland with a coaster.

On the wall to the right of the bar, a silent video looped snow falling outside a mountain cabin up in the Rockies with Pikes Peak clearly painted in. I thought that was pretty funny, given I was in Bangkok, where "winter" is what they call the time of year when your shirt only sticks to your shoulders instead of your entire torso.

I raised my glass toward the screen.

"To cabins. And poor timing," I muttered, and took a sip.

I was scribbling in my journal, lost in some overwrought and overwritten reflection, when someone slid onto the stool next to me. I caught the soft cadence of Thai as she spoke, but whatever she ordered went straight past me - and straight into action from Ert, who moved with the kind of urgency usually reserved for small fires or high-maintenance regulars.

I was still focused on my journal, trying to make my handwriting legible even to myself, when her drink arrived. It was spectacular. Smoking, glowing, layered like a Pride parade flag, but prettier - one of those cocktails that looks less like a beverage and more like something a wizard uses to summon someone from the netherworld. I should ask for one of those next!

I turned to see who warranted such a masterpiece.

And there she was. A total knockout. Radiant, poised, sipping casually like she hadn't just short-circuited my brain. I stared a beat too long - long enough that she noticed, glanced at her drink, then at me. I gave her what I hoped was a casual smile but looked more like gaping awe. Smooth.

All I could say was "*sŭai*," which means 'beautiful'.

She smiled and said, "*Khop khun kha*," and that's when I realized she thought

I'd been complimenting her. Which... fair. I had, in a roundabout way. But the praise had really been aimed at the drink - she just happened to be sitting behind it like some perfectly lit mirage.

Truth was, I didn't have any room left in my heart - or whatever part of me was supposed to house romantic feelings at that point. That space was fully occupied, and the lease wasn't up anytime soon. Still, I didn't want to be rude.

I smiled back and said, "*Yin dee*," - Thai for 'you're welcome' - because sometimes you just play along with the moment, even when you know in your heart it's not going anywhere.

I am not a barfly. Despite whatever stories you've concocted about me - and I know you have - I've never been the guy perched at the end of the bar in Armani, nursing a martini and a pickup line. Well... not never. There was a period in my late twenties when I gave that whole scene an honest go. Unfortunately, I discovered through repeated, undeniable evidence, that I was not the kind of guy women in bars were looking for. Turns out, chatting with a hot woman over a classic cocktail while quoting Byron doesn't exactly scream 'take me home sailor'.

My method, if you could call it that, involved opening with literary references, deep philosophical questions, or asking if they'd read The Brothers Karamazov. Spoiler: they had not. Not one of them. And they weren't planning on it. Somewhere between rejection number seventy and a lot of drinks, I came to terms with a simple truth: I was neither an Adonis nor even remotely skilled in the art of barroom banter, and no amount of tragic poet energy was going to change that.

Eventually, I made peace with it. If someone wasn't at least a little intrigued by metaphysics or couldn't spar with me over the finer points of Hamlet's moral paralysis, or embrace anything written by the great Hunter S. Thompson, I wasn't interested anyway.

Her English was rudimentary. At best. And I'd been down that road before.

The moment stretched, and like a cresting tsunami, memories of Charlee surged up into my chest, my spine, every nerve ending I hadn't numbed yet. Her voice, her laugh, that lasagna. All of it.

I paused. Took a breath. Wrestled briefly with the multi-car pileup in my gut, then did what I've learned to do in moments like this: I shoved it into a mental drawer labeled "*Not Now*," and resolved to be decent. Polite. Present. I smiled and engaged, even if the bigger part of me was a million miles away, still living someone who wasn't sitting next to me.

She made it easy. Without a word, she pulled out her phone and, with a raised eyebrow and the kind of look that said, "We both know the drill," opened our translator apps. The one everyone uses when pointing and pantomimes just won't cut it. I nodded, smiled, and lit up my own phone, app already running, because of course it was.

She smiled. I smiled. It was simple, light, and unexpectedly pleasant. No pressure. No awkward posturing. Just two strangers sharing a moment of modern diplomacy through glowing screens and broken grammar. And for a few minutes, it was easy to forget the pain and just be there.

She was also staying at the Asoke while in town at a convention for women's fashion and makeup artists, which - looking back - I probably should've guessed. Not just because she was beautiful, but because she was dressed like the event might be televised. Everything about her was intentional: her elegant outfit and her makeup subtle enough to seem effortless. It was clearly the work of someone who knew how to extract every ounce of effect from a few simple tricks.

She asked what I was writing, so I launched into what was a painfully long-winded explanation of my journey: documenting my travels across Thailand. I'm sure I sounded like a cross between a travel blogger and a lost philosopher - charming, right? Way to go, Larry! Now how about some Descartes?

She thought it was wonderful. Her dad was a writer too, she said, proudly. I asked what kind of books he wrote, expecting something deep and meaningful - you know, historical tomes worthy of awards, or the newest exposé, factually backed-up about the psychology of conservative mindsets, or maybe a postmodern angst review.

She placed her hand on my thigh, looked me dead in the eye, and said, "Romance novels."

Romance novels!

I took a moment to let that sink in - because nothing says literary gravitas like a lifetime spent writing about star-crossed lovers, dramatic declarations, and more plot twists than a soap opera.

It was the kind of bombshell you don't see coming when you're trying to impress someone with your own mediocre attempts at storytelling.

We bought each other a round. I threw caution to the wind and told Tee to double up whatever Mirabelle was drinking - because, why not? The night stretched out as we talked - monasteries, America, Thailand, food and cooking, makeup and fashion, tea, cars, elephants, travel, museums. A little bit of everything, back and forth. It was effortless.

It was easy. It was fun. I felt engaged and human.

But underneath it all, I was slipping into an unwelcome place - a quiet zone of regret. Did I really want this? Sex without soulful connection? That's never been my thing. One-night stands? Not my style. The few times that's happened in my life, I still carry the burden of those shallow, meaningless nights, like a bruise that won't fade.

Loveless, base, transactional - I'd rather stay home and read one of her father's romance novels. At least those come with a plot.

Normally, I would have welcomed this. She was smart, engaging, well-versed in everything from art to automobiles and incredibly hot to boot. By all rights, I should have felt something. But I didn't.

Numbness, like a thick fog settled in where feelings and the excitement of possibilities should be. And beneath it all, the sharp, definitive sense of betrayal - because no matter how enticing and engaging the company, my heart wasn't there. It was back with Charlee, tangled up in love memories mixed with regrets I hadn't fully unpacked.

She wasn't upset by my quiet rejection once I gave her the shorthand glimpse of the storm I was weathering inside. As I made my excuses to leave, she rose slowly, and with a gentleness that caught me off guard, pressed a soft kiss to my cheek.

Her eyes held a quiet kindness, a tenderness that words couldn't capture. Then, carefully, she typed into her app: "She was a very lucky woman to have found you. I'm sorry you lost her."

That simple message landed between us like a fragile thread. Delicate, sincere, and profoundly human.

Back upstairs in my apartment, curled up in bed alone, tears streaming uncontrollably down my cheeks, I couldn't stop. I found myself apologizing to Charlee, not just for the fleeting, shallow thought of hooking up with someone else, but for the desperate, aching need to fill the connection that she had built with me.

I went from quiet tears to full-on, body-wracking sobs that saw no end. The loss of my friend, my lover, crashed over me like a building collapsing, relentless and merciless, crushing my heart and soul beneath its weight.

But Charlee was more than just a friend or lover. She was the woman who had teased me, challenged me, tested me, pushed me to my limits in ways no one else ever had. And because I had passed every exam, she had rewarded me with her golden stars - adoration, admiration, and a love so rare and profound that it defies simple description.

It was still dark as I drifted slowly up from the edges of dreamland, my body heavy and still tangled in sleep, when I actually felt her - Charlee - holding me. Not just in memory, but like a warm, breath-soaked presence pressing close, her arms around me in a way that was both tender and impossibly real.

Then came her whisper, soft and clear, a voice threading through the quiet darkness: "Thank you for honoring us. She wanted to come to your bed, but all the while, your heart never left me. You are honorable and loyal, and I love you so deeply. I'll always be here, beside you, inside you, with you."

Her words hung in the air, a fragile promise wrapped in love and longing. It was both comfort and hollow ache. A reminder that some bonds outlast time, space, even absence. I lay there, feeling the weight of her presence, caught somewhere between the tangible and the ghostly, between what was lost and what remained.

It was visceral. It was physical. I woke fully from that dreamscape, sweating, heart pounding, expecting to turn and find her ghostly visage smiling softly at me with those eyes that radiated love. But no, just the quiet dark, and the stubborn ache of absence. It was my mind, my soul playing a bittersweet game, luring me back into Charlee's welcoming arms, just to feel that beautiful togetherness once again.

I drifted back into sleep knowing I'd made the right call, that honoring what I'd had was more important than chasing what might be.

It took a long time to fully awaken. I was dragging, heavy not from alcohol, but from the emotional gravity of the night. The entire encounter looped in my mind, frame by frame.

I caught myself foolishly scanning the apartment for signs. Tiny, impossible clues that Charlee had somehow crossed the veil and come to me in the night.

Was the remote angled differently than I'd left it?

Wasn't that water bottle empty when I crashed?

I could've sworn I'd tossed my clothes in the corner but now they were neatly folded and placed atop the laundry bag - something I never do, but she always did.

Stupid, I know. Desperate, definitely. But somehow, there was a faint scent in the air, Charlee's scent. Familiar, warm, yet fleeting. Something that didn't belong to memory but was fresh and alive. A lingering bouquet of her? Or maybe just my mind playing tricks, layering the longing with illusion.

Still, I held onto that trace of her, like a drowning man lunging for driftwood. I stepped into the shower and let the warmth wash over me. I closed my eyes, letting it become a meditation, on grief, on grace, on the ache of love that refuses to leave.

Yet I'll wrestle with myself every day just to keep the ache alive. Because the pain meant she was still there. And I would rather carry that weight, raw and unrelenting, than let her fade into memory. Letting go would mean losing her twice. And I couldn't bear that. Not ever.

Back in the land of the living where the water smells like diesel, I hopped the Saen Saep canal ferry, only a block and a bridge from the apartment. The boat, a very fast yet rickety, tarp-covered barge that seemed to defy both physics and modern safety standards, roared northward like it had somewhere better to be. I stayed upright, which on that thing is a minor miracle, and rode it four stops to Thonglor pier.

As I stepped off the boat, I whispered to Charlee. "Alright love. Let's go see what's out there." It was both reflex and ritual now. A quiet nod to the ghost in my machine. No tears this time. Just a gentle pang tucked away in my heart.

I had no plan. I just wanted to walk. I *needed* to walk. To discover. All the way up Thong Lo Road - Sukhumvit Road 55 for those keeping score - then right along Sukhumvit proper, then another right, taking me back down to the Asoke Residence. The goal? Rack up some kilometers, forage for breakfast and lunch like a streetwise vagabond and explore what's often touted as Bangkok's trendiest neighborhood. I'd heard Thong Lo was where Thai celebrities and nouveau riche sent their designer dogs for grooming and bought 300 Baht matcha lattes that looked like science experiments. I was in. At least from a cultural observation perspective.

Disembarking the Khlong boat with the skill of someone who's learned all the tricks, to the left of the dock was a cavernous warehouse, open to the street like a gaping mouth. Inside it was teeming with what could only be described as a junk market. This was not a tourist trap selling elephant pants and fridge magnets.

This was the real deal – purely local, unapologetically rough around the edges, and I knew the moment I stepped inside that I had crossed some invisible threshold into unfamiliar territory. The looks I got said it all: *You're not from around here, are you boy?*

Piles of used clothing were stacked in mounds. Shirts, trousers, bras, underwear, mismatched socks, most of it in tangled heaps like fabric had given up on being folded in this lifetime. The prices were so low they might have been suggestions. One of the piles had a price sign that said, in Thai, you buy not by the item, but by weight. I used the translator to figure that out. I'd never seen garments sold by weight before! Off to one side was a table of old electronics: enormous first-gen VCRs, dusty radios with dials, tangled power cords, ancient irons that probably had more rust inside than a sunken ship, and – be still my nostalgic heart – an original Sony Walkman, the kind I once clutched as a teenager like sacred treasure on long trips. I picked it up briefly, held it like a relic, and gently set it down again. There was no way that thing still worked, but it almost hurt to let it go.

Around another corner were sporting goods, if you could call them that. Battered soccer and flat basketballs, splintered cricket bats held together with duct tape, some kind of goalie assemblage, yoga mats that had clearly seen some things none of us would like to think about. This wasn't a market so much as a dingy garage sale where all the garages had flooded and no one bothered to sort the mess. And the smell – dear God, the smell! It was the kind of sour, rotten trash can, oily funk that clung to your clothes and followed you out like a stray dog.

In the back were two road-weary food carts, one with a pot of something burbling that looked like motor oil and smelled ... vile. That's the only word that truly fits. I usually orbit street carts like a meteor that's been sucked in by gravitational pull, but not this time. Whatever they were cooking back there had found a new very dark corner of the olfactory wheel, one I hope never to revisit.

Still, I lingered. Because this was life unfiltered. No camera-ready tourist angles or artful displays. Just locals going about their day, bartering over broken toasters and weathered jeans. It was raw and unfiltered, and that alone made it beautiful. Just not edible.

Wandering farther up the road and, thankfully, out of range of the chemical warfare being cooked up in that warehouse of forgotten lives, I felt the fog begin to lift. Whatever that stench had been – rancid duck fat mixed with old socks and suicidal dreams – it was now behind me, fading like a bad memory you don't want to talk about but will absolutely bring up at dinner for the gross-out factor.

I dodged a few tuk tuks and a man carrying what I hoped was a mannequin's leg, and into a side street looking for quiet. I ducked down the romantically named Thong Lo 25 Alley. They have a thing for numbered streets in Thailand.

It was there I found salvation in the form of caffeine and puffy laminated dough. Pacamara Coffee Roaster. Minimalist black-and-white signage. Industrial concrete and tinted big-pane glass with air-con cold enough to qualify as a wine cellar. So ultra-chic inside, the place practically screamed, *"We only serve people with ironic tattoos, pork-pie hats and limited-edition sneakers,"* and I was fine with that though I had none of those to offer the hipster gods. The espresso was so dense and rich it could've paid rent on a Tokyo penthouse. Perfectly extracted. No bitterness. Just that tight, tiger-striped crema that clung to the lip like a tattoo of its own. If I hadn't wiped it off, it'd still be there.

The croissant? Holy Moly! It was absurdly light, with layers so thin you could read print through them. It exploded on first bite like crystal, then gave way to a floating interior that somehow defied gravity and science. I sat there, caffeinated and quietly euphoric, reading the morning news and wondering if anyone had ever described a pastry as "explosive" without being ridiculed. I guess I'll find out.

The air was already thick with humidity, but that didn't stop the Thong Lo locals from looking sharp. A woman in full business attire strode past me like the heat was a mild inconvenience. I, on the other hand, was already sticking to myself in three places and hadn't even gotten back to the main road.

Thong Lo is a curious beast. Equal parts modern Hong Kong old-school Bangkok, and Beverly Hills on a sugar high. In one block I passed a sleek glass-fronted café called "Perception" (what does it serve? Latte's named existential dread?), a street vendor grilling skewers of foie gras, and a car dealership where the cheapest vehicle on display was a Rolls Royce Phantom.

Still, it was oddly charming. Locals bustled around. They were on a secret schedule I wasn't privy to. Expats in linen pants pretended not to care how they looked while casually angling for the best Tik Tok light. I was somewhere in the middle: sun-drenched, caffeinated, and trying not to look like I was narrating the whole thing in my head. Which I was.

And you know what? It felt good. Not profound or life-altering, but good in that subtle, "maybe I'll be okay after all" kind of way. The grief hadn't gone away. But it had loosened its grip around my soul just enough to let in a little curiosity.

And the promise of something delicious just around the corner didn't hurt either. It was lunchtime and I was on the hunt.

Back on the main drag, I wandered aimlessly. It was the kind of wandering where you're not really looking for anything, but you'll know it when you see it. The famed nightlife of Thong Lo was nowhere in sight. Daylight had a way of turning cocktail dens into shuttered mysteries and trendy restaurants into quiet storefronts with frosted windows and self-important fonts. But even in repose, you could tell why this neighborhood had a reputation. It was tidy and unnaturally new. Hipster minimalism met Bangkok gloss. Coffee shops with one-syllable names, avant-garde galleries where paintings don't have price tags, and salons so high-end you needed a stylist just to get an appointment with another stylist.

And then I saw it. Lunch. A small cluster of two-story Japanese-themed buildings sat off to my right, like someone had airlifted a corner of Kyoto and plopped it into Bangkok. I looked up. On the second floor was a modest sign in clean white font: Tsuru Home Made Udon. Below it, a Lamborghini, a Lancia, and something else expensive and aerodynamic were parked outside a luxury auto detailer.

Japanese noodles above, supercars below? I mean, who wouldn't want to slurp thick hand-cut udon while spying on someone toothbrush-clean the wheels of a hypercar?

I went upstairs and stepped inside. The place was hushed despite nearly every table being full. Each table was low to the ground with clean lines and calm aesthetics, the kind of dining arrangement that whispered discipline and posture and a slipped disc. But mercifully, someone had done us all a solid: the area beneath each table had been hollowed out. So, while it looked like you were seated demurely on a tatami mat, serene and culturally enlightened, in reality you were just sitting at the little kids' table with a leg well. A clever illusion called Horigotatsu - Zen on top, orthopedic underneath.

The menu didn't impress with design, it wasn't one of those embossed, artisanal, triple-fold affairs printed on hand-pressed rice paper in ink made with the chef's tears. No, this stunner was all content. Dish after dish that made me sit up straighter and consider what I'd been doing with my life up until now.

The Tenmusu caught my eye first - a sushi hand grenade: a plump rice boat wrapped in nori, topped with tempura shrimp so fresh it died with honor. I hadn't seen that since San Francisco at Hamano in Noe Valley - in days long past, and I wasn't about to pass up the chance to revisit that edible nostalgia.

Edamame was a no-brainer. Like peanuts at a dive bar, but for people who know what dashi is. Salty, firm, addictive, I could eat my weight in them and still consider it a palate cleanser.

Then came the main event: Hiyashi Ikura. Cold, handmade udon noodles coiled like silk ribbon beneath a riot of color and texture with translucent salmon roe that popped like tiny ocean fireworks, crispy tempura corn, dried shrimp, slivered vegetables, a confetti of umami-packed goodies. Each bite was a cold plunge into complexity, bright and briny, fat and clean all at once.

I was briefly tempted by another dish named "Bukkake Oroshi." A moment of juvenile, immature laughter flickered by. But I decided not to press my luck, or the waitress's patience. Just what was in that sauce again?

Lunch was phenomenal. If you're in the neighborhood ....

Turning right onto Sukhumvit Road I crossed to the far side. Yes, Mom, I used the crosswalk and looked both ways. I even waited for the little green man to wave me on. I could hear her voice in my head: "Do you want to get flattened by a scooter going sixty while the driver eats soup?" No mother. I do not.

I had discovered a used bookstore along that stretch, and wouldn't you know it just a few blocks down, there it was: Dasa Book Café, standing proud like a literary oasis between a Doc Martens store and a gallery. The place looked like it had survived coups, recessions, and several generations of backpackers pretending to understand Proust. My kind of shop.

With only a couple of nights left at the Asoke, tomorrow was earmarked for horizontal ambitions - lounging by the pool, catching up on writing, and reacquainting myself with the fine art of doing absolutely nothing. I'd left most of my books behind on Koh Chang. Not because I didn't like them, but because hauling around ten pounds of bound paper and ink in 100-degree heat and 200% humidity makes you question your commitment to plot development. Besides, I'd read them already.

They'd found a good home alongside the guest stash at the Kae Bae Grand View, an informal lending library of John le Carre and Danielle Steele novelettes, alongside 20 copies of Eat, Pray, Love and even more of Fifty Shades of Whatever - spines cracked and swollen like the feet of every tourist who's underestimated Thai walking distances. It was time to reload.

Preferably something with a pulse, maybe a road trip novel (sorry Jack - already read "On The Road" a dozen times,) or some coming-of-age story with a narrator who wasn't trying too hard to sound deep. A book with mileage and hopefully, a font larger than 8-point.

It wasn't The Lost Bookshop, my favorite multi-storied warren up in Chiang Mai, but Dasa was a solid runner-up. A proper used bookstore. The owner, an amiable expat with a tan the color of aged mahogany ran the place with his sharp-eyed Thai wife. You could tell they'd been at it for decades. There was a rhythm to their presence, like bartenders who'd heard every story more than twice.

I gave him some loose parameters. No trash novels, no books with embossed gold titles or cover endorsements from People magazine. He gave me a withering look over the tops of his glasses, the kind that said, "What sort of establishment do you think I'm running here, bub?" Fair enough.

To get back in his good graces, I named a few literary spirit animals: Edward Abbey, Kesey, Atwood, Thompson, Woolf, Buford, Sedaris and tossed in a few red herrings just to keep him guessing. That did the trick. He softened, nodded once, disappeared into the stacks, and returned with a few paperbacks by authors I'd never heard of. But he had the glint of a man who reads, which is different from a man who merely sells books.

I grabbed a few and made a mental note to swing back once I moved back up the road. My last week in Thailand would be spent inside the chaos of central Sukhumvit, and I had a feeling I'd want something to read that didn't involve enlightenment or instructions on how to cleanse my chakras with activated charcoal and a rub-down with fermented bean paste.

Nothing else happened. No, really. The walk back to the Asoke was uneventful. Quiet in a manner that felt like kindness. The sun was slipping lower, behind the towers of glass and steel, softening the edges of the city's energy into a gentle hum.

At the end of the alley, I stopped at the fruit cart and loaded up on skewered melons and pineapple. Mangosteens caught my eye, that nirvana fruit that once held me in rapture. Charlee and my relationship blossomed over that delicacy, and we shared mangosteens every day from the moment we met. It was our cornerstone. I gazed upon them remembering laughter over their perfumed sweetness, those moments simple and perfect, as if mangosteen was created just for us.

But today? They'd lost their sparkle. They weren't the same. Or they were, but I certainly as hell wasn't. Like so much else in life, the fruit was still there - but the magic wasn't. Sometimes, the things that once lit you up become reminders of what you can't have.

I grabbed a bag of Khao Phat and some awesome smelling Pad Krapow as well - street-cart comfort food that required no fuss, no effort beyond opening the bag (man, they wrap those red rubber bands tightly around the tops!), shoveling a spoon in and have at it. No grand gestures, just easy and delicious sustenance.

The next day unfolded slow and easy. Late morning found me sprawled poolside at the Asoke Residence, the sun pouring down in generous waves, turning the water a shimmering, hypnotic bright blue. The air was thick with the buzz of city life from down the alley, where cars and scooters were doing their thing, while the hum of conversation from nearby balconies blended into a gentle soundtrack for my reverie.

In one hand, a cold beer. Crisp, light, the kind that slides down easy and reminds you why summer days exist. In the other, a used copy of "The Lincoln Highway" by Amor Towles, its pages dog-eared, rife with stories of brothers whose road stretched out before them. The prose was rich and warm, painting Midwestern landscapes, hobo trains, vile adventures and sibling bonds with a charming tenderness that hit deep. It's an outstanding bit of writing should you be looking for something new.

I let the words wash over me, as the sunshine did, slow and steady, filling up the empty spaces left behind by restless thoughts. My shattered dreams were still there but faded, replaced by the gentle rhythm of the day, the clink of ice in glasses, the laughter of others around the pool, and the gleeful splash of kids frolicking and diving in the water. For a while, it was just my book and a blue sky and a lonely normalcy.

The fine young lads manning the front desk at Asoke had that glint in their eyes - equal parts insider knowledge and impish mischief when they told me that Srinakharinwirot University, just up the road, held a weekly night market and food fair. "It's *really* good," one of them said, with the kind of hushed emphasis usually reserved for insider trading deals.

This was the same guy who'd recommended Bombay Masala, and that young man had proven taste. So, I thought, sure, if it's terrible, I'll pivot to the yakitori shack just down the road and gnaw on some grilled chicken parts.

The market took over the university's big open quad, and it was absolutely hopping. Wall-to-wall students, music thumping from both ends, smells curling through the air like siren songs. And not another farang in sight. My hopes perked up like a street dog spotting a dropped satay skewer.

But I was worried. That market had all the trademarks of mediocrity: fancy modern carts and upscale stalls, custom neon signs, cartoon mascots bouncing around like they were promoting a new energy drink, influencers flitting about with their gimbals and filters. But beneath the razzle-dazzle, it was basically a modern remix of something ancient and wonderful - community, craziness, and food.

I immediately fell for the mushroom guy. He'd set up a long shichirin grill with row after row of hulking porcini mushrooms, their gills glistening, lined up like a fungi fashion runway over glowing Binchotan coals. He was cooking them to perfection then brushing them with a bright Yuzu juice sauce. They were incredible!

Then came the Wagyu skewers, rich and buttery and gone too fast. A woman was frying up chicken that snapped when you bit it, not from crunch but from sheer self-respect. Someone was turning out golden oyster French omelets (yes I had one,) while another cart flipped thin roti filled with banana and drizzled condensed milk like Pollock was in the back. And just when I thought I might escape with some dignity, a woman reeled me in with strawberry, blueberry, and durian custard tarts, each the size of a poker chip and twice as addictive.

And yes, I ate all of it.

But wait, there's more. Because there's always more at Thai street markets. A lot more. Local bands jammed at either end of the quad, the kind of music you don't know but instantly get nostalgic for. It looked like the entire student body, and half their professors had turned out for the shindig.

So yeah, another feather in that stylish young concierge's cap. The man was two-for-two. I might have to ask him for Thailand investment tips next.

I didn't feel like venturing too far afield, so I made a tactical retreat to WYWS. And honestly, how has no one asked me what the hell that stands for yet? WYWS. It sounds like a dental school or a boy band. But no - it's short for "Where You Wander Station." I didn't name it. I just drink there.

With that out of the way, I asked for a martini. No lecture needed, and no Himalayan bitters aged in a yak-hide barrel. Just a martini. Tee obliged, bless him.

I called it an early night. Slipped back to the apartment, caught up with Charlee over my personal hotline to heaven, watched something on Amazon Prime that I forgot ten minutes after it ended, and called it a day. A good one. Full belly, half-full heart, and just buzzed enough to sleep like a man with nothing left in that day's tank.

It was my last day at the Asoke Residence, and as I packed up early that morning, I found myself surprisingly sentimental. The place had been good to me. Quietly, steadily good. Not in any flashy, "Instagram me!" kind of way, but in the ways that mattered. Cathartic, even. It had let me heal, if even a little, stretch out, go inward, and wander outward.

Was the Asoke a five-star hotel? No. It was better. Mostly locals stayed there. The staff called me by name. I saw the same cat every morning curled under the frangipani bush. It felt lived in, honest. Real. That meant something.

I'd dropped off my laundry the day before at the little mom-and-pop place down the block and picked it up early. It smelled Downy-fresh, still warm, pressed, and bundled up ready to go. With everything zipped and packed, there was nothing left to do but go for a walk.

I made my way across the footbridge - the same one that ran above the Khlong Saen Saep canal where ferries ply the canal like coked-up sea serpents - and made for the Petchaburi BTS. One stop to Sukhumvit. I could've walked it, but I was feeling the kind of slow burn lazy that comes from knowing it's your last day and you've earned it. The best kind.

I was on one of my wandering jags, no destination in mind, just a vague craving for movement and maybe a new pair of walking shorts. Not just any shorts - something breathable, pocketed, and capable of surviving Thai humidity without welding itself to my inner thigh by midday. You know, high standards.

I got off the BTS and wandered into Terminal 21 Asok - yet another mega-mall bad-trip travesty of greed, where air conditioning and artificial light try to blind you into thinking you're having fun. Each of these shopping behemoths has its own Frankenstein personality stitched together from "influencer" wish lists and design school dropouts. T21? T21 was trying so hard to be cool it was painful. Like grandpa at Coachella in a crop top with his mullet sticking out from an ironic bucket hat. Just... no.

Every floor is themed like a different city. Rome, Tokyo, London, Istanbul - and fails miserably at the concept. It's like a passport to madness. Still, I didn't care. I was roaming, my mood set to "low expectations." I knew full well I wasn't going to find the kind of shorts I wanted. Not unless I wanted to pay luxury resort prices for the privilege of looking like a castoff from the bad RomCom third time around spin-off.

But that's the penalty for wandering into a mall where make-believe glitz and mall glamour go to die under mood controlling computerized LED lighting. I wandered on, shorts still theoretical, dignity intact, for now.

After a grueling twenty minutes - yes, a whole twenty - I couldn't take it anymore. I tapped out. Enough of the shops, which all seemed like cut-copy-paste versions of each other. Enough of the food courts trying hard to dish up authentic and failing spectacularly. I felt horrible for the shop clerks all sporting the same thousand-yard stares, endlessly refolding the same logo shirts, or obsessively rearranging artisanal soap pyramids, hoping someone - *anyone* - would wander in and ask them *anything*. I don't even think they wanted you to buy something. No, commerce was secondary. They just wanted to be seen. To feel alive. To break the slow, fluorescent chokehold of retail purgatory.

I almost walked into a shop out of pure pity, but I knew if I made eye contact, I'd never escape. I'd be guilt-sold into a cologne I'd never wear or a linen shirt that would unravel in the wash. So, I bolted.

Terminal 21: come for the air-con, stay for .... nope - can't think of a single reason.

I made my escape like a man fleeing a collapsing mine shaft - lightheaded, slightly ashamed, and covered in the psychic rot of overstimulation. Back out into the street, I took a deep breath of Bangkok smog and admired the not-so fresh air.

I wandered up toward the Nana District, that swirling human soup of confusion and consumption, where the most compacted, impacted throng of wide-eyed tourists fanned out across the zone like spilled marbles, each one slowly rolling toward their next sugar and fish sauce intersect. I had purposely been avoiding checking the area out simply because of all the tourist recommendations that said it was "crazy fun." Which means no, it isn't.

None of them knew what they wanted, which oddly made sense, because at the surface level of tourism, Bangkok doesn't really ask you to know. It just asks you to keep moving along. If you know, you know - where and how and when to get the good stuff. But Nana? Nono.

And when in doubt, eat. That's what most of them were doing anyway. Scarfing down fried things, roasted things, braised things, sweet things, skewers of mystery meats, plate after plate of mediocre tourist Pad Thai, and something that might've been alive at one point, or it might've been a shoelace. I couldn't tell, even up close. But no one seemed bothered.

And when the hoards aren't eating? They're drinking. A lot. From Tiki bars to swanky whiskey dens, everyone is drinking. Except the bar girls. Their drinks are colored water, and they'll cost you $20 a pop. That and a little love-you-long-time? That's Nana.

I strolled through it all - part spectator, part participant in the flow - letting the current pull me forward, along sidewalks, stone-laid courtyards, the Nana Plaza blazing away with neon-glazed stores, stalls and carts, past girlie and lady-boy bars. I kept moving.

I looped back toward the Asok, where the city felt less like a sales pitch and more like a well lived-in apartment where younger generations still party every night. Tomorrow, I'd move into the Rembrandt Hotel for my last eight days in Thailand - a final descent with a high thread count.

The place had character, which is just a polite way of saying the carpets had stories and the wallpaper was faded. But if it meant avoiding the gleaming towers packed with tourists who travel thousands of miles to experience a western chain hotel identical to the one back home, then yes - Rembrandt me up. I didn't need top-flight luxury. I needed a soft bed, access to great food options, a pool, and a place to quietly accept that my adventure was winding down.

That's not to say the Rembrandt didn't still carry more than a few glimmers of its former glory. Back in its heyday, it was one of the best hotels in the district - white-tablecloth fancy, elbows-off-the-bar classy. But time marches on for all and everything, and one thing I've learned along the way is that the Thai love to build. Constantly. Relentlessly. Maintenance, though? Not as sexy so that's not a part of the business plan.

And it was a killer deal on a travel site. Location and aged charm? Check. Large suites and bathrooms that didn't feel like a penalty box? Absolutely. Two pools and a deck bar to squint out at the skyline and pretend I understood anything about endings? Sold. I wasn't chasing glamour. I just needed a soft place to land while the trip folded itself onto pages and into memory.

I swung into the vast marble lobby and introduced myself, explained that I'd been staying down Asok Montri by the Saen Saep canal but would be checking in tomorrow, and - any chance of an early check-in possible? Yes! Once they found my reservation, they asked if I needed help with bags or a taxi. But by now, I knew how the city worked. I smiled, thanked them, and with the practiced ease of someone who'd earned a few Thai stripes, said, "I got it. Khop khun krab. See you in the morning."

༄

Staying in a big suite on the 29th floor, looking out over the vertical sprawl of Bangkok and down onto the high-rise pool deck and rooftop gardens felt like the proper way to wind things down. The bed wasn't just a king - it was a California King. An entire zip code of mattress.

I unpacked for the last time in Thailand, taking my time to settle in. Clothes in drawers, closet-worthy gear onto hangers, toiletries in the bathroom - what was left of them. I changed into shorts, grabbed a book, journal, and pens, and made my way to the eleventh-floor pool deck to catch a little sun. Maybe sneak in a morning nap on a chaise and order something easy poolside.

I grabbed a few towels from the deck rack and claimed the last available chaise lounge. By then, the early risers had already come down to stake their claims - towels, newspapers or a paperback left like territorial flags. One nice thing about traveling solo: there's usually that one odd-man-out spot left.

I read for a while, sipping what could technically be described as coffee, if we're going purely by color. I'd fix that situation later. The upside? So little caffeine that after a few sips and a few pages of a book that wasn't exactly setting my world on fire; I started to drift. I won't name names. The author had clearly put effort into crafting her tale but it wasn't enough. I let myself slide into dreamland beneath the mid-morning Bangkok sun.

I was woken by boisterous voices with New Zealand lilts coming my way. As they approached and saw that I was napping, the volume dropped like a DJ fading out the dance floor. I slowly surfaced, eyes still closed behind jet-black shades and gave them a cursory nod as they settled in.

I let myself drift back out onto my private ocean of sleep.

I don't know how long I was under. I'd slipped deep into a personal REM-scape; vivid, IMAX-level dreams featured a rotating cast of my ex, Charlee, my daughter, an old friend. A couple of monks dancing in and out of the sequences. All of them needed something, wanted something, urging something with the kind of intensity that makes dream logic feel like courtroom drama.

And then jostling. A voice cut through the ether: "Mate. you're gonna lobster-bake like that!"

I jerked awake, totally disoriented, skin hovering just a few degrees shy of ignition point.

Thanking the gentleman profusely, I decided a plunge would be a great way to get the blood flowing. That. Was. A. Huge. Fucking. Mistake.

I'd foolishly skipped the part where one checks the pool temp before diving in. That there wasn't ice floating on the surface was a miracle that should go into some book for posterity - oh, wait, I've got that covered.

Shrinkage? No. Shrinkage implies a measurable event. This was implosion. Internal organs retreated. Parts of me I valued wondered if they were welcome anymore.

Ice cream headache? That would've been merciful. This was full-body vascular betrayal. By the time I surfaced, gasping like someone who just survived a plane crash into the Arctic, my brain was calmly narrating: "So this is what cardiac arrest feels like."

My dive momentum had carried me through to shallow end steps, which was the only reason I didn't just sink and call it a life well lived. And any ideas of a flip turn and a heroic lap to the other side? Laughable. No thank you. That idea died on contact.

I tried to play it cool as I made my way along the curve of the kidney-shaped pool, but I was shaking and chattering like an entire grove of Aspen trees in a stiff autumn breeze. Graceful exit? Not even close.

The Kiwi chap came over, bearing a towel like it was the Holy Grail. "Bit brisk in there, mate?" he grinned, as if he hadn't just witnessed a grown man go into full aquatic convulsion.

Understatement of the century from anywhere or anytime. I wrapped the towel around me like a trauma blanket. Luckily it had been roasting in the sun and felt like it had just come out of a dryer set to "lava." I lay back down and let the blazing sun finish thawing me out. It felt incredible. I was now, without question, wide awake.

At this point, I could keep boring you with more. More tales, more street food, more wrong turns on public transportation and alley discoveries. But why? We've already walked those Sois together. You've read about the markets, the temples, the steaming bowls of soup and endless noodle slurps. You know the rhythm of it by now. The rest? You should go get lost in Thailand and find it yourself.

So, here's the short version of my final week: I wandered the enormous Chatuchak Park and lost myself in the labyrinth of the gigantic weekend market. I then spent a few tranquil hours in Benchakitti Forest Park, tucked like a vast secret right in the city's concrete chest. I saw more monitor lizards slithering through the shallows, but I didn't flinch. Charlee wasn't beside me anymore. If they wanted a piece of me, they could have it.

There were late nights, strong coffee, foot massages under flickering bulbs, the smell of grilled pork in alleys that looked dangerous until they smiled back. You know the Bangkok beat by now.

But here's a deeper truth: the soul of Bangkok is hustle.

Not the Western idea of hustle - the grind-for-status, win-at-any-cost treadmill. No. Bangkok's hustle is woven into the saffron robes of monks at dawn, walking barefoot for alms. It's in the vendor who wakes at 4AM to prep jok for the early-bird workers before traffic snarls the streets. It's in the elderly woman outside Hua Lamphong Station selling lottery tickets with a politeness so graceful it feels like a benediction.

I've never believed in heaven, hell, or an afterlife. But Dorje Rinpoche did. So did every Thai monk and lay practitioner I sat with on cushions, at a battered table with plastic stools, on a sidewalk curb or upon temple steps. For them, reincarnation wasn't a question, it was the architecture of reality. And after sitting with it through many moments of contemplation, I started to wonder: what if I'd been too quick to dismiss reincarnation? Too proud to admit there are things I don't understand that deserve a second or third look?

After all, weren't Copernicus and Newton considered madmen in their time? Einstein was told to stick to patents. And Feynman? He introduced a whole new paradigm to reality, which it seems, is always up for revision.

And then there was Namdak. All those decades ago, as we stood in that Capitola home, hugging goodbye, he whispered something that stayed with me like a string tied around my finger:

"I'll always be your friend. For all times, in every world, in all forms and rebirths. We don't end here."

I don't know if he's right. But I want him to be. I want to believe that the soul, the essence of who we are, gets another shot. That love, once kindled, doesn't vanish with the body. I want to believe in my heart that somewhere, in some form, Charlee is waiting. And if that's true - if these mysteries hold weight - I'd accept every ounce of sorrow for one more crossing.

Thailand, if not life itself, teaches you that everything cycles. People. Markets. Moods. Even the monsoons. There is a Thai saying goes: mai bpen rai - 'Never mind. Let it go.' Everything flows on. Suffering. Joy. Love. Life. That's impermanence.

And yes, the city, as is life, is a hustle. But it's not a cynical one. It's about scraping together enough. enough for a meal, a phone top-up, and a school uniform for your son. It's the kind of hustle that keeps a society running not on greed, but on grit and grace.

Because beneath it all, we all want the same things.

A safe place to sleep. A meal we don't have to beg for. A partner who holds us even after the fire of passion turns to the soft embers of loyalty. A child who eats without fear. A body that doesn't flinch at bombs, bullets or bureaucrats.

It doesn't matter if your soil is Thai or Texan, Irish or Indian. What matters is how you move through the world - how you treat the stranger at a stall, your lover in the kitchen, or your own trembling self at three in the morning.

Maybe leaving home for that quiet monastery in the misty northern mountains of Thailand was selfish. But I needed to fall apart for a while. I needed to test myself. To rebuild myself. To find out if I was right about anything or if I was clinging to beliefs that were keeping me from being truly alive.

And what I've come to believe, through monks, mangoes, and moments of connection, is that we keep turning. That the universe isn't asking us for perfection. It's asking for participation. For presence.

Every day, there are storms and gifts. Pain and balm. You don't get to choose the ratio. But you do get to show up.

So, pack a bag. Get sick. Heal. Fall in love. Lose yourself. Eat something that smells like gasoline and tastes like heaven. Sit on a bus for hours beside a stranger who offers you dried squid snacks with a grin. Smile at the faces that scare you. And watch how they smile back.

Do you hear what they're saying?

"Hey! You're just like me."

CHAPTER 18. AYUTTHAYA. LESSONS FROM A COSMOPOLITAN KINGDOM

"Arbitrary power is most easily established on the ruins of liberty abused to licentiousness." - George Washington, 1796

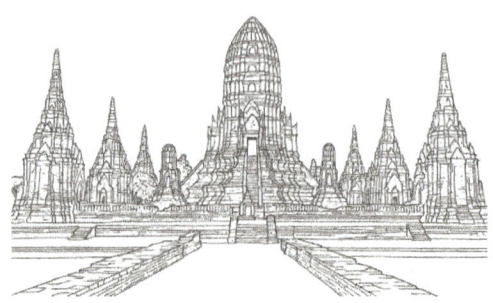

Ayutthaya would be my final frontier, the last adventure in Thailand before heading home, and I wanted to do it right. Not just postcard-right but dig-into-the-dirt and life-memory right. Three weeks out, I started researching private tour companies, hoping to avoid the kind of guide who just points at a chedi and proudly announces, "Brick. Old. Look around."

I had asked Charlee about my idea back then and she said not only was it worth the visit, but she'd happily come too, claiming it was incredible. Of course, the universe changed our plans, but I still wanted to go, to see Ayutthaya through not only my own eyes, but to imagine the wonder glowing in Charlee's as well. To honor our plans.

I found exactly what I was looking for in a guide. I'll call him Sam. A university history professor by weekday, Sam moonlighted as a private tour guide for travelers who want more than the random hookup guided by someone who has to get back by 3 to pick the kids up from school. Add to that a driver named Sira who had a marvelous smile and a comfortable luxury sedan with blessedly effective air-conditioning, and we were off.

Now, I'd love to say the trip was filled with laughs and antics, and while we shared a few good chuckles, Ayutthaya isn't *that* kind of place (I wasn't in the mood for laughs anyway.) Ayutthaya doesn't lend itself to comic relief. What those ruins offer instead is a sobering, gut-wrenching lesson in insolence, greed, brutality, and the revolting creativity of human cruelty.

"Aye-YOO-tee-uh" - say it right or be judged by Thai grandmothers everywhere - was named a UNESCO World Heritage Site in 1991. And it earned it for more reasons than I've got fingers and toes. Once one of Southeast Asia's richest and most powerful kingdoms, Ayutthaya morphed from a swampy plains trade hub to a full-blown empire, changing the continent's commercial DNA along the way.

It was wealthy - obscenely so - but it was also cosmopolitan in a way that puts most modern cities to shame. Foreign merchants weren't just welcomed, they were given their own neighborhoods: Dutch, Portuguese, Chinese, Persian, Japanese. Each with their own quarters on the far sides of the rivers, like some ancient international flea market collective, but with elephants. Cultures collided, mingled, and eventually blended, creating something new and unmistakably Thai. This wasn't just a melting pot. It was a garam masala blend from corners of the globe that had never seen each other before.

And the kingdom's real estate? Prime. As the saying goes - location, location, location! A hundred kilometers inland from the Gulf of Thailand, Ayutthaya was built on an island formed by the convergence of three rivers: the Chao Phraya, Lopburi, and Pa Sak. The choice of that geography was no accident or dumb luck. That island created a natural buttress against pirates and seaborne invasions while keeping trade flowing like cash into a casino. It also gave the kings convenient choke points for taxation. Commerce flourished. So did bureaucracy.

Before Ayutthaya was a kingdom, it was a trading post. And before it was that the future island inhabitants lived and traded in the mosquito-rich lowland plains where Prince Uthong - allegedly the son of a wealthy Chinese merchant decided to plant his flag. The origin story has a few variations, but most agree on this: in 1350AD, a plague broke out. Uthong, ever the practical visionary (and possibly immune from infectious disease because, you know, King), led his people away from pestilence and death in search of higher ground and better opportunities. After several days trekking across the plains, they arrived across the banks from a river island. Strategic. Safe. Salable.

In 1351AD, Uthong founded his new capital - Ayutthaya - and gave himself a promotion. Now King Ramathibodi I, he got busy in a big way. The name "Ayutthaya" is derived from 'Ajeyah', Sanskrit for "invincible" and referenced the mythical city of Ayodhya in the Ramayana. It was branding with intent and possibly the first genius stroke of promotional marketing.

And build he did. Using the vast resources around him - hardwood timber, clay, stone and straw, and the kind of boundless ambition that ends in either empire or disaster - he carved out his kingdom. Locally it was known as Krung Tai, "The Tai Kingdom," and for a while, it lived up to the name.

The Dutch, French, Portuguese, Chinese, Mon, Malays, Persians, Japanese, and even Armenians came to trade. You name them, they were there, hawking everything from silk, sugar, salt, ceramics, beads and shells, slaves and spices. Things went well. Until they didn't.

Enter Burma, stage left, foaming at the mouth.

By the early 1500s, Ayutthaya was not just successful, it was a glaring beacon of success across the entire southeastern continent. And nothing irritates an insecure neighbor more than someone else's thriving tax base. In 1548AD, the Burmese (technically the Toungoo Dynasty) decided they'd like Ayutthaya for themselves. You know, as a gift. To themselves. Cue the Age of War.

The prize? Not only land, slaves and riches, though there were plenty of all. Burma wanted the seal - the royal nod from China recognizing Ayutthaya as an official trading partner. That bit of diplomatic gravitas was the ancient world's green light to print as much money through trade as you could dream of. Burma wanted in.

So they invaded. And lost.

King Maha Chakkraphat (great name, got a ring to it!) rallied the troops. Fortifications were rebuilt. Mud barricades gave way to tall, thick brick walls. Cannons, courtesy of Chinese trade partners, appeared. The Diamond Fortress - Pom Phet - was constructed to keep things, and people, in check. It was not just defensive, with more than enough firepower to blow an invading armada out of the river, but an economic juggernaut as well. Ships had to stop, report, unload, and be thoroughly taxed.

Burma returned in 1569 and succeeded that time, albeit only briefly. Ayutthaya became a vassal state, though only for fifteen years. But the Thai don't mind playing the long game. They declared independence, got a little brutal and sent the invaders packing.

But it wasn't only the Burmese. The Khmer of Cambodia saw the weaknesses and damage inflicted and decided in 1570AD that war might not only be fun, but profitable as well. It didn't bode as well for them and after a short-lived siege, they were forced to retreat back to Cambodia.

So went the next century. raids, sieges, retaliation, trade, recovery. Over and over. War was a cycle, not an exception. But all the while, Ayutthaya opened new trade routes to India, Persia, and Africa. It exported rice (*So! Much! Rice!*), salt, fish and seafood, hardwoods, sugarcane, arrack (a type of rum), and ... *more* rice. But the real moneymakers? Contraband by today's standards: elephant tusk ivory, rhino horn, kingfisher feathers - sold as aphrodisiacs ("make you strong" - yeah, sure it does), bling accessories, and miracle cures. Because history repeats itself. So do scams.

To defend itself, Ayutthaya also innovated militarily. Enter Krabi Krabong - literally "sword and staff" - a form of martial arts that involved bladed weapons, flying limbs, and an Elvish flair for the dramatic. Eventually Krabi Krabong evolved into Muay Thai. Which is what happens when you remove the blades and keep the knees, feet, fists and elbows. Today Muay Thai is a revered symbol of national pride and rightly so.

And of course: war elephants.

Before nukes and drones, planes and guns, there were elephants, the tanks of ancient battlefields. Ten thousand war-trained elephants formed the backbone of Ayutthaya's defense. Towering, fast, ridiculously strong, and terrifying when armored, they trampled enemy lines like high-tide waves taking out a sandcastle. But Burma had elephants too. Battles looked like traditional warfare but with terrifying, tusked demolition walls, leaving post-skirmish fields strewn with the carnage of man and beast alike.

In 1592AD, Burma came at Ayutthaya once more, arrogantly overconfident. King Naresuan (the Great), then ruler of Ayutthaya, was already a legend in his own time, known during his lifetime for his relentless campaigns to free Ayutthaya from the Tuangoo Empire vassalage. Legend says that during the Battle of Nong Sarai, he spotted Crown Prince Mingyi Swa on the battlefield and did what any badass action-movie heroes does - charged in on elephant-back and killed him. At least that's how the romanticized tale goes. Swa did die but the mixed accounts leave a lot of truth off the table depending on who you ask.

However, the end resulted, that bold stroke ended that campaign and put a halt to the constant incursions. For a while.

What followed that glorious battlefield victory was almost a century of peace, economic boom, and cultural polish. Trade routes were expanded. The arts flourished. Grand, elaborate temples rose in every direction over the island plains. But Ayutthaya's rulers weren't naïve. They'd seen action for over four centuries and wanted security alongside the ability to earn, so they began to plan a relocation. Rivers, they discovered, were good for commerce, less great for defense. River on one side? Good. Rivers surrounding your economic juggernaut? Not so much. They were learning.

But peace never lasts. Not when the moral bankruptcy of greed and war-mongering stupidity is in play.

From 1688AD to 1767AD - almost 80 years - Burma returned to its favorite hobby: Ayutthaya invasion. This time, the gloves were off. The Burmese Konbaung dynasty (the subsequent ruling dynasty after the Toungoo) launched increasingly brutal campaigns. And in 176AD, they finally did what they'd been trying to do over centuries: they razed Ayutthaya to the ground. Torched it. Leveled the palaces. Slaughtered or enslaved every man woman and child they found. Then melted the Buddha statues for gold. Like I said - insolence and arrogance.

It was the end of the Ayutthaya Kingdom.

What's left today are silent stone stupas, grand palisades and promenades that once rang with laughter and bowed in reverence to wisdom, cultural development, and commerce. Now? Precariously leaning prangs and headless Buddhas with carrion crows for company. Walk among them and you'll hear echoes: the screams of slaughter, the cries of indentured anguish, an elephant's trumpet, bells frantically ringing through temple courtyards, all the while foreign merchants loudly negotiating that day's rice price. It's all there. If you pay attention to the brick breath.

Because history, like war, has a way of repeating itself. Especially when no one's listening.

But that was then.

My Ayutthaya began differently - with a quiet early-morning drive out of the city, no elephant required. One of those slow, unhurried departures that feels like a gentle exhale. The kind of morning where the world seems to move at half-speed, and you finally have a chance to catch up with yourself.

The Sukhumvit. Normally an electric neighborhood of movement - taxis threading through tuk-tuks; food carts ducking out of alleys getting ready for business; scooters making their own lanes through physics and prayer. It was subdued. Even the sky looked wan, a pale, washed-out blue still waking up. The air felt thick and lazy but not yet pushing towards heat. I picked up thick, cardamom and clove-spiced Turkish coffees for the three of us. We rolled east.

Eighty kilometers passed in a watercolor blur. The highway unfolded in long looping curves, flanked by low-slung buildings, roadside markets doing brisk breakfast business, and wide plots of farmland not yet swallowed by cement or industry. It was a good kind of real life in-between - between city and country, between noise and silence, between who I had been and whoever I might become. The landscape wasn't trying to impress anyone. It was simply lifescape.

The original plan? I wanted to see monkeys - because, well ... monkeys. But recently the Lopburi Monkey Temple, Wat Kai, was reading more like a simian war zone than a tourist destination. Overpopulation led to over-stimulation; over-stimulation turned to aggression with a more than a touch of ape anarchy.

Combined, this was a tinderbox for dangerous moments. Tourists fed the mayhem with ill-advised snacks and idiotic selfies (mouth-to-mouth banana feeding? *Really?*), and eventually, it spiraled. One overzealous tourist tried to selfie with a monkey who was having a bad day and was in no mood for candid photos. The tourist didn't fare so well. Then came the monkey roundups, culling of the more aggressive macaques, followed by new management policies and a whole lot of finger-pointing.

So, monkey was off the menu.

Instead, we stopped first at the Bang Pa-In Royal Palace. I'm glad we did. If you're in the neighborhood, make the time and take in a tour. It's one of those places that catches you off guard by being calmly spectacular - no chest-thumping grandeur, just grace. Sabai sabai! Tranquil. Wide boulevards were framed by broad manicured lawns. Lazy ponds rippling under pastel pavilions. The whole place felt like it was built to soothe the mind. Add buildings that don't so much clash in style as whisper to each other across cultures.

Sam knew everything and shared his knowledge with generosity and enthusiasm. We circumambulated Ho Withun Thasana, the Sages' Lookout, a vermillion and mustard yellow striped tower built like a lighthouse for royalty who never needed to navigate anything more treacherous than a formal garden party. Add to that a whole lot of gold leaf trim and you've got an eyeball party happening right in front of you. It looked like something out of a psychedelic dream; a misplaced carnival ride dropped in the tropics.

Then there was Wehart Chamrun, or Heavenly Light - a Chinese-style royal palace and throne room, constructed entirely of teak hardwood, lacquered in white and red then trimmed in gold. The latticed windows and open terraces reflecting the yin yang of Taoist balance. Built by Chinese master craftsmen as a gift from China to the Royal family of Thailand, it looked exactly like something out of the forbidden city. The smell of the wood and incense clung to the air inside, faint yet fragrant.

But the standout for me was Uthayan Phumisathian, a Victorian-style palace that looks like it had been airlifted from the Loire Valley and gently placed on Thai soil. The hall is one of the clearest examples of Siam's hybridization of Western aesthetics during the colonial era - a way of embracing modernity and signaling equality with European monarchies, while still retaining full sovereignty. That's where Czar Nikolai II, Anastasia and the rest of the Romanov clan vacationed shortly before returning home where the Bolsheviks had their nasty little photoshoot party in that Yekaterinburg basement. You can almost picture the hem of a grand Romanov dress brushing over the tiled floors in dance, a final moment of luxury before their world turned upside down.

The place was serene. Stately. Quietly astonishing. Strolling through those grounds felt like I had been invited into a world that was definitely not my own. But damn, I was hungry!

We headed to a riverside spot for lunch. Bâan Mai Rim Nam Ayutthaya. Sam knew the chef well and the menu by heart. I asked him to order the greatest hits of local classics and invited him to eat with me. At first, he hesitated. Said he'd leave me to it. But I knew how to keep him: I told him I wanted to understand the deeper stories, the real stories, and needed his help. That worked.

He smiled and sat.

Sira, ever the stoic, yet smiling chauffeur, slipped away (against my insistence that he join us), to a shady spot with his lunchbox. Something told me his wife had packed him a perfectly decent meal, possibly the Thai cousin of PB&J, a handful of chips, and something cool and fizzy.

If you've never had boat noodles, here's the rundown: it's Ayutthaya's culinary flag. A deep, dark broth made with beef stock, soy sauce, a generous inclusion of cow's blood (stay with me - if I hadn't explained that you'd be ordering your third bowl), local spices, and a fist full of herbs. Rich, pungent, slightly metallic, very beefy and totally addictive. After you experience the balance of elements you want to funnel the stuff in volume over your taste buds. We had the tendon and meatball version. Then came a spread fit for a royal feast. Stir-fried wild boar covered with bird's-eye chilies, fried snakehead fish with garlic, green-lipped mussels broiled with an herby cream sauce, crispy basil with salted egg, and a tom kha variant that brought the Thai-spice fire. Sam's eyebrows climbed halfway up his forehead when I started flop-sweating, my face almost bursting into flames. But I kept eating, spooning sticky rice into my face like it was a fire extinguisher. It hurt. It was glorious. But it was as hot as a Hades lava lake!

Lunch was fantastic, flavorful, rustic, unapologetically bold but the real gift was Sam. I don't think he's often asked to go beyond the script. But as I leaned in - really leaned in with blunt interrogations - he came alive. Names, dynasties, power plays (it's always fun to learn about the backstabbing politics of days past), architectural flourishes - it all spilled out in a way that made the past feel intimate, personal. As though those dusty ruins and forgotten royals still mattered, they still whispered their truths into the wind.

And then: Ayutthaya proper.

Ayutthaya. Once a gleaming city of a million people - larger than London or Paris in its prime, a crossroads of trade, culture and diplomacy. Now it lies in evocative decay, a place where bricks bleed memory.

The ruins rose from the earth like a nightmarish dream half-remembered. The first thing I noticed? The heads. Or rather, the lack of heads. Buddha statues, hundreds of them, all beheaded by Burmese invaders centuries ago. Some of the heads were taken as trophies, which is some seriously disrespectful bullshit vandalism. Some ended up in museums. Some were simply lost to time. All of it left a kind of sacred violence hanging in the air. There's plenty of finger pointing to go around that's completely justified. When one culture has the insolence to defile another in that manner, that is a crime against humanity and needs to be both recognized and treated as such with zero statute of limitations.

It's the kind of history that kicks you in the ass.

Wat Ratchaburana. Wat Ratchaburana was built in 1424AD **by** King Borommarachathirat II, to honor his two brothers who famously killed each other in a duel for the throne. (*That's one way to avoid a succession crisis - just skip straight to the next guy.*) It rose out of the earth. A memory made of stone. Built more than six centuries ago, it has the look of something both enduring and delicate. Time, war and fire has carved its edges, faded its surfaces, and taken a few liberties with the walls, bricks and surrounding chedi, but still, it stands bold, tall, in defiance against the insults of war. Even in its time-worn state, maybe because of it, the temple is striking. It's less a ruin than a reminder.

Sam had called a guy who knew a guy and thus we were given access to the bowels of a world heritage site. I was granted the enormous privilege to climb the steep, near-vertical steps up the prang, go inside and then down, down, down through tight, claustrophobic passages, into the central crypt. The experience delivered chills and child-like wonder to my core. Though the artifacts, relics, the gold and whatever else wasn't nailed down had been looted long ago, the frescoes that adorn the walls and ceiling were as striking as they were sophisticated. Depictions of Jataka tales (stories of the Buddha's past lives), Mount Meru, the sacred cosmic mountain of Buddhist cosmology, court life, celestial beings and mythical creatures though faded with time were breathtaking. I felt a palpable thrum of awe. It is quite special to be allowed into places normally reserved for the learned and worthy when you feel you are neither of those things. I am merely curious and that seemed enough to satisfy the guardians of the temple.

Upon our careful descent (those steps are steep and friable!) we made our way towards a more secluded area of the grounds. The grounds are enormous, so we took an hour-long stroll along paths that had seen centuries of friend and foe alike padding along them. Passing by and through the other famed towers and royal ruins, we wound up in a secluded glen, surrounded by crumbled walls of what had been a royal treasury. Sam, a living Wikipedia, made every Wat, stupa and path burst into historical relevance through knowledge and passion. He must be very popular as a lecturer at his university because he had that knack for vivid description and historical portrayal that brought everything to life.

I sat upon a tree-shaded crumbling wall that was older than me by many centuries, basking in quiet contemplation of what I had seen, when a foursome of elderly monks came into the clearing. They looked at us, surprised; it quickly became apparent they were not used to seeing people in this secluded, remote corner of the grounds.

Through Sam, I explained my journey. My brief monastic life. My quest for knowledge. My desire to experience Thailand on her terms. My love affair with Thai culture and its people. And my heartfelt longing to erase the horrors residing in the stones, the bricks, and along the paths that we had wandered.

The eldest monk gave me a smile that exuded wisdom. Through Sam, he told me that the past exists to offer lessons. That suffering, once remembered with compassion, loses its sting. Erasing it only ensures it comes again.

Another asked why I had disrobed. I said I wasn't ready yet for a life of such nobility - that I still had a lot of stupid to burn through. That received nods of understanding as I showed them pictures of my monastery days - bald, robed, trying my best to look serene and pious. They were kind about it. I mean really, what's a monk to do?

We spoke for a while. Before we parted, they invited us to their temple - Wiharn Phra Mongkhon Bophit - for a private tour and blessing. A kindness I did not expect. But then again, Thailand has had a way of opening doors when I stop knocking. I was deeply honored.

We returned to Bangkok long after the official "tour" had ended. I would have happily stayed overnight at the temple but Sam and Sira had homes and lives to return to, and their tour company required the same number of people return as departed. Maybe too many missing bodies in the past? Even so, they lingered. No one seemed in a hurry to split asunder. I'd like to believe they enjoyed the day as much as I did.

As we made our way back, I felt something relax. A kind of unburdening. Those ruins, those monks, that land - they didn't demand reverence. They simply extended wisdom like an open hand.

Places like Ayutthaya don't shout. They don't clamor for your attention the way modern monuments do. They wait, half-buried in vines, metaphorically or otherwise, and silence, for someone willing to stop long enough to hear what they've endured. And when you do, when you sit still among the scorched stone and broken relics, you feel it: the ache of impermanence, the echo of loss, the soft, insistent murmur of resilience. Ayutthaya was once a place of light and music and unimaginable beauty and bustle, but it was brought to its knees by fire, greed and arrogance. And yet, there it was - weathered, wounded, yet still whispering.

History doesn't lecture. It doesn't scold. It simply offers itself as evidence - cracked open and honest - and asks only that you see it clearly, past lies and propaganda. The suffering etched into those ruins isn't meant to make us despair. It's meant to soften us and to remind all that everything we build, everything we cherish, will one day fall away. What really matters in the end is how we hold that truth - and each other - while we still have time.

CHAPTER 19. AND IN THE END

Pay close enough attention to anything - a blade of grass, a tumbling chips bag long past its purpose, a bowl of noodles, a passing face - and the world starts whispering its secrets.

Is there such a thing as cultural perfection? Or is there some elusive societal state of grace? If so, who gets to define it? The conqueror or the quiet village? The GDP or the generosity of strangers?

Perfection implies completion, an endpoint. But culture isn't a product. It's a current - moving, merging, eddying. It thrives in contradiction. In the tension between ancient rituals and the buzz of neon. Between devotion and decadence.

So how do we measure it?

Is it in humility? The monk sweeping temple steps at dawn, never asking to be seen? Or generosity? The kind that costs nothing but kind intention. Is it in the eyes of a beautiful woman slipping fruit into your hands with a wink? Is it in humor - crude, sly, self-deprecating - telling us how a people survive history without losing themselves? Or in sadness - the collective ache of lives lost to war, famine, disease, migration, modernization, and memory? What about hope, as lanterns rise into inked night skies, carrying wishes not yet broken by the world?

And then there's desire. The motor of it all. For beauty, for recognition, for more. For less. For meaning.

Creativity follows close behind. Graffiti on a crumbling wall, calligraphy on a monk's manuscript, TikToks and temple murals, watercolors and woven silks that educate, astound and amaze.

Perspective shifts - like light in a rice field - depending on who's telling the story.

Ambition powers a city skyline. Wealth paves the roads to it. But neither tells you who smiles inside the homes.

So, is perfection found in the balance? In the willingness to keep asking, keep adapting, without forgetting the soil beneath your feet?

It's been said a thousand ways by wiser voices than mine: If you want to understand respect - not the performative kind, not the polite nod across a table - but the sincere rooted kind that lives in the bones, then you have to move. Not up, not forward. Out.

You have to travel. Not to collect visa stamps and selfies, but to be made small in the presence of something older, bigger and wiser than you. To eat food with your hands. To bow to a stranger with an open heart. To sleep on floors. To mispronounce names, words and phrases, then try again. To listen longer than is sometimes comfortable.

Respect doesn't bloom in echo chambers or airport lounges.

It grows when you let your guard down in a stranger's home.

When you don't understand the language, but you feel the meaning anyway.

When you realize *your* way is not the way.

It's just *a* way.

You begin to see that tradition isn't quaint. It's continuity.

That ritual isn't rigid. It's rhythm.

And culture isn't a museum, it's a living, breathing improvisation. A collective story constantly being written as a guiding light from the past to the future via a thousand dialects and dances.

Can cultural perfection, or some approximation of it exist? Even if it's only for the historical blink of an eye? I believe it can, though the windows of those fleeting glorious moments are small and often barely open.

Here's the thing: Strip away the passports, the rituals, the anthems, the flags, the apps and most people want the same damn thing. To be happy. To live outside the grip of constant worry. To love and be loved in return - fiercely, freely, and without footnotes or agendas. To eat well and often with laughter ringing round the table. To be healthy enough to dance at weddings and walk at sunset with the dog. To have a safe haven to rest our bodies at night, and a safer place still to rest our hearts.

Does that utopia exist? No. Not in full. Not in the way the dreamers and poets depict, or marketers promote. But there are cultures, scattered like bright beacons across the globe and throughout history that come closer than most.

Places where kindness is a reflex, not a forced performance. Where the elderly are not forgotten but honored. Where food is made to nourish, not brand. Where community isn't just a word thrown around during elections. Where the pace slows, not out of laziness, but because time is seen as a gift, not a currency.

No culture gets it all right. Every society carries its own shadows, blind spots, contradictions. But some places - some ways of living - they tilt the scale a little more toward grace. And when you find those places, even briefly, you don't want to leave. But if you must, you carry those places with you like a talisman.

But there are always the detractors. The derailers. The ones who scoff at talk of dignity, generosity, and balance because they've mistaken cynicism for wisdom. Zoom out far enough, and culture isn't just colorful dances and customs, it's a blueprint. A system. One that either prioritizes the individual ego, or collective survival. If we cede some layers of personal ambition in favor of the greater good - if we start from a place where most people have their basic needs met, where dignity isn't doled out based on wealth or status, where respect is not earned by dominance or taken by force, but offered by default, then maybe, *maybe*, we can evolve past pettiness. Past greed. Past the endless, numbing grind of "more."

Am I pitching some utopian idyll where every voice is heard, every soul seen, and the playing field is perfectly level? Don't be ridiculous. That's not how people work. People are greedy. People are needy. Some will always take more. Rise higher. Usually upon the backs of others.

And strangely enough, sometimes that's how progress happens; not because, but in spite of it. Societies adopt or reject, absorb or revolt. It's messy. And it's very human.

But what grates - what really sets my teeth on edge - are the whiny voices in both the privileged seats and the imaginarily disenfranchised. Those self-proclaimed rebels with no cause beyond attention. Entitlement in a Che Guevara T-shirt.

Because nothing screams irrelevance louder than someone who's furious the world doesn't bend to their will.

You want to change culture? Good. Start by understanding it. Then earn your outrage.

So, no. There is no perfect culture. No flawless system. No people free of contradiction, heartbreak, or hypocrisy.

But if such a thing as cultural grace exists - a near-idyll carved not from wealth or dominance, but from daily gestures of care, balance, and beauty - then Thailand comes close.

She doesn't demand your worship. She asks only that you notice. That you sit quietly with a bowl of noodles, watch a Yāy light incense, see the teenager wai the street cleaner, feel the rhythm of life flowing not in a rush, but in a tide.

Thailand doesn't hand you meaning; she invites you to earn it. In sweat, in silence, in contemplation, in humility. In alleyways filled with chili smoke and temple bells. In the way even the poorest among her offer something - a smile, a seat, a story.

She lives in balance: between restraint and pleasure, tradition and reinvention, self-respect and selflessness.

And for all her flaws, for all the changes rolling in like monsoon clouds, there's something here that whispers *"This is how it could be."*

Not perfect. but deeply, achingly human.

I hope - no, I pray to Buddha himself - that Thailand will remember me.

That in some quiet, unseen way, she carries a trace of me the way I carry her. That when I return, she'll greet me not as a stranger, but as someone who once listened. Who bowed low. Who tried to understand.

And that she'll be as thrilled to see me again as I will be to see her.

CHAPTER 19 AND IN THE END

The courtyard at Wat Pho - one of my favorite places anywhere on the planet!

ADDENDUM 1. PACK THESE AND PRAY: YOUR TECHS ROAD TO RUIN

1. Hair Dryers & Curling Irons - Unless yours is dual voltage *and* has a built-in converter, it's basically a hand-held grenade. Hotels and guesthouses almost always provide them anyway.

2. Electric Razors (Non-Dual Voltage) - These are sneaky. They look innocent, but they've claimed more sockets than a Bangkok night market has spring rolls. Bring a manual razor or buy a cheap local one if needed.

3. Blenders, Juicers, and Other Kitchen Gadgets - What are you thinking? This isn't a juice cleanse retreat in Malibu. Leave the Vitamix and bullet at home. Besides you can get a smoothy blended up every six feet along any sidewalk throughout Thailand.

4. High-Powered Hair Tools - Even dual-voltage models often behave badly overseas. They're needy, high-maintenance, and not worth the suitcase space. Do you actually need that hair straightener? Really?

5. CPAP Machines (Without Power Converter or Battery Backup) - If you need one, bring it - but make sure you've got the right voltage settings and plug compatibility, and ideally, a portable power bank designed for your model. This one is actually important so don't screw it up!

6. Surge Protectors from the U.S. - Most of these are not rated for 230v and can cause shorts or fires. Buy one locally if you really need extra outlets. Or live for the thrill of watching everything around you burn to the ground.

7. Fancy Coffee Makers - No one in Thailand wants to see your $800 espresso machine in the hostel kitchen. Great coffee is cheap and everywhere, so just enjoy the ride.

8. Old Electronics - Anything that doesn't clearly say "110-230V" isn't worth the risk. Thailand's grid won't apologize if it toasts your sentimental first-gen iPod.

ADDENDUM 2. LAURENCE RECOMMENDS: MY TOP 10 LIST

I was going to end this with a finger-wagging sermon about fast food chains and the cultural erasure they represent... but you already know that. So instead, here's a list of places that mean something to me and that I'd fly back to Thailand for in a New York minute for.

1. BEST BOWL OF NOODLES: You have to ask? Did you read the book? Up in Chiang Rai is Lanzhou Noodles. Hands down some of the greatest noodles on earth. And I've eaten a *LOT* of noodles! However, unless you're *actually* starving or have a lot of time on your hands, pass on the second helping of noodles. You can always go back! Tell Chu Larry sent you.

2. PLACES THAT MADE ME CRY: There are many places in the world that have brought me to tears through sheer beauty. But in Thailand? iMonastery is one of those places for many reasons but as a tourist, you might experience the same emotional impact by staying at iRetreat just round the bend. Sunsets on Koh Chang from Kai Bae beach? Yeah - that will do it! Wat Pho did it too! Bawled my eyes out at the serene beauty and majesty of the place.

3. MOST SPIRITUALLY TRANSFORMATIVE MANGO: Every fruit stall lining the Chiang Mai Night Bazaar. When they're in season you cannot get anything other than a life-transforming mango! Those will turn your mouth into a wonderland of appreciation.

4. RESTAURANTS THAT RESTORED MY FAITH IN ROMANCE: Sushi Masato! Romantic and unbelievable food! Sorry but the only place I dined at was with Charlee with romance in mind was Masato. Horsamut would be a *great* date place! And yet el Bario on Koh Chang comes up strong if you're with someone you're madly in love with. It may get crowded, but you'll feel both cared for and ignored in equal doses and at just the right moments.

5. BEST COFFEE IN THAILAND?: Wow - I'm thinking that those might be some fightin' words! There is sooooooo much outstanding java everywhere you go in every part of the county. However, Blue was my favorite. It's a small chain of Thai-owned slow-press coffee houses that makes syrup-consistency cappuccinos that never taste charred. You can find them in Chiang Mai and Chiang Rai.

6. FRUIT STAND THAT MIGHT CHANGE YOUR LIFE: The small store along Charoen Krung Road, just past Weed Castle. It changed mine and even though Chalermwan is no longer with me, her shop is still there, and I know there is no way her family let it slip. Incredible fruit that can be

transformative.

7. ETHICAL ELEPHANT SANCTUARY: Elephant Freedom Project is really an incredible place and an inspiration that showcases how to care for and be a part of an animal's life without being a dick. If you're in northern Thailand, you really should do the full-day package. It's life changing.

8. BEST PLACE(S) TO LAY YOUR HEAD DOWN?: The Namton Boutique in Chaing Mai is one of the most comfortable hotels I've ever stayed at anywhere in the world. In Bangkok, the Rembrandt is truly a great place to park your ass for a week or more. It's comfortable, central and the staff is fantastic. So what if it's older! Get over it.

9. BEST MEAL THAT COSTS LESS THAN A BUCK: The Sichuan pork chops in the Wat pavilion - Chiang Mai Saturday Street Bazaar! .89c and you-gotta-be-kidding-me perfection. Runner up is Rotee Pa Day cart on Tha Phae Road! They're worth the wait!!!

10. DEATHROW LAST MEAL BEFORE THE JUICE FLOWS: Horsamut. If you love Thai cuisine, and want to experience elevated interpretations of the classics, this is your place. From the food to the best booze selection, (Tequila Azul and 30-year Glenmorangie? Anyone? Class? Buhler?) I saw throughout my journeys up and down the country, plus the view? Slam dunk if your death row meal must be Thai.

11. BECAUSE SCREW LIMITS AND LISTS: THAILAND! All of it! Every god-damned bit of it. You should go. I said it before - toss away your inhibitions, your qualms and your schedule. Just do it! Oh wait - that's protected by ©. All I know is you will not be disappointed and maybe, just maybe, you'll find magic in a culture so far removed from what you know, that it absolutely will change your life.

ADDENDUM 3. ASPARAGUS, FONTINA AND PROSCIUTTO

This is for two, assuming you like the person enough to share.

One: Fat stalks only. The skinny ones are useless for this recipe. Trim the hard bottoms and peel the lower two-thirds of 8 stems. The asparagus stalks need to be uniform in length. Next: steam them just until they're just on the crispy side of al dente - about 4 minutes (they will cook further so it's important to not overcook them at this point!) Let them cool down; patience is part of the flavor.

Two: Lay out your prosciutto - two layers per bundle, about four slices each. We're making edible burritos of joy here so don't skimp.

Three: Take four stalks of asparagus, line them up next to each other like little soldiers, but top to tail (i.e. two floret heads at either end) and tuck two sticks of Fontina (or another mellow melty cheese) end to end between stalks #2 and #3. Bring 1 and 4 up and over, on top of the cheese like a Lincoln log structure. Wrap that prosciutto up and over tightly - it's got enough fat to hold everything together without twine or genuflecting to a deity.

Four: Put the bundles into a long pan and slip into the oven for a low temp warm up. You want the cheese to be just shy of melting. That'll happen in the pan.

Five: Preheat a sauté pan to medium and gently toast each side until the prosciutto crisps just enough to crackle but not enough to fight you. You do not want to overcook it and lose that fat. The cheese should just start to ooze, whispering dirty things to the asparagus.

Six: Just before serving, drizzle some really good olive oil and fresh lemon juice for that extra juju sparkle.

Serve as a side or make these a light dinner all on their own.

Salud

ADDENDUM 4. A BRIEF INTERLUDE. LAUNDRY ON THE ROAD

When you're traveling light, be prepared to run out of clothes. Fast. Even when you're doing double duty with most garments (you know the drill: yesterday's T-shirt becomes tonight's sleepwear), things get ripe quickly. So, double down on the underwear, and pack less of everything else.

In Thailand, but not only Thailand, hotel laundry services in bigger cities also tend to be overpriced. It's often better to wait, or better yet, find the nearest laundry shop and schlep your dirties there yourself. Sure, laundromats exist, there's always the option to feed coins into a spinning box and sit watching your unmentionables somersault through glass while your exploration time evaporates - but in smaller towns like Chiang Mai and Chiang Rai, the smarter move is to use the local laundry services. They are awesome, fast, dependable, and your new white shirt? It's not going to come back pink.

Here's how it works: you hand over your bag of questionable fabrics, you know, the one's holding up protest placards demanding rights and a new country, to the front desk or a nearby shop. They charge by the kilo, send it off, and the next day, like magic, your clothes return - clean, folded, and smelling like lavender and lemongrass. In Chiang Rai, I handed over a full load weighing in at 14 kilos and paid about $7 USD. That's a bargain. It's one of those underrated pleasures of slow travel: your clothes get a reset, and so do you.

You can pay (gasp) a smidgen more and have them iron your night-out-on-the-town togs too if you wish. But remember, when you're in a humid climate, just hang the stuff outside and let mother nature remove those wrinkles for you.

Acknowledgments:

To all these incredible souls who either helped me along my journey, acted as press-ganged sounding boards or ersatz editors, inspiration, or were simply there for me when I needed friends the most. I am forever in your debt.

Many merits to all of you from my heart:

Tammy Nelson, Margaret and Donn Paulk, Tobi Goff, Booth Teeters, Chris Maddox, Michael Locatti, Jim Cecil, Pinto Naravane, Lenei Jimenez, Dan and Sarah Mayhew, Jessie Hildebrandt, Spencer Sievers, Erin Miller, Sarah Mills, Ken Merrigan, Gavin Lawry, Namdak Lama, Dudjom Jigdral Rinpoche Yeshe Dorje, Joshua Lederman, Emilio le Blanc, Tan the Man Jian Wei, River Hill, Sila Samwise, Chalermwan, Jakkapan, my friends in Bangkok, Chiang Mai Chiang Rai and Koh Chang, and last but certainly far from least, my guides, my teachers, my mentors, my friends at iMonastery.

About the author:

Laurence Davidson is a writer, lifelong traveler, and practicing meditator with a taste for the absurd and a knack for well-cooked language. Based in the wine-soaked hills of Walla Walla, Washington, he's written for regional magazines and newspapers on subjects ranging from food and wine, sexuality, environmental issues and global wandering. A certified sommelier, an excellent chef (he hasn't given anyone food poisoning to date as far as he knows). An accomplished though terrible musician and unlicensed philosopher and a loving keeper of hearts and souls. He brings a unique blend of insight, irreverence, and compassion to his storytelling because PC doesn't work in his world. *The Flow* is his first book.

Want to learn more? Find out on https://laurencedavidson.com/

Want excerpts and outtakes? Check out Larryistrippin.substack.com for culled craziness and other writings.